The xVA Challenge

For other titles in the Wiley Finance Series
please see www.wiley.com/finance

The xVA Challenge

Counterparty Risk, Funding, Collateral, Capital and Initial Margin

Fourth Edition

Jon Gregory

Library of Congress Cataloging-in-Publication Data

Names: Gregory, Jon, 1971- author.
Title: The xVA challenge : counterparty risk, funding, collateral, capital
  and initial margin / Jon Gregory.
Other titles: Counterparty credit risk and credit value adjustment
Description: Fourth edition. | Chichester, West Sussex, United Kingdom :
  John Wiley & Sons, 2020. | Includes bibliographical references and
  index.
Identifiers: LCCN 2019058762 (print) | LCCN 2019058763 (ebook) | ISBN
  9781119508977 (hardback) | ISBN 9781119509028 (adobe pdf) | ISBN
  9781119509004 (epub)
Subjects: LCSH: Derivative securities—Mathematical models. | Risk
  management.
Classification: LCC HG6024.A3 G74 2020 (print) | LCC HG6024.A3 (ebook) |
  DDC 332.64/57—dc23
LC record available at https://lccn.loc.gov/2019058762
LC ebook record available at https://lccn.loc.gov/2019058763

Cover Design: Wiley
Cover Image: © Sandipkumar Patel/Getty Images

Set in 10/12pt, TimesNewRomanMTStd by SPi Global, Chennai, India.
Printed and bound by CPI Group (UK) Ltd, Croydon, CR0 4YY

C9781119508977_040324

To Ginnie, George, Christy, Flo and Luna

Contents

Section 4   The xVAs

List of Spreadsheets

One of the key features of the first and second editions of this book was the accompanying spreadsheets that were prepared to allow the reader to gain some simple insight into some of the quantitative aspects discussed. Many of these examples have been used for training courses and have therefore evolved to be quite intuitive and user-friendly. The spreadsheets can be downloaded freely from Jon Gregory's website, www.cvacentral.com, under the counterparty risk section. New examples may be added over time.

List of Appendices

The following is a list of Appendices that contain additional mathematical detail. These Appendices can be downloaded freely from www.cvacentral.com.

Acknowledgements

The first edition of this book was published about a decade ago in the aftermath of a global financial crisis and focused on the importance of counterparty credit. Since then, the area of counterparty credit risk has broadened to consider the importance of related aspects such as collateral, funding, capital, and initial margin. This area has continued to see rapid change due to regulation, accounting standards, and evolving market practice. As previously, this is much more than a new edition because most of the content has been rewritten and expanded significantly.

I hope this book can be used as a comprehensive and relatively non-mathematical reference for the subject we now generally refer to as xVA. There are other mathematical books on this subject and the book by Andrew Green (Green 2015) is recommended as a comprehensive quantitative guide to the subject.

As with previous editions, I have saved space by putting mathematical appendices together with accompanying spreadsheets on my personal website at www.cvacentral .com. Since many do not study this material in depth, this has proved to be a reasonable compromise for most readers. There is also a list of errata that can be found on this website.

I have also made use of numerous survey results and I am grateful to Solum Financial and Deloitte for allowing me to reproduce these. I am also grateful to IBM and IHS Markit who have provided calculation examples in previous editions, some of which are used here. These will all be mentioned in the text.

Finally, I would like to thank the following people for feedback on this and earlier editions of the book: Manuel Ballester, Teimuraz Barbakadze, Ronnie Barnes, Raymond Cheng, Vladimir Cheremisin, Michael Clayton, Andrew Cooke, Christian Crispoldi, Daniel Dickler, Wei-Ming Feng, Julia Fernald, Leonard Fichte, Piero Foscari, Teddy Fredaigues, Sayoko Fujisawa, Naoyuki Fujita, Shota Fukamizu, Dimitrios Giannoulis, Glen Gibson, Sergej Goriatchev, Arthur Guerin, Kazuhisa Hirota, Kale Kakhiani, Toshiyuki Kitano, Henry Kwon, Edvin Lundstrom, David Mengle, Richard Morrin, Ivan Pomarico, Yufi Pak, Hans-Werner Pfaff, Francesco Ivan Pomarico, Erik van Raaij, Kei Sagami, Guilherme Sanches, Neil Schofield, Andreas Schwaderlapp, Florent Serre, Masum Shaikh, Ana Sousa, Salvatore Stefanelli, Richard Stratford, Carlos Sterling, Norikazu Takei, Hidetoshi Tanimura, Todd Tauzer, Satoshi Terakado, Nick Vause, Frederic Vrins, Nana Yamada, and Valter Yoshida.

Jon Gregory
December 2019

About the Author

Jon Gregory is an independent expert specialising in counterparty risk and xVA related projects. He has worked on many aspects of credit risk and derivatives in his career, being previously with Barclays Capital, BNP Paribas, and Citigroup. He is a senior advisor for Solum Financial Derivatives Advisory. He is also a faculty member for London Financial Studies and the Certificate of Quantitative Finance. He currently serves on the Academic Advisory Board of IHS Markit and is a Managing Editor of the journal *Quantitative Finance*.

Jon has a PhD from Cambridge University.

Section 1

Basics

1
Introduction

In 2007, a global financial crisis (GFC) started which eventually became more severe and long-lasting than could have ever been anticipated. Along the way, there were major casualties such as the bankruptcy of the investment bank Lehman Brothers. Governments around the world had to bailout other financial institutions such as American International Group (AIG) in the US and the Royal Bank of Scotland in the UK.

The GFC caused a major focus on counterparty credit risk (CCR) which is the credit risk in relation to derivative products. A derivative trade is a contractual relationship that may be in force from a few days to several decades. During the lifetime of the contract, the two counterparties have claims against each other such as in the form of cash flows that evolve as a function of underlying assets and market conditions. Derivatives transactions create CCR due to the risk of insolvency of one party. This CCR in turn creates systemic risk due to derivatives trading volume being dominated by a relatively small number of large derivatives counterparties ('dealers') that are then key nodes of the financial system.

Post-GFC, participants in the derivatives market became more aware of CCR and its quantification via credit value adjustment (CVA). They also started to create more value adjustments, or xVAs, in order to quantify other costs such as funding, collateral, and capital. Derivatives pricing used to be focused on so-called 'exotics' with the majority of simple or vanilla derivatives thought to be relatively straightforward to deal with. However, the birth of xVA has changed this and even the most simple derivatives may have complex pricing and valuation issues arising from xVA.

Regulation has also enhanced the need to consider xVA (or XVA). Increasing capital requirements, constraints on funding, liquidity, and leverage together with a clearing mandate and bilateral margin requirements all make derivatives trading more expensive and complex. However, derivatives are still fundamentally important: for example, without them end users would have to use less effective hedges, which would create income statement volatility. The International Swaps and Derivatives Association (ISDA 2014b) reports that 85% of end users said that derivatives were very important or important to their risk management strategy and 79% said they planned to increase or maintain their use of over-the-counter (OTC) derivatives.

This book aims to fully explain xVA and the associated landscape of derivatives trading. Chapters 2 to 5 will discuss the basics of derivatives, regulation, CCR, and introduce the concept of xVA. Chapters 6 to 10 will discuss risk mitigation methods such as netting, margining, and central clearing. Chapters 11 to 15 will cover the building blocks of xVA such as exposure, credit spreads, funding, and capital costs. Finally, Chapters 16 to 20 will define the xVAs in sequence whilst also discussing their relationships to one another. Chapter 21 will discuss the 'xVA desk' and management of xVA.

The online Appendices and Spreadsheets provide more detail on various xVA calculations. This book is a relatively non-mathematical treatment of xVA. For a more mathematically-rigorous text for quantitative researchers, Andrew Green's book (Green 2015) is strongly recommended.

2
Derivatives

2.1 INTRODUCTION

Derivatives transactions represent contractual agreements either to make payments or to buy or sell an underlying security at a time or times in the future. The times may range from a few weeks or months (for example, futures contracts) to many years (for example, long-dated swaps). The value of a derivative will change with the level of one or more underlying assets or indices and possibly decisions made by the parties to the contract. In many cases, the initial value of a traded derivative will be contractually configured to be zero for both parties at inception.

Derivatives are not a particularly new financial innovation; for example, in medieval times, forward contracts were popular in Europe. However, derivatives products and markets have become particularly large and complex in the last three decades. One of the advantages of derivatives is that they can provide very efficient hedging tools. For example, consider the following risks that an institution, such as a corporate, may experience:

- *Interest rate risk*. They need to manage liabilities such as transforming floating- into fixed-rate debt via an interest rate swap.
- *Foreign exchange (FX) risk*. Due to being paid in various currencies, there is a need to hedge cash inflow in these currencies, for example, using FX forwards.
- *Commodity risk*. The need to lock in commodity prices either due to consumption (e.g. airline fuel costs) or production (e.g. a mining company) via commodity futures or swaps.

In many ways, derivatives are no different from the underlying cash instruments. They simply allow one to take a very similar position in a synthetic way. For example, an airline wanting to reduce its exposure to a potential rise in oil price can buy oil futures, which are cash-settled and therefore represent a very simple way to go 'long oil' (with no storage or transport costs). An institution wanting to reduce its exposure to a certain asset can do so via a derivative contract (such as a total return swap), which means it does not have to sell the asset directly in the market.

There are many different users of derivatives such as sovereigns, central banks, regional/local authorities, hedge funds, asset managers, pension funds, insurance companies, and non-financial corporations. All use derivatives as part of their investment strategy or to hedge the risks they face from their business activities. Due to the particular hedging needs of institutions and related issues, such as accounting, many derivatives are relatively bespoke. For example, a corporation wanting to hedge the interest rate risk in a floating-rate loan will want an interest rate swap precisely matching the terms of the loan (e.g. maturity, payment frequency, and reference rate).

Financial institutions, mainly banks, provide derivative contracts to their end user clients and hedge their risks with one another. Whilst many financial institutions trade derivatives, many markets are dominated by a relatively small number of large counterparties (often known as 'dealers'). Such dealers represent key nodes of the financial system. For example, there are currently around 35 globally-systemically-important banks (G-SIBs), which is a term loosely synonymous with 'too big to fail'. G-SIB banks are subject to stricter rules, such as higher minimum capital requirements.

During the lifetime of a derivatives contract, the two counterparties have claims against each other, such as in the form of cash flows that evolve as a function of underlying assets and market conditions. Derivatives transactions create counterparty credit risk (counterparty risk) due to the risk of insolvency of one party. Counterparty risk refers to the possibility that a counterparty may not meet its contractual requirements under the contract when they become due.

Counterparty risk is managed over time through clearing; this can be performed bilaterally, where each counterparty manages the risk of the other, or centrally through a central counterparty (CCP). As the derivatives market has grown, so has the importance of counterparty risk. Furthermore, the lessons from events such as the bankruptcy of Lehman Brothers have highlighted the problems when a major player in the derivatives market defaults. This, in turn, has led to an increased focus on counterparty risk and related aspects.

2.2   THE DERIVATIVES MARKET

2.2.1   Exchange-traded and OTC Derivatives

Within the derivatives markets, many of the simplest products are traded through exchanges. A derivatives exchange is a financial centre (Figure 2.1) where parties can trade standardised contracts such as futures and options at a specified price. An exchange promotes market efficiency and enhances liquidity by centralising trading in a single place, thereby making it easier to enter and exit positions. Exchange-traded derivatives are standardised contracts (e.g. futures and options) and are actively traded. It is easy to buy a contract and sell the equivalent contract to terminate ('close') the position, which can be done via one or more derivative exchanges. Prices are transparent and accessible to a wide range of market participants.

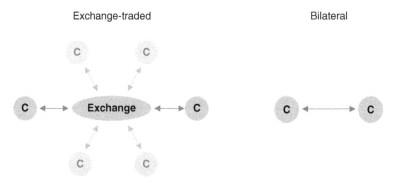

Figure 2.1   Illustration of exchange-traded and bilaterally-traded derivatives.

Compared to exchange-traded derivatives, OTC derivatives tend to be less-standard structures and are typically traded bilaterally (i.e. between two parties). Since there is no third party involved, they are traditionally private contracts and are often not actively traded in any secondary market. However, their main advantage is their inherent flexibility, as they do not need to be standardised and, in theory, any transaction terms can be accommodated. For example, a customer wanting to hedge their production or use of an underlying asset at specific dates may do so through a customised OTC derivative. Such a hedge may not be available on an exchange, where the underlying contracts will only allow certain standard contractual terms (e.g. maturity dates) to be used. A customised OTC derivative may be considered more useful for risk management than an exchange-traded derivative, which would give rise to additional 'basis risk' (in this example, the mismatch of maturity dates). It has been reported that the majority of the largest companies in the world use derivatives in order to manage their financial risks.[1] Due to the bespoke hedging needs of such companies, OTC derivatives are commonly used instead of their exchange-traded equivalents.

Customised OTC derivatives are not without their disadvantages, of course. A customer wanting to unwind a transaction and avoid future counterparty risk must do it with the original counterparty, who may quote unfavourable terms due to their privileged position. Even assigning or 'novating' the transaction to another counterparty typically cannot be done without the permission of the original counterparty. This lack of fungibility in OTC transactions can also be problematic. This aside, there is nothing wrong with customising derivatives to the precise needs of clients, as long as this is the sole intention. However, providing a service to clients is not the only role of OTC derivatives: some are contracted for regulatory arbitrage or even (arguably) misleading a client. Such products are clearly not socially useful and generally fall into the (relatively small) category of exotic OTC derivatives which in turn generate much of the criticism of OTC derivatives in general.

OTC markets work very differently compared to exchange-traded ones, as outlined in Table 2.1. OTC derivatives are traditionally privately negotiated and traded directly between two parties without an exchange or other intermediary involved (between a dealer and end user or between two dealers). OTC markets did not historically include trade reporting, which is difficult because trades can occur in private, without the activity

Table 2.1 Comparison between exchange-traded and OTC derivatives.

	Exchange-traded	Over-the-counter (OTC)
Terms of contract	• Standardised (maturity, size, strike, etc.)	• Flexible and negotiable
Maturity	• Standard maturities, typically at most a few months	• Negotiable and non-standard • Often many years
Liquidity	• Very good	• Limited and sometimes very poor for non-standard or complex products

[1] ISDA (2009). Over 94% of the World's Largest Companies Use Derivatives to Help Manage Their Risks, According to ISDA Survey. Press Release (23 April). www.isda.org.

being visible in any way (such as to an exchange). Legal documentation is also bilaterally negotiated between the two parties, although certain standards have been developed.

2.2.2   Clearing

After a transaction is executed, and before it has been settled, there is the question of clearing (Figure 2.2). An OTC derivative contract legally obliges its counterparties to make certain payments over the life of the contract (or until an early termination of the contract). These payments are in relation to buying or selling certain underlying securities or exchanging cash flows in reference to underlying market variables. Settlement refers to the completion of all such legal obligations and can occur when all payments have been successfully made or alternatively when the contract is closed out (e.g. settled in some other way or offset against another position). 'Clearing' is the process by which payment obligations between two or more firms are computed (and often netted), and 'settlement' is the process by which those obligations are affected. The means by which payments on OTC derivatives are cleared and settled affect how the counterparty risk that is borne by counterparties in the transaction is managed. Broadly speaking, clearing represents the period between execution and settlement of a transaction. One of the key aspects of clearing is, therefore, counterparty risk that arises when a party fails to perform on contractual responsibilities.

The time period for classically-exchange-traded derivatives is often no more than a few days (e.g. a spot equity transaction) or at most a few months (e.g. a futures contract). A key feature of many OTC derivatives is that they are not settled for a long time since they generally have long maturities. This is in contrast to exchange-traded products, which often settle in days or, at the most, months. For OTC derivatives, the time horizon for the clearing process is more commonly years and often even decades (and the representation in Figure 2.2 is therefore misleading since it does not emphasise the long period of clearing). This is one reason why OTC clearing is of growing importance as more such products become subject to central clearing.

Broadly speaking, clearing can be either bilateral or central. In the latter case, a third party takes responsibility for managing counterparty risk and associated components (e.g. collateralisation). All derivatives exchanges now have an associated CCP that performs this clearing function. In the bilateral case, the two parties entering a trade take responsibility for the processes and risks during the clearing process. Historically, the OTC derivatives market has been bilaterally cleared, but more recently OTC derivatives have begun to become centrally cleared (Figure 2.3).

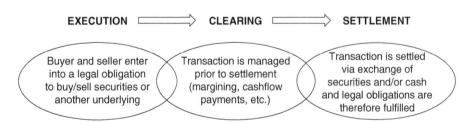

Figure 2.2   Illustration of the role of clearing in financial transactions.

Figure 2.3 Clearing in exchange-traded and OTC derivatives.

In bilateral clearing, risk management processes are dealt with bilaterally by the counterparties to each OTC contract, whereas for centrally cleared transactions, the risk management functions are typically carried out by the associated CCP.

Whilst an exchange provides efficient price discovery,[2] it also typically provides a means of mitigating counterparty risk. Since the mid-1980s, all exchanges have had such central clearing facilities. More recently, central clearing has been applied to OTC derivatives.

Central clearing can be seen as a natural extension of exchange-trading but, since it requires a certain amount of standardisation, not all OTC derivatives can be centrally cleared. Whilst the volume of centrally cleared OTC derivatives is increasing, there will always be a relatively significant portion of bilaterally cleared OTC derivatives. Other methods, such as multilateral compression (Section 6.2.4), can be used in bilateral markets and can be seen as utilising some of the functionality of central clearing.

2.2.3 Market Overview

In 1986, the total notional of OTC derivatives was slightly less than that of exchange-traded derivatives at $500 billion.[3] Arguably, even at this point, OTC markets were more significant due to the fact that they are longer-dated (for example, a 10-year OTC swap is many times more risky than a three-month futures contract). Nevertheless, in the following two decades, the OTC derivatives market grew exponentially in size (Figure 2.4) in terms of notional. This was due to the use of OTC derivatives as customised hedging instruments and also investment vehicles. The OTC market has also seen the development of completely new products (for example, the credit default swap market increased by a factor of 10 between the end of 2003 and the end of 2008). The relative popularity of OTC products is due to the ability to tailor contracts more precisely to client needs. Exchange-traded products, by their very nature, do not offer customisation.

The curtailed growth towards the end of the history in Figure 2.4 can be clearly attributed to the global financial crisis (GFC), where banks have moved away from some derivatives (for example, due to high capital charges) and clients have been less interested in some derivatives (particularly as structured products). However, the reduction in recent years is also partially due to compression exercises that seek to reduce counterparty risk by removing offsetting and redundant positions (discussed in more detail in Section 6.2.4).

OTC derivatives include the following five broad classes of derivative securities: interest rate (and inflation) derivatives, foreign exchange derivatives, equity derivatives, commodity derivatives, and credit derivatives. The split of OTC derivatives by product

---

[2] This is the process of determining the price of an asset in a marketplace through the interactions of buyers and sellers.
[3] ISDA (1986). Survey covering only OTC swaps.

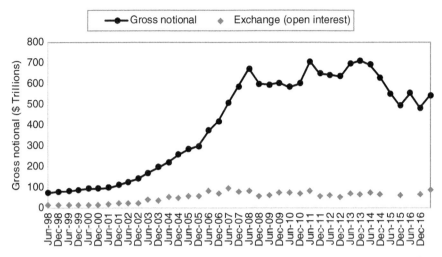

Figure 2.4   Total outstanding notional of OTC and exchange-traded derivatives transactions. The figures cover interest rate, foreign exchange, equity, commodity, and credit derivative contracts. Note that notional amounts outstanding are not directly comparable to those for exchange-traded derivatives, which refer to open interest or net positions, whereas the amounts outstanding for OTC markets refer to gross positions (i.e. without netting). Centrally-cleared trades also increase the total notional outstanding due to a double-counting effect, since clearing involves booking two separate transactions. Source: Bank for International Settlements (BIS).

type is shown in Figure 2.5. Interest rate products contribute the majority of the outstanding notional, with foreign exchange and credit default swaps (CDSs) seemingly less important. However, this gives a somewhat misleading view of the importance of counterparty risk in other asset classes, especially foreign exchange and CDSs. Whilst most foreign exchange products are short-dated, the long-dated nature and exchange of notional in cross-currency swaps mean they carry a lot of counterparty risk. CDSs not only have a large volatility component but also constitute significant 'wrong-way risk'. Therefore, whilst interest rate products make up a significant proportion of the counterparty risk in the market, one must not underestimate the other important (and sometimes more subtle) contributions from other products.

Looking at the notional of derivatives contracts can be misleading, even when doing so only on a relative basis. A key aspect of derivatives products is that their exposure is substantially smaller than that of an equivalent loan or bond. Consider an interest rate swap as an example: this contract involves the exchange of floating against fixed payments and has no principal risk because only cash flows are exchanged. Furthermore, even the cash flows are not fully at risk because, at cash flow payment dates, only the net difference in fixed and floating cash flows will be exchanged. If a counterparty fails to perform, then an institution will have no obligation to continue to make cash flow payments. Instead, the swap will be unwound based on some defined valuation. If the swap has a negative value for an institution, then they may stand to lose nothing if their counterparty defaults.[4]

---

[4] Assuming the swap can be replaced without any additional cost.

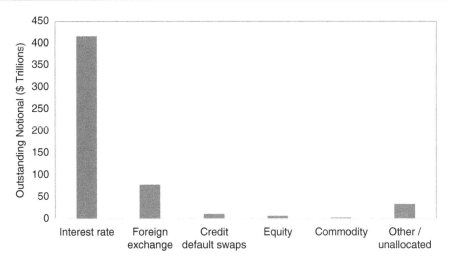

Figure 2.5 Split of OTC derivative gross outstanding notional by product type as of June 2017. Note that centrally-cleared products are double-counted since a single trade is novated into two trades in a CCP. This is particularly relevant for interest rate products, for which a large outstanding notional is already centrally cleared. Source: BIS.

It should be clear that the market value of derivatives (Figure 2.6) is a more relevant measure of the risk than the gross notional outstanding since it reflects the maximum loss that parties would incur if they all fail to meet their contractual payments and the contracts are replaced at current market prices. There are also clear incentives to reduce the gross market value of derivatives as much as possible using methods such as central clearing.[5] In recent years, central clearing has had a significant impact on OTC derivatives markets, with around 60% in notional amounts outstanding (mostly interest rate contracts) reported by dealers being centrally cleared.[6]

2.2.4 Market Participants and Collateralisation

It is useful to characterise the different players in the derivatives market and the way in which they transact. Whilst exchange-traded derivatives are effectively settled on a daily basis with margin, OTC derivatives are not usually settled in this way but may be collateralised.[7] A significant number of OTC derivatives are collateralised with parties pledging cash and securities against the value of their derivative portfolio, with the aim of neutralising the net exposure between the counterparties. Collateralisation (or settlement) can reduce counterparty risk but introduces additional legal and operational risks. Furthermore, posting collateral to meet margin requirements introduces funding costs as it is necessary to source the cash or securities to deliver. It also leads to liquidity risks in case the required amount and type of collateral cannot be sourced in the required time frame.

---

[5] There are other ways to reduce market values, such as restructuring transactions. Note that the use of collateral or margin (discussed in Section 2.2.4) is not shown in these figures.

[6] BIS (2018). OTC derivatives statistics at end-June 2016 (31 October). www.bis.org.

[7] The difference between margin and collateral will be explained in more detail in Chapter 7. The former is more associated with exchange-traded derivatives and the latter with OTC derivatives.

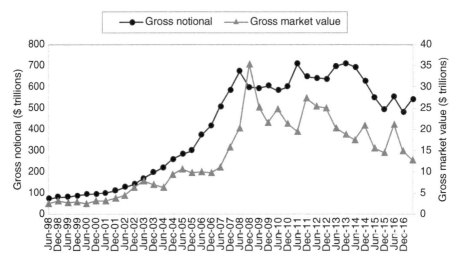

Figure 2.6 Total outstanding notional and gross market value of OTC derivatives transactions. The figures cover interest rate, foreign exchange, equity, commodity, and credit derivative contracts. Source: BIS. www.bis.org.

Broadly, the market can be divided into three groups:

- *Large player*. This will be a large global bank, often known as a dealer. They will have a vast number of derivatives trades on their books and have many clients and other counterparties. They will usually trade across all asset classes (interest rates, foreign exchange, equities, commodities, credit derivatives) and will collateralise positions (as long as the counterparty will make the same commitment, and sometimes even if they do not). They will be a member of most or all exchanges and CCPs to facilitate trading on their own account and for their clients. The OTC derivatives market is highly concentrated, with the largest 14 dealers holding around four-fifths of the total notional outstanding.[8] These dealers collectively provide the bulk of the market liquidity in most products.
- *Medium-sized player*. This will typically be a smaller bank or other financial institution that has significant OTC derivatives activities, including making markets in certain products. They will cover several asset classes, although they may not be active in all of them (they may, for example, not trade credit derivatives or commodities, and will probably not deal with more exotic derivatives). Even within an asset class, their coverage may also be restricted to a certain market (for example, a regional bank transacting in certain local currencies). They will have a smaller number of clients and counterparties but will also generally be willing to collateralise their positions. They will be a member of local exchanges and CCPs (where appropriate) and may be a member of a number of global ones.
- *End user*. Typically this will be a large corporate, sovereign, or smaller financial institution with derivatives requirements (for example, for hedging needs or investment). They

---

[8] ISDA (2010).

will have a relatively small number of OTC derivatives transactions on their books and will trade with only a few different counterparties. They may only deal in a single asset class (for example, some corporates trade only foreign exchange products, a mining company may only trade commodity forwards, and a pension fund may only be active in interest rate and inflation products). Due to their needs, their overall position will be very directional (i.e. they will not execute offsetting transactions). Often, they may be unable or unwilling to commit to margining or posting collateral or will post illiquid collateral and/or post more infrequently. Many players in the OTC derivatives market do not have strong credit quality, nor are they able to margin or post collateral to reduce counterparty risk. This counterparty risk is, therefore, arguably, an unavoidable consequence of the derivatives market.

A special case in OTC derivatives end users has been certain counterparties of exceptionally high credit quality, such as sovereigns, supranational entities, or multilateral development banks. Such entities have historically had a favourable arrangement with banks where they receive, but do not post, collateral (potentially subject to rating triggers, meaning that they may be required to post collateral if they are downgraded). Such arrangements are seen as much more costly nowadays due to the associated funding and capital requirements.

Finally, there are many third parties in the OTC derivatives market. These may offer, for example, settlement/margining/collateral management, software, trade compression, and clearing services. They allow market participants to reduce counterparty risk and the risks associated with counterparty risk (such as legal), and improve overall operational efficiency with respect to these aspects.

Broadly speaking, derivatives can be classified into several different groups by the way in which they are transacted and collateralised. These groups, in order of increasing complexity and risk are:

- *Exchange-traded*. These are the most simple, liquid, and short-dated derivatives that are traded on an exchange. All derivatives exchanges now have central clearing functions where margin must be posted against losses on a daily basis, and the performance of all exchange members is guaranteed. Due to the lack of complexity, the short maturities, and central clearing function, this has often been viewed as the safest part of the derivatives market although recent events have called this into question (Section 10.1.3). Note that exchange-traded derivatives are typically settled on a daily basis with a cash payment which is usually known as variation margin.
- *OTC centrally cleared*. These are OTC derivatives that are not suitable for exchange-trading due to being relatively complex, illiquid, and non-standard but are centrally cleared. Indeed, incoming regulation is requiring central clearing of standardised OTC derivatives (Section 2.5.4). OTC CCPs usually require a daily collateralisation in cash which, although not settlement, is still known as variation margin.
- *OTC collateralised*. These are bilateral OTC derivatives that are not centrally cleared but where parties post collateral (which may be cash or securities) to one another in order to mitigate the counterparty risk.
- *OTC uncollateralised*. These are bilateral OTC derivatives where parties do not post collateral (or post less and/or lower quality collateral). This is typically the case because one of the parties involved in the contract (typically an end user such as a corporate)

cannot commit to collateralisation. Since they have nothing to mitigate their counterparty risk, these derivatives generally receive the most attention in terms of their underlying risks.

The question is how significant each of the above categories is. Figure 2.7 gives a breakdown in terms of the total notional. Only about a tenth of the market is exchange-traded with the majority OTC. However, over half of the OTC market is already centrally cleared. Of the remainder, around four-fifths is collateralised, with only 20% remaining under collateralised. For this reason, it is this last category that is the most dangerous and the source of many of the problems in relation to counterparty risk, funding, and capital.

The majority of this book is about the seemingly small 7% (20% of the 40% of the 91% in Figure 2.7) of the market that is not well collateralised bilaterally or via a central clearing function. However, it is important to emphasise that this still represents tens of trillions of dollars of notional and is therefore extremely important from a counterparty risk perspective. Furthermore, it is also important to look beyond just counterparty risk and consider funding, capital, and collateral. This, in turn, makes all groups of derivatives in Figure 2.7 important.

2.2.5   Banks and End Users

Broadly speaking, there are two situations in which counterparty risk and related aspects such as funding, collateral, and capital arise. The most obvious (Figure 2.8) would apply to an end user transacting derivatives for hedging purposes. Their overall portfolio will typically be directional (but not completely so, as mentioned below) since the general aim will be to offset economic risk elsewhere. The result of this will be that the variation in the value of the derivatives, or mark-to-market (MTM) volatility, will be significant and any associated margin or collateral flows may vary substantially. Indeed, the fact that substantial collateral may be required over a short time horizon is one reason why many end users do not enter into collateral agreements. Another implication of directional

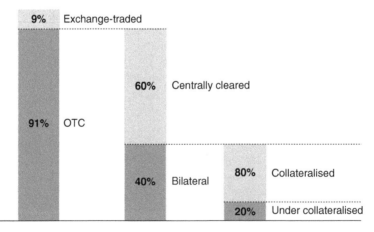

Figure 2.7   Breakdown of different types of derivatives by total notional. Source: Eurex (2014). www.eurexclearing.com.

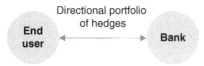

Figure 2.8   Illustration of the classic end user counterparty risk set-up.

portfolios is that there may be less netting benefit available. In practice, an end user will trade with a reasonable number of bank counterparties depending on the volume of their business and risk appetite.

Another important feature is that end users may hedge risks on a one-for-one basis – for example, the terms of an OTC swap may be linked directly to those of bonds issued rather than the interest rate exposure being hedged more generically on a macro basis. End users may find it problematic when unwinding transactions since the original counterparty will not necessarily quote favourable terms. Furthermore, if they do execute offsetting transactions (for example, certain parties may execute receiver interest rate swaps to hedge their lending,[9] whilst also using payer interest rate swaps to hedge borrowing), the terms received will be less favourable than if they macro-hedged the overall risk. This is a consequence of hedging borrowing and lending on a one-to-one basis. For a similar reason, default situations will be problematic since an end user may want to replace transactions on a one-for-one basis rather than macro-hedging their exposure to the defaulted counterparty. This will likely be more time-consuming and costly.

It is also important to understand that the hedging needs of a client may lead to certain imbalances when using derivatives. A common example is when an institution borrows money via a loan where the interest rate payment will typically be based on a floating rate (Figure 2.9). If the institution wants to hedge their interest rate risk then they may use an interest rate swap matching the terms of the loan, where they will pay a fixed rate against receiving the floating rate. However, even if they transact both the loan and interest rate swap with the same bank, they may have different practices with respect to aspects such as accounting treatment and collateralisation. From the bank's perspective, the capital treatment for the two transactions will be separate as the loan will be part of the 'banking book', whereas the swap will be a 'trading book' item.

For a bank, the classic counterparty risk situation is rather different (Figure 2.10). Banks will typically aim to run a relatively flat (i.e. hedged) book from a market risk

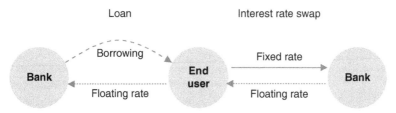

Figure 2.9   Illustration of an institution borrowing via a floating rate loan and using an interest rate swap to convert (hedge) the floating interest rate payments into fixed payments.

---

[9] This involves receiving the fixed rate and paying the floating rate.

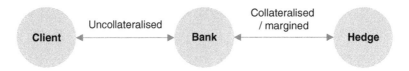

Figure 2.10   Illustration of the classic bank counterparty risk set-up.

perspective. This means that a transaction with a client will be hedged, either on a macro basis or directly ('back to back') with another market participant. This will likely lead to a series of hedges through the interbank market, possibly ending with an offsetting position with another end user. In this situation, the bank may have little or no MTM volatility or market risk. However, they do have counterparty risk to both counterparties A and B since, if either were to default, this would leave exposure for the other party.

Another important feature of this situation is that client transactions will often be uncollateralised, whereas the hedges will be bilaterally collateralised (or exchange-traded/centrally cleared). The counterparty risk problem exists mainly on the uncollateralised transactions (although there is often still a material risk on the hedges). Whilst the overall MTM is neutralised, this introduces an asymmetry in collateral flows which can be problematic. Dealers also suffer from the directional hedging needs of clients. For example, they may transact mainly receiver interest rate swaps with corporate clients. In a falling interest rate environment, the hedges of these swaps will require significant margin or collateral posting. Figure 2.10 is very important as a starting point for many different types of analysis and will be referred back to at several later points in this book.

2.2.6   ISDA Documentation

The rapid development of the OTC derivative market could not have occurred without the development of standard legal documentation to increase efficiency and reduce aspects such as counterparty risk. The International Swaps and Derivatives Association (ISDA) is a trade organisation for OTC derivatives practitioners. The market standard for OTC derivative documentation is the ISDA Master Agreement, which was first introduced in 1985 and is now used by the majority of market participants to document their OTC derivative transactions.

The ISDA Master Agreement is a bilateral framework which contains terms and conditions to govern OTC derivative transactions between parties. Multiple transactions will be covered under a general Master Agreement to form a single legal contract of an indefinite term, covering many or all of the transactions. The Master Agreement comprises a common core section and a schedule containing adjustable terms to be agreed by both parties. This specifies the contractual terms between parties with respect to aspects such as netting, collateral, termination events, the definition of default, and the close-out process. By doing this, it aims to remove legal uncertainties and to provide mechanisms for mitigating counterparty risk. The commercial terms of individual transactions are documented in a trade confirmation, which references the Master Agreement for the more general terms. Negotiation of the agreement can take considerable time, but once completed, trading tends to occur without the need to update or change any general aspects.

Typically, English or New York law is applied, although other jurisdictions are sometimes used.

From a counterparty risk perspective, the ISDA Master Agreement has the following risk-mitigating features:

- the contractual terms regarding the posting of collateral (covered in detail in Chapter 3);
- events of default and termination;
- all transactions referenced are combined into a single net obligation; and
- the mechanics around the close-out process are defined.

In relation to counterparty risk, default events lead to the termination of transactions before their original maturity date and the initiation of a close-out process. Events of default covered in the ISDA Master Agreement are:

- failure to pay or deliver
- breach of agreement
- credit support default (collateral terms)
- misrepresentation
- default under the specified transaction
- cross-default (default on another obligation)
- bankruptcy
- merger without assumption.

The most common of the above is a failure to pay (subject to some defined threshold amount) and bankruptcy.

Recent years have highlighted the need for risk mitigants for OTC derivatives. For example, the Lehman Brothers bankruptcy led to extensive litigation in relation to the ability to offset different obligations and the valuation of OTC derivative assets or liabilities (for example, refer to Figure 2.11). This illustrates the importance of documentation in defining the processes that will occur in the event of a counterparty default.

2.2.7 Credit Derivatives

The credit derivatives market grew swiftly in the decade before the GFC due to the need to transfer credit risk efficiently. The core credit derivative instrument, the CDS, is simple and has transformed the trading of credit risk. However, CDSs themselves can prove highly toxic since, whilst they can be used to hedge counterparty risk in other products, there is counterparty risk embedded within the CDS contract itself. The market has recently become all too aware of the dangers of CDSs. Credit derivatives can, on the one hand, be very efficient at transferring credit risk but, if not used correctly, can be counterproductive and highly toxic. The growth of the credit derivatives market has stalled in recent years since the GFC.

One of the main drivers of the move towards the central clearing of standard OTC derivatives is the counterparty risk represented by the CDS market. Furthermore, as hedges for counterparty risk, CDSs seem to require the default remoteness that central clearing apparently gives them. However, the ability of central counterparties to deal with the CDS product, which is much more illiquid and risky than other cleared products, is crucial and not yet tested.

2.2.8   Financial Weapons of Mass Destruction

Derivatives can be extremely powerful and useful, have facilitated the growth of global financial markets, and have aided economic growth. For example, ISDA (2014b) notes that:

- derivatives are essential to global economic activity and growth;
- thousands of companies use OTC derivatives to manage the risks arising from their business and financial activities;
- derivative users are corporations, investment managers, governments, insurers, energy and commodities firms, international and regional banks, and financial institutions;
- derivatives are transacted around the world in more than 30 currencies; and
- most of the world's 500 largest companies use derivatives to manage risk.

Of course, not all derivatives transactions can be classified as 'socially useful'. Some involve arbitraging regulatory capital amounts, tax requirements, or accounting rules. As the average person now knows, derivatives can be highly toxic and cause massive losses and financial catastrophes if misused. Some historical examples of this are Orange County (1994), Proctor and Gamble (1994), Barings Bank (1995), Long-Term Capital Management (1998), Enron (2001), and Société Générale (2008).[10]

A key feature of derivatives instruments is leverage. Since most derivatives are executed with only a small (with respect to the notional value of the contract) or no upfront payment made, they provide significant leverage. If an institution has the view that US interest rates will be going down, they may buy US treasury bonds. There is a natural limitation to the size of this trade, which is the cash that the institution can raise in order to invest in bonds.[11] However, entering into a receiver interest rate swap in US dollars will provide approximately the same exposure to interest rates but with no initial investment.[12] Hence, the size of the trade and the effective leverage must be limited by the institution itself, the counterparty in the transaction, or a regulator. Inevitably, the leverage will be significantly bigger than that in the previous case of buying bonds outright. Derivatives have repeatedly been shown to be capable of creating or catalysing major market disturbances.

As mentioned above, the OTC derivatives market is concentrated in the hands of a relatively small number of dealers. These dealers act as common counterparties to large numbers of end users of derivatives and actively trade with each other to manage their positions. Perversely, this used to be perceived by some as actually adding stability since prior to 2008 it was believed that none of these dealer counterparties would ever fail. Now this set-up is thought to create significant systemic risk: in financial terms, where the

---

[10] Hull (2015) discusses these and other examples in more detail.

[11] Although the use of a repurchase agreement ('repo') can resolve this and create leverage similar to the way in which a derivative does.

[12] Aside from initial margin requirements and bank capital requirements.

potential failure of one institution creates a domino effect and threatens the stability of the entire financial market. Systemic risk may not only be triggered by actual losses; just a heightened perception of losses can be problematic.

In 2002, the famous investor Warren Buffett described derivatives as 'financial weapons of mass destruction'. His criticisms were generally based on the following points:[13]

- their value depends on the creditworthiness of the counterparty to the contract (i.e. there is counterparty risk);
- whilst derivatives valuations should be symmetric with respect to the two parties involved, this may not be true in practice, with reported earnings on derivatives being overstated, and there are large incentives to overstate the valuation (this is referred to as 'mark-to-myth' by Buffett);
- they often have (rating) downgrade triggers requiring greater collateralisation, imposing at just the worst time an unexpected demand for cash on a company that may create liquidity problems that may even create more downgrades and lead to a death spiral; and
- they create a daisy-chain risk, thwarting prudent counterparty diversification since large receivables from interconnected counterparties build up over time.

These points were insightful with respect to events from 2007 onwards, and some of the issues captured by post-GFC regulation were foreseen by Buffett.

Criticisms of derivatives such as the above are generally aimed towards OTC derivatives, given the size and relative complexity of this market. Whereas the process by which a financial contract becomes exchange-traded can be thought of as a long journey where a reasonable trading volume, standardisation, and liquidity must first develop, OTC derivatives markets are traditionally faster moving. This has fairly obvious advantages and disadvantages, such as promoting innovation but allowing the development of large, relatively toxic risks. Prior to 2007, OTC derivatives were, to a large extent, opaque and unregulated.

Derivatives have, in many cases, become more standardised over the years through industry initiatives. Nevertheless, OTC derivative markets remain decentralised and more heterogeneous and are consequently less transparent than their exchange-traded equivalents. This leads to potentially challenging counterparty risk problems which have historically been managed through the use of various risk mitigants (discussed in later chapters).

2.2.9   The Lehman Brothers Bankruptcy

The complexity of derivatives clearing leads to potential challenges in the event that a derivatives counterparty defaults. Such a default may be directly related to or at least catalysed by losses on derivatives themselves. Defaults of major derivatives counterparties have been relatively rare, with the aforementioned cases of Barings Bank and Long-Term Capital Management being examples. Since derivatives do not trade in secondary markets and do not have an objectively-defined valuation, dealing with a major 'derivatives default' is complex.

---

[13] Berkshire Hathaway Annual Report (2002).

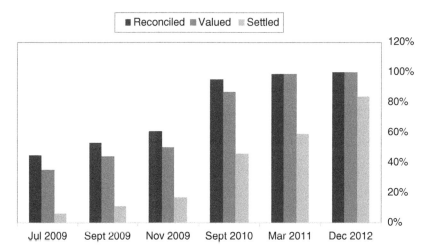

Figure 2.11 Management of derivative transactions by the Lehman Brothers estate. Source: Fleming and Sarkar (2014).

The bankruptcy of Lehman Brothers in 2008 provides a good example of the difficulty created by derivatives. Lehman had over 200 registered subsidiaries in 21 countries and around a million derivatives transactions. The insolvency laws of more than 80 jurisdictions were relevant.

In order to fully settle with a derivative counterparty, the following steps need to be taken:

- reconciliation of the universe of transactions;
- valuation of each underlying transaction; and
- agreement of a net settlement amount.

As shown in Figure 2.11, carrying out the above steps across many different counterparties and transactions has been a very time-consuming process, and the Lehman settlement of OTC derivatives has been a long and complex process lasting many years.

2.3 DERIVATIVE RISKS

An important concept is that financial risk is often not negated completely but is rather converted into different forms (for example, collateral can reduce counterparty risk but creates market, operational, legal, and liquidity risks). Sometimes these new forms of risk are more benign, but this is not guaranteed, and they may only appear so with significant hidden dangers. Furthermore, some financial risks can be seen as a combination of two or more underlying risks (for example, counterparty risk is primarily a combination of market and credit risk). Whilst this book is primarily about counterparty risk and related aspects such as funding, it is important to understand this in the context of other financial risks.

2.3.1   Market Risk

Market risk arises from the (short-term) movement of market variables. It can be a linear risk, arising from exposure to the movement of underlying quantities such as stock prices, interest rates, FX rates, commodity prices, or credit spreads. Alternatively, it may be a non-linear risk arising from the exposure to market volatility or basis risk, as might arise in a hedged position. Market risk has been the most studied financial risk over the past two decades, with quantitative risk management techniques widely applied in its measurement and management. This was catalysed by some serious market risk-related losses in the 1990s (e.g. Barings Bank), and the subsequent amendments to the Basel I capital accord in 1995 that allowed financial institutions to use proprietary mathematical models to compute their capital requirements for market risk. Indeed, market risk has mainly driven the development of the value-at-risk-type approaches to risk quantification (Section 2.6.1).

Market risk can be eliminated by entering into an offsetting contract. However, unless this is done with the same counterparty as the original position(s),[14] then counterparty risk will be generated. If the counterparties to offsetting contracts differ, and either counterparty fails, then the position is no longer neutral (for example, see Figure 2.12). Market risk, therefore, forms a component of counterparty risk. Additionally, the imbalance of collateral agreements and central clearing arrangements across the market creates a funding imbalance and leads to funding costs.

Banks generally aim to be market risk neutral so as to minimise accounting volatility and capital requirements and to comply with the regulation. The depiction in Figure 2.12 is, therefore, a useful simple example to refer to with respect to counterparty risk and related aspects.

2.3.2   Credit Risk

Credit risk is the risk that a debtor may be unable or unwilling to make a payment or fulfil contractual obligations. This is often known generically as 'default', although this term has slightly different meanings and impact depending on the jurisdiction involved. To quantify credit risk, default probability must be characterised fully throughout the lifetime of the exposure and so too must the recovery value (or equivalently the loss given default).

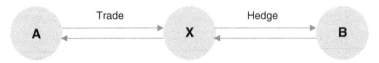

Figure 2.12   Illustration of the hedging of a transaction with counterparty A with one executed with counterparty B. Whilst the market risk may be hedged, party X is exposed to the failure of either counterparty A or party B.

---

[14] Or via a central counterparty, or later reduced via trade compression.

Although less severe than default, it may also be relevant to consider deterioration in credit quality, which will lead to a MTM loss (due to the increase in future default probability). Such deterioration can occur, for example, if a counterparty's credit rating is downgraded. In terms of counterparty risk, characterising the *term structure* of the counterparty's default probability is a key aspect. A greater chance of credit deterioration will lead to a higher future default probability.

The credit risk of debt instruments depends primarily on default probability and the associated recovery value since the exposure is deterministic (e.g. the par value of a bond or notional amount of a loan). However, for derivatives, the exposure is uncertain and driven by the underlying market risk of the transactions. Counterparty risk is therefore seen as a combination of credit and market risk.

2.3.3 Operational and Legal Risk

Operational risk arises from people, systems, and internal and external events. It includes human error (such as trade entry mistakes), failed processes (such as settlement of trades or posting collateral), model risk (inaccurate or inappropriately calibrated models), fraud (such as rogue traders), and legal risk (such as the inability to enforce legal agreements, for example those covering netting or collateral terms). Whilst some operational risk losses may be moderate and common (incorrectly booked trades, for example), the most significant losses are likely to be a result of highly improbable scenarios or even a 'perfect storm' combination of events. Operational risk is therefore extremely hard to quantify, although quantitative techniques are sometimes applied. Counterparty risk mitigation methods, such as collateralisation, inevitably give rise to operational risks, since collateral requires many operational processes in order for it to be passed from one party to another in a timely fashion.

Legal risk (often defined as a particular form of operational risk) is the risk of losses due to the assumed legal treatment not being upheld. This can be due to aspects such as incorrect documentation, counterparty fraud, mismanagement of contractual rights, or surprising decisions by courts – for example, if a party believes that they are owed a certain amount on derivatives transactions with a defaulted counterparty, but this subjective valuation is actually determined to be lower (a key component in much of the litigation with respect to the Lehman Brothers bankruptcy discussed in Section 2.2.9). Mitigating financial risk generally gives rise to legal risk due to the mitigants being challenged in some way at a point where they come into force. Defaults are particularly problematic from this point of view because they are relatively rare and so are not often tested, and they are also sensitive to the precise regional jurisdiction (sometimes courts in different countries have ruled differently on legal matters in this respect).

2.3.4 Liquidity Risk

Liquidity risk is normally characterised in two forms. Asset liquidity risk represents the risk that a transaction cannot be executed at market prices, perhaps due to the size of the position and/or relative illiquidity of the underlying market. This may lead to losses in the event that the asset is sold, with the extreme case of this being a 'fire sale'. Non-cash collateral held against derivatives exposures is prone to this type of liquidity risk since it needs to be liquidated in the event of a default. This is one of the reasons why derivatives collateral is often in cash or high-quality securities, and 'haircuts' are often required to act as a buffer against potential liquidation losses.

Funding liquidity risk refers to the inability to fund – in a timely manner – contractual outflows such as cash flows, margin, or collateral payments. In turn, this may force an early liquidation of assets and crystallisation of losses due to asset liquidity risk. Since such losses may lead to further funding issues, funding liquidity risk can manifest itself via a death spiral caused by the negative feedback between losses and cash requirements.

In general, reducing counterparty risk via margining or collateralisation comes at the cost of increased funding liquidity risk since such payments must be made in a timely fashion, usually involving tight timescales (e.g. daily). This is one of the reasons why some derivatives end users do not agree to contractual collateral-posting in bilateral OTC markets, as discussed in Section 2.2.4. Note that this is probably not related to the *amount* (since all corporations have significant assets, for example) but more the *type* of collateral. All parties have access to illiquid non-financial collateral such as property, machinery, and equipment. However, derivatives collateral commonly requires liquid financial securities that would only be held in significant quantities by financial institutions such as asset managers or pension funds. Indeed, some OTC derivatives collateral is cash only, which is restrictive even for some financial institutions.

Not surprisingly, banks find it easier to post and receive cash as derivatives collateral. Furthermore, recent bank regulation in relation to liquidity risk (see Chapter 6) penalises less liquid forms of collateral and incentivises banks to receive cash. Hence, generally, banks – due to market access – prefer to receive more liquid collateral, whilst clients prefer to post less liquid collateral.

2.3.5   Integration of Risk Types

A particular weakness of financial risk management over the years has been the lack of focus on the integration of different risk types. This is especially relevant since it has been well known for many years that crises tend to involve a combination of different financial risks. Given the difficulty in quantifying and managing financial risks in isolation, it is not surprising that limited effort is given to integrating their treatment. As noted above, counterparty risk itself is already a combination of two different risk types, market and credit. Furthermore, the mitigation of counterparty risk can create other types of risk, such as liquidity and operational risk. It is important not to lose sight of counterparty risk as an intersection of many types of financial risk, and to remember that mitigating counterparty risk creates even more financial risks.

2.3.6   Counterparty Risk

Counterparty risk is traditionally thought of as credit risk between derivatives counterparties. In the event of the non-performance (default) of a counterparty to a transaction (Figure 2.12), there is potential exposure via the market value of the transactions in question. In turn, this market value is not fixed and varies through time and is also to some extent a subjective quantity (for example, it may be derived from a valuation model). Counterparty risk, therefore, contains elements of credit risk (the default of the party) and market risk (the value of the transactions at the default time). The interaction between these components – that is to say, the relationship between the default probability and potential exposure – is often termed 'wrong-way risk'. Other aspects such as recovery value (or loss given default) and the impact of collateral are important considerations.

2.4   SYSTEMIC RISK OF DERIVATIVES

2.4.1   Overview

A major concern with respect to OTC derivatives is systemic risk, which generally refers to an uncontained crisis which may cause the failure of an entire financial system or market. Derivatives may increase systemic risk due to aspects such as their complexity, opacity, and overall volume. Derivatives may cause systemic risk episodes (for example, by a financial institution making large losses, as in the case of Barings Bank) or catalyse a crisis (as in the case of Lehman Brothers, discussed in Section 2.2.9).

Historically, the derivatives market focused on reducing the possibility of a systemic risk episode by minimising the risk of the default of a large, important market participant. However, there is clearly a balance between reduction of default risk and encouraging financial firms to grow and prosper. Derivatives markets have used processes such as netting and margining/collateralisation to minimise counterparty risk and, accordingly, systemic risk. However, such aspects create more complexity and may catalyse growth to a level that would never have otherwise been possible. Hence it can be argued that initiatives to reduce systemic risk may achieve precisely the opposite and create a source or catalyst (such as many large OTC derivative exposures supported by a complex web of collateralisation) for systemic risk.

It is useful to review some of the historical ways in which the derivatives market has sought to reduce systemic risk. Although some of these methods are somewhat obsolete, they provide a useful context for analysing more recent developments (such as central clearing).

2.4.2   Special Purpose Vehicles

A special purpose vehicle (SPV) or special purpose entity (SPE) is a legal entity (e.g. a company or limited partnership) created typically to isolate a firm from financial risk. SPVs have been used in the OTC derivatives market to isolate counterparty risk. A company will transfer assets to the SPV for management or use the SPV to finance a large project without putting the entire firm or a counterparty at risk. Jurisdictions may require that an SPV is not owned by the entity on whose behalf it is being set up.

SPVs aim essentially to change bankruptcy rules so that, if a derivative counterparty is insolvent, a client can still receive their full investment from the SPV prior to any other claims being paid out. SPVs are most commonly used in structured notes, where they use this mechanism to guarantee the counterparty risk on the principal of the note to a very high level (triple-A, typically), better than that of the issuer. The creditworthiness of the SPV is assessed by rating agencies, who look in detail at the mechanics and legal specifics before granting a rating.

SPVs aim to shift priorities so that, in a bankruptcy, certain parties can receive favourable treatment. Clearly such favourable treatment can only be achieved by imposing a less favourable environment on other parties. More generally, such a mechanism may then reduce risk in one area but increase it in another.

An SPV transforms counterparty risk into legal risk. The obvious legal risk is that of consolidation, which is the power of a bankruptcy court to combine the SPV assets with those of the originator. The basis of consolidation is that the SPV is essentially the same as the originator and this means that the isolation of the SPV becomes irrelevant. Consolidation may depend on many aspects, such as jurisdictions. US courts have a history of consolidation rulings, whereas UK courts have been less keen to do so, except in extreme cases such as fraud.

Another lesson is that legal documentation often evolves through experience, and the enforceability of the legal structure of SPVs was not tested for many years. When it was tested in the case of Lehman Brothers, there were problems (although this depended on the jurisdiction). Lehman essentially used SPVs to shield investors in complex and highly-rated transactions such as collateralised debt obligations (CDOs) from Lehman's own counterparty risk (in retrospect, a great idea).[15] The key clause in the documents is referred to as the 'flip' provision, which essentially meant that if Lehman were bankrupt, then the investors would be first in line as creditors. However, the US Bankruptcy Court ruled that the flip clauses were unenforceable,[16] putting them at loggerheads with the UK courts, which ruled that the flip clauses were enforceable. To add to the jurisdiction-specific question of whether a flip clause, and therefore an SPV, was a sound legal structure, many cases have been settled out of court.[17]

2.4.3 Derivatives Product Companies

Long before the GFC of 2007 onwards, whilst no major derivatives dealer had failed, the bilaterally-cleared dealer-dominated OTC market was perceived as being inherently more vulnerable to counterparty risk than the exchange-traded market. The derivatives product company (or corporation) evolved as a means for OTC derivative markets to mitigate counterparty risk (e.g. see Kroszner 1999). DPCs are generally triple-A-rated entities set up by one or more banks as a bankruptcy-remote subsidiary of a major dealer, which, unlike an SPV, is separately capitalised to obtain a triple-A credit rating.[18] The DPC structure provides external counterparties with a degree of protection against counterparty risk by protecting against the failure of the DPC parent. Examples of some of the first DPCs include Merrill Lynch Derivative Products, Salomon Swapco, Morgan Stanley Derivative Products, and Lehman Brothers Financial Products.

The ability of a sponsor to create their own high-credit-quality derivatives counterparty via a DPC was partially a result of improvements in risk management models and the development of credit rating agencies. DPCs usually maintained a triple-A rating by a combination of capital, margin, and activity restrictions. Each DPC had its own quantitative risk assessment model to quantify their current credit risk. This was benchmarked against that required for a triple-A rating. Most DPCs used a dynamic capital allocation

---

[15] For example, a bank may have issued a triple-A CDO which was problematic since the bank itself did not have a triple-A rating.

[16] Contiguglia, C. (2016). Flip clause ruling nets Lehman estate $3 billion. *Risk* (27 January). www.risk.net.

[17] Whittall, C. (2010). Lehman opts to settle over Dante flip-clause transactions. *Risk* (18 November). www.risk.net.

[18] Most DPCs derived their credit quality structurally via capital, but some simply did so from the sponsors' rating.

to keep within the triple-A credit risk requirements. The triple-A rating of a DPC typically depended on:

- *Minimising market risk.* In terms of market risk, DPCs attempted to be close to market risk neutral via trading offsetting contracts. Ideally, they would be on both sides of every trade, as these 'mirror trades' lead to an overall matched book. Normally the mirror trade exists with the DPC parent.
- *Support from a parent.* The DPC was supported by a parent, with the DPC being bankruptcy remote (like an SPV) with respect to the parent to achieve a better rating. If the parent were to default, then the DPC would either pass to another well-capitalised institution or be terminated, with trades settled at mid-market.
- *Credit risk management and operational guidelines.* Restrictions were also imposed on (external) counterparty credit quality and activities (position limits, margin, etc.). The management of counterparty risk was achieved by having daily MTM and margining/collateralisation.

Whilst being of very good credit quality, DPCs also aimed to give further security by defining an orderly workout process. A DPC defined what events would trigger its own failure (rating downgrade of parent company, for example) and how the resulting workout process would happen. The resulting 'pre-packaged bankruptcy' was therefore supposedly simpler (as well as less likely) than the standard bankruptcy of an OTC derivative counterparty. Broadly speaking, two bankruptcy approaches existed, namely a continuation and termination structure. In either case, a manager was responsible for managing and hedging existing positions (continuation structure) or terminating transactions (termination structure).

DPCs were created in the early stages of the OTC derivatives market to facilitate trading of long-dated derivatives by counterparties having less than triple-A credit quality. However, was such a triple-A entity of a double-A or worse bank really a better counterparty than the bank itself? The GFC essentially killed the already-declining world of DPCs. After their parent's decline and rescue, the Bear Stearns DPCs were wound down by J.P. Morgan, with clients compensated for novating trades. The voluntary filing for Chapter 11 bankruptcy protection by two Lehman Brothers DPCs, a strategic effort to protect the DPCs' assets, seems to link a DPC's fate inextricably with that of its parent. Not surprisingly, the perceived lack of autonomy of DPCs has led to a reaction from rating agencies, who have withdrawn ratings.[19]

As in the case of SPVs, it is clear that there are risks with DPCs. A DPC again illustrates that conversion of counterparty risk into other financial risks (in this case not only legal risk, as in the case of SPVs, but also market and operational risks) may be ineffective. The rating of the DPC should, therefore, be considered carefully in the context of that of the DPC parent. That said, some DPCs do still exist.[20]

2.4.4   Monolines and CDPCs

As described above, the creation of DPCs was largely driven by the need for high-quality counterparties when trading OTC derivatives. However, this need was taken to another

---

[19] Fitch withdraws Citi Swapco's ratings. *Business Wire* (10 June 2011). www.businesswire.com.
[20] Cameron, M. (2014). RBS sets up first Moody's-rated DPC in 14 years. *Risk* (14 May). www.risk.net.

level by the birth and exponential growth of the credit derivatives market from around 1998 onwards. A credit derivative, such as a CDS, represents an unusual challenge since its value is driven by credit spread changes, whilst its payoff is linked solely to one or more credit events (e.g. default). The so-called wrong-way risk in CDSs (for example, when buying protection on a bank from another bank) meant that the credit quality of the counterparty became even more important than it would have been for other OTC derivatives. Beyond single-name CDSs, senior tranches of structured finance CDOs had even more wrong-way risk and created an even stronger need for a 'default remote entity'.

Monoline insurance companies (and similar companies such as AIG)[21] were financial guarantee companies with strong credit ratings that were utilised to provide 'credit wraps', which are financial guarantees. Monolines began providing credit wraps for other areas, but then entered the single-name CDS and structured finance arena to achieve diversification and better returns. Credit derivative product companies (CDPCs) were an extension of the DPC concept discussed in Section 2.4.3 that had business models similar to those of monolines.

In order to achieve good ratings (e.g. triple-A), monolines/CDPCs had capital requirements driven by the possible losses on the structures they provided protection on. Capital requirements were also dynamically related to the portfolio of assets they wrapped, which is similar to the workings of the DPC structure. Monolines and CDPCs typically did not have to post collateral (at least in normal times) against a decline in the market value of their contracts (due to their excellent credit rating).

When the GFC developed through 2007, monolines experienced major problems due to the MTM-based valuation losses on the insurance they had sold. Concerns started to rise over their triple-A ratings and whether they had sufficient capital to justify them. Critically, monolines had clauses whereby a rating downgrade (even below triple-A, in some cases) could trigger the need to post collateral. For example, in November 2007, ACA Financial Guarantee Corporation stated that a loss of its single-A credit rating would trigger a need to post collateral, which they would not be able to meet. Although rating agencies did not react immediately, once they began to downgrade monoline credit ratings their decline was swift, as the need to post collateral essentially sent them into default. Figure 2.13 illustrates the extremely rapid decline of the monolines AMBAC and MBIA.

From November 2007 onwards, a number of monolines (for example, XL Financial Assurance Ltd, AMBAC Insurance Corporation, and MBIA Insurance Corporation) essentially failed. In 2008, AIG was bailed out by the US Government to the tune of approximately $182bn. The reason why AIG was bailed out and the monoline insurers were not was the size of AIG's exposures and the timing of their problems close to the Lehman Brothers bankruptcy and Fannie Mae/Freddie Mac problems.[22] These failures were due to a subtle combination of rating downgrades, required collateral posting, and MTM losses leading to a downward spiral. Many banks found themselves heavily exposed to the counterparty risk of monolines due to the massive increase in the value of the protection they had purchased. For example, as of June 2008, UBS was estimated to have

---

[21] For the purposes of this analysis, we will categorise monoline insurers and AIG as the same type of entity, which, based on their activities in the credit derivatives market, is fair.

[22] Whilst the monolines together had approximately the same amount of credit derivatives exposure as AIG, their failures were at least partially spaced out.

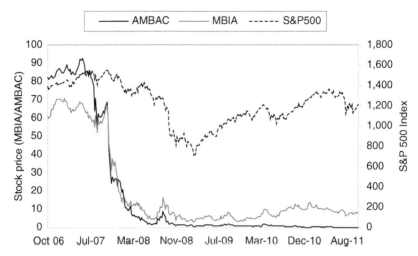

Figure 2.13   Share price (in dollars) of the monoline insurers AMBAC and MBIA (left axis) compared to the S&P 500 index (right axis).

$6.4bn at risk to monoline insurers, whilst the equivalent figures for Citigroup and Merrill Lynch were $4.8bn and $3bn respectively.[23]

The situation with AIG was more or less the same, from the joint result of a rating downgrade and AIG's positions moving against them rapidly, leading to the requirement to post large amounts of collateral. This essentially crystallised massive losses for AIG and led to potentially large losses for their counterparties if they were to fail (which is why AIG was bailed out).

CDPCs, like monolines, were highly leveraged and typically did not post collateral. They fared somewhat better during the GFC, but only for timing reasons. Many CDPCs were not fully operational until after the beginning of the GFC in July 2007; they therefore missed at least the first wave of losses suffered by any party selling credit protection (especially super senior).[24] Nevertheless, the fact that the CDPC business model is close to that of monolines has not been ignored. For example, in October 2008, Fitch Ratings withdrew ratings on the five CDPCs that it rated.[25]

2.5   THE GLOBAL FINANCIAL CRISIS AND CENTRAL CLEARING OF OTC DERIVATIVES

2.5.1   OTC Derivatives and the Crisis

The causes of the GFC were complex and related to a mixture of macro-economic events, government policies, the relaxation of lending standards by financial institutions,

---

[23] Van Duyn, A. and F. Guerrero (2008). Banks face $10bn monolines charges. *Financial Times* (10 June). www.ft.com.

[24] The widening in super senior (very-highly-rated tranches of structured credit securities) spreads was, on a relative basis, much greater than credit spreads in general during late 2007.

[25] Fitch withdraws CDPC ratings. *Business Wire* (17 October 2008). www.businesswire.com.

and the failure of regulation. However, a significant amount of blame was attributed to OTC derivatives. In 2008, the global derivatives market reached a total notional of over $700 trillion (Figure 2.4). Around nine-tenths of this amount was OTC, dwarfing exchange-traded products. In hindsight, this has been viewed as having created a dangerous mix of complexity, leverage, and interconnectedness. This is perhaps epitomised by the rapid growth of credit derivatives during the period leading up to the GFC.

Another problem was that banks trading the majority of these OTC derivatives were very large as a result of a period of mergers and takeovers. Examples include Citigroup (Citicorp, Travellers Group, Smith Barney, Salomon Brothers), JPMorgan Chase & Co. (Chase Manhattan, Bank One), and Royal Bank of Scotland (ABN AMRO). Furthermore, other large financial firms, notably AIG, had effectively become very exposed to the OTC derivatives market. This market was large, complex, opaque, and only lightly regulated.

Over the course of the GFC, governments had no easy way to deal with financial institutions whose failure could trigger the collapse of other firms through channels such as the OTC derivatives market. Central banks such as the Federal Reserve and Bank of England were forced to manage the systemic risk posed by such institutions on an ad hoc and trial-and-error basis. To prevent cascading defaults, viewed as possibly leading to a breakdown of the entire financial system, governments facilitated the sale of some large financial institutions (e.g. Bear Stearns, HBOS) and injected capital into many others (e.g. Bank of America, Royal Bank of Scotland, AIG). Whilst such actions were undesirable, the aftermath of the bankruptcy of Lehman Brothers provided ample evidence as to the potential impact of not rescuing stricken large financial firms.

The problems governments faced were not just that large financial institutions were 'too big to fail' but also that they were 'too interconnected to fail'. This interconnectedness was largely blamed on the OTC derivatives market. Regulators, therefore, believed that the GFC events demonstrated the obvious need to develop a clear regulatory framework to efficiently manage the systemic – or daisy-chain – risk posed by this market and its participants.

2.5.2   OTC Derivatives Clearing

From the late 1990s, several major CCPs began to provide clearing and settlement services for OTC derivatives and other non-exchange-traded products (such as repurchase agreements or 'repos'). This was to help market participants reduce counterparty risk and benefit from the netting benefits and fungibility that central clearing creates. These OTC transactions are still negotiated privately and off-exchange, but are then novated into a CCP on a post-trade basis.

In 1999, LCH.Clearnet (now LCH Ltd) set up two OTC CCPs to clear and settle repos (RepoClear) and plain vanilla interest rate swaps (SwapClear). Commercial interest in OTC-cleared derivatives grew substantially in the energy derivatives market following the bankruptcy of Enron in late 2001. Intercontinental Exchange (ICE) responded to this demand by offering cleared OTC energy derivatives solutions beginning in 2002. ICE now offers OTC clearing for CDS contracts.

Although CCP clearing and settlement of OTC derivatives did develop in the years prior to the GFC, this was confined to certain products and markets. This suggests that there are both positives and negatives associated with using CCPs and, in some market situations, the positives may not outweigh the negatives.

As discussed in Section 2.2.2, clearing is the process that occurs after the execution of a trade in which a CCP may step in between counterparties to guarantee performance. The main function of a CCP is, therefore, to interpose itself directly or indirectly between counterparties to assume their rights and obligations by acting as the buyer to every seller and vice versa. This means that the original counterparty to a trade no longer represents a direct risk, as the CCP to all intents and purposes becomes the new counterparty. CCPs essentially reallocate default losses via a variety of methods including netting, margining, and loss mutualisation. Obviously, the intention is that the overall process will reduce counterparty and systemic risks.

CCPs provide a number of benefits. One is that they allow netting of all trades executed through them. In a bilateral market, an institution being long a contract with counterparty A and short the same contract with counterparty B has counterparty risk. However, if both contracts are centrally cleared, then the netted position has no risk. CCPs also manage margin requirements from their members to reduce the risk associated with the movement in the value of their underlying portfolios. All of these aspects can arguably be achieved in bilateral markets through mechanisms such as portfolio compression (Section 6.2.5) and increased collateralisation (Chapter 7).

In a centrally-cleared world, the failure of a counterparty, even one as large and interconnected as Lehman Brothers, is supposedly less dramatic. This is because the CCP absorbs the 'domino effect' by acting as a sort of financial shock absorber. In the event of default of one of its members, a CCP will aim to terminate swiftly all financial relations with that counterparty without suffering any losses. From the point of view of surviving members, the CCP guarantees the performance of their transactions. This will normally be achieved not by closing out transactions at their market value but rather by replacing the defaulted counterparty with one of the other clearing members for each transaction. This is typically achieved via the CCP auctioning the defaulted members' positions amongst the other members, which provides continuity for surviving members.

However, CCPs do introduce features beyond those seen in bilateral markets. One is loss mutualisation: one counterparty's losses are dispersed across all clearing members, rather than being transmitted directly to a smaller number of counterparties with potential adverse consequences. Moreover, CCPs can facilitate orderly close-outs by auctioning the defaulter's contractual obligations with multilateral netting, reducing the total positions that need to be replaced, which may minimise price impacts and market volatility. CCPs can also facilitate the orderly transfer of client positions from financially-distressed members.

The general role of a CCP is:

- to sets certain standards and rules for its clearing members (and to some extent their clients);
- to take responsibility for closing out all the positions of a defaulting clearing member;
- to support the above, to maintain financial resources to cover losses in the event of a clearing member default:
  - o cash variation margin to closely track market movements;
  - o initial margin to cover the worst-case liquidation or close-out costs above the variation margin; and
  - o a default fund to mutualise losses in the event of a severe default; and

- to have a documented plan for the very extreme situation when all their financial resources (initial margin and the default fund)[26] are depleted – for example:
  - additional calls to the default fund;
  - variation margin haircutting;[27] and
  - selective tear-up of positions.[28]

It is important to note that some banks and most end users of OTC derivatives (e.g. pension funds) will access CCPs through a clearing member and will not become members themselves. This will be due to the operational and liquidity requirements related to becoming a clearing member. In particular, participating in regular 'fire drills' and bidding in a CCP auction are the main reasons why an institution is unable to be or decides against being a clearing member at a given CCP.

2.5.3   CCPs in the Global Financial Crisis

It is important to emphasise that even before the GFC, some OTC derivatives were being centrally cleared (most notably, interest rate swaps). Despite OTC derivatives being at the centre of the financial chaos during the GFC, one area of this market did seem to be functioning well. Even the Lehman Brothers bankruptcy did not cause huge problems for CCPs such as LCH.Clearnet ($9trn notional Lehman portfolio) and Depository Trust and Clearing Corporation (DTCC; $500m notional Lehman portfolio). CCPs acted quickly (within hours) to suspend insolvent Lehman entities from trading and therefore prevented the build-up of more risk. On the other hand, solvent Lehman entities were also identified and continued trading. The CCPs also swiftly facilitated the transfer of solvent client accounts to other clearing members. In general, the response by CCPs was seen as providing stability and safety to Lehman counterparties and clients in cleared markets. In the CCP world, this mitigated potential knock-on or systemic effects due to the bankruptcy of a major OTC derivatives player.

The best and most commonly cited example of the benefits of CCPs for OTC derivatives is LCH.Clearnet's London-based SwapClear service, which provided interest rate swap central clearing for 20 large banks including Lehman. The total SwapClear portfolio exceeded $100trn notional across 14 currencies and represented close to half the global interest rate swap market at the time.[29] LCH.Clearnet had previously experienced defaults, such as Drexel Burnham Lambert (1990) and Barings (1995). However, the Lehman failure became the biggest default in CCP history.

At SwapClear, Lehman Brothers Special Financing Inc. (LBSF) was a big player, with a $9trn OTC portfolio comprising tens of thousands of trades, which was much larger than the exchange-traded portfolios of Lehman. On 15 September 2008, LBSF did not transfer margin payments and was therefore declared in default within hours. The goal now was for LCH.Clearnet to close out the large OTC portfolio (66,390 trades) as quickly as possible without creating large losses or knock-on effects. To help achieve this, LCH.Clearnet had a substantial amount (around $2bn) of initial margin from Lehman that was held precisely for such a situation.

---

[26] Note that only the defaulter's initial margin can be used.
[27] See Elliott (2013) or Gregory (2014) for more details.
[28] See previous footnote.
[29] LCH.Clearnet Annual Report (2007). www.lch.com.

The events at LCH.Clearnet's SwapClear clearing service in the aftermath of the Lehman default were as follows:

- As required by CCP rules, clearing members were obliged (on a rotational basis) to offer representatives to assist SwapClear in dealing with the defaulted member. LCH.Clearnet formed a default management group with senior traders from a total of six banks in order to assist in the close-out process.
- In the first couple of days, hedges were applied to neutralise the macro-level market risk in Lehman's portfolio. The risk positions were reviewed daily, and further hedges were executed in response to the changing portfolio and underlying market conditions.
- The majority of Lehman client positions were transferred to other solvent clearing members within the first week.
- Auctions were arranged to sell Lehman portfolios (together with their macro-hedges) to the remaining SwapClear members. Under the CCP's rules, members had to be involved in the auction. These auctions were arranged in each of the five relevant currencies between Wednesday 24 September and Friday 3 October. All auctions were deemed successful.

The events were hailed as a success by LCH.Clearnet[30] and required only around a third of the initial margin, with the rest being returned to the Lehman administrators. It should be noted that the Lehman close-out was not without its problems. In some cases, a client's margins were returned to the administrator and frozen for many months (this was partly related to poor record-keeping by Lehman and partly due to UK law, which did not have requirements regarding customer segregation that existed in the US). Indeed, even getting access to Lehman's offices was not immediately possible (Norman 2011).

Despite the general success of SwapClear with respect to the bankruptcy of Lehman, there were some negative implications involving other CCPs. The Chicago Mercantile Exchange (CME) cleared a combination of interest rate, equity, agriculture, energy, and FX positions for Lehman and had to rely on gains from three of these asset classes to offset losses on the two others (Pirrong 2014). Furthermore, there are suggestions that the three winning bidders in the CME auction for Lehman positions made a combined profit of $1.2bn on taking over the portfolios (see later discussion in Section 10.2.2).

Also regarding the Lehman bankruptcy, in December 2008, Hong Kong Exchanges and Clearing Ltd (HKEx) disclosed a loss of HK$157m in relation to the portfolio of Lehman Brothers Securities Asia (LBSA) being closed out by the Hong Kong Securities Clearing Company (HKSCC). As a result of this, HKSCC needed to draw on resources including their HK$394m default fund and call for additional default fund contributions from their most active members. As explained later, this means that the other CCP members suffered default losses.

2.5.4   The Clearing Mandate

Prior to the events of the GFC, there was no obvious requirement by regulators for central clearing of OTC derivatives. However, from the rescue of Bear Stearns onwards, calls

---

[30] LCH.Clearnet (2008). $9 trillion Lehman OTC interest rate swap default successfully resolved. Press release (8 October). www.lch.com.

for central clearing started to emerge from regulators globally. In the US, market participants and regulators agreed on an agenda for bringing about further improvements in the OTC derivatives market infrastructure, one of the points being 'developing a central counterparty for credit default swaps that, with a robust risk management regime can help reduce systemic risk'.[31] A statement from the European Commission described a CCP for CDSs as a 'pressing need'.[32] The Lehman events of September 2008 gave further weight to such viewpoints. The rationale behind the clearing requirement seemed to be that systemic risk in the GFC was exacerbated by counterparty risk concerns that could be mitigated by CCPs.

CCPs were being seen as a kind of OTC derivatives market 'shock absorber' in the event of the default of one or more market participants, as they would allow such an event to be managed with the least disruption. A key problem in such situations was the need to replace large numbers of defaulted positions within a short time in an illiquid market. Such a requirement can clearly lead to large price moves together with increased volatilities and dependencies. In turn, the price shocks arising from the rush to replace defaulted trades can impose substantial losses that can threaten the solvency of other market participants. CCPs became widely seen as the solution to such problems by providing greater transparency and reducing risk via their margining practices. CCPs could establish and enforce the 'rules' for the OTC derivatives market.

In 2009, the G20 leaders agreed in Pittsburgh to require:

- all standardised OTC derivatives to be traded on exchanges or electronic platforms;
- mandatory central clearing of standardised OTC derivatives;
- the reporting of OTC derivatives to trade repositories; and
- higher capital requirements for non-centrally cleared OTC derivatives.

Whilst much of the initial discussion and research on risks associated with OTC derivatives was focused on credit derivatives (via credit default swaps), the clearing mandate had now been broadened to cover the whole OTC derivatives market. This was perhaps not surprising since credit derivatives made up less than one-tenth of the overall notional OTC derivatives market.

Not all OTC derivatives can be centrally cleared as clearing requires a reasonable level of standardisation and liquidity. The clearing mandate is responsible for increasing the number of cleared OTC derivatives, though (Figure 2.14).

2.5.5   Bilateral Margin Requirements

Whilst clearing is mandatory, it can be avoided by trading contracts that are not sufficiently standardised to be cleared, for example. In order to give a strong incentive for market participants to move as many OTC derivatives to central clearing as possible, regulators introduced mandatory margin (collateral) rules for derivatives that would

---

[31] Federal Reserve Bank of New York (2008). Statement regarding June 9 meeting on over-the-counter derivatives (9 June). www.newyorkfed.org.

[32] European Commission (2008). Statement of Commissioner McGreevy on reviewing derivatives markets before the end of the year (17 October). ec.europa.eu.

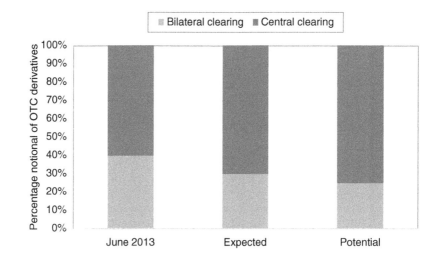

Figure 2.14   Bilateral and centrally-cleared OTC derivatives. Source: Eurex (2014).

remain bilateral. Loosely speaking, this regulation can be seen as mimicking the margining requirements under central clearing (in reality, these rules may sometimes be more punitive, as discussed in Section 4.4.2) and thus reducing any incentive for avoiding central clearing.

Following the previous 2009 agreements described in Section 2.5.4, in November 2011 in Cannes the G20 leaders agreed to add a mandate for margin requirements for non-centrally-cleared derivatives, stating:

> We call on the Basel Committee on Banking Supervision (BCBS), the International Organization for Securities Commission (IOSCO) together with other relevant organizations to develop for consultation standards on margining for non-centrally cleared OTC derivatives by June 2012, and on the FSB [Financial Stability Board] to continue to report on progress towards meeting our commitments on OTC derivatives.

The BCBS and IOSCO accordingly produced a consultative paper (BCBS-IOSCO 2012) on the subject of bilateral margin requirements.

The Working Group on Margin Requirements (WGMR) was formed in October 2011 to develop the framework for margins. The WGMR is run jointly by the IOSCO, the BCBS, the Committee on Payment and Settlement Systems (CPSS), and the Committee on the Global Financial System (CGFS).

2.5.6   CCPs in Context

The aforementioned concepts of SPVs, DPCs, monolines, and CDPCs have all been shown to lead to certain issues. Indeed, it could be argued that as risk mitigation methods they all have fundamental flaws, which explains why there is little evidence of them in today's OTC derivatives market. At the same time, there is a clearing mandate that encourages the use of central counterparties as much as possible for clearing OTC derivatives.

A CCP aims to reduce systemic risk by having the means to manage periodic failures (of their clearing members) in a controlled manner. If there is a default of a key market participant, the CCP guarantees all the contracts that this counterparty has executed through them as a clearing member. This will mitigate concerns faced by institutions and prevent any extreme actions by those institutions that could worsen the crisis. Any unexpected losses[33] caused by the failure of one or more counterparties would be shared ('loss mutualisation') amongst all members of the CCP (just as insurance losses are essentially shared by all policyholders), rather than being concentrated within a smaller number of institutions that may be heavily exposed to the failing counterparty. Loss mutualisation is a key component as it mitigates systemic risk and prevents a domino effect.

The CCP concept is different to those discussed above but shares a key characteristic, which is that the reduction of counterparty risk relies on the CCP itself being of exceptional credit quality, since a CCP failure would almost certainly create (or catalyse) a systemic risk episode. It is important to ask to what extent the flaws of SPVs, DPCs, monolines, and CDPCs may also exist within a CCP, which does share certain characteristics of these structures.

Regarding SPVs and DPCs, two obvious questions emerge. The first is whether shifting priorities from one party to another really helps the system as a whole. CCPs will effectively give priority to OTC derivative counterparties and in doing so may reduce the risk in this market. However, this will make other parties (e.g. bondholders) worse off and may, therefore, increase risks in other markets (see Sections 6.4.4 and 10.3.5 for further detail). Second, a critical reliance on a precise sound legal framework creates exposure to any flaws in such a framework. This is especially important as in a large bankruptcy there will likely be parties who stand to make significant gains by challenging the priority of payments (as in the aforementioned SPV flip clause cases). Furthermore, the cross-border activities of CCPs also expose them to bankruptcy regimes and regulatory frameworks in multiple regions.

CCPs also share some similarities with monolines and CDPCs as strong credit quality entities set up to take and manage counterparty risk. However, two very important differences must be emphasised. First, CCPs have a 'matched book' and do not take any market risk (except when members default). This is a critical difference since monolines and CDPCs had very large, mostly one-way exposure to credit markets. Second, the related point is that CCPs require margining (variation and initial margin in all situations), whereas monolines and CDPCs would essentially post only limited collateral (variation margin) and would often only do this in extreme situations (e.g. in the event of their ratings being downgraded). Many monolines and CDPCs posted no margin or collateral at all at the inception of trades. Nevertheless, CCPs are similar to these entities in essentially insuring against systemic risk. However, the term 'systemic risk insurance' is a misnomer, as systemic risk cannot obviously be diversified.

Although CCPs do not suffer structurally from the flaws that caused the failure of monoline insurers or the bailout of AIG, there are clearly lessons to be learnt with respect to the centralisation of counterparty risk in a single large and potentially too-big-to-fail entity. One specific example is the destabilising relationship created by increases in margin requirements. Monolines and AIG failed due to a significant increase in collateral

---

[33] Meaning those above a certain level that will be discussed later.

requirements during a crisis period. CCPs could conceivably create the same dynamic, which will be discussed later (Chapter 8).

Recent history has also highlighted some potential problems with central clearing, such as the default of a clearing member at the Nasdaq Nordic commodity exchange in September 2018 (see Section 10.1.3).

2.6 DERIVATIVES RISK MODELLING

2.6.1   Value-at-risk

Financial risk management of derivatives has changed over the last two decades. One significant aspect has been the implementation of more quantitative approaches, the most significant probably being value-at-risk (VAR). Initially designed as a metric for market risk, VAR has subsequently been used across many financial areas as a means for efficiently summarising risk via a single quantity. For example, the concept of potential future exposure (PFE), used to assess counterparty risk, is equivalent to the definition of VAR.

A VAR number has a simple and intuitive explanation as the worst loss over a target horizon to a certain specified confidence level. The VAR at the $\alpha\%$ confidence level gives a value that will be exceeded with *no more* than a $(1 - \alpha)\%$ probability. An example of the computation of VAR is shown in Figure 2.15. The VAR at the 99% confidence level is -125 (i.e. a loss) since the probability that this will be exceeded is no more than 1% (it is actually 0.92% due to the discrete nature of the distribution).[34] To find the VAR, one finds the *minimum* value that will be exceeded with the specified probability.

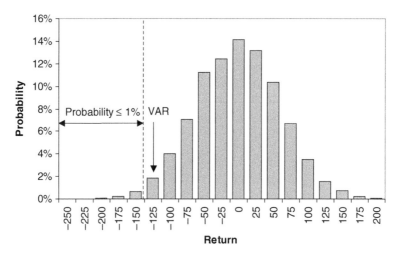

Figure 2.15   Illustration of the value-at-risk (VAR) concept at the 99% confidence level. The VAR is 125 since the chance of a loss greater than this amount is no more than 1%.

---

[34] For a continuous distribution, VAR is simply a quantile (a quantile gives a value on a probability distribution where a given fraction of the probability falls below that level).

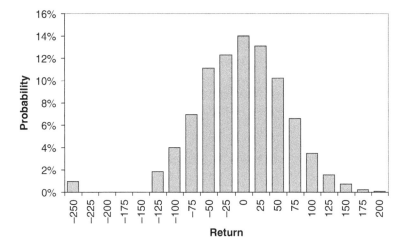

Figure 2.16   Distribution with the same VAR as the distribution in Figure 2.15.

VAR is a very useful way in which to summarise the risk of an entire distribution in a single number that can be easily understood. It also makes no assumption as to the nature of the distribution itself, such as that it is a Gaussian.[35] It is, however, open to problems of misinterpretation since VAR says nothing at all about what lies beyond the defined threshold (1%, in the above example). To illustrate this, Figure 2.16 shows a slightly different distribution with the same VAR. In this case, the probability of losing 250 is 1%, and hence the 99% VAR is indeed 125 (since there is zero probability of other losses in between). We can see that changing the loss of 250 does not change the VAR since it is only the probability of this loss that is relevant. Hence, VAR does not give an indication of the possible loss outside the confidence level chosen. Over-reliance on VAR numbers can be counterproductive as it may lead to false confidence.

Another problem with VAR is that it is not a *coherent* risk measure (Artzner et al. 1999), which basically means that in certain (possibly rare) situations, it can exhibit non-intuitive properties. The most obvious of these is that VAR may not behave in a sub-additive fashion. Sub-additivity requires a combination of two portfolios to have no more risk than the sum of their individual risks (due to diversification).

A slight modification of the VAR metric is commonly known as expected shortfall (ES). Its definition is the average loss equal to or above the level defined by VAR. Equivalently, it is the average loss knowing that the loss is at least equal to the VAR. ES does not have quite as intuitive an explanation as VAR, but it has more desirable properties such as not ignoring completely the impact of large losses (the ES in Figure 2.16 is indeed greater than that in Figure 2.15) and is a coherent risk measure. For these reasons, the Fundamental Review of the Trading Book (BCBS 2013e) requires that banks use ES rather than VAR for measuring their market risk.

---

[35] Certain implementations of a VAR model (notably the so-called variance-covariance approach that forms the basis of the SIMM approach discussed in Section 9.4.4) may make normal distribution assumptions, but these are done for reasons of simplification and the VAR idea itself does not require them.

The most common implementation of VAR and ES approaches is using historical simulation. This takes a period (usually several years) of historical data containing risk factor behaviour across the entire portfolio in question. It then resimulates over many intervals within this period how the current portfolio would behave when subjected to the same historical evolution. For example, if four years of data were used, then it would be possible to compute around 1,000 different scenarios of daily movements for the portfolio. If a longer time horizon is of interest, then quite commonly the one-day result is simply extended using the 'square root of time rule'. For example, in market risk VAR models used by banks, regulators allow the 10-day VAR to be defined as $\sqrt{10} = 3.14$ multiplied by the one-day VAR. VAR models can also be 'backtested' as a means to empirically check their predictive performance. Backtesting involves performing an *ex post* comparison of actual outcomes with those predicted by the model. VAR lends itself well to backtesting since a 99% VAR number should be exceeded once every 100 observations.

It is important to note that the use of historical simulation and backtesting are relatively straightforward to apply for VAR and ES due to the short time horizon (10 days) involved. For counterparty risk assessment (and xVA in general) much longer time horizons are involved, and quantification is therefore much more of a challenge.

2.6.2   Models

The use of metrics such as VAR relies on quantitative models in order to derive the distribution of returns from which such metrics can be calculated. The use of such models facilitates combining many complex market characteristics such as volatility and dependence into one or more simple numbers that can represent risk. Models can compare different trades and quantify which is better, at least according to certain pre-defined metrics. All of these things can be done in minutes or even seconds to allow institutions to make fast decisions in rapidly-moving financial markets.

However, the financial markets have a somewhat love/hate relationship with mathematical models. In good times, models tend to be regarded as invaluable, facilitating the growth in complex derivatives products and dynamic approaches to risk management adopted by many large financial institutions. The danger is that models tend to be viewed either as 'good' or 'bad' depending on the underlying market conditions, whereas in reality models can be good or bad depending on how they are used. An excellent description of the intricate relationship between models and financial markets can be found in MacKenzie (2006).

The modelling of counterparty risk is an inevitable requirement for financial institutions and regulators. This can be extremely useful, and measures such as PFE, the counterparty risk analogue of VAR, are important components of counterparty risk management. However, like VAR, the quantitative modelling of counterparty risk is complex and prone to misinterpretation and misuse. Furthermore, unlike VAR, counterparty risk involves looking years into the future rather than just a few days, which creates further complexity that is not to be underestimated. Not surprisingly, regulatory requirements over backtesting of counterparty risk models have been introduced to assess performance.[36] In addition, a greater emphasis has been placed on stress testing of counterparty

---

[36] Under the Basel III regulations.

risk, to highlight risks in excess of those defined by models. Methods to calculate xVA are, in general, under continuous scrutiny.

2.6.3   Correlation and Dependency

Probably the most difficult aspect in understanding and quantifying financial risk is that of dependency between different financial variables. It is well known that historically-estimated correlations may not be a good representation of future behaviour. This is especially true in a more volatile market environment, or crisis, where correlations have a tendency to become very large. Furthermore, the very notion of correlation (as used in financial markets) may be heavily restrictive in terms of its specification of dependency.

Counterparty risk takes difficulties with correlation to another level, for example, compared to traditional VAR models. Firstly, correlations are inherently unstable and can change significantly over time. This is important for counterparty risk assessment, which must be made over many years, compared to market risk VAR, which is measured over just a single day. Secondly, correlation is not the only way to represent dependency, and other statistical measures are possible. Particularly in the case of wrong-way risk (Section 17.6), the treatment of co-dependencies via measures other than correlation is important. In general, xVA calculations require a careful assessment of the co-dependencies between credit risk, market risk, funding, and collateral.

3

Counterparty Risk and Beyond

3.1 COUNTERPARTY RISK

Counterparty credit risk (often known just as counterparty risk) is the risk that the entity with whom one has entered into a financial contract (the counterparty to the contract) will fail to fulfil their side of the contractual agreement (e.g. they default).

Counterparty risk is primarily associated with the following situation:

- over-the-counter (OTC) derivatives;
- bilaterally cleared; and
- uncollateralised.

However, it is also important to consider the following cases, where some form of margining or collateralisation is always present:[1]

- exchange-traded derivatives (which are always centrally cleared and typically margined on a daily basis);
- securities financing transaction (e.g. repos), which are margined on a daily basis and sometimes centrally cleared;
- centrally-cleared OTC derivatives, which are margined on a daily basis; and
- collateralised OTC derivatives, where margining is reflected via some bespoke collateral agreement.

The above cases have less counterparty risk due to a combination of collateralisation, central clearing, and maturity dates (for example, exchange-traded derivatives and securities financing transactions are typically short-dated). Whilst some of the above cases may be thought to have relatively minor counterparty risks, this may relate to a large underlying position. The obvious example of this is centrally-cleared OTC derivatives which are generally believed to represent a small counterparty risk, but where the notional position of a bank to a central counterparty could be extremely large.

3.1.1 Counterparty Risk Versus Lending Risk

Traditionally, credit risk can generally be thought of as a lending risk. One party owes an amount to another party and may fail to pay some or all of this due to insolvency. This can apply to loans, bonds, mortgages, credit cards, and so on. Lending risk is characterised by two key aspects:

- The notional amount at risk at any time during the lending period is usually known with a degree of certainty. Market variables such as interest rates will typically create

---

[1] Margin is generally associated with exchange-traded derivatives, and collateral with OTC derivatives. Margin generally represents a requirement to settle or collateralise, whilst collateral refers to the actual cash or securities used to do this. The terms margin and collateral are often used interchangeably in the context of derivatives and related transactions.

only moderate uncertainty over the amount owed. For example, in buying a bond, the amount at risk for the life of the bond is close to par. A repayment mortgage will amortise over time (the notional drops due to the repayments), but one can predict with good accuracy the outstanding balance at some future date. A loan or credit card may have a certain maximum usage facility, which may reasonably be assumed fully drawn for the purpose of credit risk.[2]

- Only one party takes lending risk. A bondholder takes considerable credit risk, but an issuer of a bond does not face a loss if the buyer of the bond defaults.[3]

With counterparty risk, as with all credit risk, the cause of a loss is the obligor being unable or unwilling to meet contractual obligations. However, two aspects differentiate contracts with counterparty risk from traditional credit risk:

- The value of the contract in the future is uncertain, in most cases significantly so. The value of a derivative at a potential default date will be the net value of all future cash flows required under that contract. This future value can be positive or negative and is typically highly uncertain (as seen from today).
- Since the value of the contract can be positive or negative, counterparty risk is typically *bilateral*. In other words, in a derivatives transaction, each counterparty has risk to the other. Note that this counterparty risk may be asymmetric (if the transaction has an asymmetric profile,[4] or if the counterparties have significantly different credit quality and/or margining/collateralisation terms).[5]

3.1.2 Settlement, Pre-settlement, and Margin Period of Risk

A derivatives portfolio contains a number of settlements equal to multiples of the total number of transactions (for example, a swap contract will have a number of settlement dates as cashflows are exchanged periodically). There may also be a contractual exchange of collateral which is partly related to settlements because a cash flow payment may trigger a margin requirement. Historically, this led to the definition of two components covering the risk of default of the counterparty *prior to expiration* (settlement) of the contract and the risk of a counterparty default *during* the settlement process.

- *Pre-settlement risk*. This is the risk that a counterparty will default prior to the final settlement of the transaction. This is what counterparty risk usually refers to, and it is rarely referred to as pre-settlement risk nowadays (which somewhat understates its importance).
- *Settlement risk*. This arises at settlement times (and is often especially relevant at the maturity date) due to timing differences between when each party performs its obligations under the contract.

The difference between pre-settlement and settlement risk is illustrated in Figure 3.1.

---

[2] On the basis that an individual unable to pay is likely to be close to any limit.

[3] This is not precisely true in the case of bilateral counterparty risk (DVA), discussed in Section 5.2.2.

[4] For example, an option position with an upfront premium creates counterparty risk for only the option buyer.

[5] For example, one party may be required to post more collateral than the other.

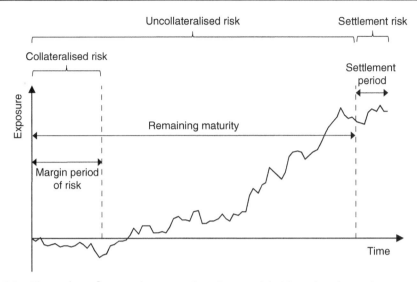

Figure 3.1   Illustration of pre-settlement and settlement risk. Note that the settlement period is normally short (e.g. hours) but can be much longer in some cases. Also shown is the margin period of risk (MPoR), which is discussed below.

Unlike counterparty risk, settlement risk is characterised by a very large exposure, potentially 100% of the notional of the transaction. Whilst settlement risk gives rise to much larger exposures, default prior to the expiration of the contract is substantially more likely than default at the settlement date. However, settlement risk can be more complex when there is a substantial delivery period (for example, a commodity contract settled in cash against receiving a physical commodity over a specified time period).

Example

Suppose an institution enters into a forward foreign exchange (FX) contract to exchange €1m for $1.1m at a specified date in the future. The settlement risk exposes the institution to a substantial loss of $1.1m, which could arise if €1m was paid, but the $1.1m was not received. However, this only occurs for a single day on expiry of the FX forward. This type of cross-currency settlement risk is sometimes called Herstatt risk (see box below). Pre-settlement risk exposes the institution to just the difference in market value between the dollar and euro payments. If the FX rate moved from 1.1 to 1.15, then this would translate into a loss of about $45,000, but this could occur at any time during the life of the contract.

Whilst all derivatives technically have both settlement and pre-settlement risk, the balance between the two will be different depending on the contract. Spot contracts have mainly settlement risk, whilst long-dated OTC derivatives have mainly pre-settlement (counterparty) risk. Furthermore, various types of netting (see Chapter 6) provide mitigation against settlement and pre-settlement risks. From now on, the term 'counterparty risk' will be used instead of 'pre-settlement risk'.

Bankhaus Herstatt

A well-known example of settlement risk is the failure of a small German bank, Bankhaus Herstatt. On 26 June 1974, the firm defaulted, but only after the close of the German interbank payments system (3:30 pm local time). Some of Bank Herstatt's counterparties had paid Deutschmarks to the bank during the day, believing they would receive US dollars later the same day in New York. However, it was only 10:30 am in New York when Bank Herstatt's banking business was terminated, and consequently all outgoing US dollar payments from their account were suspended, leaving counterparties exposed to losses.

Settlement risk typically occurs for only a small amount of time (often just days or even hours). It is therefore clearly more relevant for shorter maturity transactions such as those that are exchange-traded. Indeed, spot transactions essentially have only settlement risk. In long-dated OTC derivatives, the length of time for the settlement is very short compared to the remaining maturity, although it is important to remember that the exposure for settlement risk can be significantly higher, as illustrated in the FX example above.

To measure settlement risk to a reasonable degree of accuracy would mean considering the contractual payment dates, the time zones involved, and the time it takes for the bank to perform its reconciliations across accounts in different currencies. Any failed trades should also continue to count against settlement exposure until the trade actually settles. Institutions typically set separate settlement risk limits and measure exposure against this limit rather than including settlement risk in the assessment of counterparty risk. It may be possible to mitigate settlement risk, for example, by insisting on receiving cash before transferring securities.

Settlement risk is a major consideration in FX markets, where the settlement of a contract involves payment of one currency against receiving the other. Most FX now goes through continuous linked settlement (CLS),[6] and most securities settle using delivery versus payment (DVP),[7] but there are exceptions such as cross-currency swaps, and settlement risk should be recognised in such cases.

Another important and related component is the margin period of risk (MPoR). This refers to the risk horizon when collateralised/margined (due to the imperfect nature of this process). The standard assumption used for this value in collateralised bilateral OTC derivatives is 10 business days. Centrally-cleared OTC derivatives (which are subject to daily margining) have a shorter value of five days (see Section 9.1.2). This reduces counterparty risk because the MPoR will typically be significantly shorter than the remaining maturity of the portfolio. However, collateralised/margined portfolios still have material counterparty risk. Furthermore, there is an important interaction between settlement risk and the counterparty risk on a collateralised portfolio since each (net) settlement will change the underlying value of the portfolio. If this valuation change is positive, then the portfolio value increases, which will be uncollateralised until collateral

---

[6] A multicurrency cash settlement system, see www.cls-group.com.
[7] Delivery versus payment where payment is made at the moment of delivery, aiming to minimise settlement risk in securities transactions.

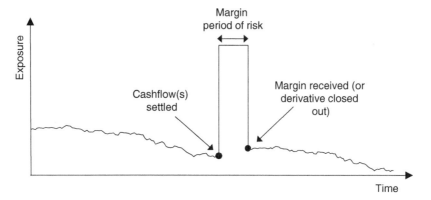

Figure 3.2 Illustration of the spike in exposure created by a cash flow payment and subsequent delay before collateral is received (or the derivative is closed out in the event of a default).

can be received. This, therefore, can intuitively create a 'collateral spike' for the duration of the MPoR (Figure 3.2). If the cash flow and collateral payments were netted, then this would not be a problem. Whilst this netting is common in exchange-traded markets, it does not occur in OTC derivatives markets, where historically the collateral has not needed to be paid in cash.

Note that, by convention, the above risk is typically characterised as counterparty risk even though it has features which are similar to settlement risk.

Certain features of margining/collateralisation can also create settlement risk. For example, central counterparties typically require margin to be posted in cash in each relevant currency. This creates currency silos across a multicurrency portfolio, which can lead to more settlement risk and associated liquidity problems, as parties have to post and receive large cash payments in different currencies.

3.1.3   Mitigating Counterparty Risk

There are a number of ways of mitigating counterparty risk. Some are relatively simple contractual risk mitigants, whilst other methods are more complex and costly to implement. Obviously no risk mitigant is perfect, and there will always be some residual counterparty risk, however small. Furthermore, quantifying this residual risk may be more complex and subjective than the counterparty risk itself. In addition to the residual counterparty risk, it is important to keep in mind that risk mitigants do not remove counterparty risk per se, but instead convert it into other forms of financial risk, some obvious examples being:

- *Netting*. Netting allows components such as cash flows, values, and margin or collateral payments to be offset across a given portfolio. There are a number of forms of netting, such as cash flow netting, close-out netting, and multilateral trade compression, which may be applied bilaterally or multilaterally, as explained in more detail in Section 6.2.4. However, netting creates *legal risk* in cases where a netting agreement cannot be legally enforced in a particular jurisdiction.
- *Collateralisation*. Collateral or margin agreements (Section 7.3) specify the contractual posting of cash or securities against mark-to-market (MTM) losses. Margining terms

are similar but are usually associated with a cash settlement or posting. There is still a residual *market risk* since exposure exists in the time taken to receive the relevant collateral amount (the MPoR defined in Section 3.1.2). Furthermore, taking collateral to minimise counterparty risk creates *operational risk* due to the necessary logistics involved, and leads to *liquidity risk* since the posting of collateral needs to be funded, and collateral itself may have price and FX volatility. Aspects such as rehypothecation (reuse) and segregation of collateral are important considerations here. Taking certain types of collateral – even cash – can create *wrong-way risk* (Section 17.6.6).

- *Other contractual clauses.* Other features, such as resets or additional termination events (Section 7.1.1), aim to reset MTM values periodically or terminate transactions early. Like margining/collateral, these can create *operational* and *liquidity risks*.
- *Hedging.* Hedging counterparty risk with instruments such as credit default swaps (CDSs) aims to protect against potential default events and adverse credit spread movements. Hedging creates *operational risk* and additional *market risk* through the MTM volatility of the hedging instruments. Hedging may lead to *systemic risk* through feedback effects (see the statement from the Bank of England in Section 13.3.6).
- *Central counterparties (CCPs).* CCPs guarantee the performance of transactions cleared through them and aim to be financially safe themselves through the margin and other financial resources they require from their members. CCPs act as intermediaries to centralise counterparty risk between market participants. Whilst offering advantages such as risk reduction and operational efficiencies, they require the centralisation of counterparty risk, significant collateralisation, and mutualisation of losses. They can therefore potentially create *operational* and *liquidity risks*, and also *systemic risk* since the failure of a CCP could amount to a significant systemic disturbance. This is discussed in more detail in Chapter 8.

Mitigation of counterparty risk is a double-edged sword. On the one hand, it may reduce existing counterparty risks and contribute to improving financial market stability. On the other hand, it may lead to a reduction in constraints such as capital requirements and credit limits and therefore lead to a growth in volumes. Indeed, without risk mitigants such as netting and collateralisation, the OTC derivatives market would never have developed to its current size. Furthermore, risk mitigation should really be thought of as risk transfer since new risks and underlying costs are generated.

3.1.4   Product Type

As already mentioned, most counterparty risk arises from bilateral OTC derivatives. In terms of asset classes, Figure 2.5 in Chapter 2 gave a breakdown of the size of this market in notional terms but commented that this could be potentially misleading in terms of defining the magnitude of counterparty risk faced in each asset class.

The above can be seen when looking at the averaged response from banks on their counterparty risk (measured by credit value adjustment, CVA) broken down by asset class in Figure 3.3. Whilst interest rate products make up a significant proportion of the counterparty risk in the market, the important (and sometimes more subtle) contributions from other products must not be underestimated. In particular, FX products have a reasonably large contribution (due to the large volatility of FX rates and potentially long maturity dates, especially of cross-currency swaps) as do CDSs (potentially due to wrong-way risk).

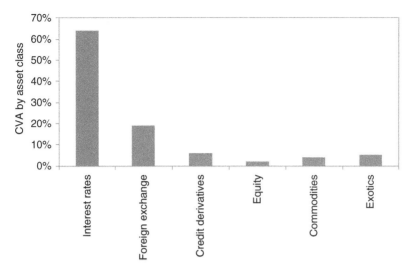

Figure 3.3 Split of CVA by asset class (average across all respondents). Source: Deloitte/Solum CVA Survey (2013).

Note that the above breakdown contains counterparty risk from OTC derivatives that are collateralised (bilaterally, at least) since, for example, all credit derivatives will be transacted under collateral agreements. It is also important to note that, whilst large global banks have exposure to all asset classes, smaller banks may have more limited exposure (for example, mainly interest rate and some FX products). End users may also have limited exposure: for example, a corporation may use only interest rate and cross-currency swaps.

Most banks do not give a breakdown of their counterparty risk, but one exception is shown in Figure 3.4, which gives a useful decomposition (of CVA) by rating and sector (i.e. counterparty type). The counterparty risk faced with high-quality credits is generally small due to the low default probability. Financial institutions also represent a relatively small part due to relatively good credit quality and the fact that most of these transactions are probably collateralised. The majority of the counterparty risk is faced with

	2016 £m	2015 £m
Ratings		
AAA	4	37
AA to AA+	22	66
A to AA-	52	49
BBB- to A-	388	293
Non-investment grade and unrated	152	329
	618	774
Counterparty		
Banks	22	18
Other financial institutions	70	126
Corporate	337	470
Government	189	160
	618	774

Figure 3.4 Example of CVA breakdown by rating and sector. Source: Royal Bank of Scotland Annual Report (2016). www.rbs.com.

respect to medium credit ratings (BBB to A-) and corporates and governments, most of which is likely to be uncollateralised. The reasonably small exposure (given their high default probability) to non-investment-grade counterparties is probably due to a partial reluctance to trade with such entities.

Over the years, the quantification of counterparty risk has developed, with one aspect being the coverage of different situations. For example, in the past a bank may have focused only on relatively poor credits and uncollateralised counterparties, ignoring the remainder for materiality reasons. This is clearly not the case in Figure 3.4. However, some aspects may receive attention over the coming years, one obvious example being the counterparty risk faced with CCPs.

3.1.5   Credit Limits

To control and quantify counterparty risk, it is first important to recognise that it varies substantially depending on aspects such as the transaction and counterparty in question. In addition, it is important to give the correct benefit arising from the many risk mitigants (such as netting and margining/collateral) that may be relevant. Control of counterparty risk has traditionally been the purpose of credit limits.

However, credit limits only limit counterparty risk and, whilst this is clearly the first line of defence, there is also a need to correctly quantify and ensure that an institution is being correctly compensated for the counterparty risk they take. This is achieved via CVA, which has been used increasingly in recent years as a means of assigning an economic value to the counterparty risk and/or complying with accounting requirements. In some cases, this CVA is actively managed, such as through hedging.

Broadly speaking, there should be three levels to assessing the counterparty risk of a transaction:

- *Trade level.* Incorporating all characteristics of the trade and associated risk factors such as the precise cash flows. This defines the counterparty risk of a trade at a 'stand-alone' level.
- *Counterparty level.* Incorporating the impact of risk mitigants such as netting and margining/collateral for each counterparty (or netting set) individually. This defines the incremental impact a transaction has with respect to the existing portfolio.
- *Portfolio level.* Consideration of the risk to all counterparties, knowing that only a small fraction may default in a given time period. This defines the impact a trade has on the total counterparty risk faced by an institution.

Credit limits (or credit lines) are a traditional tool to control the amount of counterparty risk taken over time. Counterparty risk can be diversified by limiting exposure to any given counterparty, sector, or region. This limit would naturally consider elements such as the underlying credit risk. By trading across a greater number of counterparties, sectors, and regions, an institution is less exposed. Such diversification across counterparties is not always practical due to the specialisation and relationships within an institution. In such cases, exposures can become excessively large and should be, if possible, mitigated by other means.

The basic idea of credit limits is illustrated in Figure 3.5. The idea is to characterise the potential future exposure (PFE) over time and compare this with a pre-determined limit.

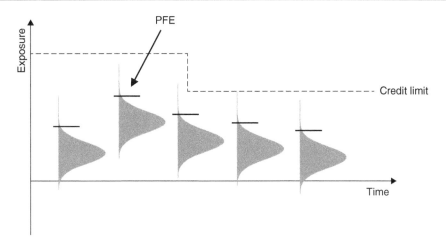

Figure 3.5   Illustration of the use of PFE and credit limits in the control of counterparty risk.

The PFE represents a bad scenario at a certain statistical confidence level. The credit limit will be set subjectively according to the risk appetite of the institution in question. It may be time-dependent, reflecting the fact that exposures at different times in the future may be considered differently.

Note that for simple lending transactions such as loans, the definition of PFE is relatively trivial since it will be approximately equal to the size of the transaction. However, for more complex transactions such as derivatives, the definition is much more complicated and will require quantitative modelling. PFE will be described in more detail in Chapter 11 but, broadly speaking, the following aspects must be accounted for in its quantification:

- the transaction(s) in question;
- the relevant portfolio being considered (typically credit limits are defined by the counterparty, but sector and regional views may also be used);
- the current relevant market variables (e.g. interest rates and volatilities); and
- contractual risk mitigants (for example, netting, collateral, and hedges).

Credit limits will often be reduced over time (as shown), effectively favouring short-term over long-term PFE. This is due to the chance that credit quality may deteriorate over a long horizon. Indeed, empirical and market-implied default probabilities for good-quality (investment-grade) institutions tend to increase over time, which suggests the reduction of a credit limit. Note that credit limits should be conditional on non-default before the point in question because the possibility of an earlier default is captured via a limit at a previous time.

Credit limits are typically used to assess trading activity on a dynamic basis. Any transaction activity (new trades, unwinding or restructuring trades) that would breach a credit limit at any point in the future is likely to be refused unless specific approval is given. From this point of view, it is the incremental change in the PFE that is relevant. The incremental PFE is the value after the new transaction is added minus the value before. Due to portfolio effects, this is smaller than the standalone PFE for the transaction in question. Indeed, for risk-reducing trades, the overall impact can be to reduce the portfolio PFE.

Note that limits could be breached for two reasons: due to either a new transaction or market movements. The former case is easily dealt with by refusing transactions that would cause a limit breach (unless special approval is given via an escalation). The latter is more problematic, and banks sometimes have concepts of hard and soft limits; the latter may be breached through market movements (but not new transactions), whereas a breach of the former would require remedial action (e.g. transactions must be unwound or restructured, or hedges must be sourced). For example, a credit limit of $10m ('soft limit') might restrict trades that cause an increase in PFE above this value and may allow the PFE to move up to $15m ('hard limit') as a result of changes in market conditions. When close to a limit, only risk-reducing transactions may be approved. Due to the directional nature of end users' activity in OTC derivatives, this is often a challenge.[8]

Credit limits allow a consolidated view of exposure with each counterparty and represent the first step in portfolio counterparty risk management. However, they are rather binary in nature, which is problematic. Sometimes a given limit can be fully utilised, preventing transactions that may be more profitable. Banks have sometimes built measures to penalise transactions (requiring them to be more profitable) close to (but not breaching) a limit, but these are generally quite ad hoc.

3.1.6   Credit Value Adjustment

Traditional counterparty risk management via credit limits works in a relatively binary fashion: the incremental risk of a new transaction is of primary importance, and its relative profitability is a secondary consideration. This can lead to the incorrect incentives being given: for example, a transaction with low (high) profitability may be accepted (rejected) because the existing credit limit utilisation is small (large).

CVA represents the actual price of counterparty risk and is, therefore, a step forward since, from an approval point of view, the question becomes whether or not it is profitable once the counterparty risk component has been 'priced in'. Put another way, CVA directly incorporates the credit risk of the counterparty and so defines a minimum revenue that should be achieved. In some sense, with credit limits, the CVA is either zero (transaction accepted) or infinity (transaction rejected).

Like PFE, an important aspect of CVA is that it is a portfolio-level – specifically counterparty-level – calculation.[9] CVA should be calculated incrementally by considering the increase (or decrease) in exposure capturing netting effects due to any existing trades with the counterparty. This means that CVA will be additive across different counterparties and does not distinguish between counterparty portfolios that are highly concentrated. Such concentration could arise from a very large exposure with a single counterparty, or exposure across two or more highly-correlated counterparties (e.g. in the same region or sector).

Traditional credit limits and CVA have their own weaknesses. CVA focuses on evaluating counterparty risk at the trade level (incorporating all specific features of the trade) and counterparty level (incorporating risk mitigants). In contrast, credit limits essentially act at the portfolio level by limiting exposures to avoid concentrations. When viewed like this, we see that CVA and credit limits act in a complementary fashion, as

---

[8] Woolner, A. (2015). Consumers exceeding bank credit lines slows oil hedging. *Risk* (2 April). www.risk.net.
[9] Strictly speaking, it is a netting-set-level calculation as there can possibly be more than one netting agreement with a given counterparty. This is discussed in more detail in Section 6.3.

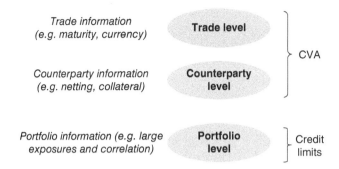

Figure 3.6 High-level illustration of the complementary use of CVA and credit limits to manage counterparty risk.

illustrated in Figure 3.6. Indeed, CVA encourages minimising the number of trading counterparties since this maximises the benefits of netting, whilst credit limits encourage maximising this number to encourage smaller exposures and diversification. Hence, CVA and credit limits are typically used together as complementary ways to quantify and manage counterparty risk. In practice, this means that the credit risk department in a bank will approve a trade (or not) and then (if approved) the 'xVA desk' will price in the CVA component before transacting.

3.1.7   What Does CVA Represent?

The price of a financial product can generally be defined in one of two ways:

- The price represents an expected value of future cash flows, incorporating some adjustment for the risk being taken (the risk premium). We will call this the *actuarial* price.
- The price is the cost of an associated hedging strategy. This is the *risk-neutral* (or market-implied) price.

The latter is a well-known concept for banks in pricing derivatives, whereas the former is more common in other areas, most obviously insurance.

On one hand, CVA is associated mainly with derivatives for which risk-neutral pricing is standard, and there are ways in which CVA can be hedged. On the other hand, credit risk in banks is often assessed in more of an actuarial framework, due to being often illiquid and unhedgeable. Historically, the practices of banks have reflected this dichotomy: in the past, it was common to see the actuarial approach being followed, where CVA was interpreted as a statistical estimate of the expected future losses from counterparty risk and held as a reserve (analogous to a loan loss reserve in a bank). More recently, CVA is typically defined in a risk-neutral fashion, interpreted as the market cost of counterparty risk and closely associated with hedging strategies. The more sophisticated and larger banks were much quicker to adopt this risk-neutral approach.

In recent years, the risk-neutral approach to CVA has become dominant. The drivers for this have been:

- *Market practice.* Larger banks, in particular those in the US, were early adopters of the risk-neutral CVA approach. This would then be seen by other banks via aspects such as prices for 'novations' (where one party contractually replaces another in a transaction).

In practical terms, this could mean that a bank stepping into another bank's shoes on a given client portfolio would price the CVA differently, which in turn would lead the original bank to question whether their CVA calculation was market standard.

- *Accounting.* FAS 157 and IFRS 13 accounting standards (Section 5.3.3) clearly reference an exit price concept and imply the use of risk-neutral default probabilities, and this has increasingly been the interpretation of auditors. Note that US and Canadian banks reporting under FAS 157 were early adopters of risk-neutral CVA at a time when many European banks (then under IAS 39 accounting standards) still used actuarial CVA. The introduction of IFRS 13 (outside the US) from 2013 has tended to create convergence here. However, the exit price concept also generally requires an institution's own credit spread to be recognised via debt value adjustment (DVA), which is generally seen as problematic (Section 17.3).
- *Basel III.* Capital rules (Section 13.3) clearly define CVA with respect to credit spreads and therefore advocate the risk-neutral approach. However, these do not permit DVA, which creates a conflict with accounting standards.
- *Regulators opinions.* Local regulators have also commented on the need to use credit spreads when calculating CVA. A typical statement is: 'it is not acceptable to have CCR [counterparty credit risk] models based on expected loss or historical calculations ignoring risk premia' and 'market-implied credit risk premia can be observed from active markets like CDSs and bonds'.[10]

The result of the above is that it is now increasingly uncommon to see historical default probabilities used in the calculation of CVA (although other historical parameters are still more commonly used). For example, even as far back as 2012, a survey by Ernst and Young commented:

Two banks use a blended approach, combining market and historical data, and four banks use primarily historical data, which is generally consistent with their Basel II reporting. Given the requirements of IFRS 13, these six banks are preparing for a potential move to a more market-driven methodology for CVA, recording a DVA on derivative liabilities, and amending their hedging policies in the near future.[11]

This does raise the question of how to define risk-neutral default probabilities when no traded credit spread is observed. This is discussed in Section 12.3.

3.1.8 Hedging Counterparty Risk and the CVA Desk

The growth of the credit derivatives market facilitated the potential hedging of counterparty credit risk. A single-name CDS is essentially an insurance contract against a certain notional value of credit risk which pays out in the event of a pre-defined credit event. One very straightforward use of hedging (Figure 3.7) could be to buy CDS protection

---

[10] Translated from FMA (2012).
[11] www.ey.com.

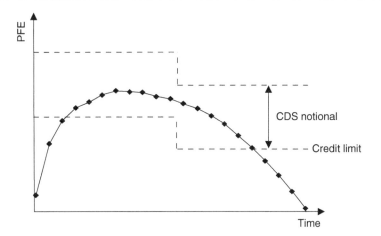

Figure 3.7   Illustration of CDS hedging in order to increase a credit limit.

on the counterparty in question so as to increase the credit limit.[12] This is often known as a 'jump-to-default' hedge. More tailored credit derivative products such as contingent CDSs (CCDSs) and risk participation agreements (RPAs) have been designed to hedge counterparty risk even more directly. CCDSs and RPAs are essentially CDSs but with the notional of protection indexed to the exposure on a contractually-specified derivative (or even portfolio of derivatives). They allow the synthetic transfer of counterparty risk linked to a specific trade and counterparty to a third party. However, whilst CCDSs and RPAs are used to share the risk of new transactions, the underlying market has never developed any significant liquidity. Even the single-name CDS market is relatively illiquid and covers only a relatively small population of reference entities.

More practically, hedging of CVA is done on a dynamic basis with reference to credit spreads (often via CDS indices, which are more liquid than single-name CDSs) and other dynamic market variables (interest rates, FX rates, etc.). This will be discussed in more detail in Section 21.2.

As CVA has become a more central concept from an accounting and regulatory point of view, and as hedging has become more practical via credit derivatives, the concept of a CVA desk in banks has emerged. Indeed, in the largest banks, this can be traced back to as early as the late 1990s. The general role of a CVA desk in a bank (Figure 3.8) is to price and potentially own the underlying counterparty risk from the originating trading or sales desk, although the precise set-up differs across different banks, especially between larger and smaller ones. Not surprisingly, this has broadened in recent years to consider other aspects such as collateral, funding, and capital, and so the term 'xVA desk' or 'central desk' has become more common.

---

[12] There are some technical factors that should be considered here, such as the possibility of wrong-way risk (Section 17.6).

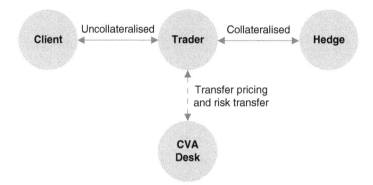

Figure 3.8   Illustration of the role of a CVA desk (xVA desk) in a bank.

3.2   BEYOND COUNTERPARTY RISK

3.2.1   Overview

In the aftermath of the global financial crisis (GFC), the perceived problems with derivatives and counterparty risk led to a significantly-increased interest in CVA, especially from regulators. At around the same time, accounting changes made CVA more of a key component of the valuation.

However, related to these changes, other aspects started to gain considerable interest, some of which are related to funding or capital costs and all of which are linked to the existence of counterparty risk:

- *Funding*. Institutions face funding costs because they need to borrow to finance their activities. Funding costs are directly related to credit and counterparty risk because the greater the risk on the balance sheet, the greater the cost of funding it will be.
- *Collateral*. Collateral posted contractually against products such as derivatives to mitigate counterparty risk may also create a cost or benefit depending on its type (e.g. currency, type of security).
- *Initial margin*. Some situations, such as central clearing, require the posting of initial margin in order to mitigate counterparty risk. This initial margin represents over-collateralisation and represents a funding cost.
- *Regulatory capital*. Banks face regulatory capital requirements for counterparty risk and CVA.

3.2.2   Economic Costs of a Derivative

We can generalise the discussion on counterparty risk to consider all relevant economic costs associated with a contract/portfolio, such as a derivative, as illustrated in Figure 3.9. In order to do this, we need to use the definition of a threshold that defines the point at which margin/collateral would be posted, and this is explained in more detail in Section 7.3.4. The explanation of the different aspects is as follows:

- *Positive value*. When the portfolio has a positive value and is 'in the money' (ITM) (above the centre line), then the uncollateralised component gives rise to counterparty

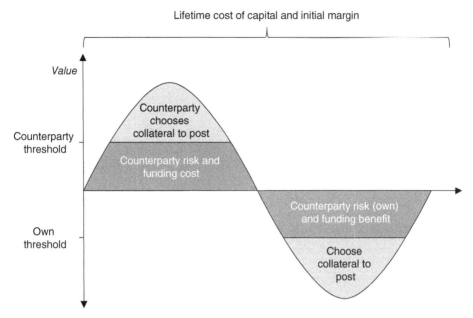

Figure 3.9   Illustration of the lifetime cost of a portfolio in relation to xVA components. Note that this representation is general, and in reality margin/collateral thresholds are often zero or infinity.

risk and funding costs. If some or all of the value is collateralised, the counterparty may be able to choose what type of collateral to post (with the range specified contractually).

- *Negative value.* When the portfolio has a negative value or is 'out of the money' (OTM), then there is counterparty risk from the party's own default and a potential funding benefit to the extent that their counterparty is uncollateralised. If margin is required, the institution may be able to choose the type of collateral to post.
- *Overall.* Whether or not the portfolio has a positive or negative value, there are costs from funding the capital that must be held against the transaction and any initial margin that needs to be posted.

Note that there are some inherent symmetries related to the symmetry in derivatives valuation (i.e. the fact that one party's positive value should be the other's negative value). An obvious example is that one party's CVA cost is the other's DVA benefit (Section 17.3). However, these symmetries are not always present: for example, capital and initial margin costs are always present and do not provide an equal and opposite benefit to the counterparties.

3.2.3   xVA Terms

Valuation adjustments (VAs) are given the generic term xVA (or XVA). An xVA term quantifies the cost (or benefit) of a component such as counterparty risk, collateral, funding, or capital over the lifetime of the transaction or portfolio in question (Figure 3.10). By convention, a cost will be associated with a positive value on the *y*-axis and benefits will, therefore, be represented by negative values. In order to compute xVA, it is necessary

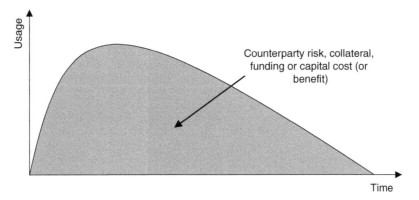

Figure 3.10   Generic illustration of an xVA term. Note that some xVA terms represent benefits and not costs and would appear on the negative *y*-axis.

to integrate the profile shown against the relevant cost (or benefit) component, such as a credit spread, collateral, funding, or cost of capital curve.

Valuation may start from a base case which may only be relevant in certain specific cases (this will be discussed in more detail in Chapter 16). Valuation adjustments correct for components ignored in the base valuation (Figure 3.11) will be defined as follows:

- *CVA and DVA.* Defines the bilateral valuation of counterparty risk. DVA represents counterparty risk from the point of view of a party's own default. These components will be discussed in Chapter 17.
- *FVA (funding value adjustment).* Defines the cost and benefit arising from the funding of the transaction. It is divided into two terms: funding cost adjustment (FCA) and funding benefit adjustment (FBA). This will be discussed in Chapter 18.

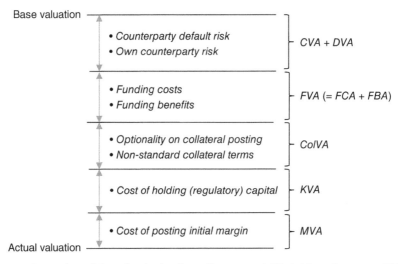

Figure 3.11   Illustration of the role of valuation adjustments (xVAs). Note that some xVAs can be benefits.

- *ColVA (collateral value adjustment)*. Defines the costs and benefits from embedded optionality in the collateral agreement (such as being able to choose the currency or type of collateral to post) and any other non-standard collateral terms (compared to the idealised starting point). This will be discussed in Chapter 16.
- *KVA (capital value adjustment)*. Defines the cost of holding capital (typically regulatory) over the lifetime of the transaction. This will be discussed in Chapter 19.
- *MVA (margin value adjustment)*. Defines the cost of posting initial margin over the lifetime of the transaction. This will be discussed in Chapter 20.

Note that the above definitions are relatively standard but are not the only ones used in the industry. Note also that, even given the definitions, there are some elements that could fit into one VA or another. For example, since collateral posting must be funded, there are components that could be defined as either FVA or ColVA. This book will aim to use the most common and logical definitions.

It is also important to note that there are potential overlaps between the above terms; for example, between DVA and FBA, where own-default risk is widely seen as a funding benefit. These overlaps are important and will be discussed where relevant.

3.3   COMPONENTS OF xVA

3.3.1   Overview

Counterparty risk represents a combination of market risk, which defines the exposure, and credit risk, which defines the counterparty credit quality. More generally, any valuation adjustment term is made up of a market component (directly or indirectly related to the base portfolio value) and a cost (or benefit) component (defining the cost of bearing the market component). This is outlined in Table 3.1.

The important components that define counterparty risk and related metrics will be outlined below.

3.3.2   Valuation and Mark-to-Market

A definition of valuation such as MTM is the starting point for the analysis of counterparty risk and related aspects. The current value does not constitute an *immediate* liability by one party to the other, but rather is the present value of all the payments an institution is expecting to receive, less those it is obliged to make. It is, therefore, the core

Table 3.1   Components of xVA terms.

	Valuation adjustment term	Market component	Cost component
Counterparty Risk	CVA/DVA	Credit exposure	Default probability
Funding	FVA	Valuation	Funding cost
	MVA	Initial margin amount	
Collateral	ColVA	Collateral amount	Collateral cost
Capital	KVA	Capital amount	Capital cost

component of valuation adjustments. With respect to the definitions in Table 3.1, the valuation defines either directly or indirectly:

- *Credit exposure*. The valuation with respect to a particular counterparty defines the net value of all positions (if positive) and is therefore directly related to what could potentially be lost today in the event of a default. This is typically defined as credit exposure.
- *Funding position*. The valuation defines the size of the asset (if positive) or liability (if negative) position and, therefore, is linked to the funding position.
- *Initial margin*. In the event that initial margin is posted, this is typically calculated based on the *variability* of the valuation.
- *Collateral amount*. Since margin is primarily determined based on the current value, there is clearly a direct link to the cost of collateral.
- *Capital*. Methodologies for defining capital are always based on the underlying valuation.

The payments that define the current valuation may be scheduled to occur many years in the future and may have values that are strongly dependent on market variables. The valuation will be positive or negative depending on the transaction(s) in question, the magnitude of remaining payments, and current market rates. Hence, all of the above components are relevant from both a current (spot) and future point of view. Essentially, characterising valuation adjustments requires answering the following two questions:

- What is the current valuation?
- What is the valuation in the future (since, for example, the counterparty can default at any point in the future)?

The first point is clearly simpler to define and needs to be done irrespective of the wish to consider valuation adjustments. The second point is naturally far more complex to answer than the first (except in some simple cases).

Valuation adjustments may also depend on risk mitigants. Where the nature of the risk mitigant is fixed through time, this may be relatively straightforward. However, when the risk mitigant itself changes over time, this is more complex. For example, margin is generally required based on a defined valuation which will change over time. It is therefore necessary to be able to calculate the future value of required margin as well as the more well-defined current margin amount. The future value of collateral securities used to fulfil margin requirements should also be quantified.

Note that there is also a potential recursive problem with the above. The valuation is an input parameter for calculating the valuation *adjustments*, and yet the correct valuation should include valuation adjustments. One solution to this is to consider a base value (without valuation adjustments) and add valuation adjustments linearly as a function of this base value. This is often used in practice, but it is only an approximation as the real problem is non-linear and recursive.

3.3.3   Replacement Cost and Credit Exposure

Default-related contractual features of transactions, such as close-out netting and termination features, refer to *replacement costs*. The base valuation is clearly closely related to replacement cost, which defines the entry point into an equivalent transaction(s) with another counterparty. However, the actual situation is more complicated. To replace a transaction, one must consider costs such as bid-offer spreads, which may be significant for highly-illiquid securities (note that even a standard and liquid contract might be non-standard and illiquid at the default time). Portfolios can be also be replaced one-for-one or macro-hedged.

Not surprisingly, documentation of derivatives in a default scenario has tended generally to aim to reference replacement costs, defined as objectively as possible, as opposed to a basic valuation. This implies that real additional costs in replacing or rehedging a portfolio can be included in the determination of the amount owed (between a surviving and defaulting party) at the default time. This will be discussed in more detail in Section 6.3.4. However, replacement costs, by their nature, may include valuation adjustment terms, such as CVA, leading to the recursive problem mentioned above.

Other aspects are important in this regard, such as the ability to net transactions in default and the possibility to adjust positions with collateral amounts. Both of these aspects are subject to legal agreements and their potential interpretation in a court of law.

Credit exposure (or simply exposure) defines the loss in the event of a counterparty defaulting. Exposure is characterised by the fact that a positive value of a portfolio corresponds to a claim on a defaulted counterparty, whereas in the event of negative value, an institution is still obliged to honour its contractual payments (at least to the extent that they exceed those of the defaulted counterparty). This means that if an institution is owed money and its counterparty defaults, then it will incur a loss, whilst in the reverse situation it cannot gain from the default by being somehow released from its liability.[13]

Exposure is relevant only if the counterparty defaults and hence the quantification of exposure is conditional on counterparty default. Having said this, it is often market practice to consider exposure independently of any default event and so assume implicitly no wrong-way risk. Such an assumption is reasonable for most products subject to counterparty risk, although the reader should keep the idea of conditional exposure in mind. We will then address wrong-way risk, which defines the relationship between exposure and counterparty default, in more detail in Section 17.6. Note that credit exposure is specific to default (and therefore CVA), and other points of view (most obviously funding-related) need not be conditional on counterparty default.

3.3.4   Default Probability, Credit Migration, and Credit Spreads

When assessing counterparty risk, one must consider the credit quality of a counterparty over the entire lifetime of the relevant transactions. Such time horizons can be extremely long. Ultimately, there are two aspects to consider:

- What is the probability of the counterparty defaulting over a certain time horizon?[14]
- What is the probability of the counterparty suffering a decline in credit quality over a certain time horizon (for example, a ratings downgrade and/or credit spread widening)?

---

[13] Except in some special and non-standard cases.

[14] The term 'defaulting' is generally used to refer to any 'credit event' that could impact the counterparty.

Credit migrations or discrete changes in credit quality, such as due to rating changes, are crucial since they influence the term structure of default probability. They should also be considered since they may cause issues even when a counterparty is not yet in default. Suppose the probability of default of a counterparty between the current time and a future date of (say) one year is known. It is also important to consider what the same annual default rate might be in four years; in other words, the probability of default between four and five years in the future. There are three important aspects to consider:

- Future default probability,[15] as defined above, will have a tendency to decrease due to the chance that the default may occur before the start of the period in question. The probability of a counterparty defaulting between 20 and 21 years in the future may be very small, not because they are very creditworthy (potentially quite the reverse), but rather because they are unlikely to survive for 20 years!
- A counterparty with an expectation of deterioration in credit quality will have an increased probability of default over time (although at some point the above phenomenon will reverse this).[16]
- A counterparty with an expectation of improvement in credit quality will have a decreasing probability of default over time, which will be accelerated by the first point above.

There is a well-known empirical mean reversion in credit quality, as evidenced by historical credit rating changes. This means that good-credit-quality (above average) firms tend to deteriorate and vice versa. Hence, a counterparty of good credit quality will tend to have an increasing default probability over time, whilst a poor-credit-quality counterparty will be more likely to default in the short term and less likely to do so in the longer term. The term structure of default is very important to consider.

We note finally that default probability may be defined as real world or risk-neutral. In the former case, the question is what is the *actual* default probability of the counterparty, and this is often estimated via historical data. In the latter case, we calculate the risk-neutral (or market-implied) probability from market credit spreads (for example, via CDSs). The difference between real-world and risk-neutral default probabilities is discussed in detail in Section 12.1.1, but it is worth emphasising now that risk-neutral default probabilities have become the standard for CVA calculations in recent years due to a combination of accounting guidelines, regulatory rules, and market practice (Section 3.1.7).

3.3.5   Recovery and Loss Given Default

Exposure calculations, by convention, will ignore any recovery value in the event of a default. Hence, the exposure (Section 3.3.3) is the loss, as defined by the value or replacement cost that would be incurred, assuming no recovery value.

Recovery rates typically represent the percentage of the outstanding claim recovered when a counterparty defaults. An alternative variable to recovery is loss given

---

[15] Here we refer to default probabilities in a specified period, such as annually.
[16] This can refer to a real expectation (historical) or one implied from market spreads (risk neutral), as discussed below.

default (LGD), which in percentage terms is 100% minus the recovery rate. Default claims can vary significantly, and LGD is therefore highly uncertain. Whilst credit exposure is traditionally measured independently, LGD is relevant in the quantification of CVA.

In the event of a bankruptcy, the holders of bilateral derivatives contracts such as derivatives with the counterparty in default would generally be *pari passu* with the senior bondholders.[17] OTC derivatives, bonds, and CDSs generally reference senior unsecured credit risk and may appear to relate to the same LGD. However, this is not always the case, and sometimes there are structural reasons why certain contracts would be assumed to have a lower LGD (higher recovery) or even vice versa.

There are timing issues with respect to LGD. When a bond issuer defaults, LGD is realised immediately since the bond can be sold in the market. CDS contracts are also settled within days of the defined credit event via the CDS auction which likewise defines the LGD. However, derivatives (unlike bonds) cannot be freely traded or sold, especially when the counterparty to the derivative is in default. This essentially leads to a potentially different LGD for derivatives. These aspects, very important in the Lehman Brothers bankruptcy of 2008, were discussed in more detail in Section 2.2.9.

3.3.6   Funding, Collateral, and Capital Costs

In addition to the cost of taking credit risk measured by a credit spread (and LGD), it is necessary to consider the costs associated with funding, collateral, and capital. Like credit spreads, these components are difficult to assess and may require a combination of qualitative and quantitative considerations. Ultimately, though, they will be key inputs in xVA quantification.

It may be helpful to consider examples where such costs will arise:

- *Funding.* Suppose an institution enters into an uncollateralised transaction[18] which requires them to make an upfront cash payment.[19] There is clearly a need to fund this payment as it relates to cash flows that will be received later. It may be necessary to borrow money (such as by issuing a bond) in order to make this upfront payment. There will be an associated cost to this, representing the compensation that lenders will require. In collateralised transactions, this will not be the cash because the margin/collateral will offset with other payments (such as the upfront cash payment in this example). Initial margin, as overcollateralisation, will not offset with any other component and will generate a funding requirement.
- *Collateral (margin).* Funding will normally be defined as the cost of raising cash in a base currency. If the collateral under a margining agreement is in a different currency or securities, then this will constitute a different interest rate, which should be reflected in the valuation. For example, receiving bonds may represent a funding benefit, but there will be a repo rate that defines the cost of converting these bonds into cash. There

---

[17] This means they have the same seniority and therefore should expect to receive the same recovery percentage.

[18] If the transactions were collateralised, then the institution would probability receive collateral to balance this, as discussed later.

[19] As will be discussed later, even transactions without upfront payments have funding considerations, but this example is an easier one to use.

may also be optionality, where the party required to post collateral to meet margin requirements may have a contractual choice over the currencies and/or securities that can be used.

- *Capital*. An institution enters into a transaction that causes an increase in its capital requirements. In order to raise share capital, the institution must pay an implicit return to shareholders via dividend payments. They should, therefore, consider the cost of the capital required when assessing the economics of the transactions.

Some of the above inputs are objective and quantifiable. For example, an institution may be able to observe where their bonds are trading in the secondary market and use this as an estimate of the cost of raising more funding. However, some aspects are more subjective, such as determining what maturity of funding is required against a transaction or what dividends will be required by shareholders in the future. More discussion of these inputs will be given in Chapter 14.

4

Regulation

4.1 REGULATION AND THE GLOBAL FINANCIAL CRISIS

Over the years, derivatives – especially over-the-counter (OTC) ones – have given institutional investors, corporates, sovereigns, and supranational organisations a flexible tool for hedging a large range of risks, and the market has grown to be very large. However, critics have accused the OTC derivatives market of triggering and amplifying the global financial crisis (GFC) and, accordingly, regulators have proposed a number of initiatives aimed at making it safer. The GFC brought about many changes to regulation as a result of experiences during the crisis, such as thinly-capitalised banks. Some of the regulatory policy has brought about alterations in existing regulatory rules, but the majority has implemented completely new requirements. Many of these changes have important impacts for the assessment of valuation adjustments as they relate to counterparty risk, funding, collateral, and capital.

Firstly, the changes in regulation can be seen as covering the strengthening of capital bases and the implementation of liquidity standards which are broadly covered by the Basel III regulation originally published in 2010 (Figure 4.1). These requirements are detailed and affect banks across many activities, not just derivatives and their associated valuation adjustments. The discussion below will focus mainly on aspects that are relevant to the scope of this book. Secondly, and specific to OTC derivatives and this topic, is the requirement to clear standardised OTC derivatives, which is backed up by the bilateral

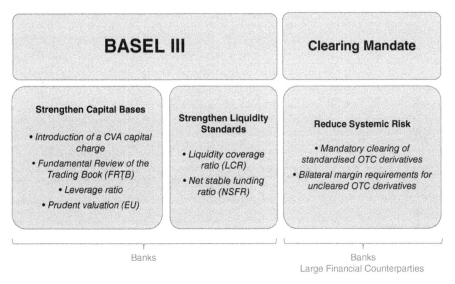

Figure 4.1 Overview of regulatory changes since the GFC that are relevant for the consideration of xVA.

margin requirements for non-centrally-cleared OTC derivatives. These requirements are potentially applicable to all users of OTC derivatives, not merely banks. However, small users will generally be exempt.

Regulatory initiatives, such as Basel III, are often global guidelines that need to be implemented into law by each region or country. Major implementations of new financial regulation include the Dodd–Frank Act in the US and the European Market Infrastructures Regulation (EMIR) in the European Union (EU). The two are similar – but not identical – in the way they treat OTC derivatives, particularly in terms of aspects such as reducing systemic risk and improving transparency.

4.2   CAPITAL REQUIREMENTS

4.2.1   Overview

The Basel II capital rules generally in force at the time of the GFC were seen as dramatically undercapitalising banks and promoting dangerous behaviour such as regulatory arbitrage prior to the GFC.[1] Defining the increased capital requirements is the job of the Basel Committee on Banking Supervision (BCBS),[2] which did this as part of Basel III (BCBS 2009b, 2010a). Basel III proposed rules to dramatically increase capital by a combination of re-parameterisation of existing methods and the addition of new requirements. Counterparty risk was a key focus for Basel III, with the view that the failure to adequately capture OTC derivatives exposure was a key factor in amplifying the GFC. In particular, the BCBS noted that only around one-third of the counterparty risk was capitalised prior to the crisis. The remaining two-thirds would be captured by a new credit value adjustment (CVA) capital charge to cover the mark-to-market (MTM) of the counterparty risk of a bank. This would capture the potential losses when credit spreads widened, even in the absence of any actual defaults. Notably, the only exemption (under Basel III at least) from the CVA capital charge for OTC derivatives trades was for those cleared with a central counterparty (CCP).[3]

The danger in calibrating risk models with relatively recent historical data is that benign and quiet periods tend to precede major crises. This means that risk measures and capital requirements are particularly low at the worst possible time. The higher leverage levels that such low-risk measures ultimately allow may increase the likelihood and severity of any crisis. This problem is typically known as procyclicality. This has led to the requirement to use stressed data to calibrate risk models. The use of the stressed period should reduce procyclicality problems by ensuring that capital does not become artificially low during quiet periods in financial markets.

Other small changes to Basel III rules have also increased counterparty risk capital requirements. For example, the margin period of risk (MPoR) used by advanced banks for computing capital requirements on collateralised/margined transactions was increased in certain situations, basically reducing the benefit from a bilateral margin agreement

---

[1] Some regions, most obviously the US, were still predominantly under the Basel I regulation at the time and had not, to a large extent, implemented Basel II.

[2] www.bis.org/bcbs.

[3] In the EU, trades with sovereign and non-financial counterparties have been exempted under CRD IV, the implementation of Basel III. However, it seems likely that some local regulators may at least partially reverse this decision by requiring more capital to be held.

(see Section 7.2.3). The overall total effect of Basel III is to increase a bank's capital requirements for counterparty risk by a significant factor, which clearly incentivises a push towards central clearing. This push is potentially made more relevant by the nature of the CVA capital charge, which penalises higher-rated counterparties in particular,[4] and by the changes to the rules for collateralised counterparties.

4.2.2   Capital Ratios

Capital acts as a buffer to absorb losses during turbulent periods and therefore contributes significantly to defining the creditworthiness of a bank. Banks strive for profits and will therefore naturally wish to hold the minimum amount of capital possible in order to maximise the amount of business they can do and risk they are able to take. There is clearly a balance to be found in defining the capital requirements for a bank: it must be high enough to contribute to a very low possibility of failure, and yet not so severe as to unfairly penalise the bank and have adverse consequences for its clients and the economy as a whole. Capital requirements govern the ratio of equity to debt, recorded on the liability side of a firm's balance sheet.

Regulatory capital is the minimum amount of capital a bank must hold as required by its regulator. This minimum capital requirement aims to ensure that banks do not take on excess leverage and become insolvent. The BCBS sets out a framework for regulatory capital standards (Pillar 1) which is generally adopted by all national regulators. This framework has evolved from Basel I in 1998 to Basel II in 2004 and finally Basel III, which has had a phased implementation since the GFC. If a bank does not meet the minimum capital requirements, then regulators may have the power to restrict dividends and remuneration policies.

Banks have also used the concept of economic capital, which is an internal measure of the capital they require. However, economic capital has become very much secondary to regulatory capital in evaluating the performance of a bank. This is mainly due to the impact of regulation increasing regulatory capital to levels where it almost certainly exceeds economic capital.

Intuitively, capital is often thought of as representing an unexpected loss (i.e. a loss that is more than expected) (Figure 4.2). The idea is that expected losses will be naturally considered and should be part of valuation (e.g. CVA is the expected loss with respect to counterparty risk). Unexpected losses, defined to some confidence level, should be absorbed by the capital of a bank. In some capital methodologies, unexpected losses are defined by a quantile of a model-generated distribution. These are generally referred to as internal model methods or approaches (IMMs or IMAs). However, some regulatory methodologies are more simple and formulaic and do not use internal models.

Regulatory capital requirements are normally expressed as a *capital ratio*, which is the percentage of a bank's capital to its risk-weighted assets (RWAs). The RWAs are defined by various methodologies across different areas and risk types. Since Basel II, it has been a requirement that the total capital ratio of a bank must be greater than 8%. There are, broadly speaking, two types of capital: Tier 1 – sometimes referred to as Common Equity Tier 1 (CET1) – and Tier 2 (there was previously a Tier 3 that has been abolished).

---

[4] Since the CVA capital charge is based on credit spread volatility and not default probability, the relative effect of a stronger rating is not as beneficial.

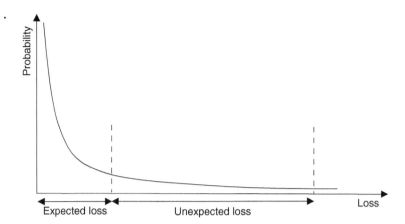

Figure 4.2   Expected and unexpected losses.

CET1 is generally 'going concern' capital and consists of common equity and some other components such as retained earnings. Tier 2 capital is generally 'gone concern' capital and consists of components such as preference shares. Going concern capital reduces the chance of insolvency, whilst gone concern capital protects depositors and senior creditors in the event of insolvency.

Regulation has increased the amount of CET1 capital that a bank must hold to 4.5% in relation to the 8% minimum capital ratio. Additionally, certain additional CET1 requirements are being introduced that will require a bank to improve its capital ratios. These are:

- *Capital conservation buffer.* This is intended to ensure that banks build up capital buffers outside periods of stress which can be drawn down as losses are incurred. The buffer is set at 2.5% above the regulatory minimum capital requirement. Banks can still operate as normal when below this requirement but are subject to constraints over distributions such as dividend payments.
- *Countercyclical capital buffer.* This aims to ensure that banking sector capital requirements take account of the economic climate, and the primary objective of the buffer is to restrict the activities of banks during periods of excess credit growth. It is intended to be set between 0% and 2.5%, and the value will change dynamically depending on the macro-economic environment, with quantities such as the deviation in the ratio of lending to gross domestic product (GDP) from the long-term trend being considered as metrics for setting the ratio.
- *G-SIB surcharge.* This is a surcharge for globally-systemically-important banks (G-SIBs). It is implemented based on a BCBS methodology that defines a bank as potentially being within one of five G-SIB buckets, with surcharge increasing from 1% to 2.5%.

The above requirements are summarised in Figure 4.3, which shows the 2019 values in the case where there is a phase-in. Note that the requirements can sometimes be region specific (i.e. regulators in one country may impose tighter standards than those in another).

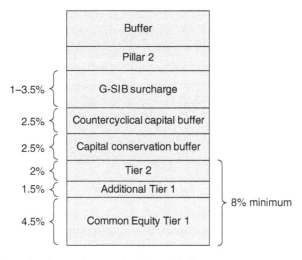

Figure 4.3 Overview of capital ratios required since 2019.

There are also two final components which should be considered:

- *Pillar 2 requirements.* Whilst Pillar 1 of the Basel Accord deals with minimum capital ratios, Pillar 2 forms a supervisory review process, with one of its aims being to address firm-specific risks that are not adequately covered by Pillar 1. National regulators can, therefore, require a bank to hold additional capital under Pillar 2.
- *Buffers.* Banks will inevitably hold more capital than the regulatory minimum to prevent having to raise more capital under tight timescales. This buffer should be considered an additional cost.

4.2.3   Risk Type

From the point of view of any valuation adjustment, it will only be relevant to consider capital requirements that apply directly to a transaction or business. Any capital requirements that cannot be allocated in this way are just general costs, like electricity or office equipment, and can only be considered implicitly.

Broadly speaking, banks must hold regulatory capital against the following risks:

- market;
- credit; and
- operational.

Accordingly, there are separate requirements within each of these areas to determine RWAs. The RWAs are a measure of the total assets, weighted for their riskiness. Whilst market and credit risk methodologies are transaction based, those for operational risk are based on much more general quantities such as net revenue. It is therefore not possible to incorporate operational risk capital costs directly into transaction-specific valuation adjustments. In contrast, it is important to understand the different capital charges for credit and market risk and how these relate back to the cost of individual transactions.

In terms of different requirements, the following are important considerations under credit and market risk capital:

- Market risk.
  - o *Market risk capital charge.* This is the capital charge for market risk across all trading desks in a bank (except the desk responsible for CVA). It has been subject to a significant rethink in recent years under the Fundamental Review of the Trading Book (FRTB). The FRTB requirements are described in BCBS (2019b).
  - o *The CVA capital charge.* This is a market risk capital charge specific to CVA trading, which is partially aligned with the FRTB rules above.
- Credit risk.
  - o *Counterparty credit risk (CCR) capital charge.* This is the specific credit risk capital charge that is relevant for OTC derivatives and other transactions subject to CCR.
  - o *Leverage ratio.* This is a general metric that aims to limit the leverage of a bank and contains the exposure (in the sense of credit risk) as a key component.

Note that capital charges are treated as mutually exclusive and additive, whereas risks may offset one another. For example, from a counterparty risk perspective, it is not easy to completely disentangle the credit risk (CCR capital) and market risk (CVA capital). Furthermore, the methodologies for market risk and CVA are separate and additive, whereas a bank may see an offset between the market risk of CVA and other market risks.

There are also two other components that are more indirect but may influence bank capital requirements. These are:

- *Bank stress tests.* Banks are subject to a variety of stress tests which assess their capability to withstand unfavourable economic conditions. Banks are typically required to maintain a certain CET1 capital ratio from these stress tests.
- *Capital floors.* Regulation imposes floors whereby banks may be forced to use standardised methodologies rather than internal models.

Most capital charges are continuous in nature – i.e. the larger the position, the bigger the capital required. Note that some of the components above are not capital charges per se but rather conditions that must be met. This applies to the leverage ratio, bank stress tests, and capital floors. This makes pricing these components more difficult, as will be discussed in more detail in Section 5.4.3.

The above components will be reviewed below. Chapter 13 will give a more detailed account of the regulatory methodologies used to define capital requirements.

4.2.4   Market Risk Capital

Banks take a significant amount of market risk in the form of interest rate, inflation, foreign exchange (FX), commodity, equity, and credit spread risks when trading derivatives and other transactions with clients. Whilst most trading desks aim to hedge most of their market risk, this is not always possible and certain residual risks remain, often in the form of more subtle components such as basis risk.

Regulation has therefore required that banks hold capital against market risk. One of the benefits of the introduction of value-at-risk (VAR) models in the mid-1990s

(Section 2.6.1) was the ability to quantify residual market risk across a portfolio that may be reasonably well balanced. VAR, or a similar metric, also allows the aggregation of different forms of market risk (e.g. interest rate and FX) in a consistent framework.

More recently, the FRTB (BCBS 2013e) is trying to define a more consistent set of market risk regulatory capital rules, balancing risk sensitivity and complexity and promoting consistency. One aspect of the FRTB is the use of expected shortfall (ES) as a replacement for VAR (Section 2.6.1) as the risk measure for market risk capital based on internal models. This is due to the view that ES is better at capturing tail risk: VAR measures only a single quantile and does not consider the loss beyond this level, whereas ES averages all losses above the confidence level. Since the ES is naturally a more conservative measure, it is proposed to replace 99% VAR with 97.5% ES (for a normal distribution the two are almost identical). The standard 10-day time horizon for VAR is also split into several categories based on the liquidity of the underlying portfolio. These changes may create larger capital requirements, especially for seemingly-well-hedged positions.

4.2.5 CVA Capital

In BCBS (2009) it is stated that, in the preceding crisis period, only one-third of counterparty risk-related losses were due to defaults, with the remaining two-thirds being driven by CVA volatility. At the time, only default losses (credit risk)[5] and not MTM (market risk) were considered. Basel, therefore, introduced the CVA capital charge to capitalise the market risk of CVA.

The CVA capital charge, in general, has been quite controversial and has attracted criticism. Some of the criticism concerns the significant increase in capital requirements, whilst some is more subtle and relates to the precise methodology. For example, the European Banking Authority (EBA 2015b) reports that the CVA capital charge as defining the potential increase in CVA is 'very conservative' as it implies that the CVA of most banks surveyed could increase between 10 and 20 times over 10 days.

Basel III defines global standards on capital requirements that are generally being implemented consistently, albeit with small differences and timescales depending on the region. However, one extremely significant divergence has occurred in Europe via the Capital Requirements Directive IV (CRD IV), which is the mechanism through which the EU implements Basel III standards on capital. In the EU, the implementation of Basel standards for CVA capital (via CRD IV) exempted banks from holding CVA capital towards sovereign counterparties.[6] This was followed in 2013 by similar exemptions covering non-financial counterparties (below the clearing threshold) and pension funds (temporarily, in line with a clearing exemption). These exemptions were themselves controversial since they meant that an EU bank would have to hold significantly less capital trading with certain counterparties than a non-EU bank would.[7] A study by the EBA reported that without the exemptions the total CVA capital of 18 banks surveyed would more than double from €12.4bn to €31.1bn, with sovereign exemptions being the most material (EBA 2015b).

---

[5] Also credit migration, as discussed in Section 13.2.2.

[6] Including public bodies, multilateral development banks, public sector entities owned by central governments, central governments, and central banks.

[7] Wood, D. (2013). UK banks face CVA exemption tension. *Risk* (28 June). www.risk.net.

There has been clear resistance by some European countries to the CVA capital exemptions. In theory, national regulators can impose additional capital charges via Pillar 2 charges (see Section 4.2.2).[8] In 2015, the EBA opined that 'EU exemptions on the application of CVA charges should be reconsidered or removed, since they leave potential risks uncaptured'.[9] However, it was suggested that this be done as part of the broader implementation of the FRTB (see Section 4.2.4).

The aforementioned FRTB process resulted in a consultative document in 2015 (BCBS 2015a) proposing changes to the CVA capital charge. Whilst these changes do make the CVA treatment generally more in line with market risk under the FRTB, the CVA capital regulation is somewhat simpler to reflect the complex nature of CVA. These changes are scheduled for implementation in 2022 (BCBS 2017).

The regulatory uncertainty over the implementation of the new CVA capital charge and the lack of clarity in the removal of the European exemption is a good example of the difficulty of pricing capital into transactions (discussed later in Section 19.2).

4.2.6   CCR Capital

CCR capital is a specific case of credit risk capital in general. Credit risk capital is defined as a product of three components, all defined by regulatory rules:

- *Probability of default (PD)*. The default probability of the counterparty in question.
- *Loss given default (LGD)*. The loss given default (or equivalently 100% minus the recovery rate).
- *Exposure at default (EAD)*. The exposure to the counterparty.

The above components are defined by various methodologies discussed in Chapter 13. For basic credit products, such as loans, the definition of EAD is trivial since it just represents the amount lent to an obligor. For products subject to counterparty risk, defining EAD is much more complex because the value of a portfolio can be both positive and negative and extremely volatile. Hence, there are specific methodologies for EAD that are relevant only for the assessment of CCR capital for derivatives and other transactions.

4.2.7   Leverage Ratio

An often-cited cause for the severity of the GFC was excessive on- and off-balance-sheet leverage of banks even when seemingly-strong risk-based capital ratios were in place. This has led to the introduction of the leverage ratio (LR) – sometimes referred to as the supplementary leverage ratio (SLR) – described in BCBS (2014a). The introduction of a simple, transparent, non-risk-based LR is designed to act as a credible supplementary measure to the risk-based capital requirements.

Although increasing capital requirements should reduce leverage, capital methodologies can be risk- and asset-type specific and are sometimes based on internal models which have been observed to vary significantly from bank to bank. Certain products

---

[8] Cameron, M. (2013). Bafin weighing CVA charge despite European exemptions. *Risk* (19 June). www.risk .net.

[9] EBA (2015). The EBA advises the European Commission on Credit Valuation Adjustment (CVA) risk (25 February). www.eba.europa.eu.

and trading strategies can effectively create extremely high leverage – collateralised OTC derivatives and repos being two examples. The LR is seen as complementing regulatory capital requirements as a fairly simple approach to limiting the overall leverage within a bank. The LR can, therefore, be seen as a backstop to capital requirements, which mitigates the inherent uncertainties in these approaches. From the point of view of capital requirements, a bank must have enough capital to meet traditional capital ratios and comply with the leverage ratio.

The LR requires that the ratio of a bank's Tier 1 capital to their exposure must be greater than a certain amount, thereby restricting leverage (which is effectively the reciprocal of this amount):

$$\text{Leverage ratio} = \frac{\text{Tier 1 capital}}{\text{Exposure}} \geq \alpha\% \tag{4.1}$$

The exposure in Equation 4.1 aims to capture the total exposure, on and off balance sheet, of the bank and includes products such as derivative exposures, securities finance transactions (e.g. repos), and other off-balance-sheet exposures. The methodology for defining the exposure for derivatives typically follows methodologies for defining minimum regulatory capital with certain restrictions (see further discussion in Section 13.4.6). It is relatively punitive for transactions such as OTC derivatives and repos and is relatively conservative in its treatment of collateral.

Note that the LR measure, by design, does not account in any way for credit quality because it only looks at exposure and not default probability (or LGD). Hence, higher-credit-quality entities will have the same impact as the same exposure to weaker credits. Since capital ratios are credit-quality sensitive, this means that transactions and businesses with good underlying credit risk are more likely to be LR-consuming (this means that the implicit capital requirement under the LR formula is higher than the usual capital requirement). LR-consuming business may eventually cause the bank to be LR constrained (close to breaching the condition, unless exposure is reduced or capital increased). The treatment of collateral also means that bilateral-collateralised and centrally-cleared transactions are more costly from an LR point of view.

A bank that is (or is close to) being LR constrained may consider this to be more relevant than its actual capital charges. However, managing business with respect to the LR is difficult since it represents a binary condition on capital rather than a continuous requirement. Furthermore, a bank must only meet the leverage requirement overall, not for a particular activity. For example, if a business grows, then their capital requirements will probably increase more or less in line with this growth and will not be related to capital requirements in the rest of the bank. This business may also catalyse its bank breaching the LR condition above, but this will happen at a discrete point and will depend on other business in the bank. It is, therefore, more difficult to envisage how the LR can be incorporated into business decisions and priced via a valuation adjustment measure such as capital value adjustment (KVA) (Section 19.2.6).

Note also that in the US, separate from Basel III, an 'enhanced supplementary leverage ratio' has been proposed for the largest banks, with a more conservative 5% minimum.

4.2.8 Capital Floors

Related to the LR is the use of capital floors based on the results of standardised approaches (BCBS 2014g). This requirement has been driven by the observation that internal models can produce large variations in capital charges across banks for the same exposure and very small capital charges in certain situations. Such results suggest significant model risk and perhaps overly-optimistic assumptions within a bank's internal models. The use of a floor based on standardised capital methodologies is intended to mitigate against excessively-low internal model numbers and limit variation between banks based on their internal models. Note that banks with internal model approval for a component (e.g. CCR capital) will also need to calculate capital under the standardised regulatory methodology.

A capital floor works by limiting a bank's aggregate calculation of RWAs (measured with methodologies including internal models) to be no lower than a certain percentage of the RWAs that would result if the bank had used only standardised methodologies. The value of the floor in this context is difficult: too high and banks will have no incentive to use internal models, but too low and it will be unlikely to have any impact.[10] The current intended final value of the floor (following a phase-in where the floor is increased gradually) is 72.5%.

A capital floor creates a similar problem as the LR for managing businesses and pricing transactions, due to the fact that it is binary and an aggregate bank measure. For example, a business may have an internal model capital requirement that is less than the standardised methodology floor, but unless this is the case at the bank level, the business's capital requirements will still be driven by its internal model.

4.2.9   Large Exposure Framework

The large exposure framework (BCBS 2014e) has been developed as a way to limit the maximum loss a bank could face in the event of a sudden counterparty failure, to prevent such an event also endangering the solvency of the bank. This is seen as complementing risk-based capital standards, which are not primarily focused around the potential default of a single counterparty. Indeed, the regulatory standards for credit risk capital under internal models (Section 13.2.2) are based on the notional of an infinitely large portfolio.

The large exposure framework is focused on the potential default of a single counterparty or group of connected counterparties. Connected counterparties – for example, where one counterparty has ownership or control over another – must be treated as a single counterparty. Large sectorial or geographical concentrations, whilst recognised as being problematic, are not considered. The only counterparties exempted from the framework are sovereigns and their central banks and public sector entities that are treated as sovereigns under capital requirements. Similarly, exposures guaranteed by such sovereign counterparties are excluded. CCPs are currently excluded, pending further observations.

A large exposure is defined as an exposure to a counterparty, or group of connected counterparties, that is larger than 10% of the bank's eligible capital base. Eligible capital corresponds to CET1 capital (Section 4.2.2). Such exposures must not be more than 25% of a bank's eligible capital base (this figure is lowered to 15% for a G-SIB's exposure to another G-SIB).

For counterparty-risk-related instruments, the exposure is defined using the Standardised Approach for Counterparty Credit Risk (SA-CCR) (Section 13.4.3). Certain risk mitigation techniques (e.g. collateral) can be accounted for in reducing the exposure.

---

[10] Maxwell, F. (2015). Basel floors must be below 75% to preserve models, banks say. *Risk* (26 January). Capital floors could spur risk-taking – Swedish FSA. *Risk* (25 March). www.risk.net.

4.2.10   Bank Stress Tests

The GFC left many banks and financial institutions severely undercapitalised. The aim of stress tests is to prevent this by analysing a bank's capability to withstand unfavourable economic circumstances. Such circumstances are defined by a series of hypothetical scenarios, generally intended to be unlikely but plausible, which may include aspects such as a fall in GDP, equity and house prices, together with an increase in unemployment and interest rates and the weakening of a local currency. Examples of regulatory stress tests are the Comprehensive Capital Analysis and Review (CCAR) and the Dodd–Frank Act Stress Testing (DFAST) in the US, and the EBA and Bank of England stress tests in Europe.

One of the key outputs of stress tests is a bank's CET1 capital ratio, which must remain above a certain defined level. This is, therefore, another binary, aggregative bank measure that must be met and may – implicitly – generate a capital requirement.

4.2.11   Prudent Valuation

Specific to the EU, Prudent Valuation (EBA 2015a) requires that financial instruments recorded at fair value from an accounting perspective (Section 5.3.3) are assessed based on their prudent (conservative) value. The prudent value aims to capture the 90% confidence level worst value. The difference between the prudent and fair values – known as additional valuation adjustment (AVA) – must be deducted from CET1 capital and can, therefore, be seen as an additional capital charge.

Amongst the components that must be assessed with AVA are:

- unearned credit spreads;
- investing and funding costs; and
- model risk.

The first component above clearly relates to CVA consideration via the credit spread inputs. Additionally, the second component above could be seen as requiring some consideration in relation to funding value adjustment (FVA) and potentially also margin value adjustment (MVA), although the reporting of these components within fair value is not yet completely standard. Finally, the last term in the list potentially relates to all valuation adjustments (to the extent that they are part of fair value) since they are all typically model driven.

4.3   LIQUIDITY

4.3.1   Overview

Banks tend to engage in activities such as funding long-dated illiquid assets (e.g. long-term loans) with short-term liquid liabilities (e.g. deposits). Such activities entail maturity transformations (borrowing money on shorter time frames than lending money out) and liquidity transformations (funding relatively illiquid assets with more liquid liabilities). Some of the high-profile failures in the GFC were directly related to these maturity and/or liquidity transformations (e.g. financing long-term lending with short-term borrowing).

One of the experiences of the GFC was that many banks, irrespective of the size and quality of their capital bases, had problems arising from not managing liquidity risk appropriately. It also became clear how quickly the liquidity of assets can decline, and how sharply the funding costs of banks can increase.

The inappropriate approach to liquidity risk by banks was broadly due to relying on short-term transactions to fund longer-term assets. This resulted in a need to refinance short-term borrowing regularly, which created liquidity risk due to the possibility that this would become more expensive or even not possible at all. Strong capital bases would not mitigate such problems, and regulators therefore saw the need to implement specific international liquidity standards for the first time, formulated in a similar way to global capital standards.

The BCBS has developed two complementary minimum standards for funding liquidity:

- *The liquidity coverage ratio (LCR).* This aims to ensure that a bank has the resources to survive a hypothetical adverse liquidity scenario of 30 days (BCBS 2013a).
- *The net stable funding ratio (NSFR).* This aims to create longer-term funding stability by ensuring that assets are financed with sources of funding that are relatively stable compared to the profiles (liquidity and maturity) of the assets. The NSFR has a time horizon of one year (BCBS 2014b).

Neither the LCR nor the NSFR aims to prevent a bank from offering various forms of maturity or liquidity transformation, but rather aims to ensure that such transformations are not extreme and that the bank has a structure of assets and liabilities that is sustainable in the long term.

Note that the LCR and NSFR have the same features as some of the capital-based regulations, such as the LR, capital floors, and stress tests, in that they are binary regulations that apply at the bank level. They also create the need to assess two separate funding strategies: the traditional one that the bank believes is appropriate, and the one that maintains compliance with the LCR and NSFR. For certain assets, the latter strategy will be different from the former. In particular, 'self-funded' products such as collateralised derivatives and repos may be thought of as requiring virtually no funding but will require implicit LCR and NSFR funding via a required stable funding component.

4.3.2   High-quality Liquid Assets

At the core of the LCR and NSFR regulation is the concept of unencumbered high-quality liquid assets (HQLAs). This generally refers to assets that can be readily converted into cash (with minimal credit and liquidity risk) to meet liquidity needs in a timely fashion.

HQLAs can consist of the following types of assets (see BCBS 2013a):

- *Level 1.* These are assets of excellent liquidity and credit quality, including cash, central bank reserves, and certain securities guaranteed by sovereign, supranational, or similar entities (subject to certain conditions). These assets can comprise an unlimited share of the pool and are not subject to a haircut.

- *Level 2A.* These are less-liquid assets, such as certain securities guaranteed by sovereign, supranational, or similar entities, corporate and covered bonds (subject to certain conditions), and commercial paper. These cannot comprise more than 40% of the total liquidity pool and have a 15% haircut applied.
- *Level 2B.* The most illiquid assets, where allowed,[11] can only comprise 15% of the liquidity pool and are subject to a 25% or 50% haircut. This includes certain corporate bonds, residential mortgage-backed securities (RMBS), covered bonds, and equities.

4.3.3   Liquidity Coverage Ratio

The LCR aims to ensure that banks have sufficient HQLAs to survive a liquidity stress event, which is associated with aspects such as increased market volatility, reduction of current funding (e.g. partial run-off of deposits), inability to access secured and unsecured funding markets, and potential outflows arising from a downgrading of the bank's external credit rating. This requirement can be expressed as:

$$\frac{\text{Stock of HQLAs}}{\text{Total net cash outflows over the next 30 calendar days}} \geq 100\% \qquad (4.2)$$

One particularly important aspect of the LCR that is particularly relevant for xVA is the liquidity needs related to downgrade triggers embedded in transactions. A bank must include in the total net liquidity outflows 100% of any additional collateral that would have to be posted, or other contractual outflows (e.g. termination), in the event of a three-notch downgrade of the bank's external credit rating.[12] This applies to derivatives transactions where there is contractual collateral posting, termination, or replacement in the event of the bank's rating deteriorating to a specified level, and can be related to both FVA (in the case of variation margin requirements being triggered) or MVA (independent amount or initial margin).

Under the LCR, banks must also consider increased liquidity needs related to changes in the valuation of derivatives or other transactions and the change in the valuation of the collateral in relation to such transactions. This can have an impact on FVA (Section 18.3.6) and MVA (Section 20.3.3).

Returning to the point about two funding strategies, suppose an A-rated bank must post a certain amount of collateral in the event that its credit rating is downgraded by three notches. The traditional funding strategy would probably consider that it would not be necessary to fund this payment prior to a downgrade (since the relatively significant downgrade to BBB is perceived to be extremely unlikely). On the other hand, the LCR implies that this contingent payment should be funded in its entirety via the requirement to hold 100% of HQLAs. However, suppose the bank has a relatively healthy LCR well in excess of 100%. Would it be relevant to impose a funding cost on originating this type of business even though it is already pre-funded via the bank's healthy LCR? We will discuss this question in more detail in Section 5.4.3.

---

[11] Some national regulators do not allow any assets to qualify as Level 2B.

[12] Note that the US implementation of the BCBS rules does not refer to a three-notch downgrade but to 100% of all additional amounts that would need to be posted. Furthermore, it specifies that changes in financial condition should not be solely defined by credit ratings. See Liquidity Coverage Ratio: Liquidity Risk Measurement Standards. Department of the Treasury, Office of the Comptroller of the Currency. www.occ.gov.

Spreadsheet 4.1 LCR Example.

4.3.4   Net Stable Funding Ratio

Whilst the LCR is relatively short term, the purpose of the NSFR is to ensure that banks hold a minimum amount of stable funding over one year to prevent excessive maturity and liquidity transformation. The NSFR is calculated by dividing a bank's available stable funding (ASF) by its required stable funding (RSF) (Equation 4.3), and uses defined weights to proxy the funding requirements of assets (receivables) and funding benefits of liabilities (payables). As with the LCR, this ratio must always be greater than 100%:

$$\frac{\text{Available amount of stable funding}}{\text{Required amount of stable funding}} \geq 100\% \qquad (4.3)$$

The NSFR requires a minimum number of stable sources of funding at a bank relative to the liquidity profiles of the assets, as well as the potential for contingent liquidity needs arising from off-balance-sheet commitments, over a one-year horizon. The NSFR aims to limit over-reliance on short-term wholesale funding during times of buoyant market liquidity and encourage better assessment of liquidity risk across all on- and off-balance-sheet items.

Most transactions for a bank are either assets or liabilities, and so the NSFR analysis is relatively straightforward. For example, if a bank funds a certain amount of residential mortgage lending (RSF of 65%) with the same amount in 'stable deposits' (ASF 95%) then its NSFR (assuming no other assets or liabilities) will be a healthy 95/65 = 146%. On the other hand, funding these same assets with funding of less than one year (typically ASF 50%) would lead to a non-compliant NSFR of 50/65 = 77%. Clearly the ASF and RSF factors and the timescale of one year are subjective, but beyond this the methodology is relatively simple.

Transactions such as derivatives are more problematic from an NSFR perspective because they can be both assets (when they have a positive value) and liabilities (when they have a negative value). They can also move from one to another as market variables such as interest rates move. With respect to collateralised transactions, the margin/collateral can either be an asset (received) or liability (posted). Overall, due to having a combination of collateralised and uncollateralised transactions, a bank may have an overall derivatives portfolio that is positive ('asset heavy') or negative ('liability heavy') even if the market risk is well hedged overall.

The NSFR, therefore, recognises that some transactions can be both assets and liabilities and that collateral may be paid in either direction. This means that gross derivatives assets are cancelled by the same amount of gross derivatives liabilities, leaving no net RSF requirement. Additionally, cash collateral received cancels with collateral posted, leaving no required funding.

However, the NSFR also takes into account (implicitly) that the balance between derivatives assets and liabilities is likely to be imperfect and also dependent on market conditions, and may therefore be transient (i.e. a bank may need to fund derivatives assets over a short timescale). There are therefore certain features specific to derivatives which receive an asymmetrical treatment:

- Whilst net derivatives assets have a 100% RSF weight and require funding, net derivatives liabilities have a 0% ASF weight. This means that a bank with a derivatives book that provides funding overall via a net surplus of liabilities over assets does not provide stable funding (i.e. generate ASF), according to the NSFR. Put another way, the NSFR assumes that collateral generated from derivatives cannot fund other parts of a bank's balance sheet. This is an important factor in FVA quantification (Chapter 18).

- Twenty percent of derivatives payables have a 100% RSF factor. This means that even funding benefits have an associated funding cost under the NSFR. The intention of this is to reflect the large variability in derivatives exposures and the fact that a funding benefit can quite quickly become a cost when negative values become positive. However, this component has been contentious, and the BCBS has communicated that regulators may, at their discretion, lower the value of this factor to no less than 5%.[13]
- Collateral (variation margin) received can only reduce the funding cost of a derivative if it is cash and it complies with certain conditions.[14] This means that collateralised trades, which may be considered to have very small funding requirements, may still have a large contribution to the NSFR if, for example, bonds are permissible as collateral.[15]

The above constraints on the way in which a bank funds its balance sheet would most obviously be a consideration for FVA quantification (Section 18.3.4).

Beyond FVA, there is the consideration of the impact the NSFR has on initial margin and MVA (Chapter 20). Received initial margin has a 0% ASF factor, which is not surprising since it is usually segregated and therefore has no funding benefit. Posted initial margin has a relatively high RSF factor of 85% (for example, as mentioned above, residential mortgages have an RSF of 65%). Therefore, if a bank is posting initial margin using securities with an ASF of less than 85%, then the NSFR introduces an additional funding cost.

Recall again that the NSFR is binary and imposed at the bank level. A given trade does not therefore, per se, have an NSFR component. Hence, it is not easy for a bank to have a robust policy on pricing such requirements and it is unclear whether a bank that is comfortably in compliance with the NSFR would feel the need to charge for RSF on new transactions.

Spreadsheet 4.2 NSFR Example

4.4   CLEARING AND MARGINING

4.4.1   Central Clearing

From 2007 onwards the GFC triggered grave concerns regarding counterparty risk, catalysed by events such as Lehman Brothers, the failure of monoline insurers, and

---

[13] BCBS (2017). Implementation of net stable funding ratio and treatment of derivative liabilities. Press Release (6 October). www.bis.org.

[14] BCBS (2014b), paragraph 35.

[15] Note that there has been a proposal in Europe to allow Level 1 assets received as variation margin to reduce the funding cost of derivatives. European Commission (2016). Proposal for a REGULATION OF THE EUROPEAN PARLIAMENT AND OF THE COUNCIL amending Regulation (EU) No 575/2013 as regards the leverage ratio, the net stable funding ratio, requirements for own funds and eligible liabilities, counterparty credit risk, market risk, exposures to central counterparties, exposures to collective investment undertakings, large exposures, reporting and disclosure requirements and amending Regulation (EU) No 648/2012. Proposal (23 November). www.eur-lex.europa.eu.

the bankruptcy of Icelandic banks. Counterparty risk in OTC derivatives, especially credit derivatives, was identified as a major risk to the financial system. There were also related operational and legal issues linked to aspects such as collateral management and close-out processes which result directly from counterparty risk mitigation. A CCP offers a potential solution to these problems as it guarantees performance, potentially reducing counterparty risk, and provides a centralised entity where aspects such as collateral management and default management are handled.

One of the largest perceived problems with bilateral OTC derivatives markets is the close-out process in the event of a major default, which can take many years and be subject to major legal proceedings (for example, see Figure 2.11). By contrast, CCPs can improve this process by establishing and enforcing the close-out rules, ensuring continuity and thereby reducing systemic risk. The default management of OTC derivatives by CCPs was viewed as being highly superior to bilateral markets in the aftermath of the Lehman bankruptcy. Although bilateral markets have made progress in certain aspects (see, for example, the adoption of the ISDA close-out protocol discussed in Section 6.3.5), they still cannot claim to be as coordinated as CCPs in this regard.

In contrast to OTC derivatives, the derivatives market that was cleared via CCPs was much more stable during the GFC. CCPs such as LCH.Clearnet coped well with the Lehman bankruptcy (Section 2.5.3) when many other elements of the OTC derivative market were operating poorly. One of the reasons for this is that, unlike most market participants, CCPs had actually envisaged and prepared for such a situation. Hence, whilst CCPs still experienced problems (such as identifying the positions of Lehman's clients), they were able, with help from their members, to transfer or close out a large volume of Lehman derivatives positions without major issues. Indeed, within a week of Lehman's bankruptcy, most of their outstanding OTC-cleared positions had been hedged, and within another week most of their client accounts had been transferred. Centrally-cleared OTC derivatives were seemingly much safer than their bilateral equivalents, although this may be questioned, especially given the recent Nasdaq default (Section 10.1.3).

In the aftermath of the GFC, policymakers (not surprisingly) embarked on regulatory changes that seemed largely aimed at moving risk away from global banks and the dangerous bilateral OTC derivatives market. This seemed to be driven generally by the view that the size, opacity, and interconnectedness of the market were too significant. One aspect of these policy changes was greater bank capital requirements for OTC derivatives. Another aspect was in relation to mandatory central clearing for certain products, with CCPs seemingly emerging as a panacea for financial markets' stability. For example:

> How do we establish good regulatory structure without destroying the incentive to innovate, without destroying the marketplace? We agree that we need to improve our regulations and to ensure that markets, firms, and financial products are subject to proper regulation and oversight. For example, credit default swaps – financial products that ensure against potential losses – should be processed through centralized clearinghouses. (George Bush, 15 November 2008)

As a part of financial reform, important legislative changes with respect to the OTC derivatives market were introduced. In September 2009, G20 leaders agreed that all standardised OTC derivatives would, in the future, need to be cleared through CCPs. This was done with the belief that a CCP can reduce systemic risk, operational risks, market manipulation, and fraud, and contribute to overall market stability. It is interesting to note that the original push towards central clearing seemed to be much lighter. The G20 meeting in 2008 defined a regulatory goal as:

> Strengthening the resilience and transparency of credit derivatives markets and reducing their systemic risks, including by improving the infrastructure of over-the-counter markets. (G20 declaration, Washington, November 2008)

Less than a year later, the clearing mandate was clear, and the focus on credit derivatives had expanded greatly to cover potentially all OTC derivatives:

> All standardized OTC derivative contracts should be traded on exchanges or electronic trading platforms, where appropriate, and cleared through central counterparties by end-2012 at the latest. OTC derivative contracts should be reported to trade repositories. Non-centrally cleared contracts should be subject to higher capital requirements. We ask the FSB [Financial Stability Board] and its relevant members to assess regularly implementation and whether it is sufficient to improve transparency in the derivatives markets, mitigate systemic risk, and protect against market abuse. (G20 declaration, Pittsburgh, September 2009)

In 2010, both Europe (via the European Commission's formal legislative proposal for regulation on OTC derivatives, CCPs and trade repositories) and the US (via the Dodd–Frank Wall Street Reform and Consumer Protection Act) put forward proposals that would commit all standardised OTC derivatives to be cleared through CCPs by the end of 2012. As a result, policymakers seemed to focus on CCPs as something close to a panacea for counterparty risk, especially with respect to the more dangerous products such as credit default swaps.

An important distinction with clearing is whether a counterparty is clearing directly (i.e. is a member of a CCP) or indirectly (i.e. is not a CCP member). In the latter case, a counterparty will have to clear through a clearing member, and the interactions in such a tri-party set-up are clearly important to understand. In general, large banks will be clearing members, and smaller participants will be non-clearing members and clear through a large bank. There will be some intermediate cases, such as smaller banks and financial institutions, where it will be necessary to weigh up the pros and cons of clearing directly and indirectly for a given asset class or product. This is discussed in more detail in Section 8.2.5.

Clearing is a process that occurs after the execution of a trade in which a CCP may step in between counterparties to guarantee performance. The main function of a CCP is, therefore, to interpose itself directly or indirectly between counterparties to assume their rights and obligations by acting as a buyer to every seller and vice versa. This means that the original counterparty to a trade no longer represents a direct risk, as the CCP to all intents and purposes becomes the new counterparty. CCPs essentially reallocate default losses via a variety of methods, including netting, margining, and loss mutualisation. Obviously, the intention is that the overall process will reduce counterparty and systemic risks.

CCPs are not a new idea and have been a part of the derivatives landscape for well over a century in connection with exchanges. An exchange is an organised market where buyers and sellers can interact in order to trade. Central clearing developed to control the counterparty risk in exchange-traded products and limit the risk that the insolvency of a member of the exchange may have. CCPs for exchange-traded derivatives is arguably a good example of market forces privately managing financial risk effectively. The two clearing structures, bilateral and central, share many common elements such as netting and margining, but also have fundamental differences. The fact that neither has become dominant suggests that they may each have their own strengths and weaknesses that are more or less emphasised in different markets.

CCPs provide a number of benefits. One is that they allow netting of all trades executed through them. In a bilateral market, an institution being long a contract with counterparty A and short the same contract with counterparty B has counterparty risk. However, if both contracts are centrally cleared, then the netted position has no risk. CCPs also manage margin requirements from their members to reduce the risk associated with the movement in the value of their underlying portfolios. CCPs also allow loss mutualisation; one counterparty's losses are dispersed throughout the market rather than being transmitted directly to a small number of counterparties with potential adverse consequences. Moreover, CCPs can facilitate orderly close-out by auctioning off the defaulter's contractual obligations with netting, thus reducing the total positions that need to be replaced, which reduces price impact. A well-managed centralised auction mechanism can be liquid and result in smaller price disruptions than uncoordinated replacement of bilateral positions during periods of pronounced uncertainty. CCPs can also facilitate the orderly transfer of client positions from financially-troubled intermediaries. The margins and other financial resources they hold protect against losses arising from this auction process.

The general role and mechanics of central clearing are:

- A CCP sets certain standards for its clearing members.
- The CCP takes responsibility for closing out all the positions of a defaulting clearing member.
- To support the above, the CCP maintains financial resources to cover losses in the event of a clearing member default:
  - o variation margin to closely track market movements;
  - o initial margin to cover liquidation or close-out costs above the variation margin; and
  - o a default fund to mutualise losses in the event of a severe default.
- The CCP also has a documented plan for the very extreme situation where all their financial resources (initial margin and the default fund) are depleted.[16] For example:
  - o additional calls to the default fund;
  - o variation margin gains haircutting; and
  - o selective tear-up of positions.

It is important to note that many end users of OTC derivatives (e.g. pension funds) will access CCPs through a clearing member and will not become members themselves. This will be due to the membership, operational, and liquidity requirements related to being

---

[16] Note that only the defaulter's initial margin can be used.

a clearing member. Some end users will also be exempt from the clearing obligation and will, therefore, be able to choose whether to clear via a CCP or not.

4.4.2   Bilateral Margin Requirements

Imposing a clearing mandate on all standardised OTC derivatives is clearly intended to encourage the central clearing of as many transactions as possible. However, for a particular product to be 'clearable' there must be enough incentive for CCPs and clearing participants to develop a clearing capability for that particular product. Obviously, if banks feel that clearing will be more expensive, then they will try and avoid this – for example, by transacting products that are not yet clearable. There are certain potential loopholes here: a clearable product can easily be made non-clearable by changing the contractual terms (for example, the maturity or reference rate). The introduction of higher capital charges (Section 4.2) for non-cleared OTC derivatives was one indirect way to promote clearing. However, a more direct way is to mandate margining/collateral practices in bilateral markets that are close to clearing. This is the aim of the bilateral margin requirements (BMR), often known as the uncleared margin rules (UMR). The rules are formulated by the Basel Committee and International Organization of Securities Commissions (BCBS-IOSCO 2012, 2013b, 2015, 2019a).

The mandatory margin regime takes into account two types of collateral:

- *Variation margin.* This covers the variability of the portfolio of transactions in question and is already relatively common in bilateral derivative markets.
- *Initial margin.* This represents extra collateral to cover costs in the event of a default and is historically uncommon (as 'independent amount') in bilateral derivative markets.

The rationale for the above rules (in particular initial margin) seems to be to reduce systemic risk (due to the fact that a large fraction of OTC derivatives will not be centrally cleared) and promote central clearing. It could be argued that high capital charges alone would achieve this objective. However, there is a key difference between initial margin and capital charges; for example, BCBS-IOSCO (2013b) notes that:

- Initial margin follows a 'defaulter pays' approach rather than a 'survivor pays' one, and therefore does not consume the financial resources of surviving entities.
- Initial margin is more 'targeted' to a specific portfolio and is furthermore adjusted over time to reflect changes in the risk of that portfolio in market conditions.

Initial margins, in terms of amount and liquidity, will be broadly in line with those required by CCPs and therefore they can be seen to promote central clearing and narrow the gap between the treatment of clearable and non-clearable OTC derivatives.

The specific details of the BMR are discussed in more detail in Section 7.4, but the key requirements are outlined below:

- Variation margin should be taken to reflect current exposure with no threshold (a threshold as described in Section 7.3.4 represents an amount below which margin is not exchanged).

- Initial margin should be taken against the potential increase in exposure in the future and should be calculated to cover a confidence level of (at least) 99%.
- A time horizon for close-out of 10 days should be assumed for initial margin calculation purposes.
- A key issue with initial margin requirements is segregation. Without any specific segregation (such as custodial or segregation agreement), a party having posted initial margin would essentially only be treated as an unsecured creditor in the event of the default of the margin receiver. Since non-segregated initial margin leads to counterparty risk (in case the receiver defaults), then initial margin segregation is required.
- Margin must be liquid, not just in normal market conditions but also in volatile periods, to the extent that it can be sold rapidly and predictably even in a time of financial stress.
- Appropriate haircuts must be taken against the value of cash or securities posted as margin.

4.4.3   Exemptions

Unlike capital and liquidity requirements, which generally apply to banks, clearing and margining regulation applies to potentially all users of OTC derivatives. However, certain relatively unsophisticated end users, who use derivatives for hedging purposes, cannot realistically be expected to clear or conform to the UMR and are therefore given exemptions. Furthermore, some products are exempt from these mandates. To determine whether a given transaction must be cleared or subject to margin requirements, the following questions must be asked:

- Are *both* parties subject to mandatory clearing or margin requirements ('covered entities')?
- Is the product itself subject to mandatory clearing or UMR?

If the answer to both the above questions is yes, then the transaction is subject to mandatory clearing or bilateral margining requirements. A transaction can, therefore, be exempt, either due to the nature of either one of the entities trading or due to the product type itself.

In general, the following entities are exempt from the mandates:

- sovereigns;
- central banks;
- multilateral development banks;
- the Bank for International Settlements; and
- other non-financial institutions that are not systemically important.

The final exemption above clearly has to be carefully defined and generally reflects end users undertaking hedging activities. However, the precise definitions are slightly different depending on the region in question:

- *Clearing exemptions under US regulation (Dodd–Frank)*. Exemptions for non-financial entities entering into transactions in order to hedge their commercial risk.

- *Clearing exemptions under EU regulation (EMIR)*. Non-financial counterparties (known as NFC-) are exempt. A counterparty is designated NFC+ when it crosses a threshold in terms of OTC derivative notional. These thresholds are set by asset class and are reviewed periodically. Entities designated as NFC+ are obliged to clear and comply with the UMRs, but NFC- entities are exempt. Pension funds are also currently given a temporary exemption, which is due to expire in 2020. This is intended to avoid dramatic shifts that could force major changes in asset allocation and gives CCPs more time to develop models for the main pension scheme products, namely interest rate and particularly inflation derivatives. Note that pension funds are not exempt from the UMR.
- *Bilateral margin exemptions (global guidelines via the BCBS-IOSCO)*. Covered entities are financial firms and systemically important non-financial entities. There is a notional threshold below which entities are exempt and a further counterparty-level threshold below which initial margins need not be posted (Section 7.4).

A significant transaction-related exemption is that of certain FX products. Market participants lobbied hard to argue that FX represents a special case since contracts are generally short-dated, and existing market practice such as CLS (continuous linked settlement) reduces risk significantly already (see discussion in Section 3.1.2 for a description of settlement risk and CLS functionality). Under EMIR, physically-settled FX forwards, FX swaps, and the FX 'leg' of cross-currency swaps are subject only to variation margin requirements (not initial margin). Similar exemptions exist in the US. Despite the clearing exemption, some non-deliverable forwards (cash-settled FX forwards) have been cleared on a voluntary basis.

Whilst physically-settled FX products create problems due to gross settlement and settlement risk (Section 3.1.2), there has been debate over the exemptions. For example, Duffie (2011) argues that whilst many contracts are short-dated, some FX transactions have significant counterparty risk due to the exchange of notional together with aspects such as the relatively high FX volatilities, fat tails, and sovereign risk. There are also potential regulatory arbitrages from categorising products differently.[17]

Another important point is that, generally, the clearing and the UMR apply only to trades done after the regulation requiring these changes was implemented and therefore only apply to new and not legacy transactions. Market participants can decide to voluntarily adopt clearing (this is referred to as 'backloading') or change their margining/collateral agreements to follow the UMR.

One potential issue, however, arises with respect to 'frontloading' of CCP trades. This requires derivatives counterparties to retrospectively clear any transaction executed between the authorisation of a CCP that clears the product and the start of a formal mandate. Once a CCP has been authorised to do business in a given region, regulators will decide if product offerings from that CCP will lead to mandatory clearing of these products. However, trades executed in the time period between CCP authorisation and this decision would need to be cleared if their remaining maturity is above a threshold. This means that a bilateral transaction may later become subject to mandatory clearing,

---

[17] Sherif, N. (2018). VM rules sound death knell for forex swaps in Europe. *Risk* (18 January). www.risk.net.

which introduces confusion as the costs of bilateral and cleared transactions are different. This will give market participants a difficult decision as, when pricing and executing the trades, they would be uncertain as to whether or not they would be hit by a clearing mandate in the future.[18]

4.4.4　CCP Capital Requirements

Given the clearing mandate, there is also a need to define capital requirements for centrally-cleared transactions. Like the bilateral market, this would have the potential to distinguish:

- the credit quality (e.g. default probability and LGD) of the CCP;
- the exposure of the portfolio; and
- the margining terms and their impact on reducing exposure.

Prior to the clearing mandate, exposure to a CCP via contracts such as derivatives (and assets held by the CCP as a custodian) were given a zero exposure under the so-called Basel II framework (2004) as long as the CCP exposures were fully margined on a daily basis.

Under current capital rules, CCP exposures are subject to capital charges in order to reflect the fact that CCPs are not risk free, and also to potentially differentiate between the quality of different CCPs. Under Basel III, a low-risk weight of 2% is applied to qualifying CCPs (QCCPs). QCCPs are recognised by local regulators as conforming to global principles and accordingly should be safer than non-qualifying CCPs (to which banks are exposed to higher capital charges). Whilst this element is not risk sensitive (i.e. the 2% applies for all QCCPs), there is another capital charge (related to the so-called default fund discussed in Section 8.2.4) which is risk sensitive. This capital charge will, therefore, be larger for a CCP that is deemed more risky.

CCP capital rules are dependent on whether clearing is done directly or indirectly. In the latter case, the 2% risk weight may be higher, but there will be no default fund-related capital charge since indirect clearers (i.e. those clearing through clearing members) do not contribute to the CCP default fund.

CCP capital charges and calculation methodologies will be discussed in more detail in Section 13.6.

---

[18] Maxwell, F. (2013). CCP frontloading: the pricing nightmare. *Risk* (22 October). www.risk.net.

5

What is xVA?

5.1 OVERVIEW

Prior to 2007 and the global financial crisis (GFC), a number of fundamental assumptions were prevalent when pricing, valuing, and managing derivatives and similar products:

- no credit risk;
- the existence of a unique, risk-free rate;
- the ability to borrow and lend at the risk-free rate (i.e. no funding costs);
- no impact of collateral/margin (i.e. collateral was purely a risk mitigant and had no value in itself); and
- no regulatory capital costs (although banks would typically impose hurdle rates with respect to economic capital usage).

Traditional derivatives pricing and valuation generally solely examined the impact of cash flows. For simple transactions, this problem was considered relatively straightforward and was often simply a question of applying the correct discount factor. The valuation was only treated as difficult where cash flows were themselves more complex, such as being non-linear, contingent, or multidimensional. These more complex payoffs or 'exotics' were difficult to value, but their vanilla equivalents were assumed to be relatively trivial.

In the years since the GFC began, these assumptions have been systematically challenged as a result of market practice (e.g. banks having material credit spreads), accounting and regulatory change. In general, this has led to a series of valuation adjustments that transform a simple valuation into the correct one by taking into account the above components.

Prior to the GFC, credit value adjustments (CVAs) and other valuation adjustments were largely unheard of. Banks may have priced the costs of counterparty risk, funding, and capital when dealing with some clients, but these costs were often not considered prohibitive to trading activity and profitability, even for the riskiest over-the-counter (OTC) derivatives. However, the events from 2007 onwards have resulted in increased costs with respect to these aspects. Additionally, accounting and regulatory standards have evolved to require certain practices around financial reporting and capitalisation, which have had significant cost implications.

Regulation has been a key driver of valuation adjustments. For example, Basel requirements around liquidity and regulatory capital have amplified the importance of funding and capital costs. In addition, the clearing mandate and bilateral margin requirements have created the need for the consideration of initial margin costs, historically rare in OTC derivatives.

5.2   ANALYSIS OF xVA

5.2.1   Definition

Before making further analysis, it will be useful to characterise valuation adjustments (xVAs) and discuss some general points of importance. A general and simple representation is:

$$\text{Actual Value} = \text{Base Value} + \text{xVA} \qquad (5.1)$$

where xVA refers to the different valuation adjustments for all relevant components. This is simply a statement that the correct value (or price) can be thought of as some base or ideal value – probably relatively simple to calculate – together with separate xVA terms.

A first implicit assumption is that of linearity, which means that the xVA components are completely separate from the actual value. In practice, this is not completely true, especially in relation to the consideration of default. This will be discussed later. In practice, the above separation will almost always be considered to be a reasonable, and necessary, approximation.

It is also useful to characterise xVA as allowing an institution to define the economic value of a given transaction. Such valuation is incremental since it represents the value after the transaction with respect to the value before. Off-balance-sheet transactions – such as derivatives – have a complex impact on valuation, which explains the significant complexity of valuation adjustments in contrast to simpler on-balance-sheet transactions such as loans. For example, if a bank lends a customer a certain amount, then they increase their credit risk by a well-defined amount and timescale, and the funding and capital implications are probably also relatively easy to understand. However, when the bank executes a derivatives transaction, the effects on credit risk, collateral, funding and capital are more subtle and complex. An obvious example of this is funding, since derivatives can be both assets and liabilities.

When we refer to value in the above context, it is important to consider what we mean by it. The value of a company can be defined as the sum of shareholder value and the value of its debt. Agency costs arise when shareholders are interested in a company following a risky strategy, since they will benefit from the entire upside whilst suffering limited downside. There is also a clear distinction in default where shareholders receive nothing, but bondholders are still paid some recovery value. These problems will be seen in valuation adjustments related to aspects such as funding where the shareholder and bondholder points of view will lead to different xVAs.

5.2.2   Components

Before making further analysis, it will be useful to characterise the different xVAs. As discussed in Section 3.2.3, the anatomy of valuation adjustments is normally defined as:

$$\text{xVA} = \text{CVA} + \text{DVA} + \text{ColVA} + \text{FVA} + \text{KVA} + \text{MVA} \qquad (5.2)$$

where the different terms refer to counterparty risk (CVA and DVA), collateral (ColVA), funding (FVA), capital (KVA), and initial margin (MVA). These are not the only definitions used by authors, although they are now relatively standard and will be used consistently throughout this book. By convention, the valuation adjustments will be represented as above, with a negative amount representing a cost (or loss) and a positive component, therefore, being a benefit (or gain). Some valuation adjustments (ColVA and

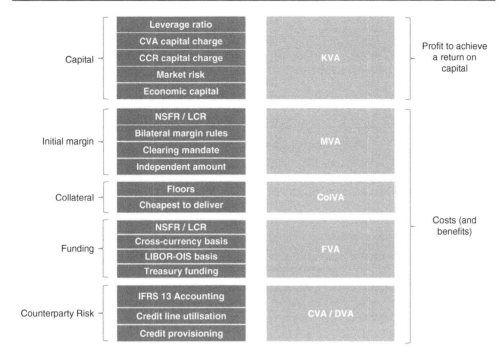

Figure 5.1   Overview of valuation adjustments.

FVA) can represent a benefit from a valuation point of view. From a pricing point of view, all valuation adjustments can represent an incremental benefit due to portfolio effects.

The valuation adjustments are also shown in Figure 5.1. Whilst not all the components have been fully explained at this point (we will refer to this figure in later chapters), note that there are three general considerations in defining a valuation adjustment:

- *Economic.* This refers to the need to value components because of due diligence and market practice. Credit provisioning – the need to provision for credit losses – is one such example. Economic capital or funding are also examples.
- *Accounting.* Distinct from economic considerations are accounting rules that may require a valuation adjustment to be included in a specific way. The obvious example here is CVA and DVA (see discussion in Section 5.3.3).
- *Regulatory.* Regulatory considerations may shape the way in which valuation adjustments are treated. The obvious example here is with capital, where regulatory capital is probably considered more relevant than economic capital, as discussed in Section 4.2.1. This is also the case with funding and liquidity requirements, such as the liquidity coverage ratio (LCR) and net stable funding ratio (NSFR) (Section 4.3).

5.2.3   Why Valuation Adjustments?

The role of xVA (Equation 5.1) is to adjust some base value (e.g. one based on simple discounting) to take into account more complex components such as credit and funding and create the actual valuation. Whilst this approach is to some extent historical (i.e.

starting from a traditional valuation), there are several reasons why the separation into valuation adjustments makes sense:

- *Complexity*. The base value may be a relatively simple calculation, perhaps only reflecting the valuation of the cash flows as in the traditional approach. It may also conform to a certain type of transaction (for example, one that is centrally cleared).[1] On the other hand, the xVA components are much more complicated and require knowledge of contractual terms together with the economic impact of credit, funding, collateral, and capital. xVA requires a number of subjective parameters (e.g. counterparty credit spread curves, volatilities, and correlations).
- *Portfolio effects*. Whilst the base valuation is typically additive across transactions, xVAs are generally portfolio-level calculations. Hence, whilst base valuations can probably be done at the transaction level, xVA terms must be calculated in a more portfolio-driven framework. Related to this, there is a question of directionality. In general, portfolios which are more unidirectional will be costlier in xVA terms, whilst more balanced positions will have lower costs.
- *Organisation*. Whilst the idealistic, cash flow-driven valuation is suited to separate trading desks specialising in, for example, asset class, market, type of client or region, the xVA component necessitates management by a single dedicated desk. Such a desk is often known as the 'xVA desk' or 'central desk' (Section 21.1).
- *Accounting and regulatory*. xVA is very much driven by specific accounting and regulatory requirements that impact the way in which various terms are treated. Knowledge of these requirements, both current and future, is a critical aspect of xVA quantification.

Whilst xVA is generally now accepted as an intrinsic part of derivatives valuation, some banks and other market participants have historically been slow to follow market practice. One of the primary reasons for this is that xVA components are generally costs and therefore have a detrimental impact on profitability over the short to medium term. Furthermore, xVA mispricing cannot generally be taken advantage of (arbitraged), and so banks pricing xVA inappropriately suffer only from an inability to correctly incentivise or disincentivise transactions in terms of their overall impact of the bank through time.

There might also be a question about where it is desirable and practical to incorporate charges such as xVA into transactions and where it is not. In general, xVA is extremely heterogeneous depending on the type of transaction, counterparty, and other aspects. It is, therefore, key to represent the costs at the transaction level for pricing and valuation purposes. This does not mean that xVA will capture all costs. However, other costs (e.g. operational expenses or capital charges that are not transaction specific, such as operational risk) are more homogeneous and therefore do not require specific attention for pricing and valuation.

5.2.4   Mark-to-market and xVA as a Cost (and Benefit)

Transactions such as derivatives are typically valued on a 'mark-to-market' (MTM) basis. MTM represents an accounting practice that involves recording the value of an asset

---

[1] At least from the CCP point of view.

or liability to reflect current market levels. MTM, therefore, means that the value is the current market price and not an alternative representation such as the historical cost. A MTM treatment is normally associated with the trading book of a bank that refers to transactions that are regularly traded or have values that can be derived from market observables that are regularly traded. By contrast, the banking book typically refers to assets that are not actively traded and are expected to be held to maturity – an obvious example being loans.

Since xVA terms are used in combination with base valuation via Equation 5.1, they are generally treated as MTM valuations even though they are not traded or based on market observables that are traded. Whilst this creates consistency in the overall valuation of derivatives, it creates inconsistency elsewhere. For example, the treatment of credit (counterparty) risk on a derivative may be different from the treatment of credit risk on a loan. Such inconsistency may be made even starker since banks may transact both products with clients (e.g. in making a floating-rate loan and providing an interest rate swap to convert this to a fixed-rate loan). Such inconsistencies are unavoidable but will provide important context for the way in which banks treat components such as CVAs.

Another important facet of MTM valuation is the treatment of revenue. Suppose a bank executes a long-maturity swap where they receive a rate slightly higher than the market rate – this difference representing their revenue. Contractually, this revenue is accrued over time, but from a valuation perspective it is all realised immediately through a higher MTM. This problem creates a fundamentally incorrect incentive in banks since the front office is potentially rewarded for looking at transactions with large MTMs, even if these have relatively high costs due to being long-dated and having high counterparty risk, collateral, funding, and capital costs.

To a degree, the incorporation of xVA in pricing and valuation can be seen to partially resolve the above dilemma since it ensures that future costs (and benefits) are correctly priced into transactions and then included in the ongoing valuation. Indeed, recent years have seen gradual incorporation of xVA components where banks have evolved from a traditional approach in which they are ignored to one in which they are treated more rigorously. In general, rather than ignoring costs altogether or accruing them over time, these costs are priced into transactions, form a part of the valuation process and are owned and managed centrally.

Table 5.1 shows a general evolution of xVA standards which has occurred at different rates. In general, CVA was the only component considered prior to the GFC, with major banks starting to adopt a more progressive CVA pricing and management approach from the late 1990s onwards. Funding and collateral were moves that started around 2010, heavily catalysed by changes in market conditions and regulation during this period. Finally, capital charges and KVA are not (yet) treated in a similar fashion to the other terms. Whilst capital is priced more rigorously than before, and hurdles are less 'soft' (in other words, it is harder to transact when the capital hurdle is not met), KVA does not form part of the valuation. Some argue that this is justified since capital is not a cost in the way the other terms are, but others argue that KVA is analogous to the other xVAs and so should be treated similarly eventually. We will discuss this further in Section 19.3.4.

Table 5.1   Evolution of xVA treatment.

	Traditional non-xVA approach	Market-standard xVA approach
Counterparty risk (CVA/DVA)	Default losses suffered as and when they occur.	CVA inception pricing, valuation, and management.
Funding (FVA/MVA)	Funding costs accrued on a daily basis with unexpected changes.	FVA inception pricing, valuation, and management.
Collateral (ColVA)	Management of operational aspects of collateral. Unexpected costs and benefits from collateral terms.	ColVA inception pricing, valuation, and central management.
Capital (KVA)	Businesses set 'soft' return on capital metrics.	KVA is priced more directly into transactions but with no valuation impact.

5.2.5   xVAs by Transaction Type

Very broadly speaking, there are four ways to transact derivatives from a counterparty risk point of view (Table 5.2):

- *Uncollateralised.* An uncollateralised transaction has no agreement for either party to post margin/collateral against their obligations. As discussed previously, many end users, especially non-financial institutions, transact in this way. This situation clearly leads to significant counterparty risk, funding, and capital considerations, and so CVA, DVA, FVA, and KVA terms are important. There is no need to consider collateral or initial margin (ColVA and MVA).
- *Strongly collateralised.* This usually means the traditional form of collateralisation in the interbank market where – generally – both parties post (receive) collateral (variation margin) based on their negative (positive) MTM value. Such collateral exchange clearly mitigates counterparty risk and funding and leads to lower capital charges, but potentially creates the need to consider ColVA.[2]
- *Overcollateralised.* In this case, which is becoming more common, there is extra collateral (initial margin) which reduces counterparty risk and capital even further but leads to costs in terms of posting initial margin. In such situations, the collateral terms are often simplified (e.g. cash in a single currency)[3] and so ColVA may be less important.

Table 5.2   Qualitative illustration of the relative importance of xVA terms in different relationships. Note that DVA adjustments are benefits and FVA adjustments can be costs or benefits.

	ColVA	CVA	DVA	FVA	KVA	MVA
Uncollateralised		✓✓✓	✓✓✓	✓✓✓	✓✓✓	
Strongly collateralised	✓✓	✓✓	✓✓		✓✓	
Overcollateralised	✓	✓	✓		✓	✓✓✓
Centrally cleared		✓			✓	✓✓✓

---

[2] For reasons discussed in Section 11.4.2, the funding contribution may practically be considered to be zero.

[3] This relates to the collateralisation (variation margin) but not to the overcollateralisation (initial margin).

- *Centrally cleared.* A centrally-cleared transaction should have minimal counterparty risk and funding requirements and low capital charges. Collateral adjustments will also likely be null due to the nature of collateralisation at a central counterparty (CCP) (cash in the currency of the transaction). However, there will be high costs of posting initial margin to the CCP.

The above analysis is simple and ignores many caveats, such as one-way collateralisation and type of collateral. The notation should not be taken literally (e.g. the MVA cost for an overcollateralised bilateral trade will not be exactly the same as for a centrally-cleared trade), but it is a general starting point for the breakdown of xVA.

An immediate consequence of the xVA differences above is that a risk conversion may occur when the transaction or counterparty terms are changed. In a sense, there is a sort of conservation of xVA where value can merely be pushed around with respect to the different components. Some obvious examples of these conversions are:

- *Collateralisation.* This can reduce counterparty and funding costs but removes beneficial components such as DVA and funding benefits and also requires an analysis of specific optionality in the collateral agreement via ColVA.
- *Central clearing and bilateral collateral rules.* The requirement to post additional collateral in the form of initial margin creates MVA but reduces CVA and KVA.
- *Hedging.* Hedging CVA for accounting purposes may create additional capital requirements and therefore increase KVA. On the other hand, reducing KVA may lead to greater CVA volatility.

It should also be noted that some conversions are not apparent within xVA terms. For example, collateralisation generally reduces counterparty risk and funding costs for both parties. But it also leads to liquidity risk for at least one party due to the need to fund uncertain collateral requirements in the future.[4] Whilst such components have no specific xVA value, they are certainly important considerations. Indeed, this is the reason why institutions benefiting from one-way margining have sometimes been reluctant to move to two-way collateralisation, even though this would reduce xVA costs (see further discussion in Section 7.6.2).

Finally, note that as some xVA terms are benefits, certain types of transactions may appear less favourable than in other situations. Consider collateral as an example: assets (i.e. lending) benefit from collateralisation, whereas liabilities (i.e. borrowing) do not. Since derivatives can be both assets and liabilities, it stands to reason that one party may see the lack of collateralisation as adding value. In a symmetric set-up this is clearly true, but it can even be true in the more realistic asymmetric set-up that xVA participants use. Put more simply, an end user may (although this is not common) actually see a better price for an uncollateralised derivative than for the same transaction executed on a collateralised basis (see Section 18.2.4).

5.2.6   Overlaps and Portfolio Effects

Some xVA terms will naturally interact. For example, capital requirements (KVA) will exist partly as a buffer against possible counterparty default, but in the event of the actual

---

[4] Banks may not consider this a liquidity risk due to the offsetting collateral requirements of their hedges, but end-users would certainly see liquidity costs attached to collateralisation.

default these will gradually reduce whilst the accounting CVA increases (see discussion on 'incurred CVA' in Section 13.4.1). This is natural as capital held against potential losses reduces as actual accounting losses are taken.

There is also a more complex interaction that is harder to quantify and manage. The definitions for xVA terms (e.g. Figure 5.1) would suggest a valuation approach via the hierarchy of components. However, the real situation is more complex due to non-linearities and overlaps between the various terms. Rather than being a series of mutually exclusive terms, xVA components may share common economic features. Hence, there is a possibility of double counting or overlap which must be considered. Such overlaps are not always obvious and are often not treated rigorously. The common representation where xVAs can be calculated separately and independently is an approximation. In reality, xVA adjustments are interdependent and should, ideally, be computed jointly. For practical reasons, the assumption of independent terms is probably a necessary one, but certain ad hoc adjustments may be made in order to correct for this. These 'overlaps' are discussed later in the relevant places. Moreover, xVA can be recursive (i.e. the value today depends on the future strategy), which can be difficult to deal with in a tractable setting.

Another problem with xVA is that it is generally a portfolio-level calculation. Portfolio in this context often applies to a given counterparty, where adjustments such as CVA and ColVA depend on counterparty-specific terms such as netting and collateral agreements. However, the portfolio may also apply to the entire book of derivatives, as is relevant for some regulatory capital calculations and funding under certain assumptions. Indeed, it could even be argued that some xVA calculations (for example, FVA or the leverage ratio) require computation vis-à-vis the entire bank portfolio. This is not surprising since the aim of xVA can be seen to be to allow an institution to fully incorporate the economic value of a given transaction (Equation 5.1). However, from a pragmatic point of view, it is often necessary to make certain simplifying assumptions so as to be able to compute xVA in a practical way for pricing and valuation purposes.

The above explains why it is critical to manage xVA centrally and make consistent decisions regarding pricing, valuation, and risk mitigation so as to optimise aspects such as capital utilisation and achieve the maximum *overall* economic benefit.

5.2.7   CVA is the Least Real Valuation Adjustment

CVA is the oldest valuation adjustment. It is an explicit component of financial reporting (Section 5.3.3), and there is now a CVA capital charge (Section 4.2.5). Other valuation adjustments are more recent and have yet to become an explicit component of financial reporting or capital rules. However, accounting and regulatory considerations aside, CVA is the least real xVA term. This is due to the fact that CVA relates purely to the possible cost arising from a default event and there are no costs unless this default occurs. Furthermore, for good-quality credits, default is a relatively unlikely event. For similar reasons, DVA is probably so unreal as to be considered inapplicable (Section 17.3).

Hence, if the counterparty never defaults, then the CVA turns out (eventually) to be zero. However, this is not true of funding, collateral, and capital costs. These are typically seen on a daily basis and are necessary 'production costs' of a transaction when the counterparty doesn't default (Figure 5.2).

The above comment on CVA should not be taken too literally, but it is an important point to keep in mind. Whilst funding, collateral, and capital are constant needs, the nature of CVA is more binary. Banks may feel that CVA is less real due to having strong

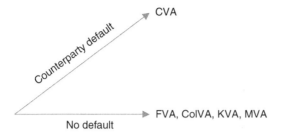

Figure 5.2   Nature of xVA with respect to default.

relationships with clients across potentially more than one business area, and will feel that the default of these clients is unlikely. Hence, they may feel that the CVA costs – as defined by accounting standards, for example – are not representative of their actual likely losses due to defaults.

One could make an analogy between CVA and a short out-of-the-money option position. Such an option is unlikely to expire in-the-money and therefore may be viewed (in the real world) as having no value. Now, suppose a trading desk has an entire portfolio of such options: perhaps the best strategy is to do nothing and wait for all the options to expire when they will hopefully be worthless. If the trader hedges the options book, then losses will be crystallised through the hedging (although this will avoid large losses in case any of the options move in-the-money). Of course, the 'do nothing' strategy is difficult to justify since the price of options will be observable in the market and will also be hedgeable (via the underlying asset), and so controls such as risk limits will force hedging. However, for CVA, such market prices do not exist, and the hedging strategy is far more difficult to execute. Hence, CVA may seem partially unreal – especially for high-quality credits – as viewed from a purely economic perspective, and may be seen more like an accounting or regulatory requirement. This is not true for other valuation adjustments that are seen on a real and continuous basis, irrespective of counterparty defaults.

The above point will be relevant for later discussion on the use of market-implied default probabilities (Section 12.1.2), the management of CVA (Section 21.2), and the overlap between CVA and KVA (Section 19.4.1).

5.3   VALUATION

5.3.1   Price and Value

Price and value are not the same thing. A price is a relatively straightforward and objective quantity as seen by a given transaction in a given market (assuming such a transaction is observed). Value is a more subjective component as it may be considered to be linked to the gain from holding an asset or by disposing of it in the market. Furthermore, accounting and regulation impact the value of a given asset due to certain requirements or restrictions in relation to holding that asset. It may be useful to define the following different versions of value:

- *Economic value*. This is often used to refer to the specific value of a derivative to a particular party. As such, it is a private valuation and can include entity-specific valuation adjustments. Economic value from a bank's point of view may well be derived from (practical) hedging considerations, including effects such as market inefficiencies. The potential to exit a transaction at some point in the future may play a role here but is probably not the primary concern.

- *Accounting value.* Accounting value is the appropriate value that a transaction should be marked at for official balance sheet purposes and as such should be general and not dependent on entity-specific considerations. This is not necessarily the same as the economic view of a given bank, although there should be a clear connection.
- *Regulatory value.* This component is increasingly important as more regulation begins to impact the derivatives market. Such regulation can essentially artificially reduce (or even increase) the value of certain transactions. For example, a bank may view a given transaction as beneficial from an economic and accounting point of view, but it may not be so beneficial in light of the underlying regulatory capital requirements or the leverage ratio (LR).

The above distinctions are important. In particular, some authors tend to focus on economic value, whilst others take more of an accounting-driven viewpoint. Arguments about the form or validity of xVA adjustments may be different when viewed from different perspectives. When the term 'value' or 'valuation' is used below, it should be assumed to be accounting driven unless otherwise stated.

The 'law of one price' states that there should be only a single price for a derivative transaction. Otherwise, arbitrageurs would simply buy and sell in different markets and remove the price difference. With respect to valuation adjustments, there could be two concerns here:

- *Asymmetry.* Valuation adjustments are generally costs and may violate the law of one price since they create a pricing framework that is not symmetric.
- *Entity-specific charges.* Some components, such as the funding and capital cost of a bank, are entity specific, meaning that different market participants will quote different prices.

The law of one price stems from no-arbitrage assumptions. However, the obvious arbitrageurs in the derivatives market with respect to valuation adjustments are end users that transact on a largely uncollateralised basis and are charged xVA components for counterparty risk, funding, and capital. However, such entities are not market makers, and their business model is not to exploit perceived inconsistencies in the pricing of banks. Moreover, it is generally not possible to trade xVA more directly – for example, in contracts such as contingent credit default swaps (Section 3.1.8).

Ultimately, xVA should be considered as a case of significant market incompleteness, and certain asymmetric and entity-specific charges (that are clearly a component of economic value) may still exist.

5.3.2   xVA Markets

It is also relevant to characterise two broad markets in which derivatives are traded:

- *Consumer market.* This refers generally to end users using derivatives to fulfil hedging or investment purposes. An end user may only transact in one direction (e.g. always paying the fixed interest rate or buying oil). End users often do not exit transactions early, and when they do the price penalties may be quite significant. Transactions in these markets are rather one-way and asymmetric and are likely to be inefficient. That said, the end users will not be set up to take advantage of arbitrage opportunities. Directionality and lack of collateralisation can make xVA components very significant in these cases.

- *Intermediary market.* This generally refers to the more sophisticated financial institutions that manage their positions with their clients via each other (e.g. in the interbank market). Some transactions will be centrally cleared. Since the players in this market are generally more sophisticated and manage two-way flows, the transactions tend to be more symmetric and efficient. Valuation adjustments will, in general, be smaller due to the use of risk-reduction mechanisms such as collateral. Arbitrage opportunities will be easier to exploit and the market will be more efficient.

The above characterisations, though general, are important since the xVA adjustments considered here originate mainly in consumer markets. Due to the nature of such markets, arguments based on considerations such as no-arbitrage and market efficiencies may be harder to apply.

5.3.3 Accounting Standards

Changes in accounting standards have been a key driver for the implementation of CVA. This has been driven by components of Financial Accounting Standards (FAS) 157, which are part of US GAAP (generally accepted accounting principles), and International Financial Reporting Standards (IFRS) 13, which are relevant for most other regions. Although there are some differences, there are many common elements between IFRS and US GAAP with respect to the measurement of fair value. These accounting standards provide principles on how to measure fair value, but this does not remove a certain level of subjectivity. In general, accounting standards are less prescriptive than regulation, such as Basel capital and liquidity requirements.

More generally, the fair price is defined as being an exit price. The wording in Financial Accounting Standards Board 157 (FASB 2006) reads:

> Fair value is the price that would be received to sell an asset or paid to transfer a liability in an orderly transaction in the principal (or most advantageous) market at the measurement date under current market conditions (ie an exit price) regardless of whether that price is directly observable or estimated using another valuation technique.

Exit price would most obviously reference the current traded price of an asset. For example, the exit price of a bond would represent the current price at which it is trading in the secondary market (assuming this is a liquid market).

Exit price creates a problem for many transactions subject to significant xVA adjustments because a market price may not be observable. Even though many OTC derivatives markets are actively traded (especially for the most common products), such prices may not be relevant for similar transactions held by the reporting entity due to the specifics of the trading relationship. For example, the price of an interest rate swap on a swap execution facility (SEF) or in the interbank market (an intermediary market) would not be reflective of the exit price of the same transaction traded on an uncollateralised basis (in the consumer market). A problem with the fair value application to xVA is that a market of some type is assumed. Kenyon and Green (2014b) go so far as to argue that an uncollateralised market price is an oxymoron.

A fair value measurement should, therefore, take into account the elements that market participants would consider when setting the price for a transaction. Counterparty risk (CVA) is clearly defined as being a component of fair value. For example, IFRS 13 (IFRS 2011) states:

> The entity shall include the effect of the entity's net exposure to the credit risk of that counterparty or the counterparty's net exposure to the credit risk of the entity in the fair value measurement when market participants would take into account any existing arrangements that mitigate credit risk exposure in the event of default.

The CVA for an uncollateralised derivative will clearly be materially greater than one that is collateralised (e.g. an interbank transaction), and this must clearly be accounted for. Although not explicitly mentioned, the concept of exit price would also indicate that other components that market participants would consider when setting a price, such as funding, should also be included in the valuation.

Related to the above point is that IFRS 13 and FASB 157 clearly define the need to include a risk premium. For example, IFRS 13 (IFRS 2011) states:

> Market participants generally seek compensation (ie a risk premium) for bearing the uncertainty inherent in the cash flows of an asset or a liability. A fair value measurement should include a risk premium reflecting the amount that market participants would demand as compensation for the uncertainty inherent in the cash flows. Otherwise, the measurement would not faithfully represent fair value. In some cases determining the appropriate risk premium might be difficult. However, the degree of difficulty alone is not a sufficient reason to exclude a risk premium.

This implies the use of market-implied (or risk-neutral) parameters (e.g. implied volatilities and credit spreads) regardless of whether such parameters can be observed directly from market prices. This clearly has a fundamental impact on the calculation of CVA and other adjustments. The most significant aspect of this is the use of credit spreads, and not historical default probabilities, in the quantification of counterparty risk (CVA), as discussed in Section 12.1.2. This is important because banks, in general, may consider historical default probabilities to be more relevant for other assets such as loans.[5]

In accounting, whilst there is the concept of credit risk applicable to the fair value of assets, there is correspondingly the concept of own credit applicable to liabilities. This creates symmetry, where the borrower considers their own credit risk in the same way as their counterparty does. Since derivatives can be both assets and liabilities, the concept of

---

[5] Although loans themselves are seeing a change in their accounting requirements through IFRS 9 (www.ifrs.org).

exit price leads to the need for an own credit component to be included, which is usually known as debt or debit value adjustment (DVA). The relevant wording is:

- IFRS 13: The fair value of a liability reflects the effect of non-performance risk. Non-performance risk includes, but may not be limited to, an entity's own credit risk.
- FASB 157: The reporting entity shall consider the effect of its credit risk (credit standing) on the fair value of the liability in all periods in which the liability is measured at fair value.

The use of DVA can be questioned since, for example, a party with a worse credit quality may achieve better terms when exiting a transaction due to their counterparty experiencing a larger cost via CVA (which is removed after exiting the transaction). Hence, a counterparty with a large CVA may pay this in order to exit, which is seen by the other party as a DVA. Collective CVA and DVA adjustments conform to the law of one price (Section 5.3.1).

However, DVA is problematic since it appears on a bank's balance sheet as a profit which increases as the credit quality of the bank deteriorates. Moreover, the benefit is in relation to the default of the bank and so – unless the bank does indeed default – this depreciates due to time decay (Section 21.1.3). Furthermore, Basel III capital requirements disallow DVA accounting benefits from a capital point of view, BCBS 2011d stating:

> Derecognise in the calculation of Common Equity Tier 1, all unrealised gains and losses that have resulted from changes in the fair value of liabilities that are due to changes in the bank's own credit risk.

This rule is to prevent a bank seeing an increase in its equity as a result of an increase in its credit risk and a reduction in the value of its liabilities.

DVA is therefore a good example of the difference between economic, accounting, and regulatory value (Section 5.3.1). Whilst it is an accounting requirement, it may not be viewed as economically meaningful and is certainly not part of the value from a regulatory point of view.

The market the exit price corresponds to should also be considered. Both IFRS 13 and FASB 157 define this as the 'principal (or most advantageous) market for the asset or liability'. This can create problems, as the following comment illustrates:

> In the case of Danske Bank, accountants are telling it that the exit price should reflect what one of its Nordic peers would pay for a trade; but Danske trades far more frequently with global dealers.[6]

From a CVA/DVA perspective, this can cause problems. For example, an institution may argue that it would exit a transaction with a counterparty who used historical default probabilities. Here, the explicit reference to components such as risk premiums would tend to suggest that this would be inappropriate. Given a smaller bank's relative inactivity in some derivatives markets, it would seem natural to view the exit price as relating more to a global dealer than a smaller peer bank.

---

[6] Becker, L. and N. Sherif (2015). FVA: How six smaller banks do it. *Risk* (2 April). www.risk.net.

5.3.4   Accounting Trends

As discussed above, accounting standards reference only CVA and DVA components directly. However, they implicitly suggest that other components should be included if they are a component of the exit price of a transaction. Indeed, it has become relatively common practice to also include funding value adjustment (FVA) in financial reporting. For example:

> … a fair-value adjustment was applied to account for the impact of incorporating the cost of funding into the valuation of uncollateralised derivatives.[7]

Regarding pricing and valuation of xVA components, banks generally want the economic value to align with official (e.g. accounting-based) numbers. The reason for this is that banks measure performance annually and base the performance of their derivatives business primarily on the basis of MTM valuation (as opposed to other measures such as return on capital). Hence, anything that a bank considers to be a real economic cost should be included in the official valuation so as to avoid reporting misleading valuations and distributing profits gross of such a cost. This may explain the motivation for banks to account for other components such as FVA. Another motivation is the overlap between DVA and FVA, which will be discussed in Section 18.2.5.

However, adjustments such as FVA lead to further complexities. Firstly, they create a framework where the law of one price – seemingly a key feature of the requirement to include DVA – no longer holds. They also create a recursive problem since one party's exit price is another's entry price, and so suggests that the funding costs should be those of the party with whom the transaction would be exited (e.g. a novation to another bank),[8] rather than the entity making the calculation. Note also that both IFRS 13 and FASB 157 state that a 'fair value is a market-based measurement, not an entity-specific measurement'. Hence, a bank seems unable to *value* with its own cost of funding, but rather with something closer to the 'market cost of funding'. It can, of course, *price* with its own cost of funding, but it may then see a deviation between price and valuation.

There have been various arguments about how to resolve the above contradictions. For example, Albanese et al. (2015) consider an exit price based on 'a competitive auction where entities of all types, including unlevered real-money funds with negligible funding costs, are allowed to participate'. Whilst exit prices permit reference to the most advantageous market – which may imply counterparties with minimal funding costs – it is not practically possible to novate derivatives transactions to such counterparties since they do not play such a role in the market. Hence, it may be argued that whilst, in theory, they should not exist, market inefficiencies may lead to real adjustments such as FVA, which are reasonable components of the actual exit price.

Whilst funding and FVA have become fairly standard adjustments in valuation, as well as pricing, other valuation adjustments such as MVA (initial margin) and KVA (capital) have not yet been treated in a similar way.[9] However, since these are clear components of

---

[7] Barclays Annual Report (2012). www.home.barclays.

[8] A novation is a legal transfer of a transaction to another party.

[9] There is some evidence of MVA being accounted for as a component of FVA by some banks, and even some profits being held back from an accounting point of view, which could be seen as a first step towards KVA accounting.

entry prices, it could be argued that it is only a matter of time before they are treated in a similar manner to FVA. This will be discussed in more detail in Sections 19.3.4 and 20.3.2.

5.3.5   Totem

IHS Markit's Totem service is a well-established utility for valuation consensus, enabling market participants to price test their own valuations for various products: each firm submits prices for specific trades and IHS Markit normalises the data and returns anonymous data to participants.[10]

One part of Totem is an xVA service that covers transactions subject to valuation adjustments involving credit risk, funding, collateral, and initial margin (at the time of writing, capital-related valuation adjustments or KVA are not considered). Only contributors see the results of the exercise, which are not public domain, and so the discussion below describes only the general approach. Products covered are mainly interest rate swaps with a variety of maturities, moneyness, and margin/collateral terms. Whilst xVAs are not seen explicitly, the coverage is comprehensive so as to allow extraction of the assumptions for pricing credit and funding in collateralised and uncollateralised trades across the anonymous list of banks.

The Totem xVA results can be used to answer questions such as:

- What general valuation adjustments (e.g. CVA, DVA, FVA) does a bank consider when pricing a transaction?
- What specific assumptions does the bank use in the calculation of a valuation adjustment (e.g. loss given default quantification)?
- What cost does the bank attach to entity-specific components (e.g. its funding cost)?
- How do banks deal with collateral in transactions given that they have a relationship to counterparty risk, funding, and collateral adjustments?

Since results are displayed bank by bank (anonymously), it is possible to see a degree of convergence in certain aspects. The prices submitted are, by convention, supposed to relate to the cost of assignment or novation (i.e. the participant is pricing the cost of stepping into an existing transaction with a given counterparty) and so have a clear notion of an entry price, which in turn implies that the aggregative data says something about the exit price.

Since the consumer market is not observable for xVA prices, Totem is the only place where certain pricing is clearly observable, and it is possible to try to extract a consensus. This may be used to defend the use of a given accounting adjustment (for example, the adoption of FVA was likely justified and driven partly by this initiative). Totem xVA has also created some convergence within xVA pricing and valuation, although there are still significant differences. Some of these differences may be expected to disappear over time as market practice becomes more well defined (e.g. with mathematical formulas and numerical implementations), but some differences might always be expected to persist (e.g. banks having different funding costs).

---

[10] www.ihsmarkit.com/products/totem.html.

Contributing to Totem can give a bank verification of its own pricing and valuation approach and may give internal and external credibility. However, there is also the potential drawback that the Totem results may indicate that a bank is an outlier with respect to certain individual assumptions, which may then need to be changed, especially if they are seen as not conservative with respect to market practice. Some example results will be shown in Section 18.2.5.

5.3.6   Contractual Terms and Value

Certain contractual terms require a definition of value in order to facilitate collateralisation or some settlement of a transaction.

- *Collateral (margin)*. Collateral exchange will require a definition of the *value* of a portfolio in order to determine the collateral amount.
- *Resets*. Some transactions, notably cross-currency swaps (sometimes called MTM swaps), have a reset feature (see Section 7.1.2) where a cash payment is made to neutralise the *value* of the transaction at pre-specified dates.
- *Termination*. Clauses may exist (Section 7.1.1) whereby the transaction may be terminated at given points, either optionally or based on certain events (e.g. a rating downgrade). In such cases, the transaction would be settled at its prevailing market *value*.
- *Close-out*. In the event of a counterparty default, the *value* of a portfolio with respect to a party defines their claim (or liability) with respect to the defaulted counterparty.

All of the above require some definition of value. From a high level, the question is, therefore, whether the value term should be defined (Equation 5.1) as being the actual value (with xVA) or the base value (without xVA).

Not surprisingly, it is base values that are generally referenced within contractual definitions. The possible exemption to this is close-out, as discussed in more detail in Section 6.3.4. The use of base value is partly for historical reasons (in the past, xVA was not seen as important) and partly for reasons of simplicity. However, this creates a potential issue: for example, a transaction being terminated will jump from its xVA-inclusive value to a value without xVA. A more theoretically-appealing solution would be, therefore, to base contractual terms on actual valuations, but this would create significant complications via more subjectivity and also a recursive problem whereby contractual terms would impact xVAs, which in turn would define contractual terms.

5.4   PRICING

5.4.1   Reality or Creating the Right Incentive?

Traditional derivatives pricing is based on so-called risk-neutral valuation principles which are directly linked to hedging. There is, therefore, a fairly direct relationship between the costs and benefits reflected in the price and those monetised as a result of the hedging strategy.

However, the costs and benefits reflected in valuation adjustments are generally more indirect, and it could be argued that a bank would not need to adjust its trading activities or capital structure every time it entered into a new transaction. However, the way in which xVA is priced will probably reflect an implicit assumption that this actually is the case. For example:

- *Credit.* The pricing of CVA may implicitly assume that a bank would immediately buy credit default swap (CDS) protection on the counterparty in question. In reality, this may not be possible, and the bank may not buy CDS protection in any form as a result of one transaction, even though it may incur additional credit risk.
- *Funding.* The pricing of FVA and MVA is linked essentially to an assumption that the bank will issue unsecured debt of some type(s) as a result of the transaction. In reality, unless the transaction is very large, the funding position will not need to be altered.
- *Capital.* The pricing of KVA or the requirement to meet a certain capital hurdle will inherently assume that the bank will need to raise more equity capital via a rights issue.

In reality, of course, alternations to a capital structure are 'sticky' as they cannot happen continuously and occur relatively discretely, and a bank will have some capacity. For example, capital buffers ensure that new business does not cause a bank to breach its regulatory capital requirements. Even hedging with illiquid transactions such as CDS must be done on a relatively discrete basis. The same is true in reverse, as transactions that 'realise' xVA may be priced as if the benefit from cost reduction can immediately be monetised by retiring debt, buying back shares, or selling CDS protection.

Why, therefore, is it important to price credit, funding, or capital into a transaction if a bank has the capacity already available and will, therefore, bear no direct economic costs? The answer is that xVA pricing is creating the right incentive and penalising (motivating) transactions that will lead to additional costs (benefits) in general. However, the lack of direct linkage to costs and benefits may lead to xVA pricing being seen as not necessarily as rigorous and well defined as otherwise might be the case.

5.4.2   Approach for Capital

An extreme case of the comments above relates to capital costs. Whilst banks have always had a notion of achieving the correct return on capital when pricing transactions and making business decisions, this may be done relatively passively. Accordingly, not meeting a capital hurdle may not necessarily mean that a transaction could not be executed, as there are other perceived benefits (such as building client relationships).

Furthermore, there is the question of whether or not capital is a cost (Figure 5.1). Buying CDS protection (CVA) or issuing fixed-rate debt (FVA/MVA) incurs fixed costs, but raising equity capital does not, since dividends paid to common shareholders that form the majority of Common Equity Tier 1 capital (Section 4.2.1) are discretionary and will depend on the performance of the bank in question. This leads to two opposing points of view:

- *Capital is not a direct cost.* Capital is not a direct cost and so need not form an explicit valuation adjustment. Imposing a fixed return on capital for all transactions and business is inappropriate, especially since banks may offer multiple services to some clients. Hence, the phrase 'return on capital' is more appropriate than KVA, and some businesses may contribute less return per unit capital but cannot necessarily be closed down as a result, since they may add franchise value. There should be no accounting adjustment in relation to capital.

- *Capital is a direct cost.* Whilst common stock dividends are discretionary, investors do implicitly require a certain return and will sell their shares if they do not achieve this. Hence, capital is another cost and the term KVA can be used to express this. If a business or transaction cannot achieve the correct KVA, then it cannot be justified and the bank should look at opportunities elsewhere. Like FVA, KVA is a component of the exit price, as all market participants require a return on capital, and so there should be an accounting KVA adjustment.

At the time of writing, it is hard to say which of the above views will prevail. Certainly, no bank has yet gone as far as making a full accounting adjustment for KVA. There are reasonable arguments in both points of view, and we will discuss this again when considering the management of KVA in Section 19.3.4.

5.4.3   Approach to Regulatory Ratios

As described in Chapter 4, the leverage ratio (LR) (Section 4.2.7) and liquidity ratios (Section 4.3) require a bank to conform to a metric which is a regulatory assessment of their capital structure with respect to capital or funding. Even if a bank prices these components into a transaction via a traditional approach to xVA, there is the question of the impact of the new transaction on these ratios and whether they will deteriorate. Of course, a bank will naturally build in a buffer and so no single transaction will cause a breach. However, in line with the discussion about pricing to incentivise (Section 5.4.1), it is natural to incentivise (disincentivise) a transaction that worsens (improves) the regulatory metric.

In general, the required ratios for capital and liquidity can be seen as being driven by a resource component, such as capital or available funding, divided by a risk component, such as exposure or required funding. We can denote these components as R and X and assume that a new transaction will cause the risk component to change by an amount ΔR, for which the bank may change the resource component by ΔX. Suppose that the bank's desired ratio is α_{req} and that its current ratio is $\alpha \geq \alpha_{req}$:

$$\frac{R}{X} = \alpha \text{ and } \frac{R + \Delta R}{X + \Delta X} = \alpha_{req}. \tag{5.3}$$

This will imply that:

$$\Delta R = \alpha_{req}\Delta X - X(\alpha - \alpha_{req}). \tag{5.4}$$

The second term in Equation 5.4 is an excess amount of the ratio that can be utilised by the new business. This means that the bank is happy for the ratio to reduce from α to α_{req}. If the bank is not happy to allow this, or equivalently if $\alpha = \alpha_{req}$, then the above formula reduces to:

$$\Delta R = \alpha\Delta X. \tag{5.5}$$

This requires that new business be charged in accordance with keeping the regulatory ratio constant. We will refer to Equation 5.5 as 'ratio invariance pricing'.

Table 5.3 Simple LR example.

	Tier 1 capital	Exposure	LR	LR-implied capital	Actual capital	Ratio
Business 1	15	200	7.5%	10	15	7.5%
Business 2	10	400	2.5%	20	15	3.75%
Total	25	600	4.2%	30	30	5%

Consider the simple example in Table 5.3. Suppose that the bank's required LR is $\alpha_{req} = 5\%$ and:

- Business 1 has a Tier 1 capital requirement (without consideration of the LR) of $R = 15$ against an exposure of $X = 200$. This leads to an implied LR of 7.5%.
- Business 2 holds less capital against an exposure $\Delta X = 400$ due to being less risky, and it has an implied LR of only 2.5%.

The bank's overall LR would be 4.2%, which is not above the required amount. For the bank to meet the LR target overall, Business 2 may be charged an extra five units (on top of 10) of Tier 1 capital based on Equation 5.4.[11] Note that Business 2 on a standalone basis has an LR of only 3.75% now, but, thanks to the position of Business 1, the overall LR of the bank is at the desired LR.

In order to price based on ratio invariance, the bank will need to charge for an increase in resources in line with the relative increase in the risk being added. For example, a NSFR invariant price would require pricing in additional funding based on the NSFR ratio, which will naturally be different from the amount of funding that would be required otherwise. An LR invariant price would price in raising enough capital to keep the bank's LR constant. Again, this will almost inevitably be different from the amount of capital the bank would assess without reference to the LR.

Whilst many assets may be assumed to be naturally LCR and NSFR compliant, i.e. their natural funding strategy would generate more available stable funding (ASF) than required stable funding (RSF), some others will not be. Some aspects of derivatives clearly fall into the latter category. Indeed, derivatives do not generate any net ASF and so cannot possibly have a standalone NSFR of more than 100% (the more derivatives liability, the worse the NSFR contribution). This is not the case for the LR which may imply capital that is either larger or smaller than the amount defined by traditional capital rules. In general, for relatively complex transactions such as derivatives, metrics such as the NSFR and LR are simple and have specific features that may be seen as being particularly conservative and even non-economic. Hence, it may be expected that maintaining invariant regulatory metrics is more expensive than more economic definitions of capital and funding. This would imply that terms such as KVA and FVA should have such metrics built in on a worst-case basis (i.e. a transaction must cover the increase in basic capital costs and maintain the bank's LR at the same or a better level).

The counterargument to the above is that a bank has many activities that can be collectively beneficial. Suppose a bank has a particular division that generates capacity in a

---

[11] $\Delta R = 5\% \times 400 - 600 \times (7.5\% - 5\%) = 5$.

given regulatory metric. One example could be lending to relatively weak credits which will incur accordingly high capital charges but will probably have a favourable effect on the LR since it is credit-quality insensitive (Section 4.2.7). It could be viewed that this area will generate 'leverage ratio capacity' that other businesses can utilise. Ultimately, there is no point in charging for the LR if there is not a material possibility that the business in question may contribute to an eventual breach of the regulatory requirement.

It is clearly important – but not trivial – for banks to decide to what extent additional LCR, NSFR funding costs, and LR costs are passed on to originating businesses. Examples of NFSR invariance (Section 18.3.4) and LR invariance (Section 19.2.6) will be given later.

5.4.4   Lack of Arbitrage

Traditional pricing of complex components such as exotic derivatives (exotics) is a useful comparison to xVA. With exotics, there is a large amount of expertise required in terms of quantitative analytics, trading, and risk management capabilities. Banks mispricing can be arbitraged by more sophisticated competitors. Traditionally, this meant that smaller banks would not try to compete in pricing certain exotic products because they lacked the economy of scale and the ability to build the required expertise.

Whilst xVA pricing shares similarities with exotics pricing in terms of quantitative techniques, the underlying environment is very different. Firstly, complex xVA adjustments arise from products that have been viewed historically as being simple, such as interest rate swaps. A bank must, therefore, approach xVA by necessity and not by choice.

There is no arbitrage in xVA markets. Banks quote prices to end user clients who mainly transact in only one direction. It is, therefore, not possible for banks to exploit the mispricing of a competitor. Since xVAs are mainly costs, a bank mispricing will therefore only suffer from a 'winner's curse' by taking on business too cheaply.[12] Such mispricings may not be immediately obvious but may potentially lead to accounting losses at some point in the future.[13] This is one reason why the adoption of market-standard xVA approaches has often been slow, especially amongst smaller and regional banks. Clearing prices for xVA-heavy products are often driven by the 'lowest common denominator', with banks incentivised to price more aggressively because competitors may ignore or underprice certain components. The herd mentality can sometimes be a strong consideration: a bank may treat something in a particular way because that is what 'market practice' represents, even if the bank believes this to be inappropriate.

It probably shouldn't be expected that, like exotics pricing, xVA prices will all converge on a well-defined value, with banks quoting very close to this value. With so much intrinsic complexity within the modelling, unobservable parameters, and potentially entity-specific costs such as funding and capital, some reasonable dispersion is not surprising. Note also that banks who are most aggressive on pricing one transaction may not be so on another. One example of this is with respect to funding: since there are both costs and benefits,

---

[12] Ivens, F. (2017). Japan CVA shift may break local banks' swaps stranglehold. *Risk* (28 March). www.risk .net.

[13] Sherif, N. (2016). ANZ's CVA loss flags challenge for regional banks. *Risk* (20 December). Becker, L. (2016). Traders shocked by $712m CVA loss at StanChart. *Risk* (15 March). Cameron, M. (2014). JP Morgan takes $1.5 billion FVA loss. *Risk* (14 January). www.risk.net.

some transactions may achieve the best price from a bank with a low funding cost, whilst others may actually be more aggressively priced by a bank with a relatively high cost of funding (see Section 18.2.4).

5.4.5   Entry and Exit Pricing

As xVAs have become more significant in recent years, transacting derivatives has generally become more expensive. Within banks, sales and trading have found xVA charges to be problematic to pass on to clients and have thus suffered from reduced profitability. However, it is also important to bear in mind that exit prices change together with entry prices.

Suppose (Figure 5.3) that a bank charges (implicitly or otherwise) a certain amount at the inception of a transaction (entry), of which some is xVA and the rest is profit. Assume that the xVA component is fully accounted for and so is not realised as profit. Now, if the transaction is exited at some point in the future (exit), then the replacement counterparty will want to charge xVA and also make some additional profit.[14] The original counterparty will be able to pay the xVA charge directly from their xVA accounting reserves, although any extra charge will result in a loss.

This illustrates that high xVA charges at inception can potentially be monetised when exiting the transaction, if the xVA charged at exit is less than the accounting xVA prior to exiting the transaction. This will be the case even if the xVA is higher than at inception because the corresponding accounting losses will have been taken (and may have been hedged), and the xVA desk will have the incentive to pay out so as to achieve xVA optimisation. Hence, whilst client relationship may be less profitable at inception, there is better

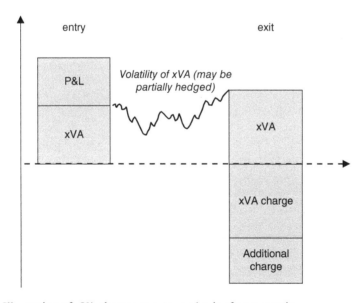

Figure 5.3   Illustration of xVA charges at entry and exit of a transaction.

---

[14] The best example of this point is a novation to another counterparty who will charge for the xVA components of the transaction that they are stepping into.

potential for gains when restructuring, unwinding, and novating transactions later. This is different from the traditional way in which client-driven derivative markets work, where initial transactions are profitable but there is little incentive for salespeople to focus effort on restructuring such transactions later.

This example may also be seen as an argument for components such as KVA being part of the accounting xVA (Section 5.4.2). If this is not the case, then it will be released as P&L at the entry of the transaction, which would suggest that exiting the transaction can only be done by taking a loss (via paying KVA to the replacement counterparty as an additional charge).

On the other hand, xVA benefits at the entry of transactions may make it harder to exit such transactions due to the loss of these benefits, although counterparties should be able to pay for these benefits (e.g. by paying for the funding generated when entering into an OTC portfolio).

5.4.6   xVA Quantification

Previously, Figure 3.10 gave a generic overview of the computation of an xVA term. A general formula for xVA can be written as:

$$xVA = \int_0^\infty C(t)D(t)E[X(t)]dt \qquad (5.6)$$

where there is an integration from the current time to the maximum maturity of the portfolio in question over the following three terms:

- *A curve, $C(t)$.* This defines the unit cost of the underlying cost or benefit. For example, a counterparty credit spread curve defines the cost of the credit risk, whilst funding and capital curves define the cost of funding or capitalising a position. This component is normally assumed to be deterministic (e.g. a funding cost is fixed).
- *A utilisation component, $X(t)$.* This defines the magnitude of the utilisation with respect to cost or benefit above. Generally, this component is not deterministic and has to be modelled. From a quantification point of view, an expected value, $E[X(t)]$, is required.
- *Discounting assumptions, $D(t)$.* Since xVA represents the present value of future costs and benefits, these need to be discounted. However, this is not trivial and may reflect credit risk as well as interest rates.

The three terms above are often assumed to be independent and/or deterministic, meaning that they can be modelled and quantified separately. However, there are some situations when recognising dependencies may be viewed as important. The most well-known of these cases, is known as wrong-way risk (WWR), which usually applies to CVA and relates to a dependency between the counterparty credit spread and the exposure. This and other situations will be discussed when relevant.

5.4.7   Special Cases

The calculation of the profile $X(t)$ in Equation 5.6 is generally a significant quantification challenge, with issues over model choice, calibration, numerical tractability, path dependency, and portfolio effects. In general, it requires the valuation of option-like pay-offs and indeed may well represent a giant option on a multi-asset portfolio. However, in certain special cases, the valuation collapses to essentially pricing forward contracts and is therefore largely model independent and separable across transactions.

These special cases arise since the value of $X(.)$ in the future equates to the future MTM of the portfolio, either due to collateralisation or because this represents the amount of the funding position. They will, therefore, be discussed later in Sections 16.2.1 and 18.2.3. These special cases can be dealt with by simply changing discounting assumptions (i.e. Equation 5.6 is not required specifically).

The special cases also relate to the starting point for xVA calculations (Equation 5.1) and may be incorporated directly into the 'base value'. There is no obvious way in which to decide on this starting point, which may relate to the easiest way to calculate and manage xVA across an organisation.

Section 2
Risk Mitigation

Netting, Close-Out, and Related Aspects

6.1 OVERVIEW

This chapter describes the role of netting and close-out in over-the-counter (OTC) derivatives markets. Netting is a traditional way to mitigate counterparty risk where there may be a large number of transactions of both positive and negative value with either a single counterparty (bilateral netting) or multiple counterparties (multilateral netting). Close-out refers to the process of terminating and settling contracts with a defaulted counterparty. The contractual and legal basis for netting and close-out and their impact in terms of risk reduction and impact on valuation adjustments (xVA) will be described. Some other related forms of risk mitigation, such as trade compression and break clauses, will also be covered.

Financial markets, such as derivatives, can be fast moving, with some participants (e.g. banks and hedge funds) regularly changing their positions. Furthermore, portfolios may contain a large number of transactions, which may partially offset (hedge) one another. These transactions may themselves require contractual exchange of cash flows and/or assets through time. Where there are multiple redundant cash flows, these would ideally be simplified into a single payment where possible. This is the first role of netting, generally called 'payment or settlement netting'. This relates primarily to settlement risk (Section 3.1.2).

Furthermore, in markets such as derivatives, the default of a counterparty – especially a major one such as a large bank – is a potentially very difficult event. A given surviving party may have hundreds or even thousands of separate bilateral transactions with that counterparty. They will need a mechanism to terminate their transactions rapidly and replace (rehedge) their overall position. The same is true for a central counterparty (CCP), which will have a large number of transactions to deal with in the event of the default of a clearing member. In such situations, it is clearly desirable for a party to be able to offset what it owes to the defaulted counterparty against what it itself is owed. This is the second role of netting, generally called 'close-out netting', and relates more directly to counterparty risk.

In order to understand netting and close-out in more detail, consider the situation illustrated in Figure 6.1. Suppose parties A and B trade bilaterally and have two transactions with one another, each with its own set of cash flows. This situation is potentially over-complex for two reasons:

- *Cash flows.* Parties A and B are exchanging cash flows or assets on a periodic basis in relation to Transaction 1 and Transaction 2. However, where equivalent cash flows occur on the same day, this requires the exchange of *gross* amounts, giving rise to settlement risk. It would be preferable to amalgamate payments and exchange only a *net* amount (see discussion on settlement risk in Section 6.2.1).

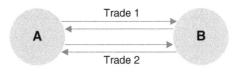

Figure 6.1   Illustration of the need for netting in bilateral markets.

- *Close-out.* In the event that either party A or B defaults, the surviving party may suffer from being responsible for one transaction that has moved against them, but may not be paid for the other transaction that may be in their favour. This can lead to uncertainty over cash flow payments or the ability to replace the transactions with another counterparty.

In general, netting can be seen as a method of aggregating obligations whilst keeping market risk constant (or close to constant), but reducing:

- settlement risk;
- counterparty risk;[1]
- operational risk;
- liquidity risk; and
- systemic risk.

We will define netting as being broadly based on either cash flows or valuations.

6.2   CASH FLOW NETTING

6.2.1   Payment Netting

Payment netting involves the netting of different payments between two counterparties that are (generally) denominated in the same currency. Such payments could have arisen from the same transaction (e.g. netting the fixed and floating interest rate swap payments due on a particular day) or different transactions (e.g. two interest rate swaps in the same currency). For example, suppose party B must pay party A 100 but also expects to receive 60 on the same day (Figure 6.2). It clearly makes sense to net these into a single payment of 40.

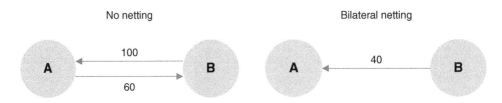

Figure 6.2   Illustration of the impact of payment netting.

---

[1] Note that the reduction of counterparty risk follows directly through the reduction of settlement risk since the future exposure is reduced.

The above netting reduces the time and costs associated with making payments, which should also reduce operational risk. It also reduces the amount that has to be delivered by both parties, which should reduce counterparty and liquidity risk. Note that the above applies in both bilateral- and centrally-cleared markets.

Bilaterally, counterparties can also extend payment netting by proactively reducing the number of transactions between them by removing redundancies such as offsetting positions. This is often known as bilateral compression. Whilst this does not reduce net exposure, there are benefits arising from reducing gross exposure, notably a reduction in operational costs and legal risk. Furthermore, certain regulatory methodologies – due to their inherent simplicity – can unfairly penalise large gross (but not net) exposures. There is, therefore, an incentive for counterparties to reduce the total notional of their positions and gross exposure even without changing their net exposure to one another. The natural extension of this to multiple counterparties is achieved through multilateral compression (Section 6.2.4).

6.2.2   Currency Netting and CLS

Payment netting mitigates settlement risk primarily in a single currency. However, settlement risk is also a major consideration in foreign exchange (FX) markets, where the settlement of a contract involves payment of one currency against receiving the other. Due to the different currencies, the payments are made in different markets and potentially at different times. Such settlement risk or 'Herstatt risk' (Section 3.1.2) occurs because of the risk of delivering the entire notional in one currency (N_{curr1}) against receiving the notional equivalent in another currency (N_{curr2}) (Figure 6.3).

The case of KfW Bankengruppe ('Germany's dumbest bank')

As the problems surrounding Lehman Brothers developed, most counterparties stopped doing business with the bank. However, government-owned German bank KfW Bankengruppe made what they described as an 'automated transfer' of €350m to Lehman Brothers literally hours before the latter's bankruptcy; not surprisingly, Lehman Brothers did not settle the swap with the required payment of $500m. This provoked an outcry, with one German newspaper calling KfW 'Germany's dumbest bank'.[2] Two of the bank's management board members (one of whom has since successfully sued the bank for his subsequent dismissal) and the head of the risk-control department were suspended in the aftermath of the 'mistake'.

Figure 6.3   Illustration of settlement risk in a physically-settled FX transaction.

---

[2] Kulish, N. (2008). German bank is dubbed "dumbest" for transfer to bankrupt Lehman Brothers. *New York Times* (18 September). www.nytimes.com.

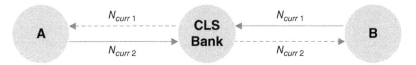

Figure 6.4   Illustration of CLS.

One way around the above problem is to use a non-deliverable forward (NDF) trans-action, where the currency exchange is cash-settled based on the difference between the NDF rate and the prevailing spot FX rate applied to the notional. This prevents the exchange of the full notional amounts in the two currencies and affects payment netting within the contractual terms of the transaction.

It is often inconvenient or impossible to settle the currencies on a net basis and so FX transactions need to be settled physically via a gross exchange of notional, as in Figure 6.3. In 2002, banks developed a continuous linked settlement (CLS) service to reduce settle-ment risk in FX transactions across a range of eligible currencies.[3] For example, Bank A delivers one currency payment to CLS Bank, and Bank B delivers the opposite currency to CLS Bank (Figure 6.4). Only after both currencies have arrived does CLS Bank make the outgoing payments to A and B. This is called payment versus payment (PVP). Parties still make the intended cash flows, but CLS ensures that one cannot occur without the other.

The use of CLS Bank can also provide operational efficiencies. For example, payments in the same currency may be netted multilaterally across multiple transactions settling on the same day.

The KfW Bankengruppe transaction that gave rise to the problem outlined above was a regular cross-currency swap, with euros being paid to Lehman and dollars being paid back to KfW. On the day Lehman Brothers declared bankruptcy, KfW made an automated transfer of €350m despite the fact that the stricken Lehman Brothers would almost certainly not be making the opposite dollar payment (at this time, this type of cross-currency swap could be safely settled via CLS). It should be noted that if they had withheld the payment, then this may have been challenged by the administrator of the Lehman Brothers estate.

6.2.3   Clearing Rings

Bilateral netting clearly works only with cooperation between two parties. However, with further cooperation, further benefits could be derived via multilateral netting. The first example of this arises through 'clearing rings', which were used on exchanges even before the development of central clearing. Clearing rings were relatively informal means of reducing exposure via a ring of three or more members who would agree to 'ring out' off-setting positions. To achieve benefits, participants in the ring had to be willing to accept substitutes for their original counterparties. Rings were voluntary, but upon joining a ring, exchange rules bound participants to the ensuing settlements. Some members would choose not to join a ring, whereas others might participate in multiple rings. In a clearing ring, groups of exchange members agree to accept each other's contracts and allow coun-terparties to be interchanged. This can be useful for further reducing bilateral exposure, as illustrated in Figure 6.5. Irrespective of the nature of the other positions, the positions

---

[3] www.cls-group.com.

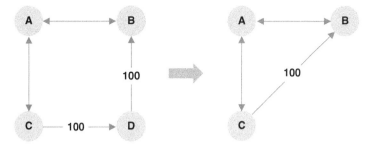

Figure 6.5 Illustration of a clearing ring. The equivalent obligations between C and D and between D and B are replaced with a single obligation between C and B.

between C and D, and D and B can allow a 'ringing out', where D is removed from the ring and two obligations are replaced with a single one from C to B. Clearing rings simplify the dependencies of a member's open positions and allow them to close out contracts more easily.

It is important to note that not all counterparties in the example shown in Figure 6.5 benefit from the clearing ring illustrated. Whilst D clearly benefits from being readily able to offset the transactions with C and B, A is indifferent to the formation of the ring since its positions are not changed. Furthermore, the positions of B and C have changed only in terms of the replacement counterparty they have been given. Clearly, if this counterparty is considered to have stronger (weaker) credit quality, then they will view the ring as a benefit (detriment). A ring, whilst offering a collective benefit, is unlikely to be seen as beneficial by all participants. A member at the 'end of a ring', with only a long or short position and therefore standing not to benefit, has no benefit to ring out. Historically, such aspects have played out with members refusing to participate in rings because, for example, they preferred larger exposures to certain counterparties rather than smaller exposures to other counterparties.

6.2.4 Portfolio Compression

Suppose parties A, B, and C need to make the same cash flows shown in Figure 6.6,[4] which may already have been reduced by bilateral netting. There is an opportunity to reduce the magnitude of the payments further, as shown, because all three parties are both paying and receiving. This would require some form of more advanced trilateral, or in general multilateral, netting scheme. Such a scheme would potentially reduce exposure further: for example, party A would have no exposure since the payment originally to be received from party B is achieved via a reduction of the amount paid to party C.

A modern-day equivalent of clearing rings in bilateral OTC derivatives markets is portfolio compression, which achieves multilateral netting benefits via the cooperation of multiple counterparties. A well-known example is TriOptima's TriReduce service,[5] which provides compression services covering major OTC derivatives products across interest rates, credit, FX, and commodities. This has been instrumental in reducing exposures in OTC derivatives markets.[6]

---

[4] This means on the same day and in the same currency.

[5] www.trioptima.com.

[6] TriOptima (2017). TriReduce's compression service surpasses $1 quadrillion in notional principal eliminated by market participants. Press release (28 June). www.trioptima.com.

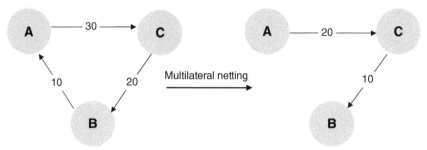

Figure 6.6 Illustration of the potential exposure reduction offered by multilateral netting. The arrows represent fungible cash flows, differing only in their size.

Portfolio compression is a risk-reduction exercise where multiple counterparties partially or entirely eliminate transactions, potentially replacing them with other transactions, with the aim of reducing the overall notional value of the transactions. Note that compression – strictly speaking – refers to the reduction of notional value and not the number of contracts, although in practice the two may well be aligned. Note also that the aim is to reduce the total notional of all parties involved and it does not necessarily follow that an individual party will experience a lower notional (although participants can specify constraints to prevent their exposures increasing, for example).

Compression has developed because OTC derivatives portfolios grow significantly through time but contain redundancies due to the nature of trading (e.g. with respect to unwinds). This suggests that the transactions can be reduced in terms of number and gross notional without changing the overall risk profile. In essence, compression can preserve the market risk position of participants whilst reducing non-market risks such as settlement and counterparty risk. It can also reduce operational costs and may also lower systemic risk by decreasing the number of contracts that need to be replaced in a counterparty default scenario.

Compression is subject to diminishing marginal returns over time as the maximum multilateral netting is achieved. It also relies to some degree on counterparties being readily interchangeable, which implies, for example, that they need to have comparable credit quality.

Broadly, a typical compression cycle works as follows:

1. Participants submit the relevant transactions.
2. The transaction details are matched according to each bilateral counterparty in the process and may also be cross-referenced against a trade-reporting warehouse.
3. An algorithm is run to determine changes to transactions that generate multilateral netting benefits, but keeping each participant's portfolio neutral in terms of value and risk. These changes are reviewed by participants.
4. Once the process is finished, all changes are binding and take effect by unwinding transactions, executing new transactions, and novating transactions to other counterparties.

An optimal overall solution to the compression cycle can involve positions between pairs of counterparties increasing or changing sign and may involve changes in mark-to-market (MTM) value and risk sensitivities. For these reasons, participants can specify constraints (such as the total exposure to a given counterparty, which may be related to the internal credit limits of a participant).

A simple example of the potential result of a credit default swap (CDS) compression exercise for one market participant is given in Table 6.1. Here, the net long position resulting from transactions with three counterparties is reduced to a single identical long position with one of the counterparties.

Portfolio compression is not without potential issues. The settlement of a CDS contract can differ depending on whether it is triggered by the protection buyer or seller. Hence, netting long and short protection positions will not definitely create the same economic value. New transactions may become subject to certain regulation (such as bilateral margining), whereas the legacy transactions that led to their creation may have been exempt from these requirements.

Basic portfolio compression by its nature requires standard contracts, which are therefore fungible, and so cash flows are essentially being netted multilaterally. A good example of producing standardisation of this type is the CDS market, where large banks together with the International Swaps and Derivatives Association (ISDA) standardised CDS contracts in terms of coupons and maturity dates to aid compression (and, indeed, facilitate central clearing). CDS contracts now trade with both fixed premiums and upfront payments, and scheduled termination dates of 20 March, 20 June, 20 September, or 20 December. This means that positions can be bucketed according to underlying reference entity (single name or index) and maturity but without any other differences (such as the previous standard where coupons and maturity dates would differ).

Standardisation of contracts to aid compression is not always possible. For example, interest rate swaps typically trade at par via a variable fixed rate. In such cases, compression is less easy because two interest rate swaps could have identical floating cash flows but different fixed cash flows (due to the different swap rates used at inception). In such cases, slightly more advanced algorithms have been developed, such as coupon blending. These will be discussed further in Section 6.2.5, which details compression at CCPs in more detail.

Recent regulation since the global financial crisis has sought to increase compression exercises. For example, European Market Infrastructure Regulation (EMIR) states that both financial and non-financial counterparties with more than 500 non-centrally-cleared derivatives contracts must have procedures in place to, at least twice a year, consider

Table 6.1 Simple illustration of trade compression for single-name CDS contracts. A party has three contracts on the same reference credit and with identical maturities but transacted with different counterparties. It is beneficial to 'compress' the three into a net contract, which represents the total notional of the long and short positions. This may naturally be with counterparty A as a reduction of the initial transaction.

Reference	Notional	Long/short	Maturity	Coupon	Counterparty
ABC index	150	Long	20/12/2023	100	Counterparty A
ABC index	75	Short	20/12/2023	100	Counterparty B
ABC index	50	Short	20/12/2023	100	Counterparty C
ABC index	**25**	**Long**	**20/12/2023**	**100**	**Counterparty A**

the potential counterparty-risk-mitigating benefit of a portfolio compression exercise.[7] Where such an exercise is not undertaken, the reasons for this must be articulated to the relevant supervisory authority. Possible reasons for not undertaking compression could be the fact that no benefit is likely (which could be the case if a counterparty has very directional positions with all other counterparties). Alternatively, compression may be avoided due to accounting, tax, or legal disadvantages. For example, an end user using an interest rate swap to hedge the risk on a loan (Section 2.2.5) may have offsetting swaps hedging their own borrowing and compression may create problems, such as in the recognition of hedge accounting.

6.2.5   Compression Algorithm

In order to understand the complexity of trade compression algorithms, consider the example 'market' represented in Figure 6.7. This shows position sizes[8] between different counterparties in certain fungible (interchangeable) products. Note that the total gross notional between counterparties (counting each transaction twice, both points of view) is 1,250.

Spreadsheet 6.1 Compression example.

Suppose that the general aim of portfolio compression is to reduce the gross notional in Figure 6.7 without changing the net position of any counterparty. This is likely to be a subjective process for a number of reasons. Firstly, it is not clear what should be minimised. An obvious choice may be the total notional, although this would not penalise large positions or the total number of positions. Alternative choices could be to use the squared notional or the total number of positions, which would reduce large exposure and interconnectedness respectively (O'Kane 2017 discusses this point in more detail). Secondly, there may need to be constraints applied to the optimisation, such as the size of positions with single counterparties. In the above example, there is no transaction between counterparties 1 and 3. It may be that one or both of them would like to impose this as a constraint. Many different algorithms could be used to optimise the market above, and commercial applications have tended to follow relatively simple approaches (for example, see Brouwer 2012). The example below, albeit for a very small market, will provide some insight into how compression algorithms work in practice.

One obvious method to reduce the total notional is to look for opportunities for netting within rings in the market. A trilateral possibility occurs between counterparties 2, 3, and 4 (as illustrated in Figure 6.8) where notionals of 60, 70, and 85 occur in a ring and can, therefore, be reduced by the smallest amount (assuming positions cannot be reversed)

---

[7] Commission Delegated Regulation (EU) No 149/2013 of 19 December 2012 supplementing Regulation (EU) No 648/2012 of the European Parliament and of the Council with regard to regulatory technical standards on indirect clearing arrangement, the clearing obligation, the public register, access to a trading venue, non-financial counterparties and risk mitigation techniques for OTC derivatives contracts not cleared by a CCP, Article 14.

[8] This will be referred to as notional, but could represent exposure or another measure as it is the relative values that are important.

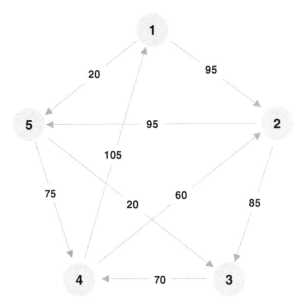

Figure 6.7   Illustration of a simple 'market' made up of positions in fungible (interchangeable) contracts.

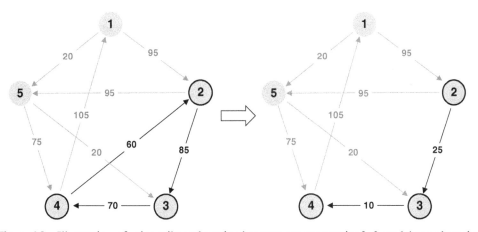

Figure 6.8   Illustration of using trilateral netting between counterparties 2, 3, and 4 to reduce the overall notional of the system shown in Figure 6.7.

of 60. This strategy corresponds to minimising the total notional (or indeed the total notional squared).

This leads to the total notional of the compressed system being reduced to 890 (from 1,250) on the right-hand side of Figure 6.8.

Continuing a process such as the one above could lead to a number of possible solutions, two of which are shown in Figure 6.9. Note that the solution on the left-hand side has reversed the exposure between counterparties 4 and 5, whilst on the right-hand side there

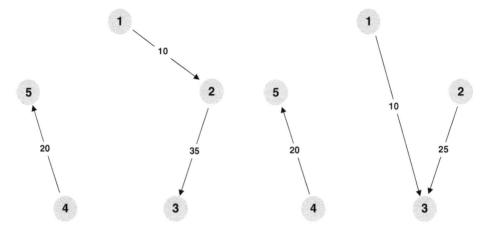

Figure 6.9 Illustration of two possible final results of compressing the original market in Figure 6.7, leading to total notionals of 130 (left-hand side) and 110 (right-hand side).

is a transaction between counterparties 1 and 3 where none existed previously. The latter solution has a lower total notional of 110 (compared to 130 for the former). However, this also illustrates that constraints imposed by counterparties (e.g. 1 and 3 not wanting exposure to one another) will weaken the impact of compression.

Figure 2.4 shows the impact of the much greater emphasis on compression in OTC derivatives in the last few years.

6.2.6   Benefits of Cashflow Netting

In general, the traditional netting approaches described above can be seen as reducing the gross value of transactions without changing the market risk profile. The immediate benefits of bilateral and multilateral netting of cash flows are relatively obvious via a reduction in settlement risk and, by extension, counterparty risk. However, there are some other benefits which may not be as obvious or intuitive:

- *Operational costs.* By reducing the number of cash flows and transactions, operational costs can be reduced.
- *Legal risks.* Portfolio compression may reduce legal risk by contractually simplifying portfolios and not relying on future risk mitigation (which may be subject to legal challenges).
- *Regulatory.* The reduction of gross notional may not always seem beneficial since the net exposure may remain the same. However, some simple regulatory methodologies are partially based on gross notional and will, therefore, appear more beneficial if these values are reduced. This mainly applies to regulatory capital requirement, a good example being the leverage ratio (Section 4.2.7), which has provided a strong incentive for portfolio compression. Some regulatory thresholds are also based on gross notional, such as in relation to central clearing (for example, see discussion on NFC+ designation in Section 4.4.3) or bilateral margin requirements (Section 4.4.2).

6.3   VALUE NETTING

6.3.1   Overview

Cash flow netting has fairly obvious restrictions since it requires cash flows (and therefore transactions) to be interchangeable. This means that the type of cash flow must be the same, suggesting the same asset class, product, payment date, and reference rate. However, many derivatives transactions with a given counterparty can be similar but not have fungible cash flows and sometimes may relate to several underlying asset classes. A more general concept is, therefore, to apply netting across the value of underlying transactions.

A related point is that bankruptcy proceedings are, by their nature, long and unpredictable processes. During such processes, likely counterparty risk losses are compounded by the uncertainty regarding the termination of the proceedings. A creditor who holds an insolvent firm's debt has a known exposure, and whilst the eventual recovery is uncertain, it can be estimated. However, this is not the case for derivatives, where constant rebalancing is typically required to maintain hedged positions. Furthermore, once a counterparty is in default, cash flows will cease, and an institution will be likely to want or need to execute new replacement contracts.

For transactions such as derivatives that can be both assets and liabilities, there is also the question of whether these can offset one another in a default event. An even broader concept is whether such an offset can be applied to different business with a given counterparty. For example, a bank may have a lending relationship with a given client but also transact OTC derivatives with them. If the client defaults, then there is a question of whether the underlying transactions should be considered independently or not.

6.3.2   Close-out Netting

Close-out netting aims to minimise counterparty risk across a portfolio of transactions with a defaulted counterparty. Parties can reduce their risk to each other via contractual terms, such as an ISDA agreement. Close-out netting comes into force in the event that a counterparty defaults, and aims to allow a timely termination and settlement of the net value of all transactions with that counterparty. Essentially, this consists of two components:

- *Close-out*. The right to terminate transactions with the defaulted counterparty and cease any contractual payments.
- *Netting*. The right to offset the value across transactions and determine a *net balance*, which is the sum of positive and negative values, for the final close-out amount.[9]

Close-out netting permits the immediate termination of all contracts with a defaulted counterparty and the settlement of a net amount reflecting the total value of the portfolio (Figure 6.10). In essence, with close-out netting, all transactions (of any maturity, whether in- or out-of-the-money) collapse to a single net value. If the surviving party

---

[9] The calculations made by the surviving party may be disputed later via litigation. However, the prospect of a valuation dispute and an uncertain recovery value does not affect the ability of the surviving party to immediately terminate and replace the contracts with a different counterparty.

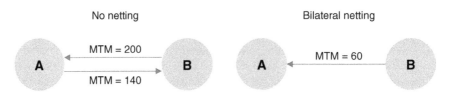

No netting   Bilateral netting

A ← MTM = 200 → B   A ← MTM = 60 B

MTM = 140

Figure 6.10   Illustration of the impact of close-out netting. In the event of the default of party A, without netting, party B would need to pay 200 and would not receive the full amount of 140 owed. With netting, party B would simply pay 60 to party A and suffer no loss.

owes money, then it makes this payment; if it is owed money, then it makes a bankruptcy claim for that amount. Close-out netting allows the surviving institution to realise gains on transactions against losses on other transactions immediately and effectively jump the bankruptcy queue for all but its net exposure, as illustrated in Figure 6.10. Note that close-out netting is completely general since it only depends on MTM values at the time of default and not matching cash flows.

Whilst payment netting reduces settlement risk, close-out netting is relevant to counterparty risk since it reduces pre-settlement risk.

Netting is not just important for reducing exposure but also for reducing the complexity involved in the close-out of transactions in the event that a counterparty defaults. In OTC derivatives markets, surviving parties will usually attempt to replace defaulted transactions. Without netting, the total number of transactions and their notional value that surviving parties would attempt to replace may be larger and hence may be more likely to cause market disturbances.

Netting legislation covering derivatives has been adopted in most countries with major financial markets. The ISDA has obtained legal opinions supporting the close-out and netting provisions in their Master Agreements in most relevant jurisdictions. (At the time of writing, they currently have such opinions covering 54 jurisdictions.) Thirty-seven countries have legislation that provides explicitly for the enforceability of netting. However, jurisdictions remain where netting is not clearly enforceable in a default scenario.[10] Note that in these scenarios, a bank may judge that netting is enforceable for pricing (and possibly accounting) purposes (and accepting the legal risk), but may not be able to reflect this in other calculations such as regulatory capital.

Note that bilateral cash flow netting (Section 6.2.1), where counterparties actively reduce the number of transactions bilaterally, is preferable to value netting because there is no legal risk as transactions are removed completely. For example, if two parties have two completely opposite positions, terminating them is preferable to relying on the enforceability of close-out netting in the event that one of them defaults.

6.3.3   Payment Under Close-out

Standard assumptions when defining counterparty risk and computing credit value adjustment are that a surviving party must still pay liabilities to a defaulted counterparty.

---

[10] Vaghela, V. (2015). Malaysia close to becoming a clean netting jurisdiction. *Risk* (16 February). www.risk.net.

This means that their post-default position is the same as that pre-default in that they must still perform on their liability. On the other hand, if a surviving party has an asset with a defaulting counterparty, then they will make some associated loss in default, depending on the amount they recover. This is a simplistic definition of the economic impact of default used in modelling, but is not often borne out precisely in practice.

For example, although no longer common, some OTC derivatives were historically documented with 'walkaway' or 'tear-up' features. Such a clause effectively allows an institution to cancel transactions in the event that their counterparty defaults. They would clearly only choose to do this in case they were in debt to the counterparty. Whilst a feature such as this does not reduce credit exposure, it does allow an institution to benefit from ceasing payments and not being obliged to settle amounts owed to a counterparty. These types of agreements, which were common prior to the 1992 ISDA Master Agreement, have been less common since and are not now part of standardised ISDA documentation. However, they have sometimes been used in transactions since 1992. Whilst walkaway features do not mitigate counterparty risk per se, they do result in potential gains that offset the risk of potential losses.

Walkaway agreements were seen in the Drexel Burnham Lambert (DBL) bankruptcy of 1990. Interestingly, in this case, counterparties of DBL decided not to walk away and chose to settle net amounts owed. This was largely due to the relatively small gains compared with the potential legal cost of having to defend the validity of the walkaway agreements or the reputational cost of being seen as taking advantage of the DBL default.

Even without an explicit walkaway agreement, an institution can still attempt to gain in the event of a counterparty default by not closing out contracts that are out-of-the-money (OTM) to them, but ceasing underlying payments. Another interesting case is that between Enron Australia (Enron) and TXU Electricity (TXU) involving a number of electricity swaps which were against TXU when Enron went into liquidation in early 2002. Although the swaps were not transacted with a walkaway feature, ISDA documentation supported TXU avoiding paying the MTM owed to Enron (A\$3.3m) by not terminating the transaction (close-out), but ceasing payments to their defaulted counterparty. The Enron liquidator went to court to try to force TXU to settle the swaps, but the New South Wales Supreme Court found in favour of TXU in that they would not have to pay the owed amount until the individual transactions expired (i.e. the obligation to pay was not cancelled, but it was postponed).

Some Lehman Brothers counterparties also chose (like TXU) not to close out swaps but to stop making contractual payments (as their ISDA Master Agreements seemed to support).[11] Since the swaps were very OTM from the counterparties' point of view, and therefore strongly in-the-money (ITM) for Lehman, there were potential gains to be made from doing this. Again, Lehman administrators challenged this in the courts. US and English courts came to different conclusions with respect to the enforceability of this, with the US court ruling that the action was improper,[12] whilst the English court ruled that the withholding of payments was upheld.[13]

---

[11] Brettell, K. (2009). Metavante to appeal swap ruling in Lehman case. *Reuters* (23 October). www.reuters.com.

[12] Bankruptcy Court for the Southern District of New York.

[13] High Court of England and Wales.

Any type of walkaway feature is arguably rather unpleasant and should be avoided due to the additional costs for the counterparty in default and the creation of moral hazard (since an institution is potentially given the incentive to contribute to their counterparty's default due to the financial gain they can make).

6.3.4   Close-out and xVA

There is an important link between the close-out and xVA. The close-out process aims to allow a surviving party to determine a reasonable valuation for their derivatives contracts so as to establish the amount payable at this point where all the underlying transactions are likely to be closed out. If the surviving party is a creditor, then such a valuation will determine their claim in the bankruptcy process. If they are a debtor, then it will determine the payment they are required to make to their bankrupt counterparty's estate.

The valuation at close-out tends to reference 'replacement costs', since a surviving party will typically replace transactions either directly or indirectly (in the latter case, by executing replacement trades, macro-hedges, or unwinding hedges). Such costs are typically perceived as being added to the value so as to compensate the surviving party.

The first problem with the above is regarding the definition of value and, generally, whether it should be the base or actual value (Section 5.2.1). The latter is clearly more relevant as it likely reflects the surviving party's current view on the actual valuation. However, unlike the base value, this requires a definition of xVA terms, which is complex and may not be objectively defined from a legal standpoint.

Assuming the surviving party has a positive valuation (i.e. they are a creditor), then the situation will be as in Figure 6.11. Note that the xVA adjustment is likely to be negative since the overall adjustment will be dominated by costs over benefits.[14] Note that, in this

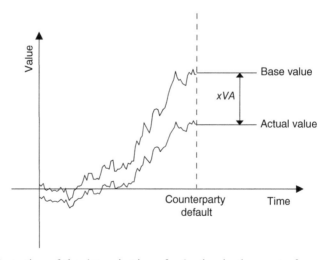

Figure 6.11   Illustration of the determination of valuation in the event of counterparty default from the surviving party's point of view and assuming they are a creditor (i.e. their valuation is positive). The xVA adjustment is assumed to be negative overall.

---

[14] This is not necessarily the case if the future profile of the transaction is very negative.

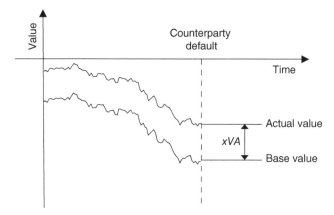

Figure 6.12 Illustration of the determination of valuation in the event of counterparty default from the surviving party's point of view and assuming they are a debtor (i.e. their valuation is negative). The xVA adjustment is assumed to be positive overall.

situation, the surviving party stands to gain by using a base valuation over the actual valuation since this will enable them to recover a higher amount as a creditor.

If the surviving party is a debtor and owes the defaulted counterparty, then the situation *might* be reversed, with the actual value being higher than the base value (Figure 6.12).[15] Note that, in this situation, the surviving party potentially gains by referencing the actual – and not the base – value.

Note that, together with xVA, there is the question of cost inherent in replacing transactions which may also be part of the defined value in default since the surviving counterparty may reasonably replace transactions (Figure 6.13). It may not be able to easily separate such costs (e.g. bid-offer costs) from xVA terms since they may both be seen as charges in executing replacement transactions.

Given the inherent problems with defining the value of a derivative in the event of a counterparty default, it may also be helpful to define a 'legal value', as shown in Figure 6.13. This is a value that might be claimed by a surviving party based on the underlying documentation, but which might be seen as being different (inflated) compared to the true value and associated costs, and might potentially lead to litigation. Clearly, documentation should aim to prevent such divergences since surviving parties may be able to gain at the expense of other creditors of the defaulted counterparty.

6.3.5   ISDA Definitions

The contractual definition regarding close-out is crucial in defining the economics of counterparty default and, as such, is a key element in defining counterparty risk and related xVA components. The default of Lehman Brothers in 2008 illustrated some of the issues with determining close-out valuations. In particular, Lehman Brothers had posted substantial amounts of collateral or security to counterparties as their credit quality deteriorated. Surviving counterparties were then incentivised to maximise their benefit

---

[15] This would be the case due to funding benefits, as will be discussed in Section 18.2.4.

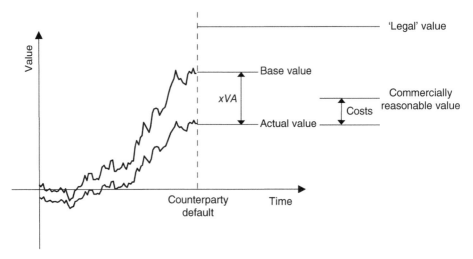

Figure 6.13 Illustration of the determination of valuation in the event of counterparty default from the surviving party's point of view, including costs (shown with respect to the actual value) and assuming they are a creditor.

under the relevant documentation in order to keep as much of this collateral as possible. The Lehman estate then had to proactively try to retrieve much of this collateral – often through the courts – in order to be fair to their creditors overall.[16] However, there are few legal precedents due to the fact that many cases have settled out of court and contradictory decisions have been made by the English and US courts.

The close-out amount represents the amount that is owed by one party to another in a default scenario. If this amount is positive from the point of view of the non-defaulting party, then they will have a claim on the estate of the defaulting party. If it is negative, then they will be obliged to pay this amount to the defaulting party. Although the defaulting party will be unable to pay the claim in full, establishing the size of the claim is important. The determination of the appropriate close-out amount is complex as parties will inevitably disagree. The non-defaulting party will likely consider their value of executing replacement transactions ('replacement cost') as the economically correct close-out amount. The defaulting party may not agree with this assessment since it will reflect charges such as bid-offer costs which it does not experience.

The ISDA Master Agreement (Section 2.2.6) is a market-standard contract used to document OTC derivative transactions, and it is important to understand the implication of the definitions with respect to the amount owing in the event of a counterparty default. There are two ISDA versions to consider – namely 1992 and 2002 – which differ in their definitions (Table 6.2).

Under the 1992 ISDA, there are two methods for defining the amount owed in default, namely 'market quotation' and 'loss', with the former often being elected as the primary

---

[16] Kary, T. (2017). Lehman, Citi Settle $2 Billion Financial Crisis-Era Dispute. *Bloomberg* (30 September). www.bloomberg.com. Note that Lehman argued in this case that Citigroup made up 'phantom transactions costs', which could be seen to equate to the 'legal value' referred to in Figure 6.13.

Table 6.2 ISDA definitions regarding the determination of the net amount owing between two parties in the event of a default of one of them.

1992 ISDA		2002 ISDA	
Market quotation	Obtain a minimum of three firm quotes for the portfolio in question and combine these quotes.	Close-out amount	Indicative quotations, public sources of price information, models.
Loss	Estimate total losses and gains reasonably and in good faith.		

method and the latter as a fallback (in case achieving a market quotation is not possible). These are characterised as follows:

- *Market quotation.* The determining (surviving) party obtains a minimum of three quotes from market makers and uses these quotations (e.g. in the case of three quotes, the middle value should be used). In the event that three quotations cannot be achieved then market quotation is deemed to have failed.
- *Loss.* The determining party is required to calculate its total losses or gains in good faith. Such an amount is intended to be representative of the amount required to put the determining party in the position that it would have been in had the contract been performed, and may include loss of bargain, funding costs, and trading-related costs (e.g. terminating or re-establishing hedges).

Market quotation is clearly designed to be a relatively objective measure, but it obviously requires a reasonable amount of liquidity in the market for the particular transactions in question. Such liquidity is not always present, especially in the aftermath of a major default (e.g. Lehman Brothers) and in more exotic or non-standard products or non-standard contractual terms (assuming the surviving counterparty aims to replicate such terms in replacement transactions). Therefore, it has sometimes been problematic to find market makers willing to price complex transactions realistically following a major default. Since 1992 there has been an increasing number of more complex and structured OTC derivative transactions, together with non-standard contractual terms (e.g. one-way margin agreements). This has led to a number of significant disputes in the determination of the market quotation amount (e.g. see Figure 2.11).

Lehman Brothers, Citigroup, and 'phantom transaction costs'

In the aftermath of the Lehman Brothers' bankruptcy, Citigroup held around $2bn in collateral and argued that most of this amount was required to cover the replacement of these transactions. The administrators of the Lehman estate argued against this and claimed that the money, in fact, should go to its other creditors and accused Citigroup of using methods such as 'phantom transaction costs' to try and justify its

> claim. Eventually Citigroup agreed to give back \$1.74bn to the estate of Lehman from a total of \$2.1bn and stated:
>
> > Citigroup says it used its best professional judgment to determine close-out amounts on the trades. The contracts, the bank said, were governed by ISDA agreements which give the non-defaulting party – in this case Citigroup – the right to assess the close-out costs as long as it uses commercially reasonable procedures.[17]

On the other hand, loss is potentially too subjective and gives too much discretion to the determining party. This implies that there may be incentives for the determining party to deliberately cause market quotation to 'fail' so as to be able to use loss as a fallback. In the event that the determining party makes gains, these would be at the detriment of other creditors of the defaulting party. The Lehman Brothers bankruptcy also gave rise to cases of this type.[18]

Because of the above problems and market developments (such as the availability of more external pricing sources), the 2002 ISDA Master Agreement introduced a new, single definition known as 'close-out amount'. On the one hand, close-out amount can be seen as a diluted form of market quotation, as it does not require actual tradable quotes but can instead rely on indicative quotations, public sources of prices, and market data and internal models to arrive at a commercially reasonable price. On the other hand, close-out amount allows for a similar calculation as loss, but with greater objectivity since the determining party must act in an objectively-reasonable manner.

The close-out amount is the only methodology provided in the 2002 ISDA contract and is intended to reflect the losses or costs/gains of the determining party in replacing or providing the economic equivalent of the material terms of the transactions under the prevailing circumstances, determined in good faith and in a commercially reasonable manner. In determining a close-out amount, the determining party may consider any relevant information, including:

- firm or indicative quotations for replacement transactions supplied by one or more third parties that may take into account the creditworthiness of the determining party and the terms of any relevant documentation (such as collateral agreement) between the determining party and a third party;
- relevant market data supplied by one or more third parties; and
- internal information, as above, from internal sources that are used by the determining party in the regular course of its business for the valuation of similar transactions.

In summary, the market quotation method is an objective approach that uses actual firm quotes from external parties. The loss method is more flexible, with the determining party choosing any reasonable approach to determine its loss or gain. The close-out

---

[17] Kary, T. (2017). Lehman, Citi Settle \$2 Billion Financial Crisis-Era Dispute. *Bloomberg* (30 September). www.bloomberg.com.

[18] Visconti, A. (2018). Lehman Bros. Intl. (Europe) (in administration) v AG Fin. Prods., Inc. *Global Legal Chronicle* (15 August). www.globallegalchronicle.com.

amount method is somewhere in between, giving the determining party flexibility to choose its approach, but aiming to ensure that such an approach is commercially reasonable.

Following the publication of the 2002 ISDA Master Agreement, some parties continued to use market quotation via the 1992 ISDA Master Agreement on the basis that it produced a more objective result. However, during the global financial crisis, the problems associated with this payment method (especially in relation to the Lehman Brothers bankruptcy) were again highlighted. As a result, there has been a growing trend towards using the 2002 close-out amount definition. In 2009, ISDA published a close-out amount protocol to provide parties with an efficient way to amend older Master Agreements to close-out amount with only one signed document, rather than changing bilateral documentation on a counterparty-by-counterparty basis. The ISDA close-out amount protocol was introduced to give market participants an efficient way to amend their 1992 ISDA Master Agreements to replace market quotation and loss with close-out amount.

Note that close-out valuations do seem implicitly or explicitly to allow xVA components to be included in the valuation to the extent that they are part of the costs associated with establishing new transactions. This is in contrast to the need for valuations for other reasons, such as collateral posting or terminating transactions which typically reference only base values (Section 5.3.6). Whilst allowing the actual value to be realised during the close-out process is more reasonable, it does create more complexity in the xVA calculation due to the recursive problem of needing to know xVA at the counterparty default time. This will be discussed in later chapters.

6.3.6   Set-off

As noted in Section 6.3.5, close-out netting under an ISDA contract is generally deemed enforceable in virtually all major jurisdictions and is therefore assumed to be an effective risk mitigant. As such, banks will usually recognise such netting benefits when calculating regulatory capital requirements and pricing new transactions.

However, some institutions trade many financial products (such as loans and repos, as well as interest rate, FX, commodity, equity, and credit products). The ability to apply netting to most or all of these products is desirable in order to reduce exposure. However, legal issues regarding the enforceability of netting arise due to transactions being booked with various different legal entities across different regions.

Bilateral netting is generally recognised for OTC derivatives, repo-style transactions, and on-balance-sheet loans and deposits. Cross-product netting is typically possible within one of these categories (e.g. between interest rate and FX transactions) since they are typically all covered by the same documentation, such as an ISDA Master Agreement (Section 2.2.6). However, netting across these product categories (e.g. OTC derivatives and loans) is not definitely possible as they are documented differently.

The case of OTC derivatives and loans is especially relevant as many banks will have lending relationships with derivative counterparties and may provide a floating-rate loan in conjunction with an interest rate swap (with terms linked to those of the loan) as a 'packaged' fixed-rate loan (Section 2.2.5). Since these products are treated completely separately within a bank, there is a question of whether their values would be netted in default (e.g. the bank is owed money on the loan but owes money on the swap). There is also the related question of access to loan collateral to cover a derivative exposure.

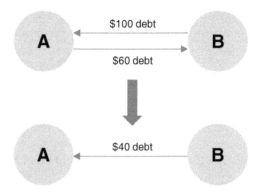

Figure 6.14   Illustration of the concept of set-off.

As with netting enforceability, banks may reflect such offsets in pricing and accounting but will not achieve benefit in terms of reduced capital requirements.

'Set-off' is a broad term that allows a party to apply an amount owed to it by the other party against amounts owed in the other direction. For example, in Figure 6.14 a right of set-off would allow party B to reduce its debt to party A from $100 to $40 via set-off against an opposite debt of $60.

There is a subtle difference between payment netting (Section 6.2.1) and set-off. Set-off recognises the existence of cross-claims between parties and allows equivalent claims in opposite directions to be extinguished. Netting results in a single contractual claim at any point in time. The economic effect is typically the same in each situation.

Typically, set-off relates to actual obligations, whilst close-out netting refers only to a calculated amount. Set-off may therefore potentially be applied to offsetting amounts from other agreements against an ISDA close-out amount representing OTC derivatives. Under the 2002 ISDA Master Agreement, a standard set-off provision is included which would allow for the offset of any termination payment due against amounts owing to that party under other agreements. It is therefore potentially possible from a legal perspective to set-off derivatives against other products such as loans. However, this will depend on the precise wording of the different sets of documentation, the legal entities involved and legal interpretation in the relevant jurisdiction. Obtaining strong legal opinions is clearly critical, but since defaults are relatively rare events, there are often no practical examples to explore the enforceability of set-off.

6.4   THE IMPACT OF NETTING

6.4.1   Risk Reduction

Close-out netting is the single biggest risk mitigant for counterparty risk and has been critical for the growth of the OTC derivatives market. Without netting, the current size and liquidity of the OTC derivatives market would be unlikely to exist. Netting means that the overall credit exposure in the market grows at a lower rate than the notional growth of the market itself. Netting has also been recognised (at least partially) in regulatory capital rules (Chapter 13), which was an important aspect in allowing banks to grow their OTC derivative businesses. The expansion and greater concentration of derivatives markets have increased the extent of netting steadily over the last decade, such that netting currently reduces exposure by close to 90% (Figure 6.15).

6.4.2   The Impact of Netting

Netting has some subtle effects on the dynamics of derivatives markets. Firstly, although the size of exposures is smaller, netted positions are inherently more volatile than their underlying gross positions, which can create systemic risk. Another problem with netting occurs when an institution wants to trade out of a position. In such a situation, the relative illiquidity of OTC derivatives may be problematic. If the institution executes an offsetting position with another market participant, whilst removing the market risk as required, they will have counterparty risk with respect to the original and the new counterparty (unless this can later be reduced by compression). To offset the counterparty risk, it is necessary to trade with the original counterparty, who, knowing that the institution is heavily incentivised to trade out of the position with them, may offer unfavourable terms to extract the maximum financial gain. The institution can either accept these unfavourable terms or trade with another counterparty and accept the resulting counterparty risk. This point extends to establishing multiple positions with different risk exposures. Suppose an institution requires both interest rate and FX hedges.

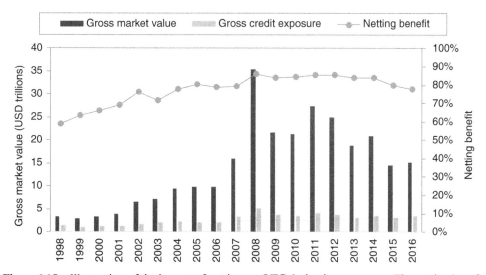

Figure 6.15   Illustration of the impact of netting on OTC derivatives exposure. The netting benefit (right-hand *y*-axis) is defined by dividing the gross credit exposure by the gross market value and subtracting this ratio from 100%. Source: Bank for International Settlements. www.bis.org.

Since these transactions are imperfectly correlated, then by executing the hedges with the same counterparty, the overall counterparty risk is reduced and the institution may obtain more favourable terms. However, this creates an incentive to transact repeatedly with the same counterparty, leading to potential concentration risk.

An additional implication of netting is that it can change the way market participants react to perceptions of increased risk of a particular counterparty. If credit exposures were driven by gross positions, then all those trading with the troubled counterparty would have strong incentives to attempt to terminate existing positions and stop any new trading. Such actions would likely result in even more financial distress for the troubled counterparty. With netting, an institution will be far less worried if there is no current exposure (MTM is negative). Whilst they will be concerned about potential future exposure and may require collateral, netting reduces the concern when a counterparty is in distress, which may, in turn, reduce systemic risk.

6.4.3   Multilateral Netting and Bifurcation

A complication to netting is created by regulatory mandates such as central clearing (Section 4.4.1) and bilateral margin requirements (Section 4.4.2).

In the case of central clearing, transactions that – from a netting perspective – would have been grouped against another bilateral counterparty are now grouped at the CCP level. This would seem to produce benefits through multilateral netting of positions held against a single CCP that would otherwise be facing multiple bilateral counterparties. Indeed, this is seen as a major advantage of central clearing.[19]

However, since not all transactions can be centrally cleared, there is a disadvantage due to the loss of bilateral netting benefits. This bifurcation between cleared and bilateral transactions can be particularly acute for market participants executing offsetting transactions (e.g. a swaption being hedged by a swap or index against single-name credit default swaps) since one product may be clearable and the other not. Clearly, there is a critical mass where enough OTC derivatives can be cleared through a reasonably small number of CCPs so as to create overall netting benefits. This has been illustrated by Duffie and Zhu (2011).

CCPs allow multilateral offset due to a clearing member facing the CCP directly on all cleared trades. As an example, consider the situation in Figure 6.16, where the arrows are probably best interpreted as cash flow or margin payments, as discussed in more detail below. This shows that although bilateral netting can reduce exposure significantly, central clearing can reduce it even more through multilateral netting.

As shown in Table 6.3, bilateral netting reduces the total exposure of the system in Figure 6.16 by a factor of three (360 to 120). This can be reduced further to 60 by central clearing, even if the exposure of the CCP is included (in practice this would be mitigated by margining).

Although the above example seems to be identical to compression (Section 6.2.4), there are important differences. For compression, trades need to be standardised, since this

---

[19] IMF (2010). 'The primary advantage of a CCP is its ability to reduce systemic risk through multilateral netting of exposures.' From: Making Over-The-Counter Derivatives Safer: The Role of Central Counterparties (Chapter 3). *IMF Global Financial Stability Report* (April). www.imf.org.

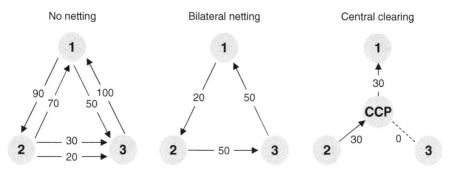

Figure 6.16   Comparison of no netting, bilateral netting, and central clearing.

Table 6.3   Illustration of the reduction in exposure from bilateral netting and central clearing, as shown in Figure 6.16.

	No netting	Bilateral netting	Central clearing
Counterparty 1	170	50	30
Counterparty 2	90	20	0
Counterparty 3	100	50	0
CCP (C)	-	-	30
Total	**360**	**120**	**60**

provides the fungibility so that contracts can be torn up to represent the result of the compression cycle. Contracts also need to be standardised for central clearing, but for different reasons relating to operational costs, margin calculations, and potential close-out in the event of clearing member default. Such differences mean that multilateral netting benefits can be seen for centrally-cleared trades that would not be achieved through trade compression. Put another way, portfolio compression can offset equivalent transactions, and possibly actual cash flows,[20] but central clearing can offset the actual value of these transactions against one another. This means that two different transactions with different counterparties that are not highly correlated (e.g. interest rate swaps in different currencies) will have a strong netting benefit under central clearing but are not appropriate for trade compression due to not being sufficiently fungible. Put another way, CCPs can compress risk, but in bilateral markets compression can only work on objectively-defined quantities such as notionals and cash flows.

When promoting central clearing, a key point made often by policymakers and regulators is that CCPs facilitate multilateral netting, which can alleviate systemic risk by reducing exposures more than in bilateral markets. Whilst multilateral netting is clearly more beneficial when all trades are covered, in reality fragmentation or bifurcation will be a problem. Two obvious sources of fragmentation are non-clearable trades (which remain bilateral) and multiple CCPs. Such a situation is illustrated in Figure 6.17, where some of the positions are assumed to be cleared outside the CCP shown.

---

[20] In the case of techniques such as coupon blending discussed later in Section 6.2.5.

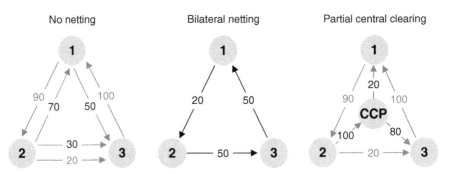

Figure 6.17   Comparison of no netting, bilateral netting, and partial central clearing where only a subset of trades (black lines as opposed to grey ones) can be centrally cleared.

Table 6.4   Illustration of an increase in overall exposure caused by multilateral netting related to central clearing of only a subset of trades, as shown in Figure 6.17.

	No netting	Bilateral netting	Partial central clearing (excluding CCP positions)
Counterparty 1	170	50	100
Counterparty 2	90	20	90
Counterparty 3	100	50	20
Total	**360**	**120**	**210**

The quantitative impact of partial multilateral netting is shown in Table 6.4, which considers the total exposure under no netting, bilateral netting and partial central clearing. Even ignoring the exposure involving the CCP itself (i.e. assuming the CCP is risk free), the overall reduction in exposure is better with bilateral netting (total exposure 120) than with partial central clearing (total exposure 210). For example, with no netting, counterparty 1 has a total exposure of 170 (70 to counterparty 2 and 100 to counterparty 3), and under bilateral netting, this is reduced to 50 (to counterparty 3 only). However, under partial central clearing, counterparty 1 gains in some multilateral netting of their positions with counterparties 2 and 3, but loses the bilateral netting of the two sets of positions.

Note that the above example could correspond to a situation where certain trades cannot be centrally cleared, or alternatively where they are cleared via a separate CCP to the one shown. The above example illustrates that the loss of bilateral netting benefits may dominate the increase in multilateral netting ones and result in central clearing, increasing the overall exposure in the market. This splitting of netting sets is analysed with some simple examples by Duffie and Zhu (2009). Their results are based on considering the netting benefit for trading a single class of contracts through a CCP as opposed to bilateral clearing. They show, using a simple model,[21] the required number of members trading through the CCP for a single asset class to achieve overall netting reduction. Overall, the Duffie and Zhu results illustrate that achieving overall netting benefits from central clearing (compared to bilateral trading) is not a foregone conclusion. Increased netting

---

[21] Simplifying assumptions of symmetry and equal variance of exposure are used in this case.

benefits can only be achieved by a relatively small number of CCPs clearing a relatively large volume of transactions.

In theory, the bilateral margin requirement does not share similar bifurcation problems as central clearing because transactions are still bilateral between the parties involved. However, since most counterparties have chosen to create new margining/collateral agreements in order to comply with such rules for new transactions, without affecting existing transactions, there is a bifurcation of collateral across these two agreements. There may even be a possibility of legal problems if such transactions would be deemed to be bifurcated across two different netting sets.

6.4.4   Netting Impact on Other Creditors

Close-out netting may seem very beneficial in OTC derivatives markets where it reduces exposure and potentially leads to easier close-outs. However, for financial markets generally, it merely *redistributes* value to OTC derivatives creditors from other creditors. Consider a generalisation of the example in Figure 6.10 to include other creditors. In Figure 6.18, party B has both derivative creditors (party A) and other creditors (OC).

Party B defaults with total assets of 180 (140 derivatives and 40 other) and total liabilities of 300 (200 derivatives and 100 other). Without netting, assuming other creditors and derivative creditors have the same seniority,[22] a recovery of 60% (180/300) would apply, and the payments would be as on the left-hand side of Figure 6.19. However, if the derivatives contracts are subject to netting, as illustrated on the right-hand side of Figure 6.18, then the liabilities become 60 and 100 for derivatives and other creditors respectively against the assets of 40. This leads to a lower recovery of 25% (40/160) for the other creditors. The derivatives creditors receive a total of 155: 140 from being able to net their assets and liabilities and 15 from a recovery amount related to their *netted* claim.

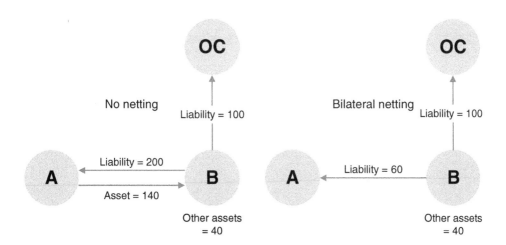

Figure 6.18   Example of bilateral derivatives netting, including other creditors.

---

[22] OTC derivatives would typically be *pari passu* with senior debt, for example.

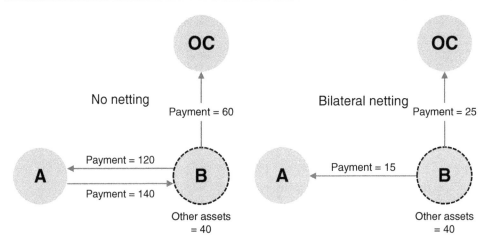

Figure 6.19 Example of bilateral derivatives netting, including other creditors, showing payments made in default of party B, assuming party A and other creditors are paid the same percentage recovery.

This leads to an overall recovery of 77.5% (155/200), whereas the other creditors receive 25% (25/100) (Figure 6.19, right-hand side).

The above example illustrates that bilateral netting of OTC derivatives increases the recovery for OTC derivatives counterparties (77.5% instead of 60%, in the above example) but reduces the recovery of other creditors (25% instead of 60%). This potentially highlights a much broader point, which is that certain benefits (netting, margining, central clearing) may be positive for OTC derivatives markets but not necessarily for financial markets in general since they merely redistribute risk (Pirrong 2014). Netting may reduce exposure to OTC derivatives counterparties but increase exposure to other creditors (e.g. bondholders). A bank may reduce its derivatives counterparty risk (and capital) through netting, but this may induce changes in other parts of the balance sheet of the bank. This could pose the question as to whether reducing systemic risk in derivatives markets at the expense of increasing systemic risk elsewhere is a worthwhile trade-off.

7
Margin (Collateral) and Settlement

Long-dated transactions such as derivatives suffer from the problem that, whilst the current exposure might be relatively small and manageable, the future exposure could increase to a relatively large, unmanageable level. An obvious way to mitigate this problem is to have a contractual feature in the transaction that permits a risk-mitigating action to reduce a large exposure.

Future exposure reduction can most obviously be achieved by having the contractual right to demand some form of security or margin (collateral) as a mitigant against that exposure.[1] Margin-posting is a periodic process that ensures continuity of the underlying transaction(s) but acts as a potential mitigant for both parties in a transaction. On an exchange, margin-posting represents a daily settlement, whereas in over-the-counter (OTC) derivatives it represents a collateralisation process.

Whilst margin has become a standard feature of exchange-traded derivatives and other simple products such as repos, it is not a standard component of OTC derivatives, especially those involving end users. Regulation is promoting more standard margin practices in OTC derivatives markets (Section 2.5), although some end users will be exempt from such regulation.

In OTC derivatives, other contractual features sometimes exist which can be seen as a more basic form of margining because they may be less periodic (such as resets) or simply cause a transaction to be terminated early.

7.1 TERMINATION AND RESET FEATURES

7.1.1 Break Clauses

A break clause allows a given transaction to be terminated, either mandatorily, optionally, or contingent on some defined event (such as a rating downgrade). Such clauses may apply to one or both parties in a transaction. Prior to the financial crisis, break clauses were typically required by banks trading with certain (often uncollateralised, i.e. non-margined) counterparties. More recently, it has become common for counterparties such as asset managers and pension funds to require break clauses linked to banks' own credit ratings due to the unprecedented credit quality problems within the banking sector during the global financial crisis (GFC).

For example, an International Swaps and Derivatives Association (ISDA) Master Agreement allows the specification of an Additional Termination Event (ATE), which permits a party to terminate transactions in certain situations. The most common ATE is in relation to a rating downgrade (e.g. below investment grade). For unrated parties such as hedge funds, other metrics such as market capitalisation, net asset value, or key person departure may be used.

---

[1] Margin is the amount of financial resources that must be deposited, whereas collateral refers to the actual financial instrument (e.g. cash or securities). Terminology will be discussed in Section 7.2.1.

ATE provisions are typically defined at the counterparty level in the ISDA schedule. However, they can be specified in a transaction confirmation. More commonly, individual transactions may reference similar terms and these are typically referred to as 'mutual puts'. Such clauses often do not reference specific events but are either mandatory (meaning the transaction will terminate at the specified break date) or optional (where the party has the right to break the transaction). It may be considered advantageous to attach such a clause to a long-dated transaction (e.g. 10 years or above), which carries significant counterparty risk over its lifetime. For example, a 15-year swap might have a mutual put in year five and every two years thereafter.

Sometimes mandatory breaks are used because a party is unable (due to internal policy such as credit limits, for example) to execute a long-dated transaction. In such cases, there may be an expectation or 'gentleman's agreement' that a new transaction will be executed at the break time. This is similar to a resettable transaction discussed in Section 7.1.2.

The exercise or triggering of a break clause does not necessarily cause a transaction to terminate, and the party against which it is exercised may have to comply with one or more of the following options:

- provide a replacement counterparty;
- provide a counterparty offering a third-party guarantee;
- terminate the transaction(s) at their current replacement value; or
- post some sort of margin.

In the event that a break clause results in a termination of a transaction(s), this is typically done at the prevailing mark-to-market (MTM) value, as determined in the documentation, typically involving pricing via a panel of banks. This is typically a base valuation (Section 5.3.6) and does not, therefore, share some of the problems with the determination of the valuation that is associated with close-out netting and xVA (Section 6.3.4), although problems sometimes still exist.[2]

An ATE is obviously designed to mitigate against counterparty risk by allowing a party to terminate transactions or apply other risk-reducing actions when their counterparty's credit quality is deteriorating. This may be considered particularly useful when trading with a relatively-good-credit-quality counterparty and/or long-maturity transactions. Over such a time horizon, there is ample time for both the value of the transaction to become significantly positive and for the credit quality of the counterparty to decline.

It is worthwhile comparing the different types of break clause with the following considerations (Table 7.1):

- *Counterparty risk reduction.* This refers to a firm's view of the counterparty risk reduction benefit, such as in consideration of credit limits. It is likely that all types of break clause will be deemed beneficial here, with some caution over the usefulness of optional and rating-based triggers.
- *Credit value adjustment (CVA) reduction.* This probably depends on the view of the CVA desk on the benefit of the break clause and their willingness to incorporate it in the price, and the associated view of whether it is appropriate to include it in CVA

---

[2] Cameron, M. (2012). Dealers call for revised language on break clause close-outs. *Risk* (5 March). www.risk.net.

Table 7.1 Illustration of the risk-mitigation benefit of different types of break clause.

	Counterparty risk reduction	CVA reduction	LCR	Capital relief
Mandatory	✓	✓	✓	✓
Optional	(✓)	✗	✓	✗
Rating-based	(✓)	✗	✗	✗

accounting assumptions. It is likely that such a desk may only see the benefit of mandatory breaks since they have no control over optional and rating-based triggers.[3]

- *Liquidity coverage ratio (LCR).* The LCR forces banks to pre-fund the requirements of rating-based triggers (Section 4.3.3).
- *Capital relief.* It is likely that capital relief will only be achievable for mandatory breaks. Even here there may be problems if a bank has a history of waiving such breaks, which may cause a regulator to question the risk-reducing benefit of the break clause. It is difficult to achieve capital relief through optional breaks, although if a bank can show that such breaks are rigorously exercised, then this might be possible. Finally, Basel capital rules explicitly rule out any capital relief from rating-based triggers (BCBS 2011b).

The problem with break clauses as a risk mitigant is that they potentially damage client relationships, and therefore salespeople in banks would be against exercising them (especially if the customer has not been downgraded and has a good credit standing), whereas the CVA desk (xVA desk) and risk management department would be in favour of making use of them wherever possible. This is essentially part of a moral hazard problem, where front-office personnel may use the presence of a break clause to get a transaction done, but then later argue against the exercising of the break to avoid a negative impact on the client relationship. Banks should have clear and consistent policies over the exercising of optional break clauses and the benefit they assign to them from a risk reduction point of view. There must not be any lack of internal clarity around who in a bank is empowered to exercise a break clause.

Behaviour around breaks has changed in recent years, with banks becoming much more willing to exercise optional break clauses and clients accordingly expecting such behaviour. This has occurred because banks are much more sensitive to the valuation impact of breaks on xVA terms and also capital costs and may put maximising profitability and reducing capital ahead of client relationship concerns.[4] Hence, it might be considered that even optional breaks should now offer CVA reductions (Table 7.1).

Recent years have highlighted the potential dangers of ATEs and other break clauses, in particular:

- *Risk-reducing benefit.* Whilst an idiosyncratic rating downgrade of a given counterparty may be a situation that can be mitigated against, a systematic deterioration in credit quality is much harder to nullify. Such systematic deteriorations are more likely for larger financial institutions, as observed in the GFC.

---

[3] It is likely that the ownership of an optional break would be with the client relationship manager and possibly also the risk management department.

[4] Cameron, M. (2012). Banks tout break clauses as capital mitigant. *Risk* (3 March). www.risk.net.

- *Weaknesses in credit ratings.* Breaks clearly need to be exercised early before the counterparty's credit quality declines significantly and/or exposure increases substantially. Exercising them at the last minute is unlikely to be useful due to systemic risk problems. Ratings are well known for being somewhat unreactive as dynamic measures of credit quality. By the time the rating agency has downgraded the counterparty, the financial difficulties may be too acute for the clause to be effective. This was seen clearly in relation to counterparties such as monoline insurers (see Section 2.4.4) in the GFC.
- *Cliff-edge effects.* The fact that many counterparties may have similar clauses may cause 'cliff-edge' effects, where a relatively small event such as a single-notch rating downgrade may cause a dramatic consequence as multiple counterparties all attempt to terminate transactions or demand other risk-mitigating actions. The near failure of AIG (Section 2.4.4) is a good example of this.
- *Modelling difficulty.* Breaks are often very difficult to model since it is hard to determine the dynamics of rating changes in relation to potential later default events and the likelihood that a break would be exercised. Unlike default probability, rating transitions probabilities cannot be implied from market data. This means that historical data must be used, which is, by its nature, scarce and limited to some broad classification. This also means that there is no obvious means to hedge such triggers. One exception is where the break is mandatory, where the model may simply assume it will occur with 100% probability.

7.1.2   Resettable Transactions

A reset agreement is a clause to periodically reset product-specific parameters determining the value of a transaction and therefore avoid either party becoming strongly in-the-money. Reset dates may coincide with payment dates or be triggered by the breach of some market value.

For example, in a resettable cross-currency swap, the MTM value of the swap (which is mainly driven by FX movements on the final exchange of notional, especially in floating-floating structures[5]) is cash-settled at each reset date. In addition, the FX rate is reset to (typically) the prevailing spot rate. The reset means that the notional on one leg of the swap will change. Such a reset is similar to the impact of terminating the transaction at its MTM and executing a replacement transaction at market rates, and consequently reduces the exposure to zero at each reset date (typically they are every quarter). An example of the impact of such a reset is illustrated in Figure 7.1, which shows the exposure over one year and the impact of quarterly resets. Figure 7.2 shows the impact of the reset on exposure over the lifetime of the transaction in a scenario where the value of the transaction would become significantly positive (in-the-money) due to a relatively large move in the FX rate.

Since resets are mandatory and not linked to any external event, they are much easier to assess and model than break clauses. One simply needs to apply the logic of the reset at each contractual date, as shown in Figure 7.1.

A reset can be seen as a weaker form of margining because the margin is usually posted on a daily basis, whilst refixes are much less frequent. Another difference is that a refix is a settlement, whereas margin (in OTC derivatives) is normally posted as security against an exposure.

---

[5] Referencing a floating rate of interest in both currencies.

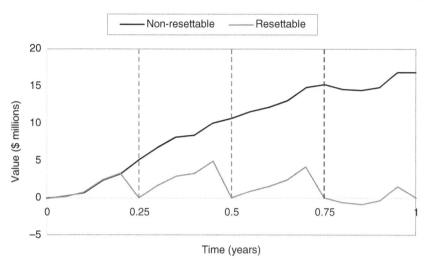

Figure 7.1   Illustration of the impact of reset features on the exposure of a long-dated cross-currency swap over the first year. Resets are assumed to occur quarterly and are shown by dotted lines.

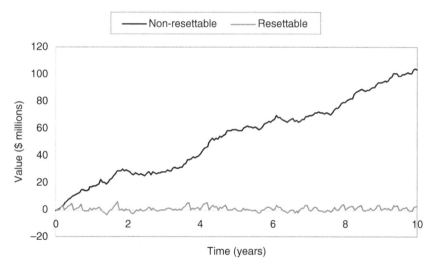

Figure 7.2   Illustration of the impact of reset features on the exposure of a long-dated cross-currency swap. Resets are assumed to occur quarterly.

7.2   BASICS OF MARGIN/COLLATERAL

7.2.1   Terminology

Historically, 'collateral' has been a term used within OTC derivatives markets and contractual agreements such as ISDA Master Agreements. However, 'margin' has been used in exchange-traded markets to represent a similar concept. Accordingly, there are terms such as 'independent amount' (OTC markets) and 'initial margin' (exchange-traded markets) that are, to some extent, interchangeable.

The industry is generally converging on the use of the term margin over that of collateral. For example, relatively recent regulatory rules for OTC derivatives are known as the 'bilateral margin requirements' (Section 7.4). The term margin will, therefore, be used from now on, with occasional references to collateral and similar terms. The terms 'collateralised' and 'uncollateralised' will still be used to define the presence, or not, of margin in OTC derivatives.

7.2.2   Rationale

Margin represents a requirement to provide collateral in credit support or settlement. In exchange-traded markets, margin acts as a daily settlement of the value of a transaction. The fundamental idea of OTC derivatives margining is that cash or securities are passed (with or without actual ownership changing) from one party to another as a means to reduce counterparty risk. This different treatment in exchange-traded and OTC markets is well-known and forms the basis of the difference between futures (exchange) and forward (OTC) contracts. ISDA (2015) estimates that there is about $5trn in margin supporting bilateral derivatives transactions, with cash becoming increasingly common.

The difference between margin as settlement (exchange-trading) and margin as a form of security (OTC markets) is important. The benefit of the latter is that it is flexible and different currencies of cash and various securities (and, in theory, even non-financial collateral) can be used. However, margin as security is not economically owned and has associated risk, such as legal challenges regarding ownership. Margin as settlement is more convenient as its value is realised immediately, but it must, therefore, be a cash payment, most obviously in the same currency as the underlying transaction. This chapter will be largely concerned with margin in bilateral OTC derivatives, with centrally-cleared OTC derivatives being the subject of Chapter 8.

Whilst break clauses (Section 7.1.1) and resets (Section 7.1.2) can provide some risk-mitigating benefit in these situations, margining is a more dynamic and generic concept. A break clause can be seen as a single payment of margin and termination of the transaction. A reset feature is essentially a periodic (infrequent) settlement payment, similar to margin, made to neutralise an exposure.

A margin agreement reduces risk by specifying that margin must be posted by one counterparty to the other to support an exposure. In OTC derivatives markets, the margin receiver typically only becomes the permanent economic owner of the margin (aside from any potential legal challenge) if the margin-giver defaults. In the event of default, the non-defaulting party may retain the margin and use it to offset any losses relating to the positive value of their portfolio. As with netting, this needs to be legally enforceable. Like netting agreements, margin agreements may be two-way, which means that either counterparty is required to post margin against a negative value (from their point of view). One or both counterparties will periodically mark all the relevant positions to market and calculate the net value. They will then check the terms of the underlying agreement to calculate whether they are owed margin and vice versa.

The basic idea of margining is illustrated in Figure 7.3. Parties A and B have one or more transactions between them and therefore agree that one or both of them will exchange margin in order to offset the exposure that will otherwise exist. The rules regarding the timings, amounts, and type of margin posted should naturally be agreed before the initiation of the underlying transaction(s). To keep operational costs under control, posting of

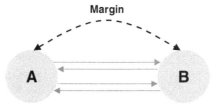

Figure 7.3   Illustration of the basic role of margin.

margin will not be continuous and will sometimes occur in blocks according to pre-defined rules. In the event of default, the surviving party may retain some or all of the margin to offset losses that they may otherwise incur.

Note that, since margin agreements are often bilateral, margin must be returned or posted in the opposite direction when exposure decreases. Hence, in the case of a positive valuation, a party will call for margin, and in the case of a negative valuation, they will be required to post margin themselves. Posting margin and returning previously received margin are not materially very different. One exception is that, when returning, a party may ask for specific securities back, whereas when posting outright, optionality may exist.

Margin posted against OTC derivatives positions is, in most cases, under the control of the counterparty and may be liquidated immediately upon an event of default. This arises due to the laws governing derivatives contracts and the nature of the margin (cash or liquid securities). Counterparty risk, in theory, can be completely neutralised as long as a sufficient amount of margin is held against it. However, there are legal obstacles to this and issues such as rehypothecation. Bankruptcies such as Lehman Brothers and MF Global have provided evidence of the risks of rehypothecation (see Section 7.5.4). It is therefore important to note that, whilst margin can be used to reduce counterparty risk, it gives rise to new risks, such as market, operational, and liquidity risk.

Margin also has funding implications. Consider the bank and end user viewpoints described in Section 2.2.5 with margin included (Figure 7.4). An end user will be directional and so when posting margin may have to source the cash or assets to post and may not naturally hold liquid resources that could be used. An end user hedging another financial instrument such as a loan will not receive margin from the loan to offset that required on the derivative.

The above is why some end users have historically been unable or unwilling to post margin. However, this creates an associated problem for a bank, since hedging an

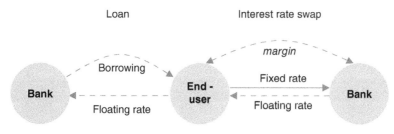

Figure 7.4   Illustration of the classic end user counterparty risk setup shown previously in Figure 2.9 with margin included.

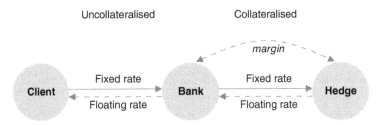

Figure 7.5   Illustration of the classic bank setup shown previously in Figure 2.10 with margin included.

uncollateralised transaction with a collateralised one will expose them to asymmetric margin-posting (Figure 7.5). These aspects require consideration of funding and funding value adjustment (FVA) (Chapter 18).

7.2.3   Variation Margin and Initial Margin

There are two fundamentally different types of margin. Primarily, margin would most obviously reflect the valuation of the underlying transactions, which can generally be positive or negative from each party's point of view. This idea forms the basis of 'variation margin'. Typically, the base valuation (i.e. without xVA, see Section 5.3.6) is typically used for variation margin calculations because it is the most obvious and easy way to define a valuation that can be agreed upon by both parties on a frequent basis. Although this base valuation is not the actual valuation, it has the benefit that it is probably symmetric (i.e. both parties can potentially agree on the valuation) and relatively easy to calculate. Furthermore, since margin has an impact on xVA, any inclusion of xVA in the valuation for margining purposes would create a recursive problem (this is similar to the discussion on close-out and xVA in Section 6.3.4).

In an actual default scenario, the variation margin is likely to be insufficient to cover the costs experienced by the surviving party. This is primarily a result of two factors:

- the inherent delay in the process between the time the party last posted margin and the time they were declared in default; and
- the associated costs in replacing and/or rehedging defaulted transactions.

The above components are often considered together as the margin period of risk (MPoR).

Due to the imperfection of variation margin in relation to the above two components, additional margin is sometimes used in the form of 'initial margin'. Historically, the term 'independent amount' has been used in association with OTC derivatives transactions under ISDA agreements. However, the term initial margin – which originated on exchanges and in central clearing – is becoming more common and will be used here. Figure 7.6 conceptually shows the roles of variation and initial margins.

ISDA (2015) reports that cash makes up around three-quarters of variation margin and just over half of the initial margin, with government securities being the next most common margin type.

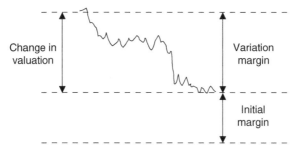

Figure 7.6 Illustration of the difference between variation and initial margins as forms of collateralisation. Variation margin aims to track the value of the relevant portfolio through time, whilst initial margin represents an additional amount that may be needed due to delays and close-out costs in the event of a counterparty default.

Historically, the bilateral OTC derivatives market has used margin almost entirely in the form of variation margin, and initial margin (independent amount) has been quite rare. Initial margin is a much more common concept on derivative exchanges and central counterparties (CCPs). However, regulation covering margin-posting in bilateral markets is making initial margin more common (Section 7.4).

7.2.4   Method of Transfer and Remuneration

OTC derivatives margin is typically exchanged by the parties directly and not held by a third-party custodian (although this is changing in part, as discussed in Section 7.4). In practice, there are two different methods of margin transfer:

- *Security interest*. In this case, the margin does not change hands, but the receiving party acquires an ownership interest in the margin assets and can use them only in the case of certain contractually-defined events (e.g. default). Other than this, the margin-giver generally continues to own the securities. This is typically the case under New York law.
- *Title transfer*. Here, legal possession of margin changes hands and the underlying margin assets (or cash) are transferred outright in terms of ownership, but with potential restrictions on their usage. Aside from any such restrictions, the margin-holder can generally use the assets freely, and the enforceability is therefore stronger. This 'outright transfer' is more common under English law.

ISDA (2015) reports that the New York law pledge agreement is most common, making up 46.8% of surveyed non-cleared margin agreements, and the English law title transfer makes up 30.1%.

The above choices can materially change the parties' rights and obligations and their position in the event of the default of the other party. In general, title transfer is more beneficial for the margin-receiver since they hold the physical assets and are less exposed to any issues such as legal risk. Security interest is preferable for the margin-giver since they still hold the margin assets and are less exposed to problems such as overcollateralisation in the event the margin receiver defaults (where, under title transfer, the additional margin may form part of the bankruptcy estate and not be returned).

The receiver of margin must pass on coupon payments, dividends, and any other cash flows. One exception to this rule is in the case where an immediate margin call would be triggered. In this case, the margin-holder may typically keep the minimum component of the cash flow (e.g. coupon on a bond) in order to remain appropriately collateralised.

The margin agreement will also stipulate the rate of interest to be paid on cash (irrespective of whether title transfer or security interest is used). Interest will typically be paid on cash margin at the overnight indexed spread (OIS) rate, for example, the Euro Overnight Index Average (EONIA) in Europe and Fed Funds in the US). Note that interest is not required on exchanges since the margin represents a settlement. Some counterparties, typically sovereigns or institutional investors, may subtract a spread on cash to discourage receiving cash margin (and encourage securities), since cash must be invested to earn interest or placed back in the banking system. Occasionally, a margin-receiver may agree to pay a rate higher than OIS to compensate for this funding mismatch or to incentivise the posting of cash.

The logic behind using the OIS rate is that since margin may only be held for short periods (due to potentially substantial daily valuation changes), only a short-term interest rate can be paid. However, OIS is not necessarily the most appropriate margin rate, especially for long-dated transactions where margin may need to be posted in substantial amounts for a long period. This may lead to a negative 'carry' problem due to an institution funding the margin posted at a rate significantly higher than the OIS rate they receive for posting the collateral. This can be considered to be the source of funding costs (FVA) (Chapter 18).

Where there is optionality in a margin agreement (e.g. the choice of different currencies of cash and/or different securities), this may be quantified via collateral funding adjustment (ColVA) (Chapter 16).

It may be that a party requires or wishes margin securities to be returned. This may be for a variety of reasons, such as:

- needing to deliver securities to a different party under either another margin agreement or repo transaction;[6]
- wanting to hold securities during the period when coupons or dividends are paid or where a party wants to exercise equity voting rights; or
- to maximise collateral optimisation ('cheapest to deliver' collateral).

In such a case, it is possible to make a substitution request to exchange an alternative amount of eligible margin (with the relevant haircut applied). The steps for doing this are:

1. the margin giver sends a notice requesting a substitution;
2. (the margin receiver consents to the substitution request);
3. the margin giver provides the new margin assets; and
4. upon receiving the new margin, the margin receiver returns the old margin within the trade settlement date.

The second step above (i.e. consent) may or may not be a requirement depending on the type of transfer being used and the election made by the parties. If consent is not required

---

[6] Note that the margin returned need not be exactly the same but must be equivalent (e.g. the same bond issue).

for the substitution, then such a request cannot be refused[7] (unless the margin type is not admissible under the agreement), although the requested margin does not need to be released until the alternative margin has been received. Whether or not margin can be substituted freely is an important consideration in terms of the funding costs and benefits of margin and valuing the 'cheapest to deliver' optionality inherent in margin agreements. This will be discussed in Section 16.2.3.

Note that substitution of margin does create additional credit risk during the short period when the margin receiver holds both the old and new margin assets. Given that this exists for a short period only, it is similar to settlement risk (Section 3.1.2).

7.2.5   Rehypothecation and Segregation

Rehypothecation and segregation are broadly opposite terms that refer respectively to the reuse and non-reuse of securities or cash margin. Each can be seen to be relevant depending on the nature of the margin, specifically whether it is variation margin or initial margin.

Due to the nature of the OTC derivatives market, where intermediaries such as banks generally hedge transactions, margin reuse can be seen to be natural, as illustrated in Figure 7.7. Note that if the transactions were settled, then the cash amounts would naturally offset. Variation margin can, therefore, be seen as 'quasi-settlement'.

Whilst cash margin and margin posted under title transfer (Section 7.2.4) are intrinsically reusable, in other situations the margin receiver must have the right of rehypothecation to allow it to be reused. Reuse means that it can be used by the margin receiver (e.g. in another margin agreement or a repo transaction). Rights of rehypothecation are generally used, as seen in Figure 7.8.

Rehypothecation is a natural concept for variation margin since this relates to a change in valuation (i.e. it is an amount that is owed) and is quasi-settlement. Rehypothecation is therefore important in OTC derivatives markets where many parties have multiple hedges and offsetting transactions, and there needs to be a flow of margin through the system. Note that these comments relate to minimising funding costs: from the point of view of funding, rehypothecation is important since it reduces the demand for high-quality collateral.

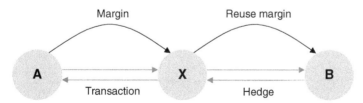

Figure 7.7   Illustration of the importance of reuse of margin. Party X transacts with counterparty A and hedges this transaction with party B, both under margin agreements. If party A posts margin, then it is natural that this is reused via posting to party B as the hedge will have equal and opposite value.

---

[7] For example, on the grounds that the original margin has been repoed, posted to another counterparty, sold, or is otherwise inaccessible.

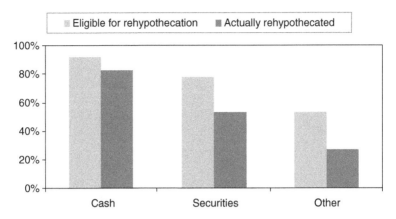

Figure 7.8   Illustration of rehypothecation of margin (large dealers only). Source: ISDA (2015).

From the point of view of counterparty risk, rehypothecation is dangerous since it creates the possibility that rehypothecated margin will not be received in a default scenario. However, for variation margin, this impact is minimal because, in the event of a counterparty default, the margin provided can be set off (Section 6.3.6) against the liability[8] (i.e. what is paid is owed based on the current valuation). There are two ways in which rehypothecation of variation margin does create counterparty risk:

- Counterparty risk is created by margin that needs to be returned against a positive change in value. However, under frequent exchange of margin (e.g. daily) this should be a relatively small problem.
- Margin assets requiring haircuts require overcollateralisation, which also creates counterparty risk due to the extra amount posted. Again, with small haircuts this is a relatively minimal effect.

Rehypothecation of variation margin is therefore not particularly problematic from a counterparty risk perspective since, by definition, it has a close relationship to the amount owed.

In contrast to variation margin, rehypothecation (or more broadly, reuse) is not a natural concept for initial margin. This is due to the fact that initial margin represents *extra* margin (overcollateralisation). Bankruptcies such as Lehman Brothers and MF Global illustrate the potential problems where rehypothecated assets were not returned. Singh and Aitken (2009) reported a significant drop in rehypothecation in the aftermath of the crisis, which is mainly related to initial margin (independent amount).

Even if margin is not rehypothecated or reused, there is a risk that it may not be retrieved in a default scenario. This risk can be mitigated by segregation, which aims to ensure that margin posted is legally protected in the event that the receiving party becomes insolvent. In practice, this can be achieved either through legal rules that ensure the return

---

[8] In other words, the negative valuation, which is the reason the variation margin has been required. Note that, as with netting, it is important to check that this would be upheld from a legal perspective.

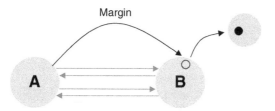

Figure 7.9 Illustration of the concept of segregation. Party A posts margin to party B, which is segregated either legally (priority rules in bankruptcy) and/or operationally (with a third party).

of any margin not required (in priority over any bankruptcy rules), or alternatively by a third-party custodian holding the initial margin. Segregation is therefore contrary and incompatible with the practice of rehypothecation. The basic concept of segregation is illustrated in Figure 7.9.

Since initial margin represents extra margin that is not owed, segregation can avoid there being additional counterparty risk in relation to the initial margin posted. Historically, rehypothecation of initial margin and co-mingling of variation and initial margins has created problems for surviving parties in default scenarios such as Lehman Brothers and MF Global. Such practices have, therefore, reduced. For example, hedge funds (as significant posters of initial margin) have become increasingly unwilling to allow rehypothecation. Whilst safer from the point of view of counterparty risk, segregation does create higher funding costs.

There are three potential ways in which segregated margin can be held:

- directly by the margin receiver;
- by a third party acting on behalf of one party; or
- in tri-party custody where a third party holds the margin and has a three-way contract with the two other parties concerned.

It is important to note that there are concepts of 'legal segregation' (achieved by all three methods above) and 'operational segregation' (achieved only by the latter two). In the MF Global default, parties had legal but not operational segregation, and due to fraudulent behaviour they lost margin that they would have expected to have had returned (see Section 10.3.1). Since cash is fungible by its nature, it is difficult to segregate on the balance sheet of the margin receiver. Hence, a tri-party arrangement where the margin is held in a designated account, and not rehypothecated or reinvested in any way, may be desirable. On the other hand, this limits investment options and makes it difficult for the margin giver to earn any return on their cash. Even if margin is held with a third- or tri-party agent, it is important to consider potential concentration risk with such third parties.

From the point of view of achieving segregation with minimal risks, the following conditions are important:

- the margin is pledged (not title transfer);[9]

---

[9] Title transfer leaves the margin giver as an unsecured creditor in the event of default of the margin receiver, since ownership of the underlying asset passes to the margin receiver at the time of transfer (and title is passed on in the event of rehypothecation).

- the margin is held with a third-party custodian that is not affiliated with the counterparty; and
- the margin cannot be reused or rehypothecated.

Note that segregation, whilst clearly the optimal method for reducing counterparty risk, causes potential funding issues for replacing margin that would otherwise simply be rehypothecated. This is at the heart of the cost/benefit balance of counterparty risk and funding that will be discussed in more detail in Section 7.6.

The above comments – that rehypothecation is natural for variation margin, whereas initial margin-posting requires segregation – is borne out in regulatory requirements over bilateral margin-posting (discussed later in Section 7.4), which generally require segregation of initial margin but not variation margin.

7.2.6   Settle to Market

As noted in Section 2.2.4, variation margin on exchanges is effectively a settlement, since it is generally required to be paid in cash and with no remuneration. On the other hand, OTC derivatives margin is not traditionally a settlement, which can be seen by the fact that an interest rate is paid to the margin giver on cash and the fact that – bilaterally – it may be possible to post margin in a range of different 'bespoke' securities or currencies of cash. This is outlined in Table 7.2.

Note that centrally cleared OTC and collateralised bilateral OTC derivatives are effectively 'collateralised to market'. In the case of bilateral transactions, this is a result of the potentially bespoke nature of the margin terms (noting that these are becoming more standard, as discussed in Section 4.4.2). In centrally-cleared OTC derivatives, the margining is equivalent to that of an exchange, but an interest rate is paid, typically known as price alignment interest (PAI); this is an interest rate used by CCPs to replicate the economics of bilateral OTC contracts.

Given that CCPs require variation margin (VM) to be in the same currency as the derivative and in cash, this margining process can be considered to be analogous to settlement. For example, the European Banking Authority (EBA 2015c) comments that, 'As cash for VM is considered the pure settlement of a claim, this should not be subject to any haircut.' Hence, some centrally-cleared OTC derivatives under variation margining are being classed as settle-to-market (STM).[10] The advantage of this is a potentially more secure legal framework in the event of default and reduced regulatory capital (including

Table 7.2 Comparison of the impact of variation margin in various derivatives markets.

	Type	Remuneration	Effect
Exchange	Cash (transaction currency)	-	Settlement
Centrally cleared OTC	Cash (transaction currency)	PAI	Collateralisation
Bilateral OTC	Bespoke	OIS	Collateralisation

---

[10] LCH.Clearnet (2017). Changes to the LCH model for Settled-to-Market FCM Contracts. Press release (11 December). www.lch.com.

leverage ratio) costs since the regulatory maturity of the derivative is effectively shortened to one day or the lowest permitted maturity bucket (discussed later in Section 13.4.3). In an STM contract, interest is still paid (to maintain economic equivalence with bilateral OTC contracts).

7.2.7   Valuation Agent, Disputes, and Reconciliations

The valuation agent is normally the party calling for the delivery or return of margin and thus must handle all calculations. Bilaterally, large counterparties trading with smaller counterparties may be valuation agents for all purposes. Alternatively, both counterparties may be the valuation agent, and each will call for (the return of) margin when they have an exposure (less negative value). In these situations, the potential for margin disputes is significant.

The role of the valuation agent in a margin calculation is as follows:

- to calculate the current value, including the impact of netting;
- to calculate the market value of margin previously posted and adjust this by the relevant haircuts;
- to calculate the total uncollateralised exposure; and
- to calculate the credit support amount (the amount of margin to be posted by either counterparty).

A dispute over a margin call is common and can arise due to one or more of a number of factors:

- trade population;
- trade valuation methodology;
- application of credit support annex rules (e.g. thresholds and eligible collateral);
- market data and market close time; and
- valuation of previously-posted collateral.

Note that for centrally-cleared transactions, margin disputes are not relevant since the CCP is the valuation agent. However, CCPs will clearly aim to ensure that their valuation methodologies and resulting margin requirements are market standard, transparent, and robust.

In bilateral markets, reconciliations aim to minimise the chance of a dispute by agreeing on valuations and margin requirements across portfolios. The frequency of reconciliations is increasing; for example, ISDA (2015) notes that most portfolios – especially large ones – are reconciled on a daily basis. Both Dodd–Frank and the European Market Infrastructure Regulation (EMIR) require more rigorous and frequent portfolio reconciliations, and there may be increased capital requirements for banks as a result of disputes (Section 13.4.5). Margin management practices are being continually improved. One example of this is the increase in electronic messaging in order for margin management to move away from manual processes (ISDA 2015).

In order to reduce operational risks and improve the efficiency of margining, various third parties also offer services around valuation, exchange of margin, dispute management, and portfolio reconciliation.

7.3   MARGIN TERMS

7.3.1   The Credit Support Annex

Traditionally, there has been no obligation in an OTC derivatives contract for either party to post margin. However, within an ISDA Master Agreement (see Section 2.2.6), it is possible to append a credit support annex (CSA) where the parties agree to contractual margin-posting. The CSA has become the market-standard margin agreement in bilateral markets.[11] ISDA (2015) reports that 34% of market participants have more than 3,000 margin agreements.[12] As with netting, ISDA has legal opinions throughout a large number of jurisdictions regarding the enforceability of the provisions within a CSA. The CSA will typically cover the same range of transactions as included in the Master Agreement, and it will typically be the net value of these transactions that will form the basis of margin requirements. Exceptions to this include instances where two parties change terms by creating a new CSA only for future transactions, leaving legacy transactions under the old CSA(s). In other words, there can be two CSAs under a single ISDA Master Agreement. This has been the general approach for banks implementing the bilateral margin requirements (Section 7.4).

Within the CSA, two parties can choose a number of key parameters and terms that will define the margin-posting requirements (credit support amount) in detail. These cover many different aspects, such as:

- method and timings of the underlying valuations;
- the calculation of the amount of margin that will be posted;
- the mechanics and timing of margin transfers;
- eligible margin (currencies of cash and types of securities);
- margin substitutions;
- dispute resolution;
- remuneration of margin posted;
- any initial margin amounts;
- haircuts applied to margin securities;
- possible rehypothecation (reuse) of margin securities; and
- triggers that may change the margin conditions (e.g. rating downgrades that may lead to enhanced margin requirements).

One important point with bilateral CSA documentation is that the underlying terms are agreed upfront on signing the CSA and can only be changed by mutual agreement through an amendment to the documentation. In contrast, a CCP can unilaterally change terms in response to market changes (e.g. some CCPs have increased and/or restricted margin requirements in illiquid and volatile markets in recent years – see Section 9.3.6).

When parties have a given CSA in place, the underlying transactions must be valued regularly (typically daily) and the impact on the required margin amount recalculated. Depending on the result of this, one party may be required to post (or return) a specific amount of margin. There need to be procedures in place to deal with disputes over the calculations, and parties may make periodic reconciliations to reduce the risk of disputes.

---

[11] Of margin agreements in use, 87% are ISDA agreements (ISDA 2013c).
[12] The respondents to this survey were 41 ISDA member firms, most of whom are banks or broker-dealers.

7.3.2   Types of CSA

The parameters of a CSA are a matter of negotiation between the two parties concerned.[13] Due to the very different nature of OTC derivatives counterparties, different margin arrangements exist. Some institutions (e.g. corporates) are unable to post margin; this is because, generally, they cannot commit to the resulting operational and liquidity requirements. Some institutions (e.g. sovereign, supranational entities, or multilateral development banks with high credit ratings) receive margin but are unwilling to post, a position partially supported by their exceptional (generally triple-A) credit quality. Non-margin-posting entities generally prefer (or have no choice) to pay xVA charges for the counterparty risk, funding, and capital requirements (KVA) they impose on a bank,[14] rather than agreeing to post margin to mitigate these charges.

Broadly speaking, three possible margin agreements exist in practice:

- *No CSA*. In some OTC derivatives trading relationships, there is no CSA, since one party cannot or prefers not to commit to margin-posting. A typical example of this is the relationship between a bank and a corporate where the latter's inability to post margin means that a CSA is not usually in place (e.g. a corporate treasury department may find it very difficult to manage its liquidity needs under a CSA).[15]
- *Two-way CSA*. For two financial counterparties, a two-way CSA is more typical, where both parties agree to post margin. Two-way CSAs with zero thresholds are standard in the interbank market and aim to be beneficial (from a counterparty risk point of view, at least) to both parties.
- *One-way CSA*. In some situations, a one-way CSA is used, where only one party can receive collateral. This actually represents additional risk for the margin giver and puts them in a worse situation than if they were in a no-CSA relationship. A typical example is a high-quality entity such as a triple-A sovereign or supranational trading with a bank. Banks themselves have typically been able to demand one-way CSAs in their favour when transacting with some hedge funds. Note that one-way CSAs are often based on a rating schedule (see Table 7.4) and would be symmetric if the party's ratings were the same. The considerations of funding and capital costs have made such agreements particularly problematic in recent years.

Note that the above are general classifications and are not identified contractually. For example, a one-way CSA would specify a threshold (Section 7.3.4) of infinity, possibly contingent on a strong rating, for the non-posting party. Hence, an endless number of different CSA agreements actually exist based on the terms that will be defined in Sections 7.3.3 to 7.3.5.

Margin-posting across the market is quite mixed depending on the type of institution (Table 7.3). In general, banks will almost always trade under CSAs, financial institutions will often use CSAs, whilst non-financial counterparties will often not trade under a CSA. Note that high-credit-quality sovereigns and similar entities under one-way CSAs will be uncollateralised from a bank's point of view.

---

[13] Although future regulatory requirements will reduce the need for negotiation (Section 7.4).

[14] Note that some xVA terms can constitute benefits overall.

[15] Some large corporates do post margin.

Table 7.3 Proportion of each type of counterparty transacting under a CSA.
Source: ISDA (2015).

Institution type	Proportion under a CSA
Dealers	90.4%
Banks and security firms	95.5%
Hedge funds	94.1%
Pension plans	75.3%
Mutual funds	68.8%
Other financial firms	70.4%
Non-financial institutions	28.6%
Government-sponsored entities/ Government agencies	42.4%
Sovereign national governments	69.0%
Local or regional government entities	75.6%

The main reasons for a party not agreeing to post margin are the liquidity needs and operational workload related to posting cash or high-quality securities under stringent margin agreements. Other aspects may include internal or external restrictions (for example, monoline insurers were only able to gain triple-A credit ratings by virtue of not posting margin, as discussed in Section 2.4.4) and the economic view that uncollateralised trading is cheaper than collateralised trading (when liquidity costs are factored in).

A margin agreement must explicitly define all the parameters of the collateralisation and account for all possible scenarios. The choice of parameters will often come down to a balance between the workload of calling and returning margin versus the risk-mitigation benefit of doing so. Funding implications, not historically deemed important, should also be considered. The following sections explain the parameters that define the amount of collateral that must be posted.

7.3.3 Margin Call Frequency

The margin call frequency refers to the contractual periodic timescale with which margin may be called and returned. A longer margin call frequency may be agreed upon, most probably to reduce operational workload and in order for the relevant valuations to be carried out. Some smaller institutions may struggle with the operational and funding requirements in relation to the daily margin calls required by larger counterparties. Whilst a margin call frequency longer than daily might be practical for asset classes and markets that are not so volatile, daily calls have become standard in most OTC derivatives markets. Furthermore, intraday margin calls are common for more vanilla and standard products such as repos and for derivatives cleared via CCPs.

Note that the margin call frequency is not the same as the MPoR (Section 7.2.3). The MPoR represents the effective delay in receiving margin that should be considered in the event of a counterparty default. The margin call frequency is one component of this, but there are other considerations also. It could, therefore, be that the margin call frequency is daily, but the MPoR is assumed to be 10 days (see Section 15.5.1 for more discussion).

7.3.4   Threshold, Initial Margin, and the Minimum Transfer Amount

The threshold is the amount below which margin is not required, leading to *undercollateralisation*. If the portfolio value is below the threshold, then no margin can be called, and the underlying portfolio is therefore uncollateralised. If the value is above the threshold, only the *incremental* amount of margin can be called for. Although this clearly limits the risk-reduction benefit of the collateralisation, it does reduce the operational burden and underlying liquidity costs of margin-posting. A threshold of zero means that margin would be posted under any circumstance,[16] and an infinite threshold is used to specify that a counterparty will not post margin under any circumstance (as in a one-way CSA, for example).

Thresholds typically exist because one or both parties can gain in operational and liquidity costs and the associated weakening of the collateralisation is worth this. Some counterparties may be able to tolerate uncollateralised counterparty risk up to a certain level (e.g. banks will be comfortable with this up to the credit limit for the counterparty in question; see Section 3.1.5). Thresholds are increasingly zero and can only be non-zero for parties that are exempt from the bilateral margin requirements (Section 7.4).

A minimum transfer amount (MTA) is the smallest amount of margin that can be transferred. It is used to avoid the workload associated with a frequent transfer of insignificant amounts of (potentially non-cash) margin. The size of the minimum transfer amount again represents a balance between risk mitigation versus operational workload. The minimum transfer amount and threshold are additive in the sense that the exposure must exceed the sum of the two before any margin can be called. We note that this additively does not mean that the minimum transfer amount can be incorporated into the threshold – this would be correct in defining the point at which the margin call can be made, but not in terms of the margin due (more details are given in Section 15.5.3).

There may also be a specified rounding of margin amounts to avoid dealing with awkward quantities. This is typically a relatively small amount and will have a small effect on the impact of collateralisation. Note that minimum transfer amounts and rounding quantities are relevant for non-cash margin where the transfer of small amounts is problematic. In cases where cash-only margin is used (e.g. variation margin and CCP), these terms are generally zero.

Initial margin is the opposite of a threshold and defines an amount of extra margin that must be posted independently from the value of the underlying portfolio. The general aim of this is to provide the added safety of overcollateralisation as a cushion against potential risks such as delays in receiving margin and costs in the close-out process (Section 7.2.3). Initial margin relates to the variability of the value rather than the value itself.

As noted above, the initial margin in bilateral OTC derivatives (known as the independent amount) was historically quite rare and was a payment in only one direction (usually from a weaker-credit-quality party to a stronger-credit-quality party). For exchange-traded derivatives and centrally-cleared OTC derivatives, initial margin is always required. However, the bilateral margin requirements (Section 7.4) are requiring that initial margin be posted in bilateral OTC derivatives also, irrespective of credit

---

[16] Assuming that the amount is above the minimum transfer amount discussed next.

quality. Initial margin is, therefore, becoming a common feature of derivatives transactions, with the exception of bilateral OTC derivatives where one party (or the product) is exempt from the bilateral margin requirements.

Unlike parameters such as thresholds which are fixed quantities, initial margin amounts typically change over time according to the perceived risk on the portfolio. Sometimes these are simple methodologies (e.g. based on notional, transaction type, and remaining maturity), but more commonly they are becoming quite complex, dynamic calculations. This is important to emphasise as the term initial margin may suggest a static quantity (this was the case when initial margin was first used, but it is not so any more). Dynamic initial margin methodologies are the subject of Chapter 9.

Note that since thresholds and initial margins essentially work in opposite directions, and an initial margin can be thought of (intuitively and mathematically) as a negative threshold, these terms are not seen together: either undercollateralisation is specified via a threshold (with zero initial margin), or an initial margin defines overcollateralisation (with a threshold of zero).

Historically, bilateral OTC derivative markets have sometimes also linked thresholds and initial margin requirements (and sometimes minimum transfer amounts) to credit quality (most commonly credit ratings).[17] An example of this is given in Table 7.4. The motivation for doing this is to minimise the operational workload when a counterparty's rating is high (the threshold is infinity at a rating of AAA), but to tighten the collateralisation terms when their credit quality deteriorates (at A+ the threshold is zero, and below this an initial margin is also required).

Prior to the GFC, triple-A entities such as monoline insurers traded through one-way margin agreements (i.e. they did not post margin), but with triggers specifying that they must post if their ratings were to decline. Such agreements can lead to rather unpleasant effects, since a downgrade of a counterparty's credit rating can occur rather late with respect to the actual decline in credit quality, which in turn may cause further credit issues due to the requirement to post collateral. This is exactly what happened with AIG (see below) and monoline insurers (Section 2.4.4) in the GFC.

Table 7.4   Example of rating-linked margin parameters. This could correspond to one or both parties.

Rating	Initial margin[a]	Threshold
AAA/Aaa	0%	∞
AA+/Aa1	0%	$100m
AA/Aa2	0%	$50m
AA-/Aa3	0%	$25m
A+/A1	0%	$0
A/A2	1%	$0
A-/A3	1%	$0
BBB+/Baa1	2%	$0

[a]Expressed in terms of the total notional of the portfolio.

---

[17] Other less common examples are net asset value, market value of equity or traded credit spreads.

The dangers of credit rating triggers

The case of American International Group (AIG) is probably the best example of the funding liquidity problems that can be induced by margin posting. In September 2008, AIG was essentially insolvent due to the margin requirements arising from credit default swap transactions executed by their financial products subsidiary AIGFP. In this example, one of the key aspects was that AIGFP posted margin as a function of their credit rating. The liquidity problems of AIG stemmed from the requirement to post an additional $20bn of margin as a result of its bonds being downgraded.[18] Due to the systemic importance of AIG, the Federal Reserve Bank created a secured credit facility of up to $85bn to allow AIGFP to post the margin they owed and avoid the collapse of AIG.

These two problems of rating linkage are now quite characterised:

- from a risk-mitigating point of view, they may be ineffectual due to the rating reacting too slowly; and
- they may create liquidity problems and cliff-edge effects for a counterparty being downgraded.

The above asymmetry is recognised by regulation. For example, Basel capital rules do not allow a capital benefit from credit rating triggers (see BCBS 2011b) and so assume – conservatively – that a counterparty will default without first being downgraded. On the other hand, the liquidity coverage ratio rules (Section 4.3.3) require a bank to pre-fund outflows such as ratings-contingent initial margin-posting. For example, based on Table 7.4, a bank rated A+ would have to fund 2% of initial margin based on a three-notch downgrade to BBB+.

7.3.5   Margin Types and Haircuts

An agreement such as a CSA specifies the assets that are admissible to be posted as margin. Cash (mostly in US dollars and Euros) is the major form of margin taken against OTC derivatives exposures (Figure 7.10). The ability to post other forms of margin is often highly preferable for liquidity reasons. Cash margin has become increasingly common over recent years – a trend which is unlikely to reverse, especially due to cash variation margin requirements in situations such as central clearing. Government securities comprise a further 14.8% of total margin, with the remaining 10.3% comprising government agency securities, supranational bonds, US municipal bonds, covered bonds, corporate bonds, letters of credit, and equities.

To the extent that there is price variability of such assets, a 'haircut' acts as a discount to the value of the margin and provides a cushion in the event that the security is sold at a lower price. The haircut will depend on individual characteristics of the asset in question. Haircuts mean that extra margin must be posted, which acts as an overcollateralisation to mitigate against a drop in the value of the asset, so that lenders will have more chance of being fully collateralised.

---

[18] AIG Form 10-K (2008).

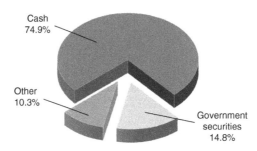

Figure 7.10 Breakdown of the type of margin received against non-cleared OTC derivatives. Source: ISDA (2014a).

Cash is the most common type of margin posted and may not attract haircuts. However, there may be haircuts applied to reflect the FX risk from receiving the margin in a currency other than the 'termination' currency of the portfolio in question.[19] Bonds posted as margin will have price volatility arising from interest rate and credit spread moves, although these will be relatively moderate (typically a few percent). Margin based on equity or commodity (e.g. gold) underlyings will clearly require much higher haircuts due to high price variability.

Haircuts are typically defined as fixed percentage amounts, although they can potentially be based on more dynamic amounts derived from a model. In bilateral markets they are specified in the agreement and cannot, therefore, be adjusted in line with changes in the market (unless both parties agree). A CCP is typically able to change contractual haircuts and eligible securities and will do so if market conditions change (e.g. a particular asset is seen to have greater market volatility, liquidity risk, or credit risk).

The haircut is a reduction in the value of the asset to account for the fact that its value may fall between the last margin call and liquidation in the event of the counterparty's default. As such, the fixed haircut is theoretically driven by the volatility of the asset and its liquidity. A haircut of x% means that for every unit of that security posted as collateral, a 'valuation percentage' of only $(1 - x)\%$ will be given, as illustrated in Figure 7.11. The margin giver must account for the haircut when posting.

Volatile assets such as equities or gold are not necessarily problematic, as relatively large haircuts can be taken as compensation for their price volatility and potential illiquidity. Assets with significant credit or liquidity risk are generally avoided as haircuts cannot practically be large enough to cover the default of the margin asset or having to liquidate it at a substantially reduced price. Some examples of haircuts, together with eligible margin types, are shown in Table 7.5.

Securities in various currencies may be specified as admissible margin but may also attract haircuts due to the additional FX risk. FX risk from posted margin can be hedged in the spot and forward FX markets, but it must be done dynamically as the value of the margin changes. If the credit rating of an underlying security held as margin declines below that specified in the margin agreement, then it will normally be necessary to replace this security immediately.

---

[19] This would refer to the currency in which the portfolio is closed out in the event of a default.

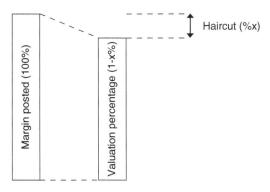

Figure 7.11   Illustration of a haircut applied to collateral.

Table 7.5   Example haircuts in a margin agreement.

	Party A	Party B	Valuation percentage	Haircut
Cash in eligible currency	X	X	100%	0%
Debt obligations issued by the governments of the US, UK or Germany with a maturity less than one year	X	X	98%	2%
Debt obligations issued by the governments of the US, UK or Germany with a maturity between 1 and 10 years	X	X	95%	5%
Debt obligations issued by the governments of the US, UK or Germany with a maturity greater than 10 years	X		90%	10%

The important points to consider in determining eligible margin and assigning haircuts are:

- time taken to liquidate the margin;
- the volatility of the underlying market variable(s) defining the value of the margin;
- default risk of the asset;
- maturity of the asset;
- liquidity of the asset; and
- any relationship between the value of the margin and either the default of the counterparty or the underlying exposure (wrong-way risk).

The last point above is often the hardest to implement in a prescriptive fashion. For example, high-quality (i.e. above some credit rating) sovereign bonds are likely to be deemed as eligible collateral. They will likely have good liquidity, low default risk, and reasonably low price volatility (depending on their maturity). However, the CSA may not prevent (for example) a bank posting bonds from its own sovereign.

An obvious way in which to derive a haircut would be to require that it covers a fairly severe potential worst-case drop in the value of the underlying asset during a given time

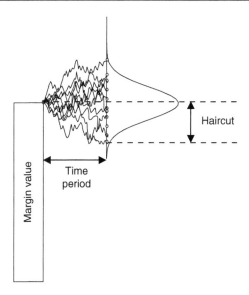

Figure 7.12   Illustration of the methodology for estimating a haircut.

period, as illustrated in Figure 7.12. The time period would depend on the liquidity of the underlying collateral, but would typically be in the region of a few days.

Under normal distribution assumptions, such a formula is easy to derive:

$$haircut = \Phi^{-1}(\alpha) \times \sigma_c \times \sqrt{\tau} \tag{7.1}$$

where $\Phi^{-1}(\alpha)$ defines the number of standard deviations the haircut needs to cover involving the cumulative inverse normal distribution function and the confidence level α (e.g. 99%). Also required is the volatility of the collateral, σ_c, and the liquidation time (similar to the MPoR concept, but typically shorter), denoted τ. For example, assuming a 99% confidence level, two-day time horizon, and an interest rate volatility of 1%, a 10-year, high-quality (i.e. minimal credit risk) government bond would have an approximate haircut of 2%,[20] which can be compared with the bilateral margin rules discussed in Section 7.4.4.[21]

Haircuts applied in this way should not only compensate for collateral volatility but also reduce exposure overall, since they should create an overcollateralisation in 99% of cases, and they will only be insufficient 1% of the time. Indeed, for a short MPoR the use of even quite volatile non-cash collateral does not increase the exposure materially, and a reasonably conservative haircut will at least neutralise the additional volatility. The major issue that can arise with respect to collateral type is where there is a significant relationship between the value of the collateral and the exposure or credit quality of the

---

[20] $1\% \times \Phi^{-1}(99\%) \times \sqrt{\frac{2}{250}} = 0.21\%$, and then multiplying by an approximate duration of 8.5 years.

[21] This should not be taken to imply that these assumptions were used to derive the results in Table 7.5, which has higher (more conservative) values.

counterparty. A sovereign entity posting its own bonds provides an example of this.[22] Note that adverse correlations can also be present with cash margin: an example would be receiving euros from European sovereigns or European banks. This will be described as 'wrong-way collateral' and discussed further in Section 7.5.3.

7.3.6   Credit Support Amount Calculations

ISDA CSA documentation defines the credit support amount as the amount of margin that may be requested at a given point in time. Due to parameters such as thresholds, minimum transfer amounts, and initial margins, this will not be the same as the value of the portfolio.

Spreadsheet 7.1 Margin calculation including thresholds and initial margins.

Consider initially that a party is only receiving margin. The relevant amount of margin considering only the threshold and initial margin will be:

$$\max(value - K_C, 0) + IM_C \tag{7.2}$$

where *value* represents the current value of the relevant transactions[23] and K_C and IM_C represent the threshold and initial margin for the counterparty respectively (note that the threshold is generally a fixed value, but the initial margin may be dynamic). The above equation shows that the threshold and initial margin act in opposite directions, and it does not make sense to include both. Indeed, when initial margins are present, the threshold will usually be zero.

More generally, including both parties, the equation defining the credit support amount for variation margin is:

$$\max(value - K_C, 0) - \max(-value - K_P, 0) - C \tag{7.3}$$

where K_P is the threshold for the party making the calculation and C represents the amount of margin held already (known as the credit support balance). If the above calculation results in a positive value, then margin can be called (or requested to be returned), whilst a negative value indicates the requirement to post (or return) margin. This is the case as long as the amount is higher than the minimum transfer amount (rounding may also be applied).

Initial margins do not depend on any of the above terms and so can be considered to be computed separately. Traditionally, variation margin is captured in the CSA, as above, by the credit support amount, and the initial margin is referred to separately as independent

---

[22] Note that there are benefits in taking margin in this form. Firstly, more margin can be called for as the credit quality of the sovereign deteriorates. Secondly, even a sudden jump to default event provides the recovery value of the debt as collateral. After this, the bank would have access to a second recovery value as an unsecured creditor.

[23] As noted in Section 7.2.3, this is typically defined as a base value.

amount. Initial margin is not netted against variation margin amounts and may also be segregated. In the case where both parties post initial margin (not common historically but required under future regulation), the initial margins themselves are not netted and are paid separately.

Note also that margin payments in OTC derivatives are not netted against cash flow payments, even if they are in the same denomination as the cash flows. This is due to the fact that margin is not a settlement. In exchange-traded markets, the settlement process means that such netting effectively does occur. In bilateral markets, this gives rise to so-called 'collateral spikes', where a large cash flow can cause a spike in the risk due to the delay in receiving margin against the change in valuation resulting from the payment (see Figure 3.2).

Table 7.6 illustrates the potential movement in the value of a portfolio and the associated margin requirements (without considering minimum transfer amounts and rounding). Important features are:

- *Time t_1*. The credit support amount is defined by the value minus the threshold amount, which means that the portfolio is only partially collateralised.
- *Time t_2*. Even though the portfolio is uncollateralised by 75, the credit support amount is -25, which corresponds to margin being returned (up to the threshold).

Note that minimum transfer amounts (MTAs) can cause *path dependency* in margin calculations, as illustrated in Table 7.7. Here, the values at times t_2 and t_3 in all scenarios are the same, but those at time t_1 are not. The result of this is that the credit support amount at time t_3 differs and can either be smaller (scenario 1) or larger (scenario 3). The amount of credit support that is required at t_3 depends on the credit support balance at t_2, which in turn depends on the previous time t_1. This shows that MTAs can cause path dependency, which can make the modelling of collateralised exposures more complicated (Section 15.5.3).

Table 7.8 illustrates the potential movement in the value of a portfolio with a zero threshold and initial margin. Some other important features are:

- *Time t_1*. The portfolio is overcollateralised due to the initial margin.
- *Time t_2*. The move in the value of the portfolio results in a margin deficit of 25 (375 - 350), but this is within the initial margin amount (in the event of default, there is the question of whether the close-out costs would be within the initial margin). The reduction of the initial margin will not be netted with the increase in variation margin.[24]

Table 7.6   Example margin calculation. No initial margin.

	t_1	t_2
Value	350	325
Threshold	100	100
Credit support balance	0	250
Credit support amount	250	−25

---

[24] Note that the initial margin amount will not depend on the value. Initial margin methodologies are discussed in more detail in Chapter 9.

Table 7.7 Example margin calculation with minimum transfer amount (assumed to be 50) and a threshold of zero and no initial margin.

Scenario 1	t_1	t_2	t_3
Value	90	110	150
Credit support balance	0	90	90
Credit support amount	90	0	60
Scenario 2	t_1	t_2	t_3
Value	40	110	150
Credit support balance	0	0	110
Credit support amount	0	110	0
Scenario 3	t_1	t_2	t_3
Value	130	110	150
Credit support balance	0	130	130
Credit support amount	130	0	0

Table 7.8 Example margin calculation with (dynamic) initial margin.

	t_1	t_2
Value	350	375
Threshold	0	0
Credit support balance	0	350
Credit support amount	350	25
Initial margin (independent amount)	50	45

7.3.7 Impact of Margin on Exposure

The impact of margin on a typical exposure profile is shown in Figure 7.13. There are essentially two reasons why margin cannot perfectly mitigate exposure. Firstly, the presence of a threshold means that a certain amount of exposure cannot be collateralised.[25] Secondly, the delay in receiving margin and parameters such as the minimum transfer amount create a discrete effect, as the movement of exposure cannot be tracked perfectly (this is illustrated by the grey blocks in Figure 7.13).[26]

Initial margin can be thought of as making the threshold negative and can, therefore, potentially reduce the exposure to zero. This is illustrated in Figure 7.14.

Margin usage has increased significantly over the last decade, as illustrated in Figure 7.15, which shows the estimated amount of margin and gross credit exposure. The ratio of these quantities gives an estimate of the fraction of credit exposure that is collateralised. The overall figure is slightly misleading since it is a combination of portfolios that may either be uncollateralised (e.g. no CSA or one-way CSA), collateralised

---

[25] Note that thresholds are increasingly zero, in which case this is not an issue.
[26] The purpose of an initial margin is to mitigate this risk by providing a buffer.

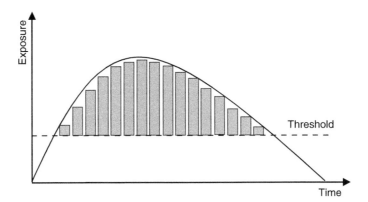

Figure 7.13   Illustration of the impact of margin on exposure without initial margin. The margin amount is depicted by grey areas.

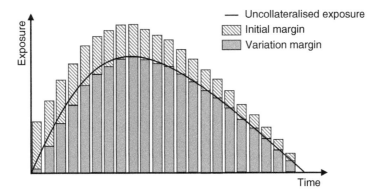

Figure 7.14   Illustration of the impact of margin on exposure, including initial margin.

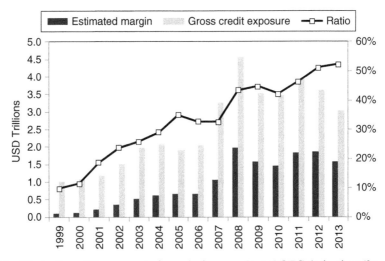

Figure 7.15   Illustration of the amount of margin for non-cleared OTC derivatives (Source: ISDA 2014a) compared to the gross credit exposure (Source: BIS 2014) and the ratio giving the overall extent of collateralising of OTC derivatives. Note that the margin numbers are halved to account for double-counting, as discussed in ISDA (2014a).

(e.g. traditional two-way CSA) or overcollateralised (i.e. including initial margin). The incoming regulatory rules on bilateral margin will increase the trend by requiring greater amounts of both variation and initial margin.

7.3.8   Traditional Margin Practices in Bilateral and Centrally-cleared Markets

In bilateral OTC derivatives, margin agreements such as CSAs are not always used, and when they are relatively bespoke, even to the extent that only one party may post margin (one-way CSA). This means that agreements are non-standard and there is a significant amount of optionality (e.g. there are many possibilities about the type of margin that can be delivered across currency, asset class, and maturity). Furthermore, initial margin (independent amount) has traditionally been rare.

On the other hand, centrally-cleared OTC derivatives are subject to much more standard margining methods that have developed over many years of central clearing of exchange-traded derivatives. Such margining involves frequent paying (receiving) of variation margin against losses (gains) in cash in the currency of the transaction and added security for the CCP in the form of initial margin. This prevents the CCP from having any FX or liquidity risk (e.g. margin in different currencies) and minimises their counterparty risk exposure.

Table 7.9 contrasts traditional bilateral and centrally-cleared OTC derivative margining practices.

There have been initiatives to attempt to standardise bilateral margining practices. Notably, the ISDA standard credit support annex (SCSA) aimed to standardise and reduce embedded optionality in CSAs, whilst promoting the adoption of standard pricing (e.g. what is now typically known as OIS discounting, discussed in Section 16.1.3). An SCSA could also be seen as changing the mechanics of the SCSA to be more closely aligned to central clearing margin practices.

In a typical CSA, a single amount is calculated at each period for a portfolio, which may cover many currencies. Cash margin may, therefore, be posted in different currencies and also typically in other securities. In addition, thresholds and minimum transfer

Table 7.9   Comparison of historical margining practices in bilateral and centrally-cleared OTC derivatives markets.

	Bilateral	Centrally cleared
Thresholds	Often non-zero	Zero
Initial margin	Rare (independent amount)	Must be posted by all parties (except CCP itself)
Type (variation margin)	Relatively flexible	Cash in transaction currency
Type (initial margin)		Cash and liquid securities
Frequency of posting	Daily or less frequently	Daily and potentially intradaily[27]
Negotiation	Bilateral	Defined by CCP

[27] Intradaily margin is likely to be required in the event of significant changes in valuation.

amounts are commonly not zero. The aim of the SCSA was to greatly simplify the process, requiring:

- cash margin only (with respect to variation margin, any initial margins will be allowed in other securities);
- only currencies with the most liquid OIS curves (USD, EUR, GBP, CHF, and JPY) to be eligible;
- zero thresholds and minimum transfer amounts; and
- one margin requirement per currency (cross-currency products are put into the USD bucket).

The SCSA did not gain in popularity due largely to the currency silo issue where each currency gives rise to a margin requirement in cash. It has been largely superseded by regulatory rules on bilateral margin-posting, which are discussed next.

7.4 BILATERAL MARGIN REQUIREMENTS

7.4.1   General Requirements

As discussed in Section 4.4.2, regulators have started to impose bilateral margin requirements, often known as the uncleared margin requirements (UMR), on most major participants when transacting non-centrally-cleared derivatives with one another. The final rules can be found in BCBS-IOSCO (2019). In general, these rules have the following aims:

- *Reduction of systemic risk*. Margin requirements are viewed as reducing 'contagion and spillover effects' by ensuring that margin is available to cover losses caused by the default of a derivatives counterparty.
- *Promotion of central clearing*. Whilst central clearing is often mandatory, the UMR will promote the adoption of central clearing by aligning costs (notably initial margin) in a bilateral market with those that will exist in centrally-cleared markets.

The concepts of variation and initial margin are intended to reflect current and potential future exposure, respectively.

The above rules apply to 'covered entities' in transactions with one another (i.e. if one party in a trading relationship is not a covered entity, then the other party does not need to comply with respect to this relationship). Parties that are exempt from the requirements include sovereigns, central banks, multilateral development banks, and the Bank for International Settlements. Other exemptions depend on the region in question (see Section 4.4.3 for more detail).

With respect to each component, standards state that covered entities for non-centrally-cleared derivatives must exchange:

- Variation margin:
  o Must be exchanged bilaterally on a regular basis (e.g. daily).
  o Full margin must be used (i.e. zero threshold).

- o The minimum transfer amount must not exceed €500,000.[28]
- o Can be rehypothecated and netted.
- o Must be posted in full from the start of the rules.
- Initial margin:
  - o To be exchanged by both parties with no netting of amounts.
  - o Should be based on an extreme but plausible move in the underlying portfolio value at a 99% confidence level.
  - o A 10-day time horizon should be assumed on top of the daily variation margin exchanged (this can be seen to align loosely with the MPoR, discussed in Section 7.2.3).
  - o Can be calculated based on internal (validated) models or regulatory tables.
  - o Must be exchanged on a gross basis (i.e. amounts posted between two parties cannot cancel), must be segregated and cannot be rehypothecated, repledged, or reused.[29]
  - o Follows a phased-in implementation (see Section 7.4.2).

Parties are required to meet strict delivery timing requirements for margin, in most cases requiring it to be provided within the same business day as the date of the calculation.[30]

The collecting counterparty must segregate the initial margin either with a third-party holder or custodian or via other legally-binding arrangements so that it is protected from the default or insolvency of the party holding the initial margin. The initial margin must be available to the posting entity in a timely manner in case the collecting party defaults. In addition, the collecting counterparty should provide the posting counterparty with the option to segregate its collateral from the assets of the other counterparties. Counterparties will need to arrange for initial margin to be provided by way of security rather than title transfer (Section 7.2.4). The collecting counterparty must not rehypothecate, repledge, or reuse the collateral collected as initial margin, although variation margin may be reused by the collecting counterparty. This is all consistent with the aim that posting initial margin – being extra margin – should not increase counterparty risk (Section 7.2.5). Firms will, therefore, have to open accounts and build connectivity with custodians.

The use of a third party to achieve segregation of initial margin is viewed as the most robust protection, although this does raise the issue of whether such entities (the number of which is currently quite small) would become sources of systemic risk with the amount of margin they would need to hold. Arrangements for segregation will vary across jurisdictions depending on the local bankruptcy regime, and would need to be effective under the relevant laws and supported by periodically updated legal opinions.

---

[28] The amounts are defined in euros and there are conversions to other currencies. The US dollar equivalent amounts are the same.

[29] Rehypothecation of initial margin is allowed in very limited situations where the transaction is a hedge of a client position, and will be suitably protected once rehypothecated, with the client having a priority claim under the relevant insolvency regime. It must be ensured that the initial margin can only be rehypothecated once and the client must be informed and agree to the rehypothecation. This is of limited benefit due to the potentially large chain of hedges that is executed across the interbank market in response to a client transaction. Sawyer, N. (2013). Industry 'won't bother' with one-time rehypothecation. *Risk* (12 September). www.risk.net.

[30] Subject to certain conditions, variation margin may be provided within two business days of calculation, under limited circumstances.

Rigorous and robust dispute resolution procedures should be in place in case of disagreements over margin amounts. This is an important point since risk-sensitive initial margin methodologies will be, by their nature, quite complex and likely to lead to disputes.

7.4.2   Phase-in and Coverage

The UMR apply to all OTC derivatives with the exception of FX swaps and forwards, which are exempt.[31] This, like a similar exemption over clearing, is controversial (Duffie 2011). On the one hand, such FX products are often short-dated and more prone to settlement risk than counterparty risk. On the other hand, FX rates can be quite volatile and occasionally linked to sovereign risk, and cross-currency swaps are typically long-dated.

Official implementation dates are shown in Table 7.10, although such timescales depend on the implementation of local regulations, which have been delayed in some cases.[32] Note that there have been changes to Phase 5 and a new Phase 6 which were not in the original regulations (see BCBS-IOSCO 2019). See ISDA-SIFMA (2018) for details of thresholds in other currencies and details on implementation in other regions.

Whereas variation margins must be posted immediately, initial margin requirements are subject to a phase-in with declining thresholds until 1 September 2021 and need only apply to new transactions executed after the relevant date (applying the initial margin requirements to existing derivatives contracts is not required). Furthermore, parties can have a threshold of up to €50m (based on a consolidated group of entities)[33] in relation to their initial margin-posting (i.e. they would only post amounts above the threshold).[34] This threshold was introduced to reduce liquidity costs as a result of the requirements.[35]

A particularly strange case for bilateral margining is a cross-currency swap. Such products have significant counterparty risk due to the large interest rate and FX volatilities and the fact that they are typically long dated. Due to the FX exemptions, the FX component of a cross-currency swap is exempt from initial margin-posting.[36] In practice, this means that there will still be material counterparty risk on such a transaction since the FX component drives the majority of the exposure. On the other hand, this component is not exempt from variation margin posting requirements.

Note that the requirements allow a party to remain exempt if they have a total notional of less than €8bn of OTC derivatives or can stay below a negotiated threshold of up to €50m with each of their counterparties.

---

[31] In the EU, physically-settled FX forwards are subject to variation margin.

[32] For example, the U.S. Commodity Futures Trading Commission (CFTC) stated that from 1 March 2017 to 1 September 2017, there would be no enforcement against a swap dealer failing to comply with the variation margin requirements subject to a 1 March 2017 compliance date. In the EU, the first date for compliance was 4 February 2017 rather than 1 September 2016.

[33] This means that if a firm engages in separate derivatives transactions with more than one counterparty, but belonging to the same larger consolidated group (such as a bank holding company), then the threshold must essentially be *shared* in some way between these counterparties.

[34] For example, for a threshold amount of 50 and a calculated initial margin of 35, no margin is required. However, if the calculated margin is 65, then an amount of 15 needs to be posted.

[35] BCBS-IOSCO (2013). Basel Committee and IOSCO issue near-final proposal on margin requirements for non-centrally-cleared derivatives. Press Release (15 February). www.bis.org.

[36] BCBS-IOSCO (2015) states 'Initial margin requirements for cross-currency swaps do not apply to the fixed physically settled FX transactions associated with the exchange of principal of cross-currency swaps'.

Table 7.10 Timescales for the implementation of margin requirements for covered entities and transactions based on the aggregate group-wide, month-end average notional amount of non-centrally-cleared derivatives (including physically-settled FX forwards and swaps), newly executed during the immediately preceding June, July, and August.

Date	Requirement
	Variation margin
1 September 2016	Exchange variation margin with respect to new non-centrally-cleared derivative transactions if average aggregate notionals exceed €3trn for both parties.
1 March 2017	As above but with no threshold.
	Initial margin
1 September 2016 to 31 August 2017 ('Phase 1')	Exchange initial margin if average aggregate notionals exceed €3trn.
1 September 2017 to 31 August 2018 ('Phase 2')	Exchange initial margin if average aggregate notionals exceed €2.25trn.
1 September 2018 to 31 August 2019 ('Phase 3')	Exchange initial margin if average aggregate notionals exceed €1.5trn.
1 September 2019 to 31 August 2020 ('Phase 4')	Exchange initial margin if average aggregate notionals exceed €0.75trn.
1 September 2020 to 31 August 2021 ('Phase 5')	Exchange initial margin if average aggregate notionals exceed €50bn.
From 1 September 2021 ('Phase 6')	Exchange initial margin if average aggregate notionals exceed €8bn.

7.4.3   Initial Margin and Haircut Calculations

As noted above, initial margin is intended to cover the potential future exposure in an extreme but plausible scenario based on a 99% confidence interval over a 10-day horizon. Such a scenario must use historical data that incorporates a period of significant financial stress. The requirement for the stress period is to ensure that a sufficiently large amount of margin is available and also to reduce procyclicality (positively correlated to the general state of the economy; see Section 9.3.5) in the margin over time.

In general, the above implies that initial margin amounts will be portfolio-based and also dynamic (i.e. they will change over time). This is in contrast to the historical use of initial margin (independent amount), which is often transaction-based and either deterministic or driven by simple formulas (e.g. a percentage of notional based on the type and remaining maturity of a transaction).

There are two methods that can be used to calculate the required amount of initial margin:

- a quantitative portfolio margin model, either an entity's own or third-party (that must be validated by the relevant supervisory body); or
- a standardised margin schedule.

There can be no cherry-picking by mixing these approaches based on which gives the lowest requirement in a given situation (although it is presumably possible to choose different approaches for different asset classes, as long as there is no switching between these approaches).[37]

The standardised initial margin schedule is shown in Table 7.11. The quantities shown should be used to calculate gross initial margin requirements by multiplying by the notional amount of each transaction and summing across all of them.

To account for portfolio effects across transactions, the following formula is used:

$$\text{Net standardised initial margin} = (0.4 + 0.6 \times \text{NGR}) \times \text{Gross initial margin} \qquad (7.4)$$

where NGR is defined as the level of the net replacement cost of the portfolio (i.e. including legally-enforceable netting agreements) over the level of gross replacement cost (ignoring netting). NGR gives a very simple representation of the future offset between positions, the logic being that 60% of the current impact of netting can be assumed for the potential future exposure. Whilst the above schedule-based approach is simplistic, there is still the question of how to treat more complex transactions which do not have easily-defined notionals (e.g. variance swaps) or maturity dates (e.g. callable or extendable structures). These will generally also have to be treated with the most realistic, conservative assumptions. The margin schedule will, therefore, likely give fairly conservative results and represent portfolio diversification badly. That said, even using a portfolio margin model, it is not permissible to benefit from potentially low historical correlations between risk factors between asset classes. The relevant asset classes – which must be treated on an additive basis – are defined as:

- currency/rates;
- equity;
- credit; and
- commodities.

Since initial margin calculations need to be agreed across many pairs of counterparties, there is clearly a need for a standard approach. This has been achieved by the ISDA SIMM (Standard Initial Margin Model), which will be described in more detail in Section 9.4.4.

Table 7.11 Standardised initial margin schedule as defined by BCBS-IOSCO (2015).

%	0–2 years	2–5 years	5+ years
Interest rate	1	2	4
Credit	2	5	10
Commodity		15	
Equity		15	
Foreign exchange		6	
Other		15	

---

[37] The precise wording from BCBS-IOSCO (2015) is 'Accordingly, the choice between model- and schedule-based initial margin calculations should be made consistently over time for all transactions within the same well-defined asset class.'

7.4.4   Eligible Assets and Haircuts

Regarding the quality of initial margin, the margin should be 'highly liquid' and, in particular, should hold its value in a stressed market (accounting for the haircut). Risk-sensitive haircuts should be applied, and margin should not be exposed to excessive credit, market, or FX risk (including through differences between the currency of the collateral asset and the currency of settlement). Margin must not be 'wrong-way', meaning correlated to the default of the counterparty (e.g. a counterparty posting its own bonds or equity).

Examples of satisfactory margin are given as:

- cash;
- high-quality government and central bank securities;
- high-quality corporate/covered bonds;
- equity in major stock indices; and
- gold.

Note that US regulations limit eligible margin for variation margin to cash (in USD, another major currency, or the 'settlement currency'), but for financial end users the same assets as permitted for initial margin are permissible.

As with initial margin, haircuts can either be based on a quantitative model or on a standard schedule (Table 7.12).

Regarding the FX component, no haircut is applied to cash variation margin, even where the payment is executed in a different currency than the currency of the contract. However, there is an 8% haircut for non-cash variation margin denominated in a currency other than the settlement currency or initial margin (cash and non-cash) under similar conditions.

As in the case of initial margin models, approved risk-sensitive quantitative models can be used for establishing haircuts, so long as the model for doing this meets regulatory approval. BCBS-IOSCO (2015) defines that haircut levels should be risk sensitive and reflect the underlying market, liquidity, and credit risks that affect the value of eligible margin in both normal and stressed market conditions. As with initial margins, haircuts should be set in order to mitigate procyclicality and avoid sharp and sudden increases in times of stress. The time horizon and confidence level for computing haircuts is not defined explicitly, but could be argued to be less (say 2–3 days) than the horizon for initial margin, since the margin may be liquidated independently and more quickly than the portfolio would be closed out.

Table 7.12 Standardised haircut schedule, as defined by BCBS-IOSCO (2015). Note that the FX add-on corresponds to cases where the currency of the derivative differs from that of the margin asset.

%	0–1 years	1–5 years	5+ years
High-quality government and central bank securities	0.5	2	4
High-quality corporate/covered bonds	1	4	8
Equity/gold		15	
Cash (in the same currency)		0	
FX add-on for different currencies		8	

7.4.5   Implementation and Impact of the Requirements

Since the above requirements are phased in and – in the case of initial margin – impact only new transactions after both parties fall in scope, there is a phasing-in effect. Of course, it is possible for parties to agree to cover all transactions, not only those in scope. ISDA has published a Variation Margin Protocol to enable market participants to put in place documentation on a standardised basis with multiple counterparties, reducing the need for bilateral negotiations. The protocol allows parties either to amend their existing credit support documents or to enter into new credit support documents, in a way which is compliant with the regulatory margin requirements. The protocol allows the following possible methods to be used (which will only take effect between two adhering parties if they agree to the method):

- *Amend method.* Terms in existing CSAs are amended as necessary to comply with the regulatory requirements of the relevant jurisdictions. Both legacy trades and new trades are covered under the amended CSA.
- *Replicate-and-amend.* A new CSA is created with the existing CSA remaining in place for legacy transactions. The new CSA is then amended to comply with the regulatory requirements.
- *New CSA.* Parties enter into a new CSA with standard terms and certain optional terms that are agreed bilaterally. This method is useful for when parties do not have an existing CSA in place.

Many covered counterparties are agreeing on new CSAs that incorporate the rules to cover future transactions but that can keep old transactions under existing CSAs. New or modified CSAs will need to consider the following aspects:

- thresholds and minimum transfer amounts;
- margin eligibility;
- haircuts;
- calculations, timings, and deliveries;
- dispute resolution; and
- initial margin calculations and mechanisms for segregation.

ISDA (2018) has surveyed the impact of the margin requirements for Phase 1 firms (i.e. those that are impacted by the €3trn threshold in Table 7.10).[38] They found that a total of around $50bn of regulatory initial margin had been posted (and received)[39] against non-cleared derivatives. They also noted that these firms had delivered about $16bn and received about $61bn of discretionary initial margin as of 31 March 2017.[40] Most variation margin was posted in cash, whilst government securities were the most popular form of initial margin.

---

[38] This survey included 18 out of the 20 Phase 1 firms, with an estimate made for the missing two participants.

[39] These numbers were roughly symmetric, as would be expected.

[40] The fact that a larger amount of discretionary initial was received is likely due to some Phase 1 firms requiring some smaller counterparties to post initial margin. Once such firms fall in scope, the larger firms will also need to post and the numbers will become more symmetric.

Clearly, the total amount of initial margin posted over time will increase as more firms become in scope. In addition to the operational and legal hurdles to comply with the regulation, there will be a growing need to understand:

- the methodologies (such as ISDA SIMM) for calculating initial margin (Section 9.4.4);
- the future costs of initial margin via margin value adjustment (Chapter 20); and
- the capital relief achievable when receiving initial margin (Section 13.4).

7.5   IMPACT OF MARGIN

Whilst margining is a useful mechanism for reducing counterparty risk, it has significant limitations that must be considered. It is also important to emphasise that margin, like netting, does not reduce risk overall but merely redistributes it. Margin also creates other residual risks, such as operational, legal, and liquidity risks. Other potential issues include wrong-way risk (where margin is adversely correlated to the underlying exposure), credit risk (where the margin securities may suffer from default or other adverse credit effects), and FX risk (due to margin being posted in a different currency). Some of these issues are outlined below. The broader issue of the link between margin and funding is discussed in Section 7.6.

7.5.1   Impact on Other Creditors

Risk mitigants such as margin are viewed narrowly only in terms of their impact on reducing exposure to a defaulted counterparty. However, more precisely, what actually happens is a *redistribution* of risk, where some creditors (e.g. derivatives creditors) are paid more in a default scenario at the expense of other creditors. Figure 7.16 shows the impact of the posting of margin against a derivative transaction. Assume that in default of party B, party A and the other creditors (OC) of B have the same seniority of the claim (*pari passu*). Party B owes derivatives creditors 50 and other creditors 100, and has assets of 100.

With respect to the amount of margin posted in Figure 7.16, it is useful to consider the following three cases:

- *No margin*. In the no-margin case, the other creditors will have a claim on two-thirds (100 divided by 150) of the assets of B, with the derivative claims of A receiving the remaining one-third. The derivatives and other creditors will both recover 67% of their claims.
- *Variation margin*. If party B posts 50 variation margin to A against their full derivative liability, then this will reduce the value received by the OCs in default. Now the remaining assets of B in default will be only 50, to be paid to the other creditors (recovery 50%). OTC derivatives creditors will receive 100% of their claim (ignoring close-out costs).
- *Initial margin*. Suppose that B pays 50 variation margin and 25 initial margin and the entire initial margin is used by A in the close-out and replacement costs of their transactions with B. In such a case, the OCs would receive only the remaining 25 (recovery 25%). It could be argued that some or all of the initial margin may need to be returned, potentially related to litigation (see Section 6.3.5), but a significant portion may be lost in close-out costs.

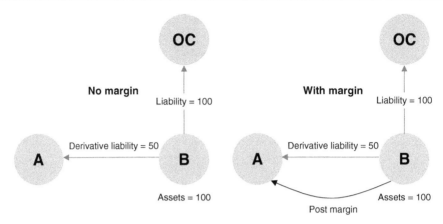

Figure 7.16 Example of the impact of derivatives margin on other creditors (OC). The margin posted (variation and possibly also initial margin) will reduce the claims of the other creditors.

Margin does not reduce risk, it merely redistributes it (although possibly in a beneficial way). Other creditors will be more exposed, leading to an increase in risk in other markets (e.g. loan market as opposed to derivatives market). Furthermore, the other creditors will react to their loss of seniority, for example, by charging more when lending money.

7.5.2   Market Risk and Margin Period of Risk

Margin can never completely eradicate counterparty risk, and it is important to consider the residual risk that remains under the margin agreement. Residual risk can exist due to contractual parameters such as thresholds and minimum transfer amounts that effectively delay the margin process. Thresholds and minimum transfer amounts can – and are increasingly being – set to zero (or very small) values. Frequent contractual margin calls obviously maximise the risk-reduction benefit at the expense of increasing operational and liquidity costs. Daily adjustment of margins is becoming increasingly standard in derivatives markets, although longer periods do sometimes exist in certain trading situations and products.

Even if margin is exchanged frequently and with zero thresholds, another important aspect is the inherent delay in receiving this collateral. This is market risk as it is defined by market movements after the counterparty last successfully posted margin. The MPoR is the term used to refer to the *effective* time between a counterparty ceasing to post margin and the time when all the underlying transactions have been successfully closed out and replaced (or otherwise hedged), as illustrated in Figure 7.17. Such a period is crucial since it defines the effective length of time without receiving margin where any increase in exposure (including close-out costs) will remain uncollateralised. Note that the MPoR is a counterparty-risk-specific concept (since it is related to default) and is not relevant when assessing funding costs (discussed in more detail in Chapter 18).

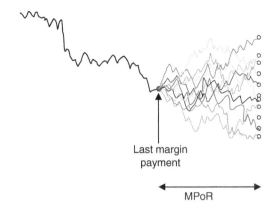

Last margin
payment

MPoR

Figure 7.17   Illustration of the role of the MPoR.

In general, for bilateral relationships (the MPoR for centrally-cleared transactions will be discussed in Section 9.1.2), it is useful to define the MPoR as the combination of two periods:

- *Pre-default*. This represents the time prior to the counterparty being in default and includes the following components:
  - *Valuation and margin call*. This represents the time taken to compute the current MTM and market value of margin already held, working out if a valid call can be made, and making that call. This should include the time delay due to the contractual period between calls.
  - *Receiving collateral*. The delay between a counterparty receiving a margin request to the point at which they release cash or securities. Clearly, recent developments such as electronic messaging are preferable to older-style approaches such as fax and email. The possibility of a dispute (i.e. if the margin giver does not agree with the amount called for) should be incorporated here.
  - *Settlement*. Margin will not be immediately received as there is a settlement period depending on the type of asset. Cash margin may settle on an intraday basis, whereas other securities will take longer. For example, government and corporate bonds may be subject to one- and three-day settlement periods respectively in some markets.
  - *Grace period*. In the event a valid margin call is not followed by the receipt of the relevant assets, there may be a relevant grace period before the counterparty will be deemed to be in default. This is sometimes known as the 'cure period'.
- *Post-default*. This represents the process after the counterparty is contractually in default and the surviving party can legally initiate a close-out process.
  - *Macro-hedging*. A party may use macro-hedges to rapidly neutralise any key sensitivities of a portfolio with a defaulting bilateral counterparty, although there may be an issue in claiming losses in the event that these hedges lose money.

- o *Close-out of transactions.* The contractual termination of transactions and representation of the future cash flow as a single MTM value.
- o *Rehedging and replacement.* The replacement or rehedging of defaulted transactions. This may be done in different ways, such as:
  - *One-to-one.* A direct replacement of each individual transaction with identical economic terms. Although potentially expensive, this would be the likely requirement for an end user of derivatives so as not to incur any additional market risk and to avoid accounting mismatches.
  - *Portfolio.* This may involve using a smaller number of transactions to neutralise the market risk of the portfolio in question. This 'macro hedge' would be more likely to be a strategy adopted by sophisticated market participants such as a bank and would be cheaper in terms of transaction costs.
- o *Liquidation of assets.* The liquidation (sale) of margin securities.[41]

Note that the MPoR will be much longer than the time taken to receive margin in normal cases and normal market conditions (which may well be small) because margin performs no function (in terms of mitigating counterparty risk, at least) in these non-default situations.[42] Instead, a party must consider a scenario where their counterparty is in default and market conditions may be far from normal. Because of this, Basel II capital requirements specified that banks should use a *minimum* of 10 business days' MPoR for OTC derivatives in their modelling.[43] The Basel III regime defines a more conservative 20-day minimum or more in certain cases. By contrast, CCPs make assumptions regarding the MPoR of around five business days (see Section 13.6.2).

The MPoR should also potentially be extended due to initiatives such as the ISDA Resolution Stay Protocol that would temporarily restrict certain default rights (by 24 or 48 hours) in the event of a counterparty default.[44] The 18 major global banks have agreed to sign this protocol, which is intended to give regulators time to facilitate an orderly resolution in the event that a large bank becomes financially distressed. Although it is intended to apply primarily to globally-systemically-important financial institutions (G-SIFIs), in time the protocol may apply to other market participants too.

Note that the MPoR is generally used as a model parameter to define the market risk arising from a collateralised exposure. It is therefore important not to take the definition too literally. For example, consider Figure 7.18, which illustrates a simplified version of the dynamics described above for bilateral markets, involving a pre- and post-default period. This shows that the risk of the portfolio will initially stay fixed and the surviving party may, therefore, be exposed to significant market risk. However, during the post-default period, the risk will decline as the close-out process is implemented.

Models are generally simpler than even the simple approach above and use only a single time step. They also implicitly assume that 100% of the risk will be present for the entire

---

[41] Note that this aspect should be included in the haircuts assigned to the margin assets.

[42] For example, in such a situation, margin may provide funding benefit.

[43] Assuming daily margin calls. If this is not the case, then the additional number of contractual days must be added to the time interval used.

[44] ISDA (2014). ISDA Publishes 2014 Resolution Stay Protocol (12 November). www.isda.org.

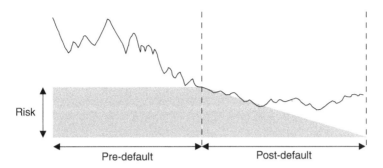

Figure 7.18 Schematic illustration of the MPoR in bilateral markets.

period assumed, whereas in reality the risk will reduce, as illustrated in Figure 7.18. One could, therefore, argue that the MPoR used in a model should be shorter due to the fact that risk will reduce during the MPoR. For example, Appendix 7A shows that under certain assumptions a 10-day exposure is equivalent to a 31-day exposure which decreases linearly through time.[45]

Another point is that the volatility of a portfolio might be expected to increase after a counterparty default (depending, of course, on the type and size of the counterparty). Models generally do not incorporate such effects, and it could therefore be argued that they should be proxied by using a longer MPoR. For example, an increase in volatility of 20% would imply an MPoR almost 50% longer.[46] This is discussed in more detail by Pykhtin and Sokol (2013).

Yet another problem for MPoR assessment is the potential for cash flow and margin payments happening within the pre- or post-default periods and the fact that these are likely to be asymmetric (i.e. a defaulting party will likely not pay, but a surviving party will). Andersen et al. (2017a, 2017b) show that this can have a significant impact.

Given all the above complexities, it is important to view the MPoR as a fairly simple estimate of the effective – not actual – period for which a surviving party suffers market risk in the event of a counterparty default. The MPoR is a rather simple 'catch-all' parameter and should not be compared too literally with the actual time it may take to effect a close-out and the replacement of transactions. The modelling of MPoR for cases where margin is present will be discussed in Chapter 15. The choice of initial margin is closely tied to the assumed MPoR, as is clearly illustrated in Figure 7.17. Indeed, as discussed in Chapter 9, initial margin methodologies will typically use a time horizon that can be seen to be consistent with the MPoR.

The MPoR is the primary driver of the need for initial margin. Assuming only variation margin is present, the *best-case* reduction of counterparty risk would be expected to be

---

[45] The formula used here, which is explained in Appendix 7A and Jorion (2007) is $\frac{n}{3} \times \left(1 - \frac{1}{n}\right) \times \left(1 - \frac{1}{2n}\right)$. The value of n is the number of days of linearly-decaying exposure, and the result of the formula gives the equivalent number of days of constant exposure.

[46] This is a result of the so-called 'square root of time rule', which is the result of independently-identically-distributed (iid) random variables. Hence, an increase of 20% increases the effective time by $1.2^2 - 1 = 44\%$.

in the region of the square root of the ratio of the maturity divided by the MPoR.[47] This would imply a reduction of $\sqrt{5 \times 250/10} \approx 11$ times for a five-year portfolio.[48] In reality, the result is worse than this estimate, as explained in more detail in Section 15.5. Hence, the only way to reduce counterparty risk to negligible levels is to have additional security in the form of initial margin.

7.5.3   Liquidity, FX, and Wrong-way Risks

Holding margin creates liquidity risk in the event that margin has to be liquidated following the default of a counterparty. In such a case, the non-defaulting party faces transaction costs (e.g. bid-offer) and market volatility over the liquidation period when selling margin securities for cash needed to rehedge their derivatives transactions. This risk can be minimised by setting appropriate haircuts (Section 7.3.5) to provide a buffer against prices falling between the counterparty defaulting and the party being able to sell the securities in the market. There is also the risk that by liquidating an amount of a security that is large compared with the volume traded in that security, the price will be driven down and a larger loss (potentially well beyond the haircut) will be incurred. Finally, there is wrong-way risk in case there is an adverse linkage between the default of the counterparty and the value of the margin securities (e.g. an entity posts bonds of its own sovereign).

When agreeing to margin that may be posted, and when receiving securities as collateral, important considerations are:

- What is the total issue size or market capitalisation posted as collateral?
- Is there a link between the margin value and the credit quality of the counterparty? Such a link may not be obvious and may be predicted by looking at correlations between variables.[49]
- How is the relative liquidity of the security in question likely to change if the counterparty concerned is in default?

Because of liquidity impacts, a concentration limit of 5–10% may be imposed to prevent severe liquidation risk in the event of a counterparty defaulting.

Margin posted in cash or securities denominated in a currency that does not match the currency or currencies of the portfolio in question will also give rise to FX risk. Even a European bank posting cash in euros will give rise to a potentially problematic linkage and wrong-way risk.

Given the above issues, it is not surprising that margin is increasingly denominated in cash in major currencies or in securities with minimal credit, market and liquidity risks. For example, ISDA (2017c) reports that, amongst the major financial institutions, 70.9% of the margin is in cash, 20.7% in government securities and 8.3% in other securities.[50] For smaller users of derivatives, a more bespoke margin arrangement still allows less liquid margin to be posted.

---

[47] This is also a consequence of the 'square root of time rule'.

[48] Assuming 250 business days in a year.

[49] In the case of the Long-Term Capital Management (LTCM) default, a very large proprietary position on Russian government bonds made these securities far from ideal as margin.

[50] This survey covers most of the firms subject to the first phase of regulatory margin-posting (Section 4.4.2). The total is 99.9% due to rounding error.

7.5.4   Legal and Operational Risks

The time-consuming and intensely dynamic nature of collateralisation means that operational risk is present, due to aspects such as missed margin calls, failed deliveries, or human error. Operational risk can be especially significant for the largest banks, which may have thousands of relatively non-standardised margin agreements with clients, requiring posting and receipt of billions of dollars of margin on a given day. As noted in Section 7.5.2, Basel III recognises operational risk in such situations by requiring a larger MPoR to be used in some cases (e.g. where the number of transactions exceeds 5,000, or the portfolio contains illiquid margin or exotic transactions that cannot easily be valued under stressed market conditions). A history of margin call disputes also requires a larger MPoR to be used. Larger MPoRs lead to higher capital requirements and therefore produce an incentive for reducing operational risk.

Receiving margin also involves some legal risk in case there is a challenge to the ability to net margin against the value of a portfolio or over the correct valuation of this portfolio. In major bankruptcies this can be an important consideration, such as the case between Citigroup and Lehman Brothers discussed in Section 6.3.5.

As already discussed above, rehypothecation and segregation are subject to possible legal risks. Holding margin gives rise to legal risk in that the non-defaulting party must be confident that the margin held is free from legal challenge by the administrator of their defaulted counterparty. In the case of MF Global (see below), segregation was not effective, and customers lost money as a result. This raises questions about the enforcement of segregation, especially in times of stress. Note that the extreme actions of senior members of MF Global in using segregated customer collaterals were caused by a desperation to avoid bankruptcy.

MF Global and segregation

The case of MF Global provides a good illustration of the potential risks of segregation. MF Global was a major derivatives broker that filed for bankruptcy in October 2011. The aim of segregation is to prevent rehypothecation and make margin safe in the event of default of the margin receiver (this applies mainly to overcollateralisation in the form of initial margin). Unfortunately, it became clear that, prior to the bankruptcy, MF Global had illegally transferred a total of $1.6bn of segregated customer margin to third parties to meet overdrafts and margin calls. As of June 2013, 89% of this had been located and returned. The violation of segregation laws resulted in private lawsuits and a civil lawsuit filed by the U.S. Commodity Futures Trading Commission against the former CEO of MF Global.[51] It is perhaps not surprising that to avoid insolvency, extreme and even illegal actions may be taken. There is obviously the need to have very clear and enforceable rules on margin segregation.

---

[51] Congressional Research Service (2013). The MF Global Bankruptcy, Missing Customer Funds, and Proposals for Reform (1 August). www.crs.gov.

7.6 MARGIN AND FUNDING

7.6.1 Overview

The traditional role of margin for bilateral OTC derivatives has been as a counterparty risk mitigant. However, there is another role which has become more important in recent years, which is a provision of funding. Without receiving margin, an institution could be owed money but would not be paid immediately for this asset. Since institutions are often engaged in hedging transactions, this can create funding problems (e.g. a bank not receiving margin on a transaction may have to post margin on the associated hedge trade, as shown in Figure 7.7). This also shows why aspects such as segregation and rehypothecation (which define the ability – or not – to reuse margin) are important.

As margin has relevance in funding as well as counterparty risk reduction, one point to bear in mind is that different types of margin may offer different counterparty risk and funding benefits. An important distinction is that margin as a counterparty risk mitigant is by definition required only in an actual default scenario. On the other hand, margin as a means of funding is relevant in all scenarios. The following two cases can be seen as extreme examples of this:

- *Counterparty posts wrong-way margin.* A counterparty posting margin such as their own bonds which have significant wrong-way risk will act as a poor counterparty risk mitigant, but will provide funding as long as the margin can be reused or rehypothecated.
- *Counterparty posts non-reusable margin.* In the event that it is not possible to reuse margin securities (e.g. corporate bonds that cannot be repoed or posted under other margin arrangements), counterparty risk will be mitigated, but a funding requirement will persist.

The Totem xVA consensus service (Section 5.3.5) makes use of the above when asking participants to price a transaction with a two-way margin agreement but where the 'counterparty posts to a segregated account'. Although this is uncommon in practice (especially since this is related to variation margin and not initial margin), it gives a case where a bank will likely include only funding in the price of a transaction without any adjustment for counterparty risk.[52]

In recent years, margin eligibility and reuse have gained significant interest as funding costs have been viewed as significant. Therefore, the consideration of the type of margin that will be posted and received is important since different forms of margin have different funding costs and remuneration rates. When posting and receiving margin, institutions are becoming increasingly aware of the need to optimise this process and maximise funding efficiencies. Margin management is no longer the work of a back-office operations centre, but can be an important asset-optimisation tool delivering (and substituting) the most cost-effective cash and securities. A party should consider the cheapest-to-deliver cash margin and account for the impact of haircuts and the ability to rehypothecate non-cash collateral. For example, different currencies of cash will pay different OIS rates, and non-cash collateral, if rehypothecated, will earn different rates on repo. Chapter 16 provides a more in-depth study of these aspects.

---

[52] Note that Totem does not include capital costs and so this example provides a means to isolate the impact of funding in the price.

7.6.2   Margin and Funding Liquidity Risk

Another important link between counterparty risk and funding is that increasing collateralisation may reduce counterparty risk, but it increases funding liquidity risk. Funding liquidity risk, in this case, is defined as the potential risk arising from the difficulty to raise required funding in the future, especially when margin needs to be segregated and/or cannot be rehypothecated. Margin agreements clearly create such risk as they require contractual margin payments over short timescales, with the magnitude of these payments typically not being deterministic (since it is related to the future value of transactions).

At a high level, the move to more intensive margin regimes can be seen as reducing counterparty risk at the expense of increasing funding liquidity risk (Figure 7.19). This occurs when moving from uncollateralised to collateralised trading via a typical CSA (two-way variation margin posting). The BCBS-IOSCO bilateral margin rules increase margin further through requiring initial margin, and central clearing takes this even further by adding default funds and potentially intraday-posting requirements (discussed in more detail in Chapter 8).[53]

The problem with margin is that it converts counterparty risk into funding liquidity risk. This conversion may be beneficial in normal, liquid markets where funding costs are low. However, in abnormal markets where liquidity is poor, funding costs can become significant and may put extreme pressure on a party.

It is easy to understand how an end user of OTC derivatives might have significant funding liquidity risk, since they use derivatives only for hedging purposes and the need to post margin is probably not offset with a similar benefit (see discussion around Figure 2.9 in Section 2.2.5). Furthermore, due to their hedging needs, end users have directional positions (e.g. paying the fixed rate in interest rate swaps to hedge floating-rate borrowing). This means that a significant move in market variables (interest rates, for example) can create substantial MTM moves in their OTC derivatives portfolio and large associated margin requirements. This is why many end users do not have CSAs with their bank counterparties. Additionally, most end users (e.g. corporates) do not have substantial cash reserves or liquid assets that can be posted as margin (and if they did, then they might rather be able to use them to fund potential projects). Some end users (e.g. pension funds)

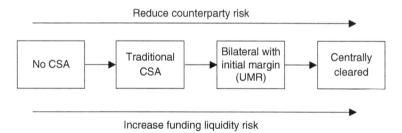

Figure 7.19   Illustration of the increasing impact of margin on counterparty risk and funding liquidity risk.

---

[53] CCPs are generally more conservative in their initial margin methodologies. This is not surprising as they do not have to post initial margin themselves, although they can be more competitive via lowering such requirements.

have liquid assets such as government and corporate bonds but hold limited amounts of cash.

In addition to the previously discussed case of AIG (Section 2.4.4), there are other examples of the problems caused by the need to post margin in derivatives (see the Ashanti case below).[54]

The Ashanti case

Ashanti (now part of AngloGold Ashanti Limited) was a Ghanaian gold producer. When gold prices rose in September 1999, Ashanti experienced very large losses of $450m on OTC derivatives contracts (gold forward contracts and options) used to hedge (possibly excessively) their exposure to a falling gold price.[55] The negative value of Ashanti's hedge book meant that its OTC derivatives counterparties were due further variation margin payments totalling around $280m in cash. Ashanti had a funding liquidity problem: it had the physical gold to satisfy contracts but not the cash to make the margin payments. To solve its liquidity crisis, Ashanti then struck an agreement that made it exempt from posting margin for just over three years.[56]

Some non-financial clients such as institutional investors, large corporates and sovereigns do trade under CSAs with banks. They may do this to increase the range of counterparties they can deal with and achieve lower transaction costs (due to reduced xVA charges). In volatile market conditions, such CSA terms can cause funding liquidity problems due to significant margin requirements. Consider a corporate entering into a collateralised five-year cross-currency swap to hedge a bond issue in another currency. The potential MTM move and therefore margin could be as much as 55% of the notional of the swap.[57] Clients entering into margin agreements need to include an assessment of the worst-case margin requirements in their cash management and funding plans and understand how they would source eligible collateral (Section 21.3.4).

End users face funding liquidity risks when posting margin since it may possibly cause them to default in a case where they are solvent but unable to meet the margin demand in eligible securities within the timescale required. In turn, their bank counterparties may carry some of the risk since they may waive the receipt of margin to avoid this, with the obvious problem that it will be converted back into uncollateralised counterparty risk and funding requirements for the banks in question. Funding liquidity risk may also mean that a rating agency may have a more negative view of a company's credit quality if they agree to post margin (note that monolines could only achieve triple-A ratings through not posting margin; Section 2.4.4).

---

[54] Unlike the AIG case, this example is not linked to any rating triggers.

[55] 'Mr. Sam Jonah, Chief Executive of Ashanti, referring to their financial problems, stated "I am prepared to concede that we were reckless. We took a bet on the price of gold. We thought that it would go down and we took a position."' From O'Connor, G. (1999). Ashanti left exposed by 'exotics'. *Financial Times* (8 November). www.ft.com.

[56] Hirschler, B. (1999). Ashanti wins three-year gold margin reprieve. *GhanaWeb* (2 November). www.ghanaweb.com.

[57] This assumes a five-year FX move at the 95% confidence level, with FX volatility at 15%.

For banks, funding liquidity issues arise due to the nature of trading with clients. Since most banks aim to run mainly flat (hedged) OTC derivatives books, funding costs arise from the nature of hedging: an uncollateralised transaction being hedged via a transaction within a CSA arrangement (Figure 7.5). The bank will need to fund the margin posted on the hedge when the uncollateralised (client) transaction moves in their favour, and will experience a benefit when the reverse happens. Many banks will have directional client portfolios, which can lead to large margin requirements. This funding problem is one way to explain the need for FVA, discussed in more detail in Chapter 18. It also explains why banks are keen for more clients to sign CSA agreements to balance the margin flows in the situation depicted in Figure 7.5.

Banks also have a problem with contingent funding requirements arising from the potential need to post more initial margin, and also as a result of any margin requirements linked to their own credit ratings. Such requirements create a need for funding under the LCR (Section 4.3.3). It is, therefore, important to consider LCR-related funding costs in the assessment of xVA funding-related components such as FVA (Chapter 18) and margin value adjustment (MVA; Chapter 20).

A key decision for market participants and regulators alike is the concentration of various trading on the spectrum represented in Figure 7.19 and the risks that this presents. Whilst pushing to the right minimises counterparty risk, it also increases opaque and complex funding liquidity risks. Indeed, the reduction of counterparty risk and CVA and KVA has been a driver for creating other funding-related xVA terms such as MVA, discussed later in Chapter 20.

8

Central Clearing

8.1 EVOLUTION OF CENTRAL CLEARING

8.1.1 Exchange Trading

In derivative markets, many transactions are exchange-traded. An exchange is a central financial centre where parties can trade standardised contracts such as futures and options at a specified price. An exchange promotes market efficiency and enhances liquidity by centralising trading in a single place. The process by which a financial contract becomes exchange-traded can be thought of as a long journey where a critical trading volume, standardisation, and liquidity must first develop.

Exchanges have been used for trading financial products for many years; futures exchanges can be traced back to the nineteenth century (and even further). A future is an agreement by two parties to buy or sell a specified quantity of an asset at some time in the future at a price agreed upon today. Futures were developed to allow merchants or companies to fix prices for certain assets and therefore be able to hedge their exposure to price movements. An exchange was essentially a market where standardised contracts such as futures could be traded. Originally, exchanges were simply trading forums without any settlement or counterparty risk management functions. Transactions were still done on a bilateral basis, and trading through the exchange simply provided a certification through the counterparty being a member of the exchange. Members not fulfilling their requirements were deemed to be in default and were fined or expelled from the exchange.

An exchange can be seen to provide several functions:

- *Product standardisation*. An exchange designs contracts that can be traded where most of the terms (e.g. maturity dates, minimum price quotation increments, the deliverable grade of the underlying, delivery location, and mechanism) are standardised.
- *Trading venue*. Exchanges provide a (physical or electronic) trading facility for the underlying products they list, which provides a central venue for trading and hedging. Access to an exchange is limited to approved firms and individuals who must abide by the rules of the exchange. This centralised trading venue provides an opportunity for price discovery.[1]
- *Reporting services*. Exchanges provide various reporting services of transaction prices to trading participants, data vendors, and subscribers. This creates greater transparency of prices.

---

[1] This is the process of determining the price of an asset in a marketplace through the interactions of buyers and sellers.

8.1.2   Evolution of Complete Clearing

The historical development of derivative exchanges led to mechanisms for risk reduction. The first was 'direct clearing', meaning that if a party has offsetting positions with the exchange, then they would be offset. For example, suppose party A makes a transaction to buy 100 contracts at a price of $105 and then at a later date executes the reverse position but at a lower price of $102 (Figure 8.1). Rather than a physical exchange of 100 contracts' worth of the underlying together with associated payments of $10,500 and $10,200, netting would be used and settlement would occur based on 'payment of difference' (in the example shown, a payment of $300). Payment of difference, rather than delivery, became common in futures markets to reduce problems associated with creditworthiness. Clearly, standardisation of terms facilitates such offset by making contracts fungible.

Direct clearing on exchanges can be seen as similar to netting in over-the-counter (OTC) derivatives (Section 6.3).

Following on from direct clearing, exchanges developed 'clearing rings' (Section 6.2.3), whereby three or more counterparties could 'ring out' offsetting positions. To achieve the benefits of 'ringing', participants in the ring had to be willing to accept substitutes for their original counterparties. In the current OTC derivatives market, portfolio compression (Section 6.2.4) offers a similar mechanism to the historical role of clearing rings.

Even with the use of direct clearing and clearing rings, counterparties are still required to fulfil obligations to each other. This would mean that the default of an exchange member would impose losses on all other members with whom they had trades, despite trading being an anonymous process. The final stage of the historical evolution of risk mitigation at derivatives exchanges was 'complete clearing' (which began in 1891), where a central counterparty (CCP) is placed centrally between all counterparties and assumes all such contractual rights and responsibilities, as illustrated in Figure 8.2.

The adoption of central clearing has not been completely without resistance: the Chicago Board of Trade (CBOT) did not have a CCP function for around 30 years until 1925 (and then partly as a result of government pressure). One of the last futures exchanges to adopt a CCP was the London Metal Exchange in 1986 (again with regulatory pressure being a factor). A proposed reason for these resistances is the fact that clearing homogenises counterparty risk and therefore would lead to strong-credit-quality members of the exchange suffering under central clearing compared to the weaker members. The reluctance to adopt clearing voluntarily certainly raises the possibility that the costs of clearing exceed the benefits, at least in some markets. Nevertheless,

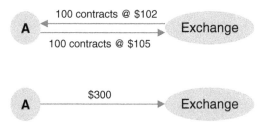

Figure 8.1   Illustration of direct clearing.

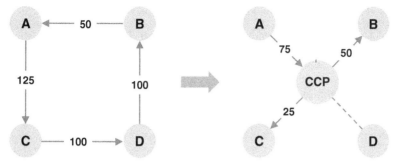

Figure 8.2   Illustration of complete clearing. The CCP assumes all contractual responsibilities as counterparty to all contracts.

all exchange-traded contracts are now subject to central clearing. The CCP function may either be operated by the exchange or provided to the exchange as a service by an independent company.

Whilst central clearing became a standard for exchange-traded markets, bilateral OTC derivatives have generally followed a bilateral clearing model. This changed in the late 1990s when SwapClear was set up as part of LCH.Clearnet to centrally-clear interest rate swaps between the major swap dealers.[2] OTC clearing is now becoming increasingly common as a result of the regulatory changes following the global financial crisis (Section 4.4.1). Centrally-cleared derivatives retain some OTC features (such as being transacted bilaterally) but use the central clearing function developed for exchange-traded derivatives. It is possible to centrally clear an OTC derivative that is not liquid enough to trade on an exchange. However, central clearing does require an OTC derivative to have a certain level of standardisation and liquidity and not be too complex. This means that many types of OTC derivatives will never be suitable for central clearing. Some market participants are not expected to centrally clear due to obstacles such as funding liquidity risk (Section 7.6.2). Nevertheless, it should be noted that a large proportion of the volume of OTC derivatives is transacted in clearable products and by participants suitable for central clearing.

At the current time, there are OTC derivatives that have been centrally cleared for some time (e.g. interest rate swaps), those that have been recently cleared (e.g. index CDSs), and those that are on the way to being centrally cleared (e.g. interest rate swaptions, inflation swaps, single-name CDSs, and cross-currency swaps). Finally, there are of course products that are a long way away and indeed may never be centrally cleared (e.g. Asian options, Bermudan swaptions, and interest rate swaps involving illiquid currencies).

8.1.3   What is a CCP?

A CCP is a particular financial market infrastructure (FMI) that represents a set of rules and operational arrangements designed to allocate, manage, and reduce counterparty

---

[2] LCH.Clearnet is now LCH Ltd.

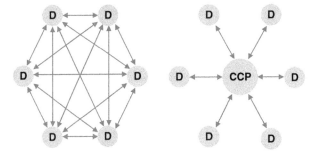

Figure 8.3   Illustration of bilateral markets (left) compared to centrally-cleared markets (right).

risk in a bilateral market. A CCP changes the topology of financial markets by inter-posing itself between buyers and sellers, as illustrated in Figure 8.3. In this context, it is useful to consider the six entities denoted by D, representing large global banks ('dealers'). Two obvious advantages appear to stem from this simplistic view. Firstly, a CCP can reduce the *interconnectedness* within financial markets, which may lessen the impact of an insolvency of a participant. Secondly, the CCP being at the heart of trading can provide more *transparency* on the positions of the members.

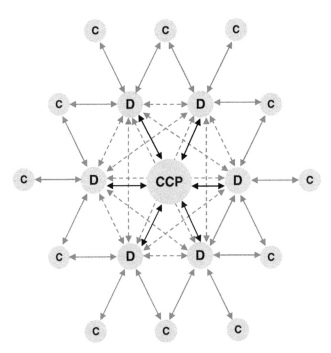

Figure 8.4   Illustration of a centrally-cleared market including bilateral transactions (dotted lines), directly-cleared transactions (black lines), and the positions of non-clearing members (C) who clear through clearing members (D) (grey lines).

The above analysis is simplistic, and although the general points made are correct, the true CCP landscape is much more complex than represented, as it ignores the following aspects:

- *Client clearing*. Parties that cannot be members of the CCP in question will have to be cleared through a 'clearing member'. This creates additional complexity regarding operational aspects such as margin transfer and what happens in a default scenario.
- *Bilateral trades*. Not all OTC derivatives are suitable for clearing, and a reasonable population will always remain as bilateral transactions.
- *Multiple CCPs*. There are clearly a number of different CCPs globally that may be implicitly interconnected – for example, via sharing members.

The first two of the above components are illustrated in Figure 8.4.

Central clearing changes the bilateral network to a hub-and-spoke-type system. Whilst this may create greater stability and transparency, it has obvious drawbacks. A CCP at the central hub constitutes a single point of failure. It reduces the possibility for diversification of errors, and a single mistake or failure at the CCP (as opposed to one of its members) has the potential to be catastrophic.

8.2   MECHANICS OF CENTRAL CLEARING

8.2.1   Landscape

Clearing trades obviously has an associated cost. CCPs cover this cost directly by charging fees per trade, and more indirectly by, for example, deriving interest from assets they hold. As FMIs and nodes of the financial system, CCPs clearly need to be resilient, especially during major financial disturbances. This may imply that a utility CCP driven by long-term stability and not short-term profits may be a preferable business model. However, it could also be argued that CCPs will need to have the best personnel and systems to be able to develop advanced risk management and operational capabilities. Moreover, competition between CCPs will benefit users and provide choice. Expertise and competition imply that CCPs should be profit-making organisations. However, this introduces the risk of a possible race to the bottom with respect to certain practices (e.g. margin calculations) that could increase the risk posed by CCPs.

A large number of CCPs will maximise competition, but this too could lead to a race to the bottom in terms of cost and the bifurcation of multilateral offset benefits. Having a small number of CCPs is beneficial in terms of offsetting benefits and economies of scale, but it increases systemic risk linked to CCP failure. Whilst a single global CCP is clearly optimal for a number of reasons, it seems likely that the total number of CCPs will be relatively large. This is due to bifurcation on two levels:

- *Regional*. Major geographical regions view it as important to have their own 'local' CCPs, either to clear trades denominated in their own currency or to clear all trades executed for financial institutions in that region. Indeed, regulators in some regions require that financial institutions under their supervision clear certain products using their own regional CCP.

- *Product*. CCPs clearing OTC derivatives have tended to act as vertical structures and specialise in certain product types (e.g. interest rate swaps or CDSs) and thus there is no complete solution of one CCP that can offer coverage of every clearable product (and regulation does not encourage this).

Mandatory clearing can potentially create more systemic risk as large banks are forced to clear only certain standardised transactions. This may have a detrimental effect on net exposure due to the bifurcation or 'unbundling' of netting between standard and non-standard contracts (Section 6.4.3). Exemptions for end users and foreign exchange transactions may also create sub-optimal outcomes and the possibility for regulatory arbitrage. The extent of bifurcation depends on how much can actually be practically cleared; for example, the International Swaps and Derivatives Association (ISDA) suggests that this value is approximately 80% for OTC derivatives.[3]

CCP ownership and operation tends to work broadly via either a vertical or horizontal set-up, with competing coexisting structures. In a vertical structure, the CCP is usually a division of, and owned by, an exchange. The CCP is then essentially tied to the exchange and provides clearing only for products traded on that exchange. This model has generally developed over the years for futures exchanges and arose as the exchanges evolved and developed a central clearing function. Another approach is horizontal, whereby a CCP is separately-owned (typically by its clearing members), has its own financial backing and can, therefore, clear trades across multiple markets and asset classes. Such CCPs generally exist as separate entities. A horizontal set-up is more natural for bilateral OTC derivatives since there is no exchange involved. Regulation appears to favour the increased competition that horizontal clearing allows, with rules calling for CCPs to be 'open'. For example, the European Commission (EC), under Markets in Financial Instruments Directive (MiFID) II Article 29, proposes to give CCPs access rights to trading venues, which would allow market participants to use a CCP other than the one defined by an exchange or other trading platform. This is seen as important to increase competition between CCPs, thereby reducing costs and improving the quality of clearing services.

Quite a large proportion of the OTC derivatives market will be centrally cleared in the coming years (and indeed quite a large amount is already cleared). This is practical since some clearable products (e.g. interest rate swaps) make up such a large proportion of the total outstanding notional. Although clearing is being extended to cover new products, this is a slow process since a product needs to have a number of features before it is clearable.

For a transaction to be centrally cleared, the following conditions are generally important:

- *Standardisation*. Standardisation of legal and economic terms is key because clearing requires the CCP to be contractually responsible for all cash flows of the product in question. Furthermore, standardisation facilitates offset and compression between identical contracts and makes it easier to replace contracts in the event that a clearing member defaults. For example, prior to 2009, there was a standardisation of CDS

---

[3] Note that ISDA (2013) reports the non-clearable fraction as 13%, as it uses the total size of the market including double-counting of CCP positions as a reference.

contracts – involving changes to standard coupons and maturities – which was a prerequisite to any migration to CCPs.

- *Complexity*. Only vanilla (non-exotic) transactions can be cleared, as they need to be relatively easily and robustly valued on a timely basis to support margin calculations and default management (Section 8.3). Exotic or complex derivatives (even if standardised) create a number of hurdles to central clearing.[4] Products that are more complex are more subjective to value for variation margin purposes, and initial margin requirements are very difficult to determine. This means that under- or over-margining is likely; the former case leading to excessive risk and the latter to high costs.
- *Liquidity*. Centrally-cleared products need to be liquid for a number of reasons. First, liquidity brings accurate pricing information for variation margin purposes and provides rich historical time-series price data to use to calculate initial margins. Second, liquid products can be more efficiently replaced in default scenarios as illiquid trades will have high bid-offer spreads and may be more likely to be subjected to large risk premiums and negative price moves in turbulent markets. It should be noted that liquidity might be *transient*, as in many OTC derivatives; liquidity tends to decline over time and yet positions are guaranteed by the CCP for their lifetime.
- *Wrong-way risk*. Ideally, centrally-cleared products would not be subject to wrong-way risk (WWR). This occurs when the default of a counterparty is linked adversely to the value of the underlying contract, which in turn means that the value of the contract will potentially decline rapidly at the time of the counterparty default. These negative implications for default management are therefore quite important. This is a subtle point in relation to CDSs, as these products catalysed the clearing mandate, and yet they are arguably the most difficult to clear centrally due to WWR.
- *Market volume*. There is a significant effort for a CCP to build the relevant processes, models, and systems to be able to clear a given product. If the size of the market for this particular product is not sufficiently large, then clearing may not be beneficial, as the CCP will be unable to recoup the expenditure in the product development process.

A list of some of the significant CCPs is shown in Table 8.1. One of the most significant players in OTC derivative clearing is LCH Ltd, the first CCP to clear significant amounts of OTC transactions through SwapClear, which is dominant in the interbank interest rate swap market. Other important OTC clearing CCPs include ICE (Intercontinental Exchange) – which offers clearing for some CDSs through ICE Clear Credit – the Chicago Mercantile Exchange (CME), and Eurex.

8.2.2   Novation

A key concept in central clearing is that of contract novation, which is the legal process whereby the CCP is positioned between buyers and sellers. Novation is the replacement of one contract with one or more other contracts. Novation means that the CCP essentially steps in between parties to a transaction and therefore acts as an insurer of counterparty risk in both directions. The viability of novation depends on the legal enforceability of the new contracts and the certainty that the original parties are not legally obligated to

---

[4] Note that an exotic product can have standard terms, but the valuation complexity would still exist.

Table 8.1   Some significant central counterparties.

US and Canada	CME Clearing US
	ICE Clear Credit
	LCH Ltd
	Int'l Derivatives Clearing Group (IDCG)
Europe	CME Clearing Europe
	ICE Clear Europe
	LCH Ltd
	Eurex Clearing AG
	LCH.Clearnet SA
	NASDAQ OMX (Sweden)
Australia	ASX Clear
Brazil	BM&FBovespa
Hong Kong	HKEx Clearing
Japan	Japan Securities Clearing Corporation (JSCC)
Singapore	Singapore Exchange Ltd (SGX)

each other once the novation is completed. Assuming viability, novation means that the contract between the original parties ceases to exist and they, therefore, do not have counterparty risk to one another.

Typically, the CCP guarantees the transaction from the point at which it is 'matched', and the CCP becomes the 'buyer to the seller and seller to the buyer'. Clearing members may therefore not need to make a counterparty risk assessment of their original bilateral counterparty. In an electronic trading environment, clearing may provide anonymity as buyers and sellers need not know each other's identity.

Because it stands between market buyers and sellers, the CCP has a 'matched book' and bears no net market risk. It does take the counterparty risk, which is centralised in the CCP structure. Put another way, the CCP has 'conditional market risk', since in the event of a member default, it will no longer have a matched book. A CCP will have various methods to return to a matched book, such as holding an auction of the defaulting member's positions. CCPs also mitigate counterparty risk by demanding financial resources from their members that are intended to cover the potential losses in the event that one or more of them defaults.

8.2.3   Multilateral Offset and Compression

A major problem with bilateral derivatives trading is the proliferation of overlapping and potentially-redundant contracts, which increases counterparty risk and adds to the interconnectedness of the financial system. Such redundancy is a natural consequence of the many users and banks in the market and their different objectives and business models.

A primary advantage of central clearing is multilateral offset. This offset can be in relation to various aspects such as cash flows or margin requirements. In simple terms, the multilateral offset is as illustrated in Figure 8.5. In the bilateral market, the three participants have liabilities marked by the directions of the arrows. The total liabilities to be paid are 180. In this market, A is exposed to C by an amount of 90. If C fails, then there is the risk that A may also fail, creating a domino effect. Under central clearing, all assets and liabilities are taken over by the CCP and can offset one another. This means that total

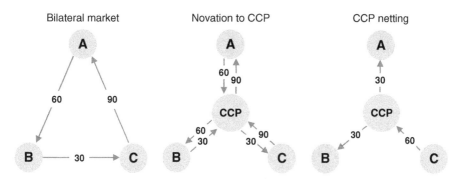

Figure 8.5   Illustration of multilateral offsetting afforded by central clearing.

risks are reduced: not only is the liability of C offset to 60, but also the insolvency of C can no longer cause a knock-on effect to A, since the CCP has intermediated the position between the two.

Note that methods such as portfolio compression (Section 6.2.4) can create multilateral offset effects such as netting. However, portfolio compression requires actual transactions (or cash flows) to be eliminated, whereas the multilateral effects at a CCP are more general. For example, if two transactions almost offset one another (such as by having slightly different reference rates or maturities), then portfolio compression may not be possible, but the CCP will still see the net market risk position as being small, leading (for example) to lower initial margin requirements. Put another away, a CCP can compress risk, whereas bilateral compression can only compress objective quantities such as cash flows.

Whilst the above representation is generally correct, it ignores some key effects: the impact of multiple CCPs, the impact of non-cleared trades, and even the impact on non-derivatives positions. These aspects will be discussed in Chapter 10.

Cleared trades can still make use of portfolio compression services. It may seem that compression of cleared trades is less relevant, as compression aims not to change the market risk characteristics of portfolios and would not (for example) be expected to lead to a reduction in margin requirements. Despite this, there are clear benefits of reducing the number of trades and the total notional cleared by a given CCP relating to efficiency, including:

- initial margin requirements (since, for example, some CCPs impose multipliers for large portfolios);
- regulatory capital (in particular the leverage ratio, as discussed in Section 13.4.6);
- operationality (e.g. cash flow payments and reporting);
- computation burden (e.g. for margin calculation); and
- simplification of the auction process (fewer trades to close out).

Compression services are therefore complementary to central clearing. An illustration of the impact of compression on clearing is given in Figure 8.6. This shows the total notional outstanding and the compressed notional for interest rate swaps cleared by the SwapClear service, together with the compressed notional that has been essentially removed. Note that, whilst there is a steady increase in notional cleared, the notional outstanding is almost constant.

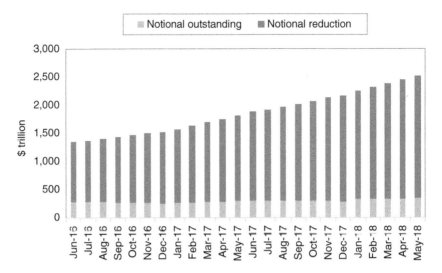

Figure 8.6 Illustration of SwapClear compression.[5]

Compression such as that shown in Figure 8.6 is gradually being expanded to cover more products and counterparties.[6] As noted in Section 6.2.4, more advanced compression approaches are also being developed, such as blended-rate compression, which enables the compression of any number of positions with varying fixed rates but the same remaining cash flow dates.[7]

8.2.4   Margin and Default Funds

The advent of complete clearing (Section 8.1.2) led to CCPs requiring both variation and initial margins (Section 7.2.3) as the primary defence against the insolvency of a clearing member. Historically, centrally-cleared markets have tended to impose standard and tighter margin requirements compared to bilateral markets, although the incoming BCBS-IOSCO bilateral margin requirements (Section 7.4) are reducing this gap.

Generally, CCPs require variation margin to be transferred on a daily (and sometimes intradaily)[8] basis and must usually be in cash. Initial margin requirements may also frequently change with market conditions and must be provided in cash or liquid assets (e.g. treasury bonds). They are calculated to high confidence levels (at least 99%) and cover the time period over which it would be anticipated to be necessary to close out the portfolio of a defaulted clearing member.

If margins are sufficient, then the central clearing follows the so-called 'defaulter-pays' approach, where a clearing member contributes all the necessary funds to pay for their

---

[5] Source: LCH Ltd. www.lch.com.

[6] TriOptima (2016). TriOptima and SwapClear include first client-cleared trades in triReduce swap compression cycle. Press release (24 October). www.trioptima.com.

[7] LCH.Clearnet (2014). LCH.Clearnet's SwapClear Launches New Blended Rate Compression Service. Press release (17 September). www.lch.com.

[8] In particular, this might be required in volatile market conditions or in the event of a significant market move.

own potential future default. Achieving this within every possible scenario is impractical, though, because it would require very high financial contributions from each member, which would be too costly. For this reason, the purpose of financial contributions from a given member is to cover losses to a high level of confidence in a scenario where they would default. This leaves a small chance of losses not following the defaulter-pays approach and thus being borne by the other clearing members.

Another basic principle of central clearing is that of loss mutualisation, where losses above the resources contributed by the defaulter are shared between CCP members. The most obvious way in which this occurs is that CCP members all contribute to a CCP 'default fund',[9] which is typically used after the defaulter's own resources to cover losses. Since all members pay into this default fund, they all contribute to absorbing an extreme default loss. Losses wiping out a significant portion of the default fund of a CCP are obviously intended to be unlikely.

Note that, in a CCP, the default losses that a member incurs are not directly related to the transactions that this member executes with the defaulting member. Indeed, a member can suffer default losses even if it never traded with the defaulted counterparty, has no net position with the CCP, or has a net position with the CCP in the same direction as the defaulter (although there are other potential methods of loss allocation that may favour a member in this situation, as discussed in Section 10.2.4).

8.2.5 Clearing Relationships

Only clearing members can transact directly with a CCP. Becoming a clearing member involves meeting a number of requirements and will not be possible for all parties. Generally, these requirements fall into the following categories:

- *Admission criteria.* CCPs have various admission requirements, such as credit rating strength and requirements that members have a sufficiently large capital base.
- *Financial commitment.* Members must contribute to the CCP's default fund. Whilst such contributions will be partly in line with the trading activity, there may be a minimum commitment, and it is likely that only institutions intending to execute a certain volume of trades will consider this default fund contribution worthwhile.
- *Operational.* Being a member of a CCP has a number of associated operational requirements. One is the frequent posting of (liquid) margin, and others are the requirement to participate in fire drills that simulate the default of a member, and auctions in the event that a member does indeed default.

The impact of the above is that large global banks and some other very large financial institutions are likely to be clearing members, whereas smaller banks, buy-side and other financial firms, and other non-financial end users are unlikely to be direct clearing members. Large regional banks may be members of only a local CCP so as to support domestic clearing services for their clients.

Institutions that are not CCP members – so-called non-clearing members ('clients') – can clear through a clearing member. Although there are different set-ups, the general

---

[9] Sometimes called a 'guarantee fund' or 'reserve fund'.

rule here is that the client effectively has a direct bilateral relationship with their clearing member and not the CCP. Whilst the position of clearing members to their clients is still bilateral, they will – to a large extent – mirror CCP requirements in their bilateral client relationships – for example, in relation to margin-posting.

Clients will generally still have to post margin but will not be required to contribute to the CCP default fund. Clearing members will charge their clients (explicitly and implicitly) for the clearing service that they provide, which will include elements such as the subsidisation of the default fund. Note also that clearing members often require more margin from their clients than is required by CCPs. Clearing members can also potentially earn returns on excess margins received (above those required by the CCP) to compensate them for the clearing service they provide and the additional risk they take in doing this. On the other hand, they must consider the cost of 'client clearing' in terms of capital requirements and the leverage ratio (Section 13.6.4).

The client clearing set-up is illustrated in Figure 8.7. Note that clients can have a clearing relationship with more than one clearing member, as shown. One reason for this is that clients may wish to 'port' their portfolio to a different clearing member. Indeed, this is the aim in a default scenario so as to provide continuity for the clients. However, the ability to achieve portability depends on the precise set-up for client clearing. In this respect, what is important is the way in which margin posted by the client is passed through to the clearing member and/or the CCP, and how it is segregated. Depending on the manner of segregation, it is possible for the client to have a risk to the CCP, their clearing member, or their clearing member together with other clients of their clearing member. In general, there are two broad account structures used for client clearing:

- *Omnibus segregation.* This refers to segregation between the account of the clearing member (the 'house account') and those of their clients (the 'omnibus account'). Typically, the margin in a house account can be used to cover the losses of a client of that member, but not vice versa. This means that a client is not exposed to losses from their clearing member's own portfolio. However, *all* assets in an omnibus account can

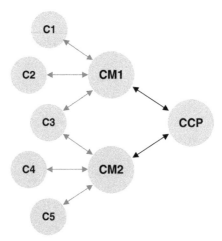

Figure 8.7 Illustration of the client clearing set-up where a client (C) accesses a CCP through one or more clearing members (CMs).

be used to meet the obligations of a defaulted client(s). This means that the clients have a risk to their clearing member and even other clients of their clearing member (this is sometimes known as 'fellow customer risk'). Note that fellow customer risk requires the default of a clearing member and one or more of their other clients, as the client defaults are otherwise the responsibility of the clearing member.

- *Individual segregation.* In this case, client accounts are segregated individually so that they cannot be used to cover the losses of other clients. This is a safer set-up as it protects against clearing member risk and fellow customer risk but is more expensive.

There are a number of other aspects that are important, such as whether or not margin is segregated by value, or if the actual assets are segregated and if the segregation is physical or just legal.[10] Other differences can relate to whether the omnibus margin is posted on a net or gross basis and what happens to any excess margin.

8.3   CCP RISK MANAGEMENT

8.3.1   Overview and Membership Requirements

A CCP stands between buyers and sellers and guarantees the performance of trades. In a centrally-cleared market, counterparty risk is centralised within the CCP that is legally obliged to perform on the contracts it clears. There is consequently no need for the original counterparties to monitor one another in terms of credit quality, as they are only exposed to the overall credit quality of the other members.[11] This clearly puts the emphasis on the operation and resilience of the CCP itself.

In order to perform counterparty risk mitigation, a CCP actually performs a number of related functions:

- *Multilateral offset.* Due to the centralisation of trades, a CCP can provide netting and/or compression benefits for trades that originated with different counterparties.
- *Loss absorbency.* A CCP will collect both variation and initial margins from its members to cover potential default losses. It will also hold default fund contributions from its members to cover possible extreme losses in excess of margins. Initial margins and default funds will be driven by factors such as volatility, correlation, and the size of the cleared portfolio.
- *Default management.* A CCP will manage a member default. This may include hedging and auctioning the underlying positions, allocating any losses in excess of the margins held, and transferring or 'porting' (Section 8.2.5) client trades to solvent clearing members.

In order to manage the risk that they take, CCPs have a number of mechanisms to ensure their continuity and resilience against counterparty and liquidity risks.

---

[10] For example, in the US, individual segregation is achieved through the model 'legally segregated; operationally commingled' (LSOC), which means that client assets are not physically segregated.

[11] There may be certain methods of loss allocation (Section 8.3.4) that lead to some sensitivity to the credit quality of a specific counterparty.

CCPs employ membership requirements to ensure clearing members do not bring undue risk to the CCP (although such restrictions should, on the other hand, not be anti-competitive). In general, membership requirements are based around:

- *Creditworthiness.* The probability of default of the clearing member, as assessed by external or internal methods.
- *Liquidity.* The ability of the member to meet liquidity requirements, such as the need to meet margin calls at short notice.
- *Operationality.* The ability to adhere to the CCP rules, such as those pertaining to auctions.

CCP members will also face requirements over the minimum capital base, default fund contributions, and default management participation.

8.3.2   Margin

Unlike a bank, which relies largely on capital to absorb losses, margin is the primary defence for a central counterparty.

Variation margining clearly requires timely and reliable price data for all cleared derivatives and, where price data is not directly available, market-standard valuation methods. Such methods may sometimes need to evolve with market practice, a good example being the move from Libor to overnight indexed spread (OIS) discounting for interest rate swaps.[12] Typically, only cash is accepted as variation margin, as it is seen – directly or indirectly – as settlement (Section 7.2.6). Variation margin and settlement amounts from clearing members' other clearing activities in a single currency may be netted, resulting in a single payment or receipt per day. Usually, there is no netting of different currencies for variation margin purposes.

Initial margin is intended to cover potential close-out losses in the event of a default by that clearing member. Typically, it is calculated using different scenarios for possible price movements over an assumed close-out period (MPoR or liquidation period), such as five days. Initial margin exists for the life of the trade and can be increased or reduced depending on market conditions and the remaining risk.

Unlike variation margin, initial margin need not necessarily be in cash. Acceptable types of margin in this context may include cash in major currencies, government treasury securities, and government agency securities. The general aim of initial margin is that, after the application of haircuts, the CCP is not exposed to significant credit, market, and liquidity risks. Securities must be sufficiently liquid, such as having price data available on a frequent basis and having low credit risk.

CCPs will hold large amounts of margin. This offers a possibility for income to balance the interest rates that CCPs may contractually agree to pay. Most CCPs will pay interest to clearing members on excess cash deposited as initial margin. Typically, this may be set at a level with respect to a short-term deposit rate such as FedFunds minus 10 basis points (bps).[13] Since CCPs will pay interest rates on some margin received, they need to

---

[12] LCH.Clearnet (2010). LCH.Clearnet adopts OIS discounting for $218 trillion IRS portfolio. Press release (17 June). www.lch.com.
[13] See the LCH Ltd definition of Client Deposit Rate (CDR). www.lch.com.

generate a return on the margin they hold. However, margin also needs to be invested extremely carefully so as to avoid creating additional risk for the CCP. CCPs may, therefore, deposit margin with central banks, commercial banks, or reverse repos, or invest it in other assets with very low credit and liquidity risks.

8.3.3   Default Scenarios and Margin Period of Risk

The main risk faced by a CCP is a default by one of its clearing members. This will lead to an unmatched book due to the contingent market risk that the CCP faces, since it will still have to pay variation margin to non-defaulters who have made a valuation gain (that would have been otherwise offset by variation margin received from the defaulting counterparty).

A CCP has greater authority and control over this process than a typical counterparty in a bilateral OTC trade. CCPs have general rights in relation to declaring a clearing member in default and subsequently managing the risk of that member's portfolio. These rights include suspension of trading, closing out positions, transferring client positions, and liquidating securities held as margin. In a default scenario, the CCP typically neutralises its exposure through a combination of the following:

- *Macro-hedging*. This aims to minimise the exposure of the portfolio to major risk factors (e.g. interest rate sensitivity) with liquid transactions. Such hedges reduce the market risk that the CCP faces. The 'default management group' has the discretion to apply relevant market risk macro-hedges in the manner they consider optimal.
- *Auctions*. After the above, the CCP auctions the portfolio amongst other clearing members by sub-portfolio (e.g. currency). The default management group has the discretion to split the portfolio into sub-portfolios in the manner they consider optimal, with the macro-hedging ensuring that they do not have significant directional risks. Surviving CCP members will submit two-way prices for sub-portfolios, and the member bidding the best price will win a given portfolio. Clearing members may have strong incentives to participate in an auction in order to collectively achieve a favourable working out of a default without adverse consequences (such as being exposed to losses through default funds or other mechanisms). There may also be individual incentives to clearing members bidding in the auction, such as any resulting losses being allocated to losing bidders first before winning bidders are affected. It should be noted that the macro-hedges executed in the previous step should be helpful in the auction process because the portfolios auctioned will be the defaulter's trades together with the macro-hedges. Since these will have less sensitivity to market moves, it should be easier for clearing members to put in reasonable bids, even in volatile markets.

A CCP also benefits from a default management group made up of key personnel from the CCP together with senior traders from member firms who may be seconded on a revolving basis. Such traders can help with tasks such as the macro-hedging of the portfolio.[14]

In order to maximise the efficiency of a potential auction, the default management process is practised via periodic (e.g. twice a year) 'fire drills', where clearing members

---

[14] There will be a firewall between seconded traders and other members of their firm.

submit prices. New CCP members will also be required to take a 'driving test' to show that they can deal with the operational requirements posed by the auction. These operational requirements revolve around the ability to process, price, and bid on relatively large portfolios of trades in a short timescale (a few hours).

Client positions are most-efficiently ported to a surviving clearing member. Indeed, clients may have agreements with backup members in place, specifically for such a purpose. However, porting requires the surviving clearing member to accept the portfolio and the associated margin in question. This in turn will depend on the way in which client margin has been charged and segregated. In the event that porting is not possible, the client trades (of the defaulted member) will be managed in the default process together with the defaulted member's own portfolio. The client's initial margin will be used to cover any losses, depending on how this is segregated (see Section 8.2.5).

In the aftermath of the Lehman Brothers bankruptcy in 2008, SwapClear reported that 90% of their Lehman risk was neutralised (macro-hedged) in one week and all 66,000 trades were auctioned within three weeks. The events were hailed as a success and required only around a third of the initial margin, with the rest being returned to the Lehman administrators.[15] The more recent Nasdaq example (discussed later in Section 10.1.3) was a less successful operation, where a substantial part of the default fund was required.

Based on the above description, the MPoR for a CCP is illustrated schematically in Figure 8.8, which can be compared to the MPoR in a bilateral market depicted previously in Figure 7.17. CCPs can be seen to reduce the MPoR by making daily and potentially also intradaily collateral calls in cash only (no settlement delays). They also have full authority over all calculations (no disputes allowed) and ensure that members can adhere to the operational requirements of posting margin, and that they guarantee to post on behalf of clients if necessary.

CCPs can also close out positions more quickly than in bilateral markets, as they can declare a member in default without any external obstructions and aim to then invoke

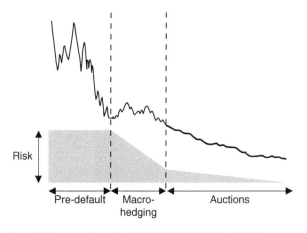

Figure 8.8   Illustration of the margin period of risk (MPoR) for a CCP.

---

[15] LCH.Clearnet (2008). $9 trillion Lehman OTC interest rate swap default successfully resolved. Press release (8 October). www.lch.com.

a swift and effective default management process thanks to a privileged position with respect to bankruptcy law. This privileged position should enhance the CCP's ability to deal with a default in an efficient manner. For example, in a bilateral market the methodology for closing out trades and the macro-hedging of the positions of a defaulted counterparty prior to close-out may be challenged by the bankruptcy administrators, as discussed in Section 6.3.5.[16] The MPoR for a CCP is therefore defined by the following three periods:

- *No action.* The 'pre-default' period (from when the clearing member last posted margin until remedial action is taken) will likely be shorter than in bilateral markets, since CCPs can declare members in default more easily and with less chance of legal challenges.
- *Macro-hedging.* The CCP may first seek to neutralise key sensitivities of the underlying portfolio via macro-hedges, which will be quite fast as the underlying hedges will be liquid. This should cause the overall risk of the portfolio to drop significantly, although the portfolio will still be subject to basis risks and bid-offer costs.
- *Auctions.* The CCP will then arrange and hold one or more auctions to trade out of the underlying portfolio. During this time, the risk will gradually drop to zero as successful auctions are completed, although the CCP may be exposed to costs in auctioning the positions.

For example, the SwapClear management of the Lehman Brothers default was described as follows:[17]

- Upon default (Monday 15 September 2008), the default management group was formed from member firms (on a rotating basis), who seconded pre-assigned and experienced traders to work alongside LCH.Clearnet's risk management team.
- The default management group applied macro-hedges to neutralise market risk on the defaulter's portfolio, with all participants adhering to strict confidentiality rules throughout the process.
- The risk positions were reviewed daily, and further hedges were executed in response to changing market conditions.
- From Wednesday 24 September to Friday 3 October, the competitive auctions of the five (currency-specific) sub-portfolios were successfully completed.

The above process lasted for three weeks, but the majority of the risk was hedged well before this. Like the MPoR for bilateral markets, it is therefore important to consider the MPoR used in risk models as a metaphorical parameter, since risk decays gradually during the CCP default management process. For OTC derivatives, CCPs generally use a value of five business days compared to the minimum 10 days used in bilateral markets (Section 7.2.3). This five-day period forms the basis of CCP initial margin calculations discussed in the Chapter 9.[18]

---

[16] For example, suppose a party hedges risk in a defaulter's portfolio, but prior to close-out these hedges lose money against gains in the value of the portfolio. The defaulting counterparty will likely claim that they should not be exposed to losses on the hedges.

[17] See Footnote 15.

[18] This period generally applies to OTC CCPs. In exchange-traded derivatives, the greater underlying liquidity means that a one- or two-day assumption is more common.

8.3.4   The Loss Waterfall

In the event of a clearing member default, the member's initial margin and default fund contributions are available to the CCP to cover costs arising from macro-hedging and the auction. In case the initial margin and default fund contributions prove insufficient, and/or the auction fails, the CCP has other financial resources to absorb and/or other mechanisms to allocate losses. In general, a 'loss waterfall' defines the different ways in which resources will be used. A typical loss waterfall is represented in Figure 8.9.

The first components of the loss waterfall are the defaulter-pays resources and include the initial margin and default fund contribution(s) of the defaulter(s).[19] After this, there is typically a 'skin-in-the-game' equity contribution from the CCP. This gives the CCP some incentive to avoid losses beyond the defaulter-pays resources.

Skin in the game

Skin in the game is not written into all CCP rules. For example, in 2014, a futures broker on the Korea Exchange (KRX) defaulted as a result of an algorithmic trading error. KRX mutualised a loss of $4.3m to the default fund contributed by its members without suffering any loss itself. The KRX rules determined that it would suffer a loss only after the default fund of around $200m had been exhausted.[20]

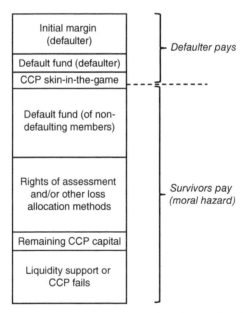

Figure 8.9   Illustration of a typical loss waterfall defining the way in which the default of one or more CCP members is absorbed.

---

[19] Note that variation margin is not mentioned here as it should offset the value of the portfolio in question. However, to the extent that the CCP may hold additional variation margin, this can be seen to be part of the defaulter-pays resources.

[20] Grant, J. et al (2014). Banks launch clearing review after Korean broker default. *Financial Times* (7 March). www.ft.com.

If the resources above are completely depleted, then the remaining default fund of the CCP is used to absorb losses. This is now a survivors-pay approach, as this forms the collective contribution of all clearing members, who now stand to make a loss. The allocation of losses in the default fund may be pro rata, or use other rules that in turn may incentivise clearing members to bid proactively in the auction (e.g. by allocating losses to winning bidders last). This is discussed in more detail in Section 10.2.3.

Losses wiping out a significant portion of the default fund of a CCP are clearly envisaged to be exceptionally unlikely. However, if this does happen, then there are other methods for absorbing losses that depend on the CCP in question. These are summarised below and discussed in more detail in Section 10.2.4.

- *Rights of assessment.* This represents an unfunded obligation to contribute additionally to a default fund that has been depleted by losses. Typically, such a recapitalisation will be invoked if a significant fraction (e.g. 25%) of the default fund is used. If this right were unlimited, then the CCP would be unlikely to fail (unless all its clearing members did so). However, this would create siginificant moral hazard and unlimited exposure for clearing members. Furthermore, it might destabilise markets as members would be required to contribute to default funds at the worst possible time. For these reasons, rights of assessment are generally capped in terms of the maximum amount in a given period.

- *Variation margin gains haircutting (VMGH).* This is probably the most common alternative loss-allocation concept (ISDA 2013b). The idea of VMGH is that losses made by a defaulting clearing member can be balanced by 'haircutting' the corresponding gains that must (due to the matched book) have been made by other clearing members. This means that clearing members whose positions have increased in value since the default will not receive the full margin to cover their gain, whilst those owing money to the CCP will still be required to pay in full. An interesting feature of this is that it mimics the economics of a bilateral market. Note also that a clearing member subject to VMGH may not have made an overall profit as their gains may be offset by losses associated with bilateral trades or those at another CCP (or they may be client trades). If a CCP can auction a defaulter's portfolio at mid-market prices, then VMGH is guaranteed to work, as the losses from the defaulter must be matched by equivalent gains for other CCP members. The obvious reason why VMGH may fail in practice is if the CCP has to close out at a significant premium to mid-market prices.

- *Tear-up.* If the resulting exposure cannot be neutralised via an auction, then one other option is for the CCP to 'tear up' unmatched contracts with surviving clearing members. The aim of the tear-up is to return a CCP to a matched book by terminating opposite trades to those of the defaulter (these could represent the original bilateral trades or just any that are suitable). All other contracts (possibly the vast majority of the total contracts cleared) could remain untouched. The major difference with tear-up compared to VMGH is that the CCP is not exposed to any risk premium in auctioning transactions. Tear-up could be partial or full; in the latter case, the CCP will obviously not fail, but the clearing members will be left with losses and the market risk that the CCP was unable to neutralise.

- *Forced allocation.* A method similar to tear-up is forced allocation, whereby clearing members are obliged to accept certain portfolios at prices determined by the CCP. This has a similar effect, since instead of tearing up an existing trade, a CCP might impose the reverse trade on a member. However, a forced allocation may be more random as any member can be allocated positions, whereas tear-up requires a member to have the appropriate trades in their portfolio. Furthermore, unlike tear-up, it would not be possible for a clearing member to pass on the impact of forced allocation to its clients.

It is also important to note that a CCP can impose losses on its members via the default fund, without being close to actually failing itself. The recent Nasdaq example (Section 10.1.3) illustrates this clearly. Note also that the default losses that a member incurs are not directly related to the transactions that they executed with the defaulting member. Indeed, a member can suffer default losses even if it never traded with the defaulted counterparty or has no net position with the CCP.

Some loss-allocation methods are theoretically infinite – i.e. the CCP would never fail, but would rather impose any level of losses on its clearing members to be able to continue to function itself. Not surprisingly, these allocation methods (e.g. tear-up or forced allocation) are fairly severe and may even cause surviving clearing members to fail.

Assuming loss allocation is finite, the remaining capital of the CCP would then be used to cover losses. At this point, assuming losses persist, the CCP will fail unless it receives some external liquidity support (via a bailout from a central bank, for example). Some CCPs may have other components in the waterfall – for example, lines of credit with banks and financial guarantees provided by insurance companies. Having such liquidity 'on tap' is costly, but this cost may be justified since CCPs could be very exposed in the event of a large negative asset price move, or the default of a clearing member and possible withdrawal of other clearing members.

Note that none of the above methods allow a CCP to use the initial margin of non-defaulting members. Initial margin haircutting has been suggested as a possible means to allocate losses (Elliott 2013), but it has not been used in practice and may not be allowed by regulators.[21] Hence, initial margin contributions are – in theory – risk free, since they do not appear in the loss waterfall. On the other hand, since other loss-allocation methods (such as tear-up) are potentially infinite,[22] this may be of limited consolation to a surviving clearing member.

8.3.5 Comparing Bilateral and Central Clearing

Table 8.2 compares bilaterally- and centrally-cleared markets. Only standardised, non-exotic, and liquid products can be cleared. CCPs allow for multilateral netting, which is potentially more efficient than bilateral netting (and portfolio compression) in bilateral markets. CCPs impose strong margin requirements on their members (although regulation in bilateral markets is becoming stricter in this respect). An important feature of central clearing is a centralised default management auction process compared to

---

[21] European Market Infrastructure Regulation article 45(4) states that 'A CCP shall not use the margins posted by non-defaulting members to cover the losses resulting from the default of another clearing member.'

[22] Meaning that an upper bound cannot be put on the loss incurred, since it relates to the cost of rehedging positions subject to tear-up.

Table 8.2   Comparing bilaterally- and centrally-cleared OTC derivative markets.

	Bilateral	Centrally cleared
Counterparty	Original	CCP
Products	All	Must be standard, vanilla, liquid, etc.
Participants	All	Clearing members are usually large dealers Other margin-posting entities can clear through clearing members
Netting	Bilateral netting agreements and portfolio compression	Multilateral netting (including compression)
Margining	Bilateral, bespoke arrangements dependent on credit quality Regulatory rules being introduced (Section 7.4)	Full collateralisation, including initial margin enforced by CCP
Close-out	Bilateral	Coordinated default management process (macro-hedges and auctions)
Loss absorbency cost	Mainly capital	Mainly initial margin (and default fund)

the more uncoordinated bilateral equivalent. In bilateral markets, costs arise mainly from capital costs (although the introduction of initial margin is changing this), whereas in centrally-cleared markets the major costs for loss absorbency are initial margin (and default fund contributions for clearing members), as capital requirements are generally quite low (see Section 13.6).

8.4   INITIAL MARGIN AND DEFAULT FUNDS

8.4.1   Coverage of Initial Margin and Default Funds

Initial margin is generally expected to provide coverage to a high degree of confidence (e.g. 99%) in the event that a clearing member defaults. However, initial margin breaches are clearly possible. Indeed, in the event that initial margin is insufficient, losses may be extremely high. For example, Bates and Craine (1999) estimated that, following the 1987 crash, the expected losses conditional on a margin call being breached increased by an order of magnitude.

The role of the default fund is to absorb extreme losses not covered by margins, as illustrated qualitatively in Figure 8.10. The distribution of losses is likely to be very heavy-tailed, meaning that if the margin is breached, then very large losses are possible. In order to provide coverage of these improbable but potentially large losses, an amount far beyond the initial margin is required. This is the classic problem of insurance and can only be mitigated by a pooling of risk. The default fund is therefore shared amongst the CCP members. The loss mutualisation inherent in the default fund is a key point since it spreads extreme losses from the failure of a single counterparty across all other clearing members. This has the potential to ameliorate systemic problems, but it also creates other risks. The size of the default fund is quantified via stress scenarios in relation to member defaults and related market conditions (Section 8.4.3).

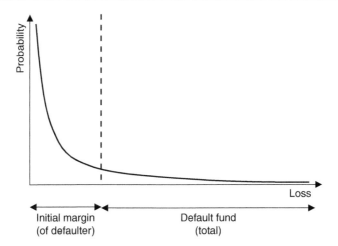

Figure 8.10   Representation of the relationship between initial margin and default fund.

8.4.2   Default Fund Versus Initial Margin

The default fund is a key component of clearing. Since it is mutualised, it provides a much higher coverage of losses than initial margin, which avoids the cost of clearing being prohibitive (since in reality paying for one's own default in all possible scenarios is not practical). Hence, the contribution to a default fund may seem reasonably small compared to initial margin requirements but will provide much greater loss absorbency due to mutualisation.

In order to understand this, consider the split of initial margins (IM) and default funds (DF) shown in Figure 8.11. In all three cases it is assumed that each of the five CCP members contributes one unit to the CCP, and the resources available to absorb the default

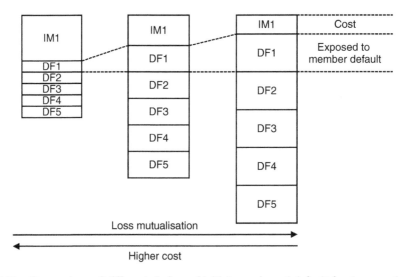

Figure 8.11   Comparison of different choices of initial margin and default fund proportions.

of one member are shown. Smaller initial margins and correspondingly-larger default funds are cheaper but increase moral hazard, as there is more chance of default fund losses and less chance of the defaulter-pays approach being followed.

Another consideration is that non-clearing members do not contribute to the default fund of a CCP. This means that clients only contribute directly to the risk of their own portfolio via the initial margin that the CCP imposes on its clearing members (which in turn will likely be imposed on the clients). Hence, default funds mutualise not only the default of clearing members but also the default of their clients. The related point is that large default funds and smaller initial margins will disincentivise clearing members from providing portability (the transfer of client positions from one clearing member to another; see Section 8.2.5). Without enough initial margin, this becomes difficult, especially since the clearing member accepting the positions may have to pay more into the CCP default fund. The balance in choice of default funds is summarised in Table 8.3.

Putting more financial contributions into initial margins generally incentivises better behaviour, whereas putting more into default funds provides greater overall loss absorbency and therefore makes clearing cheaper at the expense of moral hazard.

8.4.3   Default Fund Coverage

Losses hitting the default fund are supposed to be uncommon, in line with the high level of confidence used for calculating initial margin. To some extent, this has indeed been the case: for example, LCH reports seven defaults during its history and all of these defaults have been managed within the initial margin of the defaulter, and therefore without any impact on other clearing members or markets.[23]

That said, when CCP default funds are required, losses can potentially be large. For example, in 1987, the Hong Kong Futures Exchange made losses that dwarfed the associated default fund (see Section 10.1.2). A more recent example is the default fund losses at Nasdaq (Section 10.1.3). The potential for such losses may be considered to increase, as CCPs in the future will be larger and will have to take on more complex and risky financial products compared to the past.

Clearly, the default fund has the role of making clearing cost-effective by using loss mutualisation to cover potential tail risk over the initial margins. However, working out the appropriate size of the default fund is difficult due to the very fact that it is covering risk arising from extreme events. Calculating the potential exposure above initial margins

Table 8.3   Summary of the strengths and weaknesses between higher and lower initial margins and default funds.

	Higher initial margin Lower default fund	Lower initial margin Higher default fund
Cost	Higher	Lower
Client clearing	Clients pay for their own risk via initial margin Promotes portability	Clients do not pay for their own risk directly Portability difficult
Moral hazard	Lower	Higher

---

[23] LCH.Clearnet's Default History (20 May 2013). www.lch.com.

is plagued by problems such as fail tail behaviour, complex interdependencies, and WWR. The actual probability of a CCP exhausting its default fund is impossible to quantify with any accuracy, as it is likely linked to events involving the default of one or more clearing members together with extreme market movements and illiquidity.

For the above reasons, CCPs are typically required to calibrate the size of the *total* default fund qualitatively via pre-defined stress tests. This may then be allocated to clearing members in a relatively simplistic way, such as pro rata with initial margins (maybe averaged over a time period) or based on the total size of positions (potentially also subject to a floor). The total default fund size is typically framed in terms of the number of defaults a CCP can withstand (usually one or two). Default fund contributions are not updated as frequently as initial margins – for example, monthly.

The CPSS-IOSCO (2012) principles require that a CCP should 'maintain additional financial resources sufficient to cover a wide range of potential stress scenarios that should include, but not be limited to, the default of the participant and its affiliates that would potentially cause the largest aggregate credit exposure to the CCP in extreme but plausible market conditions'. This is typically known as a Cover 1 requirement. Additionally, it is stated that:

> In addition, a CCP that is involved in activities with a more-complex risk profile or that is systemically important in multiple jurisdictions should maintain additional financial resources sufficient to cover a wide range of potential stress scenarios that should include, but not be limited to, the default of the two participants and their affiliates that would potentially cause the largest aggregate credit exposure to the CCP in extreme but plausible market conditions.

This is known as a Cover 2 requirement.

As an example of a CCP following the guidance above, the SwapClear default fund is 'sized to cover the default of the largest two SwapClear Clearing Members (in line with the principles outlined by CPSS-IOSCO) using an updated set of extreme, but plausible, theoretical and historical stress test scenarios that are tailored specifically for the interest rates market'.[24]

The apparent 'two largest default' requirement above is potentially quite significant. For example, Heller and Vause (2012) studied dealers and estimated that CCP default funds may need to be about 50% larger to cover losses that could arise from the default of the two most important interest rate swap or CDS dealers, rather than just the single most important dealer. However, it is not surprising that OTC CCP default funds are viewed as needing to be more resilient. They would only be hit during a serious crisis when one or more clearing members had failed. It follows that the failed clearing members would quite likely be large, systemically-important financial institutions and that financial markets would be extremely turbulent at this point. Furthermore, since the failed counterparties are likely to be members of several CCPs, the chance of this causing a severe systemic disturbance is high. Only very large default funds can guarantee the financial integrity of CCPs and provide the necessary confidence and stability to prevent a major crisis in such a situation.

---

[24] Submission of Amendments to the Clearinghouse Rules to the Commodity Futures Trading Commission submitted by LCH.Clearnet Limited (16 April 2012).

8.5   IMPACT OF CENTRAL CLEARING

8.5.1   Advantages and Disadvantages of Central Clearing

CCPs offer many advantages and potentially offer a more transparent, safer market where contracts are more fungible and liquidity is enhanced. The following is a summary of the advantages of a CCP:

- *Transparency*. A CCP may face a clearing member for a large proportion of its transactions in a given market and can, therefore, see concentration that would not be transparent in bilateral markets. If a member has a particularly extreme exposure, the CCP is in a position to act on this and limit trading. These aspects may, in turn, disperse panic that might otherwise be present in bilateral markets due to a lack of knowledge of the exposure faced by institutions.[25]
- *Multilateral offset*. As mentioned above, the risk of contracts transacted between different counterparties but cleared through a CCP can be offset. This increases the flexibility to enter new transactions and terminate existing ones, and reduces costs.
- *Loss mutualisation*. Even when a default creates losses that exceed the financial commitments from the defaulter, these losses are distributed throughout the CCP members, reducing their impact on any one member. Thus, a counterparty's losses are dispersed partially throughout the market, making their impact less dramatic and reducing the possibility of systemic problems.
- *Legal and operational efficiency*. The margining, netting, and settlement functions undertaken by a CCP potentially increase operational efficiency and reduce costs. CCPs may also reduce legal risks in providing centralisation of rules and mechanisms.
- *Liquidity*. A CCP may improve market liquidity through the ability of market participants to trade easily and benefit from multilateral netting. Barriers to market entry may be reduced.
- *Default management*. A well-managed central auction may result in smaller price disruptions than the uncoordinated replacement of positions during a crisis period associated with the default of a clearing member.

For the past century and longer, clearing has been limited to listed derivatives traded on exchanges. Bilateral OTC markets have been extremely successful, and their growth has been greater than that of exchange-traded products over the last two decades. The trouble with clearing OTC derivatives is that they are more illiquid, long-dated, and complex compared to their exchange-traded relatives.

Despite the obvious advantages, the mandatory central clearing of OTC derivatives is not without criticism. The following is a summary of the disadvantages of a CCP:

- *Moral hazard*. This is a well-known problem in the insurance industry. Moral hazard has the effect of disincentivising good counterparty risk management practice by CCP

---

[25] The benefits of greater transparency should not be overstated. For example, the transparency supposedly associated with exchange-traded derivatives did not prevent the collapse of Barings Bank. Nor did the margin requirements that were required to support the large speculative positions carried by Leeson, which eventually led to the collapse of Barings. More recent rogue trader incidents such as Société Générale (2008) and UBS (2011) also involved exchange-traded products.

members (since all the risk is passed to the CCP). Parties have little incentive to monitor each other's credit quality and act appropriately because a third party is taking most of the risk.

- *Adverse selection.* CCPs are also vulnerable to adverse selection, which occurs if members trading OTC derivatives know more about the risks than the CCP itself. In such a situation, firms may selectively pass these riskier products to CCPs that underprice the risks. Obviously, firms such as large banks specialise in OTC derivatives and may have superior information and knowledge on pricing and risk than a CCP. Anecdotal evidence on this point is already apparent, with market participants aware that different CCPs are cheaper, for example, when clearing pay-fixed and receive-fixed interest rate swaps.
- *Bifurcations.* The requirement to clear standard products may create unfortunate bifurcations between cleared and non-cleared trades. This can negate the benefit of multilateral offset and increase costs.
- *Procyclicality.* Procyclicality refers to a positive dependence on the state of the economy. CCPs may create procyclicality effects by, for example, increasing margin requirements (or haircuts) in volatile markets or crisis periods. The greater frequency and liquidity of margin requirements under a CCP (compared with less uniform and more flexible margining practices in bilateral OTC markets) could also aggravate procyclicality.

CCPs perform a number of functions, such as netting, margining, transparency, loss mutualisation, and default management. Another important point to note is that some of these functions can be achieved via other mechanisms. For example, trade compression can facilitate greater netting benefits, bilateral markets can (and do) have margining mechanisms, and trade repositories can provide greater transparency.

8.5.2   Will Mandatory Clearing Kill Credit Value Adjustment?

Since CCPs ultimately mitigate counterparty risk, there is an obvious question as to whether the clearing mandate – and the associated bilateral margin requirements (Section 7.4) – will lead to a gradual reduction in credit value adjustment (CVA) – and other related components, such as funding value adjustment (FVA) and capital value adjustment (KVA) – to levels that are much less relevant than they have been historically.

To answer the above question, it is important to realise that counterparty risk, funding, and capital issues (CVA, FVA, KVA) predominantly arise from non-margined OTC derivatives with end users (see Section 5.2.5). Since such end users will be exempt from the clearing mandate, they will not move to central clearing except on a voluntary basis. Since most such end users find it difficult to post margin, such voluntary clearing (or bilateral margin posting) is unlikely.

To see this in practice, referring to the breakdown of a bank's CVA previously shown in Figure 3.4 shows that only about 15% of the CVA comes from exposures to banks and 'other financial institutions'. This is the CVA that would likely be more significantly reduced from clearing and bilateral initial margin posting. The other 85% of the CVA comes from exposure to corporates and governments who are exempt counterparties, most of whom would be unable/unwilling to centrally clear. Hence, the uncollateralised bilateral transactions that are most important from an xVA perspective will likely persist as such.

It is also important to note that central clearing and other changes, such as the incoming bilateral collateral rules, may reduce components such as CVA in certain situations, but will also increase other components (e.g. most margin value adjustment, which arises from funding initial margins, as discussed in Chapter 20). Hence, it will become even more important to consider xVA holistically to understand the balance of various effects. There will also be a growing need to assess the impact of CVA on a central counterparty, which is not yet common practice.

9

Initial Margin Methodologies

9.1 ROLE OF INITIAL MARGIN

9.1.1 Purpose

The principal aim of derivatives margin is to reduce counterparty risk, either by a settlement or by a collateralisation process. Variation margin can reduce counterparty risk significantly, but in the event that a counterparty defaults, there will be a delay since the last variation margin was received. There will then be a further delay until the portfolio has been completely closed out. The total length of time for this to happen is typically known as the margin period of risk (MPoR), which is a term that originated in bilateral over-the-counter (OTC) markets for regulatory capital purposes. A counterparty, either central or bilateral, is exposed to market risk for the length of the MPoR. The aim of initial margin is to reduce the counterparty risk over the MPoR further, such that the residual risk is small or negligible and, therefore, the 'defaulter-pays' approach is likely to be upheld.

BCBS-IOSCO (2015) defines initial margin as covering 'potential future exposure for the expected time between the last VM [variation margin] exchange and the liquidation of positions on the default of the counterparty'.

Regulatory guidance on initial margin amounts calculated by central counterparties (CCPs) is as follows:

> A CCP should adopt initial margin models and parameters that are risk-based and generate margin requirements sufficient to cover its potential future exposure to participants in the interval between the last margin collection and the close-out of positions following a participant default. Initial margin should meet an established single-tailed confidence level of at least 99 percent with respect to the estimated distribution of future exposure.[1]

Corresponding guidance for bilateral markets is as follows:

> For the purpose of informing the initial margin baseline, the potential future exposure of a noncentrally cleared derivatives [sic] should reflect an extreme but plausible estimate of an increase in the value of the instrument that is consistent with a one-tailed 99 per cent confidence interval over a 10-day horizon.[2]

---

[1] CPSS-IOSCO (2012).
[2] BCBS-IOSCO (2015).

These statements suggest that there are two critical components that go into the determination of initial margin amounts:

- *Confidence level.* Both of the above suggest a confidence level of at least 99%, which would suggest – within the assumptions of the underlying methodology, at least – that initial margin would be sufficient in at least 99 out of 100 situations. Note that some regulation specifies a higher confidence level for OTC derivatives of at least 99.5%.[3]
- *Time horizon.* The time horizon for assessing the underlying market risk is also a key component. This is linked to the MPoR concept introduced earlier. Notice that for bilateral transactions this is clearly defined as 10 days, whereas there is no specific definition for centrally-cleared transactions.

The purpose of initial margin is to cover the market risk faced when a counterparty defaults. Of course, this cannot be done with certainty, but initial margins are intended to cover a very large proportion of potential price moves (99% or more when explicitly quantified) during the MPoR. There is a clear balance in setting initial margin levels: too low will imply that the CCP or bilateral party is facing material counterparty risks, whilst too high will mean trading costs may become excessive. A CCP must balance the need to be competitive by incentivising central clearing (low margins) with maximising their own creditworthiness (high margins). Not surprisingly, high margins have been shown empirically to have a detrimental impact on trading volumes (for example, see Hartzmark 1986 and Hardouvelis and Kim 1995).

Initial margin is perhaps the key aspect that defines the effectiveness of central clearing. It represents an additional margin required to cover the largest projected loss on a given transaction or portfolio. However, determining initial margin is a complex quantitative task and represents a difficult balance: undermargined trades impose excessive risk on a CCP, whereas excessive margins raise the costs of trading OTC derivatives. The methodology and assumptions used to compute initial margins will obviously have a significant impact on margin demands, as shown, for example, by Duffie et al. (2014).

Market participants will also need – or at least wish – to be comfortable with the initial margin calculation methodologies. Whereas variation margin relates to the *current* exposure, initial margin is providing coverage for *future* exposure. Initial margin is, by contrast to variation margin, much more complex and subjective.

Note that the regulatory guidance cited above implicitly suggests that initial margin methodologies will be dynamic, with initial margin amounts changing through time. This is explicitly stated in BCBS-IOSCO (2015), which states that initial margin should be

> 'targeted' and dynamic, with each portfolio having its own designated margin for absorbing the potential losses in relation to that particular portfolio, and with such margin being adjusted over time to reflect changes in that portfolio's risk.

Dynamic and risk-sensitive initial margin methodologies are clearly desirable in terms of reacting to the current risk on a given portfolio. However, this may lead to large changes in initial margin amounts during stressful market conditions (this is typically known as 'procyclicality'). Dynamic approaches also make the prediction and quantification of the costs arising from future initial margin posting much more difficult.

---

[3] EMIR (2015).

Initial margin methodologies can be rule or risk based. Rule-based margin calculations make minimal reference to the underlying risk of the portfolio but are simple. Risk-based approaches are more complex to design and implement but have the benefit of recognising the offsetting nature of different trades in a portfolio.

Ideally, an initial margin model would take into account the following factors:

- *Forecasting*. The model can produce a reasonable forecast of potential exposures of the portfolio, accounting for all relevant risk factors and incorporating aspects such as non-Gaussian (fat-tailed) behaviour.
- *Dependencies*. Dependencies between different risk factors are modelled appropriately to capture (but not overstate) the diversification between different products. This is especially important for calculating the benefit achieved by cross-margining (Section 9.1.6).
- *Procyclicality*. The margin approach is designed to avoid procyclicality as much as possible. This may require incorporating different periods of market data, such as stressed periods.
- *Margin period of risk*. The MPoR is appropriate and based on the liquidity, market size, and specific characteristics of the product(s) in question.

9.1.2   Margin Period of Risk

Conceptually, initial margin is intended to cover potential losses during the so-called MPoR or 'liquidation period', as illustrated previously in Figure 7.6. The MPoR generally refers to the period from the point at which a defaulting party stops posting variation margin to the point at which the underlying market risk has been neutralised. It has been previously discussed for bilateral markets (Section 7.5.2) and cleared markets (Section 8.3.3).

Initial margin is generally quantified as a constant market risk for the MPoR in question and often does not make specific reference to components that may be relevant in the event of a counterparty defaulting. As such, as discussed in Section 7.5.2, it is probably not appropriate to consider the MPoR as an estimate of a literal time period, but rather as the correct value to use as an input into a quantitative model. The main problem here is one of 'wrong-way risk' (WWR). WWR refers to a linkage between default probability and exposure. This means that the MPoR should be assessed conditionally on the given counterparty being in default.

Such 'default conditioning' is not really practical for computing initial margin, as it would imply that it is not just specific to a given portfolio but also to the counterparty, and that every counterparty would have different initial margin requirements for the same underlying market risks. Such conditioning is therefore not a part of initial margin methodologies, and this is an important point to bear in mind. For example, Pykhtin and Sokol (2013) argue that the default of a more systemic party such as a bank will have a larger impact on the underlying market conditions, which would imply that more systemic counterparties should – ideally – post more initial margin.[4] Interestingly, counterparties that actively use margining (e.g. banks) tend to be highly systemic and will be

---

[4] This might be considered to be intuitively similar to the G-SIB (globally-systemically-important bank) surcharge discussed in Section 4.2.2.

subject to these problems, whilst counterparties that are non-systemic (e.g. corporates) often do not post margin anyway.

Related to the above, there are a number of aspects that may be missed from the calculation of initial margin with a basic MPoR input:

- *Volatility*. The market volatility over the period is likely to be higher than normal market volatility, especially if the counterparty in default is large and/or systemically important. For example, Pykhtin and Sokol (2013) estimate that the volatility of credit default swap (CDS) index spreads in the aftermath of the Lehman bankruptcy was around four to five times greater than over the period just prior to their failure. Extending the MPoR to compensate for this increased volatility could be significant, as a doubling of volatility would approximately equate to an MPoR four times longer (see Section 7.5.2 for further discussion).
- *Risk reduction*. During the close-out process, the actual risk of the portfolio declines due to approaches such as macro-hedging (see Section 7.5.2), which would suggest a shortening of the MPoR. For example, being exposed to a portfolio with its risk reducing linearly for 10 days is approximately equivalent to being exposed to the full portfolio for about four days.[5]
- *Downward pressure*. In addition to the market volatility, there could also be downward pressure on prices, especially if the underlying portfolio is large.
- *Costs*. Any specific bid-offer or other costs experienced in rehedging positions or during CCP auctions will contribute further losses. For example, there have been claims of profiteering by clearing members in auction processes, which imposes losses on the defaulted member and potentially also the CCP (see Section 10.2.2).

The important point is that the above effects are not *generally* modelled in specific detail for initial margin calculations. There are exceptions to this: for example, the use of stressed historical data for initial margin calculations (discussed later) could be seen as capturing the impact of higher volatility in the close-out process. The MPoR is therefore defined by the literal time between the last margin payment and the time that the market risk has been completely hedged and adjustments for effects not captured explicitly.

Clearly, estimating the MPoR for initial margin methodologies is quite complex, product-/market-specific, and subjective. However, there are, broadly, only three different MPoR values that are used in practice:

- *Exchange-traded markets (one or two business days)*. In exchange-traded futures markets, the MPoR used is generally one or two days, due to the underlying liquidity allowing for rapid close-out.
- *Centrally-cleared OTC derivatives (five business days)*. In cleared OTC products, a longer MPoR typically of five days is used, although longer periods are sometimes used (e.g. SwapClear uses seven days for client portfolios).
- *Bilateral OTC derivatives (10 business days)*. The MPoR in bilateral trades is explicitly defined as 10 days, as noted above. This is linked to the same parameter used for assessing risk in regulatory capital calculations for such transactions (Section 13.4.3).[6]

---

[5] See Section 7.5.2.

[6] Note that the MPoR for regulatory capital can sometimes be increased beyond 10 days, as discussed in Section 13.4.5, but this does not lead to any change in the MPoR for initial margin purposes.

For example, the Commodity Futures Trading Commission (CFTC 2016) states that: 'To the extent that related capital rules which also mitigate counterparty credit risk similarly require a 10-day close-out period assumption, the Commission's view is that a 10-day close-out period assumption for margin purposes is appropriate.'

Note that the choice of MPoR is partially at the discretion of the CCP in question (and will depend on the type of product being cleared), whereas initial margin requirements for uncleared bilateral trades must use a 10-day horizon. This 10-day requirement is not explicitly explained beyond the need for equivalence with the capital requirements, as mentioned above.

9.1.3   Coverage: Quantitative and Qualitative

In general, the following components are important considerations that can be seen to be assessed directly in quantitative initial margin models:

- *Volatility*. The most obvious aspect is the volatility of the portfolio in question. This is driven by the volatility of the underlying market variable(s) and the maturity. Long-dated products – such as many OTC derivatives – are likely to have significant initial margins. Likewise, more volatile asset classes should have higher associated initial margins.
- *Dependency*. A typical portfolio may consist of a variety of different trades with sensitivity to different market variables ('risk factors'), potentially in different asset classes. It is therefore important to understand the offsetting nature of such trades. If dependency between the price moves of different trades is small (or even negative), then clearly the overall portfolio is less risky, and the benefit of this is that less margin needs to be posted. However, the dependencies within and between asset classes are notoriously difficult to quantify and can change significantly through time.
- *Tail risk*. Whilst volatility typically measures continuous price variability, some products (e.g. credit derivatives) can suffer from tail risk due to jumps or gaps in the underlying market variables. Likewise, it is possible for dependency between risk factors to be non-linear and, therefore, hard to predict. For example, risk factors may show particularly high dependence in a crisis period compared to their normal relationship.

Some of the above may not raise obvious concerns over initial margin quantification since, at a confidence level of 99%, there are clearly scenarios where the initial margin is – by design – insufficient. In these relatively extreme cases, market participants have loss absorbency in the form of some sort of capital that may be utilised. Hence, whilst initial margin is intended to cover a fairly bad scenario, it may not capture some of the more extreme behaviour, such as very heavy-tailed distributions or strong dependencies. Such effects, where relevant, may be better captured by default fund contributions at CCPs or capital requirements by banks. Correspondingly, such amounts are driven by more qualitative approaches, such as stress testing and standardised models.

Margin methodologies do make use of supplementary and more qualitative approaches that may increase initial margin in certain cases. For example, they may penalise large portfolios that would be more difficult to manage in a default scenario (see Section 9.3.6).

Regulation also puts restrictions on initial margin methodologies that can be seen to mitigate some of the inherent problems that the above considerations imply in terms of model risk. Two examples of this are the requirement to use 'stressed data' as inputs to the margin methodology and the inability to gain benefit from the offsets between different asset classes (cross-margining, Section 9.1.6).

The requirement to use stressed data for bilateral trades is stated clearly in BCBS-IOSCO (2015) as requiring initial margin to be based on 'historical data that incorporates a period of significant financial stress'. Likewise, guidelines for CCPs also refer repeatedly to 'stressed market conditions' (CPSS-IOSCO 2012). By using an inherently stressed environment, initial margin will, to some extent, capture the impact discussed in Section 9.1.2 (e.g. a current definition of a stressful period may include the period immediately after the default of Lehman Brothers in 2008).

9.1.4   Haircuts

Whereas variation margins are generally cash only, both bilateral markets and CCPs allow initial margins to be posted in other securities. This raises the issue of whether the value of the initial margin assets held would decline during the close-out period. In general, this can be mitigated in two ways:

- *Eligible securities.* Securities eligible for initial margin will be restricted to those without any significant credit or liquidity risks that could cause extreme adverse price moves. Moreover, securities that might be adversely correlated to the credit quality of a clearing member would not be accepted.
- *Haircuts.* Given the above, a margin recipient should be concerned only with the market risk, which can be mitigated by the appropriate choice of haircut. Indeed, even assets such as gold and equity indices are potentially acceptable, as they have large market risks that can be mitigated by accordingly large haircuts and probably do not suffer from other sources of adverse price moves, such as liquidity.

Haircuts, as discussed previously, are generally defined to cover the majority of detrimental price moves over a representative liquidation period (e.g. a two-day price movement and a 99% confidence level). Note that the assumed period may be shorter than for initial margin calculations (MPoR) because selling margin securities is not dependent on the successful bilateral close-out or completion of a CCP auction or other default management functions. Haircuts will also be applied to cash margin with similar assumptions about the liquidation period and confidence level, and can be relatively significant.[7]

9.1.5   Linkage to Credit Quality

Initial margin is generally considered to be linked wholly to market risk and is therefore not dependent on the probability of default of the party in question. This is counterintuitive since parties with stronger credit quality often naturally expect to receive more

---

[7] For example, with the two-day time horizon and 99% confidence level and assuming a foreign exchange volatility of 15%, a haircut would be: $\Phi^{-1}(0.99) \times \sqrt{2/252} \times 15\% = 3.1\%$ (assuming 252 business days in a year).

favourable trading conditions. This also implies – to some extent – a homogeneity of parties in the market and otherwise implies that weaker ones will gain at the expense of stronger ones. Indeed, Pirrong (1998) argues that the delay in adopting central clearing on certain exchanges was related to stronger credit quality members not wishing to subsidise weaker ones.

Another reason to decouple initial margin from credit quality – in particular, credit ratings – is to avoid some of the 'cliff-edge' effects seen when a party becomes financially distressed. Such distress inevitably leads to credit rating downgrades, which in turn may trigger the requirement to post more margin at the worst possible time, and this was illustrated clearly in the global financial crisis (see Section 2.4.4). This was also relevant in the default of MF Global in 2011. MF Global was a member of several CCPs and faced increased margin requirements as its rating was downgraded. In line with these potential issues, banks now experience costs associated with credit rating triggers under the liquidity coverage ratio (LCR), as discussed in Section 4.3.3.

In the bilateral margin requirements (BCBS-IOSCO 2015), no mention is made of the credit quality of either party and, therefore, initial margin calculations are credit-quality independent. Of course, it could be argued that parties may choose not to trade with bilateral counterparties with low credit quality.

The regulatory requirements and treatment of credit quality by CCPs are more complicated. Generally, CCPs have moved away from linking initial margin to credit ratings issued by nationally-recognised statistical rating organisations (NRSROs).[8] Previous to this, SwapClear had required that initial margin for clearing members rated A–, BBB+ and BBB be multiplied by 1.1, 2.0, and 2.5 respectively (and below BBB the clearing member was required to leave).[9] Indeed, regulation explicitly forbids CCPs from linking margin to external credit ratings as required by the Dodd–Frank Wall Street Reform and Consumer Protection Act, and instead requires them to use 'other appropriate standards of credit-worthiness'.[10] CCPs do not, therefore, increase initial margin if a clearing member is downgraded.[11]

CCPs do, however, use their own internal rating systems to determine credit quality based on a number of factors, including CDS spreads, asset quality, and capital adequacy. If a clearing member's credit quality is determined by the CCP to have deteriorated to a level that does not support the volume of risk it has cleared, then it may be subject to margin multipliers and/or limitations to new business. The CCP may also assign credit limits based on its internal ratings in order to prevent counterparts with lower credit quality from building up excessive exposure.[12] CCPs may also limit membership to supervised firms.

Another aspect related to this is the linkage of haircuts to credit quality. This was illustrated quite clearly by the MF Global default. MF Global held $6.4bn of European

---

[8] There are currently 10 NRSROs, with the most significant (the 'big three') being Standard & Poor's, Moody's and Fitch Group.

[9] Cameron, M. (2012). SwapClear changes expulsion rules. *Risk* (4 May). www.risk.net.

[10] Commodity Futures Trading Commission Office of Public Affairs. Credit Ratings Q & A. www.cftc.gov. Note that this regulation applies to both clearing members or futures commission merchants (FCMs) and designated clearing organisations (CCPs).

[11] ICE Clear Europe (2018). Risk Management: Frequently Asked Questions v.6.0 (24 April).

[12] Eurex (2016). Spotlight on: CCP Risk Management (18 July). www.eurexclearing.com.

sovereign debt (which was financed through repo trades). When, due to the declining credit risk of the issuers, haircuts on these assets were increased, this created a negative asset shock that helped to catalyse the decline of MF Global. Whilst CCPs should ideally increase haircuts to mitigate declining credit risk in such situations,[13] there is a clear danger that this increases systemic risk, especially when done suddenly. Even if the CCP is better off after such a move (which is debatable, since it may push the clearing member into default), it is unlikely that the market as a whole would benefit. Such effects are less likely in bilateral markets, as a receiver of margin would typically not be able to change contractual haircuts without agreement from a counterparty.

Finally, it is worth noting that the WWR ideas in Section 9.1.2 actually suggest a completely opposite idea, in that higher (not lower) credit quality parties should be charged more initial margin, since their default would be a more unexpected event and therefore may create more turbulent market conditions and be more difficult to manage. Mathematical models for WWR typically predict this behaviour (Section 17.6). This is also true since parties with strong credit ratings are also more likely to be large and systemically-important institutions.

9.1.6   Cross-margining

Cross-margining is a general term that refers to margin calculations made on a portfolio rather than on a product-by-product basis. The advantage of this is that margins will be more competitive as they will benefit from reductions due to offsetting positions. Gemmill (1994) illustrates the diversification offered to CCPs from clearing several markets that are not highly correlated. Cross-margining offers the following inter-related benefits:

- *Lower margin costs.* Lower initial margins due to the diversification benefit between positions.
- *More efficient auctions.* In the event of a default scenario, all cross-margined positions could be liquidated together as an offsetting or hedged portfolio. This may minimise CCP auction or bilateral close-out costs and reduce the systemic impact of the default.
- *Reduced legal and operational risk.* Since initial margin represents funds not actually owed to counterparties, this also provides a reduction of exposure to losing margins in the event of non-segregation, fraud, or operational problems.

Firms and their clients will be actively looking to receive the benefits of such favourable dependencies in the form of lower initial margins. In particular, some sophisticated financial institutions use a variety of different transactions and often execute combinations of positions that are partially hedged. In such situations, the cross-margining benefits would be expected to be particularly significant.

There are a number of different ways in which cross-margining could be applied – by a CCP or in bilateral markets – that increase in complexity:

- within a given product type (e.g. different currencies of interest rate swaps);
- between products within a given asset class (e.g. fixed to floating interest rate swaps and basis swaps, or index and single-name CDSs);

---

[13] Meakin, L. (2012). LCH Raises Margin Costs for Trading Spanish Government Bonds. *Bloomberg* (20 June). www.bloomberg.com

- between centrally-cleared exchange-traded and OTC products (e.g. interest rate futures and interest rate swaps);
- between products in different asset classes (e.g. interest rate swaps and CDSs); and
- between different CCPs.

Some of the above are more challenging – for example, due to the need to develop sophisticated models to represent the dependencies in a portfolio, for operational reasons (e.g. futures versus OTC products), or due to jurisdiction differences (between CCPs in different regions). However, particularly as OTC clearing and bilateral margining become more widespread, the possibility of achieving lower margins through cross-margining will become increasingly important for market participants.

There is also some evidence that clearing multiple asset classes may be useful in default management. For example, Lehman Brothers traded a combination of interest rate, equity, agriculture, energy, and foreign exchange (FX) positions on the Chicago Mercantile Exchange (CME), and whilst they suffered losses on two out of five of these asset classes, this was covered by excess margin from the other three (Pirrong 2013), meaning that the *overall* initial margin was sufficient. LCH.Clearnet's diversified spread of business was a help in the same default, with the CEO stating, 'Without this degree of diversification it is doubtful whether we would have had the time to identify and transfer the client positions. Instead we would have had no option but to close-out all the positions in the house account, leaving many clients unhedged.'[14]

Historically, CCPs have tended to avoid extending cross-margining excessively. This is not surprising, as in the presence of cross-margining, initial margin methodologies will have to be more complex and represent dependencies and basis positions, which would not be important for silo-based portfolio calculations. However, as the use of initial margin increases (especially in the OTC derivatives space), it would be expected that cross-margining may increase as CCPs expand and cover more product types.

Probably the most difficult aspect in cross-margining is understanding and quantifying financial risk and the dependency between different financial variables. It is well known that historically-estimated correlations may not be a good representation of future behaviour, especially in a more volatile market environment. In a crisis, correlations have a tendency to become very large on an absolute basis. It is also important to represent that, unlike volatility, it is not immediately obvious how to stress a correlation value, as the underlying sensitivity of a portfolio may be positive or negative and may not even be monotonic. Therefore, whilst multidimensional modelling of risk factors can lead to increased benefits from margin offsets, it also increases the underlying model risk.

One example of the competitive benefit of cross-margining has been between exchange-traded (e.g. futures) and OTC products (e.g. swaps). For example, the CME has offered cross-margining benefits between Eurodollar and Treasury futures contracts and OTC interest rate products since 2012.[15]

---

[14] De Teran, N. (2008). How LCH.Clearnet got clear of Lehman. *Wall Street Journal* (14 October). www.wsj.com.

[15] CME Group (2016). Invoice Swap Spreads and Portfolio Margining Benefits. www.cmegroup.com.

However, such a coming together is not completely trivial.[16] Firstly, initial margin methodologies have historically differed for futures and OTC products (see discussion in Sections 9.2 and 9.3). Secondly, the assumed MPoR for more liquid futures products is shorter (typically one or two days) than their OTC counterparts (typically five or more days). Thirdly, margin account structures for these products may differ. A final potential problem could be regulatory driven – for example, in the US, where futures products are regulated by the Securities and Exchange Commission (SEC) and OTC products by the CFTC.

Regulation does restrict the extent of cross-margining that can be done, due to the view that modelling such dependencies is notoriously difficult. For bilateral transactions, BCBS-IOSCO (2015) states that:

> At the same time, a distinction must be made between offsetting risks that can be reliably quantified and those that are more difficult to quantify. In particular, inter-relationships between derivatives in distinct asset classes, such as equities and commodities, are difficult to model and validate. Moreover, this type of relationship is prone to instability and may be more likely to break down in a period of financial stress.

Requirements for CCPs are not prescriptive but do state that initial margin offsets can only be recognised between products that are 'significantly and reliably correlated' (CPSS-IOSCO 2004) with each other.

The rules for bilaterally-cleared transactions are clearer by defining that initial margin must be additive across asset classes, which are defined as currency/rates, equity, credit, and commodities (BCBS-IOSCO 2015). There can, therefore, be no cross-margining benefit between these asset classes, but the benefit can be taken within each one. This is also the approach of CCPs generally, where cross-margining occurs within asset classes (e.g. interest rate swaps and swaptions),[17] but not across different ones. This also explains why CCPs have tended to specialise and potentially dominate individual asset classes.

9.2   INITIAL MARGIN APPROACHES

9.2.1   Simple Approaches

In the early days of derivatives trading, initial margin was only used on exchanges, and the amounts were typically based on simple approaches. For example, consider a single equity position: the key inputs to determining initial margin could be considered to be the volatility (σ), the time period in question (MPoR), and the confidence level required (α). Under normal distribution assumptions, this would lead to the simple formula and example given below, where the initial margin is calculated to be 2.4% of the size of the position.

---

[16] Osborn, T. (2013). Cross-margining at CME slowed by practical challenges. *Risk* (1 August). www.risk.net.

[17] See Footnote 15.

Simple initial margin (IM) formula

$$IM = \sigma \times \sqrt{\text{MPoR}} \times \alpha$$

For example, consider:

σ (per annum) = 20%, MPoR = 1 business day, and α = 2.33 (this represents the 99% confidence level for a normal distribution).

Assuming 252 business days in a year, this would give:

$$IM = 0.2 \times \sqrt{\frac{1}{252}} \times 2.33 = 2.9\%$$

The first obvious criticism of the above approach is that it makes an assumption about the underlying risk factor distribution (e.g. normal) and therefore ignores aspects such as fat-tailed behaviour. The second problem is that it needs to be extended to other dimensions (so as to appreciate portfolio effects). This would be possible by introducing correlations between risk factors as well as their volatilities, although this would then have the problems associated with modelling dependencies. Such problems are particularly acute for balanced portfolios where the risk of positions cancels, as opposed to a directional portfolio where the risks are – more or less – additive.

Probably the biggest issue with approaches built on the above idea is that, for large portfolios, it is not clear whether the sensitivity to a given risk factor overall will be positive or negative, since there may be some positions that make money from an increase in the risk factor, whilst others lose money. Furthermore, such sensitivities can be non-linear, especially when more complex products – such as options – are included. Hence, whilst the example above essentially generates only a single scenario (since it is obvious that a long equity position is sensitive to a downward move in stock prices and vice versa), a portfolio initial margin calculation needs to consider multiple scenarios.

9.2.2   SPAN®

For exchange-traded clearing, in 1988 the CME developed a method known as Standard Portfolio Analysis of Risk (SPAN) to assess risk effectively on an overall portfolio basis.[18] SPAN was licenced by the CME, and by 2008 was being used by more than 50 exchanges and CCPs globally. Similar approaches such as the Theoretical Intermarket Margin System (TIMS) or the System for Theoretical Analysis and Numerical Simulations (STANS) have also been developed.[19]

The introduction of SPAN was revolutionary at the time, since it allowed margins for futures and options to be calculated based on the overall portfolio risk. A typical example would be the margining of a portfolio containing offsetting exposure to different equity indices (e.g. S&P 500 and Nasdaq), where the high correlation would create beneficial margin reduction.

---

[18] CME Group (2010). SPAN - Standard Portfolio Analysis of Risk. www.cmegroup.com.
[19] For more information, see www.theocc.com.

SPAN groups together financial instruments with the same underlying for analysis (e.g. futures and options on an equity index). SPAN works by evolving individual risk factors (e.g. spot price, volatility) combinatorially based on movements in either direction. Products with the same underlying will share risk factors. A series of shifts are applied to each risk factor, which is intended to be representative of one- or two-day moves in the underlying variables. Some more extreme shifts may also be applied (which may be particularly relevant – for example, for an out-of-the-money position).[20] Most SPAN exchanges and clearing organisations use 16 scenarios ('risk arrays'). The portfolio is then revalued under the different moves, and the worst scenario is normally used to define the initial margin.

The scenarios used by SPAN consider the following:

- variation of underlying price;
- variation of underlying volatility; and
- impact of time on the option price.

An example of SPAN shifts applied to an option position is shown in Figure 9.1.

An example of a SPAN calculation is shown in Table 9.1. This corresponds to a combined position in an S&P futures contract (long) and an S&P call option (short). The

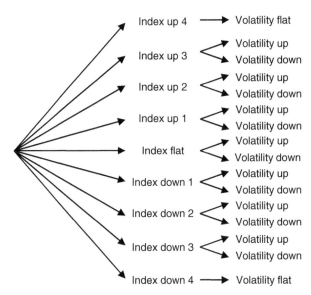

Figure 9.1 Illustration of risk factor shifts applied for determining the initial margin of an option position using SPAN. The underlying index is shifted up and down by four different amounts and single up/down volatility shifts are applied to each (note the fourth index shift is an extreme scenario intended for deep out-of-the-money options).

---

[20] Short option positions that are highly out-of-the-money near expiration represent a problem in the event that the underlying moves sharply, whereupon these positions could then be in-the-money. SPAN includes a large upwards and downwards move to consider this risk, but only a fraction of the total loss calculated is considered.

Table 9.1 Example of a SPAN calculation. The price scan range is 22,500 and the volatility scan range is 7%.[21]

Scenario	S&P move	Volatility move	Future	Option	Portfolio
1	Unchanged	Up	0	1,807	1,807
2	Unchanged	Down	0	−1,838	−1,838
3	Up 33%	Up	−7,499	7,899	400
4	Up 33%	Down	−7,499	5,061	−2,438
5	Down 33%	Up	7,499	−3,836	3,663
6	Down 33%	Down	7,499	−8,260	−761
7	Up 67%	Up	−15,001	14,360	−641
8	Up 67%	Down	−15,001	12,253	−2,748
9	Down 67%	Up	15,001	−8,949	6,052
10	Down 67%	Down	15,001	−13,980	1,021
11	Up 100%	Up	−22,500	21,107	−1,393
12	Up 100%	Down	−22,500	19,604	−2,896
13	Down 100%	Up	22,500	−13,455	9,045
14	Down 100%	Down	22,500	−18,768	3,732
15	Up 300%	Unchanged	−22,275	21,288	−987
16	Down 300%	Unchanged	22,275	−9,160	13,115

underlying movements are represented with respect to a 'price scan range' and 'volatility scan range', which are the maximum movements reasonably likely to occur over the time in question (one or two days). The change in value for the future, option, and combined (portfolio) positions are shown. Note that for the futures contract, the valuation is trivial and objective, whilst for the option position, a subjective valuation model is required.

By plotting the movements from the above table, it is possible to understand the risk of the combined position (Figure 9.2). The (long) call option makes losses when the underlying index goes down and also when volatility goes down.[22] The (short) index position gains in value when the index falls, offsetting losses on the option position.

Future and option positions' gains or losses can be combined to give the total portfolio position, shown for down and up volatility scenarios in Figure 9.3. Note that the worst-case scenario for the CME (largest gain)[23] in both volatility scenarios is the maximum down move in the S&P index, where the gains on the index position are not fully offset by the losses on the option. The volatility up scenario is worse from the CME's point of view, since the option time value is lower.

In the above example, the initial margin would be 13,115 (Table 9.1), which is the gain in Scenario 16, which is the extreme down move of 300% of the price scan range (not shown in Figure 9.3). Note that SPAN only applies a 33% weight to this scenario.

SPAN can potentially identify the risk in more subtle scenarios. For example, suppose a client clears a position which is long an index but with downside risk hedged by buying an

---

[21] See Footnote 18.

[22] Note that this is from CME's point of view, so it is the reverse of the position from the clearer's point of view.

[23] This could require the clearer to post more variation margin, which they would be expected to fail to do in the event of default.

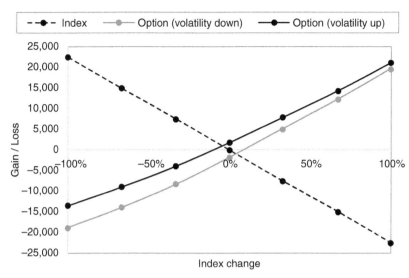

Figure 9.2 Variation for S&P future and option contracts according to the data in Table 9.1 (ignoring the extreme shifts). Note that the futures contract has no sensitivity to volatility.

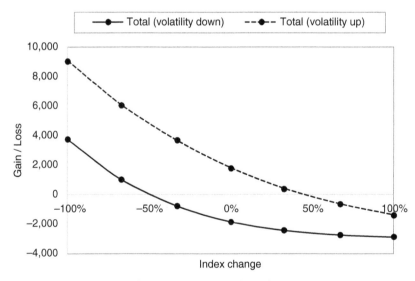

Figure 9.3 A combined move of total portfolio position in down and up volatility scenarios according to the data in Table 9.1 (ignoring the extreme shifts).

out-of-the-money put option. Figure 9.4 shows the position, from the CCP point of view. The worst scenario is not a maximum downwards move on the index, where the option is strongly mitigating client losses, but rather a more moderate move, where the option has a more limited effect. This shows that SPAN can potentially identify the worst scenario in a balanced position as not necessarily being the largest move in the underlying variable(s). However, note that because of the limited number of scenarios and the relatively large required scanning range, SPAN does not capture this point accurately.

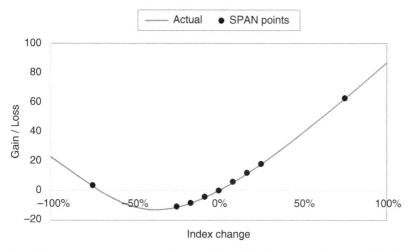

Figure 9.4   Gains and losses for a portfolio consisting of a short equity index position hedged by a long put option and SPAN points.

The strong standardisation of exchange-traded transactions (e.g. where the number of expiration dates or strikes for a given product is small) supports a relatively simple method such as SPAN. SPAN is quite well suited to risk assessment on simple portfolios such as futures and options, which are generally of low dimensionality (the above example needs only really to consider two dimensions: index level and implied volatility). Whilst SPAN-type methods work well and are tractable for simple portfolios, they have drawbacks. Most notably, they do not scale well to a large number of dimensions (as the number of combinations of moves grows exponentially).

OTC derivatives portfolios are typically of high dimensionality, with many more risk factors than for exchange-traded markets. For example, even a single interest rate swap is sensitive to the full term structure of interest rate moves, and cannot be represented as a single parallel shift in rates, since this implies unrealistically that rates for different tenors (maturity dates) are perfectly correlated. SPAN also makes relatively simplistic assumptions on implied volatility changes, normally expressed as a single volatility shift, which will not capture volatility risk in portfolios sensitive to more subtle changes in the volatility surface. SPAN approaches give results which are relatively static through time and also do not clearly attach an underlying probability to the scenario defining the initial margin, and are therefore not especially risk sensitive. Finally, the up and down moves that define the worst move of a given market variable are somewhat subjective.

For the above reasons, OTC derivatives CCPs have been moving towards more value-at-risk-like methods for initial margin calculation, as discussed below. Bilateral margining has adopted a similar, although simpler, method.

9.2.3   Value-at-risk and Expected Shortfall

As discussed in Section 2.6.1, value-at-risk (VAR) is a key approach for quantifying financial market risk that has been developed by large banks over the last two decades. A VAR number has a simple and intuitive explanation as to the worst loss over a target horizon (e.g. five days) to a certain specified confidence level (e.g. 99%). Given this definition, VAR has a natural application for defining initial margin requirements for given MPoRs and confidence levels.

One problem with VAR is that it is not a *coherent* risk measure (Artzner et al. 1999), which means that in certain (possibly rare) situations, it can exhibit non-intuitive properties. The most obvious of these is that VAR may not behave in a sub-additive fashion. Sub-additivity requires a combination of two portfolios to have no more risk than the sum of their individual risks (due to diversification). This could translate into the requirement that the initial margin when clearing a large portfolio through a single CCP would be no greater than the total initial margin when clearing the same portfolio as sub-portfolios through different CCPs.[24] Such properties cannot be guaranteed when using VAR as a risk measure.

Expected shortfall (ES) is the average loss equal to or above the level defined by VAR, and it does not suffer from the above problems. An example of the sub-additive behaviour of VAR and ES is shown in Table 9.2. Here, the 90% VAR[25] is defined by the ninth highest loss, which is higher in the combined portfolio (100) than in the sum of the two individual portfolios (80). ES is an average of the highest two values and does not exhibit this problem.

Note that VAR and ES allow the precise scenario(s) upon which the initial margin is based to be identified and that these are different for each portfolio. This is rather like the SPAN approach described in Section 9.2.2. However, unlike SPAN, VAR and ES are defined to a known statistical confidence level, as opposed to simply being the worst of a small number of scenarios. Since VAR and ES are general definitions, they can be used to define the initial margin for any portfolio.

Table 9.2   Example showing the sub-additivity properties of VAR and ES metrics. The scenarios corresponding to the VAR and ES are shown in bold. Note that all values represent losses.

	Portfolio 1	Portfolio 2	Total
Scenario 1	10	30	40
Scenario 2	30	**40**	70
Scenario 3	**40**	30	70
Scenario 4	10	**90**	**100**
Scenario 5	**80**	30	**110**
Scenario 6	35	5	40
Scenario 7	20	25	45
Scenario 8	15	35	50
Scenario 9	20	25	45
Scenario 10	10	30	40
VAR (90%)	40	40	100
ES (90%)	60	65	105

---

[24] Assuming no concentration multipliers and that the CCPs use the same initial margin approach.

[25] A low confidence level is required due to the small number of scenarios shown.

VAR models can be 'backtested' as a means to check their predictive performance empirically. Backtesting involves performing an *ex post* comparison of actual outcomes with those predicted by the model. VAR lends itself well to backtesting since, for example, a 99% number should be exceeded once every 100 observations.

Given the drawbacks of SPAN for more complex and potentially multidimensional derivatives portfolios and the general usage of VAR models for market risk applications, it is not surprising that CCPs have moved towards more risk-sensitive VAR-type approaches for initial margin calculations for OTC products. Such approaches are suited to, for example, high-dimensionality multicurrency swap portfolios.

However, VAR and ES are merely statistical measures. There is still the much bigger question of how to define them for a given portfolio. Following an approach used by banks for many years for the quantification of market risk, CCPs have generally used 'historical simulation' approaches for this. As described in Section 2.6.1, historical simulation essentially simulates how a given portfolio would have performed over a given period in history and uses the worst losses to define the VAR or ES. This has the advantage of being able to use many scenarios without the need to decide specifically on the underlying modelling of each risk factor. Historical simulation has now become a fairly standard approach for the initial margin methodologies for centrally-cleared OTC derivatives.

In the bilateral markets, historical simulation has been considered too complex an approach, since both parties need to agree on the initial margin amounts. Hence, bilateral markets are adopting the International Swaps and Derivatives Association (ISDA) Standard Initial Margin Model (SIMM^{TM}), which can be seen as a more simple and tractable version of historical simulation. Both the historical simulation and SIMM approaches will be discussed below.

9.3   HISTORICAL SIMULATION

9.3.1   Overview

The most common implementation of VAR and ES approaches is using historical simulation. This approach takes a period (usually several years) of historical data containing risk-factor behaviour across the entire portfolio in question. It then resimulates over many periods how the current portfolio would behave when subjected to the same historical evolution. For example, if four years of data were used, then it would be possible to compute around 1,000 different scenarios of daily movements for the portfolio. The 99% VAR would then be estimated as the 990th worst loss (so that 10 – or 1% – of the losses are higher).

Historical simulation can simulate, self-consistently, potential moves in all relevant risk factors by following a simple rule:

ΔRF^i(simulation i)

= previous change in risk factor over same period (at time indexed by i) in the past.

Following any simulation of risk factors, the portfolio can be valued using these new risk factor values, and the resulting change in portfolio value forms a distribution. From this distribution, a metric such as VAR or ES can be calculated. A historical simulation approach can, therefore, be summarised as follows:

1. select a set of risk-factor changes that collectively drives the value of the underlying portfolio (e.g. equity, commodity prices, interest rates, FX rates, bond yields, and implied volatilities) observed over a given historical period(s);
2. revalue the portfolio multiple times, assuming that each of the risk-factor changes happened again; and
3. calculate the statistical quantity required from the distribution of changes in portfolio value.

Inevitably, historical simulation relies on a fundamental assumption that the past is a good guide to the future. Whilst this might be criticised, it is an almost inevitable requirement for any model for assessing financial risk. There are also a number of other choices and problems when implementing historical simulation:

- *Look-back period.* The choice of how long to make the data window is subjective. A long window or 'look-back period' (e.g. 10 years) will provide more data points but *might* contain old and irrelevant data. A short window may contain more recent, relevant data but will contain fewer points overall and be subject to noise, and may cause procyclicality (Section 9.3.5). It is not necessary to use a single continuous period, which is often the case when stressed periods are included.
- *Scaling.* Since risk factors will be at a different level to where they were in the past, there is a choice to be made about how to scale past change to produce potential future changes. This inevitably requires an implicit assumption about how the underlying risk factor behaves.
- *Autocorrelation.* This refers to the fact that data over sequential time horizons may be quite dependent (such as during quiet or volatile periods). For estimating the initial margin over a period such as five days, there may not be enough data to use non-overlapping returns. Using overlapping returns presents further complications. Alternatively, the initial margin over one day could be scaled using the 'square root of time' rule or more sophisticated approaches (Danielsson and Zigrand 2003).

The above points will be analysed in more detail in the next sections.

> **Spreadsheet 9.1 Initial margin calculation of an interest rate swap using historical simulation.**

9.3.2 Look-back Period

The look-back period refers to the historical range of data used. Choosing the look-back period is quite subtle: a very long period may use old and meaningless data, whereas a short period may lead to unstable results. Banks have typically used between one and three years for the purposes of VAR models for capital calculations, and not usually more than five years. Typically, shorter look-back periods are more problematic as very volatile periods (such as the period in the aftermath of the Lehman default) drop out of the data set.

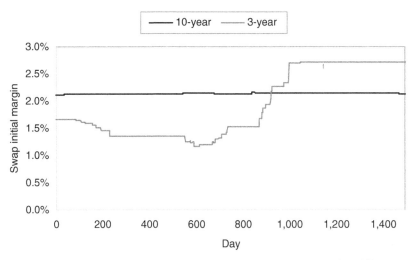

Figure 9.5 Evolution of initial margin for an interest rate swap calculated with different look-back periods.

Figure 9.5 shows the calculation of the initial margin for a single five-year interest rate swap and its evolution through time (that is to say, the initial margin is calculated repeatedly each day, as would be the case in practice) for 3- and 10-year look-back periods. Whilst the average initial margin is the same in both cases, the shorter look-back period leads to much more instability. This instability is caused because, when large moves in the risk factor drop out of the back of the look-back window ('ghost effects'), the initial margin falls. Correspondingly, as recent large risk-factor moves enter into the look-back period, the initial margin can increase rapidly. With the long look-back period, the impact of observations moving in and out of the data is damped by the much larger amount of data present (approximately 2,500 days compared to 750).

Clearly there are advantages and disadvantages to the choice of longer or shorter look-back periods: shorter may be overreactive, whereas longer may not be reactive enough. Rather than choosing a fixed look-back period where all events have recent weights, Boudoukh et al. (1998) proposed to assign more probability to recent events than those in the more distant past. This is related to volatility scaling methods and also the discussion on procyclicality in Section 9.3.5.

9.3.3   Relative and Absolute Returns

Being more explicit about the implementation of historical simulation, the simulation of risk factors can be written as:

$$x_{t+1}^s = x_t \times \frac{x_{s+1}}{x_s}$$

where x_t is the current value of the risk factor, x_{t+1}^s is its simulated value in scenario s, and x_{s+1} and x_s are the value of this risk factor at the start and end of the same time period in the past. Implicit in the above equation is the assumption that it is the relative (percentage) changes in the risk factor that are important. This is consistent with a distribution assumption such as lognormal, where the risk factor cannot change sign, and up moves (in absolute terms) can be larger than down moves. This approach is generally referred to as 'relative returns'.

Alternatively, one could consider 'absolute returns' which would correspond to the following equation:

$$x^s_{t+1} = x_t + (x_{s+1} - x_s).$$

Absolute returns are consistent with a symmetric distribution (such as a normal distribution) and do allow the risk factor to change sign.

Some risk factors are more suited to relative returns since they are naturally bounded between zero and infinity (e.g. an FX rate or a credit spread). Others may be more suited to absolute returns (e.g. interest rates, which have been seen to be negative in some cases in recent years). Other assumptions could also be used.

Relative returns have traditionally been used in historical VAR approaches. This means that a move in interest rates from 3.0% to 3.6% is interpreted as a 20.0% increase. In a low interest rate environment, where rates are 1.0%, this would translate into quite a small upwards move to only 1.2%. If instead the absolute rate change were used, then the equivalent move would be to 1.6%. This is illustrated in Table 9.3, showing two different scenarios. It is also worth emphasising that absolute returns may produce negative interest rates (which may be unrealistically large), whilst relative returns cannot (unless interest rates themselves become negative).

Whether absolute or relative scenarios are most appropriate depends on the current rates regime. Absolute moves are more conservative in a falling interest rate environment, as illustrated in Figure 9.6. On the other hand, the reverse will be true during a period of rising rates. This is a well-known problem in the area of interest rate models, where behaviour can move between normal (absolute shifts) and lognormal (relative shifts).

Figure 9.7 shows a calculation of the initial margin for a single five-year interest rate swap and its evolution through time when using relative and absolute returns. In this case, absolute returns lead to higher initial margin since the period in question is one where interest rates are generally falling. This can be seen to reverse slightly towards the end of the calculation range. Note also that absolute returns are inherently more stable since they apply the same risk factor change regardless of the current level of the risk factor. This can also be seen from Figure 9.7, where the increase in the initial margin after day 2,000 for relative returns occurs mainly due to an increase in the level of interest rates (as opposed to a change in the data being used).

Table 9.3 Comparison of historical simulation using absolute and relative returns.

	Historical data			Historical simulation	
	Initial rate	Final rate	Change	Initial	Simulated
Absolute	3.0%	3.6%	0.6%	1.0%	1.6%
Relative	3.0%	3.6%	20.0%	1.0%	1.2%
Absolute	4.0%	3.2%	−0.8%	1.0%	0.2%
Relative	4.0%	3.2%	−20.0%	1.0%	0.8%

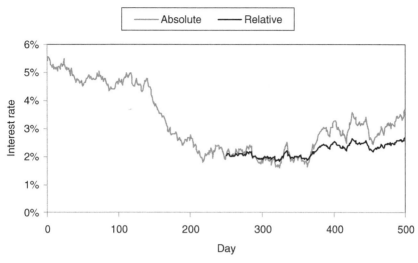

Figure 9.6 Illustration of historical simulation for an interest rate process using absolute and relative scenarios. The simulation begins at the 250-day point.

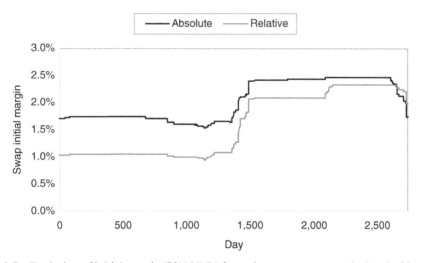

Figure 9.7 Evolution of initial margin (99% VAR) for an interest rate swap calculated with relative and absolute returns.

9.3.4 Volatility Scaling

It is well known that financial processes are not well described by a process with constant volatility. A standard historical simulation model associated with equal weights over a look-back period implicitly assumes constant volatility of the underlying risk factors. It will also be unable to produce an initial margin that is higher than that which corresponds to the worst historical move it has ever 'seen'.

Different approaches to the treatment of volatility emerged in the early days of VAR models, with the exponentially-weighted moving average (EWMA) estimation proposed in RiskMetrics (Zangari 1994; J.P. Morgan 1996). This applies a non-uniform weighting to time-series data so that a lot of data can be used, but recent data is weighted more heavily. As the name suggests, weights are based upon an exponential function, which means that large risk-factor returns will drop out of a data set gradually. It is necessary to choose the value for the 'decay factor' (RiskMetrics set it to 0.94), which defines how quickly the weight of past data decreases.

More generally, 'volatility scaling' is an approach that seeks to use an estimate of the current level of volatility to scale returns with respect to the current volatility estimate at the time they occurred. In other words, it scales the generation of possible future returns (Section 9.3.3) by a ratio of σ_T / σ_t, where σ_T is the current estimate of volatility and σ_t is the past estimate. This approach implies that current market conditions have some information: for example, if current volatility is higher than usual, then this may be indicative of market moves being larger than usual.

In general, volatility-scaled historical simulation has better backtesting properties due to it anticipating a potential increase in volatility. Accordingly, it can also produce low estimates for initial margin where there has been a period of low volatility. The result is that there is increased variability of the initial margin estimator or procyclicality (discussed in Section 9.3.5).

9.3.5   Procyclicality

Whilst initial margin models that are 'targeted' (towards a given portfolio) and dynamic (in terms of reacting to market conditions) are clearly desirable, this also raises the issue of procyclicality. CPSS-IOSCO (2014) recommends that financial market infrastructures (FMIs) such as CCPs adopt stable and conservative margin requirements to prevent procyclicality.

In times of higher market volatility, price changes are larger, so the minimum level of initial margin required to cover potential price changes must also be higher. Risk-sensitive initial margins will tend to be lower in quiet times and higher in turbulent markets. This dynamic can have a destabilising effect since it encourages high leverage in bullish market environments, leading to sudden shocks where a sharp increase in volatility can lead to additional initial margin being required from market participants. However, at this point, firms may be under stress in general and will, therefore, be required to post additional margin precisely when it becomes most difficult to raise cash or other liquid assets. Risk-sensitive margin requirements are therefore procyclical as they may amplify shocks. Whilst initial margin reduces counterparty credit risk, the procyclicality of initial margin provides a channel for the spread of contagion.

Heller and Vause (2012) estimate that without any adjustment for procyclicality, initial margins for interest rate swaps could increase by around a factor of two between a low- and high-volatility regime, and CDSs could show an impact of approximately an order of magnitude.

An alternative to the above is to try and set initial margin at higher 'through-the-cycle' levels, which are therefore less sensitive to current conditions. However, it is clearly not desirable for these levels to be excessively high or to have initial margin levels that are completely unreactive to market conditions.

This difficult balance is well articulated in the following text (ESMA 2018), which suggests the need for a balance between promoting risk sensitivity and preventing excessive procyclicality:

> It is important to recognise that it is not the intention of the regulation to prevent CCPs from revising their margins to address changes in volatility. Instead, the regulation propagates the notion that CCPs should prevent big-stepped, unanticipated calls on clearing members during periods of extreme stress. The following guidelines should therefore be read in this context.

There are a number of choices that can influence initial margin procyclicality:

- *Historical time series*. The choice of the look-back period is a key input. If the period is short, then it may arguably contain the most relevant recent data, but it will also lead to margins moving rapidly through time, as turbulent days move in and out of the data set (ghost observations) and cause rapid oscillations (see procyclical example in Figure 9.9). Using a long history will tend to smooth out such effects, as given periods will have less overall impact on the measure calculated (similar to the normal result in Figure 9.9).
- *Volatility scaling*. Certain VAR methods use various ways to capture volatility clustering in financial data. A simple example is to use EWMA historical data,[26] which means that the data points have less impact the further away they occur. Another common approach is known as filtered historical simulation (FHS). Whilst these approaches arguably all get closer to the realities of financial markets (e.g. that there are long periods of small market moves followed by short periods of strong moves), they potentially lead to greater procyclicality and would cause initial margins to increase quickly at the start of a crisis but then drop quickly as the crisis is averted.
- *Autocorrelation*. VAR approaches sometimes use overlapping returns to maximise the number of individual data points. This creates problems since overlapping data will, by definition, show dependencies, and a single extreme event will show up in several overlapping periods and have a large impact. The only simple methods to prevent autocorrelation are to use either the single worst-case loss or non-overlapping returns.
- *Risk measure*. The choice of risk measure has some impact on procyclicality. For example, suppose the worst-case scenario in a five-year window is used to calculate VAR. When this day drops out of the data window, then the initial margin will fall. If, on the other hand, the initial margin is the average of the worst few days, then one day dropping out will have a smaller impact. Figure 9.8 shows initial margin computed at the 95% and 99.5% confidence levels, with the latter being higher and more rapidly varying. Note that scaling up the 95% initial margin (assuming normal distribution quantile levels) is more stable than the 99.5% result.

---

[26] J.P. Morgan (1996).

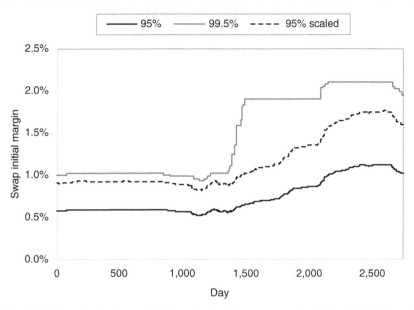

Figure 9.8 Evolution of initial margin for an interest rate swap calculated with VAR at the 95% and 99.5% confidence levels. Also shown is the 95% confidence level scaled by 1.56, which is the ratio between these confidence levels implied by a normal distribution.[27]

The impact of procyclicality on VAR is illustrated in Figure 9.9. A procyclical initial margin will change sharply with underlying market conditions. In order to avoid this procyclicality, it is necessary to have a higher initial margin most of the time. For example, Glasserman and Wu (2017) show that a non-procyclical initial margin is higher than the average procyclical initial margin and that this effect increases for higher confidence levels. Avoiding procyclicality is, therefore, costly.

An obvious way to prevent (or reduce) procyclicality is to use stressed data within the historical look-back period. For example, under the so-called Basel 2.5 changes (BCBS 2009), banks were required to include a one-year period of 'significant financial stress relevant to the bank's portfolio' in their VAR calculations. In addition, the Fundamental Review of the Trading Book (BCBS 2012a) has recommended a move from VAR to ES for bank market risk capital requirements as a more coherent risk measure (see Section 9.2.3). Both the use of stressed data and ES-type approaches have recently made their way into initial margin methodologies, as discussed in Section 9.3.6. Practically, such measures ensured that data around the global financial crisis – in particular, the Lehman bankruptcy – have remained in VAR data sets. A stressed data period could be combined discontinuously with a more recent data history.

Likewise, CCP regulations have sought to prevent procyclical initial margins. For example, in the European Union, one of the following options must be implemented (ESMA 2018):

---

[27] $\Phi^{-1}(99.5\%)/\Phi^{-1}(95\%)$.

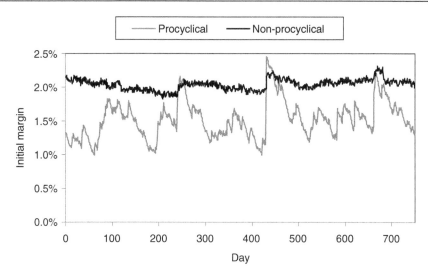

Figure 9.9   Illustration of procyclical and non-procyclical initial margin calculations through time.

- apply a margin buffer at least equal to 25% of the calculated margins which is allowed to be temporarily exhausted in periods where calculated margin requirements are rising significantly;
- assign at least 25% weight to stressed observations in the look-back period; or
- ensure that initial margin requirements are not lower than those that would be calculated using volatility estimated over a 10-year historical look-back period.

The above aspects were partly implemented on the basis that – at the time in question – the period of Lehman bankruptcy was close to dropping out of a then commonly used five-year data window.

Choosing the second of the above options as an example, Figure 9.10 shows the difference between the initial margin calculated with a three-year period, with and without an additional one-year stress period. The estimator including the stress period gives a generally more conservative estimate, but one that is more stable across time. Note also that the initial margin in this case can be seen to be (not surprisingly) driven mainly by the stress period, since it is close to the value calculated using this data alone (with a lower confidence level).

Glasserman and Wu (2017) show that the use of a stressed period is a potentially reasonable way to combat procyclicality, but they also argue that there is significant heterogeneity across asset classes, which suggests that stressed periods should be asset-class specific.

Of course, it is not possible – nor even desirable – to avoid procyclicality in initial margin entirely. Indeed, it is potentially useful that CCPs can adjust margins in response to changes in market conditions, as this limits their vulnerability (Pirrong 2011). Highly-sensitive approaches, prone to procyclicality, will also probably lead to lower average margin requirements (although these will rise significantly in a crisis). However, market conditions can change quickly, and large margin changes can influence prices through effects such as causing forced liquidations of assets. Of course, the safest

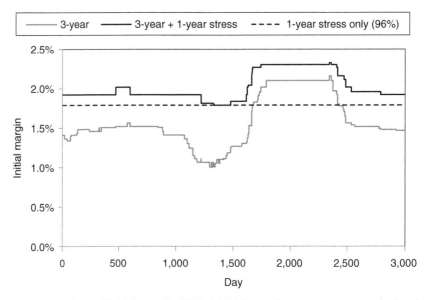

Figure 9.10 Evolution of initial margin (99% VAR) for an interest rate swap calculated with a three-year look-back period, with and without a period of stress. The 96% confidence level initial margin from the stressed period only is also shown.

approach is for initial margins to be conservative, but, as illustrated above, this is also the most expensive solution. Whilst regulation and pressure from members will prevent margin methods from becoming excessively aggressive,[28] competition between CCPs will encourage this to some degree.

Even if procyclicality is minimised, it is still important to emphasise that dynamic and risk-sensitive initial margins will change almost continuously and may exhibit significant changes over time due to:

- *Look-back period.* Old data will drop out of data windows, and new market events will be included.
- *Volatility scaling.* Changes in the current estimate of volatility.
- *CCP methodology decision.* CCPs will change their margin methodologies (e.g. changing the data window or moving from relative to absolute returns).

Given that it is important to be able to assess the cost of posting initial margin (margin value adjustment, discussed in Chapter 20), it is important to consider the potential impact of these types of effects.

As an example of the potential issues caused by the above, Table 9.4 shows estimates of the change in the initial margin for a GBP interest rate swap as a result of market moves following the 2016 United Kingdom European Union membership referendum ('Brexit vote'). The calculation assumes that the initial margin is defined by the worst six scenarios

---

[28] Cameron, M. (2012). Member revolt forces SwapClear to revamp margin model. *Risk* (5 December). www .risk.net.

Table 9.4 Estimation of the initial margin of a GBP pay-fixed interest rate swap before and after the Brexit vote in the United Kingdom on the 23 June 2016. Source: Clarus Financial Technology.[29]

23 June 2016		4 July 2016	
Scenario	P&L	Scenario	P&L
26 November 2008	−3.49	23 June 2016	−4.74
25 November 2008	−3.40	22 June 2016	−3.97
31 October 2008	−3.39	26 November 2008	−3.94
27 November 2008	−3.09	31 October 2008	−3.86
3 November 2008	−2.92	25 November 2008	−3.84
8 October 2014	−2.78	21 June 2016	−3.69
Average	−3.18		−4.01

from a 10-year data history, which is the methodology that was being used by SwapClear at the time (this is the ES at the 99.76% confidence level; see Section 9.3.6).

The large change in initial margin is due to:

- additional scenarios (21–23 June) with large negative swap rate moves being included in the look-back period;
- the use of volatility scaling (so that even the P&L change for the same historical date, such as 26 November 2008, increases due to a higher volatility estimate); and
- the lower interest rate environment (which means that the swap is slightly more sensitive to a move in interest rates, given the assumption of absolute returns).

Note that due to the second and third effects above, the initial margin of the opposite position would also increase, despite there not being any new scenarios of positive interest rate moves.

9.3.6   Current CCP Methodologies

Whilst the more straightforward exchange-traded products have maintained simpler approaches, such as SPAN for margining, historical simulation has emerged as a fairly standard approach for OTC derivatives. In general, OTC CCPs have evolved their methodologies in line with regulatory guidance and pressure from their clearing members (who themselves have experience from their own application of similar models for their market risk capital requirements). Ideally, margins should be stable through time, but they should also respond to new data and methodological advances. Certain changes may only be regarded as short-term fixes. For example, the move from relative to absolute returns becomes inappropriate when rates begin to rise.

One particularly difficult aspect of initial margin methodologies is whether to continue to extend the look-back period to the global financial crisis.[30] Whilst this was originally

---

[29] Khwaja, A. (2016). Higher Swap Margins After Brexit. Clarus Financial Technology blog (5 July). www .clarusft.com.

[30] Osborn, T. (2018). Lehman's ghost: how three CCPs anchor models to crash. *Risk* (17 September). www .risk.net.

seen, for example, in CCPs moving from five- to 10-year data windows, it now seems to have been sufficiently long ago that the events around the bankruptcy of Lehman Brothers can be ignored, despite this being the last time a major clearing member defaulted.[31]

CCPs may include additional qualitative components in the determination of initial margin. One example is the use of 'margin multipliers', which will lead to increased margins for excessive amounts of liquidity, credit, concentration, and sovereign risks. These may account for the fact that the liquidation of a reasonably large and/or complex portfolio would be subject to substantial bid-offer costs, and could move the market. Multipliers may apply based on clearing volumes exceeding certain thresholds based on the whole portfolio and sub-portfolios (e.g. currencies). Client trades may also attract a larger margin requirement. It is also important to account for FX risks for positions denominated in different currencies.

Table 9.5 contrasts the initial margin assumptions used for interest rate products at three significant OTC CCPs. It can be seen that there is a reasonable convergence on aspects such as historical simulation methods, liquidation periods, volatility scaling, and liquidity charges. Differences still exist, in terms of methods to avoid aspects such as procyclicality and autocorrelations, which are seen by the use of different data windows and measures used. Given the small differences, the methods would be expected to give

Table 9.5 Comparison of initial margin methodologies for interest rate products. Note that details of methodologies can sometimes be hard to ascertain and can change over time.

	LCH.Clearnet (SwapClear)	CME	Eurex
Name	Portfolio Approach to Interest Rate Scenarios (PAIRS)[a]	Historical value-at-risk (HVaR)[b]	Portfolio-Based Risk Management Methodology (PRISMA)[c]
Look-back period	10 years	To 1 January 2008 (fixed)	3 years + 1 year stress period and 'event scenarios'
Measure	99.7% expected shortfall (average of six worst scenarios out of 2,500)	99.7% VAR	99.5% VAR (using sub-samples to avoid overlapping effects)
Returns	Absolute	Absolute	Absolute
Volatility scaling	Yes	Yes (with volatility floors)	Yes (for non-stress scenarios)
Liquidity period	5 days (7 days for clients)	5 days	5 days
Addition charges	Credit risk and liquidity risk	Liquidity charge multipliers	Historical correlation breaks, liquidity costs, and compression adjustments

[a]www.lch.com.
[b]www.cmegroup.com.
[c]www.eurexclearing.com.

---

[31] Mourselas, C. (2019). CME no longer looking back to Lehman. *Risk* (28 August). www.risk.net.

reasonably material differences (e.g. 10–20%) on a standalone basis. However, this may be blurred by portfolio effects in the actual initial margin calculation.

The above analysis focused largely on interest rate products, which represent a large amount of OTC derivatives clearing. Another asset class worthy of special mention is credit derivatives. Calculating initial margin requirements for CDSs represents greater challenges. This is due to the sparseness of data and the fact that credit spread distributional changes can be highly complex and especially prone to aspects such as fat-tail effects. CDS clearing also has to take into account the fact that clearing members can be reference entities in CDS indices and single-name transactions.

For the above reasons, CDS initial margin methodologies tend to differ from historical simulation approaches. ICE Clear uses a proprietary Monte Carlo simulation to evaluate a large five-day decline in portfolio value based on 20,000 simulations and incorporating asymmetric distributional assumption and co-movements in relation to credit spreads.[32] Both LCH and ICE include additional components to capture effects such as bid-offer costs and concentration risks of large portfolios. CDSs with significant WWR – such as a bank selling protection on its sovereign – may be disallowed completely.

9.3.7   Computational Considerations

It is not surprising that initial margin methodologies for OTC derivatives have become broadly based on simulation methods. These methods are the most accurate as they are the only way to incorporate important effects such as irregular probability distributions, time changing volatility, and multidimensionality. They are also the only generic approaches, which makes product development and cross-margining more practical.

However, these relatively sophisticated approaches are also costly. Margin calculations are portfolio based and therefore, to calculate the initial margin on a new trade, the incremental effect vis-à-vis the entire portfolio must be calculated. Such incremental effects will be important when deciding where to clear trades and whether to backload trades to CCPs. Even with pre-computation and parallel processing, such a calculation is often not achievable in real time and therefore cannot be part of the execution process for a new trade (as discussed in Section 20.2.4, regulation may require trades to be accepted for clearing in narrow time windows such as 60 seconds). Furthermore, clearing members and clients will want to be comfortable with approaches and understand the magnitude of initial margins for various trade and portfolio combinations. One obvious way to optimise computation times is to use sensitivities ('Greeks') to approximate the change in the value of each trade, rather than resorting to a 'full revaluation'. Given the number of scenarios generated, full revaluation generally tends to be time consuming, especially for complex derivatives, which require relatively sophisticated pricing models.

Given the above, CCPs have developed tools for calculating approximate initial margins without the need for full resimulation. An example is the SwapClear Margin Approximation Risk Tool (SMART), which is also available on Bloomberg.[33] Regarding the treatment of initial margins for new trades, CCPs will either calculate these approximately in real time, or rely on initial margin buffers intended to cover the risk until the true

---

[32] www.theice.com.

[33] Bloomberg (2013). Bloomberg Integrates Margin Calculator for Swap Participants. Press release (6 August). www.bloomberg.com.

margin impact can be calculated (probably overnight). This incremental risk may also be covered by an additional component of the default fund, which could be based on the relative utilisation by a clearing member over the most recent period. This means that a member clearing large volumes of trades may have to make a relatively large additional contribution to the default fund to cover the intraday risk such trades are generating.

9.4   BILATERAL MARGIN AND SIMM

9.4.1   Overview

As discussed in Section 7.4, regulation is requiring that parties post initial margin on bilateral OTC derivatives that cannot be centrally cleared (BCBS-IOSCO 2015). Unlike initial margin at a CCP, bilateral initial margin is posted by both parties (Figure 9.11), although they will not always be symmetric (same amounts), in particular for more complex portfolios with embedded optionality.

Regulation specifies that the initial margin amounts can be either based on a 'quantitative portfolio margin model' or a 'standardised margin schedule'. In both cases, margins must be calculated separately for the following 'asset classes':

- currency/rates;
- equity;
- credit; and
- commodities.

This choice between model- and schedule-based initial margins must be made consistently by asset class, and firms cannot switch in order to cherry-pick the most favourable initial margins. However, it is possible to use model- and schedule-based approaches for different asset classes (e.g. to reflect the fact that a firm has only a small position in some derivatives).

In the case of schedule-based margins, the simple methodology is defined explicitly by BCBS-IOSCO (2015). This has the advantage of being easy to implement and unlikely to lead to disputes. However, like any simple methodology, this approach is not especially risk sensitive and will usually lead to quite conservative initial margin amounts. On the

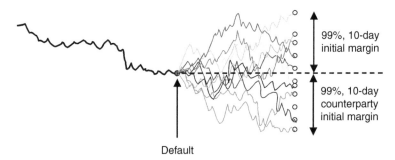

Figure 9.11   Illustration of the impact of bilateral initial margin. The party concerned holds initial margin to cover its close-out costs to a 99% confidence level over 10 days. It also posts an amount to cover the associated costs of its counterparty. These amounts will not necessarily be equal.

other hand, a model-based approach will produce lower and more risk-sensitive margins, but will require more effort in implementation and agreement with counterparties. The design of internal models is also open to substantial interpretation and would inevitably lead to disputes between counterparties and a large effort for regulatory approvals of different models.

In terms of model-based margins, there is no specific model determined by regulation, but a number of general requirements are described (BCBS-IOSCO 2015):

- the initial margin must be posted by both parties and must be based on a 99% confidence level and a 10-day MPoR;
- the model should be calibrated to a data period of no more than five years, which includes a period of financial stress (the requirement to use the stress period is aimed at avoiding procyclicality);
- the period of financial stress used for calibration should be identified and applied separately for each asset class;
- the data within the identified period should be equally weighted for calibration purposes; and
- large, discrete calls for initial margin (as could presumably arise due to procyclicality of the margin model or use of volatility scaling) should be avoided.

Together with the major banks, ISDA has developed the SIMM in order to have a single, model-based margin approach and avoid a proliferation of margin models where parties would inevitably dispute initial margin requirements.[34]

Eligible collateral assets for fulfilling initial margin requirements is relatively flexible (e.g. to include liquid equities and corporate bonds), which aligns with central clearing where CCPs accept a reasonable range of collateral assets. However, appropriate haircuts must be applied, and 'wrong-way collateral' (e.g. securities issues by the party or related entities) is not allowed. Margin assets should – after accounting for an appropriate haircut – be able to hold their value in a time of financial stress. Margin can be denominated in a currency in which payment obligations may be made or in liquid foreign currencies (again subject to appropriate haircuts to reflect the inherent FX risk involved). Collateral assets should also be reasonably diversified.

Haircut requirements should be transparent and easy to calculate, so as to avoid disputes. As in the case of initial margin models, either an approved quantitative model or a defined standardised schedule can be used to define haircuts. In the latter case, BCBS-IOSCO defines that haircut levels should be risk sensitive and reflect the underlying market, liquidity, and credit risks that affect the value of eligible margin in both normal and stressed market conditions. As with initial margins, haircuts should be set conservatively so as to mitigate procyclicality and avoid sharp and sudden increases in times of stress.

The time horizon and confidence level for computing haircuts are not defined explicitly but would likely follow those for clearing. The time horizon for computing a haircut could be argued to be less (say two to three days) than the horizon for initial margin, since the margin may be liquidated independently and more quickly than the portfolio would be closed out.

---

[34] www.isda.org.
[35] See Section 7.4.2.

Table 9.6 Comparison of initial margin methodologies in centrally-cleared and bilateral markets.

	Centrally cleared	Bilateral
Methodology	CCP model (typically historical simulation)	Quantitative model (SIMM) or schedule
MPoR	5 days	10 days
Threshold	Zero	Up to €50m[35]
Calculation and reconciliation	Calculated and called by CCP	Reconciliation and dispute-resolution process
Haircuts	CCP-defined	Quantitative model or schedule

Table 9.6 contrasts initial margin methodologies in centrally-cleared and bilateral markets.

9.4.2 Standard Schedules

The standard schedule, previously shown in Table 7.11, defines initial margin as being based on notional with pre-calibrated weights which represent a conservative estimate of the 10-day 99% move in the relevant instrument of the asset class in question. To account for portfolio effects, the well-known net gross ratio (NGR) formula is used, which is defined as the net replacement divided by the gross replacement of transactions.[36] The NGR is used to calculate the net standardised initial margin requirement via:

Net standardised initial margin = (0.4 + 0.6 × NGR) × Gross initial margin.

The NGR gives a simple representation of the future offset between positions, the logic being that 60% of the current offset can be assumed for future exposures.

Example of margin schedule calculation

Consider two four-year interest rate products with notional values of 100 and 50 and respective mark-to-market (replacement cost) valuations of 10 and -3.

Trade 1: Gross initial margin = 2 (2% × 100)

Trade 2: Gross initial margin = 1 (2% × 50)

Total gross initial margin = 3

$$\text{NGR} = \frac{\max(10 - 3, 0)}{\max(10,0) + \max(-3,0)} = 0.7$$

Net initial margin = (0.4 + 0.6 × 0.7) × 3 = 2.46

---

[36] NGR is used in bank capital requirements and the definition can be found in BCBS (2006). It is also discussed in more detail in Section 13.4.2.

Such an approach is not risk sensitive and does not properly account for netting effects and is especially punitive for hedged (balanced) portfolios. In general, this leads to an overestimate in initial margin requirements and does not give the right incentives to market participants. However, it is a simple fallback method which clearly cannot be expected to be a risk-sensitive and accurate approach.

The standardised haircuts (assuming a bank is not using a quantitative model) were previously defined in Table 7.12.

9.4.3   Variance-covariance Approaches

The standard margin schedule also likely leads to particularly large requirements (ISDA 2012 estimates over \$8trn for schedule-based margins), which suggests that applying a more sophisticated methodology for initial margin calculations could be quite important to prevent requirements being overly conservative. The SIMM has been implemented to provide a market-standard quantitative initial margin model that can potentially be used by all bilateral market participants.

An obvious starting point for a bilateral initial margin model would clearly be the models adopted by CCPs (Section 9.3). However, an important difference in bilateral markets is that parties need to agree on quantities such as initial margins (compared to centrally-cleared markets, where the CCP has the right to enforce its own calculation). More complex margin calculations methodologies, such as VAR-based methods, should be expected to lead to significant disputes. Indeed, in bilateral markets, even variation margin calculations (based on current exposure) have often led to significant valuation disputes. It is therefore inconceivable that initial margin calculations (based on future exposure estimates) would not lead to more disputes over what is, by its nature, a highly-subjective and complex estimation. It seems impractical that an institution would replicate the margin model and data set used by all of its bilateral counterparties. On the other hand, it would probably be unwilling to agree blindly to initial margin requirements generated by such a model.

The complexities of historical simulation approaches used by CCPs are related to several aspects:

- *Historical data.* The historical data for all risk factors over the entire look-back period and also including any stress periods. Issues such as market close times can cause discrepancies here.
- *Methodology.* The precise methodology used to generate the scenarios, such as the choice of absolute or relative returns and volatility scaling.
- *Revaluation.* Generally, OTC derivatives are valued using models – the same models need to be used for revaluing the underlying portfolio in all of the generated scenarios. Differences in valuation models can cause discrepancies here.

Given the complexities of the above, agreeing bilaterally on initial margins across multiple portfolios with different counterparties on a daily basis would at best represent a large operational workload. There is, therefore, a need to consider a simplified approach.

A well-known, simpler VAR-type method is a parametric approach often known as 'variance-covariance' (Jorion 2007). This involves making some assumptions about the

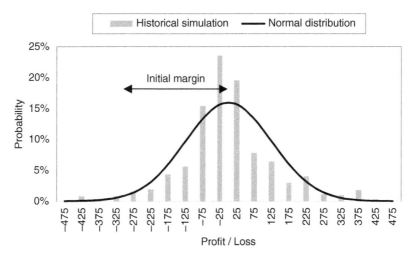

Figure 9.12   Illustration of a variance-covariance approach to approximate the portfolio profit and loss distribution.

form of the distribution of the underlying profit and loss distribution of the portfolio in question (Figure 9.12). This allows a quantity such as the initial margin to be written in terms of the moments of the underlying distribution.

A common assumption is to assume that the portfolio returns are normally distributed. This distribution has two moments, the mean and standard deviation, but commonly it is assumed that the mean of the distribution is negligibly small (which for a short time horizon is reasonable). As a result, only the standard deviation is required, and this normal distribution assumption, together with the square root of time rule (Section 7.5.2), allows initial margin to be written as:

$$IM_{\alpha,\tau} = \Phi^{-1}(\alpha) \times \sqrt{\tau} \times \sigma_P$$

where $\Phi^{-1}(.)$ represents the inverse of a standard normal distribution function. In the above representation, there are three components:

- *Scaling factor.* The scaling factor depends on the metric, confidence level, and distribution assumptions. For VAR at a confidence level of 99%, this scaling is $\Phi^{-1}(0.99) = 2.33$. Note that it is also possible to use different distribution assumptions and metrics.[37]
- *Time horizon.* The square root of time scaling, with τ representing the MPoR (e.g. 10 days). Since the volatility is typically an annual quantity, this should also be an annual quantity (e.g. $\frac{10}{252} = 0.0397$, assuming 252 business days in a year).
- *Portfolio standard deviation.* The standard deviation of the portfolio returns, estimated with some time horizon (e.g. one year).

---

[37] For example, under normal distribution assumptions, the expected shortfall is defined by $\frac{N[\Phi^{-1}(\alpha)]}{(1-\alpha)}$ where $N(.)$ represents a standard normal distribution function.

Variance-covariance initial margin calculations

Consider that the annual standard derivation of a portfolio is $100.

a) The 99% VAR for a 10-day time horizon is:

$$\Phi^{-1}(0.99) \times \sqrt{\frac{10}{252}} \times 100 = 2.33 \times 0.0397 \times 100 = 46.4$$

b) The 99% VAR for a 5-day time horizon is:

$$\Phi^{-1}(0.99) \times \sqrt{\frac{5}{252}} \times 100 = 2.33 \times 0.0198 \times 100 = 32.8$$

c) The 95% VAR for a 10-day time horizon is:

$$\Phi^{-1}(0.95) \times \sqrt{\frac{10}{252}} \times 100 = 1.64 \times 0.0397 \times 100 = 32.8$$

d) The 99% ES for a 10-day time horizon is:

$$N[\Phi^{-1}(\alpha)]/(1-\alpha) \times \sqrt{\frac{10}{252}} \times 100 = 2.67 \times 0.0397 \times 100 = 53.1$$

The main effort in a variance-covariance is the estimation of the standard deviation of the portfolio returns. This requires estimating the standard deviation of each underlying risk factor and the correlations between them (or equivalently the 'covariance matrix'). Variance-covariance approaches typically use delta approximations (as opposed to full revaluation) in order to approximate the relationship between the value of the portfolio and the change in risk factors. For portfolios with non-linear risks, it is also important to consider additional sensitivities or Greeks to capture the portfolio risk more accurately. For example, Figure 9.13 shows the profit and loss distribution of a position with optionality (a short call option with a long position in the underlying). Since this position is close to being 'delta neutral', most of the risk is second order. This means that a delta approximation is poor, but a delta-gamma approximation gives results close to full revaluation.

Variance-covariance and delta or delta-gamma approximations simplify the calculation of initial margin compared to full historical simulation (see bulleted list at the start of this section). Firstly, it is not necessary to agree on the full historical data but only on the standard deviations and correlations between the risk factors. Secondly, it is not necessary to agree on the revaluation models but only on the representation of sensitivities such as delta and gamma. This does not mean that the variance-covariance method is simple; just that it is simpler than historical simulation.

There are some drawbacks of variance-covariance. Most obviously, it potentially misses effects such as fat tails (Section 2.6.2) and complex dependencies (Section 2.6.3) and will, therefore, be expected to underestimate initial margins, especially when high confidence

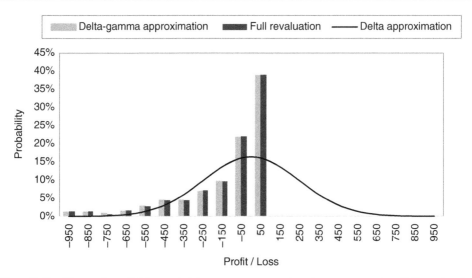

Figure 9.13 Illustration of delta and delta-gamma approximations compared to full revaluation for a portfolio with embedded optionality. The change in implied volatility is not considered.

levels, such as 99% or 99.5%, are used. One simple way to correct for such drawbacks is to be naturally more conservative when estimating the standard deviation of the portfolio returns.

Another drawback of variance-covariance is data. The correlation matrix that is required for a typical portfolio can be extremely large. For example, suppose each interest rate curve is modelled via 12 tenor points,[38] and that there are two different interest rate curves in each currency and 10 currencies overall. The resulting dimension of the correlation matrix would then be 240 × 240, requiring the estimation of a total of 28,680 correlation parameters.[39] A portfolio with sensitivity to other risk factors will clearly have an even larger underlying correlation matrix. Furthermore, in asset classes such as equities and credit, there are potentially many curves representing individual companies that increase the dimensionality further.

The potentially large correlation matrix is not only a data problem but a technical one. An estimated correlation matrix must be valid (more technically described as being 'positive semidefinite'). The larger the correlation matrix, the more likely that this will not be the case. Although there are methods to find the closest valid correlation matrix, this adds complexity to the approach.

Given the above, a simple and industrial variance-covariance approach may naturally require some sort of dimensionality reduction to create a simpler overall problem with fewer parameters and no technical problems, such as ensuring the positive semidefinitiveness of the correlation matrix.

---

[38] We will see in Section 9.4.4 that this is exactly what is done in SIMM.

[39] $\dfrac{240 \times (240 - 1)}{2}$.

9.4.4   The ISDA SIMM

Given that standardised margin schedules are too conservative, and proprietary models will lead to major dispute problems, there is an obvious need for a standard model that is risk sensitive but can be agreed by all parties across bilateral OTC markets. ISDA has pursued this idea in conjunction with the banks that were first impacted by the bilateral margin requirements (Phase 1 banks). It is worth noting that some of the inspiration for the SIMM has come from the so-called standardised approach under the Fundamental Review of the Trading Book (FRTB-SA), which defines market risk capital requirements for banks (BCBS 2019a).

The SIMM represents an initiative to develop a uniform methodology for calculating bilateral initial margins.[40] ISDA (2013e) broadly described a proposal for the structure of such a model based on the following important characteristics:[41]

- *Non-procyclicality*. Margins should not be subject to continuous changes linked to market volatility, which could exacerbate stress in volatile market conditions. It is proposed that margins are not explicitly linked to market levels or volatility and that scenarios should be updated periodically and not continuously.
- *Ease of replication*. To mitigate potential problems arising from disputes, a transparent methodology and data set must be used.
- *Transparency*. It must be possible to understand the drivers of the methodology and therefore drill down to understand discrepancies and avoid disputes.
- *Quick to calculate*. The calculation must be quick (e.g. seconds) to facilitate fast pricing checks.
- *Extensible*. It should be easy to extend to cover additional risk factors in order to facilitate the addition of new products.
- *Predictability*. Initial margin results must be predictable in order for institutions to price correctly and allocate capital.
- *Costs*. The cost to buy or build the model must not be prohibitive, so it does not restrict access.
- *Governance*. Regulators should approve the model and calibration, and review this on a periodic basis.
- *Margin appropriateness*. Margin should be risk sensitive and give an appropriate reduction for offsetting positions.

The ISDA SIMM is a variance-covariance-type approach which is simplified by:

- separation across asset classes (note that this is a regulatory requirement, as discussed in Section 7.4.3); and
- reduction of dimensionality by defining a generic set of underlying risk factors.

It can, therefore, be considered to be a sequence of small, 'nested' variance-covariance formulas, rather than a single, larger, and more complex variance-covariance formula covering all risk factors.

---

[40] Noting that this therefore does not give any opinion on initial margins calculated by CCPs.

[41] Note that this is the author's own description of the characteristics given by ISDA (2013).

It is also a sensitivity-based approach, with the sensitivities being delta, 'curvature' (gamma), and 'vega', which are defined across risk factors by asset class, tenor, and maturity. There are also base correlation requirements that apply only to certain credit positions. Note that since the bilateral margin rules apply to transactions that cannot be centrally cleared, then by definition this will need to capture the more non-standard, complex, and illiquid OTC derivatives. Hence, the curvature and vega (and base correlation) components are important. The initial margin requirements are additive across these sensitivities. Within each asset class, the initial margin requirements are then driven by:

- sensitivities to various risk factors (e.g. interest rate delta in a particular currency);
- risk weights (essentially defining the variability of a risk factor, assuming the regulatory required horizon of 10 days and confidence level of 99%);
- concentration thresholds (that penalise large positions based on the size of the position compared to the traded market volume for the relevant risk factor); and
- correlations and aggregation (defining the extent of offset between positions in the same asset class).

Additionally, to account for the fact that a given transaction may have a sensitivity to different asset classes (for example, many non-rates products have interest rate sensitivity), a total of six risk classes are defined:

- interest rate;
- credit (qualifying);
- credit (non-qualifying);
- equity;
- commodity; and
- FX.

A product can, therefore, have initial margin contributions arising from its sensitivity to more than one risk class, with aggregation rules determining how such contributions should be combined. This can be problematic in certain situations. Consider various equity transactions in different currencies hedged with FX transactions. These will be in the equity and FX asset classes, respectively, with both asset classes having FX risk. However, the FX risk will not offset as it will appear in two different asset classes that must be treated additively.

The SIMM parameters are calibrated using a three-year look-back period together with a one-year stress period.[42] The risk weights are calculated from the maximum of the 99% and 1% quantiles of this distribution (i.e. they are the worst up or down move seen at the relevant confidence level).

It is proposed that the parameters in the SIMM be recalibrated annually,[43] together with a review of the underlying methodology. As such, the methodology should have low procyclicality, at least between calibrations. Furthermore, any increases in initial margin

---

[42] The stress period is chosen as the one-year interval from January 2008, with the maximum volatility of 10-day overlapping returns.

[43] For example, version 1.0 was effective 1 January 2017 and version 2.0 was effective 4 December 2017.

Table 9.7   Calculation of weighted sensitivities for two interest rate positions.

	2 w^a	1 m	3 m	6 m	1 yr	2 yr	3 yr	5 yr	10 yr
Trade 1	0	0	0	0	1	3	291	0	0
Trade 2	1	−1	2	−4	3	−18	20	−63	−852
Net sensitivity (*s*)	1	−2	2	−4	5	−15	311	−63	−852
Risk weight (*RW*)	113	113	98	69	56	52	51	51	51
Weighted sensitivity (*WS*)	−75	146	−182	264	−132	1,072	13,797	3,191	43,427

^{a}w, week; m, month; yr, year

should be predictable and will not occur suddenly as the new methodology and calibration will be known several months ahead.[44] The calibration and methodology are defined centrally, and participants do not need access to the underlying historical data being used.

Spreadsheet 9.2 Example ISDA SIMM™ calculations.

Taking a worked example of an interest rate delta margin calculation and assuming two transactions of three-year and ten-year maturity with notional of one million each and denominated in the same currency. The first step is to calculate the underlying sensitivities, which are shown together with the relevant risk weights (which are the same for most currencies)[45] in Table 9.7.[46] The sensitivities can be netted across the products. The net sensitivities (*s*) and risk weights (*RW*) are now multipliers to generate the 'weighted sensitivities' (*WS*) for each tenor according to:

$$WS = RW \times s \times CR$$

where *CR* is the concentration risk factor, which will be one unless the position is large and above a defined concentration threshold, which is defined by currency according to market liquidity. Assuming that $CR = 1$, the weighted sensitivities are shown in Table 9.7.

The final step is to aggregate the sensitivities across tenor and sub-curve (for different reference rates).[47] Whilst the former calculation is a matrix multiplication, the majority of the contribution comes from the three- and 10-year tenors, where most of the risk exists. Hence, the simplified calculation is:

$$\text{Delta margin} = \sqrt{13{,}797^2 + 43{,}427^2 + 2 \times 84\% \times 13{,}797 \times 43{,}427} = 55{,}524$$

---

[44] Version 2.1 methodology was first published in July 2018, ahead of the implementation on 1 December 2018.

[45] These are the version 2.0 risk weights for regular volatility currencies, which are most major currencies. Low- and high-volatility current risk weights also exist.

[46] The sensitivities are defined as a prescribed set of tenors, as shown. The longer tenors (15 years, 20 years, and 30 years) are not shown.

[47] This uses a single correlation parameter of 98% to represent the relationship between different reference rates (e.g. three-month and six-month London Interbank Offered Rate or overnight indexed spread) in a given currency.

Table 9.8   SIMM delta margin for a different combination of interest rate swap trades with respect to currency and directionality.

	Directional	Anti-directional
Same currency	59,540	34,293
Different currencies	52,306	44,555

where 84% represents the correlation between the 3- and 10-year tenors. The actual calculation (including risk from all tenors) is slightly higher at 59,540.

The initial margin in the above example is relatively large because the positions are directional (same currency and positive sensitivity to the risk factor). In Table 9.8, we show the initial margins if the swaps are in different currencies and are anti-directional (sensitivities to the risk factors are of opposite signs).[48] The initial margin for different currencies is smaller due to the decorrelation that arises, which is effectively modelled by a currency correlation parameter of 23%. The anti-directional portfolio has a much lower initial margin due to the hedging effect of trades in opposite directions, which is strongest when the transaction is in the same currency. These results are risk sensitive, as would be expected.

Note that the gross initial margin under the standard schedule assuming par swaps is 60,000, which is reasonable for directional and same-currency positions, but too high for cases where the portfolio is more balanced, unless the NGR factor reduces this substantially.

For more detail on the implementation of the SIMM, the reader is referred to ISDA (2013e, 2016, 2017a, 2017b).

9.4.5   Implementation of Bilateral Margin Requirements

At the time of writing, the initial requirements are still being phased in, with only the major banks being required to post bilateral initial margin (Table 9.9). However, whilst the early phases only capture a small fraction of market participants, since these market participants are large banks, they do capture a significant amount of the total market (Condat et al. 2018).

In order to comply with the bilateral margin requirements, there is significant work on aspects such as:

- renegotiating credit support annexes;
- developing custodian relationships;
- being able to generate sensitivities for each transaction and map these onto the SIMM risk factors;
- handling any disputes over the quantity of initial margin (in either direction);
- identifying any margin shortfalls through backtesting of historical performance for each portfolio; and
- building connectivity with all counterparties in-scope for bilateral margin.

---

[48] For example, as arising from a pay-fixed and receive-fixed interest rate swap.

Table 9.9 Market participants subject to bilateral initial margin requirements. Note that due to initiatives such as compression and new trading activity, these numbers can change.

	Start date	Non-cleared notional threshold	Number of market participants (cumulative)
Phase 1	1 September 2016	€3trn	20
Phase 2	1 September 2017	€2.25trn	26
Phase 3	1 September 2018	€1.5trn	36
Phase 4	1 September 2019	€0.75trn	86
Phase 5	1 September 2020	€50bn	Hundreds
Phase 6	1 September 2021	€8bn	Thousands

The SIMM is becoming relatively standard for calculating initial margin in such situations. ISDA has defined standardised formats for the exchange of model inputs (sensitivities) and trade details via a Common Risk Interchange Format (CRIF).

In order to facilitate the required calculations, a utility called Exposure Manager, provided by AcadiaSoft in collaboration with TriOptima, is being utilised.[49] Exposure Manager is an end-to-end initial margin reconciliation, calculation, and dispute-resolution service which provides the following services:

- reconciliation of exposures, trades, and sensitivities;
- standard calculations (SIMM and schedule);
- initial margin call generation; and
- audit trail and reporting/analysis.

This can make it easier and cheaper for market participants to implement initial margin calculations with the SIMM, although there is still a concern in the industry about the many small institutions that will be captured in 2021 when the notional threshold drops to only €8bn. The standardisation of the margining process is fairly critical to allow for efficient initial margin exchange across a large number of counterparties.

There is not much evidence of the use of margin schedules or other approaches for calculating initial margin, although some banks have implemented an internal model for interaffiliate relationships where initial margin must be posted. It remains to be seen whether this will change as many more market participants become involved.

Note that, whilst all firms captured by the notional threshold must calculate initial margin between one another, this may not lead to actual posting due to the €50m threshold (Section 7.4.2) and the fact that initial margin only need be exchanged against new transactions. However, over time, the impact will clearly increase.

Regulatory initial margin is reported by ISDA as being largely made up of government securities (86.3%), which is not surprising as segregation is easier with securities. Only 13.7% of regulatory initial margin is in cash. This contrasts to variation margin, where 79.2% is reported as being in cash. Discretionary initial margin has a larger component of cash and other securities.

---

[49] www.acadiasoft.com.

As with the requirements for clearing, there are objections to initial margin requirements. These are mainly based on the fact that posting initial margin, which has to be segregated, is extremely costly and margin rules may not reduce systemic risk due to the likelihood that they may increase sharply in crisis periods (procyclicality). Additionally, Cont (2018) has argued that the liquidity horizon (MPoR) should not be fixed at 10 days but should be related to the liquidity of the instruments in question, and should take more consideration of the size of the position relative to the daily trading volume. He also argues that the ability to hedge market risk in the aftermath of a default may mean that the 10-day MPoR is too large.

Note also that, whilst the threshold of €50m would relieve the liquidity strain created via the margin requirements, it would increase the procyclicality problem as margin amounts will be even more sensitive to market conditions near this threshold.

10

The Impact and Risk of Clearing and Margining

Mandatory central clearing of over-the-counter (OTC) derivatives is not a panacea, and central counterparties (CCPs) create risks. For instance, the difficulties faced by CCPs in the stock market crash of 1987 posed a serious threat to the entire financial system. For the past century and longer, clearing has been limited to listed derivatives traded on exchanges. Bilateral OTC markets have been extremely successful, and their growth has been greater than that of exchange-traded products over the last two decades. Whilst certain OTC derivatives (notably some interest rate swaps) have been centrally cleared since 1999, the majority of OTC products have not moved to central clearing by means of natural forces.

The trouble with clearing OTC derivatives is that they are more illiquid, long-dated, and complex compared to their exchange-traded relatives. Hence, they may prove a challenge for traditional CCP risk management methods, especially with cross-border activity being so important. What is indisputable is that centralised clearing will have significant structural and behavioural effects on the management and allocation of risk in financial markets, causing a profound change in market structure and trading practices.

A first obvious and almost paradoxical problem with mandatory clearing is that CCPs clearing OTC products may become systemically important, creating a potential moral hazard if it is clear that government financial support will be forthcoming in the event of a CCP risk management failure. After all, bailing out a CCP is ultimately no better than bailing out any other financial institution. CCPs do not make counterparty risk vanish, and forcing derivatives through CCPs could create sizeable financial risks via concentrating counterparty risk within a single systemic point in the system. As CCPs clear more complex, less liquid, and longer-term instruments, their potential risks will likely increase.

A second concern is the costs and instabilities that CCPs and bilateral margin requirements will introduce through requiring a significant amount of liquid margin to be posted by members and their clients, with various estimates putting this increase in the region of trillions of US dollars. There is a question over the economic impact of such margin, which may start in terms of financial institutions being less profitable, but will eventually have an impact on economic growth in general. The more subtle problem is that margining can transmit systemic disturbances as requirements change. This can occur, for example, when firms that must meet large margin calls respond by selling assets and reducing positions in ways that exacerbate the price changes that caused the margin calls. Moreover, initial margins generally increase in volatile markets, which could have the effect of catalysing rather than resolving financial distress via a damaging, system-wide liquidity drain.

A third potential problem is related to the loss mutualisation that CCPs use, whereby any losses in excess of a member's own financial resources (mainly initial margin) are generally mutualised across all the surviving members. The impact of such a mechanism is to homogenise the underlying counterparty risk, such that all CCP members are more or less equal. The most creditworthy market participants may see less advantage to their stronger credit quality with CCP clearing. As with any form of insurance, adverse selection – when the insured know more about risks than the insurer – may be a problem and make risk-sharing costly. In a clearing context, to the extent that firms that trade OTC derivatives know more about the risks of particular cleared products than the CCP, these firms will tend to overtrade the products for which the CCP underestimates risk, and undertrade the products for which the CCP overestimates risk. CCPs could encourage excessive risk-taking compared to bilateral trading, since an institution knows that its potential losses are mutualised amongst other members.

CCPs are often touted as reducing systemic risk. Yet the clearing mandate covers OTC derivatives and so CCPs can therefore, at best, reduce systemic risk in OTC derivatives markets. Of course, based on past experience, reducing systemic risk in derivatives (aka weapons of financial destruction) may be rather close to reducing systemic risk in financial markets on the whole.

10.1   RISKS OF CENTRAL CLEARING

Regarding the general risk posed by CCPs (especially those clearing significant volumes of OTC derivatives), two obvious concerns arise:

- *Central nodes of failure.* Mandatory clearing will increase the importance of CCPs as key central nodes within financial markets. As such, their failure or even distress could initiate a major disturbance. This also creates a moral hazard and too-big-to-fail dilemma: if a CCP needs to be saved from failure, then this would likely be at the expense of the taxpayer.
- *Shock amplifiers and propagators.* Given their size and interconnections, CCPs could amplify systemic shocks and allow a financial disturbance to propagate through the market as a result of their actions (e.g. in relation to margin requirements).

10.1.1   Historical CCP Problems

There have been a number of failures of CCPs, and similar clearing-focused entities, that give some insight into the risks of central clearing

- *New York Gold Exchange Bank (1869).* Whilst not a CCP specifically, this bank did operate a clearing division and had a role insuring against default losses. Black Friday saw a large drop in the gold price which was caused by two speculators attempting to corner the gold market on the Gold Exchange. A number of speculators became insolvent, and the bank had insufficient reserves to fulfil its obligations to those that had bet on the price going down.
- *Caisse de Liquidation (1974).* Prices in the Paris white sugar market had quadrupled and were extremely volatile, partly caused by speculation. Prices then suffered a very large downward correction, and several speculators defaulted on margin calls and created losses for the Caisse de Liquidation. One member in particular – the Nataf Trading House – had a very large position. As a result of the losses of the Nataf Trading House, the Ministry of Commerce closed the sugar market and invoked a regulation which deemed that, on reopening, contracts would be settled at the average price of the last

20 days (far higher than the price when trading was suspended). This can be seen as a form of variation margin haircutting or partial tear-up (see Section 10.2.4). However, this judgement was reversed in the courts, and two of the Nataf Trading House's guarantors refused to cover sums they owed, resulting in the Caisse de Liquidation becoming insolvent. The sugar market remained closed for another 18 months.

Hills et al. (1999) outline some reasons for the failure of the Caisse de Liquidation:

o They did not increase initial margins despite the increase in sugar prices and the correspondingly-large increase in volatility, even though clearing members themselves had requested they do so. Initial margins were set based on absolute moves, which (as described in Section 9.3.3) is a problem in a rising market.

o They did not act on the relatively-large speculatory position (in comparison to the entire market) in sugar futures held by the Nataf Trading House.

o The loss allocation process in the event of the default of a clearing member was not transparent (and, as described above, there were legal problems in trying to enforce loss allocation).

- *The Commodity Exchange Inc. (COMEX) (1980)*. Not specifically a CCP failure, but COMEX was the leading gold and options exchange, which also traded silver contracts. Leading up to the problems, the Hunt brothers had been cornering the silver market, creating an order-of-magnitude increase in prices. Eventually, in response to the accumulation of a massive position, COMEX changed its rules regarding leverage. This so-called 'Silver Rule 7' placed heavy restrictions on the purchase of commodities and significantly reduced the ability of any large contract holder to use leverage to buy silver. On 'Silver Thursday' (27 March 1980), silver prices dropped significantly and, as a result of this and the leverage rule change, the Hunt brothers were unable to meet their obligations, which caused panic in the markets. Their obligations were so large that the US government forced banks to issue lines of credit totalling around $1bn to prevent a crisis. These credit lines were backed by most of the assets of the Hunt brothers who eventually, following civil charges, were declared bankrupt.

- *Commodity Clearing House (1983)*. The Kuala Lumpur Commodity Clearing House in Malaysia had only been operating for three years when it was brought down as a result of a crash in palm oil futures. Six clearing members then defaulted on a total of $70m, leading to trading being suspended. A report from the Malaysian government blamed the CCP for inactivity between the beginning of a severe squeeze on market prices and the default of the first clearing member. Officials at the CCP were also criticised for their lack of experience (Hills et al. 1999).

- *Hong Kong Futures Exchange (HKFE) (1987)*. The 1987 stock market crash was another example of an unprecedented price collapse, in this case involving the equity markets. In 1987, three separate entities were involved with the central clearing of the Hong Kong futures market:

o the exchange essentially running the futures market (HKFE);

o the CCP offering a clearing service (International Commodities Clearing House Hong Kong Limited); and

o the default fund (Hong Kong Futures Guarantee Corporation).

The above separation led to the wrong incentives. Exchange members could not participate in the management of the default fund, the CCP was responsible for monitoring positions but was not exposed to losses in the event of default, and the default fund was exposed to losses but had no say in risk monitoring or setting standards for clearing members. After a period of significant growth, on so-called 'Black Monday' (19 October 1987) the Hong Kong stock market (Hang Seng Index) dropped by almost 50%. The market was subsequently closed for the rest of the week and was expected to fall again on opening. This led to fears that margin calls would not be met and that the total losses would exceed the financial resources of the CCP. This prompted a rescue package for the CCP to be put together by the government and private institutions (Hills et al. 1999). The bailout cost the government (taxpayer) in the region of HK$1bn. One of the causes of the HKFE failure was the lack of strict margin practices, together with the fact that initial margin requirements for futures had not been increased, even though the underlying market had risen significantly in the preceding period.

- *Bolsa de Valores, Mercadorias & Futuros de Sao Paulo (BM&FBOVESPA) (1999).* BM&FBOVESPA is a stock exchange located in Brazil. A sudden foreign exchange (FX) move of the Brazilian real by around 50% with respect to the US dollar occurred in 1999, when the new president of the central bank decided to release the control over the exchange rate, triggering this massive currency devaluation. This led to the default of two banks that were clearing members, with losses that exceeded the margins and default funds held by BM&FBOVESPA. The central bank intervened and bailed out the two banks in question, thus preventing the collapse of the CCP.

Whilst not a CCP default, the recent default fund losses at the Nasdaq are also an interesting case study and will be discussed in Section 10.1.3.

10.1.2   The 1987 Stock Market Crash

Whilst HKFE represented the only CCP failure as a result of the 1987 'Black Monday' stock market crash, there are other examples of CCP distress in this period. The CCPs of Chicago Mercantile Exchange (CME), Options Clearing Corporation (OCC) and Chicago Board of Trade (CBOT) were very close to failure, and only prompt action from the Federal Reserve prevented a catastrophe (Pirrong 2010b).

Due to the very large price moves on and around Black Monday, the magnitude of margin calls was extremely large. This created a number of inter-related problems:

- Difficulties in receiving variation margin payments due from those with losing positions, despite, in some cases, multiple intraday margin calls being made.
- CCPs 'absorbing' significant amounts of liquidity by collecting some variation margin payments but not always paying out on the winning positions in a timely manner.
- Large increases in volumes of trades and unprecedented price volatility, creating operational problems such as errors and delays in confirming trades, made worse by a lack of automated payment systems in some cases. Since some trades were reconciled only at the end of the day, many leveraged positions had losses well in excess of their posted margins.
- A lack of linked clearing arrangements so that, for example, members hedging options (OCC) with futures contracts (CME) did not have gains and losses offset and were therefore caught in a 'variation margin trap'. OCC had asked CME to agree to cross-margining prior to the 1987 crash (Norman 2011).

The net result of the very heavy liquidity problems caused by the above issues was that CME came close to having insufficient margin to start trading on 20 October 1987. Failure of CME was only averted due to its bank advancing the CCP $400m just minutes prior to the market opening, so that it could make variation margin payments totalling $2.5bn (IMF 2010).

At OCC, a large clearing member had difficulties in paying margin (and only did so after an emergency loan from its bank) and OCC itself was late in making payments to clearing members and suffered a significant loss due to a clearing member default. Around three-quarters of this loss (after using retained earnings) caused a hit to the default fund, with rights of assessment used to bring the default fund to its previous level (although the default fund hit was only a fraction of the total default fund size).

Without the strong support of the Federal Reserve (both explicit and implicit in terms of liquidity injections and public statements, respectively), a large CCP failure in 1987 was a significant possibility. An interesting review of this crisis is given in Bernanke (1990).

It is important not to overstate the importance of historical CCP failures in assessing the current benefit of central clearing. On the other hand, it is also important not to overuse the previous experience as a justification for the benefits of clearing.

10.1.3   The 2018 Nasdaq Case

A recent event at Nasdaq's commodities clearing division has provided a reminder of the risks of CCPs. Nasdaq Clearing is a CCP for various products including certain commodity contracts. One of the clearing members was Einar Aas, a proprietary trader who had traded positions based on the difference in price between Nordic and German power contracts. Following a large move in these underlying markets on 10 September 2018, the value of Mr Aas's portfolio fell substantially, and he failed to make an intraday margin call. This led to Mr Aas being declared in default, and the underlying portfolio was closed out in two days following a second auction (the first having failed to produce any adequate bid). Only four clearing members were involved in this auction.[1] The result of the auction was a loss that exceeded the 'defaulter-pays' resources, which led to a loss of €7m for Nasdaq Clearing ('skin-in-the-game') and an approximate €107m loss to the segregated commodity default fund. This default fund loss was in the region of two-thirds of the total default fund, which clearing members were then contractually obliged to replenish.

The initial margin held was based on a Standard Portfolio Analysis of Risk (SPAN) methodology (Section 9.2.2) with a margin period of risk (MPoR) of two days and a confidence level of 99.2%, as well as stressed market conditions and including a buffer of 25%. The position did not trigger an initial margin add-on for concentration risk. The market move experienced was in excess of the initial margin of the defaulter, but only by about 40%. Most of the loss was, therefore, a result of the difficulty in auctioning the large position.

This episode is a cautionary tale, showing how clearing members can experience default fund losses as a result of the default of other clearing members. It highlights several potentially problematic areas of CCP risk management, notably:

- membership criteria;
- initial margin calculation methodologies and choice of parameters (such as the MPoR);

---

[1] Out of a total of well over 100, although some of these may have been unable to bid on the underlying portfolio.

- concentration add-ons for initial margin;
- the auction process; and
- the skin-in-the-game of CCPs.

For more details, see BIS (2018).

10.1.4   Risks Faced by CCPs

The primary risk for a CCP is the default of a clearing member(s) and the possible associated or knock-on effects that this could cause. Knock-on impacts could include the default or financial distress of other clearing members, failed auctions, business being moved away from the CCP, and reputational problems.

Although CCPs typically have a large number of members, the majority of clearing is concentrated amongst a much smaller number of participants. For example, Armakolla and Bianchi (2017) analyse European Union CCPs and report the proportion of total initial margin posted by the largest five clearing members ('IM5/IM'). Out of a total of 11 CCPs, this ratio is more than 50% for 8, with the largest being 73%.

CCPs could potentially suffer losses from other non-default events such as fraud, operational problems (e.g. systems failures), legal issues (e.g. if the law in a given jurisdiction does not support the rules of the CCP), or investment (of cash and securities held as margin and other financial resources, or due to a deviation from this policy (e.g. a rogue trader)).

Other risks faced by CCPs include:

- *Model risk*. CCPs have significant exposure to model risk through margining approaches. Unlike exchange-traded products, OTC derivatives prices often cannot be observed directly via market sources, so that valuation models are required to mark-to-market (MTM) products for variation margin purposes. The approaches for MTM must be standard and robust across all possible market scenarios. Initial margin requirements introduce even more complexity. Particular modelling problems could arise from misspecification with respect to volatility, tail risk, complex dependencies, and wrong-way risk. A lesson from previous CCP failures (Section 10.1.1) is that initial margin methodologies need to be updated as a market regime shifts significantly. On the other hand, such updates should not be excessive as they can lead to problems such as procyclicality (Section 9.3.5). Another important feature of models is that they generally impose linearity: model-based initial margins will increase in proportion to the size of a position. It is important in this situation to use additional components such as margin multipliers to ensure that large and concentrated positions are penalised and that risk is adequately covered (see the Nasdaq discussion in Section 10.1.3).
- *Liquidity risk*. Large quantities of cash flow through a CCP due to variation margin payments and other cash flows, and a large amount of initial margin is held. CCPs must try to optimise the investment of some of the financial resources they hold, without taking excessive credit and liquidity risk (e.g. by using short-term investments such as deposits, repos, and reverse repos). However, in the event of a default, the CCP must continue to fulfil its obligations to surviving members in a timely manner. Although CCPs will clearly invest cautiously over the short term, with liquidity and credit risk very much in mind, there is also the danger that the underlying

investments they hold must be readily available and convertible into cash. For example, CPSS-IOSCO (2012) principles require 'prearranged and highly reliable funding arrangements, even in extreme but plausible market conditions', so that bonds (including government securities) may only be counted towards a CCP's liquidity resources if they are backed with committed funding arrangements.

- *Operational and legal risk.* The centralisation of various functions within a CCP can increase efficiency but also expose market participants to additional risks, which become concentrated at the CCP. Like all market participants, CCPs are exposed to operational risks, such as systems failures and fraud. A breakdown of any aspect of a CCP's infrastructure would be catastrophic since it would affect a relatively sizeable number of large counterparties within the market. Legal challenges and litigation as a result of the default management process (e.g. see the Caisse de Liquidation case discussed in Section 10.1.1) represent a significant problem.
- *Concentration, sovereign risk, and wrong-way risk.* CCPs may hold margin in currencies and securities which are correlated to the default risks of their clearing members. For example, there may be direct exposure to the knock-on effects of a sovereign default in terms of the failure of members and the devaluation of sovereign bonds held as margin.

10.1.5   Risks Caused by CCPs

With respect to the historical cases discussed above, the common sources of failure can be identified as:

- large underlying price moves (e.g. commodities, stocks, FX);
- defaults stemming from losses in relation to large market moves;
- initial margins and default funds being insufficient to absorb losses;
- liquidity strains arising from delays in the flow of variation margin in and out of CCPs, caused by CCPs and/or clearing members (for operational reasons, as well as due to solvency problems);
- initial margin calculations making inappropriate assumptions (e.g. relative versus absolute returns, discussed in Section 9.3.3) and not being updated according to changes in market conditions (e.g. after a large asset price and associated volatility increase); and
- operational problems arising from excessive volumes and large price moves.

In summary, failures are a result of a combination of high market volatility, failure of members, and large asset price shocks, coupled with inadequate margins and default funds. There are several overall lessons to be gleaned from these derivatives CCP failures and near-failures:

- Operational risk must be controlled as much as possible.
- Variation margins should be recalculated frequently and collected promptly (intradaily in volatile markets).
- Initial margin and default funds should be resilient to large asset shocks or gaps in market variables and to extreme dependency (e.g. the concept of correlation increasing in a crisis).
- A CCP should carefully monitor positions, penalise concentration (e.g. by increasing initial margin), and act quickly in the case of excessively large positions.

10.2   ANALYSIS OF A CCP LOSS STRUCTURE

10.2.1   Review of the Loss Waterfall

Figure 10.1 shows again the loss waterfall (Section 8.3.4) and a potential liquidation scenario causing losses that exhaust the default fund over the close-out period or MPoR. In this extreme situation, the CCP needs to apply other methods of loss allocation. The definitions 'first loss' and 'second loss' are used to denote the defaulter-pays and remaining shared financial resources (survivors pay), respectively.

Mutualisation of losses can be an efficient insurance mechanism for risk sharing. It works well when risks are relatively idiosyncratic and independent (e.g. car insurance). However, it works less well as risks become more correlated and systemic, as illustrated by monoline insurers (see Section 2.4.4). Therefore, if the failure of a clearing member is an idiosyncratic event, then the loss mutualisation via the default fund of the CCP may enhance stability. However, in the case of a more systematic failure, this process may be less helpful.

Since initial margins are designed to provide coverage to a high confidence level, it is likely that any sizeable hit to the mutualised default fund would only arise due to an adverse combination of a number of underlying factors. Whilst such a scenario is by construction unlikely, there must be a well-defined allocation of losses and/or recapitalisation of the CCP as part of the CCP 'rule book'. Indeed, the mere existence of such a well-specified waterfall may add stability to the CCP, since members will be better able to measure and manage their own risk if the CCP rules are clearly defined.

The general way in which losses above the defaulter's resources are handled is either:

- to call for additional financial resources from clearing members (rights of assessment); or
- to reduce the claims of the clearing members (other loss allocation methods).

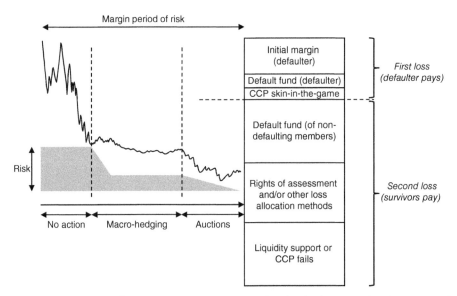

Figure 10.1   Illustration of the loss waterfall and potential risk in the event that losses exceed the primary financial resources of the CCP.

Table 10.1   Analysis of different components of the CCP default waterfall.

	Paid by	Funded or unfunded
Initial margin (defaulter)	Defaulter	Funded
Default fund (defaulter)		
CCP equity ('skin-in-the-game')	CCP shareholders	
Rights of assessment	Surviving clearing members	Unfunded
Other loss allocation methods	Surviving clearing members (and potentially their clients)	

Ideally, loss allocation rules will also create the correct incentives both before and during the default management process. The nature of the different components of the loss waterfall is shown in Table 10.1.

For a CCP to recover from a member default, it needs to re-establish a matched book. This is normally achieved by replacing the defaulter's positions – for example, by selling long positions to (or buying short positions from) surviving participants through an auction process (Section 8.3.3). In a severe scenario, an auction may not clear at prices consistent with the CCP remaining solvent. In other words, the best prices demanded by surviving clearing participants to take on the defaulter's positions may exceed the financial resources available to the CCP. In an extreme scenario, it may be that the CCP receives no bid at all for one or more sub-portfolios. Hence, other loss allocation methods may be needed (Section 10.2.4).

There are a number of inter-related reasons why a default may lead to losses that may, in turn, breach the financial contributions of the defaulted member and cause losses in the mutualised default fund (and beyond). These are:

- *Delay since last variation margin was received.* The delay before last receiving variation margin prior to the clearing member being declared in default. Due to variation margin practices of CCPs being at a minimum daily, and potentially also intradaily, this period is intended to be short. However, it should be considered how long a CCP might delay before declaring a large clearing member in default.
- *Market volatility in the hedging period.* Whilst macro-hedging the risk, the CCP will be exposed to further market volatility and potential bid-offer hedging costs for large positions. For more complex portfolios, such as OTC derivatives, such hedging costs may be significant.
- *Auction costs.* Finally, in attempting to auction the positions of the defaulted member, the CCP will be exposed to liquidation costs (although, as noted in Section 8.3.3, the above hedges should improve the auction process by creating less-directional portfolios). This could be related to bid-offer costs, but in more extreme situations there might be severe downwards price movements due to 'fire sale'-like dynamics. An extreme case of this could be a failed auction, where a CCP does not consider that it has received reasonable bids for one or more portfolios. In liquid markets, such as exchange-traded ones, even large portfolios can be closed out relatively easily. For OTC derivatives, such a resolution could take at least a few days and may even be simply unachievable.

There is a key difference between losses due to market volatility and risk premiums experienced as liquidation costs. Market volatility may lead to losses for a defaulted member, but these must lead to equivalent gains for surviving clearing members. This means that within the set of positions cleared by the CCP, there are possible ways to consider offsetting losses – for example, by not posting margin against the gains of surviving members. On the other hand, when a CCP experiences bid-offer costs and/or risk premiums, these are costs that are not balanced by equivalent gains in the opposite cleared trades. The result of this is that loss allocation is likely to be more problematic. Put another way, highly-volatile products may clearly present a challenge, but illiquid products (or those that become illiquid in the aftermath of a major default) will be even more difficult.

Loss allocation methods are typically needed in the event that the defaulter-pays resources have been exhausted. Most CCPs use 'rights of assessment', which represent an unfunded obligation to contribute additionally to a default fund that has been depleted by losses. Typically, such a recapitalisation will be invoked if a significant fraction (e.g. 25%) of the default fund is used. If this right were unlimited, then the CCP would be unlikely to fail (unless all its clearing members did so). However, this would create significant moral hazard and unlimited exposure for clearing members, and may destabilise markets as members would be required to contribute to default funds at the worst possible time. For these reasons, rights of assessment are generally capped, an example being 100% of the last default fund contribution subject to a maximum of three defaults in a six-month period (see LCH 2017; RBA 2017).

10.2.2   Impact of Default Fund Exposure

Surviving clearing members have a 'second loss' position via their default fund exposure (Figure 10.1). This means that clearing members may not be incentivised to bid aggressively within an auction if they believe that the 'defaulter's resources' (initial margin and default fund) will provide sufficient loss absorbency. Put differently, auction bidders may take on positions at a profit, knowing that the defaulter's resources that are held by the CCP will pay for such a profit. Indeed, the clearing members' optimal strategy is to utilise at least 100% of the defaulter-pays resources, which otherwise will only be returned to the bankruptcy administrator. Indeed, it is actually optimal to utilise the default fund as the winning bidder stands to gain from the entire amount of default fund lost, whereas any allocation of default fund losses via rights of assessment will be pro rata.

There is some evidence of the above optimal behaviour in practice. For example, in the Lehman bankruptcy, there were claims that CME members profited from participating in the auction,[2] although such firms seem to be immune from prosecution.[3] This may also explain the large default fund losses in the Nasdaq case (Section 10.1.3). Such effects will be a significant detriment to other creditors (Section 10.3.5).

Related to the above is the concept that a CCP waterfall may behave rather like a synthetic securitisation or collateralised debt obligation (CDO), which has been noted by a number of authors, including Murphy (2013) and Pirrong (2013). The comparison is

---

[2] Chasan, E. and A. Saphira (2010). Firms reaped windfalls in Lehman auction: examiner. *Reuters* (15 April). www.reuters.com.

[3] Bunge, J. (2010). CME, Lehman Book Bidders Likely Protected From Lawsuits. *Wall Street Journal* (15 April). www.wsj.com.

that the 'first loss' of the CDO is covered by defaulter-pays resources, and clearing members – through their default fund contributions and other loss allocation exposures, such as rights of assessment – are exposed to the second loss position on the hypothetical CDO. Of course, the precise terms of the CDO are unknown and ever changing as they are based on aspects such as the CCP membership, the portfolio of each member, and the initial margins held. However, what is clear is that the second loss exposure should correspond to a relatively unlikely event, since otherwise it would imply that initial margin coverage was too thin.

The second loss position that a CCP member is implicitly exposed to is therefore rather senior in CDO terms. Such senior tranches are known to be heavily concentrated in terms of their systemic risk exposure (see Gibson 2004; Coval et al. 2009; Brennan et al. 2009; Gregory 2014). It is well known that such structures are concentrated in systemic risk and perform very badly during large, market-wide shocks. Furthermore, a consequence of such structures is that they concentrate wrong-way risk (Gregory 2011).

The implications of the systemic and wrong-way risk concentration via the senior tranche exposure created by a CCP, by analogy to CDOs, would be:

- the risk concentrated within a CCP will be systemic in nature;
- correlation between losses from different clearing member defaults is likely to be high, as losses will hit the mutualised default fund precisely when surviving clearing members are under financial stress (wrong-way risk), and these members will be put under stress by the impact of losses of their default funds, rights of assessments, variation margin gains haircutting, and other loss allocation methods which could cause them to fail also;
- loss allocation methods increase interconnections between CCP participants during periods of stress; and
- default funds should, therefore, be very large and expensive.

10.2.3   The Prisoner's Dilemma and AIPs

If members believe that losses may exceed the defaulter-pays financial resources (Figure 10.1) and be mutualised back to them via the default fund, then this clearly incentivises better behaviour. However, once losses move into the survivors-pay region, moral hazard becomes a problem, and there is a danger of certain gaming behaviour by CCP members. The 'prisoner's dilemma' refers to a situation where it is in the individual interests of each party to take a particular course of action, but it is damaging for a large number of parties to take this route simultaneously. For example, clearing members may not participate actively in an auction process, even though collectively it is in their best interests to do this.

As long as they believe that initial margin may not be sufficient, it is collectively in the interests of the surviving clearing members to participate actively in an auction to ensure that the CCP can close out the portfolio most efficiently, so as to minimise losses to the default fund. On the other hand, an individual member potentially has the incentive not to participate actively in the auction in the hope that the other members will instead devote their time and balance sheets to ease the problem. Of course, when all members adopt this view, then the situation can become highly destabilising. Hence, the CCP should have alternative methods to close out positions and allocate the resulting losses. Ideally, these methods would also go so far as to penalise members behaving outside the bounds of the common good. This would then, in turn, incentivise good behaviour in the auction.

The first part of loss allocation involves the allocation of the finite default fund to cover losses. Some CCPs may operate separate default funds to align the losses of members with the products they clear. This would ensure, for example, that clearing members clearing only futures would be protected from default losses resulting from an OTC derivatives portfolio being cleared with the same CCP.

Furthermore, some CCPs may allocate losses within a default fund in tranches to mitigate the prisoner's dilemma and incentivise members to act in the common good. One way to achieve this is to make default fund loss allocation heterogeneous and linked to the auction bidding process. A basic form of this is to 'juniorise' the default funds of non-bidders – or bidders outside a given range – so that any losses are allocated to their default funds prior to those of other bidders. However, this introduces a related problem in that different participants may make more natural bidders in a particular auction due, for example, to their size, sophistication, or market activity in a participant type of product.[4] For example, a bank not clearing swaps in a given currency, or inflation swaps, should not be expected to bid in an auction on this particular sub-portfolio of a defaulter.

A more sophisticated approach considers a hierarchy of bids and sub-allocation of default funds in line with sub-portfolios that will likely be auctioned (e.g. currencies of interest rate swaps). An example of the above concept is provided by auction incentive pools (AIPs), used in OTC auctions by LCH.[5] With AIPs, each member's default fund contributions (pre- and unfunded) are allocated proportionally to a product and currency-specific bucket, in an amount that reflects the relative market risk that the member contributes in that currency. These currency-specific default funds will be used to absorb losses in auctions for products in each currency, respectively. If a loss exceeds the AIP in a currency, this will be allocated to the remaining default funds in other AIPs and any unallocated default funds. This means that, for example, a regional bank clearing only products in its own currency would be partially protected in the event of the default of a European bank clearing mainly euro-denominated products.

Spreadsheet 10.1 Illustration of AIP calculation.

Another feature of AIPs referring to the allocation of losses in tranches is related to members bidding in an auction for a particular currency. Losses in each LCH AIP are distributed in sequence according to the competitiveness of members bidding in the auction:

- non-bidders (who were expected to bid);
- other (unsuccessful) bidders; and
- the winning bidder.

---

[4] CPSS-IOSCO (2012) states that 'An OTC derivatives CCP may need to consider requiring participants to agree in advance to bid on the defaulting participant's portfolio and, should the auction fail, accept an allocation of the portfolio. Where used, such procedures should include consideration of the risk profile and portfolio of each receiving participant before allocating positions so as to minimise additional risk for the non-defaulting participants.'

[5] LCH Ltd Default Rules Section 2.5. www.lch.com.

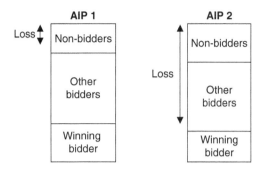

Figure 10.2   Illustration of tranching of default fund losses via auction incentive pools (AIPs).

The CCP would inform members of their relative contribution to an AIP (compared to other members). An illustration of the AIP concept is shown in Figure 10.2. This shows relatively small losses on the default fund for AIP 1 and larger losses for AIP 2. This means that all bidders on AIP 1 would be protected from default fund losses, which would be absorbed by non-bidders. Moreover, the relatively large losses on AIP 2 would not cause losses for members clearing trades only in AIP 1. However, note that the bidders in AIP 1 could experience losses in two ways: first, via larger losses on AIP 1, and second, via losses in excess of the total AIP 2 default fund. In the latter case, this is because, as mentioned above, losses in excess of an AIP can be absorbed by the remaining default fund (either unallocated or allocated to other AIPs).

The aim of the above is obviously to give clearing members the incentive to participate actively in the auction process within the subset of products they clear. Note that a member not clearing a given currency need not bid in that auction, as they will not have any default fund allocated to that AIP.

10.2.4   Other Loss Allocation Methods

In the event that rights of assessment are insufficient to absorb defaulter losses, the CCP could either fail or have other methods for allocating losses. CCP insolvency would clearly represent a highly-contagious event, and it is therefore important for there to be a robust mechanism for wind-down or recovery. In contrast to formal bankruptcy, CCP loss allocation potentially allows a timely and orderly resolution of an extreme loss event that is likely preferable to CCP failure.

The basic idea of other loss allocation methods is that defaulting members with out-of-the-money positions will be unable to pay variation margin to the CCP, and this will, therefore, be offset by some reduction in the claims of the other surviving members. This will clearly lead to a heterogeneous setup as losses will depend on the extent to which surviving members have a similar portfolio to that of the defaulter(s).

Spreadsheet 10.2 Illustration of VMGH and selective tear-up approaches to loss allocation.

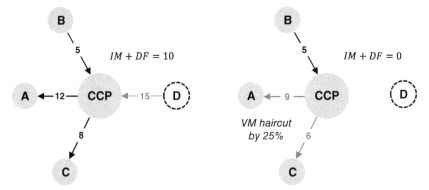

Figure 10.3 Illustration of VMGH. The diagram on the left-hand side depicts the initial situation where financial resources are not balanced, and the right-hand side represents the balancing of resources by using the defaulter's initial margin and (mutualised) default funds with VMGH.

Variation margin gains haircutting (VMGH) is probably the most common alternative loss allocation concept (see ISDA 2013b). The idea of VMGH is that gains which have accumulated since the start of the default management process can be reduced pro rata so as to absorb the amounts owing to the CCP by the defaulted member. This means that clearing members whose positions have increased in value since the default[6] will not receive the full margin to cover their gain, whilst those owing money to the CCP will still be required to pay in full.

An illustration of VMGH is shown in Figure 10.3. This shows a CCP owed variation margins of 5 and 15 by members B and D, the latter being in default. Correspondingly, the CCP owes the same total (20) of variation margin to two other members (A and C) in the amounts 12 and 8. Since the defaulter's initial margin and default fund contributions (10) are exceeded by the net amount owed (15), then the CCP must allocate a loss of 5. In the absence of any rights of assessment (or after such rights have been exhausted), this could be allocated via haircutting the variation margin owed to members A and C on a pro rata basis, as shown.

There may possibly be a cap on the variation margin haircut that can be applied. For example, LCH Ltd (LCH 2017; RBA 2017) caps VMGH at £200m or twice a participant's default fund contribution, and the loss distribution process is limited to 10 days. Surviving members vote if the cap or time horizon is likely to be breached.

Another interesting feature of VMGH is that it mimics the economics of insolvency in bilateral markets since parties with claims on the defaulter lose in a pro rata fashion. It may be argued that clearing members on the other side of the defaulter's trades – and therefore more likely to incur VMGH – may more actively bid in auctions to avoid this. However, it may not be fair to penalise a member just because they were on the correct side of a market move (e.g. their positions may be hedges).

If a CCP can auction a defaulter's portfolio at mid-market prices and suffer no other losses, then uncapped VMGH is guaranteed to work, as the losses from the defaulter must be matched by equivalent gains for other CCP members. This may be seen as particularly

---

[6] Strictly speaking, the last point at which the defaulted member paid variation margin.

relevant if the underlying portfolio is liquid and the default has been associated with a large market move, creating some large 'winners' and 'losers', as may be the case in exchange-traded markets (as seen from some historical CCP failures, Section 10.1.1).

The obvious reason why VMGH may fail in practice is if the CCP has to close out at a significant premium to mid-market prices. In such a case, unless the risk premium required can be covered by the member's initial margin and default fund contribution, then VMGH will fail. Any non-default losses or caps in VMGH may create the same effect. One more drastic approach in such a situation is 'tear-up' with a similar method being 'forced allocation'.

Tear-up involves cancelling contracts with surviving clearing members that represent the opposite position to that of the defaulter. Such contracts could be terminated with a cash settlement based on the current mid-market price, or the equivalent price when the default occurred or when variation margin was last exchanged. There may also need to be a pro rata reduction if the CCP is unable to pay such prices in full. The aim of the tear-up is to return a CCP to a matched book by terminating the other side of a defaulter's trades (or at least those that cannot be auctioned). All other contracts (possibly the majority of the total contracts cleared) could remain centrally cleared. As with VMGH, this option as a backstop may incentivise active bidding in an auction if members fear they may otherwise have contracts torn up.

The major difference with tear-up compared to VMGH is that the CCP is not exposed to any risk premium in auctioning transactions as it pays (at most) only the current market value of the transaction. To understand this, consider the illustration in Figure 10.4, which is similar to the VMGH example in Figure 10.3, except that it is assumed that in the auction there is a risk premium of 25 charged (represented as a payment to the market – M). This risk premium means that VMGH will fail since, even if the haircut is 100%, the CCP's total financial resources (15 + 5 = 20) are insufficient to pay the risk premium. In this scenario, an alternative would be to tear up all the underlying trades with members A and C and avoid the risk premium. Note that the CCP can pay the full (mid-market) amount owed to A and C without any haircut or other reduction (such as using a valuation when margin was last posted).

A CCP may reasonably attempt to tear up the smallest subset of trades that will return it to a matched book and allow it to continue operating. In the above example, if there were an additional 5 of financial resources (e.g. if the CCP had a larger mutualised default fund), then it would only be necessary to tear up 80% of the positions.[7] Furthermore, if the CCP pays out less than the current market value of the contracts being torn up, then the tear-up fraction can be lower.

Tear-up represents a dramatic loss allocation process and has a number of important disadvantages:

- *Unlimited liability*. Non-defaulting members theoretically face an unlimited liability since the amounts they are paid for torn-up trades will differ from the market prices at which these members can enter into replacement transactions.
- *Replacement impact*. Whilst tear-up avoids the CCP needing to replace trades via the auction, a similar dynamic may occur where clearing members have to hedge their risk

---

[7] This assumes linearity but, in reality, the close-out of a smaller portfolio may be easier and the resulting risk premium smaller.

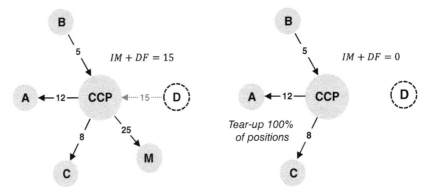

Figure 10.4 Illustration of partial tear-up. The diagram on the left-hand side depicts the initial situation where financial resources are not balanced, and the right-hand side represents the balancing of resources by using the defaulter's initial margin and (mutualised) default funds together with tear-up. M denotes the auction market where a risk premium of 25 is included in the price and therefore represents an extra cost for the CCP. Tear-up prevents the need to pay this risk premium.

from trades subject to tear-up. Such replacement hedges could create market instability, especially since the CCP has failed to execute similar trades via the auction. A clearing member could even be sent into default because of tear-ups.

- *Portfolio bifurcation*. Partial tear-up may alter the balance of surviving members' portfolios and therefore the exposure to the CCP. This, in turn, may trigger additional initial margin or capital requirements if the tear-up results in a less diversified portfolio.

There are other loss allocation methods that are similar to tear-up. One is 'forced allocation' or 'invoicing back', where clearing members are obliged to accept certain portfolios at prices determined by the CCP. This has a similar effect since instead of tearing up an existing trade, a CCP might impose the reverse trade on a member. However, forced allocation may be more flexible as any member can be allocated positions, whereas tear-up requires a member to have the appropriate trades in their portfolio. Unlike tear-up, it may not be possible for a clearing member to pass on the impact of forced allocation to its clients.

Most CCPs use rights of assessment (capped) together with VMGH and/or tear-up as possible loss allocation methods. Other approaches, such as initial margin haircutting, have been suggested (Elliott 2013) but have not been used in practice, and also regulation may prevent them – for example, European Market Infrastructure Regulation forbids CCPs from using initial margin of non-defaulted members to cover default losses.[8] Note that regulation may incentivise clearing members to pass on aspects of loss allocation to their clients.[9]

Pirrong (2011) notes that a CCP could be *solvent* but *illiquid* due to struggling to meet the immediate requirements to pay margin. In such a situation, a CCP would require

---

[8] EMIR article 45(4): 'A CCP shall not use the margins posted by non-defaulting members to cover the losses resulting from the default of another clearing member.'

[9] For example, under the EU's Capital Requirement Regulation article 306(1)(c), a clearing member will have to pass on the impact of actions such as VMGH to get appropriate capital relief.

access to external liquidity. This implies that a liquidity injection from a central bank is the only way to avoid a potentially catastrophic, liquidity-induced CCP failure. Not surprisingly, regulators view this liquidity support as a last resort and may require them to have facilities such as lines of credit in place to avoid this necessity.[10]

10.3   IMPACT OF MARGIN

10.3.1   Background and Historical Examples

Mandatory clearing and bilateral margining requirements will have one stark impact on the OTC derivatives market: a significant increase in margin requirements. Whilst it is not surprising that post-GFC regulation was focused on the reduction of counterparty risk, a concern is that the related funding and liquidity impacts of such regulation are in danger of being overlooked. Assessing the impact of increased margin requirements is difficult because it will be driven by subtle aspects such as the quality of margin required, segregation, and the functioning of margin transformation trades (e.g. repo markets). Nevertheless, it is important to characterise the impact of the increase in margin as a balance between reducing counterparty risk and increasing funding liquidity risk.

During the GFC, the reliance of financial institutions on short-term debt made them particularly vulnerable to the outbreak of problems in longer-dated markets (such as sub-prime mortgages). Excessive reliance on short-term funding markets has been cited by many as an important contributor to the severity of the GFC. It is therefore important to consider the funding liquidity risk created by clearing and margin requirements. Generally, it is relevant to consider two broad effects that arise from both clearing and bilateral margining requirements:

- increases in *variation margin* requirements due to the tighter requirements compared to bilateral markets; and
- the impact of the additional *initial margin* requirements.

The operation of margining mechanisms relies heavily on the extension of credit (Bernanke 1990). This could imply that in certain cases margining may be irrelevant or even lead to problems that would not exist in a non-margined world. There are some historical examples that shed light on these aspects:

- *American International Group (AIG).* The example of AIG (Section 2.4.4) is a well-known example of the funding liquidity problems that can be induced by margin posting. In September 2008, AIG was essentially insolvent due to the margin requirements arising from credit default swap trades executed by its financial products subsidiary (AIGFP). Due to the systemic importance of AIG, the Federal Reserve Bank created a secured credit facility of up to $85bn to allow AIGFP to post the margin it owed and avoid the collapse of AIG. In this example, one of the key aspects was that AIGFP posted margin as a function of its credit rating. This created a

---

[10] Sourbes, C. (2013). BoE's Carney: liquidity support for CCPs is a 'last-resort' option. *Risk* (28 November). www.risk.net.

'cliff-edge' effect as a downgrade of AIG led to a very large margin requirement. Linkages of margin requirements to ratings have generally been removed or diluted in recent years in both bilateral and centrally-cleared markets.

- *The BP Deepwater Horizon oil spill.* In 2010, British Petroleum (BP) experienced the largest accidental marine oil spill in the history of the petroleum industry. This caused loss of life, severe environmental problems, and financial losses for BP itself. Not surprisingly, in the aftermath of these problems, some of BP's trading partners (including banks trading OTC derivatives) had credit risk concerns which were compounded after BP's credit rating was downgraded by the major rating agencies (Moody's, Standard & Poor's, and Fitch) and its credit spreads widened significantly. There is some anecdotal evidence of banks giving flexibility in terms of margin posting to prevent BP from suffering further problems. BP then borrowed a total of $5bn from banks to ease its liquidity problems as a result of additional margin demands arising from the aforementioned credit rating downgrades.[11] One interpretation of this is that banks were reabsorbing the credit risk of BP that had been previously transferred to BP as funding liquidity risk via margin requirements. Furthermore, this was being done at the very time when the margin arrangements were most important.[12]
- *Ashanti.* Ashanti (now part of AngloGold Ashanti Limited) was a Ghanaian gold producer. When gold prices rose in September 1999, Ashanti experienced very large losses of $450m on OTC derivatives contracts (gold forward contracts and options) used to hedge its exposure to a falling gold price. Market participants commented that Ashanti had hedged an unusually high proportion of its total reserves. The negative value of Ashanti's hedge book meant that its OTC derivatives counterparties were due variation margin payments totalling around $280m. Ashanti had a funding liquidity problem: it had the physical gold to satisfy contracts, but not the liquid assets to make the interim variation margin payments. Ashanti then struck an agreement, making it exempt from posting margin for just over three years.[13] This is another example of liquidity risk being converted into credit risk as margin agreements are deemed impractical, which in turn takes place at the time that they are most important. It could be argued that this is a good argument for exemptions for end users hedging with derivatives. However, it seems to be generally believed that Ashanti went too far in using derivatives as a risk management tool and hedged excessively (around 10 times its annual gold production at the time).[14]
- *MF Global.* MF Global entered into trading strategies that it was unable to fund. Due to having insufficient liquidity to sustain its investment strategies (despite, allegedly, resorting to segregated customer funds, as discussed in Section 7.5.4), MF Global defaulted in October 2011 (see Heckinger 2012).

---

[11] Kelly, K. (2010). Collateral Demands Growing for BP. *CNBC* (28 June). www.cnbc.com.

[12] It could be argued that the credit risk could at least be appropriately priced with respect to the creditworthiness of BP at the time. However, this illustrates that a margin agreement can expose an institution to volatility arising from its own credit risk, which is a risk that may be more effectively managed by banks.

[13] Hirschler, B. (1999). Ashanti wins three-year gold margin reprieve. *GhanaWeb* (2 November). www.ghanaweb.com.

[14] 'Mr. Sam Jonah, Chief Executive of Ashanti, referring to their financial problems, stated "I am prepared to concede that we were reckless. We took a bet on the price of gold. We thought that it would go down and we took a position."' From O'Connor, G. (1999). Ashanti left exposed by 'exotics'. *Financial Times* (8 November). www.ft.com.

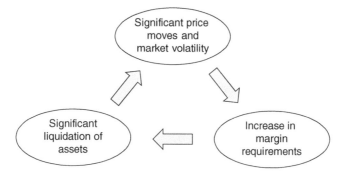

Figure 10.5   Illustration of a potential feedback loop involving margin posting.

Margin has the potential to cause feedback effects in volatile markets, as illustrated in Figure 10.5. This could be driven by the risk sensitivity (and in the extreme, procyclicality) of initial margins leading to larger requirements in volatile markets, in turn creating liquidations and large price moves. Such problems may spill over into other markets, as if CCP members have to meet unexpected margin calls in one market, they may sell assets in another and therefore drive prices down. Of course, methodologies for initial margin calculation that produce stable results can reduce these problems.

10.3.2   Variation Margin

It can be argued that variation margin is not expensive since it only represents a settlement (actual or proxy, see Section 7.2.6) of running profit and loss, and as such is a zero-sum game (one party's loss of variation margin is another's gain). This zero-cost variation margin idea has been expressed in various ways – for example:

> In the case of variation margin, the BCBS and IOSCO recognise that the regular and timely *exchange of variation margin* represents the settlement of the running profit/loss of a derivative and *has no net liquidity costs* given that variation margin represents a transfer of resources from one party to another. (BCBS-IOSCO 2013b, emphasis added)
>
> The variation margin payments, on the contrary, should not have a first-order effect on the demand for collateral, as variation margin is a one-way payment and hence does not affect the net demand for collateral [margin] assets. (CGFS 2013)

These statements suggest that margin costs and benefits are symmetric and/or that the 'velocity of margin' is infinite. In reality, this is not true, due to a frictional drag on margin from operational delays between margin posting and settlement, and also since institutions may have to hold excess funds to fulfil potential variation margin calls. Large derivatives players have hundreds of margin calls per day in both directions, representing potentially hundreds of millions of dollars in cash and securities.[15] Margin velocity

---

[15] ISDA Margin Survey (2013b, Table 4.5).

is also subject to resistance, as margin flow (especially high-grade liquid margin) within the financial system has fallen significantly and adversely influenced global liquidity in recent years. Singh and Aitken (2009b) show that counterparty risk during and in the aftermath of the GFC resulted in a decrease of up to $5trn in high-quality margin due to reduced rehypothecation, decreased securities lending activities, and the hoarding of unencumbered margin.

It can be argued that variation margin is not without additional liquidity costs for two reasons. Firstly, variation margin must be paid in relatively liquid securities or cash (CCPs typically only allow the latter), whilst some market participants will only have access to illiquid non-eligible assets.[16] This could lead to a large liquidity squeeze in the event of a large market movement catalysing large variation margin requirements. This might be especially difficult if standard methods for transforming assets into cash, such as the repo market, become more strained in such situations. This could be a good example of why, for an end user carrying out hedging trades, these trades should be exempt from clearing and margin requirements. This is highlighted by the following quote:

> The economic effect of the requirement to provide cash collateral [margin] is to convert the primary risk for companies from that associated with counterparty exposure into liquidity risk. Non-financial companies are highly experienced in managing their counterparty risk with financial institutions; managing liquidity risk in collateral requirements is substantially more difficult for them and is less efficient.[17]

A second problem with variation margin is the inherent delay caused by non-immediate posting (which can be days or at least hours). This interrupts the flow of variation margin through the system and causes funding liquidity risk. This effect will be particularly strong in volatile markets and even more so when there is a large asset price shock. CCPs have a privileged position with respect to margin exchange and may, therefore, interrupt margin flow significantly for their own benefit (if not that of the market in general). Here is a statement that seems to support the view that variation margin has high liquidity costs (at least in a crisis):

> The following discussion of CME cash flows emphasizes variation margin payments because, as will be discussed, these payments placed the greatest stress on the financial system during the week of October 19 (Brady 1988).

Heller and Vause (2012) quantify the potential impact of variation margin calls in stressed markets. One of their conclusions is: 'Variation margin calls on G14 dealers from CCPs that cleared all of their IRS [interest rate swap] or CDS [credit default swap] positions could cumulate over a few weeks to a substantial proportion of their current cash holdings, especially under high market volatility.' Pirrong (2013) argues that variation

---

[16] For example, consider an airline hedging its exposure to the price of aviation fuel via an oil swap or forward contract. The airline will make (lose) money on those hedges in the event of high (low) fuel prices, which will be balanced economically by higher (lower) fuel costs over the period of the hedge. However, when margin is brought into this picture, cash margin against losses on a derivative cannot be funded by cheap fuel price benefits, which accrue over time. The result of this is that the airline may have liquidity problems in relation to using derivatives with associated variation margins.

[17] European Association of Corporate Treasurers (2011). Open Letter to the Commissioners of the European Union (7 November).

margin has the potential to contribute to financial stress. The mechanism of MTM and (sometimes very large) variation margin posting on a daily (and sometimes intradaily) basis leads to a very tight coupling between parties. During stressed periods, rigid variation margin requirements can lead to substantial spikes in short-term liquidity needs. The size and timescale of these requirements could be billions of dollars during a period of hours. This arises from the non-perfect velocity of variation margining in the financial system. Furthermore, this velocity may slow in a crisis period as institutions may attempt to hold on to margins for longer, due to liquidity needs and worries about credit quality. At the same time, the ability to obtain short-term credit is likely to be at its most difficult. Variation margin requirements can also lead to feedback effects. Large price moves and their associated variation margin requirements may lead to fire sales that in turn may lead to further price moves in other markets. Hence, the very mechanism that is intended to reduce counterparty risk can potentially create systemic risk.

In the event of a clearing member default, the short-term liquidity requirements of variation margin on a CCP could be severe, as CCPs will need to pay out variation margin against losses incurred by the defaulter. Heller and Vause (2012) note that this would require a CCP to have access to short-notice liquidity backstops worth several billion dollars. Without this, a CCP may struggle to meet the variation margin requirements given the time horizons (hours) involved.

One important feature of variation margin is that it exposes market participants to MTM volatility, which in turn may increase their likelihood of default (as in the case of monolines and AIG, Section 2.4.4). This is also shown by Kenyon and Green (2013), who refer to a 'virtual default' as one which is created by the forced MTM effect of margining which otherwise would be avoided. Whether virtual defaults are correct or not is another matter. However, the likelihood is that tighter coupling to MTM via methods such as variation margining would create more, not fewer, defaults.[18]

It is important not to lose sight of a key benefit of variation margin, which is that it prevents excessive exposures and leverage from building up in the first place. With respect to the aforementioned cases of AIG and monoline insurers, the resulting losses would likely have never happened since it would not have been possible for the institutions to have built up such large losses.

10.3.3 Initial Margin

Even if variation margin is zero cost and should, therefore, be a natural consequence of OTC derivatives trading, the same is not true of initial margin. Initial margin represents overcollateralisation and moves away from a zero-sum-game market. This is especially true since initial margin requires segregation not to create counterparty risk of its own.

Additionally, initial margin calculations are subjective and complex due to their need to assess future (rather than current) exposure at some arbitrarily-defined confidence level and time horizon. Initial margins can also be procyclical.

Unlike variation margin, initial margin can at least be posted in non-cash securities. However, the admissibility of such securities represents a difficult balance. On the one

---

[18] Carney, J. (2012). Here's What That Deutsche Bank Trade Was Really All About. *CNBC* (7 December). www.cnbc.com. This example is of an *alleged* avoidance of MTM losses that may have otherwise led to a default or government bailout.

hand, if a party allows a wide range of securities to be posted, then this relieves the liquidity strain of posting. On the other hand, having liquid and high credit-quality margin that retains its value even in a crisis period implies a more narrow range of eligible securities. Competition between CCPs may also lead to more relaxed margin restrictions, which ultimately increases the risk of failure.

10.3.4   Cost and xVA

With respect to variation margin, there is generally no xVA cost component. Variation margin is close to settlement and therefore simply offsets a valuation (or equivalently offsets cash flow payments). For this reason, a case of 'perfect collateralisation', which relates to frictionless variation margin exchange, does not lead to any xVA components, as discussed in more detail in Chapter 16. It is rather the lack of variation margin that leads to a valuation adjustment, normally known as funding valuation adjustment (FVA), as shown previously in Figure 2.12 and discussed in more detail in Chapter 18.

This does not mean that variation margin has no cost, but rather that this cost is not easy to quantify in line with some of the risks discussed in Section 10.3.2. Put another way, the costs are not related to the absolute amount, but rather are second order and relate to the underlying volatility of the variation margin requirements. From a bank's perspective, variation margin costs are contingent liquidity costs and may relate to the requirements under liquidity regulations such as liquidity coverage ratio and net stable funding ratio (Sections 4.3.3 and 4.3.4). For end users, variation margin costs may be more obvious due to the fact that their derivative positions are directional (see Figure 2.9). This can be seen in the behaviour of entities such as multilateral development banks (MDBs) who – thanks to their strong credit quality – have typically enjoyed the benefits of one-way credit support annexes (CSAs) (Section 7.3.2) when trading with banks. However, this leads to charges for credit, funding,[19] and capital (CVA, FVA, and KVA) that in recent years have increased substantially due to the tighter funding and regulatory environments in which such banks are operating. An obvious way to reduce these large charges would be for MDBs to post variation margin via entering two-way CSAs. Whilst there is some evidence of this,[20] there has not been a wholesale change in market behaviour, which suggests that the inherent costs (liquidity) outweigh the benefits (more favourable pricing). As with banks, these costs are probably considered largely to be contingent, such as the potential need to fund a large amount of variation margin requirements after a large price move in stressed market conditions.

Since initial margin represents overcollateralisation and must be segregated, its costs are more direct. The term margin value adjustment (MVA) is generally used to define initial margin costs, whether these may arise in bilateral or cleared environments. The volatility of initial margin can also be thought of as representing an additional cost on top of the average initial margin requirements.

From an xVA perspective, the reduction of counterparty risk and increase in funding liquidity risk discussed in Section 7.6.2 can be seen via a reduction in counterparty risk

---

[19] Including charges for any initial margins (independent amount) that the MDB may also hold.
[20] Pollack, L. (2012). The Bank of England gets economical with its derivatives. *Financial Times* (22 June). www.ft.com.

Table 10.2 Indicative comparison of counterparty risk, funding, and capital costs under different margin terms.

	Bilateral (no margin)	Bilateral (variation margin)	Bilateral (initial margin)	Centrally-cleared
Counterparty risk (CVA and KVA)	High	Medium	Low	Low
Initial margin funding (MVA)	None	None	High	High

(CVA) and related capital costs (KVA), and an increase in initial margin costs (MVA), as shown in Table 10.2.

When posting and receiving margin, institutions are becoming increasingly aware of the need to optimise their margin management as, during the GFC, funding efficiencies emerged as an important driver of margin usage. Margin management is no longer a back-office cost centre, but can be an important asset optimisation tool, delivering the most cost-effective margin. An institution must consider the 'cheapest-to-deliver' cash margin and account for the impact of haircuts and the ability to rehypothecate non-cash margin. For example, different currencies of cash will pay different overnight indexed spread rates, and non-cash margin, if rehypothecated, will earn different rates on repo. The optimisation of margins posted across both bilateral and centrally-cleared trades (where there is optionality) will also become increasingly important (e.g. increasing bilateral margin usage of non-CCP-eligible securities). This is discussed later in Section 16.2.3.

10.3.5 Seniority

As shown in Sections 6.4.4 and 7.5.1, netting and margining do not eliminate risk. What they actually achieve is the redistribution of risk by changing the seniority of various creditors: the creditors benefiting from netting and margining (e.g. derivatives counterparties) become more senior, whilst other creditors are effectively demoted. As noted by Pirrong (2013), it is also important to look beyond the impact of clearing on OTC derivatives markets only. OTC derivatives make up only a subset of an institution's balance sheet.

It may be realistic to make OTC derivatives more senior and demote others since these other creditors may be less systemically important. However, it is important to foresee the potential changes brought about by clearing. Faced with a deleveraging in derivatives markets, market participants will likely find other ways to create leverage and obtain alternative forms of credit to support the increase in the required margin. These changes in capital structures, in turn, may create risks in areas of financial markets that have previously been viewed as relatively benign. It could be that regulation is too focused on OTC derivatives and is therefore blinkered to other possible dangers.

10.3.6 Bilateral and Cleared Markets

Table 10.3 contrasts some high-level differences between traditional bilateral clearing and central clearing (and to some extent bilateral clearing with initial margin). Traditional bilateral clearing follows a survivors-pay approach, where parties hold capital against

Table 10.3 Comparison of bilateral versus central clearing. Note that bilateral initial margins correspond more closely to the central clearing characteristics.

	Traditional bilateral clearing (no initial margin)	Central clearing or bilateral clearing with initial margin[21]
Margining	Variation margin or none	Variation and initial margin
Model	Survivors pay	Defaulter pays
Primary loss absorbency	Capital	Initial margin (and default funds)
Risk horizon	~ 1 year	~ 5 days
Risk view	Long term (e.g. based on fundamental credit analysis and ratings)	Short term (e.g. dependent on short-term market risk)
Credit quality sensitivity	Strong	Weak/none
Market risk sensitivity/ procyclicality	Small	Potentially large (although reduced by using stressed data, for example)
Incentive	Losses aligned to risks	Loss mutualisation and potential moral hazard
Default close-out	Uncoordinated bilateral close-out	Coordinated auctions
Segregation	None	Initial margin segregation required

possible losses when their counterparties default. Such capital is typically calculated based on a one-year time horizon and is sensitive to credit quality (e.g. a bank would need to hold more capital against a weaker-rated counterparty). As a result, the risk sensitivity and potential procyclicality of this capital is small. In theory, incentives are strong as losses are borne in general by those taking risks, although the process in the event of default is uncoordinated, with each party closing out transactions individually. In a bilateral market, variation margin may be used, but typically not initial margins (historically).

Central clearing (and in terms of many characteristics, bilateral initial margining) is very different and follows a defaulter-pays approach. The main loss absorbency is provided by initial margins. These are based on a short time horizon (e.g. five days for an OTC CCP or 10 days for bilateral margining requirements) and are usually relatively insensitive to credit quality. This can potentially make initial margins much more sensitive to market factors, which in the extreme can lead to procyclicality (which in turn can be mitigated by aspects such as using long time horizons and stressed data periods). Loss mutualisation via default funds (and capital for default funds) is used to absorb large losses, but potentially creates adverse incentives. There are centralised auctions for closing out a defaulter's portfolio, which may be more efficient than close-outs in bilateral markets.

The above table should illustrate that central clearing and initial margining has both advantages and disadvantages which may be difficult to define precisely (e.g. risk sensitivity is probably a good thing, but in the extreme can lead to procyclicality, which is clearly not). What is also clear is that central clearing changes many aspects of OTC derivatives trading and the underlying risks.

---

[21] This shares many of the characteristics of central clearing but does not involve loss mutualisation or coordinated auctions.

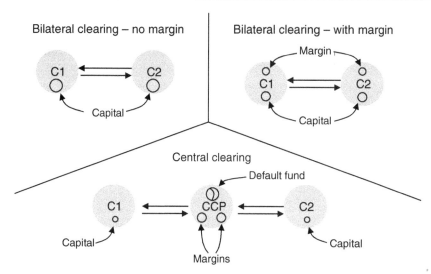

Figure 10.6 Comparison of loss allocation in bilateral (no margins), bilateral with margin, and centrally-cleared markets.

It is also interesting to compare the loss absorbency in different setups (Figure 10.6). In a bilateral market with no margining, this is based only on capital held by each party, whereas in a bilateral market with margins,[22] loss absorbency is provided jointly between capital and margins. However, in a centrally-cleared market, a single capital amount is replaced by margins, mutualised default funds, and the associated capital requirements for both these components.[23] The important point is that regulation must try to create the correct incentives. For example, the capital requirements in a bilateral market should be smaller as initial margin is posted, or a CCP with a larger default fund should impose lower capital requirements on its members. This is particularly difficult to do, especially with a relatively simple methodology for determining capital requirements. This is covered in more detail in Chapter 13.

---

[22] Variation margin and potentially also initial margin.

[23] There are two distinct types of capital covering trade exposure and default fund exposures, as described in Section 13.6.

Section 3
Building Blocks

11

Future Value and Exposure

The concept of future value is a key determinant in xVA because it represents the potential value of a transaction or portfolio in the future. The utilisation components (Section 5.4.6) of all xVA terms are related – simply or otherwise – to the future value, and it is therefore a common component of all xVA adjustments. This chapter will be concerned with defining future value in more detail and explaining the key characteristics. We will focus initially on credit exposure – the core component of credit value adjustment (CVA) – including the important metrics used for its quantification. Typical credit exposure profiles for various products will be discussed, and we will explain the impact of netting and margin on credit exposure. We also describe the link between future value and funding costs, which are driven by similar components but have some distinct differences, especially when aspects such as segregation are involved. This leads us on to define the economic impact of funding, which is similar to the definition of exposure but has some distinct differences. The calculation of funding value adjustment (FVA) will then be similar to that of CVA.

11.1 CREDIT EXPOSURE

11.1.1 Positive and Negative Exposure

A defining feature of counterparty risk arises from the asymmetry of potential losses with respect to the value of the underlying transaction(s).[1] In the event that a counterparty has defaulted, a surviving party may close out the relevant contract(s) and cease any future contractual payments. Following this, the surviving party may determine the net amount owing between itself and its counterparty and take into account any margin that may have been posted or received. Note that margin may be held to reduce exposure, but any posted margin may have the effect of increasing exposure.

Once the above steps have been followed, there is a question of whether the net amount is positive or negative. The main defining characteristic of credit exposure (hereafter referred to just as exposure) is related to whether the net value of the contracts (including margin) is positive (in a party's favour) or negative (against it), as illustrated in Figure 11.1:

- *Negative value.* In this case, the party is in debt to its counterparty and is still legally obliged to settle this amount (it cannot walk away from the transaction(s) except in specific cases (see Section 6.3.3)). Hence, from a valuation perspective, the position appears largely unchanged. A party does not generally gain or lose from its counterparty's default in this case.
- *Positive value.* When a counterparty defaults, it will be unable to undertake future commitments, and a surviving party will have a claim on the (positive) value at the time of

---

[1] The definition of 'value' is more clearly defined later.

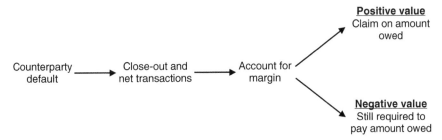

Figure 11.1   Illustration of the impact of a positive or negative contract value in the event of the default of a counterparty.

the default, typically as an unsecured creditor. The surviving party will then expect to recover some fraction of its claim, just as bondholders receive some recovery on the face value of a bond. This unknown recovery value is, by convention, not included in the definition of exposure.

The above feature – whereby a party loses if the value is positive and does not gain if it is negative – is a defining characteristic of counterparty risk and CVA. The definition of positive exposure is:[2]

$$Positive\ exposure = \max(value, 0) \qquad (11.1)$$

Exposure is therefore directly related to the current and future value of a counterparty portfolio, and calculating this future value is, therefore, key to determining the exposure. Note that the quantification of future value must take into account the relevant netting across different transactions and also any margin that may be held against the exposure.

A key feature of counterparty risk is that it is bilateral, as both parties to a transaction can default and therefore both can experience losses. For completeness, we may need to consider losses arising from both defaults. From a party's point of view, its own default will cause a loss to any counterparty to whom it owes money. This can be defined in terms of negative exposure, which by symmetry is:

$$Negative\ exposure = \min(value, 0) \qquad (11.2)$$

A negative exposure will lead to a gain, which is relevant since the counterparty is making a loss.[3] This is defined as 'own counterparty risk', which is represented by debt value adjustment (DVA).

11.1.2   Definition of Value

The amount represented by the term *value* in the above discussion is dependent on the value of the individual transactions in question at each potential default time of the

---

[2] Sometimes authors may define this simply as 'exposure', but we will be explicit on 'positive exposure' and also define the concept of 'negative exposure'.

[3] This is a symmetric effect where one party's gain must be another's loss. There may be reasonable concern with defining a gain in the event of an institution's own default. This will be discussed in more detail in Section 17.3.5.

counterparty (or the party itself). It must also account for the impact of risk mitigants, such as netting and margin. However, there is a question of whether this is the 'base value' or 'actual value', as discussed in Section 5.2.1. Whilst the base value would be a more appealing definition, this is not the one typically defined by documentation (Section 6.3.5) and therefore is unlikely to be the value agreed with the counterparty (the administrators of their default).

From one perspective, a party would wish for the relevant documentation and legal practices to align the actual value – agreed bilaterally after the default – to its own unilateral view prior to any default. Without this, there would be a jump in the valuation at the point at which the counterparty defaults (Figure 6.11). However, this actual value does not conform to a definitive, objective representation due to the complexity of valuation adjustments and close-out effects. Furthermore, the actual value contains xVA components, which therefore creates a recursive problem, discussed in Section 6.3.5.

Quantification of exposure and xVA will, therefore, rely on relatively clean measures or base values which can readily drive quantitative calculations. However, it should be remembered that documentation will tend to operate slightly differently. For example, recall that International Swaps and Derivatives Association (ISDA) documentation (Section 6.3.5) specifically references that the 'close-out amount' may include information related to the creditworthiness of the surviving party. This implies that an institution can potentially reduce the amount owed to a defaulting counterparty, or increase its claims in accordance with CVA charges it experiences in replacing the transaction(s) at the point where its counterparty defaults. Such charges may themselves arise from the xVA components that depend on exposure in their calculation. The result of this is a recursive problem where the very definition of current exposure depends on potential xVA components in the future. However, note that it is general market practice to link exposure quantification to the concept of base value, which is relatively easy to define and model, and that any errors in doing this are usually relatively small.

When quantifying exposure and other xVA terms, Equations 11.1 and 11.2 are fundamental starting points and will typically rely on a definition of value which may come from a standard valuation model. Whilst this theoretical definition of value cannot practically include aspects such as the type of documentation used, jurisdiction, or market behaviour at the time of default, it will be hoped that issues such as these will only constitute small uncertainties.

A final point to note about the above problems in determining close-out amounts is the time delay. Until an agreement is reached, an institution cannot be sure of the precise amount owed or the value of its claim as an unsecured creditor. This will create particular problems for managing counterparty risk. In a default involving many contracts (such as the number of OTC derivatives in the Lehman bankruptcy), the sheer operational volumes can make the time taken to agree on such valuations considerable. This risk may be taken by the xVA desk in a bank (Section 21.1).

11.1.3   Current and Potential Future Exposure

A *current* valuation of all relevant transactions and associated margin will lead to a calculation of current value and exposure (admittedly with some uncertainty regarding the actual close-out amount, as noted in Section 11.1.2). However, it is even more important to characterise what the exposure might be at some point in the future. This concept is

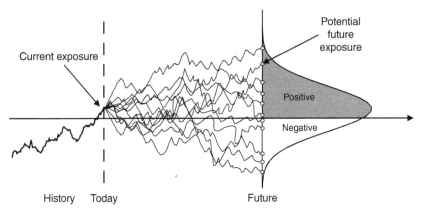

Figure 11.2   Illustration of potential future exposure. The grey area represents positive values and the white area negative values.

illustrated in Figure 11.2, which can be considered to represent any situation from a single transaction to a large portfolio with associated netting and margin terms. Whilst the current (and past) exposure is known with certainty, the future exposure is defined probabilistically by what may happen in the future in terms of market movements, contractual features of transactions, netting, and margining, all of which have elements of uncertainty. Hence, in understanding future exposure, one must define the *level* of the exposure and also its underlying *uncertainty*.

Quantifying exposure is complex due to the long periods involved, the many different market variables that may influence the future value, and risk mitigants such as netting and margin; this will be the subject of Chapter 15. This chapter focuses on defining exposure and intuitively discussing the impact of aspects such as netting and margin, and the related concept of funding.

11.1.4   Nature of Exposure

Counterparty risk creates an asymmetric risk profile, as shown by Equation 11.1. When a counterparty defaults, a surviving party loses if the value (from its point of view) is positive, but does not gain if it is negative. The profile can be likened to a 'short' option position,[4] since from the surviving party's perspective, the defaulting counterparty has the option not to pay them. Familiarity with basic options-pricing theory would lead to two obvious conclusions about the quantification of exposure:

- since exposure is similar to an option payoff, a key aspect will be volatility (of the value of the relevant contracts and margin); and
- options are relatively complex to price (compared with the underlying instruments at least), so quantifying exposure, even for a simple instrument, may be quite complex.

By symmetry, an institution has long optionality from its own default (this is related to the term 'DVA').

---

[4] The short option position arises since exposure constitutes a loss.

We can extend the option analogy further – for example, by saying that a portfolio of transactions with the same counterparty will have an exposure analogous to a basket option, and that a margin agreement will change the *strike* of the underlying options. However, thinking of xVA as one giant exotic options-pricing problem is correct but potentially misleading. One reason for this is that, as already noted in Section 11.1.3, we cannot even write the payoff of the option, namely the exposure, down correctly (since we cannot precisely define the *value* term in Equation 11.1). Furthermore, xVA contains many other subjective components, such as credit and funding curves (Sections 12.2 and 14.3) and wrong-way risk (Section 17.6). At the core of exposure calculation there is an options-pricing-type problem, but this cannot be treated with the accuracy and sophistication normally afforded to this topic, due to the sheer complexity of the underlying options and the other components that drive xVA. Treating xVA quantification as a purely theoretical options-pricing problem tends to underemphasise other important but more qualitative aspects.

There is another way to look at exposure quantification. In financial risk management, value-at-risk (VAR) methods (Section 2.6.1) have, for almost two decades, been a popular methodology for characterising market risk and have more recently been applied to methodologies for initial margin (Chapter 9). Such approaches aim to characterise market risk over relatively short horizons, such as 10 days.[5] As illustrated in Figure 11.2, the characterisation of exposure is a similar problem since it involves quantifying the market risk of a portfolio. This is indeed true, although we note that in quantifying exposure there are additional complexities, most notably:

- *Time horizon*. Exposure needs to be defined over multiple time horizons (often far in the future) so as to understand the impact of time and the specifics of the underlying contracts. There are two important implications of this:
  - Firstly, the 'ageing' of transactions must be considered. This refers to understanding a portfolio in terms of all future contractual payments and changes such as cash flows, termination events, exercise decisions, and margin postings. Such effects may also create path dependency, where the exposure at one date depends on an event defined at a previous date. In VAR models, due to the short horizon used (e.g. 10 days), such aspects can often be neglected.
  - Secondly, when looking at longer time horizons, the trend (also known as the 'drift') of market variables (in addition to their underlying volatility and dependence structure) is relevant (as depicted in Figure 11.2). In VAR-type approaches the drift can be ignored, again since the relevant time horizon is short.
- *Risk mitigants*. Exposure is typically reduced by risk mitigants such as netting and margin, and the impact of these mitigants must be considered in order to estimate future exposure appropriately. In some cases – such as applying the correct netting rules – this requires knowledge of the relevant contractual agreements and their legal interpretation in the jurisdiction in question. In the case of future margin amounts – especially

---

[5] Traditional market risk capital models use a horizon of 10 days (Section 2.6.1), which is similar to the bilateral margin requirements (Section 4.4.2). CCP methodologies for initial margin typically use an even shorter horizon – for OTC derivatives – of five days. Note that the Fundamental Review of the Trading Book (BCBS 2019b) requires longer time horizons of up to 120 days, depending on the underlying asset class.

dynamic initial margin (Section 9.3) – another degree of subjectivity is created, since there is no certainty regarding the type of margin and the precise time that it will be received. Other contractual features of transactions – such as termination agreements (Section 7.1.1) – may also create subjectivity, and all such elements must be modelled, introducing another layer of complexity and uncertainty.

- *Application.* Traditional approaches for market risk and initial margin quantification are risk-management approaches. However, exposure must be defined for both risk management and pricing (i.e. xVA). This creates additional complexity in quantifying exposure and may lead to two completely different sets of calculations: one to define exposure for risk-management purposes ('real world') and one for pricing purposes ('risk neutral'). This is discussed in more detail in Section 15.3.3.

11.1.5 Metrics

This section defines the measures commonly used to quantify exposure. The different metrics introduced will be appropriate for different applications and xVA terms. The most common definitions will be used; sometimes the nomenclature used for the terms defined below can differ – in particular, in regulatory definitions (BCBS 2005b) and in previous editions of this book. Such differences will be highlighted below.

Note that the definitions given below are general and can apply to any underlying transaction or groups of transactions. In practical terms, there will also be the question of the aggregation level, which is a group of transactions that must be considered together. For example, for counterparty risk, the obvious aggregation level is all transactions with the counterparty in question, or more specifically all that are covered by a single legal agreement such as a 'netting set'. Aggregation is discussed in more detail in Section 11.3 and need not be a consideration for the definitions below, where we will simply use the term 'portfolio' to refer to the relevant transactions and associated risk mitigants.

Considering first the definition of exposure metrics for a given time horizon, the first definition is expected future value (EFV).[6] This component represents the forward or expected value of the portfolio at some point in the future. As mentioned above, due to the relatively long time horizons involved in measuring counterparty risk, the expected value can be an important component, whereas for traditional market risk quantification (involving only short time horizons) it is not. EFV at time zero is, by definition, the current value. At other times, EFV represents the expected (average) of the future value calculated with some probability distribution in mind (to be discussed in Chapter 15). EFV may vary significantly from current value for a number of reasons:

- *Cash flow differential.* Cash flows in some transactions may be significantly asymmetric. For example, early in the lifetime of an interest rate swap, the fixed cash flows will typically exceed the floating ones (assuming the underlying yield curve is upward sloping, as is most common). Another example is a cross-currency swap, where the payments may differ by several percent annually due to a differential between the associated interest rates. The result of asymmetric cash flows is that a party may expect a transaction in the future to have a value significantly above (below) the current one due to paying

---

[6] Sometimes referred to as 'expected mark-to-market' (EMTM) or 'expected exposure' (EE).

out (receiving) cash flows. Note that – in a portfolio context – this can also apply to transactions maturing due to final payments (e.g. cross-currency swaps), which has an impact on the future value of the remaining portfolio.

- *Forward rates.* Forward rates can differ significantly from current spot variables. This difference introduces an implied drift (trend) in the future evolution of the underlying variables in question (assuming one believes that this is the correct drift to use, as discussed in more detail in Section 15.3.3). Drifts in market variables will lead to a higher or lower future value for a given portfolio even before the impact of volatility. Note that this point is related to the point above on cash flow differential, since this is a result of forward rates being different from spot rates.
- *Asymmetric margin agreements.* If margin agreements are asymmetric (such as a one-way margin posting), then the future value may be expected to be higher or lower, reflecting unfavourable or favourable margin terms, respectively.

In risk management, it is natural to ask what is the worst exposure at a certain time in the future. Potential future exposure (PFE) (Figure 11.2) will answer this question with reference to a certain confidence level. For example, the PFE at a confidence level of 99% will define an exposure that would be exceeded with a probability of no more than 1% (100 minus the confidence level). PFE is an equivalent metric to VAR.

The pricing of some xVA terms requires both expected positive exposure (EPE) and expected negative exposure (ENE), which are the averages of the positive and negative exposures defined previously in Equations 11.1 and 11.2. Note that these definitions are not the average of only the positive (EPE) or negative (ENE) values, but rather the average across all values, but where the negative or positive ones are set to zero. So, for example, when calculating the EPE, only positive values contribute to the total, but zero and negative values contribute in terms of their probability (this may be best understood in the example below).

The above metrics are summarised below and in Figure 11.3.[7]

- *Expected future value (EFV).* The average across all exposure values. Note that this can differ significantly from zero, which represents a more significant positive or negative expected value.
- *Potential future exposure (PFE).* The highest (or lowest) exposure calculated to some underlying confidence level.[8]
- *Expected positive exposure (EPE).* The average of all of the positive exposures (noting that some will be zero). Note that this term, like the PFE, is sensitive to the variability of the distribution (e.g. the volatility). This term is sometimes known as expected exposure (EE).
- *Expected negative exposure (ENE).* The average of all of the negative exposures (noting that some will be zero). This represents the positive exposure from the counterparty's point of view. This term is sometimes known as negative expected exposure (NEE).

---

[7] Note that the normal distribution used to depict the distribution of future values does not need to be assumed.

[8] Note that the PFE can be defined at low confidence levels, which would show on the left side of the distribution (white area). This represents the counterparty point of view.

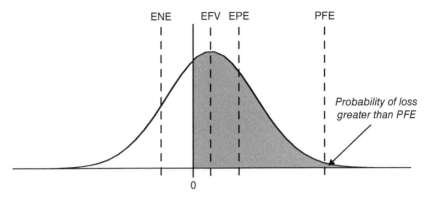

Figure 11.3   Illustration of exposure metrics for a single time horizon. PFE is assumed to be calculated at a high confidence level.

Spreadsheet 11.1 Simple exposure metric calculation.

Example.

Suppose the future exposure is defined by only five different scenarios, each with an equal probability of occurrence. The metrics defined above would then be as in the table below. The calculation of the PFE assumes that the confidence level is more than 80% (in which case it is the highest exposure number).

	Future exposure	Calculation
Scenario 1	70	
Scenario 2	50	
Scenario 3	30	
Scenario 4	−10	
Scenario 5	−30	
EFV	22	$(70 + 50 + 30 - 10 - 30)/5$
PFE	70	The highest value (in this case)
EPE	30	$(70 + 50 + 30)/5$
ENE	−8	$(-10 - 30)/5$

Appendix 11A gives formulas for the exposure metrics for a normal distribution.

Spreadsheet 11.2 EPE and PFE for a normal distribution.

Example. Suppose future value is defined by a normal distribution with mean 2.0 and standard deviation 2.0. As given by the formulas in Appendix 11A, the EFV, PFE, EPE, and ENE (at the 99% confidence level) are:

EFV	= 2.0 (by definition)
PFE (99%)	= 6.65
EPE	= 2.17
ENE	= 0.17

For a larger standard deviation of 4.0:

EFV	= 2.0
PFE (99%)	= 11.31
EPE	= 2.79
ENE	= 0.79

Note the aforementioned sensitivity of the EPE, ENE, and PFE to the standard deviation. The ENE increases by almost five times when the standard deviation is doubled. Using the options pricing analogy, this is because it represents an out-of-the-money position.

A final metric will approximate exposure over time. Average EPE is defined as the average exposure across all time horizons. It can, therefore, be represented as the weighted average of the EPE across time, as illustrated in Figure 11.4. If the EPE points are equally spaced (as in this example), then it is simply the average. Note that the average EPE is sometimes known simply as EPE, which can cause confusion with the definition of EPE used here. As noted above, the most common definitions are being used, and the Basel definitions (Section 13.4.5) do differ.

This single average EPE number is often called a 'loan equivalent', as the average amount effectively lent to the counterparty in question. It is probably obvious that expressing a highly-uncertain exposure by a single EPE or loan-equivalent amount can represent a fairly crude approximation, as it averages out both the randomness of market variables and the impact of time. However, it will be shown later that EPE has a strong theoretical basis for assessing regulatory capital (Section 13.4.5) and quantifying xVA (Section 17.2.3).

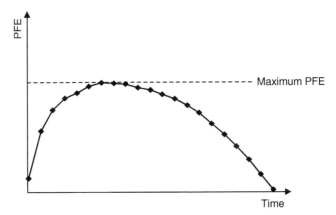

Figure 11.4   Illustration of average EPE, which is the weighted average (the weights being the time intervals) of the EPE profile.

11.2   DRIVERS OF EXPOSURE

We now give some examples of the significant factors that drive exposure, illustrating some important effects, such as maturity, payment frequencies, option exercise, roll-off, and default. The aim here is to describe some key features that must be captured; Chapter 15 will give actual examples from real transactions. In the examples below, exposure is shown as a percentage (i.e. assuming a unit notional of the transaction in question). In most cases, the initial value will be assumed to be zero, but the impact of a positive or negative current value will also be shown. Unless stated, the profile shown is the EPE; in most cases, the PFE will have the same behaviour but simply be a larger value. The current time will be represented by t and the maturity of the transaction by T.

Although not generally characterised as counterparty risk, the exposures of debt instruments such as loans and bonds can usually be considered almost deterministic and approximately equal to the notional value. Bonds typically pay a fixed rate and therefore will have some additional uncertainty, since, if interest rates decline, the exposure may increase and vice versa. In the case of loans, they are typically floating-rate instruments, but the exposure may decline over time due to the possibility of pre-payments.

In contrast to the above, products such as derivatives can have complex exposures due to their inherent complexities and the complex impact of risk mitigants such as margin.

11.2.1   Future Uncertainty

The first and most obvious driving factor in exposure is future uncertainty. Some derivatives – such as forward contracts – are usually characterised by having just the exchange of two cash flows or underlyings (potentially netted into a single payment) at a single date in the future (the maturity date of the contract). This means that the exposure is a rather simple, monotonically increasing function, reflecting the fact that, as time passes, there is growing uncertainty about the value of the final cash flow(s). Based on fairly common assumptions,[9] the exposure of such a profile will follow a 'square-root-of-time' rule, meaning that the exposure will be proportional to the square root of the time (t):

$$Exposure \propto \sqrt{t} \ (t \leq T) \tag{11.3}$$

This is described in more mathematical detail in Appendix 11B, and such a profile, which is roughly illustrative of a foreign exchange (FX) forward, is illustrated in Figure 11.5. We can see from the above formula that the maturity of the contract does not influence the exposure (except for the obvious reason that there is zero exposure after this date). For similar reasons, much the same shape is seen for vanilla options with an upfront premium, although more exotic options may have more complex profiles (see Section 11.2.6).

11.2.2 Cash Flow Frequency

Many OTC derivatives include the periodic payment of cash flows, which has the impact of reversing the effect of future uncertainty. The most obvious and common example here is an interest rate swap, which is characterised by a peaked shape, as shown in Figure 11.6. The shape arises from the balance between future uncertainties regarding payments, combined with the roll-off of fixed against floating payments over time. This can be represented approximately as:

$$Exposure \propto (T - t)\sqrt{t} \ (t \leq T) \tag{11.4}$$

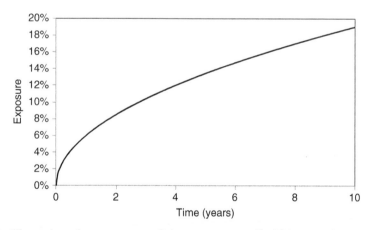

Figure 11.5 Illustration of a square-root-of-time exposure profile. This example assumes volatility of 15% and the calculation of EPE under normal distribution assumptions.

---

[9] Specifically, that the returns of the underlying market variable (e.g. FX) are independently identically distributed (iid).

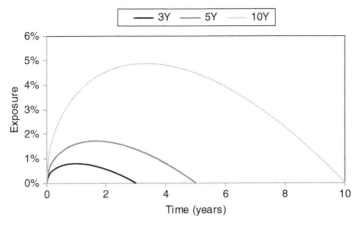

Figure 11.6 Illustration of the exposure of swaps of different maturities. This example assumes volatility of 1% and the calculation of EPE under normal distribution assumptions, which is roughly illustrative of interest rate swaps.[10]

where T represents the maturity of the transaction in question. This is described in more mathematical detail in Appendix 11B. The function shown in Equation 11.4 initially increases due to the $\sqrt{t}$ term, but then decreases to zero as a result of the $(T - t)$ component, which is an approximate representation of the remaining maturity of the transaction at a future time t. It can be shown that the maximum of the above function occurs at $\frac{T}{3}$ (see Appendix 11B) – i.e. the maximum exposure occurs at a date equal to one-third of the maturity.

As seen in Figure 11.6, a swap with a longer maturity has much more risk, due to both the increased lifetime and the greater number of payments due to be exchanged. An illustration of the swap cash flows (assuming equal semiannual payment frequencies) is shown in Figure 11.7.

An exposure profile can be substantially altered due to the more specific nature of the cash flows in a transaction. Transactions such as basis swaps, where the payments are made more frequently than they are received (or vice versa), will then have more (less) risk than the equivalent equal payment swap. This effect is illustrated in Figure 11.8 and Figure 11.9.

11.2.3   Curve Shape

Another impact the cash flows have on exposure is to create an asymmetry between opposite transactions. In the case of an interest rate swap, this occurs because of the different cash flows being exchanged. In a 'payer swap', fixed cash flows are paid periodically at a deterministic amount (the 'swap rate'), whilst floating cash flows are received. The value of future floating cash flows is not known until the fixing date, although, at inception, their (risk-neutral) discounted expected value will typically be equal to that of the fixed cash

---

[10] We will see below that the shape of the yield curve can have an important impact and, in a more sophisticated calculation, that mean reversion of interest rates is important (Section 15.6.1).

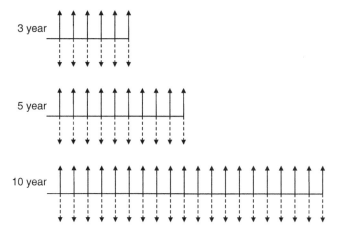

Figure 11.7 Illustration of the cash flows of swap transactions of different maturities (semiannual payment frequencies are assumed). Solid lines represent fixed payments and dotted lines floating payments.

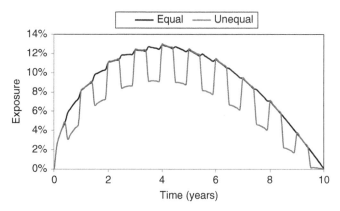

Figure 11.8 Illustration of the exposure for swaps with equal and unequal payment frequencies. The latter corresponds to a swap where cash flows are received quarterly but paid only semiannually.

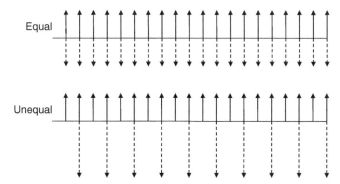

Figure 11.9 Illustration of the cash flows in a swap transaction with different payment frequencies. Solid lines represent fixed payments and dotted lines floating payments.

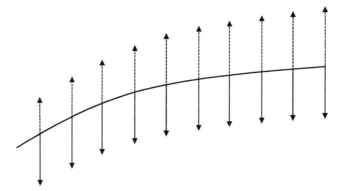

Figure 11.10   Illustration of the floating cash flows (dotted lines) against fixed cash flows in a swap where the yield curve is upward sloping. Whilst the (risk-neutral) expected value of the floating and fixed cash flows may be equal, the projected floating cash flows are expected to be smaller at the beginning and larger at the end of the swap.

flows ('par swap'). The value of the projected floating cash flows depends on the shape of the underlying yield curve.[11] In the case of a typical upwards-sloping yield curve, the initial floating cash flows will be expected to be smaller than the fixed rate paid, whilst later in the swap the trend is expected to reverse. This is illustrated schematically in Figure 11.10.

The net result of this effect is that the EPE of the receiver swap is lower due to the expectation of receiving positive net cash flows (the fixed rate against the lower floating rate) in the first periods of the swap, and of paying net cash flows later in the lifetime (Figure 11.11). The ENE is correspondingly more negative. Another way to state this is that the EFV of the swap is negative (by an amount defined by the expected net cash flows). For the opposite 'payer swap', this effect would be reversed, with the EPE being higher, the ENE less negative, and the sign of the EFV reversed.

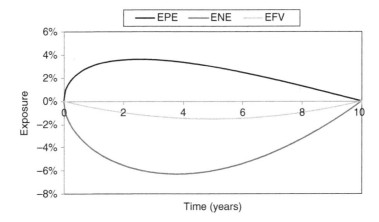

Figure 11.11   Illustration of the EFV, EPE, and ENE for a receiver interest rate swap.

---

[11] By 'projected' we mean the risk-neutral expected value of each cash flow.

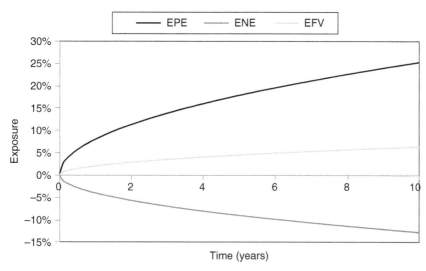

Figure 11.12   Illustration of the EFV, EPE, and ENE for a cross-currency swap where the payment currency has a higher interest rate.

The above effect can be explained in three different ways, all of which are related:

- the cash flow differential, as discussed above;
- the fact that the yield curve is (usually) upwards sloping, suggesting a market-implied view that interest rates will rise; and
- the fact that the forward swap rates will be higher than the current swap rate (and therefore a forward starting swap receiving the swap rate will have a negative value).

This will be discussed in more detail in Section 15.6.1.

The above effect can be even more dramatic in cross-currency swaps, where a high-interest-rate currency is paid against one with lower interest rates, as illustrated in Figure 11.12. The overall high interest rates paid are expected to be offset by the gain on the notional exchange at the maturity of the contract,[12] and this expected gain on the exchange of notional leads to significant exposure for the payer of the high interest rate. In the reverse swap, when paying the currency with the lower interest rates, it is increasingly likely that the future value of the swap will be negative. This creates a negative drift, making the exposure much lower.

The impact of cash flow differential or – equivalently – drift is particularly important in xVA calculations, as will be seen later.

11.2.4   Moneyness

The previous examples have all shown par transactions where the initial value is zero. However, another consideration is 'moneyness', where a transaction could be

---

[12] From a risk-neutral point of view.

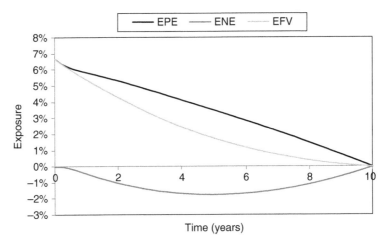

Figure 11.13   Illustration of the EFV, EPE, and ENE for an ITM receiver interest rate swap.

in-the-money (ITM) (positive value) or out-of-the-money (OTM) (negative value). Figure 11.13 shows the exposure profiles for an ITM interest rate swap. Not surprisingly, the ENE is small due to the smaller likelihood of the future value being negative. The EPE is large and quite close to the EFV and therefore is more predictable in its form. This is analogous to an ITM option being more deterministic and having lower sensitivity to volatility.

11.2.5   Combination of Profiles

Some products have an exposure that is driven by a combination of two or more underlying risk factors. An obvious example is a cross-currency swap, which is essentially a combination of an interest rate swap and a FX forward transaction.[13] This would, therefore, be represented by a combination of the profiles shown in Figure 11.5 and Figure 11.6, and is described in more mathematical detail in Appendix 11C. Figure 11.14 illustrates the combination of two such profiles. Cross-currency swap exposures can be considerable due to the high FX volatility driving the risk, coupled with the long maturities and final exchanges of notional. The contribution of the interest rate swap is typically smaller, as shown. We also note that the correlation between the two interest rates and the FX rate is an important driver of the exposure (in Figure 11.14 a relatively low correlation is assumed, as often seen in practice, which increases the cross-currency exposure).[14]

Spreadsheet 11.3 Simple example of a cross-currency swap profile.

---

[13] Due to the interest rate payments coupled with an exchange of notional in the two currencies at the end of the transaction.

[14] The impact of correlation can be seen in Spreadsheet 11.3.

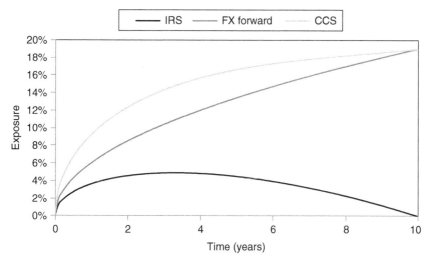

Figure 11.14   Illustration of the EPE of a cross-currency swap (CCS) profile as a combination of an interest rate swap (IRS) and FX forward.

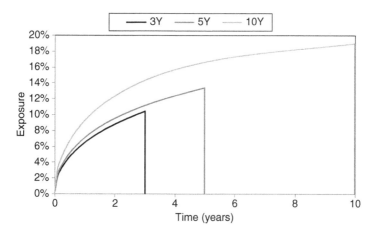

Figure 11.15   Illustration of the exposure for cross-currency swaps of different maturities.

Figure 11.15 illustrates the exposure for cross-currency swaps of different maturities. The longer-maturity swaps have slightly more risk due to the greater number of interest rate payments on the swap.

11.2.6   Optionality

Although some options have relatively straightforward exposures (Section 11.2.1), the impact of exercise decisions can create some complexities in exposure profiles, since after the exercise date(s) the underlying transaction will have a certain probability of being 'alive' or not. This is particularly important in the case of physical settlement. As an example, Figure 11.16 shows the exposure for a European-style interest rate swaption that

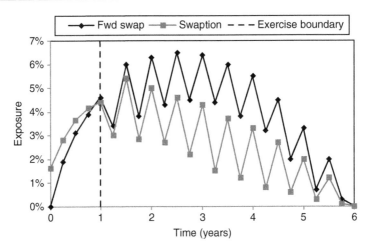

Figure 11.16 Exposure (PFE) for a swap-settled (physically-settled) interest rate swaption and the equivalent forward swap. The option maturity is one year and the swap maturity five years.

is physically settled – rather than cash settled[15] compared with the equivalent forward starting swap (as can be seen, the underlying swap has different payment frequencies). Before the exercise point, the swaption must always have a greater exposure than the forward starting swap,[16] but thereafter this trend will reverse, since there will be scenarios where the forward starting swap has a positive value but the swaption would not have been exercised. This effect is illustrated in Figure 11.17, which shows a scenario that would give rise to exposure in the forward swap but not the swaption.

The above example is based on the base value of the underlying swap. This means that the valuation paths illustrated in Figure 11.17 will be the same for both cash- and physically-settled swaps and the exposure can be calculated directly from the future values of the swaption. To use the 'actual value' in the calculation would be more complicated, since the future value, exposure, and exercise decision would become linked. Another way of stating this is that, in exercising the option, one should naturally incorporate future xVA adjustments. This, therefore, leads to a recursive problem for the calculation of xVA for products with exercise boundaries,[17] which is similar to the recursive problem discussed in Section 11.1.2.

11.2.7   Credit Derivatives

Credit derivatives represent a challenge for exposure assessment due to wrong-way risk, which will be discussed in Section 17.6. Even without this as a consideration, exposure profiles of credit derivatives are hard to characterise due to the discrete payoffs of the instruments. Consider the exposure profile of a single-name credit default swap (CDS),

---

[15] The cash-settled swaption has an identical exposure until the exercise date and then zero exposure thereafter. Physically-settled swaptions are standard in some interest rate markets. Depending on the currency, either cash or physical settlement may be most common.

[16] The option to enter into a contract cannot be worth less than the equivalent obligation to enter into the same contract.

[17] It also implies that where multiple exercise decisions should be taken at a given time, all possible combinations should be considered.

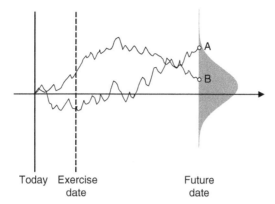

Figure 11.17 Illustration of exercise of a physically-settled European swaption showing two potential scenarios of future value for the underlying swap. Scenario B corresponds to a scenario where the swaption would be exercised, giving rise to exposure at a future date. In scenario A, the swaption would not have been exercised, and hence the exposure would be zero. The exercise boundary is assumed to be the *x*-axis (in reality it would not be constant).

as shown in Figure 11.18 (long CDS protection), for which the EPE and PFE are shown. Whilst the EPE shows a typical swap-like profile, the PFE has a jump due to the default of the reference entity. This is a rather confusing effect (see also Hille et al. 2005), as it means that the PFE may or may not represent the actual credit event occurring and is sensitive to the confidence level used.[18] Using a measure such as expected shortfall partially solves

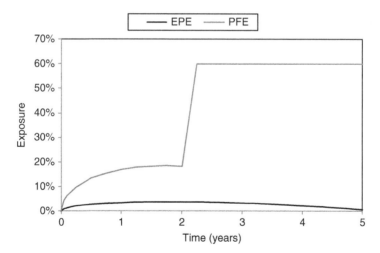

Figure 11.18 EPE and 99% PFE for a long-protection single-name CDS transaction. A PFE of 60% arises from default with an assumed recovery rate of 40% when the probability of default of the counterparty is greater than one minus the confidence level (i.e. 1%).

---

[18] We comment that the above impact could be argued to be partly a facet of common modelling assumptions, which assume default as a sudden unanticipated jump event with a known recovery value (40%). Using more realistic modelling of default and an unknown recovery value gives behaviour that is more continuous.

this problem.[19] This effect will also not be apparent for CDS indices due to a large number of reference credits where single defaults have a less significant impact.

Spreadsheet 11.4 Simple calculation of the exposure of a CDS.

11.3   AGGREGATION, PORTFOLIO EFFECTS, AND THE IMPACT OF COLLATERALISATION

The aggregation of transactions across a particular portfolio has an important impact on exposure. One example of aggregation is close-out netting (Section 6.3.2), which effectively allows the future values of different transactions to offset one another thanks to a contractual agreement. This requires that all transactions under a given netting agreement with a counterparty be added together for the purposes of determining exposure.[20] Netting set aggregation is important for counterparty-specific quantities such as CVA.

There are also other levels at which aggregation may need to be done which relate to aspects such as funding and capital and the corresponding metrics (e.g. FVA and KVA). The discussion below will be generic and consider only the general impact of aggregation on exposure. There are several different aspects to contemplate before understanding the full netting impact on overall exposure.

11.3.1   The Impact of Aggregation on Exposure

Figure 11.19 illustrates the general impact of aggregation. Since the exposure profiles are partly offsetting – meaning that one is positive whilst the other is negative – when aggregated, they produce a reducing effect. This means that the exposure (positive or negative) of the aggregated profile is smaller than the sum of the exposures of each transaction (indeed, the negative exposure is zero since, when aggregated, there is no negative contribution). It is this reduction which is the rationale for risk mitigants such as close-out netting.

Spreadsheet 11.5 Simple two transaction example of netting effects.

Table 11.1 illustrates the impact of aggregation on exposure using a simple example with five scenarios and a single point in time. Note firstly that the EFV is additive across the two transactions,[21] which should be expected since it is simply the average of the values. The EPE and ENE, on the other hand, are not additive, which is a consequence of their definitions including only positive or negative values (Section 11.1.1): the aggregated EPE

---

[19] Expected shortfall is recommended by the Fundamental Review of the Trading Book (BCBS 2019a) instead of VAR which, as a quantile measure, can create problems such as this. Note that EPE is similar to expected shortfall and therefore does not suffer from the same problem as the PFE shown.

[20] Noting that there may be more than one netting agreement with a given counterparty.

[21] $10 - 5 = 5$

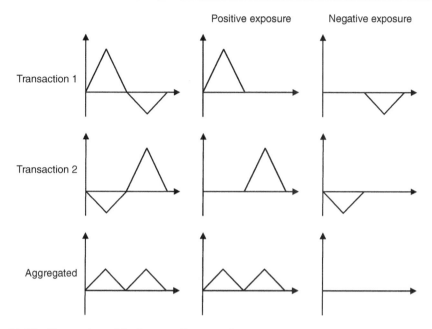

Figure 11.19   Illustration of the impact of aggregation on exposure.

Table 11.1   Illustration of the impact of aggregation when there is a positive correlation between values. The exposure metrics are shown, assuming each scenario has equal weight.

	Transaction 1	Transaction 2	Aggregated
Scenario 1	50	15	65
Scenario 2	30	5	35
Scenario 3	10	-5	5
Scenario 4	-10	-15	-25
Scenario 5	-30	-25	-55
EFV	10	-5	5
EPE	18	4	21
ENE	-8	-9	-16

or ENE is always less (in absolute terms) than the sum of the individual components.[22] This is a general result that the aggregated EPE or ENE cannot be larger (in absolute terms) than the sum of the individual components.[23]

Aggregation can be seen to produce a diversification effect. When considering the aggregation benefit of two or more transactions, the most obvious consideration is, therefore, the correlation between their future values (and therefore their exposures

---

[22] The EPEs of the transactions are 18 and 4 respectively, whereas the aggregated EPE is 21. The ENEs of the transactions are -8 and -9 respectively, whereas the aggregated ENE is -16.
[23] This follows mathematically from the fact that $\max\left(\sum_i value_i, 0\right) \leq \sum_i \max(value_i, 0)$.

also). A high positive correlation between two transactions means that future values are likely to be of the same sign. This means that the aggregation benefit will be small or even zero, as is the case in Table 11.1, where the diversification effect is small. Aggregation only produces a reduction in exposure in scenarios where the values of the transactions have opposite signs, which occurs only in scenario 3. The aggregated EPE and ENE – compared to the sum of the individual values – are only reduced by a small amount.[24]

On the other hand, negative correlations are clearly more beneficial as values are much more likely to have opposite signs, and hence the aggregation benefit will be stronger; this is illustrated in Table 11.2.

Appendix 11D gives a simple formula for the impact of aggregation on the exposure of a portfolio. It shows that the exposure reduction increases with the size of the portfolio and as the correlation between individual transactions reduces.

11.3.2   Off-market Portfolios

Offsetting effects in the aggregation are not always driven by the *structural* correlation between the future values of different transactions, but also by relative moneyness – for example, the extent to which the current value of a portfolio is significantly positive (ITM) or negative (OTM).

Figure 11.20 illustrates the impact of an OTM portfolio on the exposure of a new trans-action. The OTM (negative value) portfolio is unlikely to have positive exposure unless the value of the transactions moves significantly. This, therefore, damps the positive exposure contribution of a new transaction in aggregate.[25]

An ITM portfolio can also produce a beneficial aggregation effect on positive exposure, as shown in Figure 11.21. The negative value of a new transaction will have an impact on

Table 11.2   Illustration of the impact of aggregation when there is a negative correlation between values. The exposure metrics are shown, assuming each scenario has equal weight.

	Transaction 1	Transaction 2	Aggregated
Scenario 1	50	−25	25
Scenario 2	30	−15	15
Scenario 3	10	−5	5
Scenario 4	−10	5	−5
Scenario 5	−30	15	−15
EFV	10	−5	5
EPE	18	4	9
ENE	−8	−9	−4

---

[24] Note that the correlation of values (columns two and three in Table 11.1) is 100%, but the correlation of the exposures (only the positive or negative parts of these values) is less than 100%, which explains the small aggregation benefit. In practical terms, this effect could correspond to otherwise identical transactions which have different current values due to having a different reference rate. This is also discussed in Section 11.3.2.

[25] As noted in footnote 24, this can be thought of as the exposures being less correlated than the futures values.

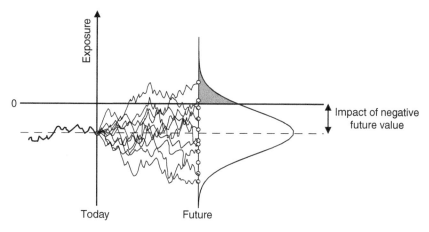

Figure 11.20   Schematic illustration of the impact of a negative future value on netting.

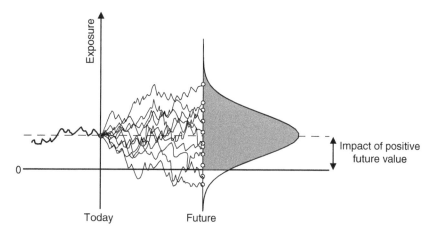

Figure 11.21   Schematic illustration of the impact of a positive future value on netting.

offsetting the positive exposure of the ITM portfolio. Put another way, the ENE of a new transaction is offset by the ENE of the portfolio.

The above effects are important since they show that even directional portfolios can have significant aggregation effects. They will help us to understand the behaviour of xVA at a portfolio level in later examples.

11.3.3   Impact of Margin

In general, margin has the effect of reducing exposure, and it can, therefore, simply be subtracted from the value of the portfolio to determine the positive and negative exposures. Equations 11.1 and 11.2 therefore become:

$$Positive\ exposure = \max(value - margin, 0) \tag{11.5}$$

$$Negative\ exposure = \min(value - margin, 0) \tag{11.6}$$

Table 11.3 Illustration of the impact of margin on exposure. The exposure metrics are shown, assuming each scenario has equal weight.

	Value (no margin)	Margin amount	Value (with margin)
Scenario 1	25	20	5
Scenario 2	15	12	3
Scenario 3	5	3	2
Scenario 4	−5	−3	−2
Scenario 5	−15	−16	1
EPE	9		2.2
ENE	−4		−0.4

Margin that is received is positive in the above equations and will, therefore, reduce positive exposure and increase negative exposure. Posted margin will do the opposite. This is in line with the fact that receiving margin mitigates counterparty risk, but posting margin may create counterparty risk (to the extent that it is not offset by the value). Concepts such as segregation (Section 11.4.3) will complicate the above description.

A simple example is given in Table 11.3, loosely assuming two-way collateralisation without initial margin. In scenarios 1–3, the positive exposure is significantly reduced since margin is held. The exposure is not perfectly collateralised, which may be the case in practice due to factors such as a rapid increase in value, or contractual aspects such as thresholds and minimum transfer amounts (Section 7.3.4). In scenario 4, the value of the portfolio is negative, and margin must, therefore, be posted, but this does not increase the positive exposure (again, in practice, due to aspects such as thresholds and minimum transfer amounts). Finally, in scenario 5, the posting of margin *creates* positive exposure.[26] In comparison with the benefits shown in the other scenarios, this is not a particularly significant effect, but it is important to note that margin can potentially increase as well as reduce exposure. Overall, both the EPE and ENE are reduced due to the two-way collateralisation. These effects will be seen in actual cases in Section 15.6.5.

Margin typically reduces exposure, but there are many (sometimes subtle) points that must be considered in order to assess the true extent of any risk reduction. To correctly account for the real impact of margin, parameters such as thresholds and minimum transfer amounts must be properly understood and represented appropriately. Furthermore, the margin period of risk (MPoR) must be carefully analysed to determine the true period of risk with respect to margin transfer. Quantifying the extent of the risk-mitigation benefit of margin is not trivial and requires many, sometimes subjective, assumptions.

To the extent that collateralisation is not a perfect form of risk mitigation, there are three considerations, which are illustrated in Figure 11.22:

• Firstly, there is a granularity effect, because it is not always possible to ask for all of the margin required due to parameters such as thresholds and minimum transfer amounts. This can sometimes lead to a beneficial overcollateralisation (as seen in Figure 11.22), where the margin amount is (for a short time) greater than the exposure. Note that the analysis of exposure should consider the impact of posted, not just received, margin.

---

[26] In practice, this can happen when previously-posted margin has not yet been returned as required.

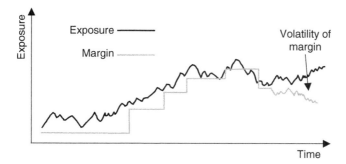

Figure 11.22   Illustration of the impact of margin on (positive) exposure, showing the delay in receiving margin and the granularity of receiving and posting margin amounts discontinuously. Also shown is the impact of the volatility of margin itself (for ease of illustration, this is shown in the last period only).

- Secondly, there is a delay in receiving margin, which involves many aspects such as the operational components of requesting and receiving margin or the possibility of margin disputes. These aspects are included in the assessment of the MPoR (Section 7.2.3).
- Thirdly, we must consider a potential variation in the value of the margin itself (if it is not cash in the currency in which the exposure is assessed).

We also emphasise that the treatment of margin is path dependent, since the amount of margin required at a given time depends on the amount of margin called (or posted) in the past. This is especially important in the case of two-way margin agreements.

Figure 11.23 shows the qualitative impact of collateral on exposure for three broadly defined cases:

- *Partially collateralised.* Here, the presence of contractual aspects such as thresholds means that the reduction of exposure is imperfect. A threshold can be seen as approximately capping the exposure.

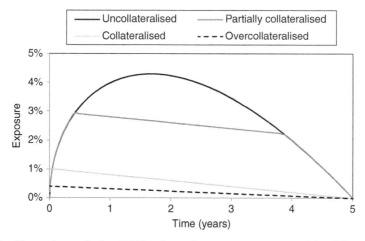

Figure 11.23   Illustration of the EPE of an interest rate swap with different levels of collateralisation.

- *Strongly collateralised.* In this case, it is assumed that parameters such as thresholds are zero, and therefore the exposure is reduced significantly. We assume there is no initial margin and the MPoR leads to a reasonably material exposure.
- *Overcollateralised.* In this case, we assume there is initial margin, and therefore the exposure is reduced further compared to the strongly collateralised case (and potentially to zero if the initial margin is large enough).

The impact of margin on exposure is discussed further in Section 15.5.

11.4   FUNDING, REHYPOTHECATION, AND SEGREGATION

11.4.1   Funding Costs and Benefits

Over recent years, a market consensus has emerged that uncollateralised exposures that give rise to counterparty risk and CVA also need to be funded and therefore give rise to additional costs. Such funding costs are generally recognised via funding value adjustment (FVA). It is, therefore, appropriate to discuss exposure from the point of view of funding.

The more detailed explanation and arguments around funding costs will be discussed in Chapter 18, but a basic explanation is as follows. A positive value represents an asset that needs to be funded, whilst a negative value represents a funding benefit (Figure 11.24). To some extent, funding costs and benefits cancel out since it is only necessary to consider them at a portfolio level (e.g. it is not necessary to fund transactions individually). The precise discussion of what 'portfolio' means in this context is discussed later in Section 18.3.2.

Note that not all assets give rise to funding costs. For example, it is possible to repo many bonds with good liquidity and low credit risk (e.g. treasuries). The receipt of cash from the repo transaction to a large extent offsets the funding cost of buying the bond. On the other hand, assets – such as derivatives – that cannot be 'repoed' in this way may be considered to have a funding cost.

Similar to the repo example above, if margin is received against an asset, then it may mitigate the funding cost, as long as it is reusable. Accordingly, margin that needs to be posted against a liability will likely negate any funding benefit. Hence, it is generally the portfolio value less the margin posted or received that determines the funding position. Loosely, the funding position is defined as:

$$funding = value - margin \tag{11.7}$$

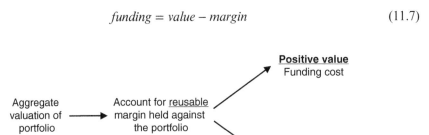

Figure 11.24   Illustration of the impact of a positive or negative value and margin on funding.

There is a funding cost when the above term is positive, and a funding benefit when the term is negative. Posted margin will be negative and so create a positive funding cost, whilst received margin will be positive and represent a benefit.

11.4.2   Differences Between Funding and Credit Exposure

The concept of funding costs and benefits can, therefore, be seen to have clear parallels with the definitions of positive and negative exposure given earlier (compare Figure 11.24 with Figure 11.1). A positive exposure is at risk when a counterparty defaults, but is also the amount that has to be funded when the counterparty does not. A negative exposure is associated with own default and is also a funding benefit (we will see later that these two components are generally thought to overlap). Accordingly, any margin held against a positive exposure reduces both counterparty risk and the associated funding cost. Margin posted against a negative exposure reduces own counterparty risk and the funding benefit.

However, whilst positive and negative exposures defined for counterparty risk (CVA and DVA) purposes have clear parallels with funding positions, there are some distinct differences that must be considered:

- *Definition of value*. The definition of *value* in the equations defining positive and negative exposure depends on close-out assumptions, since they only arise in default scenarios. Such valuations are subjective and need to be agreed between both the defaulting and surviving parties, based on the documentation and possibly subject to legal challenge (Section 6.3.5). With respect to funding, this can be considered to be an objective measure made by the party in question, since funding arises in non-default scenarios. However, the potential recursive problem (Section 6.3.4) with respect to the definition of value and the calculation of xVA (FVA in this case) does still exist.
- *MPoR*. The MPoR is a concept that is defined assuming the default of the counterparty and is relevant for credit exposure. In assessing the equivalent funding delay in receiving margin against a derivatives portfolio, a more normal (i.e. not contingent on counterparty default) margin posting frequency (which is likely much shorter) should be assumed. As discussed in Section 18.2.5, this is one reason why the FVA of a collateralised derivative may be considered to be zero, even though the equivalent CVA is not.
- *Aggregation*. Close-out netting is a concept that applies in a default scenario and hence credit exposure is defined at the netting set level (which may correspond to or be a subset of the counterparty level). On the other hand, funding may apply at the overall portfolio level, since values for different transactions are additive, and margin received from counterparties may be reused.
- *Wrong-way risk (WWR)*. Wrong-way risk is generally (although not always) a concept applied in relation to credit exposure as it relates to a linkage between the event of default and the underlying value of a portfolio. WWR, therefore, is less important to consider in the case of funding (although it will be discussed in Section 18.3.7).
- *Segregation*. As discussed in Section 11.4.3, segregation has different impacts on credit exposure and funding because it prevents the reuse of margin.

Despite the above differences, credit, debt, and funding value adjustments (CVA, DVA, and FVA) have many similarities and are usually quantified using shared methodologies.

11.4.3   Impact of Segregation and Rehypothecation

Margin in derivative transactions can be seen to serve two purposes: it has a traditional role in mitigating counterparty risk, but it can also be seen as neutralisation funding. This is why margin can be considered to impact both credit exposure and funding costs.[27] Historically, the primary role of margin in OTC derivatives was to reduce counterparty risk. One way to observe this is in the prominence of one-way margin agreements (Section 7.3.2) for counterparties with excellent credit quality, meaning that the counterparty risk is low. In a more funding-sensitive regime, such margin terms are more costly because the associated funding costs may not be seen to be driven by the credit risk of the counterparty, but rather by the cost of raising funds by the party itself.

Whilst the traditional use of margin is to reduce counterparty risk, its role in defining funding costs and benefits has become increasingly important in recent years as funding has received closer consideration. Margin may, therefore, be complementary in mitigating both counterparty risk and funding costs. For example, receiving margin from a counterparty against a positive value has a two-fold benefit.

- *Counterparty risk reduction.* In the event of the counterparty defaulting, it is possible to hold on to (or take ownership of) the margin to cover close-out losses.
- *Funding benefit.* The margin can be used for other purposes, such as being posted against a negative value in another transaction.[28] Indeed, it could be posted against the hedge of the transaction.

However, as Table 11.4 illustrates, the type of margin must have certain characteristics to provide benefits against both counterparty risk and funding costs. Firstly, in order to maximise the benefits of counterparty risk mitigation, there must be no adverse correlation between the margin and the credit quality of the counterparty (WWR). Note that wrong-way margin does still provide some benefit as a mitigant as long as it retains some value when the counterparty defaults. A second important consideration is that, for margin to be used for funding purposes, it must be reusable. This means that margin must not be segregated and must be reusable (transferred by title transfer or allowed to

Table 11.4   Impact of margin type on counterparty risk and funding. In this context, WWR refers to an adverse relationship between counterparty default and the value of the margin (e.g. a counterparty posting its own bonds).

	Margin can be used	Segregated or rehypothecation not allowed
No WWR	Counterparty risk reduction Funding benefit	Counterparty risk reduction No funding benefit
WWR present	Limited counterparty risk reduction Funding benefit	Limited counterparty risk reduction No funding benefit

---

[27] As in Equations (11.5) and (11.7).
[28] As long as it does not need to be segregated and can be rehypothecated.

be rehypothecated). In the case of cash margin, this is trivially the case, but for non-cash margin, rehypothecation must be allowed so that the margin can be reused or pledged via repo.

Consider the counterparty risk mitigation and funding benefit from various types of margin under certain situations:

- *Cash that does not need to be segregated.* As discussed above, this provides both counterparty risk and funding benefits.
- *Securities that can be rehypothecated.* As above, as long as the haircuts are sufficient to mitigate against any adverse price moves and also the corresponding haircuts associated with reusing the securities (e.g. the repo market or the margin terms for another transaction).
- *Cash or securities that must be segregated or cannot be rehypothecated.* These provide a counterparty mitigation benefit since they may be monetised in a default scenario, but they do not provide a funding benefit since they cannot be reused in a non-default scenario. Note that this is one of the scenarios used in the Totem xVA consensus pricing service (Section 18.2.5), where it can be seen as a means to separate counterparty risk and funding-related costs.
- *Counterparty posting own bonds (that can be rehypothecated).* These provide a questionable counterparty risk-mitigation benefit since they will obviously be in default when needed.[29] However, as long as they can be rehypothecated (and the haircuts are sufficient for this purpose), then they provide a funding benefit.

One example of the above balance can be seen in the recent behaviour of sovereigns, supranationals, and agencies (SSAs) counterparties, who have traditionally enjoyed one-way credit support annexes (CSAs) with banks and not posted margin due to their high credit quality (typically triple-A). SSAs have begun to move towards two-way margining, sometimes in the form of their own bonds.[30] This is because the traditional one-way agreement creates a very significant funding obligation for the banks, which is, in turn, reflected in the cost of the swaps SSAs use to hedge their borrowing and lending transactions. As banks have become more sensitive to funding costs, which in turn have become higher, the move towards a two-way margining means that a counterparty can achieve a significant pricing advantage (see later example in Section 21.3.4). Posting own bonds may be seen as optimal for a high-credit-quality counterparty because it minimises the liquidity risk it faces from posting other margin. Furthermore, thanks to its strong credit quality, the counterparty risk it imposes is less significant than the funding costs, and hence it most obviously needs to reduce the latter (put another way, it is focusing on minimising costs via the bottom left of the four scenarios in Table 11.4).[31]

---

[29] Note that they will provide some counterparty risk-reduction benefits. Firstly, if the bonds decline in value, then it is possible to request more margin and, secondly, the bonds will be worth something in default. However, a rapid default of the counterparty coupled with a low recovery value will make this form of margin almost worthless.

[30] Wood, D. (2011). KfW now using two-way CSAs, dealers claim. *Risk* (2 February). Wood, D. and J. Rennison (2014). Bank of England to post collateral in OTC derivatives trades. *Risk* (22 June). www.risk.net. IFR (2014). Europe's SSAs embrace two-way collateral. *IFR SSA Special Report 2014* (16 April).

[31] As discussed in Chapter 19, the capital requirements for counterparty risk (KVA) may still be quite significant, even if the counterparty risk charge itself (CVA) is not.

11.4.4   Impact of Margin on Exposure and Funding

Given aspects such as rehypothecation and segregation, when considering the benefit of margin on exposure, it is important to carefully define the exposure and funding components with reference to the nature of the underlying margin. In general, margin should be subtracted (added) to the exposure when received from (posted to) the counterparty. However, segregation and rehypothecation create distinct differences. From the more general Equation 11.5, the positive exposure from the point of view of counterparty risk is:

$$Positive\ exposure = \max(value - margin^R + margin^P_{NS}, 0), \qquad (11.8)$$

where $margin^R$ is the value of the total margin received from the counterparty,[32] and $margin^P_{NS}$ is the margin posted to the counterparty that is *not* segregated. Any margin received, irrespective of segregation and rehypothecation aspects, can be utilised in a default situation. However, if margin posted is not segregated, then it will create additional counterparty risk, since it cannot be retrieved in the event that the counterparty defaults.[33]

On the other hand, the funding position (generalised from Equation 11.7) is:

$$funding = value - margin^R_{RH} + margin^P \qquad (11.9)$$

where $margin^R_{RH}$ represents the margin received that can be rehypothecated (or, more generally, reused), and $margin^P$ represents all margin posted, irrespective of segregation and rehypothecation aspects.

Finally, to make these definitions more precise, we can distinguish between the two general types of margin (Section 7.2.3):

- *Initial margin.* As seen from Equation 11.8, to minimise counterparty risk this needs to be segregated, otherwise posting initial margin will increase positive exposure. Furthermore, if initial margin is both posted and received, then the amounts will offset one another (in practice, initial margin received could be simply returned to the counterparty!). Two-way initial margin must, therefore, be segregated (as required by bilateral margin rules; Section 7.4),[34] and unilateral initial margin should ideally be segregated.[35]
- *Variation margin.* From Equation 11.9, we can see that variation margin should be rehypothecable (or reusable) so as to reduce funding costs. Whilst this potentially creates more counterparty risk when posting, since variation margin is typically already owed against a negative value, this should not be a major concern. Variation margin is never segregated and can typically be rehypothecated, since it is posted against a negative valuation and does not represent overcollateralisation.

---

[32] Noting that WWR could reduce this value substantially.

[33] Note that negative exposure is defined differently, since this is relevant in the case that the institution itself defaults (DVA): *Negative exposure* $= \min(value + margin^P - margin^R_{NS}, 0)$.

[34] Except for the one-time rehypothecation of initial margin mentioned in Section 7.4.1.

[35] There are still situations in which parties not subject to regulatory margin posting hold non-segregated unilateral initial margin ('independent amount'), but this is becoming increasingly uncommon.

Making the above assumptions regarding initial and variation margins, we can write the above formulas more specifically as:[36]

$$Positive\ exposure = \max(value - VM - IM^R, 0), \tag{11.10}$$

$$Funding = value - VM + IM^P \tag{11.11}$$

The exposure for counterparty risk purposes can be offset by variation margin (which may be positive or negative), and initial margin received (IM^R). The funding position is fully adjusted by variation margin and increased by initial margin posted (IM^P). Note finally that in the absence of initial margin, the formulas above become similar, with caveats from the first four points in Section 11.4.2. Note that there are also some other points that may need to be considered above. For example, initial margin received may be considered to have a funding cost due to the need to segregate it with a third-party custodian.

Whilst both variation and initial margin impact funding, it is convenient to separate their effects into FVA and MVA (margin value adjustment) terms. This will become more obvious in the example below.

Spreadsheet 11.6 Impact of variation and initial margin on exposure and funding.

Example. Suppose the current value of a portfolio is 20, and 18 of variation margin is held together with 3 of (unilateral) segregated initial margin. Ignoring close-out costs:

$$Positive\ exposure = \max(20 - 18 - 3, 0) = 0$$

$$Negative\ exposure = \min(20 - 18, 0) = 0$$

$$Funding = 20 - 18 = 2$$

The current counterparty risk exposure is zero, since the initial margin makes up the gap between the value and variation margin (this gap could be a result of the value increasing before more margin can be received), whereas the amount that has to be funded is 2, since the initial margin held does not provide a funding benefit.

Example. Suppose the current value of a portfolio is 20, 15 of variation margin is held and 3 of segregated initial margin is posted bilaterally. We have:

$$Positive\ exposure = \max(20 - 15 - 3, 0) = 2$$

$$Negative\ exposure = \min(20 - 15 + 3, 0) = 0$$

$$Funding = 20 - 15 + 3 = 8$$

---

[36] As before, note that the concept of negative exposure for counterparty risk purposes is defined as $Negative\ exposure_{CCR} = \min(value - VM + IM^P, 0)$, with posted variation margin being negative. The funding exposure can be positive or negative and is defined directly by Equation (11.9).

There is positive exposure due to the initial margin being insufficient to cover the difference between the value and variation margin. The amount that has to be funded is 8, which is partially uncollateralised value (2) and partly the initial margin that is posted (5).

Suppose the current value of a portfolio is -20, 15 of variation margin has been posted and 3 of initial margin is posted bilaterally. We have:

$$Positive\ exposure = \max(-20 + 15 - 3, 0) = 0$$

$$Negative\ exposure = \min(-20 + 15 + 3, 0) = -2$$

$$Funding = -20 + 15 + 3 = -2$$

The positive exposure is zero, since the amount of variation margin posted is less than the (negative) value. There is negative exposure, since the initial margin does not completely cover the variation margin gap. There is a funding benefit arising from the variation margin that has not been posted (5) less the initial margin posted (3).

12

Credit Spreads, Default Probabilities, and LGDs

This chapter discusses default probabilities and recovery rates, or equivalently loss given default (LGD), which are key inputs to define credit value adjustment (CVA) and debt value adjustment (DVA) in counterparty risk quantification. Default probability (Section 3.3.4) defines the likelihood of counterparty default, whilst recovery rates (Section 3.3.5) define the amount lost in the default scenario. The difference between real-world and risk-neutral default probabilities will be discussed, together with the use of the latter in CVA/DVA quantification. This, in turn, leads to the need to define credit spreads, which often need to be estimated from the relatively scarce underlying data.

12.1 DEFAULT PROBABILITY

12.1.1 Real World and Risk Neutral

There is an important difference between so-called real-world and risk-neutral default probabilities that has been at the heart of the increased importance of CVA in recent years. Real-world default probabilities are often estimated from historical default experience via some associated credit rating. Alternatively, they may be based on quantitative models using balance sheet information. A risk-neutral (also known as 'market-implied') default probability is derived from market data, using instruments such as bonds or credit default swaps (CDSs).

It would be expected that risk-neutral default probabilities would be higher than their real-world equivalents since investors are risk averse and demand a premium for accepting default risk. This is indeed observed empirically – for example, Altman (1989) tracks the performance of portfolios of corporate bonds for a given rating and finds that the returns outperform a risk-free benchmark (which is a portfolio of treasury bonds). This outperformance shows that the return on the corporate bonds is more than adequate to cover the default losses experienced, and that bond investors are being compensated for material components above expected default rates and recoveries.

We depict the difference between a real-world and a risk-neutral default probability in Figure 12.1. The risk-neutral default probability is typically larger due to an embedded premium that investors require when taking credit risk. There has been research based on understanding the nature and behaviour of the risk premium depicted in Figure 12.1 (see Collin-Dufresne et al. 2001, Downing et al. 2005, and Longstaff et al. 2005).

The difference between real-world and risk-neutral default probabilities has been characterised in a number of empirical studies. For example, Giesecke et al. (2010) used a data set of bond yields that spanned a period of almost 150 years from 1866 to 2008, and found that average credit spreads (across all available bond data) have been about twice as large as realised losses due to default. This would suggest that the two

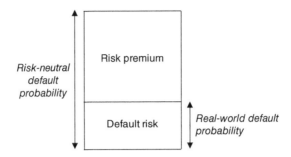

Figure 12.1   Illustration of the difference between real-world and risk-neutral default probabilities.

Table 12.1   Comparison between real-world and risk-neutral default probabilities in basis points.

	Real world	Risk neutral	Ratio
Aaa	4	67	16.8
Aa	6	78	13.0
A	13	128	9.8
Baa	47	238	5.1
Ba	240	507	2.1
B	749	902	1.2
Caa	1690	2130	1.3

Source: Hull et al. (2005).

components in Figure 12.1 are, on average, approximately equal. Studies that are more specific include Fons (1987), the aforementioned work by Altman (1989), and Hull et al. (2005). For example, Fons found that one-year risk-neutral default probabilities exceed actual realised default rates (in absolute terms) by approximately 5%. The difference between real and risk-neutral default probabilities from Hull et al. (2005) is shown in Table 12.1 as a function of credit rating. Note that the relative difference can be large, especially for better-quality credits.

12.1.2   CVA and Risk-neutral Default Probabilities

In the early days of counterparty risk assessment, it was common for firms to use real-world default probabilities (usually based on historical estimates and ratings) in order to quantify CVA, which was not universally considered a component of the fair value of a derivative. This treatment is broadly consistent with the quantification of credit risk across a bank (e.g. for its loan book). Some firms (typically small banks and non-banking firms) may still do this, but it is increasingly less common in the industry. This is highlighted in the following text, which references the implementation of CVA capital charge under Basel III:

> In contrast, accounting practices were much more diverse when the Basel Committee, in reaction to CVA losses observed during the crisis, initiated discussions on the implementation of a prudential framework for CVA. Accounting for CVA was

not universally fair valued through P&L [profit and loss] and, in many instances, relied almost exclusively on the use of historical default probabilities.[1]

Many small banks still use – either partially or completely – historical default probabilities.

The use of historical default probabilities has probably been the largest driver in the disparity in accounting for CVA across market participants. This was one of the reasons that the Basel III capital requirements for CVA, first introduced in 2010 (Section 4.2.5), were outlined with a risk-neutral-based CVA concept, irrespective of whether or not the bank in question actually accounted for its CVA in this fashion.

As discussed in Section 3.1.7, it has been increasingly common in recent years for risk-neutral default probabilities to be used. For example, in an Ernst & Young survey in 2012,[2] 13 out of 19 participating banks used risk-neutral information ('market data') for default probability estimation. The move to risk-neutral has been catalysed by accounting requirements and Basel III capital rules. International Financial Reporting Standard 13 (IFRS 2011; see also Section 5.3.3) requires entities to make use of observable market inputs wherever possible, and Basel III makes explicit reference to the credit spread in the underlying CVA formula (Equation 13.9). Some small regional banks still use real-world default probabilities, but this is becoming increasingly rare and harder to defend to auditors and regulators. For example, Ernst & Young (2014) states 'The use of historical default rates would seem to be inconsistent with the exit price notion in IRFS 13.'

The use of risk-neutral default probabilities changes the interpretation of CVA to be a market price of counterparty risk, rather than an actuarial assessment of expected future losses due to counterparty defaults. In some sense, this is not surprising given the development of the CDS market and the fact that CVA hedging has become more commonplace. On the other hand, it is important to emphasise that many counterparties are 'illiquid credits' in the sense that there is no direct market observable from which to define a risk-neutral default probability. This is particularly true for banks, which may have thousands of counterparties, many of whom are relatively small and do not have bonds or CDSs referencing their own credit risk. The problem of illiquidity is also more significant in regions outside Europe and the US, where CDS and secondary bond markets are more illiquid and sometimes non-existent. Furthermore, many liquid credits are large financial institutions which typically post margin and are therefore less important from a CVA perspective. Non-margin-posting counterparties, such as corporations and small and medium-sized enterprises (SMEs), are almost always illiquid credits but are very important from a CVA perspective.

The requirement to use risk-neutral default probabilities for illiquid credits creates a further problem with hedging: risk-neutral probabilities suggest the existence of a hedge, but without a liquid CDS on the counterparty in question, such a hedge does not exist. This is problematic since CVA will generally be much larger and more volatile (compared to using historical default probabilities), but without the availability of the natural hedging instruments to manage this volatility. For these reasons, banks have sometimes attempted to follow an intermediate approach, such as using a blend of historical and

---

[1] EBA (2015). Report on CVA (February). www.eba.europa.eu.

[2] Ernst & Young (2012). Reflecting credit and funding adjustments in fair value Insight into practices A survey https://otcmarket.news/QDownloads.aspx?guid=4d8ab547-a9c6-49a2-9761-36b213e32dfd www.ey.com.

risk-neutral default probabilities (including two banks from the aforementioned 2012 Ernst & Young survey). Another approach has been to use risk-neutral default probabilities for 'liquid credits' (i.e. those with an active CDS market or equivalent) and historical or blended probabilities for illiquid credits.

However, regulators and auditors generally do not support the deviation from risk-neutral default probabilities, even in cases of illiquid credits. For example, the CVA challenger model imposed by the European Central Bank (ECB) states:[3]

> The CVA challenger model then calculates an estimate of the CVA based on Benchmark PD [probability of default] parameters estimated from current index CDS curves and a market standard LGD parameter. The source of any significant deviations should then be understood.

Basel III capital rules impose similar requirements for capital allocation against CVA, requiring CDS spreads to be used where available, and for non-liquid counterparties stating that a reasonable estimate ('proxy') should be used (BCBS 2011b):

> Whenever such a CDS spread is not available, the bank must use a proxy spread that is appropriate based on the rating, industry and region of the counterparty.

Using the current credit environment (via CDS spreads) as a reference would seem to be preferable to a backwards-looking and static approach using historical data. However, the large non-default (risk premium) component in credit spreads, the inability to define CDS spreads for most counterparties, and the underlying illiquidity of the CDS market does create problems with such an approach. Furthermore, the unintended consequences of the use of CDS-implied default probabilities has potentially unintended adverse consequences, such as a 'doom loop', where CVA hedging can cause an increase in the cost of buying CDS protection (see Section 13.3.6). Some authors (e.g. Gregory 2010) have argued against this requirement and noted that banks do not attempt to mark-to-market much of their illiquid credit risk (e.g. their loan books). However, whilst using subjective mapping methods to determine a credit spread may seem rather non-scientific, it is generally a necessary process for banks to value illiquid assets, such as bonds and loans, held on their trading books. Accordingly, regulators clearly see risk-neutral default probabilities as a fundamental building block for CVA calculations, and they are clearly the basis for defining exit prices for fair value accounting purposes.

In line with the above, market practice (especially in the larger banks) has converged on the use of risk-neutral default probabilities. For example, the European Banking Authority (EBA 2015b) states:

> The CVA data collection exercise has highlighted increased convergence in banks' practices in relation to CVA. Banks seem to have progressively converged in reflecting the cost of the credit risk of their counterparties in the fair value of derivatives using market implied data based on CDS spreads and proxy spreads in the vast majority of cases. This convergence is the result of industry practice, as well as a consequence of the implementation in the EU of IFRS 13 and the Basel CVA framework.

---

[3] European Central Bank (2014). Asset Quality Review (March). www.ecb.co.uk.

12.1.3   Defining Risk-neutral Default Probabilities

Risk-neutral default probabilities are those derived from credit spreads observed in the market. There is no unique definition of a credit spread, and it may be defined in slightly different ways and with respect to different market observables, such as:

- single-name CDSs;
- asset swaps spreads;[4]
- bond or loan prices;[5] or
- using some proxy or mapping method.

All of the above are (broadly speaking) defining the same quantity, but the CDS market is the most obvious clean and directly available quote. In contrast, to calculate a credit spread from a bond price requires various assumptions, such as comparing with some benchmark such as a treasury curve. Where observable, the difference between CDS- and bond-derived credit spreads (the 'CDS-bond basis') is significant. The analysis below will discuss the calculation of a risk-neutral default probability, and the definition of credit spreads will be discussed in Section 12.2.

Spreadsheet 12.1 Calculating risk-neutral default probabilities.

Appendix 12A gives more detail on the mathematics of deriving risk-neutral default probabilities. For quantifying a term such as CVA, we require the default probability between any two sequential dates. A commonly used approximation for this is:

$$PD(t_{i-1}, t_i) \approx \exp\left(-\frac{s(t_{i-1}) \times t_{i-1}}{LGD}\right) - \exp\left(-\frac{s(t_i) \times t_i}{LGD}\right) \tag{12.1}$$

Where $PD(t_{i-1}, t_i)$ is the default probability between t_{i-1} and t_i, $s(t)$ is the credit spread at time t, and LGD is the assumed LGD (discussed below). Note that the PD in Equation 12.1 is unconditional (i.e. it is not conditional upon the counterparty surviving to t_{i-1}). Table 12.2 illustrates this for a simple example using annual default probabilities. To obtain a more granular representation, the most obvious solution would be to interpolate the credit spreads.

Table 12.2   Annual default probabilities for an example credit curve using Equation (12.1). The LGD is assumed to be 60%.

Time	Credit spread	PD
1 year	100 bps	1.65%
2 years	125 bps	2.43%
3 years	150 bps	3.14%
4 years	175 bps	3.79%
5 years	200 bps	4.34%

---

[4] An asset swap is essentially a synthetic bond, typically with a floating coupon.
[5] Note that loans are typically more senior than CDSs and bonds.

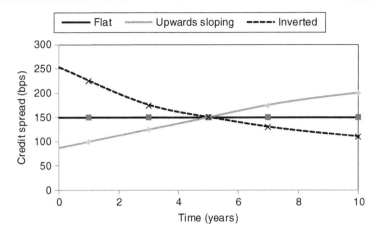

Figure 12.2   Three different shapes of credit curve, all with a five-year spread of 150 bps.

Equation 12.1 is only an approximation because it does not account for the shape of the credit spread curve prior to the time t_{i-1} (and the more sloped the curve is, the worse the approximation). In Spreadsheet 12.1, it is possible to compare the simple formula with a more accurate calculation.

Suppose we take three different credit curves: flat, upwards sloping, and inverted, as shown in Figure 12.2. The cumulative default probability curves are shown in Figure 12.3. Note that all have a five-year credit spread of 150 bps and assumed LGD of 60%. The only thing that differs is the shape of the curve. Whilst all curves agree on the five-year cumulative default probability of 11.75%, the precise shape of the curve up to and beyond this point gives very different results. This is seen in Figure 12.4, which shows annual default probabilities for each case. For an upwards-sloping curve, default is less likely in the early years and more likely in the later years, whilst the reverse is seen for an inverted curve. In order to calculate risk-neutral default probabilities properly, in addition

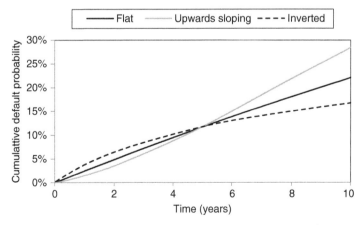

Figure 12.3   Cumulative default probabilities for flat, upwards-sloping, and inverted credit curves. In all cases, the five-year spread is 300 bps and the LGD is assumed to be 60%.

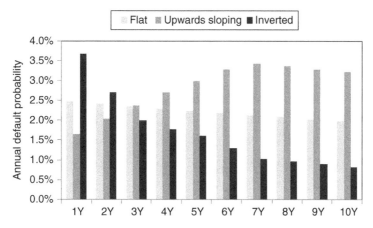

Figure 12.4 Annual default probabilities for flat, upwards-sloping, and inverted curves, as described in the text. In all cases, the five-year spread is 150 bps and the LGD is assumed to be 60%.

to defining the level of the credit curve, it is also important to know the precise curve shape. Extrapolation to the 10-year point, if that information is not available, is very sensitive.

12.1.4   Loss Given Default

In order to estimate risk-neutral default probabilities, an assumption for the LGD is typically required. The LGD refers to the percentage amount that would be lost in the event of a counterparty defaulting (all creditors having a legal right to receive a proportion of what they are owed). Equivalently, this is sometimes defined as one minus the recovery rate. LGD depends on the seniority of the over-the-counter (OTC) derivative claim – normally this ranks *pari passu* (of the same seniority) with senior unsecured debt, which in turn is referenced by most CDS contracts. However, sometimes derivatives may rank more senior (typically in securitisations) or may be subordinated, in which case further adjustments may be necessary.

Historical analysis on recovery rates shows that they vary significantly depending on the sector, the seniority of the claim, and economic conditions. As an example, Table 12.3 shows some experienced recovery values for financial institutions, which span the whole range from virtually zero to full recovery. For CVA computation, if the seniority is *pari passu* to that of the observable credit instruments and so the estimate is not of primary importance due to a cancellation effect. In situations where the LGD is expected to be higher or lower than that of other creditors (e.g. due to structural seniority), the estimation is more important. We discuss this more in Section 12.2.3.

A final point on recovery is related to the timing. CDSs are settled quickly following a default and bondholders can settle their bonds in the same process (the CDS auction) or simply sell them in the market. However, more complex contracts such as derivatives cannot be settled in a timely manner. This is partly due to their bespoke nature and partly due to netting (and margin), which means that many transactions are essentially aggregated into a single claim and cannot be traded individually. The net claim (less any margin) is

Table 12.3 Recovery rates for CDS auctions for some credit events in 2008. The Fannie Mae and Freddie Mac subordinated debt traded at higher levels than the senior debt due to a 'delivery squeeze' caused by a limited number of bonds in the market to deliver against CDS protection.

Reference entity	Seniority	Recovery rate
Fannie Mae	Senior	91.5%
	Subordinated	99.9%
Freddie Mac	Senior	94.0%
	Subordinated	98.0%
Washington Mutual		57.0%
Lehman		8.6%
Kaupthing Bank	Senior	6.6%
	Subordinated	2.4%
Landsbanki	Senior	1.3%
	Subordinated	0.1%
Glitnir	Senior	3.0%
	Subordinated	0.1%
Average		38.5%

then often quite difficult to define for the portfolio of trades (see Figure 2.8). This potentially creates two different recovery values:

- *Settled recovery*. This is the recovery that could be achieved following the credit event by trading out of a claim – for example, by selling a defaulted bond.
- *Actual recovery*. This is the actual recovery received on a more complex portfolio (e.g. including derivatives) following a bankruptcy or similar process.

In theory, settled and actual recoveries should be very similar, but in reality, since bankruptcy processes can take many years, they may differ materially. This is illustrated in Figure 12.5. It should be possible to agree on the claim with the bankruptcy administrators prior to the actual recovery, although this process may take many months. This would allow an institution to sell the claim and monetise the recovery value as early as possible. In the case of the Lehman Brothers bankruptcy, the settled recovery was around 9%, whereas some actual recoveries traded to date (e.g. derivatives portfolios) have been substantially higher (in the region of 30–40%).

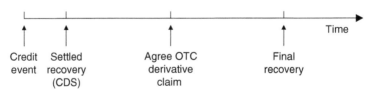

Figure 12.5 Schematic illustration of recovery settlement after a credit event. The settled recovery rate is achieved shortly after the credit event time (e.g. by participating in the CDS auction). The final recovery occurs when the company has been completely wound up. The actual recovery for a derivative claim may be realised sometime between the settled and final recoveries via trading out of the claim.

It should also be noted that recoveries on derivatives may be improved due to offsetting against other claims or other assets held (e.g. see the discussion on set-off in Section 6.3.6). These components may not be included in CVA but may give some additional benefit in a default workout process (discussed in Section 21.1.4).

12.2   CREDIT CURVE MAPPING

12.2.1   Overview

A credit curve is a key but often subjective input into a CVA calculation. Banks will have many hundreds or even thousands of counterparties, which will be entities such as corporates, SMEs, financial institutions, and SSAs (sovereigns, supranational entities, and agencies). The vast majority of these counterparties will not have liquid CDS quotes, bond prices, or even external ratings associated with them. End users of derivatives will be in a somewhat different situation, with only a relatively small number of (bank) counterparties. However, even then CDS quotes for some counterparties may be illiquid or unavailable. All firms, therefore, face some sort of credit curve mapping challenge.

No standard method exists for defining a credit curve for a given counterparty. This is not surprising given the subjectivity of the problem, and although some basic principles apply, there are many different approaches to credit curve mapping. Much of the regulatory guidance is quite broad and only makes reference to general aspects such as the rating, region, and sector being considered when determining the appropriate credit spread. One more detailed example is a publication by the EBA (2013) that discusses the determination of credit spreads for CVA purposes. Some of the general issues to be faced with credit curve mapping are:

- *Reference instrument.* As noted above (Section 12.1.3), there are a number of potential sources of credit spread information, such as CDSs or bonds.
- *Tenor.* It is also important to define fully the term structure of credit spreads up to the maturity of the counterparty portfolio in question. Available market data may mean that some tenors may be easier to map than others. Defining long-dated tenors (e.g. above 10 years) is particularly challenging.
- *Seniority.* It may be that the instrument used to define the credit spread has different seniority to that of the potential derivative claim with the counterparty.
- *Liquidity.* Some instruments, such as CDS indices, will be more liquid but less appropriate from a fundamental point of view for mapping a given credit. Other more relevant sources may be rather illiquid. A certain threshold for market liquidity (e.g. the number of entities quoting a price and the frequency of trading) needs to be established for a given quote to be used.
- *Region.* Whilst European and US debt markets may provide a reasonable amount of liquidity, other regions (e.g. Asia) are generally much more limited. Regional banks may, therefore, face an even greater challenge for determining credit spreads.
- *Hedging.* Related to the above liquidity comments, some reference instruments may provide reasonable mapping information but may not facilitate the hedging of counterparty risk. This could be due to a lack of liquidity or for practical reasons (e.g. not being able to short a corporate bond).

- *Capital relief.* Related to hedging will be the potential capital relief that will be available from various hedges, which can sometimes create problems. For example, proxy single-name CDSs may be considered good hedges,[6] but under current capital rules they achieve no capital relief (Section 13.3.6).[7] Index hedges do allow capital relief, but the magnitude of this may not align with the view of the bank and/or the accounting CVA.

The above will lead to some rather difficult and subjective decisions over the choice of mapping methodology – for example, whether it is appropriate to map to an illiquid bond price observed in the secondary market for the counterparty in question, or to use a CDS index that is much more liquid and can provide a hedge. Another difficult decision might be whether a firm should use a single-name CDS on a similar credit, which is believed to represent an excellent reference point but under regulatory rules does not attract any capital relief as a hedge.

12.2.2   The CDS Market

There are a few hundred reference entities with liquid single-name CDS quotes, mainly large financial institutions and sovereigns, although the liquidity of this market has not been improving in recent years. There are also credit indices, which are generally more liquid. Figure 12.6 gives an overview of the main CDS instruments available for mapping purposes. The indices are managed by IHS Markit.[8] Reading from the bottom, the first choice would obviously be to map to a single-name CDS or a relevant proxy such as a

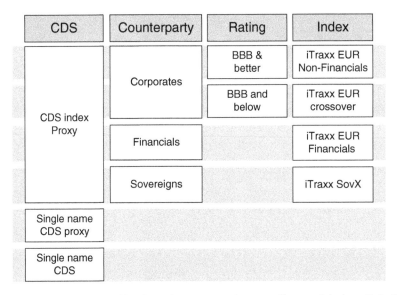

Figure 12.6   Illustration of classification of counterparties according to global credit indices.

---

[6] A single-name proxy is one that is viewed as giving a good representation of the credit spread in question. This may be a similar company, parent company, or sovereign entity.

[7] Note that this will change with the introduction of FRTB-CVA scheduled for 2022 (see Section 13.3.5).

[8] www.ihsmarkit.com.

parent company. If such information were not available, then the counterparty would be mapped to the relevant index depending on whether it is a corporation, financial, or sovereign entity. Corporations may be further sub-divided according to credit quality. For example, the European Crossover index and CDX High Yield indices contain non-investment-grade names.

Table 12.4 lists some characteristics of credit indices globally. Generally, indices reference liquid credits that trade in the single-name CDS market or secondary bond market. Note that more detailed classifications exist that are not shown. For example, iTraxx SovX is sub-divided into various regions (Western Europe, CEEMEA – Central and Eastern Europe, Middle East and Africa – Asia Pacific, Global Liquid Investment Grade, G7, BRIC – Brazil, Russian, India, and China – and Latin America). The main non-financials index is sub-divided into sectorial indices (TMT – technology, media, and telecommunications – industrials, energy, consumers, and autos). Whilst these sub-divisions potentially give a more granular representation, they have to be balanced against the available liquidity in the CDS market, which is poor beyond the iTraxx and CDX main indices. The liquid indices trade at maturities of 3, 5, 7, and 10 years, whilst for the less liquid ones the 5- and 10-year tenors are the most traded. In general, the 5-year CDS quote for any reference entity or index is the most liquid.

There are some additional technical issues with using CDSs to derive credit spreads for calculating CVA. First, the credit events under an International Swaps and Derivatives Association (ISDA) standard CDS are failure to pay, bankruptcy, or restructuring. Restructuring is specific to CDS agreements in Europe and emerging markets and is not considered a credit event in CDSs referencing North American credits.

Table 12.4 The universe of key credit indices globally.

	Index	Size	Comment
iTraxx Europe	Main	125	Most actively traded investment-grade names
	Non-financials	100	Non-financial credits
	Financials senior	25	Senior subordination financial names
	Financials sub	25	Junior subordination financial names
	Crossover	40	Sub-investment-grade credits
	High volatility	30	Widest spread credits from the main index
	LevX	30	European first lien loan CDSs
CDX	Main	125	Most actively traded investment-grade credits
	High vol	30	High-volatility investment-grade CDSs
	High yield	100	High-yield credits
	Crossover	35	CDSs that are at the crossover point between investment grade and junk
	Emerging markets	14	Emerging markets CDSs
	Emerging markets diversified	40	Emerging markets CDSs
	LCDX	100	First lien leverage loans CDSs
iTraxx Asia	Asia	50	Investment-grade Asian (ex-Japan) credits
	Asia HY	20	High-yield Asian (ex-Japan) credits
	Japan	50	Investment-grade-rated Japanese entities
	Australia	25	Liquid investment-grade Australian entities

From the perspective of hedging CVA, it is important that a counterparty failing to make a payment in a derivative contract would trigger a payment on the underlying CDS used for hedging. Ideally, there would therefore be a 'cross-default' of these obligations in the documentation so that a derivatives default will trigger the CDS contract. Indeed, sometimes CDSs do include such a trigger explicitly, although they are inevitably more expensive. A recent development in the CDS market has also been to add a new credit event triggered by a government-initiated bail-in.

The definition of restructuring as a credit event is quite complex but intends to cover a circumstance where a reference entity (due to a deterioration of its credit) negotiates changes in the terms with its debtors as an alternative to formal insolvency proceedings. However, in 2012 the restructuring of Greek debt avoided triggering CDSs via a restructuring credit event (potentially so as to ensure the stability of major European banks selling protection on Greece). A similar problem has occurred more recently with Banco Popular Español SA.[9]

Another important aspect of CDSs is a 'succession event', which could refer to proceedings such as a merger, demerger, transfer of assets or liabilities, or another similar event in which one entity assumes the obligations of another entity. For banks, ring-fencing and bad-bank-type restructuring are important considerations. A potential problem is 'orphaning', where a restructuring process leaves CDS contracts referencing an old entity and not referencing any outstanding debt, meaning that they become worthless.[10]

Note also that the deliverable in a CDS contract is typically a bond or loan, and not a derivative receivable. This leaves a potential basis risk between the LGD on the derivative and the payout on the CDS, as discussed in Section 12.1.4. Contingent CDSs, which do reference derivatives transactions or portfolios directly, are very illiquid.

Liquidity in the single-name CDS market has fallen since the global financial crisis, although some indices have become more liquid. There is a general issue with the depth and liquidity of the single-name CDS market and the calculation and management of CVA. Despite this, there is still a requirement to reasonably estimate credit spreads in order to calculate CVA for any counterparty.

12.2.3   Loss Given Default

Ideally, LGDs would be derived from market prices, but this is not generally possible since the relevant market information does not exist. Generally, a credit spread curve can be used to estimate risk-neutral default probabilities, with an assumed LGD value being an important part of the process (Equation 12.1). It is not possible to estimate market-implied LGDs unless different seniorities of credit spread are traded by the same reference entity (which is rarely the case). A 'recovery lock' or 'recovery swap' is an agreement between two parties to swap a realised recovery rate (when/if the relevant recovery event occurs) with a fixed recovery rate (fixed at the start of the contract and generally the same as the standard recovery rates outlined above). Recovery locks do not generally trade, except occasionally for distressed credits. Likewise, a 'fixed recovery CDS' (when

---

[9] 'ISDA EMEA Credit Derivatives Determinations Committee (2017). Banco Popular Español SA Governmental Intervention and Restructuring Credit Events (9 June). www.isda.org.

[10] Smith, R. (2017). Credit default swaps: a $10tn market that leaves few happy. *Financial Times* (25 July). www.ft.com.

compared to a standard CDS) would allow information on implied recovery rates to be observed, but these typically do not trade either.[11]

There are defined LGDs in the trading of CDS contracts (e.g. in order to value transactions) which depend on the underlying reference entity (e.g. 60% for iTraxx Europe and CDX NA). However, these LGD values only represent a convention and are not, therefore, truly market-implied or risk-neutral values. Generally, these standard LGDs, where known, are used to derive risk-neutral default probabilities. The choice of LGD is therefore driven by market convention but is not implied directly from market prices.

Sometimes, more favourable (lower) LGDs may be used to reflect aspects such as (in order of ease of justification):

- *Structural seniority of the portfolio* – for example, derivative transactions with securitisation special purpose vehicles.
- *Credit enhancements* or other forms of credit support, such as collateral available either directly (although margin specific to the contracts in question should generally be modelled within the exposure simulation, as discussed later in Section 15.5) or as a result of a broad relationship with a client. In the latter case, legal opinion as to whether the collateral can be used will be important.
- *The assumption of a favourable workout process*, based on past experience. Often banks may have actual recovery rates on their derivative portfolios which are generally higher than the standard recovery rates, even though in terms of seniority they should be the same. One reason for this is the Lehman case mentioned in Section 12.1.4. Auditors and regulators may not accept such assumptions without stronger evidence.

An example of a bank commenting on the use of the first approach above is 'estimated recovery rates implied by CDS, adjusted to consider the differences in recovery rates as a derivatives creditor relative to those reflected in CDS spreads, which generally reflect senior unsecured credit risk'.[12] The above arguments may sometimes be hard to justify, especially for regulatory capital purposes (e.g. the incoming FRTB-CVA capital requirements only seems to allow, with evidence, the first case; see Section 13.3.5).

12.2.4 General Approach

The most obvious observable market price to determine a credit spread is generally accepted to be that of a CDS, as this instrument cleanly references credit risk without other effects (such as a significant interest rate component in a bond). Not surprisingly, CDSs are viewed as being the primary source of credit spread information. Note, however, that regulation does tend to allow other liquid trading credit risk instruments (such as bonds) where CDSs are not available, as long as such spreads correspond to the appropriate rating, region, and industry combination.[13]

---

[11] Unlike a standard CDS, a fixed recovery CDS in the instance of a credit event settles at a pre-specified fixed recovery. In theory, a recovery swap can be reproduced by buying protection on a fixed recovery CDS and selling protection on the standard CDS (in practice, there may be some differences relating to settlement).

[12] J.P. Morgan Annual Report (2015).

[13] EBA (2017) states 'Article 383 of the CRR explicitly requires the use of the CDS spread of the counterparty, where the spread is available, even where credit spread data stemming from bonds are available too'.

In general, there are three different sources of credit spread information for a given counterparty:

- *Direct observables*. In this situation, the credit spread of the actual counterparty in question is directly observable in the market. Note that even when this data exists, there may only be one liquid tenor (e.g. typically five years for a single-name CDS), which is a clear problem, especially for long-dated portfolios. If it is possible to short the credit (e.g. buy CDS protection), then it may be possible to hedge and gain capital relief.
- *Single-name proxies*. This is a situation where another single reference entity trades in the market, which is viewed as a good proxy for the counterparty in question. This may be a parent company or the sovereign of the region in question, and may be used directly or have an additional component added to the credit spread to reflect greater riskiness. Hedging with such a name may provide a spread hedge but not a default hedge, and capital relief will not be achieved under current regulatory rules.[14]
- *Generic proxies*. This is the case where there is no defined credit spread that can be readily mapped directly, and some sort of generic mapping via rating, region, and sector is required. CDS indices do not provide default protection[15] but may be used as macro credit spread hedges, which will provide partial capital relief.

More discussion of the capital relief of various credit hedges will be given in Section 13.3.6. In particular, future regulation will recognise single-name credit hedges that either are linked through the legal entity or share the same sector.

A summary of the above approaches is given in Table 12.5.

If there is no relevant credit spread information available, then it may be acceptable for credit spreads to be constructed more indirectly using historical default probabilities and risk premium components (Figure 12.1), although it is clear that credit spreads should be in line with market levels.[16] For example, the EBA (2017) states:

> When no time series of credit spreads is observed in the markets of any of the counterparty's peers due to its very nature (eg project finance, funds), a bank is allowed to use a more fundamental analysis of credit risk to proxy the spread of an illiquid counterparty. However, where historical PDs ('probabilities of default') are used as part of this assessment, the resulting spread cannot be based on historical PD only – it must relate to credit markets.

Table 12.5 Comparison of different credit spread approaches.

	Liquidity	Hedging	Capital relief
Direct observables	Poor	Spread and default hedge	High
Single-name proxies	Medium	Partial spread hedge only	None[a]
Generic proxies	Good		Partial

[a]Future regulatory rules will provide partial relief; see Section 13.3.6.

---

[14] See Footnote 7.

[15] Unless the counterparty is one of the reference entities in the index.

[16] EBA (2017) states 'the proxy spread should reflect credit spread markets even where historical PDs are used as part of the alternative credit quality assessment'.

The future FRTB-CVA capital rules (BCBS 2017) make a similar statement:

> When no credit spreads of any of the counterparty's peers is available due to the counterparty's specific type (eg project finance, funds), a bank is allowed to use a more fundamental analysis of credit risk to proxy the spread of an illiquid counterparty. However, where historical PDs are used as part of this assessment, the resulting spread cannot be based on historical PD only – it must relate to credit markets.

Any credit spread mapping needs to be implemented via some sort of decision tree, as illustrated in Figure 12.7. The typical benchmark choice is a CDS where available, and other instruments such as bonds will normally only be considered where the single-name CDS is not liquid. Other quotes, such as bond spreads, will have to be derived using some methodology and then potentially basis-adjusted to attempt to estimate the equivalent CDS value. Single-name proxies may attract a small spread adjustment to account for a perceived higher (or lower) credit risk. This spread adjustment could be because a parent company is being used as a proxy (but does not offer an explicit guarantee and the child company is viewed as riskier). Sovereign CDSs are also quite common proxies, especially in markets where single-name CDSs are limited, and a spread will be added to

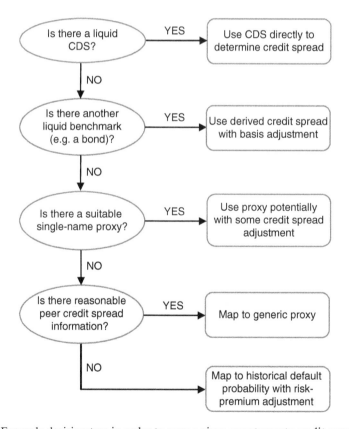

Figure 12.7 Example decision tree in order to map a given counterparty credit spread.

reflect the additional idiosyncratic risk with respect to the sovereign credit quality. Clearly, if a significant spread adjustment needs to be made, then this suggests that the proxy is not a particularly good choice. Is it also important to note that single-name proxies may increase volatility, since any idiosyncratic behaviour of the proxy will be incorrectly reflected in the mapped credit spread. Using historical data may only be justifiable when no relevant credit spread data on similar credits is available.

An important consideration in the decision tree above is what constitutes a liquid CDS quote. Banks may define a certain threshold for this by considering, for example, the average number of CDS quotes for the reference entity over a certain period of time. Alternatively, a third-party source could be used – for example, IHS Markit defines CDS liquidity scores of 1–5, with 1 being the most liquid and 5 being the least liquid, based on aspects such as bid-ask spreads, number of active market makers, and number of quotes.[17] Fitch Ratings also offers a similar service, where each entity is given a score across the global CDS universe.[18]

With respect to the decision tree in Figure 12.7, it is important to note that a typical bank will end up with many generic proxies. This is due to the likelihood of having many clients who have relatively small balance sheets (e.g. corporates, SMEs) and therefore not having liquid instruments traded in the credit markets. Although the individual exposure to each of these clients may be relatively small, collectively the total exposure is likely to be very significant, and therefore the construction of general curves as proxies is important.

12.3   GENERIC CURVE CONSTRUCTION

12.3.1   General Approach

The aim of generic credit curve mapping is to use some relevant liquid credit spread quotes to estimate a general curve based on observable market data, as illustrated in Figure 12.8. Some methodology will be required to combine points at a given tenor (perhaps with some underlying weighting scheme also used to bias towards the more liquid quotes). Some other and possibly separate approach will be required to interpolate between tenors.

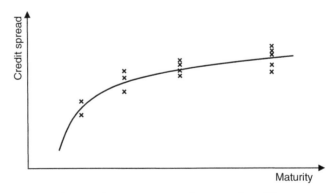

Figure 12.8   Illustration of a generic curve construction procedure. The crosses represent observable credit spreads as a function of maturity.

[17] www.ihsmarkit.com.
[18] www.fitchratings.com.

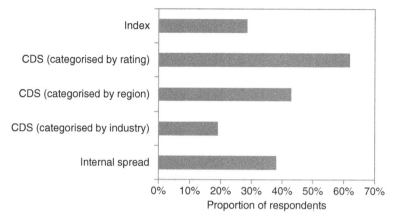

Figure 12.9   Market practice for marking non-tradable credit curves. Source: Deloitte/Solum CVA Survey (2013).

Granularity is an important consideration in generic curve construction. A very granular definition will be problematic as relevant data may not be available to define various components. On the other hand, a very coarse approach may not define specific credit spreads well. Clearly, in regions such as the US and Europe the most granular definition may be possible, whereas in smaller regions industry classification will almost certainly need to be excluded. Counterparties such as municipalities may represent a particular challenge, with limited credit spread information, apart from that of the sovereign, being available.

Figure 12.9 illustrates market practice for the construction of generic curves for non-tradable credits. In addition to the obvious use of indices, it can be seen that bespoke curves are generated as a function of rating, region, and industry. Not surprisingly, whilst classification via rating is common, the use of region and industry grouping is less common. In other words, banks will classify by all three if possible and drop the industry and possibly also the regional categorisation if necessary. Internal spread corresponds to using some internal spread estimation, potentially from the pricing of loans to the same or similar counterparties. This is clearly less in line with the concept of defining spreads with respect to external pricing and market observables.

Regulators generally propose a mapping based upon rating, region, and industry; they necessarily accept more sparse representation when data does not clearly allow this. Even within these categories, the classification is generally kept fairly narrow – for example, EBA (2013) states that, 'where a CDS for a counterparty is not available, institutions shall use a proxy spread that is appropriate having regard to the rating, industry and region of the counterparty' and suggest the following classification as a minimum:[19]

- A pre-defined hierarchy of internal and/or external credit ratings. Note that for non-externally rated names, banks will typically use their internal rating mapped to external ratings.

---

[19] Note that this guidance is specific to the determination of credit spreads for the purposes of capital calculations for banks using the 'advanced CVA capital charge' methodology, which is discussed in Section 13.3.4. However, there is no reason why it would not also be useful guidance for determining credit spreads for other purposes (such as calculating accounting CVA numbers).

- Industry, based on:
  - o public sector;
  - o financials; and
  - o others.
- Region, based on:
  - o Europe;
  - o North America;
  - o Asia; and
  - o rest of the world.

Despite the relatively general definitions above, it is recognised that firms may have to depart from the minimum granularity if there is insufficient data.

The approach to classification may differ between firms. For example, a large global bank may believe it has an exposure that is not concentrated from a regional or sectorial point of view. On the other hand, a local bank will necessarily have a more geographically-concentrated exposure and may be more exposed to certain industry sectors that are more active in its own region.

In general, there are two general approaches that have become popular for defining generic credit curves:

- *Intersection (or 'bucketing') approach*. This is a basic approach that takes a measure such as the average or median across all liquid names in the relevant rating, region, and sector sub-categories to imply the generic credit spread. Whilst simple, this suffers from the sparseness of the underlying data, with some sub-categories having no data whatsoever. As such, it would be expected not to be robust and to be potentially unstable.
- *Cross-section methodology*. This is a more sophisticated approach, based on a multidimensional regression across rating, region, and industry sector. The use of regression avoids problems that arise from a lack of data.

These approaches will be outlined in more detail below.

12.3.2   Intersection (Bucketing) Approach

In the intersection methodology, the proxy spread for a given obligor shall be determined by aggregating data across the relevant rating, region, and sector sub-categories forming a bucket. If this classification is rather broad (e.g. a single-A European financial services counterparty), then there will be a large number of data points but less distinction between different counterparties. In contrast, a more granular classification (e.g. a single-A Asian utility company) distinguishes better between different counterparties but provides less data for each curve calibration. Mapping has to consider granularity carefully; more granular mapping is preferable only if there are sufficient data points for each categorisation. With few data points, there is a danger of the idiosyncratic risk of a particular credit creating unrealistic and undesirable volatility.

Chourdakis et al. (2013) illustrate the problems with an intersectional approach by considering the following classification:

- *Regions (five)*. North America, Europe, Japan, Asia ex-Japan, and rest of the world.
- *Rating (six)*. AAA/AA, A, BBB, BB, B, and CCC.
- *Sectors (five)*. Financial services, non-financial services, industrial production, raw material, and other sectors.

Note that even the above broad classification gives a total of $5 \times 6 \times 5 = 150$ possible combinations. Not surprisingly, there are data issues with this classification. Whilst these authors observe 1,551 CDS quotes available across the defined universe, making an average of 10.3 quotes per sub-category, the data is concentrated in certain regions, and there are 42 sub-categories without a single CDS quote. For example, Figure 12.10 shows a breakdown of the quotes for financial services firms by rating and region, illustrating that the majority of the data is North American and European credits and intermediate (A and BBB) credit ratings.

A potential process for generic curve construction based on an intersectional methodology could be as follows:

1. Define the universe of available CDSs via a minimum liquidity threshold.
2. Bucket this universe by the agreed-upon classification (rating, region, and sector).

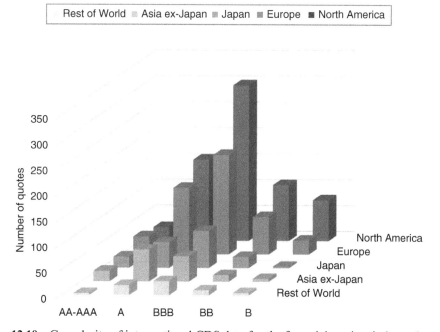

Figure 12.10   Granularity of intersectional CDS data for the financial services industry by credit rating and geographic region. Source: Chourdakis et al. (2013).

3. Depending on the data available, potentially exclude outliers in each bucket according to some given metric, such as more than a certain number of standard deviations from the median (this clearly requires a reasonable number of observations).
4. Define the resulting generic curve(s) via an average of the relevant points or a weighted average depending on the relative liquidity of different points.
5. Fill in missing data points via various rules, interpolation, and extrapolation methods.

The main advantage of the above approach is its simplicity and ease of understanding and implementation. Clearly, without a more liquid underlying CDS market, it is not a robust approach and will require override, interpolation, and extrapolation assumptions in order to be able to define generic credit spreads for each sub-category.

12.3.3   Cross-section Methodology

The intersectional approach has drawbacks driven by the limited liquid credit spread data available in the market. A very broad definition of generic curves is less descriptive, whereas a detailed categorisation is limited by the illiquidity of the CDS market, meaning that buckets will have limited or no data points. As a result, there will be potentially large jumps in credit spreads due to the idiosyncratic behaviour of names in a given bucket. This behaviour will be particularly adverse for buckets with fewer CDS quotes to which to calibrate.

An alternative approach to credit spread mapping is proposed by Chourdakis et al. (2013) and is based on a cross-section methodology using a multidimensional linear regression.[20] This approach still uses a categorisation based across rating, region, and sector (and potentially other categories), but it generates the spread via a factor approach rather than a direct mapping to the names in a given bucket. A given spread is generated as the product of several factors, such as:

- global (M_{glob});
- industry sector (M_{ind});
- region (M_{region});
- rating (M_{rating}); and
- seniority (M_{sen}).

Each factor will contain several sub-categories (e.g. different credit ratings), for which the coefficients need to be estimated. The spread is defined by:

$$S_i^{generic} = M_{glob} \times M_{ind} \times M_{region} \times M_{rating} \times M_{sen} \qquad (12.2)$$

or equivalently by:

$$\log(S_i^{generic}) = \log(M_{glob}) + \log(M_{ind}) + \log(M_{region}) + \log(M_{rating}) + \log(M_{sen}) \qquad (12.3)$$

---

[20] This approach is proposed in relation to the specific risk model required as part of the advanced CVA capital charge (Section 13.3.4) and not for the quantification of CVA for accounting purposes, although there is no obvious reason why it might not be considered useful for the latter.

which is a linear regression problem from which the coefficients can be estimated. A key assumption behind such a methodology is that CDS spreads can be defined by a set of factors that are independent of the other components (e.g. there is a single multiplicative credit spread factor for all European credits, which is independent of the sector, rating, and seniority of those obligors). This means that the estimate of a BBB Asian credit spread, for example, will use all BBB data and all Asian data, rather than just the data intersecting the two-dimensional classification. This credit spread can be estimated even if there are no BBB Asian reference points, as long as there are separate points for BBB and Asia.

Spreadsheet 12.2 Example cross-sectional methodology for credit spreads.

The calibration of the factors above to liquid credit spread data is straightforward, as it involves a linear regression which is the result of minimising the squared differences in log spreads. The advantage of a cross-sectional approach is that there will be much more data available to calibrate each of the factors. This would be expected to give rise to smoother and more reasonable behaviour (such as credit spreads changing monotonically across the credit rating spectrum), as is shown by Chourdakis et al. (2013).

A simple example of cross-sectional regression coefficients and resulting credit spreads is shown in Table 12.6. This example ignores seniority and has a limited granularity over industry and region.

There are a number of ways to check the accuracy of this type of approach. One is to examine the residuals (the deviation of observed credit spreads compared to those implied

Table 12.6 Example coefficients and implied credit spreads for a simple example. Note that the credit spread is in basis points per annum.

	Sub-category	Coefficient
$\log(M_{glob})$	Global	−5.90
$\log(M_{rating})$	AAA	0.00
	AA	0.63
	A	1.11
	BBB	1.42
	BB	2.37
$\log(M_{ind})$	Financials	0.00
	Non-financials	−0.05
$\log(M_{region})$	US	0.00
	Europe	0.16
	Asia	0.23

	Global $\log(M_{glob})$	Rating $\log(M_{rating})$	Industry $\log(M_{ind})$	Region $\log(M_{region})$	Proxy credit spread
European AA financial	−5.90	0.63	0.00	0.00	51.4 bps
US AA financial	−5.90	0.63	0.00	0.07	55.2 bps
US BBB non-financial	−5.90	1.42	−0.05	0.07	115.6 bps
US BB non-financial	−5.90	2.37	−0.05	0.07	299.0 bps

by the regression formula), which is an 'in-sample' test. Alternatively, an 'out-of-sample' test could be used to examine the prediction of data (e.g. CDS spreads) not used in the regression. Weak and distressed credits can be a particular problem in this type of approach, since their behaviour is quite idiosyncratic and may not be well explained by the model in Equation 12.2. For example, CCC credits can have particularly high or low spreads as a result of industry and region coefficients that are mainly driven by other ratings.

EBA (2015b)[21] shows some time series of generic spreads for various hypothetical and real credits for banks using the advanced CVA capital charge methodology (Section 13.3.4).[22] These results illustrate the variation between the methodologies of different banks and the differing stability of different approaches.

It should be possible to improve cross-sectional approaches by extending them across factors other than liquid CDS spreads to produce more reliable and stable results. For example, Sourabh et al. (2018) show that the additional use of equity returns produces more accurate estimates of CDS spreads. Depending on the amount of data available, it may also be useful to include other credit spread information from loans and bonds, with appropriate representation of aspects such as seniority and basis.

12.3.4   Curve Shape, Interpolation, and Indices

Quite often, generic curve methodologies may only characterise a single liquid point, and indices can be used to fill in missing points. For example, suppose a generic credit spread is defined at only a single point (e.g. five years). It is then necessary to imply the curve shape: an obvious solution is to use a representative index and to scale this shape to fit the defined point, as shown in Figure 12.11. Due to the importance of term structure

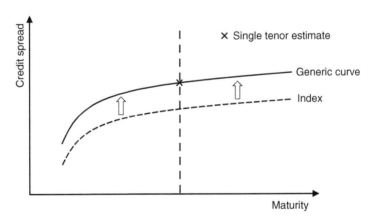

Figure 12.11   Illustration of defining a curve shape based on the shape of the relevant index. The cross shows a single (e.g. five-year) point that is assumed to be known for the curve in question.

---

[21] See Figures 30–35 in EBA 2015b.

[22] The hypothetical credits are a UK insurer rated AA, a Swiss municipality of more than 100,000 inhabitants rated A, and a Japanese airline company rated BB. The actual credits are the Government of Turkey, Berkshire Hathaway Inc., and Tata Motors Ltd.

noted in Section 12.1.3, it is essential not to make crude assumptions. Indices can also be used to fill in missing rating points. For example, one may look at the ratio of single-A to triple-B spreads in iTraxx or CDX and use this ratio to infer one rating curve from another in the more granular generic curve representation.

12.3.5   Third-party Providers

A potential source of generic credit spread curves is a third-party provider. This may offer a potentially cheaper solution compared to a firm implementing its own method-ology and is also independent (which may be desirable from an auditor's perspective). On the other hand, there are potential drawbacks, such as the methodology being rigid and producing unexpected behaviour beyond the control of the user (e.g. the volatility of hedged CVA).

A non-exhaustive list of third-party providers providing generic credit spread informa-tion is as follows:

- *IHS Markit CDS Enhanced Sector Curves.*[23] This provides generic CDS curves for all tenors across seven regions, eleven sectors, and seven rating classes (Table 12.7), using end-of-day CDS prices and a 'multivariate factor value model' (cross-sectional-type approach). CVA computation is a key motivation for the provision of this service.
- *Standard & Poor's Credit Default Swap Market Derived Signals (CDS MDS).*[24] This uses CDS spread data in a linear regression model against rating, sector,[25] corporate/sovereign classification, CDS documentation type (credit event definitions), and CDS currency denomination. This allows the determination of generic benchmark CDS spreads across these classifications.
- *Moody's Fair Value CDS (FVS-CDS) spreads.*[26] These are CDS spreads derived from an expected default frequency (EDF^{TM}) measure published daily.[27] Because the under-lying model is based on balance sheet information (e.g. equity prices), it can be used directly rather than to generate generic credit spread curves.
- *Fitch.* Fitch provides a Bank Credit Model, which is a statistical model producing a daily implied CDS spread for over 9,500 banks globally, and CDS Benchmark Curves to support the pricing of illiquid names using average CDS values calculated by rat-ing, sector, and region for the full-term structure across each currency, seniority, and restructuring.[28]
- *Kamakura Risk Information Services (KRIS).* KRIS provides quantitative measures of creditworthiness such as implied CDS spreads for 40,000 global companies.

---

[23] www.ihsmarkit.com.

[24] Standard & Poor's (2013). How Standard & Poor's Arrives At Credit Default Swap Market Derived Signals (September). www.sprating.com.

[25] Known as Global Industry Classification Standard (GICS), which is a categorisation by Standard & Poor's of all public companies into 11 sectors, 24 industry groups, 68 industries, and 157 sub-industries.

[26] www.moodysanalytics.com.

[27] Moody's Analytics (2016). CDS-Implied EDF^{TM} Measures and Fair Value CDS Spreads – At a Glance (2 November). www.moodysanalytics.com.

[28] www.fitchratings.com.

Table 12.7 Regions, sectors, and ratings for IHS Markit CDS Enhanced Sector Curves.

Region	Sector	Rating
North America	Basic materials	AAA
Europe	Consumer goods	AA
Eastern Europe	Consumer services	A
Middle East	Energy	BBB
Japan	Financials	BB
Asia ex-Japan	Government	B
Oceania	Healthcare	CCC
	Industrials	
	Technology	
	Telecommunications services	
	Utilities	

Source: www.ihsmarkit.com.

12.3.6 Hedging

An important consideration in the choice of mapping methodology is the potential hedging of CVA. Here, the appropriate strategy depends on the liquidity of the counterparty. For liquid counterparties, the single-name CDS is the most obvious hedging instrument. For illiquid counterparties, proxy single-name hedges may be less liquid and do not currently allow capital relief (Table 12.5). Credit indices are, therefore, the most efficient macro-hedges. Whilst a more granular mapping methodology may be considered to more accurately reflect the underlying economic behaviour, it may make hedging less effective.

Ultimately, mapping and hedging can be self-fulfilling prophecies since the mapping mechanism ultimately defines the effectiveness of the hedge. For example, consider a European firm that intends to hedge its CVA using the iTraxx Europe index. It is likely that using only the single-name CDSs contained within this index for a generic curve construction methodology will lead to lower volatility (of the hedged CVA). However, this ignores other reasonably liquid European credits that – whilst not liquid and/or large enough to be part of the index – may be expected to provide useful credit spread information. Whether or not such an approach is acceptable would be up to the firm's auditors and regulators.

In order to macro-hedge credit risk under a generic curve approach, it is necessary to construct a 'beta mapping' to a given index or set of indices. This involves performing a regression of the generic curve against the index to obtain the optimum hedge ratio. There is no definitive consensus as to over what time period such regression should be performed; longer shows will be less noisy, but shorter periods may be more accurate. Another important consideration is the recalibration frequency; daily recalibration minimises the potential for large discrete changes but may be operationally cumbersome. From a practical perspective, a periodic (e.g. monthly) recalibration may be more appropriate but will lead to potentially significant changes, leading to mark-to-market impacts and required adjustment of hedges. Some banks actually map to the beta-adjusted indices directly, which produces more stability in between recalibration dates but may be harder to defend to regulators and auditors. CVA hedging is discussed in more detail in Section 21.2.

13

Regulatory Methodologies

13.1 OVERVIEW

The Basel Committee for Banking Supervision (BCBS) is a committee of banking supervisory authorities. One of the functions of the BCBS is to set global standards for minimum capital requirements for banks. Since the advent of minimum regulatory capital requirements for banks, it has been necessary to develop regulatory methodologies to define such amounts. This chapter will discuss the methodologies that are specific to counterparty credit risk, both for bilateral and centrally-cleared trades.

Most regulatory capital methodologies apply to a particular class of risk (e.g. credit, market, operational) and are specific to that application. This is problematic for counterparty credit risk (CCR), which contains elements of both market and credit risk. For example, the primary emphasis of the Basel framework for credit risk is basic financial instruments such as loans. There is generally a need to fit more complex transactions – such as derivatives – into these frameworks in a consistent and relatively simple fashion. The primary issue for derivatives here is defining the exposure at default (EAD), which, loosely speaking, represents the exposure that should be assumed in the event of the counterparty defaulting. In contrast to simple lending instruments, where the EAD is a trivial and contractual amount, the EAD for derivatives is conceptually complex. This is because of the randomness of the underlying exposure and its potentially strong time dependence.

Even looking just at derivatives, the relevant methodologies tend to be fairly numerous for the following reasons:

- there are different setups (Figure 10.6) where loss absorbency is held differently, and therefore the size of required bank capital differs;
- there are requirements covering both credit and market risk, with each often needing a particular calculation methodology;
- new regulations often give rise to the need for new methodologies (e.g. the credit value adjustment – CVA – capital charge, see Section 13.3.1);
- whilst large and sophisticated banks have the economies of scale to develop and maintain more sophisticated methodologies (such as internal models), smaller banks require more simple approaches that are easier to implement; and
- regulatory methodologies may be improved over time, either to better reflect the underlying risks or take account of changes in market practice – for example, the standardised approach for CCR (SA-CCR), discussed in Section 13.4.3.

Recent years have seen a period of rapid regulatory change with respect to changes in existing capital rules (e.g. the SA-CCR) and new requirements (e.g. the leverage ratio). Furthermore, there is a secondary effect from new regulations creating the need for new or improved capital methodologies. For example, the clearing mandate (Section 4.4.1) has led to the need to define bank capital requirements when facing central counterparties, which will be discussed in Section 13.6. Furthermore, the bilateral margin requirements (Section 4.4.2) have created a need for methodologies that incorporate the risk-mitigating nature of (received) initial margin in regulatory capital quantification. These two aspects have been a key driver in relation to the development of the SA-CCR (Section 13.4.3).

Note also that standards on banking regulation, such as those issued by the BCBS, are not always adopted universally, and there can be regional differences due to national regulators implementing standards at a different pace or with different specifications. For example, at the time of writing, the SA-CCR is scheduled for implementation in some regions in 2020, but other regions have not yet set a date. Unless otherwise stated, the discussion in this chapter will refer to global standards and the envisaged timescales. Actual timescales can often be materially later than these.

Figure 13.1 gives an overview of the development of regulatory capital methodologies for counterparty risk-related requirements, with more specific details given in Sections 13.3, 13.4, and 13.6. Some of the timescales shown are subject to change and may differ across regions.

Note that most of the following discussion applies to the calculation of minimum capital requirements or risk-weighted assets (RWAs), with Section 13.4.6 discussing the leverage ratio specifically.

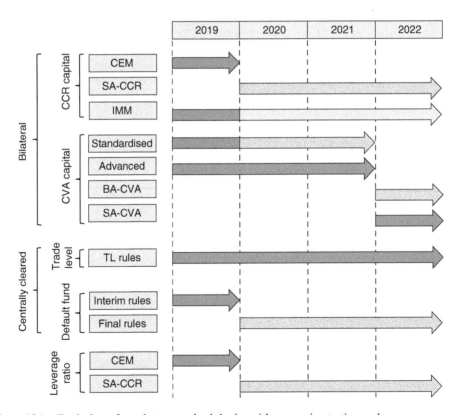

Figure 13.1   Evolution of regulatory methodologies with approximate timescales.

13.2   CREDIT RISK (DEFAULT RISK) CAPITAL

CCR capital in Figure 13.1 is based on more general capital rules to capitalise the default risk on typical credit risk instruments, such as loans. Since 1995, banks have had the option of using internal models for defining market risk capital requirements via value-at-risk (VAR), which is being enhanced under the Fundamental Review of the Trading Book (FRTB) (Section 4.2.3). However, internal models have not been generally allowed for credit risk. Such a limitation can be put down to the increased complexity of modelling credit risk, together with the limited data and longer time horizons involved.

Credit risk capital is defined by three terms, specifically the EAD, probability of default (PD), and loss given default (LGD), in a multiplicative formula. There are various methodologies that are used to define these terms. The methodologies for PD and LGD are described below, whilst EAD is discussed in Section 13.4. There are two broad methodologies for calculating capital requirements for credit risk (PD and LGD in Figure 13.2). Firstly, the standardised approach assigns standardised risk weights to exposures based on external ratings (in jurisdictions that allow the use of external ratings for regulatory purposes). The second approach is the internal ratings-based (IRB) approach, which allows banks to use their internal rating systems for credit risk, subject to the explicit approval of the bank's supervisor. There is no internal model approach to credit risk as such, but internal models can be used for defining EAD.

Note that credit risk capital requirements – both standardised and IRB – are defined at the counterparty level, and there is no portfolio effect across many counterparties.

13.2.1   Standardised Approach

In this simple approach, banks assess the risk of their exposures using external ratings. BCBS (2006) provides tables that specify a capital charge for each risk bucket. The risk weights depend on asset class and are generally linked to external ratings. There are changes to this approach scheduled for implementation in 2022 (BCBS 2017). Example risk weights are given in Table 13.1.

$$EAD \times PD \times LGD$$

CEM	Standardised
IMM	F-IRB
SA-CCR	A-IRB

Figure 13.2   Approach to credit risk capital charge for counterparty credit risk instruments. The terms are defined in more detail in Sections 13.2.1, 13.2.2, and 13.4.

Table 13.1   Example risk weights under the standardised approach for credit risk.

External rating of counterparty	AAA to AA–	A+ to A–	BBB+ to BBB–	BB+ to BB–	Below BB–	Unrated
Sovereign	0%	20%	50%	100%	150%	100%
Corporate	20%	50%	75%	100%	150%	100%

13.2.2   Internal Ratings-based Approach

Under the IRB approach, banks can use their internal rating systems for credit risk, subject to the explicit approval of their respective supervisors.

The IRB approach still uses a relatively simple formula, although the origins of this formula have a theoretical basis. The theory rests on the large homogeneous pool (LHP) approximation described in Appendix 13A. This is used to define a conditional loss (based on a confidence level) under the LHP assumptions of Vasicek (1997) and the granularity adjustment formula of Gordy (2004), with a confidence level set at 99.9%. Under the advanced IRB approach, regulatory capital (RC) for a given instrument is defined by the following formula:

$$RC = EAD \times LGD \times (PD_{99.9\%} - PD) \times MA(PD, M)$$ (13.1)

with the following definitions:

EAD the exposure at default (e.g. the notional of a bond or loan).

LGD the expected loss given default in relation to the EAD (estimated conditionally on an economic downturn).

PD the obligor's probability of default.

$PD_{99.9\%}$ the obligor's probability of default (subject to a floor of 0.03%), with $PD_{99.9\%}$ representing an unexpected probability of default at the confidence level of 99.9%.[1] This incorporates an asset correlation parameter which may penalise more correlated or systemic exposures and is higher for financial institutions.[2]

M the regulatory maturity which is the maturity of the transaction capped at five years.

MA a maturity adjustment factor which partially accounts for the fact that an obligor's credit quality may deteriorate (credit migration via a rating downgrade, for example) and that this effect may be more significant for high-quality obligors.

The above formula is intuitive; the capital should depend on the size of the position concerned (EAD), and on the PD, LGD, effective maturity, and correlation within the portfolio concerned. From the point of view of counterparty risk, the above formula makes up what will be referred to as the 'default risk capital charge'.

There is also a scaling factor of 1.06 applied to IRB capital requirements calculated by the above formula. This scaling factor is being removed in changes to IRB capital requirements scheduled for implementation in 2022 (BCBS 2017).

There are two IRB approaches:

- *Advanced IRB (A-IRB)*. Banks use their internal estimates of the PD, LGD, and EAD parameters.
- *Foundation IRB (F-IRB)*. Banks use only their internal estimates of PD.

---

[1] The probability of default is subtracted from the worst-case probability of default here, as explained in Appendix 13A.

[2] Due to the view that financial firms are significantly interconnected, Basel III increased the correlation parameter in the Basel II IRB formula by a multiplier of 1.25 for regulated financial institutions whose total assets are greater than or equal to $100bn, and also unregulated financial institutions.

The aforementioned IRB changes (BCBS 2017) include certain enhancements to and constraints on the application of IRB approaches for certain asset classes. This includes the removal of the possibility of using the A-IRB method for certain asset classes and counterparties, and the modification of floors for PD and LGD values.

It is beyond the scope of this book to discuss the IRB methods in more detail, and the reader is referred to BCBS (2006) and BCBS (2017) for more information.

13.2.3   Guarantees

Suppose credit risk is hedged with a product, such as a credit default swap, or otherwise guaranteed by a third party. There should be capital relief due to this risk reduction since there is now only risk in the case where both parties (the original counterparty and the party providing the guarantee) default. In general, under the IRB approach, it is possible for banks to reduce the PD or LGD parameters (the latter for A-IRB banks only) to reflect the guarantee. This reduction is defined – broadly speaking – via a substitution approach (the credit quality of the guarantor is substituted for that of the original obligor). Assuming the guarantor has a better credit quality, this will cause some reduction in risk. The previously allowed 'double default' formula (BCBS 2005b) is no longer allowed.

13.3   CVA (MARKET RISK) CAPITAL

13.3.1   The CVA Capital Charge

As noted in Section 4.2, post-GFC (global financial crisis) regulation introduced a CVA capital charge to capitalise the market risk of CVA. This capital charge is separate, and generally additive, with respect to the credit risk capital requirements discussed in Section 13.2. Although CVA capital represents a market risk capital charge, it is treated separately from all other market risk capital. The CVA capital charge only covers the volatility of CVA and not any other terms, such as debt value adjustment (DVA) or funding value adjustment (FVA). Although DVA is an accounting requirement (Section 5.3.3), it must be explicitly derecognised from capital (to ensure that an increase in the credit risk of a bank does not achieve an increase in its common equity due to a reduction in the value of its liabilities; see BCBS 2011d). The derecognition of DVA is perhaps not too surprising and problematic since most banks consider FVA to be a more relevant adjustment (Section 18.2.5). However, the lack of consideration of FVA here is difficult since it may be part of a bank's accounting adjustment alongside CVA, but may not be capitalised in an equivalent way.

There are currently two methodologies for computing CVA capital, which are planned to be replaced by two new methodologies from 2022 onwards (BCBS 2017). These methodologies (Table 13.2) can be broadly characterised as basic (to be used by any

Table 13.2   Methodologies for the CVA capital charge.

	Current	Future
Basic	Standardised CVA risk capital charge	BA-CVA (basic)
Advanced	Advanced CVA risk capital charge	SA-CVA (standardised)

bank) and advanced (requiring specific regulatory approval). The naming of these methodologies may be confusing (since the current basic methodology is referred to as standardised, but in the future the more advanced methodology will be standardised).

Note that, unlike the credit risk capital charges (Section 13.2), the above methodologies are all portfolio-level calculations. In other words, they calculate a single capital number across all counterparties. On the one hand, this is advantageous because the capital requirements (per counterparty) reduce the larger the portfolio is. On the other hand, this makes pricing capital more challenging (Section 19.2.5).

13.3.2   Standardised CVA Risk Capital Charge

The presentation below will not follow BCBS (2009b) precisely, so as to maintain some consistency with the BA-CVA approach discussed in Section 13.3.3. More details are given in Appendix 13B. The standardised CVA risk capital charge can be written as:

$$K = 2.33.\sqrt{h}.\sqrt{\left(0.5\sum_c (S_c - S_h^{SN}) - \sum_{ind} S^{ind}\right)^2 + 0.75\sum_c (S_c - S_h^{SN})^2} \qquad (13.2)$$

with the following definitions:

2.33 a multiplier that corresponds to a 99% move for a normal distribution.
h a time interval (which is set to one year).

The terms S_c, S_h^{SN}, and S^{ind} can be interpreted as being related to the EAD and the single-name (SN) and index (ind) hedges respectively:

$$S_c = w_c.M_c.EAD_c^{total}$$
$$S_h^{SN} = w_c.M_h^{SN}.B_h^{SN}$$
$$S^{ind} = w_{ind}.M^{ind}.B^{ind}$$

with:

w_c a weight depending on the rating of the counterparty i. The weights are 0.7%, 0.7%, 0.8%, 1.0%, 2.0%, 3.0%, and 10.0% for AAA, AA, A, BBB, BB, B, and CCC ratings respectively. This is most obviously interpreted as representing the (annual) credit spread volatility of the counterparty, with worse ratings having higher volatility. Note that since the Dodd–Frank Act does not allow the use of credit ratings, under US rules these weights are related instead to default probabilities.

M_c the effective maturity (see Appendix 13A) of transactions with respect to the counterparty, which approximately represents the duration of the exposure to the counterparty (a longer duration will mean more volatility).

EAD_c^{total} the total exposure, including netting and margin for the netting set in question for the counterparty, defined according to whatever methodology is used (see Section 13.4).

M_h^{SN} maturity of single-name credit default swap (CDS) hedge with notional B_h^{SN}.

B_h^{SN} notional of single-name CDS.
w_{ind} weight of the index hedge, based on the average spread of the index.
M^{ind} maturity of index CDS hedge (see Appendix 13A) with notional B^{ind}.
B^{ind} notional of index CDS.

Equation 13.2 can be interpreted as a simple representation of the worst-case move in the CVA with a confidence level of 99% over a time horizon of one year. Both single-name and index CDS hedges are included and can, therefore, allow capital relief. The former must be hedged on the correct legal counterparty, and proxy hedges (single-name CDSs that reference a related counterparty) are not allowed. The first and second terms in Equation 13.2 can be interpreted as being systematic and idiosyncratic. The factors 0.5 and 0.75 above effectively assume that a given counterparty is correlated by 50% to a credit index and the systematic term can, therefore, be reduced with an index CDS (with adjustments for maturity effects).[3] Index hedges only provide partial capital relief, since they reduce only the systematic term and not the idiosyncratic one. Single-name CDSs can reduce both terms and hence, in theory, can make the capital for a given counterparty zero if the notional is chosen so as to make the $(S_c - S_h^{SN})$ term equal zero. Note, though, that overhedging, like underhedging, will increase the capital charge. This penalises an open position (as seen from the formula, at least) due to the hedge position being too large. Examples showing the capital relief achievable with single-name and index hedges are shown later in Section 13.5.3. The reader is also referred to Pykhtin (2012) for an analysis of the standardised formula.

13.3.3   BA-CVA

The BA-CVA requirements were first introduced in BCBS (2015a) and modified and developed further in BCBS (2017). The BA-CVA capital charge can be seen as a modification of the standardised CVA capital charge discussed above, with the following main differences:

- The 2.33 factor (which is the 99% VAR for a standard normal variable) is replaced by a factor of 2.34 (which is the 97.5% expected shortfall for a standard normal variable). This factor is also absorbed into the risk weights and does not appear explicitly; nor does the one-year time horizon previously specified by the parameter $h = 1$.
- The EAD term is divided by the 'alpha multiplier' (see Section 13.4.5) to improve the approximation.
- Proxy single-name hedges (that do not reference the counterparty directly) are incorporated via a correlation parameter that represents the relationship between the counterparty credit spread and the credit spread of the name referenced by the hedge.
- An explicit treatment of counterparties with multiple netting sets and multiple single-name hedges of the same counterparty is introduced in the formula.
- The risk weights (RW) are no longer based on ratings (see the definition of w in standardised CVA risk capital charge), but instead are defined via credit spread buckets depending on the industry sector. Credit quality is represented by different risk weights for investment-grade and one for speculative-grade counterparties.

---

[3] The correlation of 25% between spreads can be seen as being 50% × 50%, since each spread process is driven by a 'global' index in a one-factor model.

There are two versions of BA-CVA that can be chosen by a bank:

- *Reduced version.* A simple version with no recognition of hedges which must be calculated by all banks.
- *Full version.* A version with recognition of credit spread hedges for banks that hedge CVA. Note that the reduced version is also used here as a conservative means to restrict hedging efficiency.

Under the reduced version, the capital charge is defined as:

$$K_{reduced} = \sqrt{\left(\rho . \sum_c SCVA_c \right)^2 + (1 - \rho^2) . \sum_c SCVA_c^2} \qquad (13.3)$$

Where ρ is the supervisory correlation (50%) between the credit spread of a counterparty. This is the same as the standardised formula without hedges shown in Section 13.3.2, with the correlation seen by the values of 0.5 and 0.75 and the 2.33 multiplier and time horizon being dealt with now within the new risk weights. In this formula, $SCVA_c$ represents the standalone CVA capital for counterparty c and is given by:

$$SCVA_c = \frac{1}{\alpha} . RW_c . \sum_{NS} M_{NS} . EAD_{NS} . DF_{NS} \qquad (13.4)$$

with:

α	the alpha multiplier (see Section 13.4.5), which is equal to 1.4.
RW_c	the supervisory weight for counterparty c.
M_{NS}	the effective maturity of the netting set NS, without any maturity cap applied.
EAD_{NS}	the EAD (Section 13.4) of the netting set NS, calculated in the same way as for the CCR capital charge (Section 13.2).
DF_{NS}	a supervisory discount factor which is 1 for internal model method (IMM) banks (see Section 13.4.5) and equal to $\frac{(1-\exp(-0.05.M_{NS}))}{(0.05.M_{NS})}$ otherwise.

The risk weights are given in Table 13.3.

In the full version of BA-CVA, eligible hedges are recognised. These hedges are defined as being for the purpose of mitigating the counterparty credit spread component of CVA and can be single-name CDSs, single-name contingent CDSs,[4] and index CDSs.

The capital, including eligible hedges, is defined as:

$$K_{hedged} = \sqrt{ \left(\rho . \sum_c (SCVA_c - SNH_c) - IH \right) + (1 - \rho^2) \sum_c (SCVA_c - SNH_c)^2 + \sum_c HMA_c } \qquad (13.5)$$

---

[4] A contingent CDS is similar to a normal CDS, but the notional may be linked to a quantity such as the value of a transaction or portfolio.

Table 13.3   BA-CVA supervisory risk weights (RW_c).

Risk bucket	Investment-grade	Non-investment-grade or not rated
Sovereigns, including central banks, multilateral development banks	0.5%	3.0%
Local government, government-backed non-financials, education, and public administration	1.0%	4.0%
Financials, including government-backed financials	5.0%	12.0%
Basic materials, energy, industrials, agriculture, manufacturing, mining, and quarrying	3.0%	7.0%
Consumer goods and services, transportation and storage, administrative, and support service activities	3.0%	8.5%
Technology, telecommunications	2.0%	5.0%
Health care, utilities, professional, and technical activities	1.5%	5.0%
Other sector	5.0%	12.0%

where the correlation parameter (ρ) and standalone CVA ($SCVA_c$) are defined as in the reduced version above. As with the two terms in the standardised formula (Equation 13.2), the first two terms in Equation 13.5 can be seen as representing the systematic and idiosyncratic risks. The third term - the hedging misalignment parameter (HMA) - represents the idiosyncratic risk of (non-perfect) single-name CDS hedges (if any are present).

The quantity SNH_c represents single-name CDS hedges and is defined by:

$$SNH_c = \sum_{h \in c} r_{hc} . RW_h . M_h^{SN} . B_h^{SN} . DF_h^{SN} \tag{13.6}$$

with:

r_{hc} the correlation between the credit spread of counterparty c and the credit spread of a single-name hedge h of counterparty c. This is set at 100% if the hedge directly references the counterparty, but at less than 100% otherwise (see Table 13.4).

RW_h the supervisory risk weight for single-name hedge h that reflects the credit spread volatility.

M_h^{SN} the remaining maturity of single-name hedge h.

B_h^{SN} the notional of single-name hedge h.

DF_h^{SN} a supervisory discount factor for the single-name hedge calculated as $\frac{(1-\exp(-0.05.M_h^{SN}))}{(0.05.M_h^{SN})}$.

As noted above, the correlation between a counterparty credit spread and the systematic factor that drives all indices (ρ) is set to 50%. The correlation between the credit spread of a counterparty and its single-name hedge is defined in Table 13.4.

Table 13.4 The correlation between the credit spread of a counterparty and the credit spread of its single-name hedge (r_{hc}).

Single-name hedge h of counterparty c	r_{hc}
References counterparty c directly	100%
Has legal relation with counterparty c	80%
Shares sector and region with counterparty c	50%

Note that the treatment of single-name proxy hedges (where the correlation is 80% or 50%) actually incentivises overhedging as the optimal hedge amount (in terms of reducing capital) increases as the correlation term r_{hc} reduces (Gregory 2019).

The term *IH* represents index hedges used to hedge CVA risk, and is defined (with parameters analogous to those in Equation 13.6 as:

$$IH = \sum_i RW_i.M_i^{ind}.B_i^{ind}.DF_i^{ind} \tag{13.7}$$

Finally, as noted above, the full BA-CVA capital is defined using the reduced version so as to limit the capital relief from hedges with the value of the β parameter being 0.25:

$$K_{full} = \beta.K_{reduced} + (1 - \beta).K_{hedged} \tag{13.8}$$

13.3.4   Advanced CVA Capital Risk Charge

The current advanced CVA capital risk methodology allows a bank to use internal models for CVA capital computation. This approach is relevant for banks that have the following separate regulatory approvals:[5]

- *IMM approval.* Whether or not the bank has IMM approval for counterparty risk (see Section 13.4.4).
- *Specific risk approval.* Whether a bank has the approval to use a specific risk VAR model, which would allow a joint simulation of credit spreads of counterparties which is clearly relevant in the case of quantifying CVA capital.

Note that for banks using the advanced CVA capital change, the credit spread mapping methodology (Section 12.2) must be consistent with the specific risk model used for simulating credit spreads.

The advanced CVA capital charge defines CVA as follows:

$$CVA = LGD_{mkt} \sum_{i=1}^{T} PD(t_{i-1}, t_i) \left(\frac{EE_{i-1}D_{i-1} + EE_i D_i}{2} \right) \tag{13.9a}$$

$$PD(t_{i-1}, t_i) = max \left(0; exp \left(-\frac{s_{i-1}t_{i-1}}{LGD_{mkt}} \right) - exp \left(-\frac{s_i t_i}{LGD_{mkt}} \right) \right) \tag{13.9b}$$

---

[5] This is according to the Basel guidelines. Some regulators (e.g. US) may allow advanced banks to use the standardised formula.

With the following definitions:

LGD_{mkt} the loss given default of the counterparty.
$PD(t_{i-1}, t_i)$ the probability of default in the interval $[t_{i-1}, t_i]$.
s_i the counterparty spread at time t_i.
EE_i the expected exposure at time t_i – note that the BCBS definition of EE is equivalent to the definition of expected positive exposure (EPE) used in the industry (see Table 13.10).
D_i the discount factor at time t_i.

The above can be seen as an approximate representation of a one-dimensional integral defined by $[t_0, t_1, \ldots .., t_n]$ and is similar to the market-standard CVA formula discussed in Section 17.2.2. The default probability $PD(t_{i-1}, t_i)$ is an approximation based on the spreads at the beginning and end of the interval, and is floored at zero since it is a probability (see Section 12.1.3 for more discussion). CVA is very clearly defined as a market-implied quantity referencing credit spreads. The loss given default LGD_{mkt} is also supposed to be based on market expectations and not historical estimates that might be used for other capital charges. Note also that the same LGD must usually be used in both the numerator and denominator of the above formula, although BCBS (2017) notes that when the underlying derivatives have a different seniority, different values may be used.

It is worth emphasising that the CDS spread defined by s_i in the Basel III CVA definition is clearly defined as a market-implied parameter. Indeed, BCBS (2011b) states 'Whenever the CDS spread of the counterparty is available, this must be used. Whenever such a CDS spread is not available, the bank must use a proxy spread that is appropriate based on the rating, industry sector and region of the counterparty.' Another point to note is that the EE in Equation 13.9a is the one calculated by an approved capital model (IMM) and not defined by accounting purposes when calculating CVA. This is likely to lead to efforts to align this exposure calculation with the one used by the CVA desk when pricing and hedging.

A simplifying assumption is that the exposure (EE_i in Equation 13.9a) should be held fixed, and only the impact of credit spread changes is considered. This avoids a potentially extremely costly calculation, but is a significant approximation because parameters such as interest rates, foreign exchange (FX) rates, and volatilities are assumed to be fixed and therefore have no impact on CVA volatility. This also means that any exposure (as opposed to credit) hedges will not provide capital relief, just as in the more basic standardised and BA-CVA methodologies described above. The eligible hedges are, therefore, single-name CDSs (or single-name contingent CDSs),[6] other equivalent hedges referencing the counterparty directly, and index CDSs which need to be simulated. Only hedges used for the purpose of mitigating CVA risk, and managed as such, are eligible (i.e. if a bank happens to have bought CDS protection on a counterparty for other purposes, then it is not eligible). Eligible hedges may be removed from the standard market risk calculation. Proxy hedges (i.e. where a bank has bought single-name protection on a different but highly-correlated name) are not eligible for capital relief.

---

[6] Short bond positions are allowed if the basis risk is captured.

With the above definition of CVA, the advanced approach requires a bank to use its VAR engine to calculate 'CVA VAR' directly, with the aforementioned simplification of fixed exposure. Formulas for delta and gamma of the CVA similar to the above are also provided for banks that calculate their VAR using these approximations. The approved specific risk model gives the ability to simulate the credit spreads that are required in order to calculate CVA, as in Equation 13.9a. Such approaches tend to simulate spreads for generic or proxy curves, generally defined via ratings and potentially also regions and sectors. Hence, this is approximately aligned with the mapping procedures already required to estimate credit spreads for CVA valuation purposes (Section 12.3).

The advanced CVA capital charge methodology is illustrated in Figure 13.3. Generally, the methodology is analogous to market risk VAR, which requires a 99% confidence level, a 10-day horizon and a multiplier of 3 to be used (this multiplier can be increased by local regulators and may also depend on the performance of the model with respect to backtesting). In addition, the aforementioned changes require an additional calculation with the simulation of stressed market data. The stressed market data corresponds to both the calculation of exposure with the CVA formula and the simulation of credit spread, and the final number is the sum of the normal and stressed calculations.[7] The choice of this stress period is subjective. BIS (2015b) reports that most banks use a period around 2008–2009, giving a stressed CVA VAR which is between three and four times higher than the normal VAR, whilst some use a period around 2010–2012 and report a corresponding increase of between 1 and 2.5. Hence, the choice of stress period can clearly have a major impact on capital costs. Note finally that, despite the similarity to the general market risk VAR methodology of a bank, the advanced CVA capital calculation must be run separately.

With index CDS hedges, the basis between the counterparty CDS and the index spread must be simulated in the calculation. The extent to which this spread is correlated to the relevant index then defines the benefit through hedging. The index may be modelled as a linear combination of its components. However, 'If the basis is not reflected to the satisfaction of the supervisor, then the bank must reflect only 50% of the notional amount of index hedges in the VaR' (BCBS 2011b). This suggests that high correlations that lead to better hedging performance may be questioned by regulators.

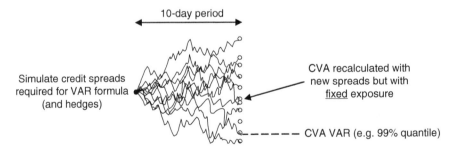

Figure 13.3   Illustration of advanced CVA capital methodology.

---

[7] But does not include the incremental risk charge (IRC), which measures the impact of effects such as default and credit migration risk over a one-year time horizon and is therefore similar to the Basel II IMM approach.

13.3.5   SA-CVA

In the original proposals for a new CVA capital charge (BCBS 2015a), it was proposed that there would be an internal model approach (IMA-CVA), which could have been seen as a more sophisticated version of the advanced approach described in Section 13.3.4. However, the decision was then taken to remove this option, which left only the standardised approach (SA-CVA) as more sophisticated compared to the BA-CVA (BCBS 2017). The SA-CVA is an adaptation of the standardised approach for trading book market risk (SA-TB) under the FRTB (BCBS 2019a). Compared to SA-TB, SA-CVA has reduced granularity of market risk factors, and does not include default risk and curvature risk. To balance this, SA-CVA uses a more conservative risk aggregation and a multiplier which can be increased by the bank's local regulator if it determines that the bank's CVA model risk warrants it. One specific example cited is if the dependence between the bank's exposure to a counterparty and the counterparty's credit quality is not taken into account in its CVA calculations often known as wrong-way risk (WWR).

The SA-CVA approach is based on transaction-level sensitivities of 'regulatory CVA' to counterparty credit spreads and other market risk factors. In order to use this approach, a bank must be able to model exposure and calculate, on at least a monthly basis, CVA and CVA sensitivities to the required market risk factors. The bank must also have a CVA desk (or other dedicated function) responsible for the risk management and hedging of CVA.

The aforementioned regulatory CVA must be calculated under the assumption that the bank is default risk free (i.e. no DVA or survival probability used; see Section 17.3.3). The default probabilities must be estimated from credit spreads observed in the market, with proxies used (Section 12.3) for names where credit spreads are not observable. Credit spreads of illiquid counterparties must be estimated from credit spreads observed in the markets of the counterparty's liquid peers via an algorithm that discriminates on at least three variables: a measure of credit quality, industry, and region. There are also two specific cases where credit spreads can be defined differently:

- In certain cases, mapping an illiquid counterparty to a single liquid 'proxy' credit spread. An example given is the mapping of a municipality to the credit spread of the underlying sovereign credit spread (potentially plus a premium). Such cases must be individually justified.
- Using an estimated default probability, derived from a fundamental analysis of the underlying credit risk (e.g. the historical default rate for the rating category), together with a market-derived risk premium component.

When calculating regulatory CVA, the market LGD must be the same as the one used to calculate the default probabilities, unless the bank can demonstrate that the seniority of the derivative exposure differs from the seniority of senior unsecured bonds. BCBS states explicitly that collateral provided by the counterparty does not change the seniority of the derivative exposure (Section 12.2.3) although it is not clear whether this refers to derivatives specific collateral (margin) or more general collateral that might be part of a lending arrangement.

All material market risk factors must be simulated as stochastic processes for an appropriate number of paths defined on an appropriate set of future time points extending to the maturity of the longest transaction. The exposure simulation model of the bank for calculating CVA for pricing and accounting purposes must be used and, if relevant, adjusted to define the exposure for regulatory CVA. The model calibration process (with the exception of the MPoR) and market and transaction data must be the same as those used for the accounting CVA calculation. In other words, the regulatory CVA must follow closely the bank's actual accounting CVA methodology. This implies that the regulatory requirements may have a significant impact on accounting CVA numbers.

Regarding calibration of market risk factors:

- the drifts must be calibrated to market-implied (risk-neutral) data;
- volatilities and correlations must be market implied if sufficient data exists, and can be historically calibrated otherwise; and
- the distribution of modelled risk factors must account for the possible non-normality of the distribution of exposures, including the existence of fat tails, where appropriate.

The first two points are quite common in CVA calculations, although there may be questions over the use of proxies and choices around interpolation and extrapolation (Section 12.3.4). The final point is more open ended as some CVA models are relatively simplistic and are often calibrated mainly to at-the-money (ATM) volatility, and may not capture features such as volatility skew and stochastic volatility.

Where relevant, margin is permitted to be recognised as a risk mitigant under appropriate MPoR modelling (Section 15.5). The exposure simulation must capture the effects of margin along each exposure path. All the relevant contractual features (frequency of margin calls, type of margin, thresholds, independent amounts, initial margins, and minimum transfer amounts) must be appropriately captured by the exposure model.

For transactions with a significant level of dependence between exposure and the counterparty's credit quality (WWR), this dependence should be taken into account.

SA-CVA allows both counterparty credit spread and exposure component hedges to be recognised, with only a minority of hedges (such as tranched or basket CDSs) being ineligible.[8] For CVA hedges that are subject to curvature risk, a default risk charge or the residual risk add-on under the FRTB, there are certain conditions that must be met in order for the hedge to be considered eligible. If the CVA desk executed the hedge internally with a trading desk that in turn executed a back-to-back transaction with an external counterparty, this would meet the criteria of eligibility. In this case, some components of the CVA hedge (e.g. delta, vega) would be recognised within the CVA capital calculation, and others (e.g. curvature) would be recognised within the general market risk calculation. This ensures that these more complex components are not understated in terms of market risk quantification.

Although there is a hedging disallowance term, most hedges should otherwise reduce SA-CVA capital perfectly through cancellation of sensitivities (assuming these sensitivities do match). The main exception is credit spread hedges which do not reference the counterparty directly (proxies or indices). These hedges produce partial capital relief based on a prescribed regulatory correlation with the counterparty. The overall capital relief achievable will depend on the following factors (see later example in Section 13.5.3):

- the overall size and concentration of the portfolio (which determines the extent to which idiosyncratic risk is diversified);

---

[8] Instruments that cannot be included in the internal model approach for market risk under the FRTB cannot be eligible CVA hedges.

- the correlation parameter (which depends on the nature of the relationship between the counterparty and the hedge); and
- (for index hedges) the sectorial balance between the counterparty portfolio and the index (in terms of the industry sector buckets defined in SA-CVA).

The SA-CVA capital requirement is calculated as the sum of the capital requirements for delta and vega (not curvature) risks calculated for the entire CVA portfolio and including eligible hedges. The capital requirement for delta risk is calculated as the sum of delta capital requirements for the following six risk types:

- interest rate;
- FX;
- counterparty credit spreads;
- reference credit spreads (i.e. credit spreads that drive exposure);
- equity; and
- commodity.

The capital requirement for vega risk is calculated as the sum over the same risk types, but not including counterparty credit spreads (i.e. there is no vega capital requirement for counterparty credit spread risk). Within each risk type, there are buckets (e.g. each currency in the case of interest rates) over which the risks are aggregated.

For a given bucket k, the calculated CVA sensitivities (s^{CVA}) and sensitivities of eligible hedges (s^{Hdg}) are used to define 'weighted sensitivities' (WS) according to:

$$WS_k^{CVA} = RW_k \cdot s_k^{CVA} \tag{13.10a}$$

$$WS_k^{Hdg} = RW_k \cdot s_k^{Hdg} \tag{13.10b}$$

$$WS_k = WS_k^{CVA} + WS_k^{Hdg} \tag{13.10c}$$

where the risk weights (RW) for each risk type are given in BCBS (2017). The weighted sensitivities are then aggregated to produce a capital charge in each bucket b according to:

$$K_b = \sqrt{\left[\sum_{k\in b} WS_k^2 + \sum_{k\in b}\sum_{l\in b, l\neq k} \rho_{kl} \cdot WS_k \cdot WS_l\right] + R\sum_{k\in b}[WS_k^{Hdg}]^2} \tag{13.11}$$

with regulatory defined correlation parameters (ρ_{kl}) and a 'hedging disallowance' parameter (R) that is set at 0.01 and prevents the possibility of perfect hedging of CVA risk, even if the sensitivities are perfectly offset by those of hedges (in such a case, there would still be other risks, such as curvature or gamma, which are not captured by the SA-CVA formula). Example risk weights and correlations for interest rate delta are shown in Table 13.5.

The counterparty credit spread risk weights are the same as those in the BA-CVA (Table 13.3), and the correlations are similar but more granular due to the presence of tenors (Table 13.6). The impact of CDS hedges is captured via these correlations and will depend on the relationship between the counterparty credit spread and the hedge (e.g. same entity, legal related, or unrelated).

Table 13.5   Correlations and risk weights for the interest rate delta risk class in SA-CVA.

Correlation (ρ_{kl})	1 year	2 years	5 years	10 years	30 years
1 year	100%	91%	72%	55%	31%
2 years		100%	87%	72%	45%
5 years			100%	91%	68%
10 years				100%	83%
30 years					100%
Risk weight (RW_k)	1.59	1.33	1.06	1.06	1.06

Table 13.6   Correlations for the counterparty credit spread delta risk class in SA-CVA.

Correlation	Same tenor	Different tenors
Same entity	100%	90%
Legally related	90%	81%
Unrelated entities, same credit quality (investment grade / high yield)	50%	45%
Unrelated entities, different credit quality (investment grade / high yield)	40%	36%

The bucket-level capital charges are then aggregated across buckets within each risk type:

$$K_b = m_{CVA} \cdot \sqrt{\sum_b K_b^2 + \sum_b \sum_{c \neq b} \gamma_{kl} . K_b . K_c} \qquad (13.12)$$

with further correlation parameters defined by γ_{kl} and a multiplier with a default value of $m_{CVA} = 1.25$. The multiplier is intended to compensate for a higher level of model risk in the calculation of CVA sensitivities in comparison to sensitivities of the market value of trading book instruments. As noted previously, this can be increased by a national regulator to compensate for aspects such as WWR.

Figure 13.4 shows an example of the SA-CVA capital charge for uncollateralised and collateralised interest rate swaps, broken down by the different risk classes. The counterparty credit spread delta is the most significant component, followed by the

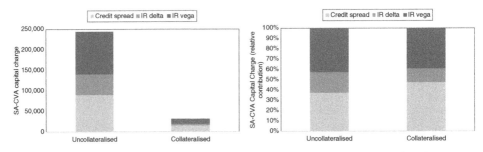

Figure 13.4   Example CVA capital charges for an uncollateralised and collateralised interest rate swap.

interest rate vega and then interest rate delta. For the collateralised swap, all three components reduce substantially, especially the interest rate delta. Note that for portfolios, delta components other than counterparty credit spread may tend to offset against different trades and contribute less overall. This is not true for counterparty credit spread delta and vega contributions, which are almost always in the same direction (the CVA generally increases with an increase in the counterparty credit spread or any implied volatility) and will therefore not tend to offset as much at the portfolio level.

13.3.6   Capital Relief and EU Exemptions

A summary of the potential hedging benefit for the different CVA capital methodologies is given in Table 13.7. The current methodologies for CVA capital (standardised and advanced) and the future BA-CVA methodology only allow capital relief to be achieved for credit spread hedges. Any other market risk hedges are not represented and potentially create a 'split hedge' issue, where these hedges must be represented in the bank's market risk capital and may increase, rather than reduce, the overall capital charge. Hence, a bank is given regulatory capital incentives *not* to hedge the market risk components of CVA. US and Canadian regulators have moved to exempt CVA-related market risk hedges and thus resolve this issue, and other regions may be expected to follow this lead (see EBA 2015b).[9] Note that some banks have tried to resolve this problem by including their CVA sensitivities in their market risk models.

Table 13.7   Capital relief for CVA hedges under different methodologies.

	Current regulation		Future regulation	
	Standardised	Advanced	BA-CVA	SA-CVA
Single-name CDS	Relief via EAD offset depending on notional and duration match	Yes, via full simulation	Relief via EAD offset depending on notional and duration match and with a penalty to prevent perfect hedging	Most hedges treated via a sensitivity-based approach with regulatory risk weights, correlations, and aggregation rules
Index CDS	Partial relief via EAD offset, as above, assuming a correlation of 50%	Yes, as above, but the basis must be modelled	As above, with regulatory prescribed correlation inputs	
Proxy single-name CDS	No relief	No relief	No relief	
Other market risk hedges	No relief	No relief	No relief	

---

[9] Although, strangely, EBA (2015b) reports that only three out of 18 banks reported a material benefit if such hedges were exempted, and several banks would actually see a negative impact from this exemption (i.e. the hedges offset other risks in their trading books).

As noted in Section 4.2.5, the European Union (EU) exempted EU banks from holding CVA capital to certain counterparties (predominantly non-financial end users of derivatives), which remains a controversial topic. The exemptions were likely driven – at least partially – by the potentially adverse consequences of CDS hedging by CVA desks. For example, the Bank of England second quarter bulletin in 2010 stated:

> … given the relative illiquidity of sovereign CDS markets a sharp increase in demand from active investors can bid up the cost of sovereign CDS protection. CVA desks have come to account for a large proportion of trading in the sovereign CDS market and so their hedging activity has reportedly been a factor pushing prices away from levels solely reflecting the underlying probability of sovereign default.[10]

The potentially adverse impact of CDS hedging by CVA desks has sometimes been referred to as the 'doom loop' (Murphy 2012). Where a bank has an exposure to an uncollateralised end user counterparty, it can achieve capital relief – under any of the aforementioned methodologies – by using single-name CDS hedges. The related hedging activity could then artificially inflate CDS spreads. The reduction in liquidity in the single-name CDS market – see Callsen and Hill (2018) – has amplified this problem. There have also been questions about the validity of the doom loop argument (IMF 2013), and some European regulators do not agree with the form of the exemptions.[11] The exemptions have not been applied in any other region,[12] and, at the time of writing, it seems they may be reversed in Europe at some point.[13]

It is therefore particularly beneficial that the SA-CVA capital charge gives capital relief from all hedges, not solely CDS ones. It would seem likely that most banks with CVA desks will want to use this over the more advanced BA-CVA methodology when they are implemented. Indeed, this may also provide an added incentive for a bank to set up a dedicated CVA desk.

13.4   EXPOSURE CALCULATION METHODOLOGIES

13.4.1   Exposure at Default

The methodologies for credit risk (Section 13.2) and market risk (Section 13.3) are broadly focused on default risk and credit spread volatility, respectively. In general, most of the underlying methodologies utilise a, separately-defined, concept known as EAD. The one exception to this is the future SA-CVA methodology which does not require a separate EAD specification and is therefore defined uniquely according to the discussion in Section 13.3.5. With this exception, a key component of the aforementioned regulatory methodologies is, therefore, EAD (Equations 13.1, 13.2, and 13.4).

---

[10] Bank of England (2010). Quarterly Bulletin (Q2). www.bankofengland.co.uk.

[11] Cameron, M. (2013). Bafin Weighing CVA Charge Despite European Exemptions. *Risk* (19 June). www.risk.net.

[12] Cameron, M. and L. Becker (2013). No CVA exemptions in US Basel III rules. *Risk* (3 July). www.risk.net.

[13] Maxwell, F. (2014). Corporate CVA exemption should be removed, says EBA. *Risk* (5 December). www.risk.net.

EAD is calculated at the netting set level. A netting set is a group of transactions with a single counterparty subject to a legally-enforceable bilateral netting agreement that satisfies certain legal and operational criteria, described in Annex 4 of BCBS (2006). Each transaction that is not subject to a legally-enforceable bilateral netting agreement is interpreted according to its own netting set. The interpretation of a netting set according to Basel II is therefore consistent with the earlier definition of close-out netting (Section 6.3.2).[14]

The definition of EAD for a derivative portfolio is challenging due to the inherent uncertainty of the underlying exposure, which is driven by:

- changes in risk factors, such as interest and FX rates and their correlations; and
- legal terms defining risk mitigants such as netting and margin.

The above factors are complex and therefore difficult to represent realistically in a simple regulatory formula.

The Basel II framework (BCBS 2006) developed a choice of methods for banks to use when calculating EAD for each counterparty they faced.

There are three methods mainly relevant for computing EAD under Basel rules (see Figure 13.1):

- *Current exposure method (CEM)*. This is a simple and prescriptive method which has been used as the basic methodology for many years for banks without internal models.[15] It also forms the basis of the current capital requirements for exposures to central counterparties (CCPs) (Section 13.6). From 2019 onwards, it is being replaced by the SA-CCR approach.
- *Internal model method (IMM)*. The IMM involves sophisticated modelling of all the underlying risk factors, and IMM approval is therefore costly to achieve (and maintain). For this reason, only the largest banks have IMM approval for counterparty risk. There is also a simpler methodology, often known as the IMM shortcut method, for collateralised counterparties only, which is being phased out with the implementation of the SA-CCR.
- *Standardised approach for CCR (SA-CCR)*. This is a new, more risk-sensitive approach that replaces the CEM and aims to balance simplicity and risk sensitivity with treatment of more recent developments such as initial margin (BCBS 2014c). Note that IMM banks must also compute SA-CCR requirements which may constitute a floor. The SA-CCR is also utilised in other regulations, including the future CCP capital requirements (see Section 13.6).

Note that the CEM and SA-CCR approaches are objective since they are based on prescribed formulas, whilst the IMM is subjective since it is based on a complex set of modelling assumptions.

---

[14] Although, situations do occasionally arise where a bank considers that it has sufficient legal opinion to assume that close-out netting is enforceable but its regulator does not allow this for capital purposes.

[15] Note that there is another approach as an alternative to the CEM, known as the standardised method (SM), which is rarely used and not allowed by some national regulators (e.g. US and Canada). There are also separate approaches to handle repo transactions (see Appendix 13A).

IMM approval brings a number of benefits, such as having a more risk-sensitive methodology tailored to the actual risks that a bank takes. This methodology can not only be used for computing exposure for regulatory capital purposes, but also for other purposes – for example, regulators normally require that an IMM bank uses the same model for credit limits management. On the other hand, IMM approaches are very subjective, and it may be feared that they may artificially lead to lower capital charges in certain cases. This is one of the reasons for the implementation of capital floors (Section 4.2.8), meaning that IMM banks must also compute SA-CCR capital numbers, which may limit any incremental benefit of IMM approval.

Note that some local regulators have expressed different opinions on the relative advantages and disadvantages of using the more sophisticated IMM approach. For example, in 2014, the Office of the Superintendent of Financial Institutions (OSFI) in Canada stated that it had implemented both the CEM and IMM (BCBS 2014f) and that domestic systemically-important banks (D-SIBs) may use the latter with OSFI's approval. Since this time, at least one Canadian bank has received approval to use the IMM approach. On the other hand, the Australian regulator does not allow the IMM to be used within its prudential framework (APRA 2016).

As discussed in Section 13.3.4, a bank with IMM approval may also use the advanced CVA capital risk charge as long as it also has the relevant regulatory approval for modelling specific risk. If it does not have one or both of these approvals, then it uses the standardised CVA capital charge. Note that the current standardised CVA capital charge relies on the definition of EAD, which may make IMM approval even more desirable, since a more simplistic EAD approach such as CEM will drive both the CCR and CVA capital charges. However, this will cease to be the case when BA-CVA and SA-CVA are implemented, at which point IMM approval will only impact the CCR capital charge.

Note that it is possible to reduce EAD by what is defined as 'incurred CVA', which is the CVA value on the balance sheet of a firm, and a loss that has already been accounted for. This could be best understood by considering a counterparty close to default: the CVA will be quite large, but the capital charge will be largely unnecessary since most of the anticipated default loss will be factored into the CVA. By removing the CVA from the EAD, the capital charge will, therefore, be correspondingly reduced. This reduction of EAD by incurred CVA losses does not apply to the determination of the CVA capital charge (Section 13.3.1), but only to the determination of the credit risk capital charge. Pykhtin (2012) discusses this in more detail.

13.4.2   Current Exposure Method

Whilst the CEM is being phased out, it provides a useful historical context, and is also useful to understand since the SA-CCR is based upon the same basic idea.

The CEM is based on the fundamental idea that EAD arises from two components, the current exposure (CE) and the potential future exposure (PFE), as illustrated in Figure 13.5. The CE is obviously relatively easy to define, whilst the PFE is more complex as it represents the possible exposure in the future (Section 11.1.3).

Under the CEM rules (see BCBS 2006), the EAD for a given transaction is computed according to:

$$EAD_{NS} = RC_{NS} + AddOn_{NS} \qquad (13.13)$$

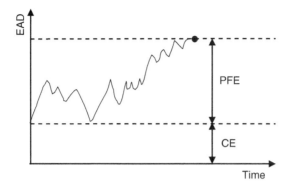

Figure 13.5 Illustration of the CEM approach to defining exposure at default (EAD) via current exposure (CE) and potential future exposure (PFE).

where RC (replacement cost) is used to define the CE and is typically defined as the CE or positive value of the portfolio summed over the relevant transactions,[16] i.e. $RC = \max\left(\sum_i value_i, 0\right)$, as long as the transactions in question are covered by a legally-enforceable bilateral netting agreement.

$AddOn_{NS}$ is the estimated amount of PFE over the remaining life of the contract. This is defined, initially at the transaction level, as the product of a notional and an add-on factor. The add-on is defined prescriptively based on the remaining maturity and the type of underlying instrument (e.g. interest rates, FX, etc.), according to Table 13.8. For example, a six-year interest rate swap with a notional of $10m would have an add-on of 1.5%, and therefore an EAD of $10,000,000 \times 1.5\% = \$150,000$.

There are a number of special cases that are defined under the CEM. For example, for contracts that settle at pre-defined dates (such as resettable swaps), the maturity is defined by the time until the next reset date.

In a settle-to-market (STM) treatment of centrally-cleared trades (Section 7.2.6) then it may be possible to use a maturity of one day, this being the time until the next exchange of variation margin on the contract. The conditions for doing this are that the STM contract settles any outstanding exposure on the contract and terms are reset so that fair value of the contract is zero. This reduction in maturity can provide a benefit to capital requirements when using methodologies such as the CEM.

Table 13.8 Add-on factors (%) for the CEM by the remaining maturity and type of underlying instrument.

Remaining maturity	Interest rates	FX and gold	Equities	Precious metals (except gold)	Other commodities
< 1 year	0.0	1.0	6.0	7.0	10.0
1–5 years	0.5	5.0	8.0	7.0	12.0
> 5 years	1.5	7.5	10.0	8.0	15.0

---

[16] This is not clearly stated, but BCBS (2006) defines current exposure as 'the larger of zero, or the market value of a transaction' and states that this is often called the replacement cost.

In terms of aggregating the transaction-level EADs into the netting set level, the CEM provides recognition of close-out netting, but does so in quite a simple way. The add-on for a netting set of n transactions (again, under the assumption of legal enforceability) is given by:

$$AddOn_{NS} = (0.4 + 0.6 \times NGR) \times \sum_{i=1}^{n} AddOn_i \qquad (13.14)$$

where $AddOn_i$ is the add-on for transaction i and NGR (net gross ratio) is a quantity that determines the current impact of netting in percentage terms (an NGR of zero implies perfect netting, and an NGR of 100% implies no netting benefit). The NGR is defined as the ratio of the current net exposure to the current gross exposure for all transactions within the netting set:[17]

$$NGR = \frac{RC_{NS}}{\sum_{i=1}^{n} \max(value_i, 0)} \qquad (13.15)$$

Equation 13.15 can be viewed as giving 60% of the current netting benefit to future exposure. This is a compromise, since the benefit of netting can change significantly over time as the values of individual transactions change. In order to understand this, consider two transactions that net perfectly today since they have equal and opposite values. Only if they are completely opposite transactions will the netting be perfect in the future. Essentially, giving only 60% of the current netting benefit recognises the fact that some netting benefit will be structural (such as hedges), but some will occur only transiently and by chance. This treatment seems conservative as it assumes that the current netting benefit will decay over time, whereas the reverse can also occur. In general, for directional portfolios (where netting is not particularly strong), banks find that the above treatment is not particularly punitive. However, it can appear so for more balanced portfolios with stronger netting.

The treatment of margin (collateral) in the CEM is generally defined as (see BCBS 2005b) subtracting the 'volatility adjusted collateral' from the EAD term. The volatility adjustment haircuts the current value of margin downwards to proxy a potential price decline. This recognises that margin currently held (subject to haircuts) reduces the exposure. However, this does not consider the potential to receive more margin in the future in the event that the CE increases, or recognise overcollateralisation.

The CEM has a number of drawbacks, mostly arising due to its inherent simplicity:

- Whilst the CEM approach clearly captures, in essence, the differing exposure profiles for derivatives based on their asset class and maturity, it is not especially risk sensitive (e.g. a two-year and a five-year interest rate swap have the same add-on).
- The treatment of netting is very simple and may underestimate (or possibly overestimate) the impact of netting on the PFE.
- Since the RC is defined at the current exposure or positive value of the portfolio, the benefit of a portfolio with a negative value is not captured. In reality, such a portfolio should have a lower PFE due to the offsetting effect of the negative value. Under the CEM, a transaction with a negative value will have the same EAD as one with a zero value (in both cases the RC is zero, and the add-on will be the same).

---

[17] The definition of NGR can be found in Annex 4 of BCBS (2006).

- The CEM does not account for a situation of overcollateralisation (very uncommon in OTC derivatives at the time it was designed), where the margin may exceed the replacement cost and the EAD could become negative. Since CEM allows the amount of margin to be subtracted from the exposure then, EAD will be reduced by initial margin, often to zero. If initial margin is not allowed to offset exposure in this way, then the EAD will not be reduced at all. The inability to reproduce the risk-mitigating impact of initial margin properly is especially problematic given the dramatic increase in the use of initial margin that is prescribed under the incoming bilateral margin rules (Section 4.4.2). Indeed, this is one of the major reasons for the implementation of the SA-CCR.

13.4.3 Standardised Approach for Counterparty Credit Risk

As noted above, the CEM has a number of shortcomings in its estimation of EAD:

- the percentage add-on factors (Table 13.8) were calibrated many years ago and did not reflect volatilities observed over more recent stress periods, especially during the GFC;
- the recognition of netting benefits is simplistic and may produce estimates that are rather conservative for netting sets with strong netting benefit (offsetting and hedging transactions);
- the treatment of margin is also simplistic and does not account for the benefit of receiving margin in the future and overcollateralisation (e.g. initial margin); and
- the methodology does not capture the fact that off-market (negative value) portfolios should have a lower exposure than the equivalent par transactions (this is similar to the impact of initial margin).

In order to address the above points, the SA-CCR was developed to replace the CEM (and SM)[18] methodologies and to provide a backstop for IMM methodologies. The SA-CCR was originally intended for implementation in January 2017, but this date has been significantly delayed.

Broadly speaking, the aim of the SA-CCR can be seen to be to introduce more risk sensitivity without introducing significantly greater complexity. The SA-CCR has also been (conservatively) calibrated to IMM results benchmarked from banks.

The benefits of the SA-CCR over the CEM are:

- a smoother representation of EAD as a function of maturity;
- a better recognition of netting (although the netting benefits are still somewhat limited);
- a more risk-sensitive treatment of margin, in particular, initial margin; and
- recognition of negative value.

The above points will – generally – tend to reduce capital, but since there has been a reappraisal of the underlying calibration, the SA-CCR will potentially give higher capital requirements due to the use of more conservative parameters such as higher add-on factors and the alpha factor (α) of 1.4.

This section gives an overview of the key components of the SA-CCR, and the reader is referred to BCBS (2014c) for more details.

---

[18] See Footnote 15.

The SA-CCR methodology – like the CEM – treats the EAD as a combination of the CE or replacement cost (RC) and PFE:

$$EAD = \alpha \times (RC + PFE) \tag{13.16}$$

where the factor α is used to be consistent with the IMM methodology and is therefore set to 1.4. Whilst this maintains some consistency, it has the unpleasant effect of inflating the RC by 40%.

For uncollateralised transactions, the RC is defined by the netted value of the underlying contracts, as in the CEM. The PFE is essentially linked to add-on factors, again like in the CEM, but these add-ons are specified differently by:

$$AddOn_i = SF_i \times SD_i \tag{13.17}$$

where SF_i is a supervisory factor depending on the asset class and intended to capture a loss over a one-year period, and SD_i is an approximate measure of the duration.[19] For example, a six-year interest rate swap with a notional of $10m would have a SF of 0.5% and a SD of 5.18, leading to an EAD of $10,000,000 \times 0.5\% \times 5.18 = \$249,182$. Note that this is already significantly higher than the equivalent value for the CEM (Section 13.4.2) even before application of the alpha factor of 1.4. This illustrates the generally more conservative underlying calibration of the SA-CCR.

The treatment of netting in the SA-CCR is more sophisticated than the basic NGR formula in the CEM (Equation 13.14). It is based on the concept of a hedging set, which is a representation of transactions with similar risk sensitivities. Within a hedging set, either full or partial netting is allowed depending on the asset class, risk factor, and maturity. The hedging sets and offsets are defined within each of five asset classes as follows:

- *Interest rate*. Hedging sets are defined by currency and three maturity buckets: up to one year, one to five years, and over five years. Full offset is given to transactions in the same maturity bucket, whilst partial netting is achieved for transactions in different buckets. This partial netting is defined by correlations of 70% between the adjacent buckets and 30% otherwise.[20]
- *FX*. A hedging set is defined by all transactions referencing the same currency pair. Full netting is available within each hedging set and is zero otherwise.
- *Credit and equity*. Each of these asset classes represents a hedging set. Full offset is allowed between transactions referencing the same name or index. Partial offset is allowed between other transactions with correlations of 64% (index, index), 40% (index, single-name), and 25% (single-name, single-name).
- *Commodity*. There are four hedging sets (energy, metals, agriculture, other). Within a hedging set, full netting applies to transactions referencing the same commodity, and partial netting applies otherwise (with a correlation of 16%).

Note that with respect to the correlations above, BCBS (2014c) essentially defines a systematic factor for each netting set, which must be multiplied to get the correlation (e.g. for single-name and index equity, this gives $80\% \times 50\% = 40\%$). Supervisory factors

---

[19] Similar to the BA-CVA method, $SD_i = [1 - \exp(-0.05 \times M_i)]/0.05$ with M_i being the maturity.

[20] These correlations were calibrated to a continuous representation of correlation, but this bucketing approach is used for tractability.

Table 13.9 SA-CCR parameters.

Asset class	Sub-class	Supervisory factor	Correlation	Supervisory option volatility
Interest rate		0.50%	N/A	50%
FX		4.00%	N/A	15%
Credit (single-name)	AAA	0.38%	50%	100%
	AA	0.38%		
	A	0.42%		
	BBB	0.54%		
	BB	1.06%		
	B	1.60%		
	CCC	6.00%		
Credit (index)	IG	0.38%	80%	80%
	SG	1.06%		
Equity (single-name)		32%	50%	120%
Equity (index)		20%	80%	75%
Commodity	Electricity	40%	40%	150%
	Oil/Gas	18%		70%
	Metals	18%		70%
	Agricultural	18%		70%
	Other	18%		70%

for defining the PFE are defined for each of the hedging sets above, with those for credit further divided by rating, in Table 13.9.

The above correlations specify the netting effect but must be combined with the direction of the underlying transactions, which is done via a delta adjustment. For linear transactions (not options),[21] the delta is either +1 or -1 depending on whether or not the transaction is long or short in the primary risk factor.[22] Delta, therefore, serves two purposes:

- it specifies the *direction* of the trade with respect to the primary risk factor; and
- it serves as a scaling factor for trades that are non-linear in the primary risk factor (e.g. options).

For options, the precise calculation of delta is covered in more detail in BCBS (2014c). The volatility is determined by supervisory parameters shown in Table 13.9.

The SA-CCR treatment of margin accounts for the presence of both variation and initial margins in different ways. Haircuts are applied to convert non-cash margin into cash equivalents; these haircuts reduce (increase) the value of margin received (posted). A key component is the net independent collateral amount (NICA), which defines a net amount of additional margin that will be available in default (it does not include variation margin). NICA does not include margin that a bank has posted to a segregated, bankruptcy-remote

---

[21] There is also a provision for tranches of collateralised debt obligations (CDOs).

[22] Long (short) meaning that the value increases (decreases) as the primary risk factor increases.

account, and therefore represents any margin (segregated or unsegregated) posted by the counterparty less the unsegregated margin posted by the bank. Referring to Equation 11.9 and the related discussion in Section 11.4.4:

$$NICA = margin^R - margin^P_{NS} \qquad (13.18)$$

which is the margin received ($margin^R$) less the non-segregated margin posted ($margin^P_{NS}$). Any segregated margin posted to the counterparty is ignored since it is assumed to be bankruptcy remote and returned in a default scenario. NICA will typically be initial margin, but BCBS (2014c) does not define it as such due to the different terminologies used (such as independent amount). Note that NICA can be negative if a relatively large amount of initial margin is posted and not segregated. However, under bilateral margin rules (Section 7.4), posted initial margin must be segregated and therefore NICA would correspond only to the initial margin received.

In the presence of margin, the first question is how to define the replacement cost. This is taken to be the higher value of:

- the current collateralised exposure (including variation margin and NICA) defined by the term C; and
- the maximum possible uncollateralised exposure, which is the highest exposure that would not trigger a variation margin call – taking into account thresholds (TH), minimum transfer amounts (MTA), and NICA.

Furthermore, the RC cannot be negative and so:

$$RC = \max(V - C, TH + MTA - NICA, 0) \qquad (13.19)$$

where V represents the portfolio value. As an example, assume that $V = 7$, $C = 0$, $TH = 10$, $MTA = 1$, and $NICA = 0$. Although the current exposure is 7, the RC is 11 to represent the fact that the exposure could get to this level without variation margin being received (note that TH and MTA are treated as being additive in a margin agreement; Section 7.3.4). The above representation can be quite conservative where the relatively large threshold and/or minimum transfer is in place, but bilateral rules (Section 7.4) specify these to be zero and €500,000, respectively.

The impact of being able to receive variation margin in the future is to reduce the time horizon for an exposure (Section 7.5.2) to approximately the MPoR. SA-CCR proxies this by introducing a multiplicative factor of:

$$\frac{3}{2}\sqrt{MPR/250} \qquad (13.20)$$

where the MPoR is typically 10 business days for bilateral OTC derivatives (see discussion in Section 9.1.2). The above factor adjusts for the shorter risk horizon for collateralised transactions.

For the example of the interest rate swap mentioned above, the PFE would reduce from \$259,182 to \$77,755[23] (the CEM equivalent would be unchanged at \$150,000 since no benefit for future margin is recognised).

---

[23] Calculated from multiplying by $1.5 \times \sqrt{10/250} = 0.3$.

Whilst the above does recognise that the impact of variation margin is effectively shortening the risk horizon of a trade from its maturity to the MPoR, the benefit is limited by the arbitrary one-year horizon on which the PFE in the SA-CCR calculation is based. This means that for long-dated trades, the risk mitigation impact of variation margin may not be fully recognised.

Note that SA-CCR requires that, if multiple margin amounts cover a single netting set, then the netting set must be divided into sub-netting sets that align with their respective margin agreements. This can lead to a conservative treatment (compared to the real economics of the situation) when banks have more than one margin agreement with one another, due, for example, to the bilateral margin rules (Section 4.4.2).

A final component of the SA-CCR is the recognition of overcollateralisation (initial margin) and netting sets that are out-of-the-money (negative current value). Note that these two effects are similar because, in both cases, an increase in value may not cause an increase in exposure. SA-CCR allows this to be recognised via a multiplier of:

$$\min\left(1; Floor + (1 - Floor) \times \exp\left(\frac{V - C}{2 \times (1 - Floor) \times AddOn^{aggregate}}\right)\right) \tag{13.21}$$

where $Floor$ is 5% and $AddOn^{aggregate}$ is the total add-on for the netting set after application of the rules described above. The term $V - C$ can be negative due to an uncollateralised netting set and/or the presence of initial margin in the total margin determined by C. This will then cause a reduction in the add-on. Note that positive value benefits (Section 11.3.2) are not recognised and the presence of the floor means that the capital cannot go to zero, even in the case of a very large initial margin or extremely negative value. The multiplier is illustrated in Figure 13.6 for an aggregate add-on of unity. Note that the initial margin, for example, would have to be several multiples of the add-on to reduce the EAD to near zero, and even then this is restricted by the 5% floor.

Spreadsheet 13.1 Implementation of SA-CCR.

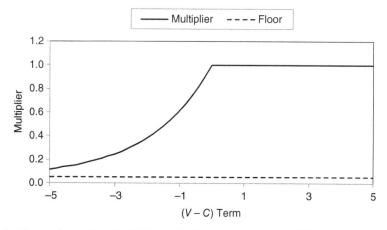

Figure 13.6 Illustration of the SA-CCR multiplier that reduces the PFE when there is overcollateralisation (through the term $V - C$ being negative).

13.4.4   Broader Impact of SA-CCR

It is important to emphasise the potential impact that the new SA-CCR methodology will have on the regulatory capital for banks and clearing members, and in defining derivatives regulation in general.

As discussed in Section 13.4.3, SA-CCR is generally conservative in its representation of EAD, and whilst more risk sensitive than the previous standardised method for EAD (CEM), it has some notable drawbacks. For example:

- a relatively conservative calibration of 'supervisory factors', in particular for certain asset classes (e.g. equities);
- the inclusion of a conservative alpha multiplier of 1.4;
- limited netting benefit due to the fairly granular definition of 'hedging sets';
- a conservative and limited recognition of received initial margin; and
- the splitting of netting sets when there is more than one margin agreement.

The relative conservatism of SA-CCR compared to IMM and the lack of risk sensitivity with respect to certain aspects is important since the methodology is used in a number of different places within the new regulatory framework:

- *Regulatory capital.* Minimal regulatory capital requirements for derivatives for non-IMM banks will be determined by the SA-CCR.
- *Capital floors.* Even IMM banks will have to compute SA-CCR capital numbers and may be subject to a capital floor if the result of this and other standardised approaches is materially more than their actual capital requirements (Section 4.2.8).
- *The leverage ratio.* The leverage ratio (Section 4.2.7) exposure calculation for derivatives uses the SA-CCR (for all banks, including those with IMM approval).
- *The large exposure framework.* The SA-CCR is used to define derivatives exposures in the large exposure framework (Section 4.2.9).
- *CCP capital requirements.* The capital requirements for CCP default fund exposures will be determined with reference to the CCP methodology, which will determine the 'hypothetical capital requirement' of the CCP (Section 13.6.3).

In the context of the above, any drawbacks of SA-CCR will potentially have multiple impacts across a bank. For example, the alpha multiplier may be seen to gross up leverage ratio exposures and create 40% of extra receivables on a bank's balance sheet. The same will be true of the large exposure framework. Indeed, a large derivatives exposure could be likely to originate from an in-the-money uncollateralised position, where the alpha multiplier becomes even more irrelevant since the position is more dominated by the replacement cost, which should not be arbitrarily made 40% higher. Where SA-CCR is particularly conservative with respect to a type of transaction (e.g. equities or transactions with received initial margin), such transactions may be subject to high capital requirements under any trading relationship (bilateral, centrally cleared) and generally discouraged. This may, in turn, lead to the wrong incentives for banks.

The above concerns may be one of the reasons why US regulators have removed the alpha factor for 'commercial end-user counterparties' – Federal bank regulatory agencies finalize rule to update calculation of counterparty credit risk for derivative contracts, Board of Governors of the Federal Reserve System, Federal Deposit Insurance Corporation, Office of the Comptroller of the Currency, Press Release, 19 November 2019. www.federalreserve.gov.

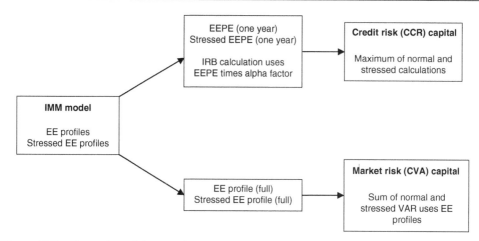

Figure 13.7   Illustration of the use of IMM-calculated effective expected positive exposure (EEPE) in both credit and market risk capital calculations.

13.4.5   The Internal Model Method

The internal model method (IMM) is the most risk-sensitive approach for EAD calculation available under the Basel framework. Under IMM, the EAD is calculated from a bank's own internal model for PFE, which must be approved by the bank's national supervisor(s).

Note that IMM models currently form the basis of both credit and market risk capital methodologies (Figure 13.7). In the former case, the normal and stressed EEs up to one year form the basis of the EAD in the IRB approach (Section 13.2.2), and the maturity adjustment factor as required by Equation 13.1 can also be calculated. In the latter case, the full profile of normal and stressed EEs is an input in the advanced CVA capital charge calculation (Equation 13.9). This second application of internal models will be redundant when the BA-CVA and SA-CVA methodologies (Sections 13.3.3 and 13.3.5) are implemented.

Banks with IMM approval generally make capital savings compared to using more basic methodologies such as SA-CCR. There is also the benefit of capital being more risk sensitive and so being better aligned to actual economic risks.

Broadly speaking, an IMM implementation permits:

- accurate modelling of all underlying risk factors and their dependencies to generate the resulting future exposure of all transactions;
- full netting across asset classes, as long as certain legal and operational requirements have been met; and
- margin benefit, including aspects such as thresholds and the modelling of future margin received.

The IMM method allows the calculation of an accurate exposure distribution at the counterparty level. However, since the CCR capital charge for counterparty risk requires a single EAD value per counterparty, a key aspect of the IMM method is representing this distribution in a simple way.

The key basis for defining EAD was provided by Wilde (2001), who showed that it could be defined via the average EPE (Section 11.1.5) under the following conditions:

- an infinitely large portfolio (number of counterparties) of small exposures (i.e. infinite diversification);
- no correlation of exposures;
- no wrong-way or right-way risk.

Whilst this is only relevant as a theoretical result, it implies that the average EPE is a good starting point. Picoult (2002) therefore suggests accounting for the deviations from the idealistic situation above by using a correction.[24] This correction has become known as the alpha (α) multiplier and corrects for the finite size and concentration of the portfolio in question. Banks using IMM have an option to compute their own estimate of alpha with a methodology that is approved by their regulator and subject to a floor of 1.2 (BCBS 2005b). However, this is relatively uncommon, and most banks with IMM approval use a supervisory value, which has a default value of 1.4 but can be increased by national regulators. BCBS (2015b) reports that, out of 19 banks (from 10 jurisdictions) surveyed, only one calculates its own alpha, whilst three are subject by their supervisory authority to a higher alpha. The default alpha of 1.4 is the reason for this adjustment in SA-CCR discussed in Section 13.4.3.

Note that regulation defines the alpha factor as conditioning EPE on a 'bad state' of the economy, in addition to accounting for aspects such as granularity described above. The alpha multiplier is also viewed as a method to offset model error or estimation error (BCBS 2005b).

As discussed in Section 11.1.5, Basel regulation has typically used the term EPE to define what is defined here – and more commonly in the industry – as average EPE. Unless stated, the more common definitions will be used (Table 13.10), with Basel terms referred to explicitly (e.g. 'Basel EPE').

Spreadsheet 13.2 Calculation of 'alpha' factor.

Regulators have made one other modification under IMM by requiring banks to use effective EPE (EEPE), which is, by definition, the same or higher than the EPE. The motivation for EEPE (BCBS 2005b) is as a more conservative version of EPE that deals with the following two problems:

- Since Basel EPE represents an average of the exposure, it may neglect very large exposures that are present for only a short time.

Table 13.10 Exposure definitions used by BCBS (2005b) compared to the more common definitions used here.

Basel definition	More common definition (used here)
EE	EPE
EPE	Average EPE
EEE	N/A
Effective EPE	N/A

---

[24] According to Picoult (2002), alpha 'expresses the difference between calculating economic capital with full simulation and with a simulation assuming the exposure profile of each counterparty can be represented by a fixed exposure profile'.

- Basel EPE may underestimate exposure for short-dated transactions and not properly capture 'rollover risk'.[25] This arises from current short-dated transactions that will be rolled over into new transactions at their maturity. This is particularly true for portfolios such as, for example, short-dated FX positions.

For the above reasons, EEPE was introduced for regulatory capital purposes. It is the average of the effective EE (EEE), which is simply a non-decreasing version of the EPE profile.[26] These terms are shown in comparison with EPE in Figure 13.8. Loosely speaking, EEPE assumes that any reduction in the EE profile is a result of a maturing transaction that will be replaced.[27] Note, that due to the definition of regulatory capital calculations, only a one-year time horizon is relevant in the EEPE definition. It could be argued that EEPE may sometimes be unnecessarily conservative. For example, a profile with a spike in exposure for a very short period (due, for example, to large cash flows) will create an EEPE that is much higher than the Basel EPE.

> **Spreadsheet 13.3 EPE and EEPE example.**

Finally, the EAD under an IMM approach is defined as:

$$EAD = \alpha \times EEPE \tag{13.22}$$

where α is the previously described alpha parameter with a default value of 1.4.

For collateralised counterparties, Basel III introduced requirements that the MPoR must be increased from the minimum of 10 days for OTC derivatives. These situations are as follows:

- For all netting sets[28] where the number of trades exceeds 5,000 at any point during a quarter, a longer 20-day period should apply for the following quarter.

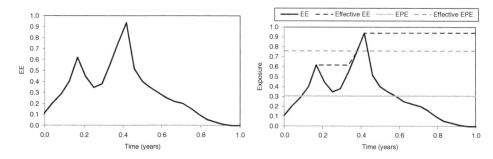

Figure 13.8   Illustration of effective EE (EEE) and effective EPE (EEPE).

---

[25] It could also be seen as assuming some worst-case default time within the one-year interval considered.

[26] Under regulatory terminology this is defined as the EE profile.

[27] The regulatory formula essentially assumes that any reduction in exposure is a result of maturing transactions. This is not necessarily the case.

[28] The MPoR applies to netting sets and not at the counterparty level (unless there is only one netting set).

- For netting sets containing one or more trades involving either illiquid margin or an OTC derivative that cannot easily be replaced.
- If there have been more than two margin call disputes on a particular netting set over the previous two quarters that have lasted longer than the original MPoR (before consideration of this provision), then the period must be at least doubled.

It is also not possible to model any reduction in EPE arising from contractual clauses relating to credit quality (e.g. a counterparty posting margin in the event that they are downgraded). This can be seen as a worst-case scenario in assuming that a counterparty *will not* trigger such a clause prior to default. Note that the liquidity coverage ratio takes a similar worst-case scenario that a bank itself *will* be downgraded (Section 4.3.3).

Whilst some banks have been using IMM approaches since before the GFC, Basel III rules brought about more stringent requirements for such approaches (BCBS 2009b, 2011b).

To limit procyclicality (Section 4.2.1), IMM approaches must calculate EEPE with parameters calibrated based on stressed data. These stressed inputs must use three years of historical data that include a one-year period of stress (typically defined as increasing CDS spreads) or, alternatively, market-implied data from a stressed period. This stressed period must be used in *addition* to the 'normal' period of at least three years of historical data, which itself should cover a full range of economic conditions (EBA 2015b notes that most banks use a stress period around 2008–2009). The highest EEPE (stressed or normal) must be taken on a portfolio (not counterparty-by-counterparty) basis.[29] The use of stressed EEPE is also envisaged to capture general WWR, as the dependencies that contribute to this may be more apparent in stressed periods. Otherwise, the treatment of general WWR as EEPE multiplied by the α factor is unchanged, except for some points related to the robust calculation of α.[30]

It has been observed that the IMM approaches of different banks can result in materially different results. For example, BCBS (2015b) notes a very substantial variation in EEPE values for individual trades, but with less variation for diversified and realistic netting sets (typically most banks are within 50% and 150% of the median). IMM variation can be a result of many aspects, including the choice of model and calibration, and also numerical issues such as the time grid used.[31] This model risk is one motivation for the requirement for banks still to use standardised approaches and be subject to capital floors (Section 4.2.8).

Another mitigant for model risk is backtesting. Basel III also introduced a requirement for the backtesting of IMM models which follows similar standards for market risk capital approaches. Backtesting involves testing a predictive model on (objective) historical data, and is illustrated in Figure 13.9. A quantile measure, such as PFE (Section 11.1.3), is straightforward to backtest; assuming independence of daily forecasts implies that the number of exceedances or violations of a 99% PFE over an annual period (250 business days) would be 2.5 and, to a 95% confidence level, violations above six or below one are rejected.[32]

---

[29] This is in contrast to market risk requirements (e.g. the CVA capital charge), where the sum of stressed and non-stressed capital charges must be used.

[30] In particular, it seems that banks cannot attain IMM approval without modelling WWR in some way.

[31] Due to the definition of EEPE, more time points would generally be expected to lead to a higher value.

[32] This can be shown via the relevant binomial probabilities or more robustly using the two-tailed approach of Kupiec (1995).

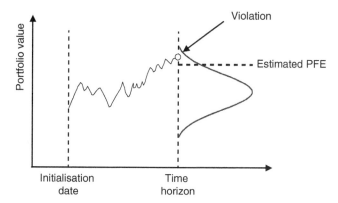

Figure 13.9   Illustration of backtesting via comparing a realised path, at some time horizon, to the estimated PFE.

Some challenges in backtesting IMM methodologies are:

- Multiple time horizons must be considered, which require more data to be stored and processed. The need to look at longer time horizons implies that a much larger historical data set is used and creates problems with effects such as ageing. It is also necessary to keep track of the quarterly recalibration of EPE models.[33]
- Backtesting must be done for different portfolios of trades, as EPE is defined at the counterparty (or netting set) level. However, such portfolios cannot be assumed to be independent. For example, if one portfolio contains the hedges of another, then they will never be expected to have a high exposure at the same time.
- Measures such as EPE are based on expectations and not – like PFE – on a quantile. Non-quantile-based quantities are harder to backtest.

There are a number of considerations that are necessary to cope realistically with the above (see also the discussion in BCBS 2010b). One example is the use of overlapping windows. However, it is then important to deal with the dependence of data (e.g. exceeding an exposure in one period leads to a greater likelihood of exceedance in an overlapping period). This leads to difficulties, as most simple statistical tests are based on the assumption of independent observations.

Backtesting can first be done at the risk-factor level. The aim of this is to test the distributional assumptions for each risk factor individually and avoid the potential for these to be diluted or masked at the portfolio level. Secondly, backtesting must be done at the netting set or portfolio level. Assuming the risk-factor backtesting shows acceptable results, then the portfolio-level backtesting is relevant for testing the ability to capture important co-dependencies between different risk factors.

Backtesting must involve multiple time horizons, up to at least one year, and multiple initialisation points. Furthermore, using different quantiles can effectively test across the whole exposure distribution. To simplify the workload, given the millions of transactions that may exist within a typical large OTC derivatives book, it is possible to backtest

---

[33] For example, a three-month and six-month distribution generated today will be inconsistent with the three-month distribution generated three months from now, since a recalibration of the model will be performed.

'representative portfolios'. Such representative portfolios must be chosen based on their sensitivity to the significant risk factors and correlations to which a bank is exposed. This could be done via regression methods, principal components analysis or maybe in a rather more ad hoc way (e.g. based on the largest counterparties, exposures, or overall capital contributions). Once representative portfolios have been chosen, a typical backtesting exercise may use, for example, tenors defined at one week, two weeks, one month, three months, six months, one year, and two years and test 1%, 5%, 25%, 75%, 95%, and 99% quantiles with weekly initialisation points. The data and systems implications of doing this are considerable. In addition, representative portfolios should presumably be reviewed on a periodic basis. Whilst a typical portfolio will not change materially over the short term, any large market move or significant trading in a particular asset class may create sensitivities in a bank's portfolio that need to be included in the representative portfolios.

Finally, Basel III introduced an increased focus on the stress testing of counterparty risk exposures generated by IMM methodologies, such as the need to stress, individually and jointly, all principal market risk factors (interest rates, FX, equities, credit spreads, and commodity prices) and to assess material non-directional risks, such as curve and basis risks, at least quarterly. A high-level framework for a counterparty risk stress-testing program may also focus on credit risk stresses, co-movement of market and credit risk (WWR) and margin. The results of various stress tests can be shown in a number of different ways, such as through valuation changes, capital changes, and impact on margin requirements.

13.4.6   The Leverage Ratio

Methodologies such as CEM and later SA-CCR form the basis of EAD to be used in defining the minimum capital ratios (or RWAs) of a bank. The same methodologies generally define the EAD to be used in the leverage ratio numerator (Section 4.2.7). It is worth emphasising the differences between minimum capital requirements and the leverage ratio and the impact they may have (Table 13.11).

The main difference is that the leverage ratio considers exposure only, and not credit quality, which generally makes business with low credit risk 'leverage ratio constraining'. Another important impact is that an IMM approach cannot be used in the leverage ratio exposure calculation, even if the bank uses IMM to define its minimum capital requirements.

Table 13.11   Comparison between minimum capital requirements and the leverage ratio.

	Minimum capital requirements	Leverage ratio
Credit quality	Capital depends on credit quality	Driven only by exposure and not credit quality
Methodology	Internal models or standardised approaches	Standardised approaches only
Treatment of collateralised portfolios	Received margin recognised in all methodologies	Only cash margin recognised
Moneyness	Out-of-the-money portfolios (negative value) will have reduced EAD under SA-CCR	No benefit

There are further differences that can be attributed to the specific calculation of EAD for minimum capital requirements compared with the exposure defined in the leverage ratio. In the treatment of collateralised portfolios, whilst minimum capital requirements allow the exposure to be reduced by received margin, this is not generally the case for the leverage ratio, except if the margin is in cash. A recent change to the leverage ratio treatment of client-cleared derivatives (BCBS 2019b) allows both cash and non-cash margin to reduce the exposure. In the leverage ratio, it is also not possible to recognise an out-of-the-money portfolio as reducing the exposure.

Some of the above features may contribute to a bank being more leverage ratio constrained, as opposed to RWA constrained. This may depend on the general business and asset base of the bank, with banks with low-risk assets more likely to be constrained by the leverage ratio. However, it may also be driven by aspects such as the regulatory treatment of exposure shown in Table 13.11.[34]

13.4.7   Wrong-way Risk

Wrong-way risk (WWR) is the term generally used to describe positive co-dependency between exposure and the credit quality of the counterparty (i.e. the exposure increases as the PD of the counterparty increases). Regulators have generally characterised two broad forms of WWR:

- *General WWR*. This is driven by macro-economic behaviour (e.g. the fact that credit spreads and interest rate moves exhibit co-dependency).
- *Specific WWR*. This is related to the structural nature of individual trades or counterparty exposures (e.g. a company writing put options on its own stock).

For IMM banks, general WWR is viewed as being partly captured by the stressed EPE calculation. However, on top of this, it may be necessary to incorporate modelling of general WWR, driven by macro-economic factors such as correlations between exposure drivers and credit spreads in IMM exposure simulation (WWR models are discussed in Section 17.6). Since the alpha multiplier is partly intended to capture general WWR, a bank's regulator has the ability to impose a higher α if it is not comfortable with the coverage of general WWR elsewhere.

Whilst non-IMM banks are not required to implement any modelling of WWR, there is a greater burden in terms of identification and management, including the following with respect to general WWR:

- identification of exposures that give rise to a greater degree of general WWR;
- the design of stress tests and scenario analysis that specifically include WWR factor evolution (e.g. credit spreads strongly correlated with interest rates or FX moves);
- continuous monitoring of WWR by region, industry, and other categories; and
- generation of reports for appropriate senior management and board members explaining WWR and mitigating action being taken.

---

[34] Rennison, J. and L. Noonan (2017). Deutsche Bank walks away from US swaps clearing. *Financial Times* (9 February). www.ft.com.

Basel III seems to view specific WWR as often being due to badly-designed transactions, which potentially should not even exist. It requires that there be procedures in place to identify, monitor, and control cases of specific WWR for each legal entity. Transactions with counterparties where specific WWR has been identified need to be treated differently when calculating the EAD for such exposures:

- each separate legal entity to which the bank is exposed must be separately rated, and there must be policies regarding the treatment of a connected group of entities for the identification of specific WWR; and
- instruments for which there exists a legal connection between the counterparty and the underlying issuer, and for which specific WWR has been identified, should not be considered to be in the same netting set as other transactions with the counterparty.

Furthermore, for single-name credit default swaps, where there exists a legal connection between the counterparty and the underlying issuer, and where specific WWR has been identified, the EAD should be 100% less any current losses accounted for (e.g. via CVA). This is applied for other products also, such as equity derivatives, bond options, and securities financing transactions that reference a single company which has a legal connection to the counterparty. In such a case the EAD must be defined assuming a default of the underlying security.[35]

13.5   EXAMPLES

In this section, we will give examples of the different regulatory approaches and their impact on capital. Comparison of capital methodologies is difficult due to the different asset classes and a number of different effects to consider (e.g. moneyness, netting, and margin). For this reason, we will base the results below on a simple interest rate swap portfolio, but will consider a number of important risk mitigation effects.

Note also that the more advanced approaches (e.g. IMM and SA-CVA) are subject to particular implementations for modelling exposure and calculating sensitivities, and the approaches chosen are intended to be representative of a typical implementation (the currency chosen was US dollars). By contrast, the more basic approaches (e.g. SA-CCR) are prescriptive and currency independent.

Whilst the examples will be for simple trades/portfolios, some general statements will be made around the relative conservativeness of the various approaches. We will start with a comparison of EAD methods and then compare capital requirements directly.

13.5.1   Comparison of EAD Methods

We first show the EAD of a par (zero-value) interest rate swap with a notional of 1,000 as a function of maturity in Figure 13.10. Both uncollateralised and collateralised examples are shown. In the latter case, only variation margin (a two-way credit support annex – CSA – with a zero threshold, a zero minimum transfer amount, and an MPoR of 10 business days), and not initial margin, is included. The discrete behaviour of the

---

[35] The LGD must be set to 100%, regardless of using a lower value elsewhere.

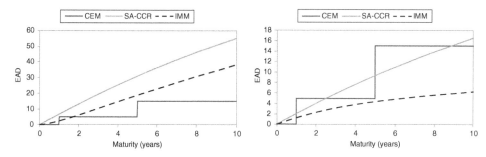

Figure 13.10   EADs for uncollateralised (left) and collateralised (right) 10-year USD par interest rate swaps with a notional of 1,000 as a function of maturity for three possible regulatory capital approaches. Note the difference in scale (*y*-axis).

CEM approach is due to the granularity of the add-ons (Table 13.8). SA-CCR shows a more realistic shape due to the use of the supervisory duration (Section 13.4.3), which is comparable to the more sophisticated IMM method. Also noticeable is the more conservative nature of SA-CCR calibration.

In the collateralised case, IMM and SA-CCR results reduce substantially – in the former case due to full margin modelling, whereas in the latter it arises due to the factor of 0.3 specified by Equation 13.20. The reduction in the IMM approach is stronger than SA-CCR, especially for long-dated trades, since it recognises the benefit of reducing the time horizon from the final maturity to the MPoR, rather than just one year to the MPoR (Equation 13.20). The CEM approach gives no benefit for future margin received, and therefore the results are unchanged (since the value of the swap is zero, the current margin is not relevant).

As noted above, the SA-CCR has a multiplier that gives benefit for both off-market (negative value) trades and initial margin. These effects are, from an exposure point of view, similar because they both lead to overcollateralisation. Figure 13.11 shows the impact of overcollateralisation, in each case assuming a two-way CSA with a minimum transfer amount of zero (and zero threshold posting in the case of the initial margin). CEM does not have any mechanism for capturing these effects. SA-CCR does

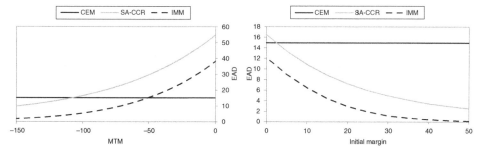

Figure 13.11   EAD for an uncollateralised 10-year USD off-market interest rate swap with a notional of 1,000 as a function of value (left) and the equivalent collateralised par swap with initial margin (right) for three possible regulatory capital approaches.

a reasonable job of reproducing the IMM behaviour, although it is high in comparison; this is due to the relatively conservative add-on and floor included in Equation 13.21.

Finally, we consider the impact of netting by using two interest rate swaps that are offsetting (i.e. one paying and the other receiving the fixed rate) in the same and different currencies. We hold the maturity of one swap fixed at 10 years and vary the other between zero and 20 years to see the netting impact in each of the three methodologies (Figure 13.12). In the case of the same currency, the CEM approach is very poor since it gives a 60% netting regardless of the maturity mismatch, and therefore shows the wrong behaviour entirely. SA-CCR gives netting benefit since the swaps are in the same hedging set and it matches the IMM results quite well. A noticeable aspect is the discontinuities at one and five years due to the three maturity buckets used by SA-CCR. SA-CCR does not recognise the decorrelation of tenors when the second swap has a maturity above 10 years,

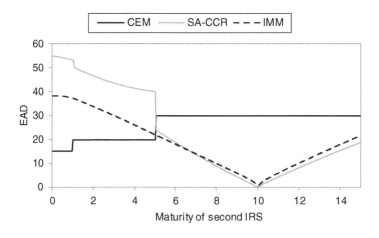

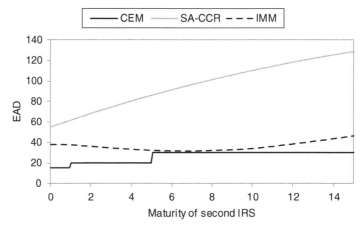

Figure 13.12   EAD for two offsetting interest rate swaps in the same currency (top) and different currencies (bottom), each with a notional of 1,000 as a function of the maturity of one swap (the other has a maturity of 10 years) for three possible regulatory capital approaches.

which may be why the IMM results are higher in this region. For the swaps in different currencies, SA-CCR appears too conservative compared to IMM due to treating them in different hedging sets and giving no netting benefit.

The above examples show some general trends. The CEM results are generally poor due to a lack of risk sensitivity, which illustrates one reason for replacing this approach with SA-CCR. Comparing SA-CCR with IMM, it can be seen that SA-CCR is more risk sensitive but generally more conservative than IMM. The basic parameters of SA-CCR tend to lead to higher EADs, and the impact of netting and margin is not as strong as would be expected, and in some cases there is no benefit at all (e.g. different currencies, as shown above).

In general, the SA-CCR results tend to be significantly higher (e.g. double) compared to the IMM ones. For example, using a hypothetical portfolio, the International Swaps and Derivatives Association and Association for Financial Markets in Europe (ISDA-AFMR 2017) reports SA-CCR EAD to be about 2.5 times that of an IMM approach, and more than three times for margined counterparties. In the presence of initial margin, the increase is closer to an order of magnitude.

This can have a strong influence on capital costs and also in other areas that SA-CCR is used for (Section 13.4.4). Additionally, SA-CCR can produce some counterintuitive results – for example:

- two offsetting interest rate swaps with different reference rates but in the same maturity bucket would lead to zero EAD (e.g. a basis swap could be structured as two offsetting interest rate swaps); and
- FX triangles (e.g. USD/EUR, GBP/USD, EUR/GBP FX positions that are perfectly offsetting) would give rise to capital costs on each of the three trades.

13.5.2 Comparison of Capital Charges

Spreadsheet 13.4 Comparison of capital costs across different methodologies.

A comparison of total capital costs across different methodologies is challenging due to the different methodologies and parameter choices. However, it is possible to make some general statements regarding the different methodologies using the examples below. The IMM and advanced CVA capital methodologies will not be considered, as they are quite subjective and specific to a bank's individual implementation. However, the general observation that IMM capital numbers are often materially lower than those with SA-CCR is relevant.

The following methodology choices corresponding to credit risk (CCR)/market risk (CVA) capital will be examined:

- *CEM + standardised.* This represents the current approaches for banks without IMM approval prior to the implementation of SA-CCR.
- *SA-CCR + standardised.* This represents the impact of the implementation of SA-CCR.
- *SA-CCR + BA-CVA.* This represents the impact of the basic option under the FRTB rules (BA-CVA) using the current regulatory parameterisation of this approach.

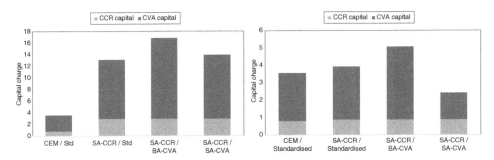

Figure 13.13 Capital calculations using different methodology choices for an uncollateralised (left) and collateralised (right) 10-year interest rate swap, each with a notional of 1,000, with a BBB manufacturing company (basic materials, energy, industrials, agriculture, manufacturing, mining, and quarrying sectorial risk bucket).

- *SA-CCR + SA-CVA*. This represents the impact of the more advanced option under the FRTB rules (SA-CVA) using the current regulatory parameterisation of this approach.

The impact is shown for a single 10-year par interest rate swap on both an uncollateralised and collateralised basis. Two counterparties are considered: a BBB (triple-B) telecommunications company and an A (single-A) financial institution.

Figure 13.13 shows the capital requirements for the BBB manufacturing company. The first observation is that CEM/standardised charges are very small in the uncollateralised case due to the relatively small weights, discussed in Section 13.4.2. This is not the case in the collateralised case due to the fact that CEM does not account for the future benefit of margin. In the uncollateralised case, the standardised CVA capital charge together with the future BA-CVA and SA-CVA approaches give similar results. In the collateralised case, the more advanced SA-CVA approach gives significantly lower numbers due to the better representation of the impact of future collateralisation (compared to the relatively crude approach in SA-CCR shown in Equation 13.20).

Figure 13.14 shows the capital requirements for the A financial institution. An important additional aspect to note here is that the weight under the BA-CVA approach

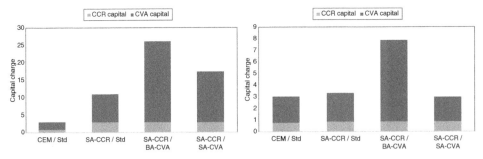

Figure 13.14 Capital calculations using different methodology choices for an uncollateralised (left) and collateralised (right) 10-year interest rate swap, each with a notional of 1,000, with an A financial institution (financials, including government-backed financials risk bucket).

is particularly high in this case (Table 13.3), due to the relatively high volatility of the credit spreads of financial institutions that have been observed during and since the GFC. Note that the current standardised methodologies are parameterised by rating and not counterparty type (Section 13.3.2). This makes the SA-CVA approach seem particularly beneficial.

Note that a further benefit of the SA-CVA approach is the better recognition of CVA hedges, as discussed in Section 13.5.3.

13.5.3   Impact of Hedges

As discussed in Section 13.3.6, CCR- and CVA-related capital charges provide a means to include certain hedges as risk mitigants. This is important since it incentivises risk-controlling and -reducing activities such as CVA hedging.

CCR-related capital relief is relatively simple, as discussed in Section 13.2.3, and simply involves a substitution of the credit quality of the original exposure with that of the guarantor (e.g. CDS counterparty) for the EAD in question. Since this capital relates only to defaults (and potentially credit migrations), then only single-name CDSs (or equivalent) referencing the counterparty are eligible as hedges. A point that is important to make here is that the notional of the single-name hedge will need to equal the defined EAD of the counterparty in order to achieve maximum capital relief. Since regulatory methodologies are, in general, relatively conservative, this may require banks to *overhedge* their exposures to achieve the best capital relief. For example, the use of the relatively conservative alpha multiplier in IMM approaches (Section 13.4.4), and the use of this same multiplier and other conservative assumptions in SA-CCR (Section 13.4.3), would be expected to increase the amount of hedge required to provide the best capital relief.

Under the simpler standardised CVA capital charge and BA-CVA approach, only CDS hedges can be taken into account, but this includes indices and proxies (BA-CVA only). In order to understand the impact of hedges, it is useful to plot a simplified version of this formula. Removing the multipliers and hedges from Equation 13.2, or equivalently considering directly the BA-CVA formula in Equation 13.3, gives:

$$\sqrt{\left(\rho.\sum_c SCVA_c\right)^2 + (1 - \rho^2).\sum_c SCVA_c^2} \qquad (13.23)$$

Assuming an equally-weighted portfolio of n counterparties and dividing by n to generate a per counterparty charge further simplifies the formula to:

$$\sqrt{\frac{(n.\rho.SCVA)^2 + n(1 - \rho^2)SCVA^2}{n}} = SCVA^2\sqrt{\rho^2 + \frac{(1 - \rho^2)}{n}} \qquad (13.24)$$

The term $\sqrt{\frac{\rho^2 + (1-\rho^2)}{n}}$ provides a portfolio effect, so that the capital cost per counterparty reduces as the portfolio becomes larger. This function is illustrated in Figure 13.15 for different levels of correlation. As the portfolio becomes large, the multiplier will tend towards the value of ρ (i.e. 50% reduction for $\rho = 50\%$). Note that the portfolio in this example is equally weighted. In reality, a large but concentrated portfolio will behave like a smaller portfolio due to the lack of granularity.

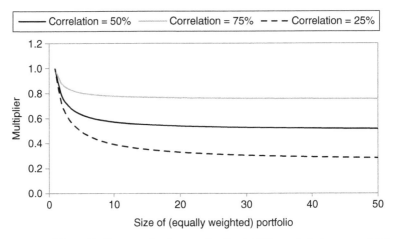

Figure 13.15 Implicit multiplier term in the standardised CVA capital charge and BA-CVA for different levels of correlation.

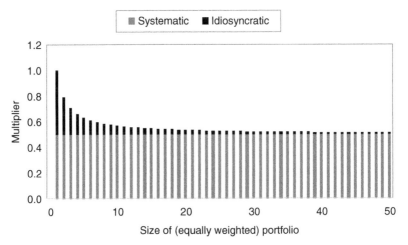

Figure 13.16 Split of the implicit multiplier term in the standardised CVA capital charge and BA-CVA for 50% correlation into systematic and idiosyncratic terms.

Another way to look at the above multiplier is that it represents a diversification of idiosyncratic risk as the portfolio increases in size (Figure 13.16). This is particularly relevant for hedging with a CDS index since the systematic component is reduced by index hedges, and so the hedging benefit is greater when the idiosyncratic component is smaller for a more diversified portfolio.

In terms of the value of correlation, there are a number of cases to consider (Figure 13.17):

- *100% correlation no penalty*. In the case of single-name CDSs, the standardised CVA capital charge allows a potentially perfect offset if the weighted and maturity-adjusted

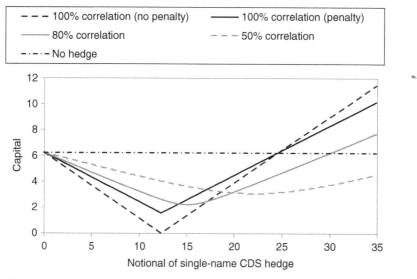

Figure 13.17   Impact of single-name CDS hedges on CVA capital under the standardised CVA capital charge (100% correlation with no penalty) and BA-CVA approach.

EAD is offset by the similarly weighted and maturity-adjusted notional of the single-name hedge (terms S_c and S_h^{SN} in Equation 13.2). This is shown in Figure 13.17 and corresponds to the case with 100% correlation and no penalty.

- *100% correlation with hedging penalty.* In the BA-CVA approach,[36] the hedging limitations (HMA in Equation 13.5 and also the effect of Equation 13.8) means that hedging cannot be perfect. This is, therefore, the case of a single-name CDS referencing the counterparty, and is similar to the above but with a minimum above zero.
- *80% correlation.* In the BA-CVA approach, proxy single-name CDS hedges with a legal connection (Table 13.4) are given a lower correlation of 80%, which allows less capital relief and (unusually, as discussed in Section 13.3.5) incentivises overhedging.
- *50% correlation.* This is similar to the case above for proxy single-name hedges in the same sector, and provides less capital relief and incentivises an even larger hedge.

The above results for single-name hedging do depend marginally on the size and granularity of the underlying portfolio. The case of index hedges is even more portfolio specific. The reason for this is that index hedges, as discussed in Section 13.3.2, only impact the systematic term in these formulas and not the other idiosyncratic term. As discussed above, this means that a more diversified portfolio can be more effectively hedged via indices, as shown in Figure 13.18. Note also that the hedging penalty term in the BA-CVA approach reduces the benefit achievable compared to the standardised CVA capital charge, which does not contain this component.

Recall that under the basic approaches for CVA capital described above, there is no capital relief for hedging other than single-name and index CDS positions. All other market

---

[36] For the purposes of this example, the capital charges in the standardised CVA approach and BA-CVA have been aligned to give the same value, which would not be the case in practice.

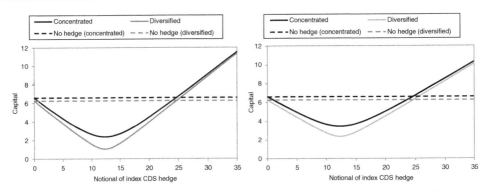

Figure 13.18 Impact of index CDS hedges on CVA capital under the standardised CVA capital charge (left) and BA-CVA approach (right).

risk hedges not only do not provide any capital reduction but may also consume capital, as discussed in Section 13.3.6.

Under SA-CVA, most CVAs are eligible for capital relief with the following restrictions:

- only entire transactions used for the purpose of mitigating CVA risk (e.g. executed by the CVA desk) are eligible; and
- hedging instruments that cannot be included in the internal model approach (IMA) for market risk (e.g. tranched credit derivatives) are not eligible.

Under the SA-CVA approach, CVA sensitivities and the equivalent sensitivities of hedges are aggregated according to Equation 13.10c. This means that the contribution of any risk factor in SA-CVA could be zero if the sensitivities (CVA and hedge) cancel perfectly. By extension, this could mean that a set of hedges could be executed that would reduce the SA-CVA capital charge to zero. There are two general problems with this:

- the SA-CVA approach only considers a certain range of risk factors (reduced even according to the SA-TB approach for general market risk, as described in Section 13.3.5) and CVA risk will exist, which is not captured by these risk factors; and
- hedges will have sensitivities other than those aggregated within SA-CVA, and these will give rise to additional risk.

As noted previously, SA-CVA contains a simplistic hedging disallowance parameter (R in Equation 13.11), which prevents the possibility of perfect hedging of CVA risk and can be seen to correct for the above factors. The hedging disallowance can be seen to be driven by 10% of the gross sensitivities of the hedges.[37]

An example of the capital charge for the interest rate delta risk class of an interest rate swap is shown in Figure 13.19. Note that the presence of the hedging penalty means that it is not possible to reduce capital to zero and the optimal hedge is slightly less than 100% of the CVA sensitivities.

---

[37] Given by the square root of R, which is 0.01.

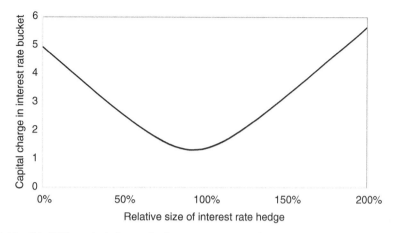

Figure 13.19 SA-CVA capital charge for interest rate delta risk class of an interest rate swap as a function of the size of the hedge (100% corresponds to perfect hedging of all sensitivities).

Single-name CDS hedges will aggregate exactly with the corresponding CVA sensitivities according to the correlations previously shown in Table 13.6. This gives correlations of 100%/90% for the same entity for same tenor/different tenor. The equivalent numbers for legally-related entities are 90%/81%, which are slightly more favourable than the BA-CVA equivalent number of 80%.

For index hedges, sensitivities to all risk factors in the index must be calculated separately. The benefit of the index hedge will depend on the sectorial composition of the index compared with that of the underlying portfolio across the industries (risk buckets) in Table 13.3. This is illustrated in Figure 13.20, which shows the impact of hedging with indices that are aligned (similar sectorial composition) and misaligned (different sectorial composition) with the underlying portfolio. With the aligned index (a reasonable but

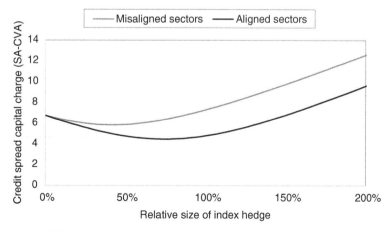

Figure 13.20 SA-CVA capital charge for the counterparty credit spread delta bucket for an interest rate swap as a function of the relative size of the hedge, assuming a misaligned and aligned index hedge.

not perfect match with the portfolio sector composition), about a 33% reduction in CVA capital can be achieved. When an index is misaligned it will not reduce the risk optimally in some sectors (underhedge) and increase risk in other sectors (overhedge). The result of this may be that the index cannot produce any material capital relief and may increase capital overall. This suggests that the development of sectorial indices would be a useful development and provide better capital relief for banks using the SA-CVA approach.

Note that at the time of writing there is a consultation (BCBS 2019c) that would allow the treatment of credit index hedges via an addition sector which would not require a decomposition as described above. In such a case then the sectorial misalignment may be less of an issue.

13.6   CENTRAL COUNTERPARTY CAPITAL REQUIREMENTS

13.6.1   Background

Central clearing is seen as reducing counterparty risk, but CCPs do represent some default risk to their clearing members (and their clients) via a potential default of either the CCP itself or one or more clearing members (for example, refer to the recent Nasdaq example in Section 10.1.3). Prior to Basel III, regulatory capital requirements allowed all CCP-related exposure to be given (explicitly or not) a zero-capital charge. The introduction of mandatory clearing led to the need to have a formal capital charge for CCP exposures. Moreover, the methodology for computing the capital charges should be coherent (e.g. if a CCP increases the size of its default fund, then the capital requirements for its members should reduce in line with their decreasing risk). There should also be a distinction between different CCPs, which will have different levels of riskiness.

At the time of writing, capitalisation of CCP exposures is covered by the so-called 'interim rules' (BCBS 2012b). These rules are soon to be replaced by the 'final rules' (BCBS 2014d). The final rules incorporate the SA-CCR methodology (Section 13.4.3) and so are also linked to this implementation. The forthcoming discussion will cover both sets of rules.

The Basel committee has broadly identified two types of risk, and therefore capital charges, associated with clearing members' CCP exposures:

- *Trade exposure*. This is direct exposure to the CCP default and consists of any current exposure (portfolio value and variation margin), a PFE, and (non-segregated) initial margin.
- *Default fund exposure*. This is a more indirect exposure to the default of the other clearing members of the CCP and is associated with the current default fund contribution, future contributions to the default fund ('rights of assessment'), and other loss-allocation methods (Section 8.3.4).

A key determinant in capital rules is whether or not a CCP has qualifying status. A qualifying CCP (QCCP) complies with the CPSS-IOSCO (2012) principles[38] and is licensed to operate as a CCP (including via an exemption) in relation to the clearing services

---

[38] Committee on Payment and Settlement Systems (CPSS) and the Technical Committee of the International Organization of Securities Commissions (IOSCO).

offered. Exposures to QCCPs receive preferential capital treatment. There is, therefore, a strong incentive for a CCP to maintain qualifying status. This creates the possibility of a 'cliff-edge' effect due to a large jump in capital if a CCP loses its qualifying status. Most of the discussion below concerns QCCPs, with reference made to non-QCCPs where relevant.

13.6.2   Trade Exposure

Trade exposure is defined as being represented by the following components:

- *Current exposure.* The current portfolio value adjusted for variation margin posted or received (if positive).
- *Potential future exposure (PFE).* The potential increase in the exposure in the future, calculated in a similar way to other bilateral (collateralised) derivatives positions.
- *Initial margin.* The initial margin posted to the CCP, unless this has been posted in a manner which makes it bankruptcy remote. This includes margin given to a CCP in excess of the minimum amount required where the CCP may prevent the return of this margin.

Capital requirements for trade-related exposures are defined in a simple and non-risk-sensitive way. For a QCCP, this component attracts a capital charge based on a relatively low-risk weight of 2% due to the perceived safety of such a counterparty. With the standard 8% minimum capital ratio this equates to a 0.16% ($8\% \times 2\%$) capital charge. In the case of initial margin being bankruptcy remote (e.g. held with a third-party custodian), and therefore being remote from CCP default, a 0% risk weight can be applied to this component.

Regarding the calculation of PFE, a clearing member must use the same method it uses to calculate EAD for bilateral exposures (Section 13.4). In these methodologies, the CCP exposure can be treated as collateralised in the usual way, with a 10-day MPoR being applied (the potential increases in MPoR for bilateral trades discussed in Section 13.4.4 are generally not applicable).

A clearing member trading with a non-qualifying CCP is required to capitalise its exposure in accordance with the bilateral framework for calculating capital. This will result in a minimum 'standardised' risk weight of 20% (the lowest risk weight under Basel capital rules, others being 50% and 100% - see Table 13.1).

13.6.3   Default Fund Exposure

A CCP default fund exposure broadly consists of two components:

- the current or pre-funded contribution, which is known; and
- rights of assessment of other unfunded loss-allocation methods, which are more uncertain.

In general, CCP default fund capital requirements are defined by the following stages:

- calculation of the hypothetical capital for the CCP;
- calculation of the aggregate capital requirements of the CCP; and
- allocation of aggregate capital to clearing members.

Under the current ('interim') rules (BCBS 2012b), banks may choose between two approaches:

- *Method 1*. A 2% risk weight against the trade exposure (as discussed in Section 13.6.2) and pre-funded default fund multiplied by a 'c-factor', which is calculated by, and specific to, the CCP in question.
- *Method 2*. The maximum of either a 2% risk weight against the trade exposure plus a 1250% risk weight against the pre-funded default fund contribution, or a 20% risk weight against the trade exposure.

For Method 1, CCPs are required to calculate and publish the required c-factor at least on a monthly basis to enable members to calculate their capital requirements. In order to calculate the c-factor, a CCP must calculate its derivatives exposures to all of its clearing members and their clients (CCP counterparties). For this purpose, the CCP uses a risk weight of 20% (at least) and the CEM methodology (Section 13.4.2) for determining EAD.[39] For the purposes of netting, the 60% factor in the CEM formula (Equation 13.14) is increased to 85% to reflect the diversification that may be present in cleared portfolios. The initial margin and default fund of each CCP counterparty are subtracted from the calculated exposure, as it is the loss above these amounts that is at risk in the event of a clearing member default. This results in a calculation of the 'hypothetical capital' (K_{CCP}), which is compared to the actual available default fund of the CCP in order to determine the c-factor. The bigger the available default fund of the CCP compared to K_{CCP}, the smaller the c-factor and the lower – on a pro rata basis – the clearing member capital charge. The precise formula is given in BCBS (2012b).

Method 2 does not require such a disclosure or calculation but requires a one-for-one (1250% times the standard 8% capital ratio) capital charge on the default fund, although this method is capped by 20% of the trade-related exposure (relevant in the case that the default fund contribution is rather large compared to the initial margin). See BCBS (2012b) for more details.

In the so-called 'final rules' that are scheduled for implementation around the time of publication of this book, the default fund capital calculation will change to use:

- the SA-CCR (instead of CEM) methodology for determining the hypothetical capital of the CCP; and
- a different calculation of the clearing member capital requirement as a function of the above, based on a simple ratio of the hypothetical capital to actual default fund (but floored at 2% risk weight, which prevents this falling below the initial margin requirement).

13.6.4   Client Clearing

In the case that an entity clears trades through another intermediary ('client clearing'), there are two situations:

- *Clearing member point of view*. The clearing member has exposure to both the client and the CCP. As such, there is the question of the capitalisation of these two exposures and the resulting impact on the leverage ratio.

---

[39] This applies to derivatives transactions. For securities financing transactions such as repos, standard supervisory haircuts apply.

- *Client point of view.* The client position (assuming, of course, that the client is a bank and subject to capital charges) and whether they are exposed to the CCP or the clearing member (or both).

Regarding the latter situation, under certain conditions, if a bank is clearing through another clearing member, it may capitalise the transactions as a CCP exposure (rather than a bilateral one). The conditions required for this treatment to apply are:

- The transactions must be identified by the CCP as client transactions.
- Margin to support the transactions must be held by the CCP and/or the clearing member such that the client is protected from the insolvency of the clearing member and any of the clearing member's other clients. Legal opinions must support this margin protection.
- The relevant transactions are highly likely to continue to be transacted through the CCP in the event of the insolvency of the clearing member. This refers to the likelihood that the transactions can be 'ported' (see Section 8.3.3) to another surviving clearing member in such a default scenario.

Where the above conditions are met, but a client is not protected from losses in the case that the clearing member and another client of the clearing member jointly default ('fellow customer risk'; see Section 8.2.5), a higher risk weight of 4% is applied. If the conditions are not met, then the client must assume a bilateral capital charge to its clearing member.

Turning to the clearing member point of view, a clearing member must capitalise its exposure to its client as well as that to the CCP. These capital charges will be calculated as follows:

- *Client trade.* This must be treated as a usual bilateral trade (irrespective of whether the clearing member guarantees the trade or simply acts as an intermediary between client and CCP), as the CCP provides no support in the case of the client defaulting. These capital charges may be reduced by the margin (including initial margin) that the client is obliged to post (the benefit will depend on which capital model the bank uses for counterparty risk). The only difference compared to a pure bilateral trade is that it is possible to use a smaller MPoR, which can be reduced from a minimum of 10 days to five days to reflect the shorter close-out periods for cleared transactions. This reduction can either be modelled directly or by a simple multiplier of $\sqrt{\frac{5}{10}} = 0.71$.
- *CCP trade.* A clearing member must also apply the 2% capital charge to its trade exposure to the CCP, even for a client trade. This is relevant if the clearing member is generally obligated to cover any losses the client would face due to the failure of the CCP. The clearing member will also have a charge on any additional contribution to the default fund that is required due to its client trades (although often CCPs do not require this).

Finally, the leverage ratio is particularly penalising with respect to centrally-cleared transactions, since the margin provided by the client cannot, in general, be used to reduce the exposure to the CCP.

14

Funding, Margin, and Capital Costs

14.1 BANK FINANCING

Banks and other firms must fund their assets with various sources of financing. There are two main types of financing: debt and equity. In general, a bank's cost of this financing reflects the compensation that investors and depositors demand in exchange for funding the bank's activities. Banks have a range of possible sources of funding available to them, including retail funding (e.g. deposits) and wholesale funding (e.g. unsecured or secured bonds), as well as the bank's equity (capital) base.

The Modigliani–Miller (MM) theorem (Modigliani and Miller 1958) is a well-known result of capital structure theory. It states that, in an efficient market and in the absence of taxes, bankruptcy costs, agency costs, and asymmetric information, the value of a firm is unaffected by how that firm is financed. This, therefore, implies that the mix of equity and debt used to finance a bank is irrelevant. To some extent this can be seen in practice. For example, an increase in equity capital for a bank can be seen to lead to a reduction in risk and a corresponding lowering of the required return on equity.

Whilst a helpful result, the MM theorem is nevertheless based on some strong assumptions which do not hold in practice. This can lead to effects that may cause banks to find a particular capital structure more attractive. For example, the cost of default or financial distress may make equity financing appealing, whilst the tax deductibility of interest expenses would favour more debt financing.

The MM theorem suggests that banks should be indifferent to the proportion of equity capital they hold. Whilst high equity capital would reduce return in good times, it would also increase returns in bad times. This stabilisation of returns and reduction of risk would suggest that the 'equity risk premium' investors require in order to effectively provide capital would reduce, and the required return on capital should be lower. However, banks do generally consider equity capital to be expensive and believe they are most profitable when they operate at a high leverage with relatively low capital bases.

Correspondingly, the cost of bank failure can mean that having banks with larger capital bases is more socially advantageous, as the capital serves as a buffer that absorbs losses and reduces the probability of bank default. This, in turn, protects bank creditors and (in systems with explicit or implicit public guarantees) taxpayers. This is one reason for regulation to define minimum capital requirements for banks.

In general, the cost of funding is associated with various xVA terms (Figure 14.1), specifically funding value adjustment (FVA) and margin value adjustment (MVA) for the cost of debt financing ('cost of funding'), and capital value adjustment (KVA) for the cost of equity financing ('cost of capital').

In general, banks consider funding and capital costs to be different components and assess their costs separately. This is only an approximation of the overall balance sheet financing required, due to the clear linkage and potential for an optimal balance sheet financing strategy in a world where not all of the MM assumptions hold.

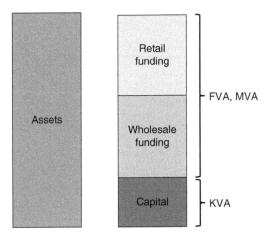

Figure 14.1   Simple illustration of funding and capital costs and their relationship to xVA terms.

Furthermore, the treatment of balance sheet financing costs via xVA adjustments may need simplifying in relation to the following aspects:

- *Different types of financing instruments.* There are a multitude of funding sources in terms of both debt and equity funding.
  - o *Debt funding.* Retail deposits, unsecured wholesale funding (e.g. bonds), and secured wholesale funding (e.g. covered bonds).
  - o *Equity funding.* Common equity, contingent capital, preferred shares, and subordinated debt.
- *Marginal cost of financing.* For assessing new transactions or businesses, it is the marginal cost of financing that represents the financing cost of the opportunity. However, this is rather hard to assess, and the current financing costs may be used as a proxy.
- *Financing should be asset specific.* Related to the above, financing is asset specific. It should be cheaper to fund an asset with better credit quality and also to fund a more liquid asset (e.g. it might be possible to repo certain liquid securities). However, financing costs may not always be accurately assessed based on credit quality and liquidity.

Another important aspect is that regulation around capital, funding, and liquidity means that banks must comply with multiple metrics when financing their balance sheets. Different banks may be more or less sensitive to these metrics, and a single metric may be the primary determinant of costs (Table 14.1). For example, a bank may be leverage ratio constrained, even when having met its required total loss-absorbing capital (TLAC) ratio. A bank's debt funding strategy may not be consistent with the liquidity coverage ratio (LCR) or net stable funding ratio (NSFR), which may require additional funding of high-quality liquid assets (HQLAs) and/or longer-term funding. Some banks may be more or less sensitive to the various metrics due to their natural client base and financing (e.g. size of deposit base and general credit quality of borrowers). Furthermore,

Table 14.1 Key regulatory metrics for capital and funding.

Capital	Minimum capital ratios
	Total loss-absorbing capital
	Capital stress tests
	Leverage ratio
Funding	Liquidity coverage ratio
	Net stable funding ratio
	Liquidity stress tests

certain types of transactions (e.g. derivatives) may have certain behaviours with respect to the metrics which should ideally be captured. It may not be easy to assess how much additional capital, funding, and contingent liquidity should be represented in terms of assessing new opportunities.

Since a bank finances itself via both debt and equity, the cost of each should be calculated based on its underlying costs, together with the type of transaction, identity of counterparty, and consideration of the above metrics. The cost of debt requires consideration regarding the underlying maturity and funding liabilities used (e.g. deposits and wholesale funding). The cost of such liabilities is to a large extent known (e.g. the spread from issuing a bond). The deductibility of tax on interest rates paid should also be a consideration. The cost of capital is more subjective since it is the return paid to shareholders, which is a policy decision by the bank, but it must deliver a satisfactory return from the shareholder point of view (or they will sell their shares). However, the cost of capital mainly arises from common equity and so, unlike debt funding, does not require the consideration of many different securities or maturities.

14.2 CAPITAL

14.2.1 Minimum Capital Ratios and Capital Costs

Capital (equity) has a number of different definitions:

- it is the accounting value that remains after subtracting a bank's (fixed) liabilities from its assets;
- it is what is owed to the bank's owners – the shareholders – after liquidating all the assets at their current value; and
- it is the buffer that protects the bank from insolvency.

The cost of capital reflects the perceived risk of a company's equity to investors and the bank will seek to outperform this return via a defined return on capital (ROC). Whilst this cost is not an explicit and contractual payment, the ROC is a real cost of raising equity. Banks will make some assessment of the ROC on a given transaction given the underlying revenue and other costs. Historically, this assessment revolved around a bank's own assessment of its required capital, often known as economic capital.

Table 14.2 Regulatory capital requirements pre- and post-GFC.

		Pre-GFC	Post-GFC
Quantity	Minimum capital	8%	10.5%
	Countercyclical capital buffer	N/A	0–2.5%
	G-SIB surcharge		1–3.5%
Tests	Leverage ratio	N/A	Yes (3–6%)
	Stress tests		Yes
Type	Minimum CET1	2%	7%
	Minimum Tier 1	4%	9%
	Hybrid capital	Eligible	Ineligible

Prior to the global financial crisis (GFC), banks were subject to general regulatory standards requiring a minimum capital buffer equal to 8% of risk-weighted assets (RWAs). To protect the taxpayer against future bank bailouts, this minimum capital ratio has been gradually raised to 10.5%, with the inclusion of a mandatory capital conservation buffer of 2.5% (Table 14.2). Furthermore, there are potential additional requirements due to a countercyclical capital buffer and globally-systemically-important bank (G-SIB) surcharge. The TLAC of G-SIB banks must be at least 16% (rising to 18% from January 2022). Furthermore, the quality of the capital base is also required to be better, with more capital needing to be common equity and not other Tier 1, Tier 2, or hybrid securities. There is also a separate leverage ratio (LR) with a minimum of 3% (and higher for G-SIB banks) and stress tests that may become the binding constraints for some banks (in the event that they need to raise capital ratios further so as to meet these requirements).

The regulatory changes over the past few years have generally made banks focus less on economic capital and more on regulatory capital. This has arisen because the regulatory-defined minimum capital ratios are almost certainly higher than any economic capital requirements a bank may calculate. Regulatory capital, as defined by minimum capital ratios, the LR, and stress tests, is the binding constraint for most banks. The higher minimum regulatory capital ratios and need for Common Equity Tier 1 (CET1) capital (Section 4.2.2) have meant that banks have had to focus less on actual profits from their derivative activities and more on the ROC. Certain areas of a bank that have relatively high capital requirements may tend to focus more on the ROC. In general, even before recent regulation this was the case for some derivatives businesses.

Higher capital ratios have been contentious. On the one hand, they are supported by the risks associated with high bank leverage and the social costs of a financial crisis. Indeed, there are arguments that bank capital ratios should be even higher: the Minneapolis Plan calls for a minimum CET1 capital ratio of 23.5% of RWAs for the largest banks, achieved over a period of five years, with G-SIB banks then having to increase the ratio further to 38%. On the other hand, opponents of higher capital requirements argue that these may significantly increase the cost of bank credit and slow economic growth.

It is certainly now clear that when banks have to increase their capital ratios quickly, they are likely to constrain the supply of credit. The underlying transition costs can be lower when the capital adjustment is staggered (as has been the case) and/or takes place in the upswing of the credit cycle. Nevertheless, there is evidence that the equilibrium costs of higher bank capital are relatively small. This is supported by the MM theorem and can be seen since, for example, banks with weaker capital positions tend to face higher funding costs (Dagher et al. 2016).

Specific components such as the alpha factor (Section 13.4.5) and methodologies such as the standardised approach for counterparty credit risk (SA-CCR) (Section 13.4.3) create additional credit risk capital costs due to grossing up the value of a position, and can be particularly acute for certain transactions, such as in-the-money uncollateralised ones.[1] This may have led some banks, even pre-GFC, to focus more on capital costs in derivatives businesses. Furthermore, in addition to the overall capital ratios, post-GFC regulation has also raised the quantity of RWAs in some specific areas (that the capital ratios are calculated against). This has been particularly important for derivatives due to:

- the introduction of a credit value adjustment (CVA) capital charge (Section 4.2.5);
- the need to use stressed data when calibrating internal model method (IMM) models (Section 13.4.5);
- the need to use a larger margin period of risk (MPoR) in certain situations (Section 13.4.5); and
- the capitalisation of central counterparty default funds (Section 13.6.3).

There is also the fact that there are a number of imminent regulatory changes impacting derivatives RWAs specifically, such as the SA-CCR (Section 13.4.3) and basic CVA/standardised CVA (BA-CVA/SA-CVA) (Section 13.4) approaches. Finally, there is the fact that derivative regulatory RWAs can be quite volatile due to positions moving in- and out-of-the-money (this will be shown in Section 19.3.2). All of this has led to the need to focus more heavily on capital costs for derivatives, often known as KVA.

14.2.2   Leverage Ratio

As discussed in Section 4.2.7, the LR is a measure that is intended to complement capital ratios by restricting a bank from being excessively leveraged (according to certain definitions of capital and exposure). The LR implies that exposure must – on average – be supported by a certain percentage of (Tier 1) capital. Of course, exposures will already be supported by some amount of capital based on various requirements (market risk, credit risk, operational risk, counterparty risk). If this amount of capital is less than the LR percentage (α in Equation 5.3) then this could be defined as LR constraining business since it will tend to reduce the bank's LR.

An obvious solution to the above problem is to price the capital as the maximum of the normal capital requirements and the LR-implied requirement. However, if the bank is not LR constrained – shown by the case where $\alpha \geq \alpha_{req}$ in Equation 5.4 – then this may be considered unnecessary.

---

[1] An in-the-money derivatives portfolio can be seen to behave similarly to an amortising loan, but would require approximately 40% extra capital, with an alpha factor of 1.4. Since alpha is a general adjustment across all positions, the alpha in this context is clearly too high.

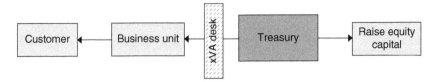

Figure 14.2   Simple illustration of charging capital requirements to originating businesses.

14.2.3   Cost of Capital

Cost of capital is usually quantified via a benchmark percentage ROC that should ideally be achieved in order to pay a return to the investors who have provided the capital.
Banks' derivatives businesses, like any other, are typically subject to capital hurdles due
to the associated costs. The given ROC applied is an internal and somewhat subjective
parameter, with around 8–10% being a commonly used base assumption. However, since
profits generating an ROC will be taxed, an effective tax rate (for the region in question)
will also be incorporated, leading to a higher effective rate. The number may be grossed up
further by other costs, and so the gross ROC that banks aim for on their over-the-counter
(OTC) derivative activities is probably more in the region of 15–20%. Traditionally, capital hurdles have represented guidelines but are now becoming more rigorously priced in
via KVA (Chapter 19).

The increasing sophistication around quantifying costs (and benefits) such as CVA and
FVA in banks and charging (paying) them to the originating business has also led to a push
towards a more active KVA approach in line with this. It is therefore natural that the xVA
desk may be responsible for correctly passing on the capital costs to a derivatives business
unit (Figure 14.2).

Whilst it is certainly reasonable that the *size* of the capital requirements could be accurately calculated with reference to the underlying regulation, the cost component (ROC)
remains a more subjective component that would need to be assessed on the basis of the
minimum required return by shareholders. This should also consider MM-type considerations that a higher capital would, in turn, lead to a lower required return for shareholders.
It may also consider other qualitative components, such as franchises and other relationships with the same clients. Ultimately, a bank may wish to look at the ROC by client (or
even group of clients) and not impose the cost on all client activities separately. All of the
above makes the correct assessment of the ROC more difficult and subjective. Banks may
accept that the ROC for derivatives will be low but partially subsidised by revenues from
other business with the same – or even different – clients.

14.3   FUNDING

14.3.1   Overview

Historically, banks and other financial institutions did not – explicitly – consider funding
costs in the valuation of derivatives. This was for a number of inter-related reasons:

- banks could fund rather easily via deposits or raising money in the wholesale
  market;

- through the above, banks could fund at a rate close to Interbank Offered Rates (IBORs) or better, and an IBOR was viewed as being a close proxy for the risk-free rate; and
- banks generally treated derivatives (from a funding point of view) as short-term assets and therefore considered only short-term funding costs where relevant.

Funding costs and associated funding risk were rarely considered in relation to derivatives, even those that were very long-dated.

Prior to the GFC, bank funding costs largely moved in line with 'risk-free' interest rates set by central banks. All of this changed with the onset of the GFC: some sources of funding evaporated rapidly, and other funding sources became materially more expensive. Some banks, such as those with low capital ratios or the inability to accept deposits and funded mainly via wholesale markets, were particularly sensitive to this increase.

Whilst funding costs have eased in the years since the GFC, they are still high compared to pre-crisis, and the market has experienced a regime shift and funding costs are now of greater importance. Additionally, some of the regulatory response to the crisis will make funding of positions, especially derivatives, increasingly costly. For example:

- *Liquidity coverage ratio.* This requires banks to have sufficient HQLAs to withstand a 30-day stressed funding scenario and will restrict the use of short-term funding, again creating additional cost. Downgrade triggers, sometimes used in derivatives contracts, are especially penalised (Section 4.3.3).
- *Net stable funding ratio.* This requires banks to use more stable sources of funding, which again will be more expensive. Derivatives suffer due to having a zero net funding benefit and other costs (Section 4.3.4).
- *The clearing mandate.* The requirement to centrally clear standardised OTC derivatives will create significant funding costs due to the requirement to post initial margins and default funds to central counterparties (CCPs) (Section 4.4.1).
- *Bilateral margin rules.* The requirements to post margin (collateral) against non-clearable OTC derivatives (Section 4.4.2) will increase funding requirements, again predominantly through initial margin.

All of the above has led banks to become much more aware of the need to quantify and manage funding costs alongside more traditional areas such as counterparty risk. In derivatives businesses, such funding is usually defined by the need to post and receive margin. Since variation margin is a two-way payment, this gives rise to both costs and benefits, which are generally defined within FVA. Initial margin – due to the required segregation – gives rise only to funding costs which are associated with MVA. Both FVA and MVA create a clear need to define funding curves, just as credit curves are required for CVA.

It may be hard to separate general funding costs from the need to hold HQLAs in order to meet requirements such as the LCR. This is because holding a large HQLA buffer may reduce funding costs overall, and it may not be completely clear how much of the HQLA should be apportioned to a given business. Likewise, the NSFR may cause a bank to fund its balance sheet more conservatively, but it may not be able to define precisely the additional cost of doing this. Such costs may, therefore, be borne implicitly across the bank or transfer pricing more heterogeneously (Section 14.3.6). However, there are components (e.g. the need to pre-fund ratings downgrades under the LCR) that may be easier to capture heterogeneously and charge to the originating business.

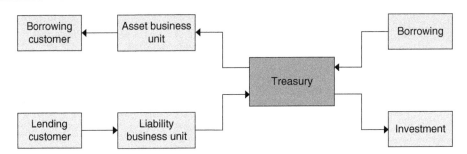

Figure 14.3 Simple illustration of charging and remunerating funding requirements to originating businesses.

Most banks have funds transfer pricing (FTP) frameworks (Figure 14.3). The Treasury charges business units that require funding to buy assets, and remunerates business units that attract funds via liabilities. The internal price of funding is based on the market price for funds for the relevant maturity and currency, and is traditionally transferred on an accrual basis. The Treasury then manages aggregate mismatches in the balance sheet through an asset-liability management (ALM) strategy.

A problem with derivatives in the above set-up is that they can be both assets and liabilities and therefore represent both costs and benefits. Furthermore, since derivatives are typically mark-to-market (MTM), it makes sense to do the same with the associated funding costs and benefits, rather than just accruing them over time. It therefore makes sense for the xVA desk to act as an intermediary between the derivatives business and the treasury to appropriate, own, manage, and transfer the costs and benefits of funding. The precise relationship between the treasury and the xVA desk will be important and discussed in more detail in Section 21.3.1.

Recent years have seen the incorporation of funding costs into the pricing and valuation of uncollateralised derivatives trades. Aside from anecdotal evidence and the observation of clearing levels, the clearest manifestation of FVA is via Markit's Totem consensus pricing service (Section 5.3.5). Generally, FVA is an adjustment alongside CVA that accounts for the net funding cost or benefit of the trade in question. Banks have generally moved from charging funding on an accrual basis to a more upfront FVA approach (Figure 14.4). Key catalysts for this have been significantly-increased costs of funding and the requirement to rely less on short-term funding.

FVA has, therefore, become a key component of the clearing price for derivatives and will be routinely priced into uncollateralised (and potentially some collateralised) trades by most banks (Chapter 18), especially those that are long-dated (Figure 14.5). Banks may also pay special attention to cases such as one-way margin agreements or in-the-money portfolios.

Although this will be discussed in more detail in Section 18.2.5, it is useful to characterise the approximate relationship between CVA, debt value adjustment (DVA), and FVA (Figure 14.6). FVA is generally made up of funding cost adjustment (FCA) and funding benefit adjustment (FBA). This is analogous to bilateral CVA (BCVA) (Section 17.3.3) which consists of CVA and DVA. CVA and FCA are related to expected positive exposure (EPE), whilst DVA and FBA arise from expected negative exposure (ENE). A threshold in a margin agreement should have the effect of reducing FCA and FBA (just as it does

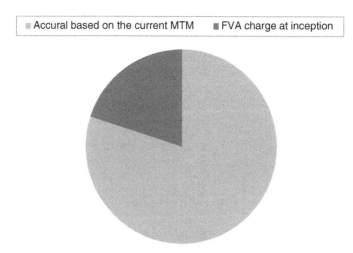

Figure 14.4   Market practice on pricing funding. Source: Deloitte Solum CVA Survey (2013).

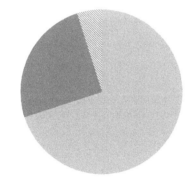

Figure 14.5   Market practice on pricing FVA into trades. Source: Solum FVA Survey (2014).

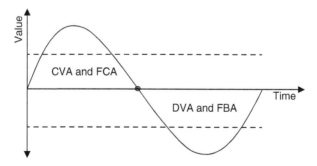

Figure 14.6   Illustration of the relationship between bilateral CVA (CVA and DVA) and FVA (FCA and FBA). The dotted lines represent thresholds in the margin agreement for each party.

for CVA and DVA). Note that this may be asymmetric: for example, it would be expected that a one-way margin agreement acting against a party would remove their FBA (since they must post margin against any negative value) but leave the FCA unaffected.

Note that FVA may present an immediate discrepancy between pricing and valuation. For pricing purposes, a bank would presumably wish to use its own funding costs, but for accounting purposes, the exit price implies that the bank should rather reference a market cost of funding.

Some have argued that FVA should not be considered in the pricing or valuation of derivatives.[2] The industry has largely ignored such arguments, which imply significant structural changes to the current treatment of funding.[3] Indeed, these arguments are now more in relation to the accounting treatment of FVA than to the consideration of funding when pricing.[4]

14.3.2   Cost of Funding

The cost of funding of derivatives could be linked to (at least) three inter-related aspects:

- uncollateralised market values;
- cash flows; and
- margin flows.

It is important to capture all relevant aspects but also to avoid double-counting. For example, an in-the-money uncollateralised derivatives portfolio will generally require margin to be posted on the hedges. Furthermore, cash flow payments on collateralised derivatives will be largely offset by margin flows in the opposite direction. Given that most bank's derivatives books are mainly hedged from a market risk point of view, the main source of funding requirements on a day-to-day basis will be margin moves. The assessment of margin will usually, therefore, be the primary determinant of funding costs (and benefits). However, it is also important to capture large cash flows (e.g. novating into a large in-the-money derivatives portfolio) and uncollateralised market values (e.g. a relatively profitable transaction).

It also makes sense to charge a business for funding on a net, or portfolio, basis. This means that funding benefits (e.g. receiving margin or a negative market value) will tend to offset funding costs. However, there is also the question of what to do if the total funding position is beneficial for a given business. There may be inherent asymmetry: a net derivative asset will probably be considered to require long-term unsecured funding, but a net derivative liability may not be considered to represent an equivalent benefit. The NSFR treatment of derivatives also reflects this view, where net derivative assets incur a 100% required stable funding (RSF) charge, whereas net derivatives liabilities represent 0% available stable funding (ASF). Indeed, it may be appropriate to incorporate derivatives more fully in the ALM process so that, for example, short-term derivatives liabilities

---

[2] Hull and White (2012a, 2012b).

[3] For example, requiring that the internal treasury of a bank should not charge a derivatives desk a funding cost and should lend to them at the OIS rate.

[4] Andersen et al. (2016) came to the same conclusion as Hull and White for valuation, but argue that a bank can price using FVA to maximise shareholder value.

are not considered as fully funding longer-term derivatives assets. These aspects are at the heart of the definition of FVA and will be discussed in more detail in Section 18.3.2.

There is also the need to incorporate correctly the costs arising from contingent funding. The LCR forces banks to hold HQLAs against potential liquidity shocks. Such HQLAs will produce relatively low returns which will not offset the funding costs. Furthermore, any returns from HQLAs will likely be due to the inherent credit and liquidity risk and should not, therefore, be seen as reducing the underlying funding cost. A good FTP framework will allocate contingent liquidity costs to the originating businesses.

The cost of funding differs from the cost of capital (Section 14.2.1) in a number of ways:

- it can be partially observed via the spreads of securities (e.g. bonds) trading in the secondary market and issuance levels in the primary market;
- whilst more observable, it arises from multiple different instruments with different characteristics (secured/unsecured, maturity, and availability); and
- it is not asset specific, and so whereas capital charges differ across transactions and clients, the cost of a unit of funding may be seen as the same, irrespective of the use of the funding.

In general, the funding cost of a bank may be seen as the combination of four components (Figure 14.7):

- *Risk-free rates.* Central banks implement monetary policy by setting their own short-term borrowing and lending rates, which in turn define short-term market interest rates. These interest rates can be viewed as 'risk free' given that the risk of the central bank defaulting is generally considered to be very low. Longer-term rates reflect market participants' expectations of future central bank policy. Because risk-free rates are a common component of funding costs for all types of bank funding, it is common to refer to a bank's 'funding spreads' as the difference between funding costs and an appropriate risk-free rate at a given maturity.

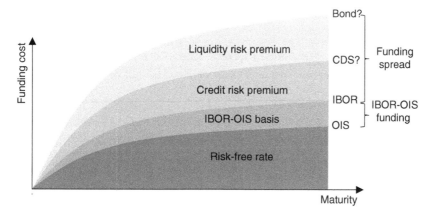

Figure 14.7   Illustration of the funding cost for a bank.

- *IBOR-OIS basis.* This is the difference between the most reasonable proxy for the risk-free rate (overnight indexed spread, OIS) and the reference for defining funding spreads (typically an IBOR). This component has existed for technical reasons and may disappear with the transition away from IBORs (Section 14.3.4).
- *Credit risk premium.* When buying bank debt, investors will demand compensation for bearing the credit risk that the bank may default on its debt. The credit risk premium will be largely for more risky and less well-capitalised banks. An individual bank's credit risk premium may increase if investors consider it to be riskier. The credit risk premium of the banking sector may increase if investors believe that all banks are more risky. The credit risk premium will also depend on the maturity of the borrowing and other characteristics such as whether it is unsecured or secured, with the latter being lower credit risk.
- *Liquidity risk premium.* Investors will also factor in liquidity when they decide on the price they will pay and/or the return they will demand for an investment. Investors will demand compensation in the form of a liquidity risk premium in exchange for investing in illiquid assets. A key determinant of the liquidity risk premium is the maturity of an asset, with longer-dated assets requiring a higher return than shorter-dated ones. This is demanded in return for the inconvenience of not being able to access these funds for a longer period of time. Liquidity risk premiums may depend on both idiosyncratic and macro risk factors. The idiosyncratic component may depend on factors such as how frequently a bank's debt is traded in secondary markets. The macro component may be driven by confidence in the banking sector in general.

In the above, the funding cost of the bank is represented as the sum of all components. The credit default swap (CDS) market may be expected to include all components except the liquidity risk premium, which would, therefore, be observable via the so-called CDS-bond basis. The additional liquidity premium would compensate a bondholder for potential illiquidity when selling a bond (Longstaff et al. 2005). This represents (by convention) a negative CDS-bond basis (bond spreads higher than CDS spreads), although this does not necessarily have to be the case, nor has it always been the case historically.

14.3.3   The Risk-free Rate, IBOR, and OIS

Historically, IBORs were thought to be largely free of credit risk due to the extremely small default probabilities of banks and short tenor (three or six months).[5] An alternative risk-free proxy has been the yields of triple-A treasury bonds, again considered to be largely free of credit risk due to the extremely high-quality rating of the sovereign issuer. IBORs were generally thought to be preferable to treasury bonds due to better liquidity, the lack of problems with technical factors (such as repo specialness and tax issues), and the close links between IBORs and funding costs. Hence, pre-2008, the market standard discount (or funding) curve was the three- or six-month IBOR curve.[6]

---

[5] For example, a typical quote from a paper discussing derivative pricing prior to the crisis states: 'LIBOR is not a risk-free rate, but it is close to it as the participating banks have very strong credit ratings.'

[6] Depending on the currency, the most liquid point may have been either maturity. However, the differences between the IBOR at different tenors was extremely small.

The OIS rate is generally the (unsecured) interest rate that banks use to borrow and lend from one another in the overnight market. There are conceptual similarities between OIS and IBORs. Both are unsecured, and whilst the former reflects a single-day time horizon, the latter is longer (e.g. three months). Furthermore, OIS rates are averages from actual transactions, whereas an IBOR is just the average (with the highest and lowest submissions removed) of banks' stated opinions.

Before the GFC, the basis between OIS and IBORs was tight (less than 10 basis points). However, the crisis caused the IBOR-OIS basis to widen dramatically, as can be seen from Figure 14.8 for Fed Funds and the USD three-month London Interbank Offered Rate (LIBOR). Whilst the basis is much tighter than during the worst point of the GFC, it is still material. This effect can be seen in other ways, such as via basis swap spreads, which represent the exchange of rates in the same currency. For example, the three-month Euro Interbank Offered Rate (EURIBOR) versus the six-month EURIBOR basis swap spread went from less than 1 bp to over 40 bps in October 2008 after the Lehman Brothers bankruptcy. This represents the additional unsecured credit risk in the six-month tenor versus the three-month tenor. When banks were perceived as risk free, such differences did not exist, but as soon as this myth dissolved, basis swap spreads blew up dramatically. The difference or 'spread' between the IBORs and OIS rates is an important measure of risk and liquidity. A higher spread is typically interpreted as an indication of decreased willingness to lend by major banks. Whilst this basis has tightened in recent years, the use of IBORs as a ubiquitous risk-free rate is considered wrong.

The historical situation where IBORs were seen as a good proxy for the risk-free rate drove this rate to be used as a common funding reference in transactions such as loans, deposits, floating-rate notes, and derivatives. The use of IBORs as a reference represents

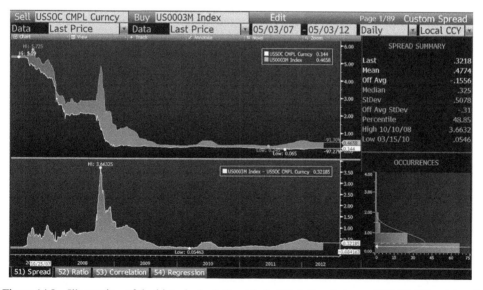

Figure 14.8   Illustration of the historical relationship in US dollars between OIS (Fed Funds) and three-month LIBOR. The top graph shows the respective levels, whilst the bottom line shows the difference between the two. Source: Bloomberg, reproduced with permission. www.bloomberg.com.

a problem in a market where an IBOR cannot be reasonably used as a proxy for the risk-free rate. In derivatives, another problem with the use of IBORs in defining funding is that collateralised derivatives usually specify the relevant OIS for the remuneration of cash margin. The presence of the IBOR-OIS basis, therefore, causes a technical problem in terms of defining funding and xVA adjustment.

Due to their short tenor and unbiased submission process, OIS rates would seem to be a more logical risk-free rate. The daily tenor of such transactions means they should carry a minimal amount of credit risk. The transition away from IBORs will, therefore, simplify the definition and application of xVA adjustments.

14.3.4 IBOR Transition

First published in 1986, LIBOR fixings and other related IBORs have been important reference rates in the derivatives market. Historically, IBOR rates have been used as a measure of credit risk, since they reflect the confidence banks have in each other's credit quality. IBOR rates are also hardwired into many areas of the financial markets as a reference rate. An IBOR is typically constructed by taking quotes from a range of banks on how much they would be charged in interest to borrow money on a short-term basis from another bank. The outliers are excluded and an average is taken. LIBOR rates have historically been published across five currencies and over a range of tenors. LIBOR fixings are intended to represent the interest rate charged on short-term (unsecured) loans made between banks. IBORs are very important to financial markets due to the fact they are extensively referenced in derivative, bond, and loan documentation, and in a wide range of consumer borrowing and lending instruments such as deposits, mortgages, and loans.

IBOR rates represent indicative unsecured lending between banks, and they are the rates charged (determined daily) for banks to borrow from other banks, usually for terms of three months on an uncollateralised basis. An IBOR is risky in the sense that the lending bank loans cash to the borrowing bank on an unsecured basis, albeit for a relatively short period. An IBOR is supposed to represent an average interest rate that a bank would be charged if borrowing from other such banks.

An IBOR was always understood not to be truly risk free, but was seen as a robust benchmark with a relevant grounding in the extensive market of interbank lending, which prior to the GFC was seen as very low risk. In the aftermath of the GFC, there was a series of fixing scandals in relation to IBORs which damaged their reputation as being objective benchmarks.[7] Furthermore, at the same time, activity in the market on which IBORs are based – unsecured interbank term borrowing – declined substantially. This was partly in response to regulation (such as NSFR) that treated interbank borrowing as unstable.

In February 2013, the G20 commissioned the Financial Stability Board (FSB) to review the major interest rate benchmarks, as a result of concerns regarding the reliability and robustness of these IBOR benchmarks. The FSB (2014) recommended their general replacement with so-called risk-free rates (RFRs). Whilst IBOR rates will not be banned, regulators globally have given a clear signal that firms should transition away from IBORs towards alternative overnight RFRs.

---

[7] BBC (2013). Timeline: Libor-fixing scandal (6 February). www.bbc.co.uk.

Table 14.3   Example RFRs.

Currency	RFR	Abbreviation
USD	Secured Overnight Financing Rate	SOFR
JPY	Tokyo Overnight Average Rate	TONAR
GBP	Sterling Overnight Index Average	Reformed SONIA
CHF	Swiss Average Rate Overnight	SARON
EUR	Euro Short Term Rate	ESTER

RFRs are generally overnight secured or unsecured rates and are defined on a currency-by-currency basis, with no uniform definition nor method for their calculation used across all currencies. They are generally required to represent actual market funding rates based on reliable data. They should also be robust to changes in market structure and subject to appropriate controls and governance. Some examples are shown in Table 14.3. For example, the Sterling Overnight Index Average is calculated as the weighted average of the interest rates charged for all unsecured loans (of more than £25m) reported by market participants in the London market.

Unlike IBORs, RFRs do not – generally – reflect the credit risk of the borrowing institution, since they are intended to be risk free. The other main difference is that RFRs have no term structure (yet, although term RFRs are not yet being proposed) as they only reference overnight rates, unlike IBORs, which are defined by various terms. RFR-based transactions will accrue interest over the relevant time period and, by necessity, will be calculated in arrears.

The transition to RDRs is complex and requires significant work given the vast number of transactions specifying IBOR rates. Current fallbacks to IBOR (such as using the last known rate) only envisage that a rate is temporarily unavailable rather than permanently withdrawn. If this 'same rate' persisted indefinitely then it could be very disadvantageous to one party during a period of significant interest rate change. The industry is, therefore, working on better transition mechanisms for each RDR. Since RDRs are generally lower than the IBORs they replace, this would imply replacing the IBOR reference in a contract with the relevant RDR plus a spread. However, since the spread between IBOR and RDR rates is not fixed, this would not lead to economically equivalent contracts.

Despite the transitional changes, the move to RFRs will simplify derivatives and the definition of funding costs by removing IBOR-OIS basis risks currently seen in collateralised trades. It will also tend to align the margin remuneration rate more closely with the standard reference rate (although it is unclear whether the margin remuneration rates will be standardised to the defined RFR in all regions).

14.3.5   Funding Spreads

Derivatives, due to their dynamic nature and the funding approach of banks, are not term funded. Traditionally, the funding has been generally considered to be short term, but regulation (e.g. LCR and NSFR) is pushing banks to rely less on short-term funding.

In general, the funding spread or term liquidity premium (TLP) will define the relevant funding curve for a bank. In terms of quantifying this funding curve, a starting point would be the range of funding sources used by a bank, such as:

- deposits (e.g. current accounts);
- unsecured money market (e.g. commercial paper);
- secured money market (e.g. repo);
- unsecured capital market (e.g. bonds); and
- secured capital market (e.g. covered bonds).

The above have different positives and negatives in terms of their characteristics, such as cost, duration (contractual or behavioural), and availability. These are often subjective judgements: for example, customer deposits have a very short term (typically one day). However, they are typically quite 'sticky', in that a bank's deposit base will not reduce substantially over a short period (especially due to depositor guarantee schemes that may reduce the chance of a bank 'run'). This can be seen as a 'behavioural adjustment', where the statistical maturity is not the same as the contractual maturity. Whilst this provides a reasonably stable and cheap source of funding, it may be difficult for banks to increase funding in this way by attracting more deposits, and some banks – for example, investment banks – cannot rely on a natural deposit base as a source of funding.

Furthermore, secured funding can only be achieved with sufficient liquid assets to use as margin, and the money market funding is short term (e.g. commercial paper has a fixed maturity of no more than 270 days). This leaves unsecured capital market funding as the most obvious benchmark for assessing new funding costs, since this would be the obvious place for a bank to raise money if required. There is also the question of whether to look at secondary or primary markets. The secondary market defines the current long-term unsecured funding cost, but the primary market may represent a more realistic basis for the marginal cost of raising new funding.

It may also be that CDS quotes are useful indicators of the funding costs of banks. Whilst they do not represent issuance levels, they may generally be more liquid than the secondary bond market.

Derivatives assets can be effectively used for margin for other derivatives liabilities (through netting), but they cannot be used as security against borrowing (e.g. repoed). This also suggests that an unsecured term funding rate would be more applicable for assessing the underlying funding costs.

Another consideration is the term: although to some extent funding should be priced according to its maturity and the underlying cost of borrowing money, it may be acceptable not to charge as if all assets were to be term funded. This may be implemented qualitatively by a flattening of the funding (TLP) curve. NSFR regulation should be a consideration on this point as a bank would only improve its NSFR by issuing funding beyond one year, and would presumably look significantly beyond this in order to create a stable NSFR. Hence, even short-term assets may need to be charged longer-term funding costs.

A bank's FTP curve for internal pricing of funding will, therefore, be set on a blended basis with all of the above considerations taken into account. Ultimately, the assessment of a funding curve will be – like the credit curve mapping in Section 12.2 – subjective and open to debate.

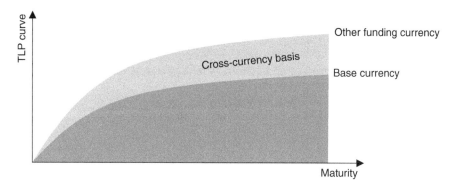

Figure 14.9 Illustration of cost of funding in different currencies and the cross-currency basis.

In terms of defining costs of funding in different currencies, a bank may issue in either a single currency or multiple currencies. It may, therefore, be possible to define the TLP curve in different currencies directly (Figure 14.9). Alternatively, a bank may need to use the foreign exchange (FX) markets to transfer funding via cross-currency basis swaps. These two methods should produce broadly similar results. Another post-GFC effect is that funding in certain currencies can be materially more expensive than others.

As noted previously, funding costs are asset specific. For example, a high-quality treasury bond can be repoed fairly easily, and it is, therefore, the financing cost via the repo market (haircut and spread) that is relevant. The existence of the repo market means that it is not necessary to consider the cost of borrowing money on an unsecured basis to buy the bond (which would be considerably higher). The funding of an asset should also depend on the credit quality of the asset itself, as lenders will charge funding rates that inevitably depend on the quality of the balance sheet of the borrower. For example, a bank trading with a triple-A counterparty should have lower marginal funding costs than if it were doing the same business with a lower-rated counterparty, since it will have a more beneficial effect on the credit spread premium in Figure 14.7. Whilst it is not practical to have many separate funding curves, it may be relevant to adjust FTP policy in certain cases (e.g. triple-A counterparties) so as to create the right incentive.

Given that funding references margin, the underlying remuneration will also be an important consideration. Typically, cash margin will be remunerated in the associated overnight rate in the relevant currency (e.g. Fed Funds). Since this will typically align as a good proxy for the risk-free rate in Figure 14.7, this creates self-consistency. However, if remuneration of margin is less than OIS (e.g. in the case of cash initial margin posted to a CCP), then the overall funding cost should be higher: even funding at OIS may be seen as costly. Indeed, segregation may be seen to create additional funding costs: initial margin received may be costly to segregate and may not earn a return.

Where there is clear value in the margin management process, such as being able to post non-cash margin and/or having a choice over the type of cash/securities, this may be seen as an additional cost (benefit) when receiving (posting) margin. The relevant haircuts in different markets (derivatives through the margin agreement and the current levels in the repo market) must also be factored in. Such benefits may be defined more explicitly as collateral value adjustments (ColVA) outside the main funding framework.

14.3.6   NSFR and LCR

Suppose a bank has an NSFR of 95% as a result of 950 ASF and 1,000 RSF. Assume that the bank has a desired NSFR of 105% and so raises additional long-term funding of 125 in five-year bonds with an average ASF ratio of 80%[8] and retires short-term debt with an ASF of 0%. This results in a higher cost of funding of 100 bps, this being the difference between the rate on the new long-term debt compared to the retired short-term debt. It may seem natural for the bank to charge the additional cost of the funding on a pro rata basis to businesses with RSF requirements, the logic being that the reason for raising the new funding was solely to improve the NSFR. This will clearly penalise businesses with high RSF compared to their natural funding costs.

Some RSFs – a good example being the charge for 20% of derivatives liabilities – do not require any normal funding (e.g. cash is not required). It may be argued that charging for these components may feel unnatural and may penalise an RSF-generating business that does not require additional funding, potentially to the detriment of shareholders. On the other hand, not charging the RSF will tend to deteriorate the bank's NSFR. An NSFR invariance pricing approach will lead to charges for components such as the 20% liability RSF charge. This will be discussed in more detail in Section 18.3.4.

A similar effect will occur with respect to the LCR and the need to hold HQLAs for various contingent liquidity stress events. To the extent that this requires additional funding beyond the normal strategy, this additional cost of HQLA should probably be transfer priced. If this is not the case, then new business will tend to deteriorate the bank's LCR as the incremental cost of additional HQLA will not be priced. A good example of this is the need to fund margin requirements (e.g. posting initial margin) for a three-notch rating downgrade. It is unlikely that, in the absence of the LCR, any funding would be put in place for this contingent liquidity. An LCR invariance pricing policy may, therefore, transfer price the full cost of funding the additional HQLA requirement. However, this does assume that there are no other benefits to having a strong LCR, such as lower funding or capital costs.

14.3.7   Accounting

Since FVA and MVA are reported in the financial statements of banks, it is also relevant to consider the cost of funding that would be used for such adjustments. As discussed in Section 5.3.3, from an accounting point of view, it is the exit price that drives the valuation, and entity-specific components cannot be included. It follows that the funding curve should reference the cost of funding of other market participants. There is also the question of whether the full contractual maturity of a transaction should be used, or some shorter period based on the fact that the transaction could be exited early if required. However, this could become difficult since an entity might argue that it would tactically exit certain transactions with parties with different funding costs depending on the characteristics of the transaction at the time (e.g. whether it is in-the-money and the tenor).

---

[8] This is the weighted average ASF for five-year debt, given that the ASF is 100% for maturities greater than one year and 0% for those less than one year.

All the above points have left market participants, accountants, and regulators in much debate over defining the cost of funding. Some of the questions that arise when incorporating funding into pricing are:

- the instruments a funding cost should be calibrated to (e.g. primary issuance, secondary bond trading, CDS quotes, or internal assessment of the cost of funding);
- whether a party should use its own cost of funding, the cost of funding of a counterparty (with whom it might exit the transaction if required), or a curve that is blended based on the cost of funding of market participants in general; and
- whether term funding should be assumed using the final contractual maturity of a transaction, or if a shorter tenor should be assumed, based on the fact that term funding is not required and/or that the transaction may be terminated early.

This will be discussed in more detail in Section 18.2.7.

15

Quantifying Exposure

15.1 METHODS FOR QUANTIFYING EXPOSURE

15.1.1 Overview

This chapter will present the various methods used to quantify exposure and other utilisation components, focusing mainly on the most common and generic approach of Monte Carlo simulation. The methodology for exposure quantification, including a discussion of the approaches to modelling risk factors in different asset classes and their co-dependencies, and also the computational aspects, will be explained. By way of illustration, a number of examples will be shown, looking in particular at the impact of aspects such as model choice and calibration, as well as the effect of netting and margin.

In general, counterparty risk is defined by future exposure, which is usually expressed in the form of potential future exposure (PFE), expected positive exposure (EPE), and expected negative exposure (ENE). These components are determined directly from knowing the distribution of the future value of the relevant portfolio. More generally, xVA calculations require the quantification of a 'utilisation' component, as discussed in Section 5.4.6 (Equation 5.6), which may represent aspects such as funding or capital. All such components can be seen as being directly, or indirectly, linked to the same distribution of future value (Table 15.1). For credit, funding, and margin, the utilisation component is directly linked to the value, with potential consideration of issues such as rehypothecation. For capital and initial margin, the expected capital profile (ECP) and expected initial margin profile (EIM) are more complex calculations but are also functions of the future value of the relevant portfolio. Hence, the problem of quantifying exposure can be broadened into the problem of quantifying the utilisation components (although we will refer to it as quantifying exposure).

Exposure quantification generally involves a long-term portfolio calculation and cannot be tackled by more short-term approximations. There are many complexities in exposure quantification that must also be dealt with, such as:

- *Model choice.* It is necessary to choose a model for each underlying risk factor, usually across multiple asset classes. Pragmatically, it is important to use relatively simple and tractable models to avoid the implementation and performance being inadequate. Note that it is necessary to use a generic model definition as xVA is generally a portfolio-level problem, and the underlying transactions must be treated in a self-consistent way.
- *Calibration.* The practical calibration of the chosen model to market and/or historical data is generally challenging given the large number of risk factors, lack of data for some components (e.g. volatility), and large number of correlation parameters. Numerical methods may be required for calibration to market prices.
- *Numerical implementation.* The choice of implementation of the model is important as it will impact performance and accuracy. Furthermore, the optimal implementation for one xVA component may not be the case for another.

Table 15.1   Utilisation components of different xVA terms. See Glossary for definitions.

Area	xVA term	Utilisation component	Calculation
Credit	CVA	EPE	max($value$, 0)
	DVA	ENE	min($value$, 0)
	n/a	PFE	Quantile of $value$
Funding (and margin)	FVA	EFV	$value$
	FCA	EPE	max($value$, 0)
	FBA	ENE	min($value$, 0)
Capital	KVA	ECP	Function of $value$
Initial margin	MVA	EIM	

- *Ageing.* In a long-term portfolio calculation, it is necessary to correctly 'age' a portfolio by taking into account cash flow payments, contract expiration, and cancellation features.
- *Path dependency.* Path dependencies can also be important, most commonly when it is necessary to treat termination clauses, margin, and physically-settled options.

As a result of the above, the practical calculation of exposure inevitably involves choosing a balance between sophistication and resource considerations.

15.1.2   Parametric Approaches

These approaches are not model-based but instead aim to parameterise exposure based on a number of simple parameters that have potentially been calibrated to more complex approaches. Their advantage is that they are simple, but they are not particularly risk-sensitive and often represent more complex features poorly.

The simplest such approach is the current exposure method (CEM), used historically in counterparty risk capital calculations, as discussed in Section 8.2. The new standardised approach for counterparty credit risk (SA-CCR) for capital (Section 13.4.3) is more sophisticated, although a bit more complicated. These approaches approximate future exposure as the current positive exposure plus an 'add-on' component that represents the uncertainty of the PFE. At the transaction level, the add-on component should account for:

- the specifics of the transaction in question (moneyness, currency, nature of cash flows, and maturity); and
- the volatility of the underlying asset class.

For example, longer time horizons will require larger add-ons, and volatile asset classes – such as foreign exchange (FX) and commodities – should attract larger add-ons. At the portfolio level, such approaches should also aim to capture:

- netting; and
- margin (both variation and initial margin).

Such effects are often difficult to incorporate accurately and often use fairly crude rules, although more sophisticated methodologies have been proposed (e.g. Berrahoui et al. 2019). These may still be attractive to small banks and market participants, who need a basic and easy-to-implement methodology for PFE, credit value adjustment (CVA), or xVA.

15.1.3   Semianalytical Methods

Semianalytical methods are generally more sophisticated than the simple parameter approaches as they are model-based. Their advantage lies in avoiding the time-consuming process of Monte Carlo simulation. A semianalytical method will generally be based on:

- making some simple assumptions regarding the risk factor(s) driving the exposure;
- finding the distribution of the exposure as defined by the above risk factor(s);
- calculating a semianalytical approximation to a risk metric for that exposure distribution.

Some very simple and general semianalytical expressions were described in Section 11.1.5 and formulas can be found in Appendix 11A. One product-specific and well-known semianalytical formula can be found in Sorensen and Bollier (1994), who show that the exposure of an interest rate swap (IRS) can be defined in terms of a series of interest rate swaptions.[1] The intuition is that the counterparty might default at any time in the future and, hence, effectively cancel the non-recovered value of the swap, economically equivalent to exercising a swaption.

The swaption analogy is illustrated in Figure 15.1, with more mathematical details given in Appendix 15A. The EPE of the swap will be defined by the interaction between two factors: the swaption payoff and the underlying swap duration (these are the two components in the simple approach given in Section 11.2.2, Equation 11.4). These quantities

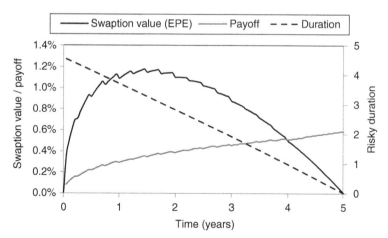

Figure 15.1   Illustration of interest rate swap EPE as defined by swaption values, which are given by the product of the swaption payoff and the risky duration value (shown on the secondary *y*-axis).

---

[1] We note that these semianalytical formulas are generally concerned with calculating risk-neutral exposures using underlyings such as traded swaption prices. Such approaches can also be used for real-world calculations (as is usual for PFE), but this is not as straightforward.

respectively increase and decrease monotonically over time. The overall swaption value, therefore, peaks at an intermediate point.

Spreadsheet 15.1 Semianalytical calculation of the exposure for a swap.

This approach naturally captures effects such as the asymmetry between payer and receiver swaps (Figure 15.2) and unequal payment frequencies, such as in a basis swap. In the former case, the underlying swaptions are in-the-money (ITM) or out-of-the-money (OTM) for payer and receiver swaps respectively. In the latter case, the strike of the swaptions moves significantly OTM when an institution receives a quarterly cash flow whilst not needing (yet) to make a semiannual one.

The Sorensen and Bollier formula gives a useful insight into exposure quantification: specifically that the exposure calculation of terms such as EPE will be at least as complex as pricing the underlying product itself. To quantify the EPE of a swap, one needs to know about swaption volatility (across time and strike), components far beyond those needed to price the swap itself. The value of the swap does not depend significantly on volatility, and yet the EPE for the swap does. The above intuition will also be useful when discussing the calibration of volatility in exposure models (Section 15.4).

The above analogy can be extended to other products, since any non-path-dependent transaction can be represented as a series of European options. A semianalytical approach would clearly be the method of choice for evaluating the exposure of a single transaction, although some cases such as cross-currency swaps, and more exotic products, will still be problematic. In some circumstances, semianalytical approximations can also be extended beyond the single transaction level to, for example, a portfolio of IRSs in a single currency, as discussed by Brigo and Masetti (2005b). The ability to do this may often be useful, as some end user counterparties may trade a rather narrow range of underlying products, the

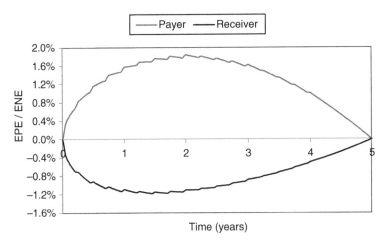

Figure 15.2   Illustration of the EPE for a payer interest rate swap as defined by the swaption values and the ENE for the same swap (or the EPE for the equivalent receiver swap).

exposure of which may be modelled semianalytically. However, multidimensional portfolios will typically need to be treated in a more generic approach.

Obvious drawbacks of such semianalytical approaches are:

- They depend on simplifying assumptions made with respect to the risk factors involved. Hence, complicated distributional assumptions cannot typically be incorporated. Put another way, the model(s) chosen must allow analytical tractability.
- Path-dependent aspects (exercises, breaks) will be hard to capture, as will margin, which is path-dependent, although approximations for collateralised exposures may be easier to formulate, as discussed in Section 15.5.
- It may be possible to incorporate netting or, more generally, portfolio effects at some level. For example, Brigo and Masetti (2005b) consider an approach for a portfolio in a single currency. Note that the above approaches are risk neutral by their nature and therefore would not naturally support the use of real-world calibrations (although this may not be a major concern).
- Such approaches may not be future-proof. In particular, the need to incorporate new products and changes in market practice (e.g. the increasing use of initial margins) may be hard to capture.

Whilst there will be situations where analytical calculations may be possible (e.g. quantifying the CVA of a counterparty trading in only a single currency), the fact that such calculations are not generic is difficult from an operational point of view.

Note also that certain cases where the EPE is equal, or approximately equal, to the expected future value (EFV) can be treated more easily, potentially without the need for complicated calculations. Two examples are:

- *ITM portfolios.* Where the EPE is close to the EFV (see Figure 15.3).
- *Options with upfront premiums.* Where EPE is equal to EFV.

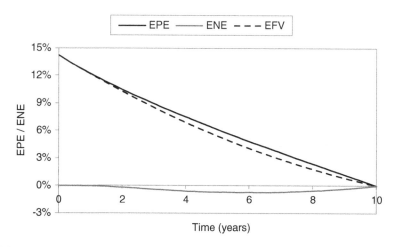

Figure 15.3   EPE, ENE, and EFV for an ITM portfolio.

15.1.4   Monte Carlo Simulation

Monte Carlo simulation, whilst the most complex and time-consuming method to quantify exposure, is generic and copes with many of the complexities, such as transaction specifics, path dependency, portfolio effects, and collateralisation. It is the only method that in the case of a high-dimensionality portfolio can realistically capture the relatively large number of risk factors and their correlations.

A generic approach also provides flexibility as market practice and regulation changes. For example, initial margins have been rare in the past but are becoming increasingly important (although incorporating dynamic initial margins into Monte Carlo simulation is complex, as discussed in Section 15.6.6).

Whilst add-on and analytical approaches still sometimes exist, Monte Carlo simulation of exposure has been considered state-of-the-art for some time. Banks generally use Monte Carlo implementation across all products and counterparties, even when analytical approximations may be achievable in some cases.

It is important to note that, whilst Monte Carlo simulation is generic, it will still pose a challenge in terms of implementation and computational time. It is therefore important to consider the choice of model, calibration, and framework to avoid unnecessary workload. Additionally, whilst it is possible to include aspects such as initial margin, these often create even higher workloads due to their inherent complexity.

Monte Carlo simulation is also a challenging technique to use when it is required to calculate sensitivities (Greeks) for calculating hedges and explaining profit and loss (P&L) changes. This is because the inherent noise may cause real problems operationally. This will be discussed later in Section 21.2.2.

15.2   EXPOSURE ALLOCATION

15.2.1   Overview

Since xVA is generally a portfolio-level calculation, it will be necessary to have methods for allocating exposure back to individual transactions. This may be required for pricing new trades or for making accounting adjustments. There are generally two methods that could be used for exposure allocation, depending on the purpose. Incremental allocation looks at the incremental effect of transactions sequentially and is forward looking. Marginal allocation is backwards looking and allocates back the total exposure to each transaction. Each of these methods will be illustrated with a simple example below and then used later in the examples in Section 15.6.

It is clear from the above examples that netting benefits can be substantial. It is not clear, though, how to allocate these benefits to the individual transactions. If the EPE (and ENE) of the transactions are considered on a standalone basis, then this will overstate the actual risk. However, there is no unique way to distribute the netted exposure amongst the transactions.

15.2.2   Incremental and Marginal Exposure

Consider two exposures defined by normal (Gaussian) distributions with different means and standard deviations, as illustrated in Figure 15.4. The distributions have different

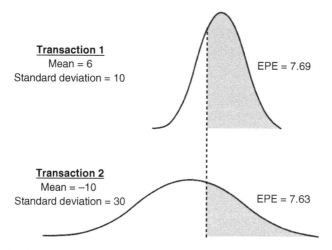

Figure 15.4 A simple example of two different normal distributions with similar EPEs.

moments: the first has a positive mean and a smaller standard deviation, and the second has a negative mean but a larger standard deviation. The result of this is that the EPEs are similar: 7.69 and 7.63 for transaction 1 and transaction 2, respectively.[2] Assuming zero correlation, the total EPE of both transactions would be 10.72.[3]

Now the question is how to allocate the EPE of 10.72 between the two transactions. The most obvious way to do this is to ask simply in which order they arose. If transaction 1 came first, then by definition it would contribute an EPE of 7.69 at that time. By simple subtraction, transaction 2 would then have to represent only 3.03. If the order were reversed, then the numbers would be almost the opposite. This will be referred to as 'incremental exposure', since it depends on the incremental effect, which in turn depends on the ordering. Incremental allocation is usually most relevant because the nature of trading is sequential. This is consistent with pricing transactions at their inception.[4]

The incremental exposure is defined via:

$$EPE_i^{incremental}(u) = EPE_{NS+i}(u) - EPE_{NS}(u).$$ (15.1)

In other words, it is the exposure of the netting set with the new transaction added $(NS + i)$, minus that of the netting set alone (NS). A similar formula applies for other metrics such as ENE and PFE, and for calculations requiring another type of aggregation. Moreover, this does not have to represent the addition of a transaction but could also be removal (e.g. unwind) or other restructuring.

In risk management, it is common and natural to ask the question of from where the underlying risk arises. Risk managers and xVA desks may find it useful to be able to 'drill

---

[2] These EPE numbers can be computed using the formula in Appendix 11A. This effect is similar to an ITM option having a similar value to an OTM option with a greater underlying volatility.

[3] Since the distributions are independent, we can calculate the combined mean and variance as $6 - 10 = -4$ and $10^2 + 30^2 = 1,000$, respectively, and then use the formula in Appendix 11A.

[4] This leads to a transfer pricing concept for xVA at trade inception, where a hard payment is made to the xVA desk.

down' from a number representing total exposure and understand which transactions are contributing most to the overall risk. This can be important information when considering whether to unwind transactions or enter into more business. Marginal exposure is useful in this context since, just because transaction-level (standalone) exposures are similar, it does not mean that the contributions to the total netted exposure are also similar. Marginal exposure (e.g. EPE) will naturally lead to the definition of marginal xVAs.

Instead of looking at EPEs sequentially, it might be desirable to find a fair breakdown of exposure, irrespective of the order in which transactions were originated. This could be relevant if two transactions are initiated at the same time (e.g. two transactions with the same counterparty on the same day) or for analysing exposure to find the largest contribution. One could simply pro rata the values in line with the standalone EPEs. Whilst this may seem reasonable, it is not theoretically rigorous. A more robust way to do this is via marginal exposure.

Marginal risk contributions are well-studied concepts due to the need to allocate risk measures back to individual constituents. For example, they have been described by Arvanitis and Gregory (2001) for credit portfolios, and a discussion on marginal value-at-risk can be found in Jorion (2007). In most situations, a marginal EPE contribution can readily be calculated as the derivative of the risk measure with respect to its weight (Rosen and Pykhtin 2010). Hence, it is necessary to numerically calculate the derivative of the total EPE with respect to each constituent exposure in order to know the marginal EPEs. This will be described more intuitively below. The marginal EPEs will, under most circumstances,[5] sum to the total EPE as required. More mathematical details are given in Appendix 15B.

The marginal EPEs under the assumption of independence between the two exposure distributions are summarised in Table 15.2 and compared also to incremental exposure and the crude pro rata approach.[6] We can see that the marginal EPE of transaction 2 is actually quite significantly higher than that of transaction 1, even though the standard EPE is lower. The distribution with a smaller expected value and a larger standard deviation is more 'risky' than the one with the opposite characteristics.

Spreadsheet 15.2 Example marginal exposure calculation.

Table 15.2 Summary of different EPE decompositions for the simple example in Figure 15.4, assuming independence between exposures.

	Incremental (1 first)	Incremental (2 first)	Pro rata	Marginal
Transaction 1	7.69	3.09	5.38	3.95
Transaction 2	3.03	7.63	5.34	6.77
Total	10.72	10.72	10.72	10.72

---

[5] One obviously difficult case is where there is a margin agreement with a non-zero threshold or an initial margin. This is discussed in more detail by Rosen and Pykhtin (2010).

[6] In the case of normal distributions, the analytical expression makes the calculation of marginal EPE quite easy without the need for simulation, as shown in Spreadsheet 15.2.

There are two obvious reasons why marginal exposure might be a meaningful measure. Firstly, the situation where two or more transactions happen simultaneously (or within a short time interval) and incremental allocation would, therefore, be inappropriate (and arbitrary); and secondly, when it is important to allocate the exposure back to constituents in order to make some decision, such as which transactions to terminate or restructure. So, whilst incremental exposure is clearly useful for quantifying new individual transactions, marginal exposure can also be a useful measure in other situations.

In summary, incremental exposure is relevant when exposure is built up sequentially, which is usually the case in practice. It is potentially unfair, in that incremental exposure depends on the timing as well as individual characteristics. Marginal allocation is fair but changes each time a new exposure is added, which is not appropriate for charging to the originator of the risk (directly via xVA, or indirectly via PFE and credit limits). In order to illustrate this, consider adding a third exposure based on a normal distribution with mean 7 and standard deviation 7 (again, with a similar standalone EPE of 7.58). The numbers change, as shown in Table 15.3. Whilst the marginal EPEs seem fairer, the impact of the third exposure is to change the magnitude of the first two (indeed, the first is increased and the second is reduced). By construction, the incremental exposures do not change.

Section 15.6 will give some more real examples of incremental and marginal exposure and discuss how they are both useful in practice.

15.2.3 Impact of Dependency

An important aspect in relation to allocation is the underlying dependency – or correlation – in the portfolio. It will be useful to define broadly three possible types of portfolio:

- *Directional*. This is a situation of similar trades with high underlying dependency (high positive correlation). End users will often be in this situation, as they may be executing a narrow range of transactions for hedging purposes (e.g. swapping floating to fixed rates in a single currency). A regional bank trading with a global bank may also lead to a directional portfolio.
- *Balanced*. A portfolio with different types of transaction, either of different underlying (e.g. currencies) or asset classes, would tend to be more balanced. This may be the case for an end user with broader hedging needs or the relationship between two banks.
- *Offsetting*. In this situation, a portfolio would have trades in both directions (e.g. paying and receiving fixed). This may be the case between two banks, or for more active clients (such as hedge funds) who may execute certain transactions in both directions (e.g. buy or sell a commodity) and put on offsetting trades to (partially) lock in profits or losses.

Table 15.3   As Table 15.2, with a third transaction added.

	Incremental (1 first)	Incremental (2 first)	Pro rata	Marginal
Transaction 1	7.69	3.09	4.86	4.45
Transaction 2	3.03	7.63	4.82	5.67
Transaction 3	3.76	3.76	4.79	4.36
Total	14.48	14.48	14.48	14.48

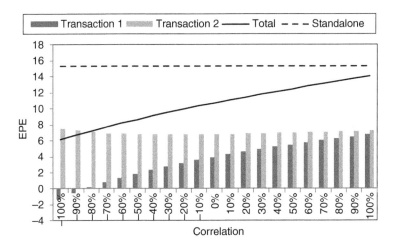

Figure 15.5   Marginal EPEs for the simple two-transaction example shown in Figure 15.4 as a function of the correlation between the normal distributions. The total is the sum of the marginal EPEs. The total standalone EPE is also shown for reference.

In order to understand the impact of the type of portfolio on exposure allocation, the simple exercise in Figure 15.4 is repeated for a range of correlation values, as shown in Figure 15.5 (these calculations can be seen in the aforementioned Spreadsheet 15.2). The total EPE is smallest at -100% correlation and increases with the correlation as the overall netting benefit is reduced. The breakdown of total EPE into marginal components depends very much on the correlation. At zero correlation, as already shown above, transaction 2 has a larger contribution to the overall EPE. With a negative correlation, the more 'risky' transaction 2 has a positive marginal EPE that is partly cancelled out by transaction 1 having a negative marginal EPE. At high correlations, the marginal EPEs are both positive and of almost equal magnitude (since there is little or no netting benefit).

The point being emphasised here is that for portfolios with low or negative correlation, marginal EPEs are particularly important to understand. The marginal EPE of a transaction depends on the relationship of that transaction to others in the netting set. A transaction which is risk reducing (negative marginal EPE) in one netting set might not have the same characteristic in a different netting set.

With respect to the consideration of new transactions, we can again characterise three different situations:

- *Risk increasing.* A directional transaction would be in the same direction as the existing (directional) portfolio. In this situation, exposure allocation is of limited interest because the exposures will be largely additive, as shown in Figure 15.5 (high positive correlation).
- *Neutral.* In this situation, a new transaction has a relatively neutral impact on the existing portfolio (e.g. it is an FX trade in a portfolio dominated by interest rate trades). The incremental contribution of this new transaction would be expected to be small.
- *Offsetting.* If a new transaction is in the opposite direction to (dominant risk factors in) the existing portfolio, then it will tend to reduce exposure. The incremental contribution of this new transaction would be expected to be of the opposite sign (i.e. negative for EPE), indicating a benefit (EPE) or cost (ENE).

Risk-increasing transactions will tend to increase the overall xVA, and risk-reducing transactions will reduce xVAs. Neutral transactions will have a relatively small impact on xVA terms. In this context, it is important to keep in mind that some xVA terms can represent costs and benefits: a risk-reducing transaction is advantageous in the former case and disadvantageous in the latter.

15.3   MONTE CARLO METHODOLOGY

15.3.1   Basic Framework

Despite being a relatively expensive technique from a computational standpoint, Monte Carlo simulation is a completely general methodology which can, therefore, cope with high dimensionality (e.g. multiple currencies and FX pairs) and path dependency (e.g. margin modelling). Monte Carlo involves generating scenarios based on the underlying risk factors in the portfolio, with each scenario being a joint realisation of risk factors at a given point in time. Scenarios need to be self-consistent for a given portfolio, since it must be possible to see portfolio effects such as netting. Strictly speaking, this 'scenario consistency' is not required across different portfolios, but for various reasons, most implementations will effectively consider only one portfolio.

Exposure simulations are normally implemented via a path-wise generation of exposure on a fixed grid (Figure 15.6), which generates an entire possible trajectory. The calculation of xVA would then be done as a one-dimensional integral over this grid. A path-wise approach has certain advantages, such as more efficient generation of risk factors and treatment of path-dependent features such as margin. It is also more natural when calculating and visualising PFE. However, this approach is less efficient from a convergence point of view and also leads to additional P&L noise (and difficulties in 'P&L explain') due to the grid moving across discrete features such as cash flows for calculations on sequential days.

In a 'direct' simulation approach, the time grid need not be fixed and default times are not bucketed. For xVA calculations, where only a single value – and not a full profile, as in the case of PFE – is required, a direct approach will require more simulation effort

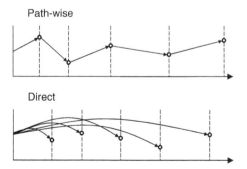

Figure 15.6   Illustration of the difference between path-wise and direct simulation. Note that the direct simulation may be more time consuming and be problematic with respect to capturing path dependence because adjacent points are independent. In the direct approach, the time points are not fixed and can be chosen arbitrarily.

but fewer portfolio revaluations. This can lead to a better convergence (Section 17.2.2), greater stability of CVA over time, and theta P&L explain (Section 21.2.7). It is also more naturally linked to the implementation of wrong-way risk (WWR) models (Section 17.6).

Both path-wise and direct methods should converge to the same underlying result, notwithstanding numerical errors in the path-wise discretisation. The path-wise method is more suitable for PFE calculations and also for path-dependent derivatives, derivatives with Bermudan features, and margin modelling. For pure xVA calculations of vanilla products, a direct approach may be preferable.

Typically, in the order of 10,000 simulations are used, with quasi-random sequences used for variance reduction. It may be necessary – or at least desirable – to use more simulations for the calculation of Greeks.

In a path-wise implementation, it is first necessary to use a grid for the simulation, as illustrated in Figure 15.7. The number of grid points must be reasonably large to capture the main details of the exposure, but not so large as to make the computations unfeasible. A typical value is in the region of 50–200.

Note that the spacing of the above dates need not be uniform for reasons such as roll-off (discussed below) and identifying settlement risk. In addition, since intervals between simulation points are often greater than the length of the margin period of risk (MPoR), it may be necessary to include additional 'look-back' points for the purposes of simulating the impact of margin (Section 15.5.3).

When exposure is calculated at only discrete points, as in a path-wise simulation, it is possible to miss key areas of risk. Profiles can be highly discontinuous over time due to maturity dates, option exercise, cash flow payments, and break clauses. The risk of missing jumps in exposure caused by these aspects is called 'roll-off risk'. Such jumps may be small in duration but large in magnitude. These components are typically considered by regulators to be counterparty risk (and not settlement risk) (for example, see BCBS 2015b). The impact of roll-off risk is shown in Figure 15.8, which shows a PFE calculation using simulations with different levels of granularity. Whilst roll-off risk manifests itself in PFE terms via the profile having an incorrect and rapidly-changing structure, for xVA calculations it will lead to additional noise in day-to-day calculations.

Roll-off risk can be controlled by using time-heterogeneous time grids (as in Figure 15.7), at least providing a better definition as discrepancies become closer. However, this can mean that xVA and PFE quantities can change significantly from day to day due to exposure jumps gradually becoming engulfed within the more granular short-term grid. A better approach is to incorporate the critical points where exposure changes significantly (e.g. due to maturity dates, settlement dates, and cash flow payment dates) into the time grid. However, this would need to be done separately for each portfolio. This may also be beneficial to provide the ability to change grids to reflect different maximum maturity dates, margin terms, and underlying product type. However, in a generic xVA framework, this may be impractical due to the definition of 'portfolio' being specific to the value adjustment (VA) being calculated.

Time

Figure 15.7 Illustration of time grid for exposure simulation.

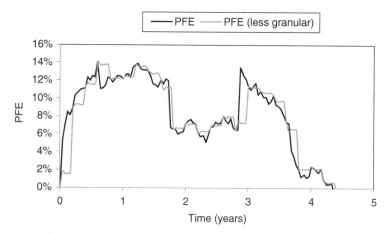

Figure 15.8 PFE for a counterparty calculated at different levels of granularity. In the normal case, the time intervals are spaced by 10 business days, whilst in the less granular case, the interval is five times greater.

15.3.2   Revaluation, Cash Flow Bucketing, and Scaling

The calculation of xVA is computationally demanding due to the use of Monte Carlo simulation and the need to evolve the portfolio across the entire lifetime of trades (which in turn requires full revaluation). Suppose the total population of transactions and exposure calculation involves:

- 10,000 simulations;
- 100 time steps (path-wise simulation);
- 250 counterparties; and
- 40 transactions with each counterparty (on average).

Then the total number of trade revaluations would be $10,000 \times 100 \times 250 \times 40 = 10,000,000,000$ (10 billion). This has very significant implications for the computation speed of pricing models, as this step usually represents the bottleneck of a PFE or xVA calculation. On top of the above, Greeks calculated via 'bump-and-run' approaches which calculate finite-difference sensitivities will add a potentially linear computational burden with respect to computation time and the total number of sensitivities required.

The above will also be sensitive to the total portfolio under consideration. In the past, a CVA calculation may have been done on only the uncollateralised counterparties, with no other xVAs considered. This reduced scope meant that the problem was more manageable, as the potentially large number of collateralised transactions would not need to be captured and simulated. However, it is now common to consider collateralised counterparties for the calculation of CVA (see Section 3.1.4), which – even ignoring the additional complexity in modelling margin discussed in Section 15.5 – requires the simulation of a much larger universe, including interbank counterparties. Furthermore, other xVA terms are not only related (solely) to uncollateralised transactions (e.g. capital value adjustment – KVA, margin value adjustment – MVA) and therefore require a much larger portfolio to be handled.

The first implication of the above is that pricing functions must be highly optimised, with any common functionality (such as calculating fixings) stripped out to optimise the calculation as much as possible. Whilst such pricing functions are usually relatively fast, the sheer volume of vanilla products makes this optimisation important.

For more complex products, whilst there may be fewer of them in a typical xVA portfolio, pricing often involves lattice-based or Monte Carlo methods that may be too slow. There are various ways to get around this problem, for example:

- *Approximations.* Sometimes crude, ad hoc approximations may be deemed of sufficient accuracy – for example, approximating a Bermudan swaption as a European swaption (which allows an analytical formula).
- *Grids.* Grids giving the value of a transaction can be used as long as the dimensionality of the problem is not too large. Such grids may be populated by front-office systems and therefore be in line with trading desk valuation models. The PFE/xVA calculation will look up (and possibly interpolate) the relevant values on the grid rather than performing costly pricing.
- *American Monte Carlo methods.* This is a generic approach to utilising future Monte Carlo simulations to provide good approximations of the exposure at a given point in time, in a path-wise simulation approach.[7] Examples of this and related approaches can be found in Longstaff and Schwartz (2001), Glasserman and Yu (2002), and Cesari et al. (2009). This may be the best solution for xVA quantification, but may not be as relevant for PFE and risk management.

For both vanilla and more complex transactions, it may be useful to use techniques such as machine learning to evaluate such pricing functions (and their Greeks) very rapidly, as discussed later in Section 21.3.3.

It is usually reasonable that xVA calculations do not perfectly represent the underlying value of transactions. This is different from, for example, incoming market risk capital requirements, which for internal model approval require an exact, or very close, alignment of front-office and risk models due to the so-called 'P&L attribution test' (BCBS 2019a), which compares theoretical predicted P&L with actual P&L changes. The potential for slight misalignment in xVA means that if a pricing function can be speeded up significantly with only a small loss of accuracy, then this will be worthwhile.

Another important optimisation is to bucket cash flows in a single currency so as to reduce the number of pricing evaluations (Figure 15.9). Given the inherent approximation of using a relatively large discrete time step, this should not represent a further significant approximation. In a path-wise approach, cash flow bucketing may not represent any further approximation since the integral has already been discretised.

Inevitably, even for simple products, there are valuation differences between the exposure calculation and the official valuation. These differences are sometimes corrected by applying shifts, as illustrated in Figure 15.10. For example, multiplying all paths by $\frac{Valuation\ Difference \times (T-t)}{T}$ (where t represents the current time and T the final maturity) would affect an amortising scaling. For forward contracts and cross-currency swaps (or contractual mismatches, such as the misspecification of a cash flow), a fixed scaling

---

[7] This can be used for both xVA and PFE applications, although the accuracy in the latter case is typically worse. Furthermore, being a generic approach, this will not match front-office valuations exactly.

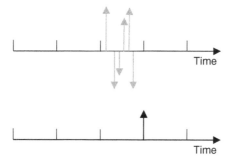

Figure 15.9 Illustration of cash flow bucketing in a single currency. The cash flows between the dates shown (top) can be realistically combined into a single payment (bottom) whilst preserving the overall valuation and potentially other aspects such as the sensitivity.

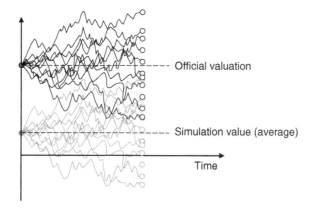

Figure 15.10 Illustration of the use of a proportion shift to correct an exposure simulation to the official valuation.

is more appropriate. Ideally, since different transactions vary significantly in terms of their contractual features and valuation methodologies, shifts should be applied at the transaction level.

15.3.3   Risk-neutral or Physical Measure

Scenario generation for risk-management purposes and arbitrage pricing theory tend to use different 'measures'. Arbitrage-based pricing uses the so-called risk-neutral measure, which is justified through hedging and arbitrage considerations. For example, in a risk-neutral framework, interest rate volatilities (and associated parameters such as mean reversion) would be derived from the prices of interest rate swaptions, caps, and floors, rather than estimated via historical time series. In addition, the drift of the underlying variables (such as interest rates and FX rates) will need to be calibrated to forward rates, rather than coming from some historical or other real-world analysis.[8] Parameters (and

---

[8] As described below, risk-neutral drift may often be used anyway for calculating exposure for risk-management purposes.

therefore probability distributions) such as drifts and volatilities are market implied and need not correspond to the real distributions (or even comply with common sense).

On the other hand, in a risk-management application, one does not need to use the risk-neutral measure and may focus rather on the real-world or physical measure, estimated using, for example, historical data. Models calibrated using historical data predict future scenarios based on statistical patterns observed in the past and assume that this previous behaviour is a good indicator of the future; such models are sometimes slow to react to changes in market conditions. Models calibrated to market prices tend to be more forward looking, but contain components such as risk premiums and storage costs that introduce bias. Furthermore, they may produce exposures that jump dramatically – for example, during a period of high volatility.

The question of risk-neutral or physical measures is quite easy to answer in the case of CVA. Risk-neutral approaches have become standard for quantification of CVA (and FVA). This has been catalysed by the more active management of such components and accounting standards. Parameters are generally risk neutral, to the extent that this is possible. The estimation of non-observable parameters in this context is discussed in Section 15.4.5.

The need for CVA to be based on a risk-neutral simulation is summarised by BCBS (2017) and relates to using the most advanced approach under the Fundamental Review of the Trading Book (FRTB) CVA capital charge (Section 13.3.5). BCBS (2017) makes the following statements:

- Drifts of risk factors must be consistent with a risk-neutral probability measure. Historical calibration of drifts is not allowed.
- The volatilities and correlations of market risk factors must be calibrated to market data whenever sufficient data exists in a given market. Otherwise, historical calibration is permissible.

Where a difference in market practice exists, this relates more to PFE (credit limits) and regulatory capital calculations using the internal model method (IMM) (Section 13.4.5). Here it is probably best to consider the calibration of drift, volatilities, and correlations as separate topics.

Drift (or trend) is an increasingly-important parameter as the exposure simulation time horizon becomes longer since it has an approximately linear effect, whereas volatility has more of a square root impact. In other words, the *drift* of an underlying variable can be just as important as its *uncertainty*. Futures (or equivalently forward) prices have long been an important mechanism of price discovery in financial markets, as they represent the intersection of expected supply and demand at some future point in time. Forward rates can sometimes be very far from spot rates, and it is important to understand whether or not this is truly the 'view of the market'. Some important technical factors are:

- *Interest rates*. Yield curves may be upwards sloping or downwards sloping (and a variety of other shapes) due to the risk appetite for short-, medium-, and long-term interest rate risk and the view that rates may increase or decrease.
- *FX rates*. Forward FX rates are determined from an arbitrage relationship between the interest rate curves for the relevant currency pair. The expectation of future FX rates

may have an influence on the current interest rate curves in the corresponding currencies. However, there has long been doubt regarding the ability of long-term forward FX
rates to predict future spot FX rates. See, for example, Meese and Rogoff (1983) and a
review by Sarno and Taylor (2002).

- *Commodity prices.* In addition to market participants' view of the direction of commodity prices, storage costs (or lack of storage), inventory, and seasonal effects can move
commodities futures apart from spot rates. For high inventories, the futures price is
higher than the spot price (contango). When inventories are low, commodity spot prices
can be higher than futures prices (backwardation). However, non-storable commodities (e.g. electricity) do not have an arbitrage relationship between spot and forward
prices, and therefore the forward rates might be argued to contain relevant information
about future expected prices.
- *Credit spreads.* Credit curves may be increasing or decreasing either due to demand for
credit risk at certain maturities or the view that default probability will be increasing or
decreasing over time. Historically, the shape of credit curves has not been clearly seen
to be a good predictor of future credit spread levels.

There has been much empirical testing of the relationship between spot and futures
prices across different markets. It is a generally held belief that the futures price is a
biased forecast of the future spot price. On the other hand, choosing a historical drift
may be inappropriate: for example, in a falling interest rate environment, it will produce
more simulations where rates decline, which may be precisely opposite to the expected
economic behaviour. Using a drift of zero may, in certain situations, be argued to be most
appropriate and subject to the least bias.

Using a different drift tends to offset the exposure distribution, as illustrated in
Figure 15.11. In this example, since the interest rate curve is upwards sloping (long-term

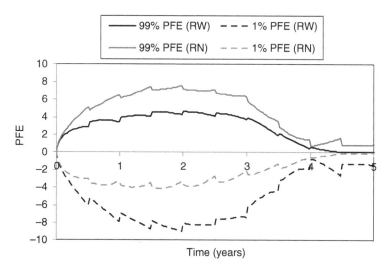

Figure 15.11   Illustration of the PFE for a five-year interest rate swap computed with both
real-world (RW) and risk-neutral (RN) simulations for the drift. Note that, in order to isolate the
drift impact, historical volatility has been used in both cases.

interest rates are higher than short-term rates), the risk-neutral drift is positive, leading to the 99% PFE being higher than the 1% PFE, as explained in Section 11.2.3.

Regarding volatility, historical estimates make the implicit assumption that the past will be a good indication of the future. It is also necessary to decide what history of data to use; a short history will give poor statistics, whereas a long history will give weight to 'old', meaningless data. In quiet markets, the lack of variability in historical time series will give misleadingly low volatility. Using historical data from stress periods (as required in IMM approaches, see Section 13.4.5) can alleviate this, but then yet more subjectivity is introduced in choosing the correct period of stress.

In many markets, there is also implied volatility information, potentially as a function of the strike and the maturity of the option. However, implied volatility will not be observed for OTM options and long maturities. The use of implied volatility (which will react quickly when the market becomes more uncertain) may be justified via the 'market knows best' view (or at least, the market knows better than historical data). However, risk premiums embedded in market-implied volatilities will lead to a systematic over-estimation of the overall risk. It has been argued that implied volatility is a superior estimator of future volatility (Jorion 2007, Chapter 9) compared with historical estimation via time-series approaches. The stability of the volatility risk premium and the fact that an overestimation of volatility will always lead to a more conservative risk number give greater credence to this idea.[9] One example of risk-neutral volatility calibrations being preferable is in the case of pegged currencies where the historical FX volatility is small, but option prices can provide information on the likelihood of the peg breaking, leading to a much higher volatility regime (Clark 2016).

Larger volatility will increase EPE, ENE, and PFE in absolute terms. Figure 15.12 shows the PFE of a cross-currency swap under both real-world and risk-neutral volatility assumptions. Here the main impact is simply that risk-neutral volatilities tend to be higher than real-world ones and hence both the EPE and ENE are bigger.

When using risk-neutral volatility, the term structure is also important, as shown in Figure 15.13. An upwards-sloping volatility term structure leads to a higher exposure at longer maturities.

Another difference between historical and implied volatility is the term structure impact (including aspects such as mean reversion in models). A volatility skew across time (e.g. long-dated volatility being higher than short-dated volatility) means that forward volatility is higher than spot volatility. However, empirical evidence does not always support forward volatility being predictive of actual future volatility.

Whilst it is at least conservative to assume volatilities are high, the same is not true of correlation inputs. When estimating a correlation for modelling exposure, there may not be an obvious way of knowing whether a high or low (or positive or negative) value is more conservative. Indeed, in a complex portfolio it may even be that the behaviour of the exposure with respect to correlation is not monotonic.[10] Implied correlations are sometimes available in the market. For example, a quanto option has a payoff in a different currency and thus gives information on the implied correlation between the

---

[9] Using implied volatility might be expected to produce an upwards bias due to a risk premium, leading to higher (more conservative) risk numbers.

[10] Meaning, for example, that the worse correlation may not be equal to 100% or -100%, but somewhere in between.

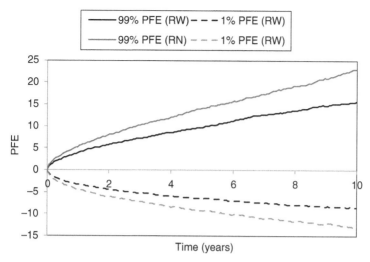

Figure 15.12 Illustration of the PFE for a 10-year cross-currency swap computed with both real-world (RW) and risk-neutral (RN) simulations for the volatility. Note that, in order to isolate this impact, risk-neutral drift (forward rates) has been used in both cases.

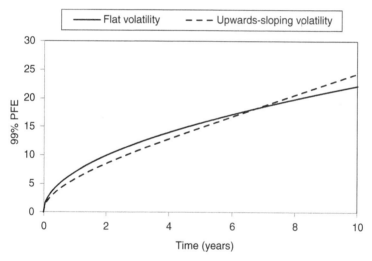

Figure 15.13 Illustration of the PFE for a 10-year cross-currency swap computed with flat and upwards-sloping volatility term structures.

relevant FX rate and the underlying asset. One key aspect of correlation is to determine WWR: a quanto credit default swap (CDS) – a CDS where the premium and default legs are in different currencies – potentially gives information about the correlation between the relevant FX rate and the credit quality of the reference entity in the CDS (Section 17.6.4). Whilst implied correlation can sometimes be calculated, for most quantities no market prices will be available and so historical data will typically be used.

BCBS (2015b) reports that, out of 19 participating banks, only one used a risk-neutral (market-implied) calibration for all risk factors in its IMM model. A further five banks were reported to use a combination of risk-neutral and historical data for calibration (e.g. drifts calibrated to market-implied data and volatilities to historical data). The remaining banks used only historical data. Many large banks have separate implementations for xVA quantification and counterparty risk assessment (PFE and IMM) across the front office, and risk functions which will usually follow broadly risk-neutral and real-world approaches, respectively.

Using a risk-neutral calibration for an IMM does have various advantages. It potentially allows alignment with xVA calculations, which may provide better internal assessment of trades and hedging performance. However, this is not without problems: regulatory capital requirements under a risk-neutral IMM are still typically required to use stressed calibrations (e.g. stressed-implied volatility from a period in the past), which will be misaligned with the xVA desk view of current market-implied volatility. Furthermore, the use of risk-neutral calibrations may make backtesting results (Section 13.4.5) harder to interpret.

A more subtle problem with the separation between physical and risk-neutral approaches is illustrated in Figure 15.14. Revaluation of transactions at future dates needs to be done using risk-neutral valuation (the so-called 'Q-measure'), as this is what happens in reality. Simulating using the physical ('P-measure') can lead to inconsistency and implementation difficulties (e.g. in using American Monte Carlo methods, as discussed above). On the other hand, also simulating in the Q-measure, as is the case for CVA (and typically also FVA), makes the setup self-consistent. Using a risk-neutral calibration within an IMM approval would also create self-consistency.

However, valuation adjustments that look at the capital (KVA) and initial margin (MVA) are not solely based on risk-neutral valuations but also on historical data:

- *Capital.* Internal model methodologies typically (although not always, as discussed above) use historical data to calibrate, and standardised methodologies (e.g. SA-CCR) use weights based on historical calibration.

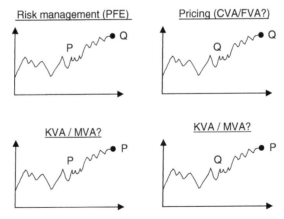

Figure 15.14   Illustration of the different requirements from scenario models for risk management and pricing/valuation. For risk management, simulations tend to be done under the real-world (P-) measure, whilst revaluations must be risk neutral (Q-measure). For pricing purposes, both scenarios and revaluations are risk neutral. For capital and initial margin (KVA and MVA), the underlying calculation is based on the P-measure.

- *Initial margin.* Central counterparty (CCP) methodologies for over-the-counter (OTC) derivatives use historical simulation (Section 9.3) based on historical data, Standard Portfolio Analysis of Risk (SPAN) (Section 9.2.2) uses spanning ranges based on historical experience, and the International Swaps and Derivatives Association's Standard Initial Margin Model (ISDA SIMM™) (Section 9.4.4) uses parameters calibrated to historical data.

The above implies that KVA and MVA may need to be calculated in a region more like the two shown at the bottom of Figure 15.14. For example, the initial margin that a CCP would charge at some point in the future would, strictly speaking, require a simulation under the physical measure, as CCPs use historical and not market-implied parameters in their calculations. There are therefore questions as to whether a KVA or MVA calculation should use the physical or risk-neutral measure. The former would be consistent with assessing the likely real-world costs of capital and initial margin, but would require a separate calculation. The latter would be consistent with CVA/FVA and could be included in the same simulation methodology. An example of this for KVA will be shown in Section 19.2.4.

Some of the above problems have been discussed in the recent literature. For example, Hull et al. (2014) discuss a 'joint measure model', representing the single forward-looking movement of interest rates under both the P- and Q-measures. Sokol (2014) discusses the challenges of long-term simulation in general, and Kenyon and Green (2014b) discuss the problem with regulatory methodologies being defined in the P-measure, meaning that pricing of components such as MVA and KVA can no longer be considered risk neutral. Kenyon, Green, and Berrahoui (2015) discuss the appropriate measure to use for PFE computation in more detail.

15.3.4   Aggregation Level

It is worth emphasising that xVA is, in general, a portfolio-level calculation (Section 5.2.6). Whilst this will be discussed in more detail in the relevant Chapters (17–20), Figure 15.15 illustrates a possible hierarchy. The main point to emphasise at this point is that it may be necessary to aggregate xVA components at different levels. For example, CVA – for obvious reasons – is a counterparty-level (or netting-set level) quantity. However, other components such as funding and capital are not necessarily counterparty specific and may need to be considered at a different level and aggregated accordingly. This, in turn, requires large computational power and data science methods to cope with running calculations at the correct aggregation level (e.g. for pre-deal pricing). However, realistic shortcuts are often acceptable.

In general, it is possible to represent exposure simulation data in three dimensions corresponding to the transaction (k), simulation (s), and time step (t), leading to a future value represented as $V(k, s, t)$. Assume that transactions $k = 1, K$ need to be aggregated. The future aggregate value is characterised by the matrix:

$$V_{Agg}(s, t) = \sum_{k=1}^{K} V(k, s, t) \qquad (15.2)$$

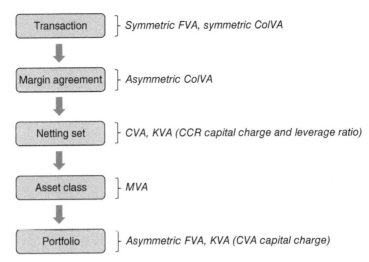

Figure 15.15 Illustration of the portfolio hierarchy for xVA calculations which will be covered in more detail in later chapters. Note that the margin agreement and netting set may be the same, although it is possible to have more than one margin agreement covered by the same netting agreement. See Glossary for definitions.

It may not be necessary to store all of the individual transaction information, $V(k, s, t)$, although this might be needed for calculating certain quantities (see the discussion on marginal exposure in Section 15.2.2).

Related to the aggregation level is the need to treat margin differently. From a counterparty risk (CVA) perspective, margin only needs to be available in a default scenario, whereas for funding (FVA), it has to be available in all situations and rehypothecable. This can require different exposure simulations (discussed later in Section 18.3.2).

15.4   CHOICE OF MODELS

15.4.1   Overview

This section will give an overview of the commonly-used models in exposure simulation and xVA quantification. Given that this is a cross-asset class problem, the number of different model choices and total number of risk factors can be substantial. It is ultimately important to choose relatively simple models for reasons of tractability and stability. There are also 80/20-rule-type considerations. For example, it may be necessary to build a model to cover a relatively small number of products in some asset classes (e.g. some banks have only a limited number of inflation or commodity products). Additionally, some asset classes – typically equity and credit – often have short-dated and/or mainly collateralised transactions for which xVA is less important. The discussion below will reflect this, with interest rate and FX models discussed in more detail since they tend to be most used by uncollateralised counterparties such as corporates.

It is important to strike a balance between a realistic risk factor model and one that is parsimonious. For example, there are 50–60 or more risk factors defining an interest rate curve, whereas the simplest interest rate models involve only one factor. A model involving two or three factors may represent a compromise. Such an approach will capture more of the possible curve movements than would a single-factor model, but without producing the unrealistic curve shapes and arbitrageable prices that a model for each individual risk factor might generate. A more advanced model will also be able to calibrate more accurately and to a broad range of market prices (e.g. swaption volatilities). Models must obviously not be too complex, as it must also be possible and practical to simulate discrete scenarios of the risk factors using the model. Typically, many thousands of scenarios will be required at many points in time, and hence there must be an efficient way in which to generate these many scenarios.

It is important to emphasise that the simulation model must be generic to support consistent simulation of the many risk factors that would be required to value a quite complex netting set. Calibrations also tend to be generic, rather than netting set or transaction specific. This is very different from classical modelling of derivatives, where many models (and individual calibrations thereof) are typically used. This leads to unavoidable differences (hopefully small) between current valuation, as seen from the xVA system, and the relevant front-office systems, as discussed previously in Section 15.3.2. The need to use a generic approach across asset classes creates inevitable cross-dependencies: for example, all other asset classes will exist in a model where interest rates are stochastic.

Another reason for simpler underlying models for risk factors is the need to incorporate dependencies (correlations) in order to capture the correct multidimensional behaviour of the netting sets to be simulated.[11] The correct description of the underlying risk factors and correlations leads to a significant number of model parameters. A balance is important when considering the modelling of a given set of risk factors (such as an interest rate curve) and the correlation between this and another set of risk factors (such as an interest rate curve in another currency). There is no point in having sophisticated univariate modelling and naïve multivariate modelling.

Ultimately, exposure simulation modelling choices will depend on the nature of the problem at hand, important considerations being:

- *Complexity of portfolio*. As noted above, a simple portfolio with mainly vanilla transactions will not warrant a more sophisticated modelling approach, and it is more appropriate to focus on the correct treatment of vanilla products (e.g. a reasonable volatility calibration).
- *Collateralisation*. Collateralised positions also suggest more simple models can be used, since the nature of margin is to shorten time horizons and neutralise positive and negative portfolio values. Furthermore, the choice of MPoR dominates in importance over the choice of exposure simulation model. Margin (collateral) modelling is discussed in Section 15.5.
- *Dimensionality*. High dimensionality (e.g. several interest rate and/or FX risk factors for a given counterparty) may suggest simpler models due to the importance of considering the modelling of the underlying co-dependencies.
- *Wrong-way risk*. If WWR models (Section 17.6) are to be implemented, then it is even more important to keep the basic setup simple.

---

[11] Correlation is often the specific way in which dependency is represented, and it is very commonly used. We will use correlation from now on, but note that there are other ways to model dependency, as discussed further in Chapter 17.

- *Computational workload.* Due to the likely need for rapid pricing, Greeks, and scenario analysis, it is important that the modelling framework chosen does not lead to excessive hardware requirements.

By necessity, exposure simulations may not incorporate complex features such as stochastic volatility and stochastic basis, and may not calibrate fully to features such as volatility skews.

There are different ways to implement Monte Carlo simulation on a grid. The first is the so-called Euler scheme, which generates step-wise diffusions sequentially and is subject to 'discretisation bias'. An alternative approach that aims to eliminate this bias is to use 'integrated diffusions'. However, such a technique requires integral expressions to be calculated. Using relatively simple models means that such expressions are closed form.

The discussion below is concerned primarily with risk-neutral exposure models which would be most relevant for xVA calculations. This is an important point since real-world and risk-neutral approaches may lead to different modelling choices. For example, when modelling interest rates using historical data, an approach such as principal component analysis (PCA) may be preferred as a means to capture historical yield curve evolution. However, a risk-neutral interest rate model would more naturally be an arbitrage-free term structure approach. For PFE/IMM implementations, other considerations also come into play. For example, specifications of mean reversion, together with other aspects such as models allowing negative rates, can be particularly problematic for PFE, as a high quantile may be viewed as defining an economically unreasonable event. Sokol (2014) discusses these topics in more detail.

For more mathematical details on the implementation of risk-neutral exposure simulation, the reader is referred to books by Cesari et al. (2009) and Brigo et al. (2013) for details on the underlying mathematical framework, and Green (2015), who discusses both this and specific modelling choices for each asset class.

15.4.2   Interest Rates

For most xVA applications, the interest rate is the most important risk factor simulation. This is because interest rate products often dominate other asset classes in terms of importance, and also because other asset classes will have a sensitivity to interest rates through discounting. The simplest interest rate model used is the one-factor Hull–White (HW1F) model, which is usually formulated as a short-rate Gaussian model (Hull and White 1990). Such models have a large amount of analytical tractability due to being Markovian (no memory), allowing closed-form calculations of discount factors and volatility products (caps, floors, and swaptions). This allows an efficient calibration to the initial yield curve and volatility term structure, and also allows a fast determination of the yield curve in future states. Together with the Markovian property – which means that the simulation is not path dependent – this makes Monte Carlo simulation more straightforward. Short-rate models also have the advantage that they are typically easier to combine with models for other asset classes.

The most obvious drawbacks of the HW1F model are:

- the inability to calibrate to all implied volatilities (caps/floors and swaptions);
- the strong correlation between rates of different tenors; and
- the fact that the model allows negative rates.

Whilst negative interest rates may not be a concern as long as there is a reasonable fit to the yield curve and volatility term structure, they can create technical challenges (e.g. if a Black model is used for pricing caplets). In such cases, using the simulation model (e.g. HW1F) for pricing caplets and implementing a scaling approach may be the most practical solution. The inability of a single-factor model to realistically model the relationship between tenors is problematic if there exist significant positions of this type (e.g. pay and receive swaps or constant maturity products), and would support the use of a two- or multifactor HW model, in which there is still reasonable analytical tractability.

Spreadsheet 15.3 Simple simulation of an interest rate swap exposure.

When pricing exotic interest rate instruments such as Bermudan swaptions, so-called 'market models' have become a standard for pricing and allow calibration to the entire at-the-money (ATM) volatility term structure. Methods such as SABR (stochastic alpha beta rho) (Hagan et al. 2002) can be used to introduce a 'skew' and therefore price swaptions of different strikes. However, market models, whilst more flexible in terms of calibration to instruments such as caplets and swaptions, are less analytically tractable, non-Markovian, and require simulation with a large number of state variables and complicated drift terms. For xVA applications – which are already by their nature computationally demanding and also require the modelling of other asset classes – market models are often (but not always) deemed too complex, and a HW1F model is more common.

Where it exists, the overnight indexed spread (OIS) or risk-free rate (RFR) curve of a given currency is usually the curve chosen for diffusion purposes. However, in most currencies there exist multiple interest rate curves which can be characterised by their tenor (e.g. OIS, 1M LIBOR, 3M LIBOR, 6M LIBOR, and 12M LIBOR). The divergence between these curves in 2008 (often known as the OIS-LIBOR basis, discussed in Section 16.1.3) suggested a need to model the basis between these curves reasonably. Such 'dual curve' pricing would then use different curves for discounting (e.g. OIS) and projection (e.g. LIBOR). Ideally, an interest rate model would individually calibrate to all observable interest rate curves in a given currency and model the relationship between these curves in an arbitrage-free setting. Achieving the latter is challenging due to the fact that different basis curves will likely be highly, but not perfectly, correlated and that basis spreads will likely, but not always, be positive (in the sense that longer tenors will have higher interest rates). There is also the problem that the instruments that would be needed to calibrate a stochastic basis model – such as options on basis swaps – are very illiquid. These points may be simplified after the IBOR transition (Section 14.3.4).

Given the difficulties in modelling stochastic basis, exposure simulation models normally assume a deterministic basis. In such a model, the different rates are correctly calibrated using fixed spreads, but are assumed to be driven by the same random component and are therefore perfectly correlated. This will miss some potential optionality, the materiality of which will depend on the underlying portfolio (e.g. the number of basis swaps).

The interest rate swaption market is large, due to the fact that many fixed-income securities and structured products embed swaption-like optionality, and the fact that there are many market participants (e.g. corporations swapping callable debt). European swaptions are common calibration instruments for exposure simulation models.

The European swaption market is defined by three dimensions:

- the maturity of the underlying swap (e.g. 2, 5, 10, 20, and 30 years);
- the expiry of the option (e.g. 1, 3, 6, and 9 months and 1, 2, 5, and 10 years); and
- the strike (e.g. ATM plus or minus 25, 50, 100, 150, 200, 300, and 400 basis points).

The US dollar and Euro markets are by the far the most liquid, but many other major currencies have a reasonable range of observable swaption prices.

The terms 'diagonal' or 'co-terminal' refer to a group of swaptions where the option and swap maturities sum to a constant number. For example, the set of swaptions with option and swap maturities defined by 2Yx8Y, 4Yx6Y, 5Yx5Y, 6Yx4Y, and 8Yx2Y are the 10-year co-terminal swaptions. Bermudan swaptions are typically hedged with the underlying co-terminal European swaptions.

Co-terminal swaptions are also interesting from an exposure simulation point of view. For example, the work of Sorensen and Bollier (1994) discussed in Section 15.1.3 is helpful since it shows that the EPE profile of an IRS can be defined as a series of European co-terminal swaptions corresponding to the swap maturity. This is logical since the exposure from the potential default on the swap is economically driven by the exercising of a European swaption on a swap with the remaining life of the original swap at the default time. For example, the four-year discounted EPE on a 10-year swap is equivalent to the price of a 4Yx6Y swaption today.

Whilst the Sorenson–Bollier analogy would seem to suggest that a co-terminal calibration strategy to the ATM T-year co-terminal swaptions would accurately represent the EPE of a T-year IRS, this is not true due to moneyness. The swaptions traded in the market would have to be all at the prevailing swap rate whilst, in reality, the ATM swaptions will trade at the forward swap rate. There is also, therefore, the question of which co-terminal swaptions to use for a portfolio of swaps of different maturities and the calibration of skew.

In the HW1F model, the volatility and mean reversion parameters will determine the volatility structure produced by the model. Both of these parameters can be made time dependent without any loss in tractability. Swaption-implied volatility[12] within the model generally decreases monotonically with tenor, although it can increase if mean reversion is negative. By extension, it is possible to produce a hump in volatility – as is sometimes seen in the market – if a term structure of mean reversion is used.

The mean reversion parameter in the HW1F model strongly affects the correlation between rates of different tenors. This can have a large impact for portfolios where there is a big sensitivity to the movement between such tenors (e.g. a portfolio with paying and receiving fixed at different tenors). This is similar to the impact of mean reversion on the pricing of exotics such as Bermudan swaptions.

A common strategy when calibrating the HW1F model for exposure simulation is to use a fixed mean reversion parameter and calibrate to a set of co-terminal swaptions (e.g. 20 years), which is relatively straightforward via a 'bootstrap' procedure. Mean reversion can be very unstable over time when calibrated to swaptions of one maturity (likely due to the model being overspecified), but is more stable if two or more maturities (e.g. 10-year and

---

[12] This typically refers to the implied volatility of the forward swap rate in a Black model.

20-year co-terminals) are used. Calibrating mean reversion can also more easily adapt to large changes in the volatility surface that are sometimes observed through time. Calibrating to all swaptions with time-dependent mean reversion may be considered more accurate than the co-terminal approach, although such a calibration is necessarily a global process.

Many implementations fix mean reversion at a level such as 0.01 or 0.03 (depending on the currency) due to the possible stability issues otherwise, and calibrate to a chosen co-terminal swaption maturity. This is fairly robust when using a piece-wise constant volatility and bootstrap procedure. As noted above, such an approach does not fit the full ATM volatility surface especially well. For example, Figure 15.16 shows swaption-implied volatilities for a HW1F model with fixed mean reversion calibrated to the 20-year co-terminal swaptions. Whilst the co-terminals (e.g. 5Yx15Y and 10Yx10Y) are matched closely, the model underestimates the left side of the diagonal (e.g. 1Yx5Y) and overestimates the right side (e.g. 10Yx20Y). This will lead the exposure of swaps – especially those not of 20-year maturity – to be incorrect, as will be shown below (Section 15.6.1).

As discussed above, market models allow a better calibration to the ATM volatility surface, and with methods such as SABR can produce a better representation of the skew. However, this comes at the expense of additional computational costs and potential instabilities. Cheyette models (Cheyette 2001; Andersen and Piterbarg 2010b) can also be useful for xVA purposes as they are Markovian and have analytical tractabilities, whilst allowing volatility skew to be calibrated.

15.4.3   Foreign Exchange

The standard FX model used for exposure simulation tends to be a relatively simple lognormal approach with (piece-wise constant) time-dependent volatility. Whilst this may seem overly simplistic, it is important to note that, due to the necessary interest

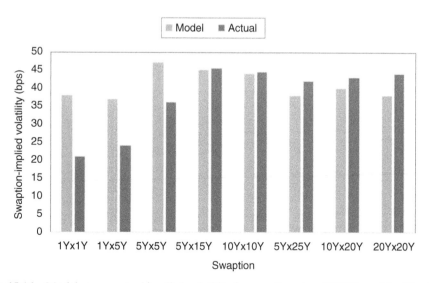

Figure 15.16   Model versus actual implied volatility for swaptions in a HW1F model calibrated to the 20-year co-terminal swaptions.

rate modelling, this will already constitute a stochastic interest rate environment. This effectively means that the overall FX model is this assumption for FX together with a HW1F model (for example) for each of the (domestic and foreign) interest rate processes. The relatively simple choice keeps the multidimensional exposure simulation (i.e. n interest rates and n-1 FX rates) reasonably straightforward. Forward FX models are more convenient for option calibration, but spot FX models are more convenient for (historical) correlation estimation.

Given that an exposure simulation model is multicurrency, it is necessary to define a base or 'domestic' currency, which is most obviously the main and/or reporting currency of the bank in question. Only FX pairs involving the base currency need be simulated, since other pairs can be derived via 'currency triangles'.

Whilst FX spot processes have no term structure as such, the appropriate construction of market FX forwards is essentially a drift calibration. Within the joint hybrid simulation, there are conceptually two types of FX forwards:

- Model-implied, 'risk-free' forwards that are constructed from the relevant spot FX and interest rate curves and are internally consistent. However, FX forwards constructed in this manner are not consistent with market FX forwards, since they will not incorporate the corresponding cross-currency basis spreads observed in FX forwards or cross-currency swap basis swaps. The risk-free FX forwards would be used solely internally within the model for model-consistent, no-arbitrage conversion of units of value from one currency to another.
- Risky FX forwards that are consistent with market-observed FX forwards which, for example, correctly reprice cross-currency basis swaps. Similar to interest rate modelling, this is typically achieved through a constant basis. As with the single currency basis, cross-currency basis spreads are derived from market instruments (FX forwards and cross-currency swaps) during construction of the respective cross-currency discount curves.

Pegged currencies are also challenging to model as volatilities will typically be small, but there will be a risk of the peg breaking, accompanied by a substantial jump and/or increase in volatility. Jump-diffusion processes have often been used to characterise emerging markets or pegged currencies. The shorter the time horizon, the greater the importance of capturing such jumps (e.g. Das and Sundaram 1999). As noted in Section 15.3.3, the options market may provide interesting information regarding such probabilities, although it will be important to consider the calibration scheme carefully (the likelihood of the exchange rate regime changing may be seen first in the price of OTM options).

A typical volatility calibration would calibrate across a set of ATM FX option prices within the underlying three-factor (i.e. stochastic interest rate) model. Using a piece-wise constant volatility function in a lognormal FX model, together with two HW1F models, is a simple bootstrap procedure with analytical pricing formulas. Using more sophisticated interest rate and FX models will make calibration and simulation more difficult.

In general, FX options on 'cross-FX rates' (not involving the base currency) will not be correctly reproduced. This is because, for example, the USD/GBP FX process will be uniquely defined by the USD/EUR and USD/GBP processes. In some cases, this may not be material due to the nature of the underlying portfolio. Otherwise, a potential solution is to use the correlations between the FX rates to calibrate to the correct volatility term structure for the cross-FX rate (as discussed in Section 15.4.5, such correlations would otherwise typically be defined by historical estimates). Strictly speaking, the correlations would need to be time dependent to allow an accurate fit. This could either be a bespoke process to calibrate to important FX rates or a global calibration to attempt to fit all FX option volatilities. In reality, the complexity that this introduces may not be worthwhile.

15.4.4   Other Asset Classes

Exposure simulation models for asset classes other than interest rate and FX will generally be of lower importance depending on the portfolio in question. For example, credit products are typically always collateralised, and many equity, commodity, and inflation derivatives will be transacted by financial counterparties on a collateralised basis and not used much by uncollateralised counterparties such as corporates. The following approaches are generally taken:

- *Inflation.* A common approach here is a three-factor representation of the inflation process (lognormal) and the real and nominal rates (HW1F), sometimes known as the Jarrow-Yildirim model (Jarrow and Yildirim 2003). This approach is based on a foreign-currency analogy, where real and nominal rates are modelled, and the inflation rate is seen as an 'FX rate' connecting these rates. The real rate volatility may be set as a multiplier to the nominal rate volatility with fixed mean reversion and a high correlation between real and nominal rates. The drift of the inflation rate can be calibrated to zero-coupon inflation swaps, and the volatility to inflation caplets for the most liquid strike (no skew). Given that most xVA implementations will already use a multicurrency framework, this is a natural approach to fit within the same framework.
- *Commodities.* Some commodities tend to be highly mean reverting around a level, which represents the marginal cost of production (see Geman and Nguyen 2005 and Pindyck 2001). Furthermore, many commodities exhibit seasonality in prices due to harvesting cycles and changing consumption throughout the year. Commodities trading as spot (e.g. precious metals) may use a lognormal assumption similar to FX or equity. Forward-based commodities may use what is sometimes referred to as a Gabillon (1992) model, which is an analytically-tractable two-factor model for the (positively-correlated) spot and long-term prices. Most common calibration instruments are commodity swaps and swaptions (see Geman 2009).
- *Equity.* Whilst less important due to being short-dated and/or collateralised/exchange-traded, a common equity approach is a lognormal (Black–Scholes) with dividends. A factor model may be used to avoid simulation of a large number of equity underlyings.
- *Credit.* Credit models are required for two reasons: to represent the exposure of credit derivatives and also to model WWR. A CIR++ model (Brigo and Mercurio 2001) is quite common for credit derivatives, although it should be noted that all such counterparties will probably be collateralised. WWR is discussed in more detail in Section 17.6.

15.4.5   Correlations, Proxies, and Extrapolation

A typical exposure simulation will require a large number of correlation estimates between underlying risk factors. For example, assuming a one-factor interest rate representation, simulating 20 interest rates would lead to 19 FX rates (involving the base currency) and then $\frac{39 \times 38}{2} = 741$ correlations. Even for a single transaction, this dependency can be important: a cross-currency swap has risk to the FX rate and the two interest rates, and hence, at a minimum, three risk factors, and the three correlations between them must be accounted for. However, individual correlations will have very different importance in defining future exposure. For two IRSs in different currencies, the correlation between the interest rates may be a very important parameter. However, the correlation between, for example, the price of oil and an FX rate may be unimportant or completely irrelevant. It will be informative to make a distinction between *intra-* and *inter-*asset class correlations.

The nature of a lot of client business for banks is asset class-specific by counterparty. For example, interest rate products may be traded with one counterparty, and commodities with another. Intra-asset class dependencies will be important components. For example, to specify the future exposure of two interest rate transactions in different currencies, the correlation between the interest rates is important. Indeed, it may be a more important factor than the impact of subtle yield curve movements, which justifies the use of a relatively parsimonious (e.g. HW1F) interest rate model. Intra-asset correlations can be estimated from time series and may also be observed via the traded prices of products such as spread options, baskets, and quantos.

In some cases, the population of transactions with a given counterparty will cover two or more asset classes or contain cross-asset-class transactions such as cross-currency swaps. The inter-asset class correlation between the risk factors must then be considered carefully. Inter-asset-class correlations are harder to estimate from historical time series as the correlations are more likely to be unstable due to the more subtle relationship across asset classes. Furthermore, inter-asset correlations are less likely to be able to be implied from the prices of market instruments. However, such correlations, especially for uncollateralised counterparties, can often be less important due to single-asset-class transactions. Having said that, even a relatively simple end user of derivatives, such as an airline, could in theory trade across commodities, FX, and interest rate products, creating a future exposure dependent on many inter- and intra-asset-class correlation parameters.

In general, it is not possible to imply such correlations from market prices (with the exception of the FX volatility case mentioned in Section 15.4.3), and so they are typically estimated historically. The estimation generally uses a reasonably large data history and may avoid estimation methods such as exponentially-weighted moving average (EWMA, Section 9.3.4), which could lead to instability in correlation numbers. The historical correlations may only be updated periodically (e.g. quarterly).

When using an integrated diffusion scheme, it is necessary to generate integrated correlation matrices for propagating the simulation, so as to maintain the correct joint multidimensional correlation structure. These integrated correlation matrices are generated from the incremental co-variances and variances associated with each time step period via numerical integrals of the deterministic (piece-wise constant) volatility term structure functions for each respective process, and the corresponding instantaneous pairwise correlation value.

Where risk factors have no underlying developed option market, it may be appropriate to use proxies to define the volatility term structure. An alternative is to use historical estimates on volatility, although in such cases it is important to consider the impact of mean reversion. In situations such as interest rates, a constant (e.g. historical) volatility together with mean reversion can create low volatility for long-term horizons. On the other hand, where there is no mean reversion (e.g. FX), the risk factor distribution over long-term horizons may be excessively broad.

Related to the above point, volatilities often need to be extrapolated beyond the last observable point, which will obviously require relatively simple assumptions. However, applying flat extrapolation to FX and interest rate model volatility parameters leads to monotonically-increasing implied FX forward volatilities, potentially leading to excessively high long-dated volatility, which would impact instruments with long-dated FX risk such as cross-currency swaps. It may be relevant to provide some ad hoc adjustment, such as reducing volatilities beyond a certain point, to control such problems.

15.5 MODELLING MARGIN (COLLATERAL)

15.5.1 Overview

In order to deal with collateralised counterparties, exposure simulation models require the modelling of the *future* risk-mitigation effect of margin on the underlying credit exposure to a particular counterparty. Since metrics such as EPE depend on the entire exposure profile, it is necessary to quantify the impact of the future margin that would be held in each given scenario at a future date. Margin modelling is important in the following situations:

- bilateral derivatives with margin agreements;
- exchange-traded and centrally-cleared trades; and
- repos and securities financing trades.

Bilateral derivatives represent the most important category above. However, it is also important to model margin in cases such as centrally-cleared trades, both to assess the capital requirements to the CCP (Section 13.6) and also to determine the risk when acting as a clearing member. Repos and securities financing trades are generally low risk due to being short-dated.

Uncollateralised exposure should be considered over the full time horizon of the transaction(s) in question. Long-term distributional assumptions, such as mean reversion and drift, are important and the specifics of the transactions, such as cash flow dates and exercise times, must be considered. In general, margin partially changes this by transforming a risk that should be considered usually over many years into one that is primarily relevant over a much shorter period. As discussed previously (Section 7.5.2), this period is commonly known as the MPoR. The impact of the MPoR is illustrated in Figure 15.17, which shows some future point at which a position is strongly collateralised (e.g. no threshold in the margin agreement), and hence the main concern is the relatively small amount of risk over the MPoR. Note that, due to the length of the MPoR, aspects such as drift and the precise details of the transaction may not be important. Indeed, some of the intricacies of modelling exposure can often be ignored, as long as the counterparty is well collateralised. The problem now becomes a short-term market risk issue and therefore shares some commonalities with market risk value-at-risk (VAR) methodologies (Section 2.6.1).

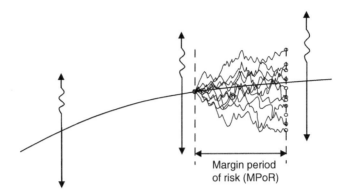

Figure 15.17   Schematic illustration of the impact of collateralisation on future exposure.

Whilst the above is generally true, the overall impact of margin is not always straight-forward and may not reduce the exposure as much as might be expected. Furthermore, certain contractual terms can be more difficult to assess and quantify. Note also that, whilst margin may leave residual market risk that is only a fraction of the uncollateralised risk, it will be more difficult and subjective to quantify and indeed hedge.

It could be argued that, in some situations, modelling margin over the entire life of a portfolio is unnecessary, and that the current risk for a short period equal to the MPoR can be used as a proxy for this. Indeed, in certain situations it might be misleading to model the entire life of the portfolio: for example, a client portfolio of short-dated derivatives that are being constantly hedged and replaced. Regulatory capital methodologies have historically recognised this through the use of the so-called 'shortcut' method (Section 13.4.1).

However, going forward, such simple approaches do not appear to be recognised. Regulators generally require internal models to make full multiperiod calculations of margined exposures,[13] rather than use single-period approximations (e.g. the shortcut method – is being removed as a possible regulatory capital calculation, as discussed in Section 13.4.1). The need to fully model margin in regulatory capital calculations is emphasised by the incoming rules for standardised CVA (SA-CVA) (Section 13.3.5), with BCBS (2017) stating:

> For margined counterparties, the exposure simulation must capture the effects of margining collateral that is recognised as a risk mitigant along each exposure path. All the relevant contractual features such as the nature of the margin agreement (unilateral vs bilateral), the frequency of margin calls, the type of collateral, thresholds, independent amounts, initial margins and minimum transfer amounts must be appropriately captured by the exposure model.

---

[13] European Banking Authority (EBA) Capital Requirements Regulation states 'The model shall estimate EE [EPE] at a series of future dates t1, t2, t3, etc.' EBA Capital Requirements Regulation > Part Three > Title II > Chapter 6 > Section 6 > Article 284. www.eba.europa.eu.

With respect to different transactions and trading relationships, regulation only treats them differently in the choice of the MPoR, where the following rules generally apply:[14]

- the MPoR should be five business days for repurchase transactions (repos), securities- or commodities-lending or -borrowing transactions, and margin-lending transactions;
- the MPoR should be five business days for centrally-cleared transactions;
- the MPoR should be 10 business days for all other (generally bilateral OTC) derivatives;
- the MPoR shall be at least 20 business days for netting sets involving either illiquid margin or an OTC derivative that cannot be easily replaced; and
- the MPoR must be increased by $N - 1$ days for a contractual remargining period of N which is greater than one day.

There is, therefore, a general need to capture margining in any exposure simulation.

15.5.2   Margin Period of Risk

The close-out process in the aftermath of a default will not occur instantaneously, but rather will be a gradual process involving a combination of:

- delay before the counterparty is deemed or assumed to be in default;
- macro-hedging, replacement/unwinding of hedges; and
- liquidation of non-cash margin.

As noted in Section 7.5.2, it is important to realise that the MPoR is a model parameter and – since the exposure simulation modelling will be necessarily simplistic – will not align with the actual time taken in a default scenario. There are a number of effects that exposure simulations will ignore or simplify and it is important that the chosen MPoR accounts for these. Some examples are:

- *Risk reduction*. At some point during the default process, risk will be gradually reduced as a result of hedging, replacing, and unwinding positions. This would tend to shorten the risk horizon, as discussed in Section 7.5.2 and shown in Appendix 7A.
- *Conditionality*. Exposure quantification generally assumes implicitly that after a counterparty default, the economic conditions will remain unchanged. In reality, market conditions in the aftermath of a default may be different; most obviously, there may be increased volatility. This will be particularly significant for a large financial counterparty. Indeed, in the aftermath of the Lehman Brothers bankruptcy, the volatility in the CDS market was five times greater than in the preceding period (Pykhtin and Sokol 2013). Counterparties that post margin generally tend to be larger financial institutions and have larger OTC derivatives exposures. The impact of their default, notwithstanding any margin considerations, may be considered to be significant. This would tend to increase the required MPoR unless modelled directly. Following the 'square root of time' rule (Section 7.5.2), in order to mimic the impact of volatility doubling in the aftermath of a default, it would be necessary to *quadruple* the MPoR.

---

[14] EBA Capital Requirements Regulation > Part Three > Title II > Chapter 6 > Section 6 > Article 285. www.eba.europa.eu.

- *Disputes.* In the case of a dispute, the undisputed amount should be transferred, and then the parties involved should enter into negotiations to agree on the disputed amount. The latter procedure may take significant time and would suggest an increase in the MPoR. Indeed, this is one of the aspects under Basel III that can lead to an increase in the regulatory MPoR (Section 13.4.5).
- *Cash flows and margin flows.* Although the MPoR is a relatively short period, for some portfolios there may be cash flows that would occur during this interval. There is also the question of whether both parties or merely the defaulting party will cease to make margin payments during the MPoR.

The discussion above should illustrate that the MPoR is a parameter that may incorporate many effects and it should not be interpreted as being precisely related to the actual time to close out a portfolio in a counterparty default scenario. A typical exposure simulation model effectively assumes that the whole portfolio will be closed out and replaced at the end of the MPoR, and ignores many or all of the above effects.

Very little attention has been given to the precise modelling of the events during the MPoR. One recent exception looking at the impact of cash flow payments is Andersen et al. (2015). It is important to balance the incremental benefit of more advanced margin modelling against the fact that the MPoR is by nature very hard to quantify. The MPoR is a ubiquitous parameter that captures the general uncertainty and delay inherent in the margin process. However, it does express many uncertain aspects, such as margin disputes and increased market volatility in a single variable.

Note finally that the MPoR is used for modelling credit exposure and for the purpose of quantifying components such as PFE and CVA. It is not relevant for modelling margin for the purpose of calculating collateral and funding value adjustments. However, such adjustments may still need to quantify a collateralised exposure, as will be discussed in Section 15.5.3.

15.5.3   Modelling Approach

The obvious output of an exposure simulation is the value of the portfolio at each point in time and in each scenario, which will be denoted as *value$_t$*. This allows quantities such as EPE to be calculated easily and there is, therefore, no need to store any intermediate information, such as cash flows or calculations that led to the evaluation of this value at a given point in time.

Knowing *value$_t$* will allow various other features to be included after the original calculation of the uncollateralised exposure. For example, a mandatory break clause would be assumed to lead to the portfolio value being zero at all points in time after the break. A resettable transaction can be treated by resetting the value to zero and changing the contractual rate at each of the reset dates. Since clauses such as resets and mandatory breaks are transaction level, this would need to be done prior to aggregation of the portfolio value.

Margin, at first glance, is fairly easy to include. Since margin will typically apply at the portfolio level, it is not necessary to retain information on individual transactions. The uncollateralised portfolio value along a given simulation path can simply be used together with the logic to determine, at each point, how much margin would be posted. This amount, in turn, would determine the collateralised portfolio value. Examples of how to do this were presented in Section 7.3.6. Traditional margin agreements are usually treated separately, independently, and after the quantification of uncollateralised exposure, since they generally depend on the value of the underlying portfolio and portfolio-specific fixed contractual terms (such as thresholds). However, there are caveats to this which will be discussed below.

Spreadsheet 15.4 Simple margin simulation based on portfolio value.

In order to deal with collateralised counterparties, exposure simulation models must incorporate the implicit delay caused by the MPoR (Figure 15.18). To quantify the collateralised exposure at a given time t, it is necessary to know information regarding how much margin would have been requested previously up to time $t - MPoR$.

The simplest way to modify an exposure simulation to include margin is, therefore, to include additional points to determine the amount of margin that would be called prior to the start of the MPoR. This could use either a look-back approach with single points, or a more continuous approach[15] simulating at all points, with a time step equal to the MPoR (Figure 15.19). The former approach is clearly simpler and allows an easily-configurable MPoR without changing the main time step of the simulation. The latter approach, whilst more expensive, does allow any path dependency in margining to be represented.

Generalising the previous definition of credit exposure (Section 11.1.1, Equation 11.1) to include margin, but ignoring aspects such as segregation for now, gives:

$$Positive\ exposure_t = \max(value_t - C_{t-MPoR}, 0), \tag{15.3}$$

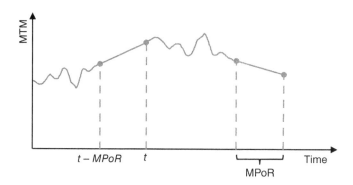

Figure 15.18   Schematic illustration of the use of MPoR to model the impact of margin.

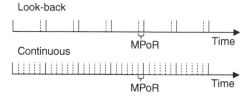

Figure 15.19   Illustration of time grid for exposure simulation, with additional points included for margin calculations.

---

[15] Continuous with respect to the MPoR unit.

This – seemingly reasonably – defines the collateralised exposure as being determined by the portfolio value at the current time less the amount of margin required at a *previous* time $t - MPoR$. In this situation, a positive value for C_{t-MPoR} would indicate margin received, whilst a negative value would indicate margin posted.

One possible problem with the above is that it assumes that the amount of margin at a given time can be calculated knowing only information available at that time. This is generally true but not always, one example being minimum transfer amounts (MTAs). Take the following example: the current portfolio value is $value_t = 150$ and the value at a point in the past corresponding to the MPoR is $value_{t-MPoR} = 110$. It may, therefore, be reasonable to assume that $C_{t-MPoR} = 110$, resulting in a positive exposure of $\max(150 - 110, 0) = 40$. However, this would assume that whatever margin was required at time $(t - MPoR)$ was above any minimum transfer amount. Table 7.7 in Section 7.3.6 illustrates that the value could be either lower or higher than this depending on the size of the MTA and the values prior to the point $t - MPoR$. To model this path dependency properly would require more time steps, as in the 'continuous' sampling shown in Figure 15.19. Given that MTAs are typically small, this may not be considered important, and unless there is any strong path dependency (e.g. a large minimum transfer amount), then a look-back approach is a reasonable approximation.

Equivalently, there is the question of whether or not there is a difference between margin held that needs to be returned and margin that needs to be posted outright. Again, a distinction does not often have to be made, but there are situations where this is important, such as in the consideration of 'cheapest-to-deliver' optionality (Section 16.2.3).

Assuming a simple modelling of a collateralised exposure via Equation 15.3 makes the following assumptions:

- the defaulting party will make any contractual margin payments up to the time $t - MPoR$, but cease doing so after this point;
- the surviving party will also stop making margin payments at the same point; and
- both counterparties will continue to pay cash flows during the MPoR period (which will be captured by the change between $value_{t-MPoR}$ and $value_t$).

The above is probably unreasonable as the (defaulting) counterparty will likely cease any cash flow payments at the same time as stopping the posting of margin. Furthermore, the surviving party may at some point cease to make contractual payments (cash flows and margin), but only when it is aware of the default and/or is confident in the legal basis for stopping payments. Using the previous definitions of pre- and post-default, it is possible to propose more realistic assumptions ('improved model') compared to the 'classical model' (Table 15.4).

The improved model – or some variation of it – would be necessarily more complex than the classical model. In particular, it would require an extra time point to be included that would represent the point at which the counterparty is known to be in default, and so the surviving counterparty may cease to make payments. It would also require the (non-netted) cash flows to be known precisely, rather than being represented implicitly via the evolution of the term $value_t$ in Equation 15.1.

Note that regulation only specifies the length of the MPoR and does not define what precise assumptions should be made during this period. Regulation does not, therefore, prescribe a more complex modelling approach to be taken. It is also clear that banks

Table 15.4 Assumptions used in classical and improved models for modelling margin within the MPoR.

		Classical model		Improved model	
		Pre-default	Post-default	Pre-default	Post-default
Defaulting party	Cash flows	Continue		Stops	
	Margin	Stops		Stops	
Surviving party	Cash flows	Continue		Continue	Stops
	Margin	Stops		Continue	Stops

are using different modelling assumptions within their internal models (BCBS 2015b). Clearly, it is important to consider whether improved assumptions, with their additional complexity, are required.

It is also important to distinguish between MPoR modelling for capital purposes and for CVA calculations. In the former case, it could be argued that a better – and possibly more prudent – modelling of the MPoR is advantageous to avoid portfolios being under-capitalised. For CVA calculations, this may be seen as less relevant since it may not be possible to charge CVA to many collateralised counterparties, and the accounting CVA is not supposed to represent prudent – but rather fair – assumptions. However, given that future regulation (BCBS 2017) is aligning regulatory capital with accounting CVA, this point may not apply at some point in the future.[16]

15.5.4 Initial Margin

The historical approach to modelling margin was relatively simple because – assuming a classical model for the MPoR – the approach only relied on the portfolio value at each time step in the simulation. This is because variation margin is directly related to the portfolio value and the contractual terms in the margin agreement. The only complexity in modelling margin would have been in relation to an improved modelling of the MPoR, as discussed in Section 15.5.3.

However, the growing presence of initial margin being held against bilateral OTC derivatives due to the 'bilateral margin requirements' (Section 7.4) is requiring more advanced methods for modelling the amount of future margin held to quantify correctly the risk-reducing impact of initial margin. Whilst such additional margin is not completely uncommon historically, its impact prior to the bilateral margin requirements has been of less concern for the following reasons:

- In bilateral derivatives, the additional margin was often based on simple metrics such as percentage of notional, which are easy to model.
- In centrally-cleared derivatives, where a party was acting as a clearing member (and therefore facing clients bilaterally), there may have been less concern over residual risk since the portfolios would typically be short-dated.

---

[16] The alignment of accounting and regulatory CVA is part of the SA-CVA approach described in Section 13.3.5.

- Traditional non-internal model methods for quantifying capital, notably CEM described in Section 13.4.2,[17] did not treat initial margin or other overcollateralisation specifically. This actually led to a rather favourable treatment and would often lead to capital charges (via the exposure at default) being zero. This is no longer the case due to the replacement of CEM with SA-CCR, which does treat such components (known as the 'net independent collateral amount') directly but in a rather conservative fashion, as described in Section 13.4.3. So, for non-IMM banks, the regulatory capital treatment of initial margin has become less favourable.

Considering the modelling of collateralised exposure in a general way, the calculation of the future amount of margin held can be considered – in order of increasing complexity – to be a function of the following:

- deterministic characteristics of the portfolio (e.g. the notional or time to maturity of a transaction) that do not depend on the market conditions;
- quantities dependent on the market state at the time point in question (e.g. variation margin linked to the portfolio-level, or possibly transaction-level, value, and contractual quantities such as thresholds);
- as above, but requiring additional calculations (e.g. sensitivities and aggregation rules as required for the ISDA SIMM, as described in Section 9.4.4); and
- as above, but also requiring the time series of variables up to the future time point in question (e.g. CCP initial margin methodologies using historical simulation).

The first two points above are relatively easy since – in addition to the appropriate time-step modelling for the MPoR mentioned above – it requires only basic information and calculations. This applies mainly to the general discussion in Section 15.5.3. The third and fourth situations above introduce dramatically more difficult calculations and data requirements, such as:

- reproduction of the necessary calculations that may only be usually done at time zero (e.g. sensitivities and VAR);
- the reconstruction and generation of all the required data (e.g. historical time series); and
- the provision of adequate computational resources in order to accomplish the above.

Due to the number of simulations and time steps in a typical exposure calculation, the above represents a significant computational requirement, especially since it likely covers a very large universe of transactions. For example, to include, without approximation, the risk-mitigation benefits of initial margin calculated under ISDA SIMM in an exposure simulation would require:

- the ability to determine which trades are subject (including partially)[18] to bilateral initial margin requirements and to allocate the €50m threshold to each portfolio;

---

[17] This is also the case for the so-called 'standardised method' that was mentioned briefly during the explanation of CEM.

[18] For example, the FX component of cross-currency swaps is currently exempt from initial margin.

- the ability to calculate dynamically the trade sensitivities (in addition to trade values) in all future scenarios (this is both an implementation and computation challenge);
- the incorporation of SIMM parameters and aggregation rules into the exposure simulation (and the provision of subsequent updates of these on an annual basis); and
- the ability to reconstruct the time series of returns for each risk factor so as to be able to determine how SIMM would recalibrate at a given future date.

Typically, there are a number of different methods that have been proposed to overcome such challenges. These approaches are similar to the need to calculate future initial margin for the calculation of MVA, discussed later in Section 20.2.4, and include:

- *Simple approximations.* Approaches based on normal distribution assumptions have been described by Andersen et al. (2017) and Gregory (2016).
- *Proxies.* The use of approximate pricing formulas (and their sensitivities) that are much faster to compute (e.g. Zeron and Ruiz 2018).
- *Adjoint algorithmic differentiation (AAD).* For fast calculation of sensitivities, as required by ISDA SIMM.
- *Regression techniques.* The use of information on risk factor evolution within the exposure simulation to approximate the initial margin (e.g. Anfuso et al. 2016 and Caspers et al. 2017).

It is important to balance carefully the effort in building a complex and accurate methodology for initial margin calculation against using a simpler but more conservative approach (that may produce, for example, less capital relief but be much easier to put into production). Not surprisingly, banks have not found it easy to get approval to incorporate the risk-reducing benefit of future initial margin into their IMM capital calculations (Figure 15.20).

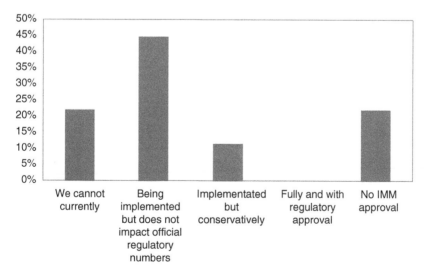

Figure 15.20 Incorporation of initial margin into IMM capital approaches. Source: McKinsey/ Solum Survey (2017).

15.6   EXAMPLES

15.6.1   Interest Rate Swap Example

Spreadsheet 15.5 HW1F model for exposure for interest rate products.

The first example will show the standalone exposure profiles for a pay fixed IRS with a notional of 1,000 using a HW1F model which can be reproduced with Spreadsheet 15.5. Figure 15.21 shows the interest rate curve to which the model is calibrated (in terms of the 'zero rates'). Also shown are the values of co-terminal forward starting swaps. Note that the value of the forward starting swaps is equal to the discounted EFV profile since, by arbitrage, the discounted expected value of the swap at some point in the future must be equal to the current price of a swap starting at that future point. This calculation of EFV is relatively simple and – unlike EPE or ENE – can be calculated without simulation. Note that the EFV is positive when paying the fixed rate, as discussed in Section 11.2.3. The equivalent receiver swap would have an equal and opposite EFV.

It is possible to use Monte Carlo simulation to calculate the exposure distribution of the swap.[19] First, it is necessary to simulate the interest rate paths, which are approximately centred around the forward rates as shown in Figure 15.22. A flat volatility of 1% and mean reversion parameter of 0.01 were used. Since the swap cash flows are paid on a quarterly basis, this same discretisation is used for the path-wise simulation of interest rates.

Given the interest rate simulations, it is possible to revalue the swap at each future date via the analytical formulas for discount factors. The resulting future value paths of the swap are shown in Figure 15.23. This expands into an envelope, but then contracts due to the ageing effect of cash flows (Section 11.2.2). Also shown are PFEs at the 5% and 95% confidence levels and the EPE and ENE.

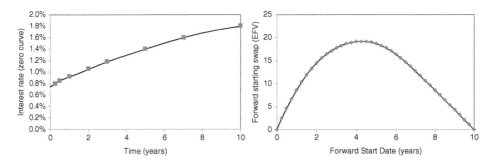

Figure 15.21   Interest rate curve and forward values of co-terminal forward starting swaps.

---

[19] A total of 5,000 simulations were used for all the examples.

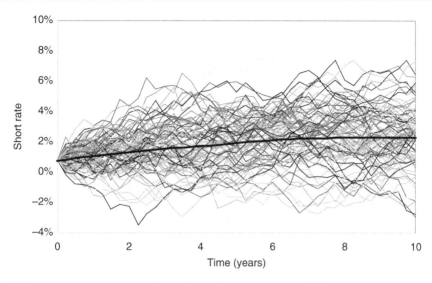

Figure 15.22   Interest rate paths with the forward rates shown (solid line).

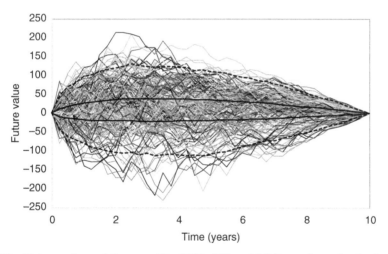

Figure 15.23   Future values of the swap. The PFEs (5% and 95%) are shown by the dotted black lines and the EPE and ENE are shown by the solid black lines.

Finally, Figure 15.24 shows the EPE, ENE, and EFV of the swap. Note that the sum of the EPE and ENE is approximately equal to the EFV, which is shown. The exact EPE and ENE are also shown via the valuation of the appropriate co-terminal swaptions (Section 15.4.2), which in this interest rate model can be evaluated analytically.

Figure 15.25 shows profiles for four variations on the above swap. First, a swap with unequal cash flow payment dates (receive quarterly, pay semiannually) which shows a jagged profile due to the unequal payment dates. Second, an ITM swap receiving a higher fixed rate. Note that the fact that the swap is ITM means that the exposure

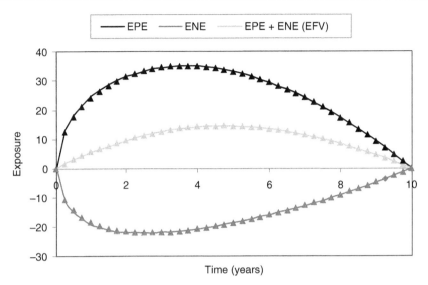

Figure 15.24 EPE, ENE, and EFV of the swap from Monte Carlo simulation. Also marked are the analytical results from valuing the forward start swaption (EFV) and appropriate co-terminal swaptions (EPE and ENE).

profile is more predictable: in the swaption analogy (Section 15.1.3), this is because the underlying swaption is either ITM (EPE) or OTM (ENE) and therefore less sensitive to volatility. Third, a three-year into seven-year (3Yx7Y) forward starting swap that shows a slightly different structure due to the absence of cash flows during the forward start period. Finally, a long physically-settled swaption based on the same forward starting swap. Note that the swaption is – like the ITM swap – reasonably predictable but does have some negative exposure after the exercise date, as discussed previously in Section 11.2.6.

The above example used a constant volatility assumption. As discussed in Section 15.4.2, volatility calibration is a challenge, especially when using relatively simple models. Figure 15.26 shows the EPE of a 20-year swap with a rate (not par rate) equal to that of the 10Yx10Y forward starting swap and a volatility function calibrated to the 20-year co-terminal swaptions. By construction, the 10Yx10Y swaption is reproduced almost exactly, but the EPE does not match precisely the other co-terminal swaptions due to the different market rates.

15.6.2   Trade-level Exposures

The examples in this section will use a number of real transactions, which are as follows:[20]

- *7Y payer IRS*. Seven-year pay fixed USD interest rate swap.
- *5Y payer IRS*. Five-year pay fixed USD interest rate swap.
- *5Y receiver IRS*. The opposite (i.e. receiver) of the above.

---

[20] I am grateful to IHS Markit for providing the simulation data for these examples.

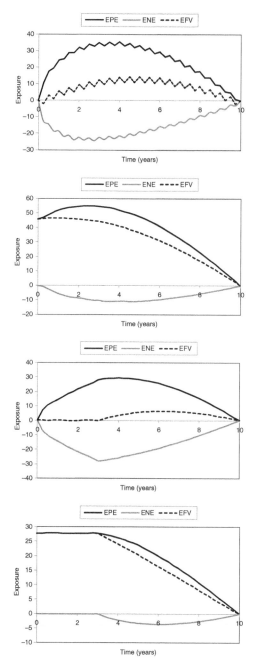

Figure 15.25 EPE, ENE, and EFV for (top to bottom) a swap with unequal cash flows, an ITM swap, a forward starting swap (3Yx7Y), and a physically-settled swaption (3Yx7Y).

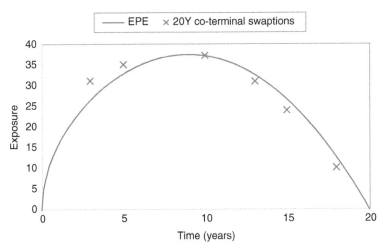

Figure 15.26   EPE for a 20-year swap with a fixed rate equal to the 10Yx10Y forward starting swap compared to 20-year co-terminal swaption values.

- *5Yx5Y long payer swaption.* Five-year long swaption on five-year pay fixed USD interest rate swap with physical delivery.
- *5Y USDJPY XCCY.* Five-year pay USD, receive JPY cross-currency swap.

All transactions have a notional of $100, except the cross-currency swap, which has a smaller notional of ¥10,000.[21] The exposures have been simulated at time intervals of three months, with a total of 2,000 simulations. The transaction-level EPE/ENE and PFE profiles (both positive and negative) are shown in Figure 15.27. All the results below will be reported in US dollars.

The interest rate and cross-currency swaps show the characteristic shapes discussed in Sections 11.2.2 and 11.2.1, with drift effects determined by the shape of the yield and interest rate differential respectively. The swaption exposure profile is more complex due to the fact that it is physically settled. During the first five years, the exposure can only be positive due to the long optionality, but there is some chance of negative exposure for the last five years where a swap may be present. However, on many paths where the swap would be OTM, the swaption would not have been exercised, and so the negative exposure (ENE or 5% PFE) is relatively small. The exposure profile of options was discussed previously in Section 11.2.6.

15.6.3   Portfolio Exposures

Spreadsheet 15.6 Illustration of the impact of netting.

---

[21] This is to prevent the inherently riskier cross-currency swap dominating the results. The USD notional was $43.50.

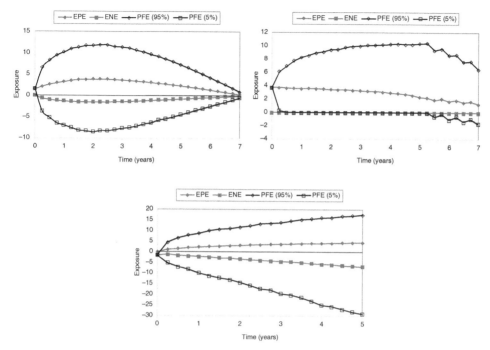

Figure 15.27   EPE, ENE, and PFE profiles for the 7Y payer IRS (top left), 5Yx5Y long payer swaption (top right) and 5Y USDJPY XCCY (bottom).

Portfolio effects cause exposures to be non-additive such that each transaction contributes less than its standalone exposure to the total exposure. One way to see this impact is by calculating the incremental exposure of a new transaction with respect to the existing portfolio. As discussed in Section 15.2.2, the impact of the portfolio effect depends on the interaction between the new transaction and the existing portfolio. Figure 15.28 shows the standalone and incremental exposure (EPE and ENE) for a directional trade.[22] In this case, there is only a relatively small reduction in EPE and ENE due to the fact that the exposure is almost additive.

Figure 15.29 shows a similar example, but where the new trade can be considered to be neutral or offsetting.[23] In this case, the reduction in EPE and ENE is large as a result of the strong cancellation effect between the portfolio and the new trade. Note that the effect is relatively complex: although the absolute reduction in EPE and ENE is similar, the ENE profile actually changes sign. Note also that there is no incremental effect for the EFV (which is the sum of the EPE and ENE): the incremental EFV is the same as the standalone EFV.

---

[22] This trade is the 7Y payer IRS described in Section 15.6.2, with the existing portfolio assumed to be made up of the 5Yx5Y long payer swaption. This is directional since both the swap and swaption are in the same currency and paying the fixed rate.

[23] This trade is the same 7Y payer IRS, but the existing portfolio is assumed to contain the 5Y USDJPY XCCY. There is no definitive definition of neutral or offsetting. In this case, the EPE effect is more neutral, since it reduces but stays mainly the same sign, whereas the ENE changes sign and so would be better defined as offsetting.

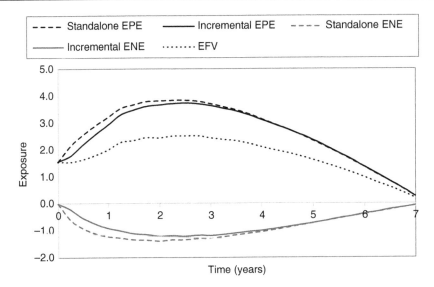

Figure 15.28 Standalone and incremental exposures for the case of a directional trade.

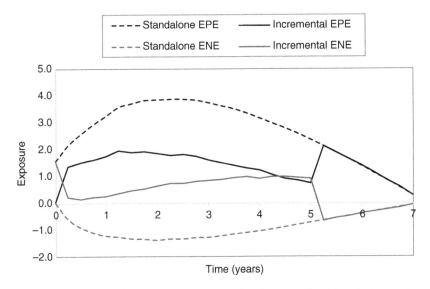

Figure 15.29 Standalone and incremental exposures for the case of a risk-reducing trade.

We now compare incremental and marginal exposures for two different trades: a cross-currency swap (XCCY Swap) and an IRS.[24] Figure 15.30 shows the EPE allocated incrementally (in both ways) and marginally. Note that the top line is the same in all cases, as this represents the total EPE. The second transaction allocated incrementally has a relatively small exposure, to the detriment of the first transaction. The marginal

---

[24] This corresponds to the 5Y USDJPY XCCY and 7Y payer IRS.

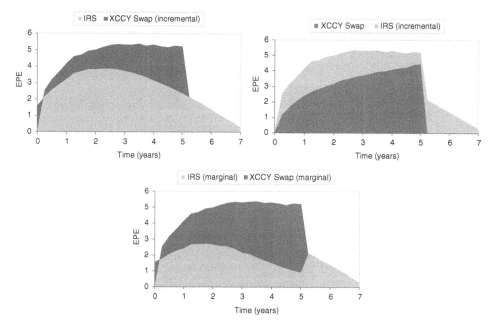

Figure 15.30 Illustration of the breakdown of the EPE of the interest rate and cross-currency swaps via incremental (interest rate swap first), incremental (cross currency swap first), and marginal allocation.

allocation is more balanced and would be appropriate if the transactions occurred at the same time.[25] The respective CVA and FVA numbers for this example will be shown later in Sections 17.4.2 and 18.3.3.

Marginal exposures can be materially different from standalone exposures. The marginal allocation of EPEs for the five transactions[26] is shown in Figure 15.31 and compared to the standalone contributions (which are significantly larger due to the lack of portfolio effects). The marginal allocation is very different compared to the standalone contributions. Most obviously, the receiver IRS has a negative marginal EPE contribution due to being risk reducing with respect to the payer IRS (which has an equal and opposite marginal EPE) and the swaption.

Spreadsheet 15.7 Marginal EPEs.

Marginal EPEs will translate directly into marginal xVA (and PFE) contributions, which will be revisited in Sections 17.4 and 18.3.3. Marginal allocations may be useful

---

[25] There is still some problem of allocation here since, for trades occurring at the same time, we wish to allocate marginally, whilst the total impact of the trades should be allocated incrementally with respect to existing trades in the netting set. An obvious way to get around this problem is to scale the marginal contributions of the trades so that they match the total incremental effect.

[26] Defined at the start of Section 15.6.2.

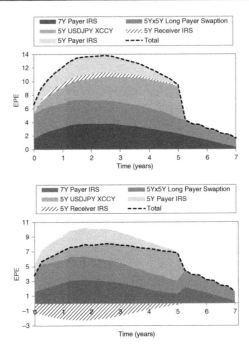

Figure 15.31 Illustration of the standalone (top) and marginal (bottom) EPE of the five transactions. Note that in the latter case the total reflects the subtraction of the negative contribution for the receiver interest rate swap.

to analyse when attempting to reduce the overall exposure of the transactions in order to comply with the credit limit[27] or to optimise xVA. All other things being equal, the transaction with the higher marginal EPE (or PFE) is the most relevant to look at. There are two points of interest here. Firstly, the marginal allocation is not homogeneous with time and so, depending on the horizon of interest, the highest contributor will be different. Secondly, it is not always easy to predict, *a priori*, which transaction will be the major contributor.

15.6.4 Notional Resets

Notional resets are similar to collateralisation, with the following differences:

- they are typically defined at the transaction rather than portfolio level;
- the reset is a settlement paid in cash; and
- the reset is periodic (e.g. quarterly), and therefore the risk reduction is weaker compared to the shorter MPoR (e.g. 10 days).

---

[27] In such a case, PFE, rather than expected positive exposure (EPE), would be the appropriate metric to consider. Whilst the marginal PFE numbers are systemically higher than the EPEs shown, there is no change in the qualitative behaviour.

A common example of a reset is in a cross-currency swap. In a standard cross-currency swap, as the FX rate moves, one party will be ITM and the other will be OTM with respect to the exchange of notional at the end of the transaction. This can create a large exposure, as shown in Figure 15.27. In a notional resetting cross-currency swap, the notional of one leg resets on every coupon period to rebalance the FX exposures in the transaction. The mark-to-market difference at each reset is settled from the OTM to the ITM party.

Spreadsheet 15.8 Notional resetting cross-currency swap.

Figure 15.32 shows the exposure of standard and notional resetting cross-currency swaps (quarterly coupons). The exposure is clearly reduced by the reset, which brings the value back to zero at each quarterly date.

15.6.5   Impact of Variation Margin

As discussed in Section 15.5.3, modelling variation margin is relatively straightforward as it is generally related directly to the value of the underlying portfolio, together with any relevant parameters such as thresholds. This means that the impact of margining can be accounted for after the simulation of exposure, under the assumption that the margin agreement depends only on the net portfolio value and not on other market variables.[28] This has been described previously in Sections 11.3.3 and 15.5.3.

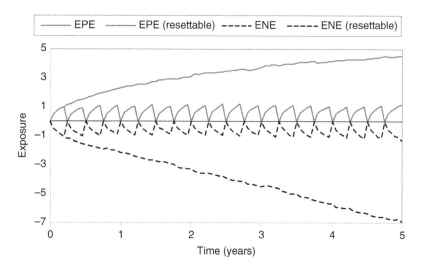

Figure 15.32   Exposure of standard and notional resetting cross-currency swaps.

---

[28] There are situations where this assumption may not be entirely appropriate – for example, margin parameters may be defined in different currencies to the deals to which they apply. In practice, this means some FX translations may be required when the margin parameters are applied within the simulation. However, in the majority of situations the assumptions made will be valid and will greatly simplify the analysis of collateralised exposures.

> **Spreadsheet 15.9 Quantifying the impact of margin on exposure.**

The examples below use a portfolio of three interest rate swaps and one cross-currency swap with a total notional of £325. More details can be found in Spreadsheet 15.9.[29] The exposure simulation is done with a 'continuous' grid (Figure 15.9) with a time step of 10 days and uses a 'classical' model (Table 15.4). This means that the MPoR can be assumed to be an integer multiple of this amount. The thresholds and MTAs are assumed to be zero. There is assumed to be no market risk on the margin itself (i.e. it is paid in cash in the portfolio base currency).

In general, for a strongly-collateralised position (variation margin, zero threshold, and assumed MPoR of 10 days), the amount of margin will track the value of the portfolio with an inherent delay due to the modelled MPoR. This is illustrated in Figure 15.33 which shows a single simulation path. Note that there is material noise due to the MPoR and that this noise is present even when the portfolio value is negative (Section 11.3.3). This is due to the need to post margin against a negative portfolio value, which creates risk in case the portfolio value increases and the counterparty defaults.[30]

The overall impact of margin on EPE and PFE (the latter at the 95% confidence level) is shown in Figure 15.34. There is still a significant exposure due to the MPoR: although the 10-day MPoR is significantly shorter than the portfolio maturity (125 times),[31] the risk reduction will be more approximated by the square root of time (approximately 11 times).

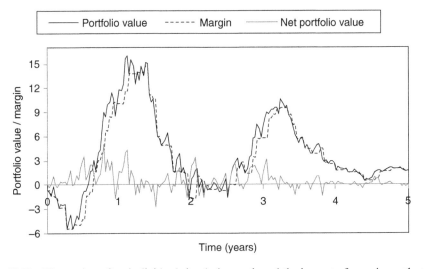

Figure 15.33   Illustration of an individual simulation path and the impact of margin on that path.

---

[29] I am grateful to IBM for providing the underlying portfolio simulations which were first used in the second edition of this book.

[30] This is because variation margin is not segregated (Section 11.4.3).

[31] Five years divided by 10 days, assuming 250 days in a year.

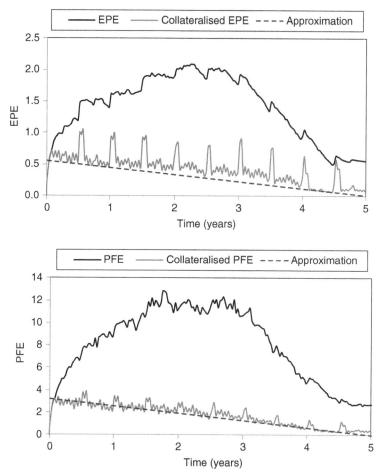

Figure 15.34 Illustration of EPE (top) and 95% PFE (bottom) calculated with and without collateralisation.

Furthermore, the collateralised exposure also shows 'collateral spikes' (Section 7.3.6) due to the payment of cash flows (for which margin is not received immediately). These spikes represent an increase in the exposure for a length of time corresponding to the MPoR. The collateral spikes are not as pronounced for the PFE since this represents an extreme scenario, whereas the cash flow payment is the same in all scenarios. Note also that the relative reduction in the PFE is better, since not all simulations contribute equally to the PFE, and those with the most contribution (when the exposure is high) are precisely the ones where the most margin is taken. Note that margin spikes are considered by regulators to be part of counterparty risk and should not be treated separately as settlement risk (see BCBS 2015b).

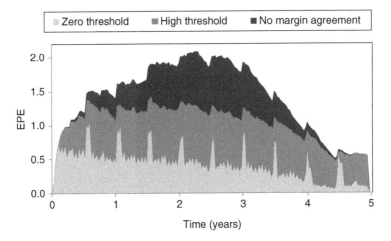

Figure 15.35   Illustration of EPE calculated with different threshold assumptions.

It is possible to approximate the collateralised EPE and PFE quite well, as shown in Figure 15.34 (see Appendix 15C for more details). The PFE approximation is better since it is less sensitive to effects such as margin spikes.

The discretisation of the exposure simulation is clearly important in terms of correctly capturing the impact of cash flows. Furthermore, the precise modelling assumptions within the MPoR can have a significant impact on quantities such as EPE. This has been discussed by Andersen et al. (2017).

The above example of a strongly-collateralised portfolio is relevant for the consideration of EPE and PFE and also later CVA (and possibly DVA). It is probably not relevant for funding (FVA) considerations where the MPoR would be assumed to be negligible since this does not correspond to a default scenario (Section 11.4.2).

One situation where funding would be a consideration is if there is a significant threshold in the margin agreement, although this is becoming increasingly uncommon. Figure 15.35 shows the EPE in a high-threshold margin agreement compared to the case of a zero-threshold or no margin agreement (i.e. infinite threshold). As expected, the exposure with a high threshold is intermediate between the other cases.

15.6.6   Impact of Initial Margin

Although initial margin is historically quite rare, receiving it against bilateral derivatives portfolios is becoming increasingly common due to the bilateral margin requirements (Section 7.4). Clearly, received initial margin can potentially reduce exposure to negligible levels if it is substantial enough. Note that the initial margin posted should not increase the exposure, as long as this is appropriately segregated.

One way of looking at an initial margin is that it converts counterparty risk into 'gap risk'. The gap risk is defined in this case by the chance of the exposure 'gapping' through the initial margin during the MPoR. Quantifying the residual exposure now becomes more difficult since it is driven by more extreme events and will be very sensitive to modelling assumptions. When assessing gap risk, one should be more concerned about distributional assumptions such as fat tails, jumps, and extreme co-dependency.

The modelling of received initial margin can be a challenge depending on the underlying methodology used to define the amount. Traditional 'independent amounts' based on simple metrics such as percentage of notional or the standardised margin schedule (Section 7.4.3) are easy to capture since they depend on known quantities within the exposure simulation (such as the remaining maturity for a given transaction). Whilst this does require transaction-specific information to be retained for a portfolio exposure calculation, this is relatively straightforward and not computationally demanding. More sophisticated initial margin methodologies, such as ISDA SIMM (Section 9.4.4), represent a more difficult challenge because (in addition to transaction-level information) they are model-based calculations. This means that (ideally) the full model-implied initial margin will be replicated within the exposure calculation. Put another way, as discussed in Section 15.5.4, SIMM-based initial margin is scenario dependent and will be different in each exposure simulation at the same point in time.

Since the initial margin is taken to a high confidence level (e.g. 99%), there is the question of whether a full modelling of exposure is actually required. At such high coverage, it would be expected that the residual exposure would be immaterial. Indeed, in a simple example (Appendix 15D), it is possible to show that 99% initial margin would reduce the exposure by over two orders of magnitude. However, this type of stylised analysis ignores features such as collateral spikes, which are typically not captured by an initial margin methodology (as such methodologies typically only consider market risk and not quantities such as cash flows). Furthermore, there are several reasons why the initial margin held against a portfolio will not equate to a true 99% coverage:

- the requirement to post initial margin (IM) - where it applies - only impacts new transactions, and so legacy trades will not have initial margin held against them (although this effect will fade over time until all legacy trades have matured);
- there is a threshold of up to €50m that can be applied to the IM amount; and
- there are exempt transactions (e.g. some FX).

Figure 15.36 illustrates some of the above points by showing the EPE in the presence of a 99% IM and compared to the case with only the variation margin (shown previously in Figure 15.34). Also shown is the case of partial coverage where IM is not taken against all of the underlying transactions.[32]

Figure 15.36 shows that even with a full 99% IM, the residual risk is material, which is mainly due to the collateral spikes. When IM provides only partial coverage, the residual exposure is larger still.

---

[32] Since the portfolio in question contains a cross-currency swap for which the FX portion is exempt from initial margin (Section 7.4.2).

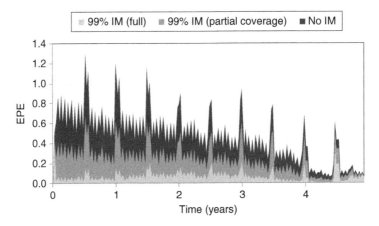

Figure 15.36   EPE with and without IM.

It will clearly be increasingly important in the future to model accurately the impact of dynamic IM. This is a very challenging computational task since it requires a calculation of the future IM that would be held at every single scenario in the exposure calculation.

Section 4
The xVAs

16

The Starting Point and Discounting

16.1 THE STARTING POINT

16.1.1 Basic Valuation

Before making a valuation *adjustment*, it is clearly necessary to define a valuation. Section 5.2.1 defined xVA as being an adjustment to what was defined as the 'base value'. The first question will be to define this base value. Whilst there is no unique choice, an obvious choice for this is a collateralised transaction in a mature market, such as the interbank market, or the valuation defined by a central counterparty (CCP).

Another definition of base value could be in relation to the historical view of this valuation, prior to the birth of valuation adjustments. Pricing derivatives has always been relatively complex. However, prior to the global financial crisis (GFC), pricing of vanilla products was believed to be well understood, and most attention was paid to more complex products ('exotics'). Credit, funding, and capital were ignored since their effects were viewed as negligible. The old-style framework for pricing financial instruments has undergone a revolution which is generally defined by the birth of xVA adjustments.

However, the concept of base valuation has also changed. Primarily, Interbank Offered Rates (IBORs) such as LIBOR (London Interbank Offered Rate) (Section 14.3.4) was traditionally seen as the appropriate discount rate for cash flows. For many years, LIBOR was seen as a good proxy for the risk-free rate, which was used to discount cash flows. It is important to note that both the time value of money and the concept of a risk-free rate are essentially theoretical constructs. Furthermore, traditional LIBOR discounting of risk-free cash flows, so standard for many years, was generally used with two key assumptions in mind:

- LIBOR is (or at least is a very good proxy for) the risk-free interest rate; and
- there are no material funding considerations that need to be considered – i.e. an institution can easily borrow and lend funds (including for margin purposes) at LIBOR.

The two above points are seen as being generally incorrect and so, irrespective of the move away from LIBOR as a benchmark, there has been a move away from using LIBOR as a discount rate.

Since concepts such as 'risk free' are becoming increasingly difficult to define, it is also important to define base value objectively and straightforwardly. Whilst, as mentioned above, there is no unique starting point, the base value would naturally conform to a number of principles:

- it would be a transaction-level (not portfolio-level) calculation;
- the calculation – at least for vanilla products – would be relatively simple (e.g. just requiring the discounting of cash flows), without any xVA adjustments (by definition); and
- it would require only knowledge of the transaction in question and no other quantities (such as the identity of the counterparty).

Associated with the starting point in valuation is the role of an xVA desk. In general, banks are set up with trading desks broadly concerned with the base value, and xVA desks responsible for valuation adjustments. A trading desk will have expertise in a given asset class, such as interest rates, foreign exchange (FX), or commodities. The trading desk may price, value, and manage at a base value that may ignore any counterparty risk, funding, margin (collateral),[1] and capital effects. The xVA desk will act as a centralised resource to deal with some or all of these components. Whilst this may be a setup driven by historical development rather than the optimal structure, it does require the notion of base value and separate xVA adjustments.

It is also important to note that certain special cases of xVAs related to funding and margin simply involve changing discounting assumptions. In these situations, it may be a matter of choice to define the base value.

16.1.2   Perfect Collateralisation

In order to provide a starting point, we will define the concept of 'perfect collateralisation' as the case where a transaction can be valued without any further xVA adjustments. Such a concept is largely theoretical (except perhaps from the point of view of a CCP) but is a convenient base case. Perfect collateralisation would correspond to the following factors:

- The transaction is covered by a symmetric (two-way) margin agreement based on the value of the underlying transaction, with zero threshold, minimum transfer amount, and rounding (i.e. the exact amount of required variation margin is received or posted at any time).
- There is no requirement to provide overcollateralisation (e.g. initial margin).
- Variation margin is transferred continuously (i.e. there is no delay in paying or receiving margin) and the underlying value does not change discontinuously.
- The margin period of risk (MPoR) is also zero (i.e. the transaction can be closed out and replaced with no associated cost).
- Margin can be reused and is not segregated.
- A single type of margin is used with a known remuneration rate (typically this will be cash in the currency of the transaction).

Under the above assumptions, the amount of margin received or posted will be at all times identical to the value of the transaction and denominated in the same currency. If there were an xVA formula, then it would involve the expected future value (EFV), which is a relatively simple metric to calculate (Section 11.1.5). However, there is no need for an xVA adjustment, as in this situation a perfectly-collateralised transaction can be valued by discounting with a rate equal to the contractual return paid on the margin (Piterbarg 2010).

'Collateral discounting' is illustrated qualitatively in Figure 16.1, showing symmetry between the accumulation of the margin (collateral) amount versus the discounting of

---

[1] The term 'margin' will generally be used, as in previous chapters, but the term 'collateral' will often be used to denote valuation adjustment terms. The terms 'margin' and 'collateral' can be considered largely interchangeable.

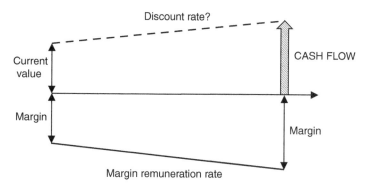

Figure 16.1   Illustration of the concept of 'collateral discounting'.

the cash flow. Since the cash flow is perfectly collateralised, the amount of margin at the end must be equal to the cash flow amount. Accordingly, the amount of margin currently held must be equal to the value of the cash flow. The only way to achieve this is for the discount rate used to value the cash flow to be equal to the margin remuneration rate. Note that this is the case even if this contractual rate is zero (i.e. there is no discounting) or negative (i.e. discount factors greater than zero). It also follows that if the margin is in a different currency, then the remuneration rate in *this* currency (converted to the currency of the cash flow) is the correct discount rate. It is also possible that the cash flows may be in different currencies, in which case the same argument will hold. This may be inconvenient since, for example, the margin against an FX transaction must be in only one currency. However, to allow margin to be posted in more than one currency will create optionality, as discussed in Section 16.2.3.

The only counterparty in the market that enjoys perfect collateralisation (or something very close to it) is a CCP. CCPs impose on their members (and their clients) margin requirements that are close to perfect collateralisation (e.g. the CCP can potentially make intraday margin calls). To the extent that this is not perfect (e.g. there are discontinuities in margin or valuation), then the CCP has initial margin to absorb losses. Note that CCP members are not perfectly collateralised primarily due to the need to fund financial resources (initial margin and default fund) paid to the CCP (against which they must also hold capital).

The other situation which is close to perfect collateralisation is a typical interbank transaction which is usually strongly two-way collateralised, although some valuation adjustments for counterparty risk, margin, and capital may still be relevant. Incoming bilateral margin rules (Section 7.4) will, on the one hand, improve this – for example, by requiring zero thresholds and incentivising or requiring cash margin. However, these rules also require bilateral initial margin posting, which reduces counterparty risk further but also creates extra funding costs and, consequently, the need for more valuation adjustments.

16.1.3   Collateral or OIS Discounting

The margin remuneration rate that defines the discounting rate need not be associated with any economic properties (such as being the 'risk-free rate'); it merely needs to be deterministic and known. However, the standard remuneration rate specified in a margin agreement is the overnight index spread (OIS) rate (Section 14.3.3). This is not because OIS is the risk-free rate, but rather because (with daily calls) margin is only guaranteed to be held for one day (although in practice it can be held for much longer, which is an important consideration). Hence, in this situation 'OIS discounting' is the correct base valuation. Since OIS is a good proxy for the risk-free rate, it turns out that collateral discounting is close to the traditional concept of 'risk-free valuation'. However, this is not a requirement: OIS is an appropriate discount rate because it is the margin remuneration rate, not because it is a proxy for the risk-free rate. In cases where another rate is referenced in the margin agreement, this is most obviously the appropriate discount rate. If it is not, then a separate – and potentially unnecessary – valuation adjustment will need to be made. This is discussed in more detail in Section 16.2.1.

Given the above, many transactions have seen a move from LIBOR to OIS discounting.

Even without the intervention of the GFC, OIS discounting should always have been the more correct way to approach valuation. However, prior to the crisis, the difference between this and traditional LIBOR discounting was not particularly material, as shown in Figure 14.8 in Chapter 14. There has been a gradual shift from LIBOR to OIS discounting for valuing collateralised transactions in recent years, although the extent of this move depends on the underlying product and region (see ISDA 2014).

Another driver for adopting OIS discounting is the move away from IBORs (Section 14.3.4). In this context, the appropriate discount rate will probably be the relevant risk-free rate as defined for the currency in question, assuming this aligns with the contractual remuneration rate. Note that such rates are not defined in a completely consistent fashion (e.g. some are secured rates and some are unsecured rates).

Prior to the IBOR transition discussed in Section 14.3.4, the use of LIBOR rates complicates valuation since there is one rate for discounting (OIS) and another for the projection of cash flows (LIBOR). This is often known as 'dual curve' pricing, which means that pricing and risk management of a single-currency interest rate swap involves multiple curves and basis risks.

Traditional interest rate curve building typically follows the following steps:

1. Select a set of liquid securities (cash deposits, futures, and swaps).
2. Make decisions on overlapping, interpolation, etc.
3. Fit a single curve via a 'bootstrap' procedure, which solves sequentially to fit market prices or a more complex algorithm.

Dual curve pricing complicates this process. LIBOR-OIS swaps are generally more liquid than OIS swaps, and so OIS and basis curves[2] have to be built simultaneously from these market prices together with standard LIBOR-based swaps. In this calibration, discounting is assumed based on OIS, whilst cash flows are projected in the relevant rate (OIS or LIBOR). This dual curve problem means that standard simpler bootstrap methods are not applicable. However, this remains a base valuation problem and does not need to be considered to be an xVA problem. More details on these issues can be found in, for example, Morini and Prampolini (2010), Kenyon (2010), and Mercurio (2010). The IBOR transition will generally remove these dual curve issues and potentially align the projection and discount rates via the chosen risk-free rate.

---

[2] This defines the basis between the LIBOR and OIS.

16.2   ColVA AND DISCOUNTING

16.2.1   Definition of ColVA

Suppose that a transaction denominated in one currency (Curr1) is collateralised in another currency (Curr2). This is a real situation in some markets, where local currency transactions are collateralised in USD, and there is, therefore, no reference for a local currency transaction collateralised in the local currency. Following the above discussion on collateral discounting, the obvious base valuation for this transaction is to discount the cash flows using the relevant remuneration rate (Curr2) converted back into the cash flow currency (Curr1) at the relevant forward FX rates (as observable from FX forwards and cross-currency basis swaps).

Suppose that, instead of the above, the base valuation was defined with respect to a discounting in Curr1. This is not necessarily incorrect – and it is an example of where there is no clear definition of base valuation – but it must be associated with a correction for the difference between the relevant rates in Curr1 and Curr2. This correction can be defined as a collateral value adjustment (ColVA).

Spreadsheet 16.1 ColVA calculation.

A simple ColVA can, therefore, be defined as the difference between discounting at a rate given by r_X compared with using some base rate r:

$$ColVA(r_X, r) = value(r_X) - value(r). \tag{16.1}$$

It is possible to show that, for a set of fixed cash flows, the above is equivalent to (Appendix 16A):

$$ColVA = -\sum_{i=1}^{T} DF(t_{i-1})ECB(t_{i-1})[\exp(-s_X(t_{i-1}) \times t_{i-1}) - \exp(-s_X(t_i) \times t_i)] \tag{16.2}$$

where $DF(t_{i-1})$ represents discount factors according to the base rate, and the spread $s_X = r_X - r$ represents the difference between the two rates. The term ECB represents the expected collateral balance in the future. For a perfectly-collateralised transaction, the ECB will be exactly equal to the EFV. This is a transaction-level quantity which is relatively easy to calculate (Section 11.1.5). This is not surprising since the ColVA is representing the difference between valuation using two different discounting rates. The above can be considered to be a discretised version of the following integral, which follows the general definition of an xVA calculation in Section 5.4.6:

$$ColVA = -\int_0^\infty DF(t)ECB(t)s_X^f(t)dt \tag{16.3}$$

where $s_X^f(t)$ is now the difference between the forward rates. The above integral can be calculated via other routes (see Green 2015).

To give an example of the above, consider the interest rate swap profile previously shown in Figure 15.23 (Section 15.6.1) with a notional amount of 100 million. This is a swap

Table 16.1   Illustration of ColVA calculation.

	Pay fixed	Receive fixed
Swap value discounted at base rate	−23,968	23,968
Swap value discounted at alternate rate	−33,401	33,401
Difference (Equation 16.1)	−9,433	9,433
ColVA formula (Equation 16.2)	−9,433	9,433

paying a rate which is slightly more than the par rate, and so the current value is negative. Suppose instead that the relevant margin rate was higher than the discount rate used (in the example shown, a flat spread of 10 bps is used). Discounting the cash flows at the higher rate leads to a more negative valuation (Table 16.1) since the floating payments to be received are larger for later dates, and the heavier discounting reduces their value by slightly more than those of the fixed payments to be paid. The same result can be achieved by using the ColVA formula. Here, the intuition as to the negative ColVA is that the ECB is positive, for which the received margin would have to be remunerated at a higher rate. The receive fixed swap shows the opposite behaviour (calculations shown in Spreadsheet 16.1).

The definition of ColVA above may seem unnecessary and circular since it merely corrects for a base valuation that has been done with the 'wrong' discount rate. However, there may be situations where this is helpful from an operational point of view, where a given transaction is valued at a default rate r (without any knowledge of the margin agreement) and a ColVA adjustment is made elsewhere to capture the correct rate r_X (with knowledge of the margin agreement). Such situations could apply to the following cases:

- *Different currencies.* Where the valuation and margin remuneration currencies are different – for example, a local transaction is by default valued by discounting in local currency and then an adjustment is made for the fact that the margin agreement requires (for example) USD cash.
- *Different remuneration rates.* Where the valuation and margin remuneration rates are different – for example, a transaction is discounted in OIS, but the margin agreement actually specifies a rate of OIS plus or minus a spread and so a ColVA adjustment is made to capture the spread differential.

Note that the choice of whether to discount with the correct rate or make a separate ColVA adjustment is probably a matter of choice and may depend on systems constraints and organisation responsibilities.

16.2.2   Asymmetry

The treatment in Section 16.2.1 assumed that a transaction was strongly (strictly speaking, perfectly) collateralised. In this case, with zero thresholds and small minimum transfer amounts, the ECB will closely track the EFV of the transaction (note that since this scenario is not default related, there is no need to consider an MPoR concept). The EFV is quite easy to calculate, and the ColVA is also a transaction-level calculation in line with the fact that it is simply representing a change of discount rate. The above treatment would also – trivially – treat an uncollateralised transaction where the ECB, and therefore the ColVA, would be zero. Note that the above treatment is, by design, symmetric in that it requires the remuneration rate on margin posted and received to be equivalent, and also that the transaction is strongly collateralised.

There are, however, more complicated cases that may need to be dealt with:

- *Partially collateralised.* In this case of undercollateralisation, the ECB will depend on the size of contractual terms such as thresholds which tend to decrease this value.
- *One-way collateralised.* In a one-way margin agreement, margin will be posted in only one direction, and the ECB will only be either positive or negative.
- *Asymmetric remuneration rates.* In this situation, the remuneration rates (or indeed eligible margin)[3] would be different.

Whilst the above situations are relatively uncommon, they do give rise to a more complex ColVA formula, which can be written as an extension of Equation (16.3) in terms of collateral received adjustment (ColRA) and collateral posted adjustment (ColPA):

$$ColVA = ColRA + ColPA = -\int_0^\infty DF(t)PCB(t)s_X^P(t)dt - \int_0^\infty DF(t)NCB(t)s_X^N(t)dt$$
(16.4)

with *PCB* and *NCB* being the positive collateral (margin) balance and negative collateral balance, respectively, and s_X^P and s_X^N representing the relevant spreads when the collateral balance is positive and negative, respectively. In the special case of perfect collateralisation, the PCB and NCB equal the uncollateralised expected positive exposure (EPE) and expected negative exposure (ENE), respectively, and the spreads are equal (Figure 16.2). Since EPE + ENE = EFV, this then returns to the special (discounting) case of Equation 16.3.

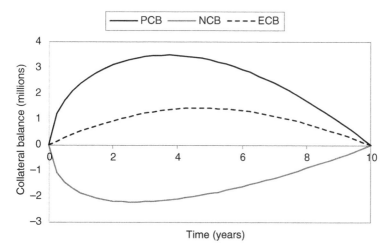

Figure 16.2   Illustration of PCB and NCB for a fully-collateralised interest rate swap. Note that these terms are analogous to the EPE and ENE for an uncollateralised swap (Figure 15.24).

---

[3] This also requires a discussion of cheapest-to-deliver margin in Section 16.2.3.

Table 16.2   Illustration of ColCA and ColBA calculation.

	Pay fixed
Difference (Equation 16.1)	−9,433
ColRA (Equation 16.4)	−24,226
ColPA (Equation 16.4)	14,799
ColRA + ColPA	−9,427

Table 16.2 shows the example of using the explicit ColVA expression for the fully-collateralised interest rate swap example shown previously. The ColRA (ColPA) term can be seen as the cost (benefit) of a higher remuneration rate when receiving (posting) margin. The sum of these two terms equals (with some Monte Carlo noise) the difference when discounting with a higher rate.[4]

In order to show the potential importance of the more complex ColVA formula, a real portfolio is used, and the following cases considered (Figure 16.3):

- *Strongly collateralised ('strong')*. A strong two-way margin agreement.
- *One-way collateralised in favour ('receive')*. A one-way margin agreement where the margin is only received. In this case, the PCB will be required.
- *One-way collateralised against ('post')*. A one-way margin agreement where margin is only posted. In this case, only the NCB will be required.
- *Partially collateralised ('weak')*. A two-way margin agreement with a relatively high bilateral threshold.

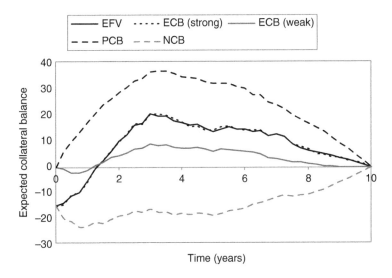

Figure 16.3   Illustration of the collateral balance terms and EFV for the portfolio.

---

[4] 50,000 simulations were used.

Table 16.3   Illustration of ColVA calculation.

	ColVA	ColRA	ColPA	Value
Valued at base rate		N/A		−14.900
Valued at adjusted rate		N/A		−14.689
Strong two-way	0.211	0.584	−0.373	−14.689
One-way (receive)	0.584	0.584	–	−14.316
One-way (post)	−0.373	–	−0.373	−15.273
Weak two-way	0.090	0.252	−0.162	−14.810

A symmetric spread of $s_X^P = s_X^R = -25$ bps is assumed. This could correspond to a situation where the margin remuneration is OIS minus 25 bps, and the transaction has been valued using OIS discounting. Alternatively, it could be considered similar to a situation where LIBOR (instead of OIS) discounting has been used.[5] For all but the first cases above, it is necessary to use an exposure simulation to calculate the ECB.

The ECB terms are shown in Figure 16.3, and the associated ColVAs and valuations are shown in Table 16.3. Note that the ECB for the strongly-collateralised case is very close to the EFV, as before (any difference being only Monte Carlo noise). The current value of the portfolio valued with the base interest rate is -14.900. Normally, discounting a payable (liability) position with a lower rate (due to the negative spread of 25 bps) would be expected to lead to a more negative valuation. However, given that the profile of the portfolio over the entire maturity is predominantly positive, the discounted value at the adjusted rate is higher (less negative) due to the benefit of paying a lower return on the margin received over most of the lifetime. This more beneficial valuation under the adjusted rate can be seen to correspond exactly to the ColVA adjusted for the strong two-way agreement, which is 0.211. This figure, in turn, is made up of -0.373 of collateral posted and 0.584 of collateral received components.

In the one-way margin agreements, these cost and benefit terms exist in isolation and make the portfolio more (less) valuable when receiving (posting) margin under a one-way agreement. Finally, the two-way margin agreement with large thresholds has a smaller ColRA and ColPA due to less margin being received and posted, the net result being slightly positive.

16.2.3   Cheapest-to-deliver Optionality

Margining arrangements are historically quite flexible. A typical agreement will allow a range of cash and other assets to be posted as collateral. This range of eligible assets will comprise some or all of the following (in approximate decreasing order of likelihood):

- cash in different currencies;
- government bonds;
- covered and corporate bonds;
- equities;
- mortgage-backed securities (MBSs); and
- commodities (e.g. gold).

---

[5] In this situation, the LIBOR-OIS basis would not be constant, but the calculation is no more difficult.

There will also be contractual haircuts specified for all of the above (cash in major currencies may be zero). This creates a choice for the giver of margin, who should pick the most optimal margin to post. This optimal choice will depend on:

- the return paid on the margin (as usually specified by the OIS rate in the currency in question);
- the haircut required in the margin agreement (generally only for non-cash securities);
- the repo rate and associated haircut (for securities where such a market exists);
- the availability of the margin in question (although if repo or reverse repo markets exist, then this is less of a concern as the assets in question can be readily acquired or lent).

The above optionality creates a valuation problem linked to the ability to optimise the margin posted by a given party, noting that their counterparty holds a similar option for the margin that they post. The market volatility experienced as a result of the GFC exposed – in dramatic fashion – the potential margin optionality value embedded within the contractual margin definitions. As a result, parties (especially the more sophisticated ones) began to value and monetise this embedded optionality. Collateral management, which used to be mainly a reactive back-office function, has moved on to become a proactive front-office process. Banks and some large financial institutions have become fairly optimal in managing the margin they post and the associated valuation issues. However, it is a great challenge to value and hedge the future impact of margin optionality, essentially monetising value that is effectively embedded in contractual terms.

For portfolios where the ECB is generally positive, the cheapest-to-deliver (CTD) valuation would be expected to be lower due to the counterparty posting margin requiring a higher return. Higher valuations would generally arise when the ECB is negative. The overall effect will depend on the CTD curve and the ECB profile. Asymmetric terms (such as in a one-way margin agreement) would also be expected to be important.

We will deal with optionality around different currencies of cash first. Assume that a party has to post a certain amount defined in a base currency. They can either:

- post this currency directly and be remunerated at the relevant rate; or
- exchange the amount via an FX transaction into an alternative currency and post this currency instead, receiving the remuneration at a different rate, which is then exchanged into their base currency again.

Return on cash margin is tied to the remuneration rate in the corresponding currency, such as the Euro Overnight Index Average (EONIA), the Sterling Overnight Index Average (SONIA) or Fed Funds. Assuming they have availability for all such currencies, a party should optimally choose to post margin in the currency which is remunerated at the highest rate. This is often called the CTD currency, which is the highest-yielding currency at a given time. The CTD currency can be calculated by comparing yields (implied by forward rates) earned in other currencies after exchanging them back into the base currency at the relevant forward FX rates. This adjustment is typically made by adjusting with cross-currency basis spreads which – for some currency pairs in particular – can be significant. The counterparty should be expected to follow the same optimal strategy in terms of their own optionality over posting. Clearly, this is a dynamic process, since the CTD currency may change through time.

The above represents a very challenging valuation problem due to the following factors:

- It requires a model for the co-movement of the OIS (or other) curves in each currency that represents the remuneration rates and the underlying FX rates to convert between currencies. As noted in Section 15.4.2, exposure simulation models generally assume that these curves are perfectly correlated and do not model the basis between them. Even if such a model exists, the calibration of parameters such as the volatility of the basis between different remuneration currencies will be challenging.
- It may be a path-dependent problem, since the amount of margin to be posted at a given time depends on the amount that was posted in the past. For example, there may be a difference between a party needing to post margin outright (where they have the optionality) and where margin needs to be returned (where the counterparty may have the optionality to request the return of a specific currency or asset). A key question here is whether margin can be substituted, since this will give greater value to the party posting because they can replace the posted margin with a more optimal choice (e.g. if the OIS in one currency widens with respect to another). Margin agreements not allowing substitution (or requiring consent)[6] should have less optionality, but a party can still optimise to some degree.

A common simplification is to assume that the underlying remuneration curves are static and also that margin can be freely substituted. The former assumption means that the CTD currency at any point in time stays fixed over the lifetime of the portfolio. The latter point means that path dependency is unimportant since a party can either post CTD margin outright or substitute it for the current margin. In this simplified approach, it is possible to form a CTD curve, as illustrated in Figure 16.4. The projected margin return in each currency (forward rate for the curve in question) is converted into some base reference (currency 1 is used in this case), and then the maximum is calculated. The CTD curve is then a composite of all the admissible curves, with an FX adjustment derived from cross-currency basis spreads.

The above CTD curve can either be used to discount the collateralised transactions in question directly, or to define a spread in order to calculate the appropriate ColVA adjustment from Equation 16.2. A specific ColVA adjustment will only be required in asymmetric cases, as discussed in Section 16.2.2, and in other cases discounting will give the same result. Assuming that currency 1 is used as the base currency, this relevant 'CTD basis' is shown in Figure 16.5.

In order to illustrate the above, we consider a receive fixed interest rate swap under a strong (two-way) and also a one-way (in favour of the party) agreement. The ECB profiles for these two cases are shown in Figure 16.6. Note that the ECB for the two-way margin

---

[6] Since the counterparty's optimal strategy would be not to give consent.

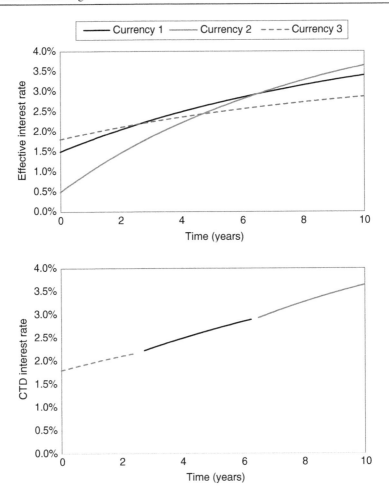

Figure 16.4   Construction of a CTD curve.

agreement is equal to the EFV. For the one-way agreement, there is only a PCB term as the margin is only received. This term is similar to the EPE of the equivalent uncollateralised swap, as noted previously.

Under the above assumptions, the valuation results in Table 16.4 can be generated. The valuation using different curves for discounting is different, reflecting the different remuneration rates. The CTD valuation is the largest, which is expected since the ECB (two-way margin agreement) is negative, and therefore the party in question is expected to be posting margin and receiving a higher return. The ColVA calculation using the spread in Figure 16.5 and the two-way ECB profile in Figure 16.6 is the same as the difference in valuation (between currency 1 and CTD). Under the one-way margin agreement, the ColVA is negative, reflecting the fact that margin can only be received and the party in question is short optionality.

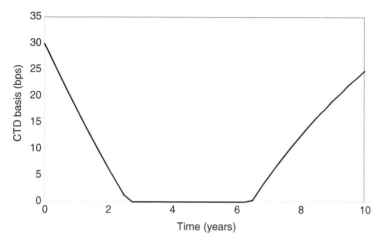

Figure 16.5   CTD basis implied from Figure 16.4 using currency 1 as the base currency.

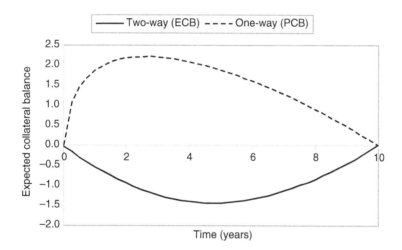

Figure 16.6   ECB for a swap under a two-way and one-way margin agreement.

Table 16.4   CTD valuations using discounting and ColVA adjustments.

	Value	ColVA
Value (currency 1 discounting)	38,594	
Value (currency 2 discounting)	22,598	
Value (currency 3 discounting)	20,398	
Value (CTD discounting)	42,547	
Difference (CTD vs currency 1)		3,953
ColVA (two-way)		3,953
ColVA (one-way)		−7,669

The above treatment, whilst relatively simple, makes two very important implicit assumptions:

- It assumes that margin is always posted in full in the currency that earns the highest remuneration rate. This requires margin to be freely and immediately substituted into the CTD currency. In practice, it may be necessary for consent to be given for such a substitution. If the party wishing to switch currency finds it optimal, then the counterparty's optimal action is to refuse such consent. The assumptions here may also be jurisdiction specific: for example, substitution rights are generally viewed as enforceable under New York but not British law. However, anecdotal evidence suggests that there is a 'gentleman's agreement' not to refuse such requests. Even then, switching margin gives rise to settlement risk and may cause associated trading and hedging costs. It may not be optimal to substitute relatively small amounts of margin.
- It captures only the intrinsic value of the margin optionality and does not price the time value of the optionality due to potential curve co-movements over time. Indeed, in many situations, the intrinsic value of the optionality is zero (i.e. the adjusted curves do not cross, as in Figure 16.4).

Since the above components have value for both parties, it is not clear whether the above approximations lead to a value which is too high or too low. It should also be noted that pricing via a CTD curve may result in complex risk management considerations, since even relatively small movements can result in dramatically different risk profiles (e.g. EUR exposure shifting to USD exposure on any given day).

As shown in Figure 16.7, the intrinsic CTD valuation method described above is common, although some banks do use a more sophisticated option-based valuation. This component is challenging to deal with as it requires a model for the joint evolution of all eligible currencies for the lifetime of the transactions in question. Note also that a more sophisticated representation of the substitution of margin is a path-dependent problem for a given margin balance; it must be known how much of the margin has already been posted (and would, therefore, need to be substituted) and how much needs to be posted (for which the optimal currency can be chosen). More sophisticated pricing of optionality has been discussed, for example, by Fuji and Takahashi (2011) and Piterbarg (2012 and 2013).

Note that there have been some problems in margin agreements where reference interest rates have become negative. Whilst remunerating margin at a negative return (i.e. the margin giver effectively pays the return) may appear unfair, flooring this rate will give rise to a much more complex pricing treatment, requiring the modelling of the dynamics of the remuneration curves.

16.2.4   Non-cash Margin

In the case of non-cash collateral, rates for transforming between cash and securities (e.g. repo rates) and associated haircuts must be considered. Suppose a party has to post margin of X and can choose between posting cash and securities both denominated in a given currency (with the multiple currency case being dealt with in Section 16.2.3). They can either:

- post cash and earn the corresponding remuneration rate for the currency in question; or

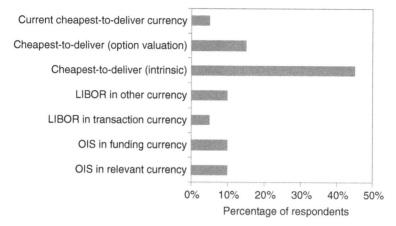

Figure 16.7   Market practice around the discounting curve used for collateralised transactions. Source: Solum FVA Survey (2015).

- reverse repo this amount of cash into a larger notional amount $X(1 + H_{repo})$ of securities, where H_{repo} represents the current repo rate, and then post $X(1 + H_{CSA})$ worth of such securities, where H_{CSA} represents the haircut specified for these securities in the margin agreement.

The above implies that it is more efficient to post securities if the repo rate times $\frac{(1+H_{repo})}{(1+H_{CSA})}$ are higher than the remuneration rate on the cash. A given security will become more advantageous to post as its repo haircut increases and its margin agreement haircut decreases. This ratio will change as haircuts in the repo market change compared to the relatively static contractual haircuts in margin agreements. Note also that technical factors and balance sheet considerations may also be important: there may be a benefit in posting non-cash margin that cannot easily be repoed, and aspects such as the leverage ratio (Section 4.2.7) may also be relevant. Additionally, not all parties may have the same access to the repo market.

16.2.5   The End of ColVA

Dealing with pricing, valuation, and hedging when there is optionality over margin types is clearly a complex problem depending on many aspects such as the future exposure, OIS rates in different currencies, cross-currency basis swap spreads, haircuts, and substitution criteria. Even then, methods such as CTD valuation make inherent simplifications.

Many transactions are close to the theoretical ideal of OIS discounting, especially through interbank and centrally-cleared trades, as mentioned above. There is also clearly a push towards this standard of perfect collateralisation and OIS discounting through the following aspects:

- *Renegotiation.* Market practice over recent years has been to renegotiate margin agreements such as credit support annexes (CSAs) bilaterally, often aiming to bring them closer to some of the perfect characteristics given in Section 16.1.2. This may involve having a more frequent exchange of margin (e.g. daily), reducing thresholds and minimum transfer amounts, and restricting the cash and securities that can be delivered.

- *Bilateral margin rules.* The incoming bilateral rules discussed in Section 7.4 require frequent margin exchange, a zero threshold, and a minimum transfer amount of no more than €500,000. They also penalise certain types of margin through haircuts, in particular, when cash is posted in a currency different from that of the transaction (see Table 7.12). The US rules restrict variation margin in some cases to cash only. The requirement to negotiate new agreements to comply with the bilateral margin requirements has also catalysed a simplification of terms (such as variation margin in USD only). These simplifications restrict some of the embedded value and optionality inherent in margin agreements and tend to reduce ColVA.
- *Clearing mandate.* Typically, CCPs require variation margin to be posted in the currency of the underlying transaction and do not allow netting across different currencies (Section 4.4.1). Cross-currency products are close to being centrally cleared, with one of the main hurdles to this being the currency of the underlying margin. For these reasons, CCPs consider the valuation of single-currency products such as swaps to be relatively simple, as they are – more or less – perfectly collateralised and OIS discounting is the valuation method used by the CCP.

The above comments generally apply to banks and other financial institutions who have already engaged in two-way margin agreements and are not exempt from the bilateral margin rules or clearing mandate. They are less relevant for end users who transact without a margin agreement or with a one-way agreement in their favour. However, through the pricing they receive from banks, such end users are also under pressure to move closer to the perfect collateralisation ideal.

However, this reduction of ColVA will not be absolute. Single-currency margin agreements create additional challenges, such as settlement risk. Many end users (e.g. pension funds) will struggle to move to post cash margin since they prefer to post directly the assets they hold. Problems will also remain with multicurrency products (e.g. cross-currency swaps).

Note also that collateral optionality adjustments may be present in other situations, such as those involving posting initial margin. Both bilateral markets and CCPs permit initial margin to be posted in a variety of different assets, and there is similar optionality to that described above for variation margin. However, in these situations, any optionality may be incorporated in the determination of the underlying funding costs, rather than being adjusted directly. This will be dealt with in Chapter 20.

16.3   BEYOND PERFECT COLLATERALISATION – xVA

16.3.1   Overview

We return to the problem of defining the starting point for valuation adjustments, as discussed previously in Section 5.2.1:

$$\text{Actual Value} = \text{Base Value} + \text{xVA} \qquad (16.5)$$

In collateral discounting (Section 16.1.3), the discount rate arises according to the remuneration rate on the margin and not for any other reason, such as that it is a good proxy for the risk-free rate. It therefore does not necessarily follow that collateral discounting would be the appropriate starting point for an uncollateralised transaction where, by design, there is no margin remuneration rate.

However, there are a number of reasons why it may be relevant to use the same collateral discounting (e.g. OIS) for all transactions, irrespective of whether or not they are collateralised:

- *Risk-free proxies.* Margin remuneration rates do tend to be good proxies for the risk-free rate.
- *Backwards compatibility.* This approach may be close to the historical approach used.
- *Operational.* Using 'risk-free' discounting may be the easiest starting point as it requires (at most) knowledge only of the underlying margin agreement and not of any other components, such as the identity of the counterparty or the funding cost of the organisation. Related to this, client transactions and their hedges may lead to a completely flat book (in terms of market risk with respect to the base value) for the originating trading desk.
- *xVA desk setup.* Related to the above point, the role of the xVA desk becomes better defined. An originating trading desk can value transactions at a base price which will ignore any counterparty risk, funding, and capital effects. The xVA desk will then act as a centralised resource and centre of expertise to deal with some or all of these components, and assume the related pricing, market volatility, and capital implications.

One could also argue that this is a reasonable starting point for all transactions, and additional xVA components can then be added on to this base case as required. This is not always the case in practice: for example, even after the general move to OIS discounting, some trading desks continued to use LIBOR discounting for uncollateralised transactions. Such choices – whilst in line with historical approaches – are often sub-optimal for the management of xVA.

One starting point could, therefore, be that all transactions be valued using risk-free rate discounting in the currency of the cash flows, with default choices for cross-currency trades. This has the advantage that the base valuation only requires knowledge of the cash flows and nothing else in line with the historical – pre-GFC – view of valuation (Section 5.1). However, this may also lead to some strange cases, as discussed in Section 16.2.1, with a transaction collateralised in a currency that is not the same as the transaction currency. In this situation, a purist approach might be to discount the transaction in the cash flow currency (even though this has no relevance for valuation) and then make a ColVA adjustment. However, it might be considered preferable (from an operational, pricing, valuation, and risk management perspective) to discount the transaction directly with the margin remuneration rate, which would then not require a separate valuation adjustment.

Another important point is that regulatory capital requirements for market risk treat the base value and xVA adjustments separately. This can, therefore, mean that different approaches to base valuation can have different capital impacts. This will be discussed further in Chapter 21.

From now on, the general view will be that all transactions should use the concept of perfect collateralisation as their base value and that xVA adjustments should then be made with respect to this value. There are two important cases where it may be desirable to deviate from this: one is the collateralised case discussed in Section 16.2.1, and another relates to funding and funding value adjustment, which will be discussed later in Section 18.2.3.

16.3.2   Definition of xVA Terms

Starting from the case of perfect collateralisation, it is useful to discuss xVA adjustments reflecting deviations from this ideal:

- *ColVA*. Collateral adjustments due to deviations from a perfect collateralisation, in terms of margin type and remuneration, as discussed above.
- *CVA (credit value adjustment) and DVA (debt/debit value adjustment)*. The bilateral valuation of counterparty risk. CVA is in relation to the counterparty default, and DVA is related to a party's own default. Note that DVA will be defined as being specific to own default, as distinct from being a funding benefit.
- *FVA (funding value adjustment)*. Defines the cost and benefit arising from the funding effects of being uncollateralised, or partially uncollateralised. This may include contingent liquidity provisions, such as when a bank needs to hold a buffer of high-quality liquid assets against certain contractual clauses.
- *KVA (capital value adjustment)*. Defines the cost of holding capital (typically regulatory) over the lifetime of the transaction.
- *MVA (margin value adjustment)*. Defines the cost of posting initial margin over the lifetime of the transaction. Default fund contributions (for clearing members) could also be captured under this same definition.

Note that both FVA and MVA are funding costs, but the former is the cost of being *undercollateralised*, whereas the latter is the cost of being *overcollateralised*. From this point of view, it is probably easiest to treat them as separate terms.

Note that, like the problem in defining base value, there may be different ways to define certain valuation adjustments. For example, consider a transaction in USD for a bank that considers its funding costs to be in EUR. There are (at least) two possible similar ways to consider an FVA:

- a single FVA calculated with respect to USD funding (i.e. raising cash in USD); or
- an FVA calculated with respect to EUR funding and a collateral adjustment calculated with respect to transforming EUR cash into USD cash (ColVA).

The choice of which of the above to use may be a matter of preference and may also be driven by operational aspects. For example, an institution could fund itself directly in USD, or alternatively fund itself in EUR and use the FX market to convert this into USD. Overall, there should not be significant differences in the final result (in terms of the total xVA), as long as the approach chosen is consistent.

Clearly, different xVA adjustments will arise in different situations. Table 16.5 outlines the different components that are relevant in various common situations in over-the-counter (OTC) derivatives. Note that this is general and there can always be special cases: for example, if margin is hard to repo, then a collateralised transaction may be considered to have an FVA.

Table 16.5   Illustration of the various components of different types of margin arrangement.

	Uncollateralised	Collateralised	Collateralised with initial margin	Central clearing
Credit (CVA)	✓✓✓	✓✓	✓	✓
Funding (FVA)	✓✓✓	✓		
Collateral (ColVA)		✓✓	✓	
Capital (KVA)	✓✓✓	✓✓	✓	✓
Initial margin (MVA)			✓✓	✓✓

The above is obviously only a general qualitative treatment, but some of the choices in Table 16.5 are explained as follows:

- *Uncollateralised.* Uncollateralised transactions have significant credit, funding, and capital adjustments, but contractually do not include any collateral or initial margin adjustments.
- *Collateralised.* Collateralised transactions have a reduced CVA and little or no FVA due to the variation margin. They may have ColVA components, and the capital requirements will be generally lower but still material.
- *Collateralised with initial margin.* Initial margin should – in theory – mean that there is no significant CVA contribution, although in practice this may not always be the case (Section 15.5.4). There may be ColVA adjustments, but these may be less impactful due to the inherent standardisation of the underlying margin agreement. Capital requirements will typically be lower due to the presence of initial margin. Initial margin costs through MVA will be an important consideration.
- *Central clearing.* CVA may be considered insignificant, although the thinking is changing around this point (Section 17.6.7). There will be no FVA due to the variation margin requirements. The capital costs will be small, but again initial margin costs will be important.

One of the problems with xVA definition is that it may be important to consider the hedges of transactions. Since the originating transactions may be client transactions, a bank may naturally consider not only the xVA of this transaction but also the associated material adjustments for hedges. For example, an uncollateralised transaction with a client may have an associated MVA component due to the necessity to post initial margin on the hedge.

17

CVA

17.1 OVERVIEW

This chapter will introduce the first members of the xVA family, namely credit or counterparty value adjustment (CVA) and debt or debit value adjustment (DVA). It will be shown that, under fairly standard assumptions, CVA and DVA can be defined in a straightforward way via credit exposure, default probability, and loss given default (LGD). We will then discuss computational aspects and show example calculations.

CVA has become a key topic for banks in recent years due to the volatility of credit spreads and the associated accounting (e.g. IFRS[1] 13, Section 5.3.3) and capital requirements (Basel III). However, whilst CVA calculations are a major concern for banks, they are also relevant for other financial institutions and corporations that have significant numbers of over-the-counter (OTC) derivatives to hedge their economic risks.

A key and common assumption made initially in this chapter will be that credit exposure and default probability are independent.[2] This involves neglecting wrong-way risk (WWR), which will be discussed in Section 17.6. We will also discuss CVA and DVA in isolation from other xVA terms, which will then be dealt with in more detail in Chapters 18 to 20. This is an important consideration since xVA terms cannot, in reality, be dealt with separately and possible overlaps should be considered.

CVA was originally introduced as an adjustment to the risk-free value of a derivative to account for potential default. Rather than using the term 'risk-free value', it is possible to define CVA as being the difference between the value with and without counterparty default. Historically, CVA was seen as a 'credit charge' for pricing and a 'reserve' or 'provision' for financial reporting purposes. Such calculations were often made with historical parameters (e.g. volatilities and default probabilities). More recently, accounting requirements (Section 5.3.3) have meant that CVA has become defined via an 'exit price' concept and computed with market-implied (risk-neutral) parameters.

In general, CVA is computed with market-implied parameters where practical. Such an approach is relevant for pricing since it defines the price with respect to hedging instruments and supports the exit price concept required by accounting standards. Risk-neutral exposure simulation (Section 15.3.3) is relatively natural due to the parallel with option pricing (e.g. Section 15.1.3) and the fact that many parameters (e.g. forward rates and volatilities) can be derived from market prices. Of course, certain parameters cannot be market-implied since they are not observed in the market (e.g. correlations), or may require interpolation or extrapolation assumptions (e.g. long-dated volatilities). Risk-neutral parameters such as volatilities may generally – but not always – be higher than their real-world equivalents (e.g. historical estimates).

---

[1] International Financial Reporting Standards.
[2] As well as the recovery value.

A more controversial issue is the default probability component of CVA. Obtaining market-implied default probabilities in most cases requires proxy credit spread curves to be defined (Section 12.3). As for exposure, the use of market-implied parameters is relevant for pricing purposes. However, the use of market-implied default probabilities may be questioned for a number of reasons:

- market-implied default probabilities are significantly higher than their real-world equivalents (Section 12.1.1);
- a default cannot, in general, be hedged since most counterparties do not have liquid single-name credit default swaps (CDSs) referencing them; and
- the business model of banks is generally to 'warehouse' credit risk, and therefore they are only exposed to real-world default risk.

The above arguments are somewhat academic, as most banks (and many other institutions) are generally required by accounting standards to use credit spreads when reporting CVA. There are, however, cases where historical default probabilities may still be used in CVA calculations today, such as in the case of smaller regional banks with less significant derivatives businesses, who may argue that their exit price would be with a local competitor who would apply a similar approach.

In situations such as the above, which are increasingly rare, banks may see CVA as an actuarial reserve and not a market-implied exit price.

17.2   CREDIT VALUE ADJUSTMENT

Standard early reference papers on the subject of CVA calculation include Sorensen and Bollier (1994), Jarrow and Turnbull (1992, 1995, and 1997), Duffie and Huang (1996), and Brigo and Masetti (2005a).

17.2.1   CVA Compared to Traditional Credit Pricing

Pricing the credit risk for an instrument with one-way payments, such as a bond, is relatively straightforward – one simply needs to account for default when discounting the cash flows, and add the value of any payments made in the event of a default. However, many derivatives instruments have fixed, floating, or contingent cash flows or payments that are made in both directions. This bilateral nature characterises credit exposure and makes the quantification of counterparty risk significantly more difficult. Whilst this will become clear in the more technical pricing calculations, a simple explanation is provided in Figure 17.1, which compares a bond to a similar swap transaction. In the bond case, a given cash flow is fully at risk (a portion of its value will be lost entirely) in the event of a default, whereas in the swap case only part of the cash flow will be at risk due to partial cancellation with opposing cash flows. The risk on the swap is clearly smaller due to this effect.[3] However, the fraction of the swap cash flows that is indeed at risk is hard to determine, as this depends on many factors such as yield curve shape, forward rates, and volatilities.

---

[3] It is also smaller due to the lack of a principal payment, but this is a different point.

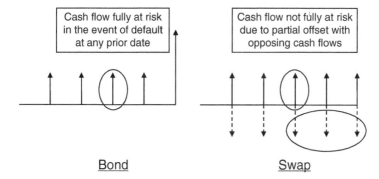

Bond   Swap

Figure 17.1   Illustration of the complexity when calculating the CVA on a derivative instrument such as a swap, compared with pricing credit risk on a debt instrument such as a bond. In the bond, the cash flow circled is fully at risk (less recovery) in the event of default of the issuer, but in the swap the equivalent cash flow is not fully at risk due to the ability to partially offset it with current and future cash flows in the opposite direction (the three dotted cash flows shown circled).

The above will be illustrated in more detail in Section 17.2.4.

17.2.2   Direct and Path-wise CVA Formulas

CVA can be seen as being driven by three separate terms:

- Does the counterparty default?
- If the counterparty defaults, what is the exposure at that time?
- How much of the exposure is lost?

The standard unilateral CVA (UCVA) formula (which assumes the party making the calculation cannot default) can be written as the following expected value (Appendix 17A):

$$UCVA(t) = -E[I(\tau \leq T).V(t, \tau)_+.LGD] \qquad (17.1)$$

where t represents the current time, T the (maximum) maturity of the portfolio, and τ the default time of the counterparty. The terms inside the expected value are as follows:

- $I(\tau \leq T)$ is the indicator function, which takes the value 1 if the default time of the counterparty is within the maturity in question ($\tau \leq T$) and zero otherwise. The expected value of this indicator function should be the cumulative default probability of the counterparty in the interval $[t, T]$.
- $V(t, \tau)_+ = \max[V(t, \tau), 0]$ is the exposure in the event of default discounted to time t. The expected value of this at a given default time is the expected positive exposure (EPE), as defined in Section 11.1.5.
- LGD is the loss given default. This is the percentage amount of the exposure expected to be lost if the counterparty defaults. Note that sometimes the recovery rate (R) is used with $LGD = 100\% - R$.

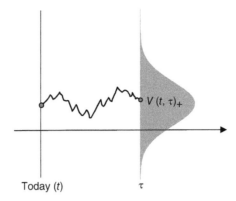

Figure 17.2   Illustration of a direct CVA calculation.

Note that the above three components may be dependent within the calculation specified by Equation 17.1. The above formula could be implemented with a scheme as follows:

1. Simulate a random time of default, τ, consistent with the underlying credit spread curve (does the counterparty default?).
2. Simulate a value of the portfolio at the future default date discounted back to time t, $V(t, \tau)$ and from this define the exposure at default $V(t, \tau)_+$ as simply the positive part of this term (if the counterparty defaults, what is the exposure at that time?).
3. Simulate an LGD value (how much of the exposure is lost?).
4. Multiply the above terms.
5. Repeat and average.

The above process is greatly simplified by assuming that the default time, the exposure at default, and the LGD are independent (no WWR), which also means that only a single average LGD need be used. This will be referred to as a 'direct CVA calculation' (Figure 17.2). Note that it is consistent with the direct approach to exposure simulation described in Section 15.3.1, since it is only necessary to evaluate the value of the portfolio at a single potential default date in the future. It is also efficient only to simulate default times that are in the interval $[t, T]$ and then multiply the final result by the counterparty default probability in this interval.

Spreadsheet 17.1 Direct CVA calculation for an interest rate swap.

Another way to write the CVA expression is via a one-dimensional integral over time:

$$UCVA(t) = -LGD \int_t^\infty \lambda_C D_{r+\lambda_C}(t, u) EPE(t, u) \qquad (17.2)$$

where λ_C is the instantaneous default probability, $D_{r+\lambda_C}(t, u) = \int_t^u \exp(-(r + \lambda_C)ds)$ is a 'risky discount factor', and $EPE(t, u) = E[V(t, u)_+]$ is the EPE.

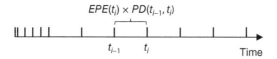

Figure 17.3 Illustration of CVA formula. The component shown is the CVA contribution for a given interval. The formula simply sums up across all intervals and multiplies by the LGD.

The above formula is typically approximated as a discrete sum:

$$UCVA(t) \approx -LGD \sum_{i=1}^{m} EPE(t, t_i) \times PD(t_{i-1}, t_i) \tag{17.3}$$

The UCVA depends on the following components:

- *LGD*. The loss given default, as described above.
- *EPE*. The discounted EPE for the relevant dates in the future given by t_i. Although discount factors could be represented separately, it is usually most convenient to apply (risk-free) discounting during the computation of the EPE.[4]
- *Probability of default (PD)*. The default probability for the interval $[t_{i-1}, t_i]$, as previously discussed in Section 12.1.3.

The above formula is an alternative way to compute CVA and can be seen as a weighted average of the EPE profile, as illustrated in Figure 17.3. Since the LGD was not assumed to have any time behaviour, it is a simple multiplier.

The above formula is quite intuitive since it represents CVA as a product of the EPE (market risk) and PD (credit risk). Note that default enters the expression via default probability only following the assumption of independence (no WWR). In this approach, whilst one may require a simulation framework in order to compute EPE, it is not necessary to simulate default events. Spreadsheets 17.1 and 17.2 can be used to show that the CVA calculated via Equations 17.1 (with no WWR) and 17.3 is the same.

Spreadsheet 17.2 Path-wise CVA calculation for an interest rate swap.

At first glance, it probably seems that the best method for computing CVA is the path-wise formula, rather than the direct approach. One reason for this is that the path-wise formula in Equation 17.3 is intuitive in representing CVA as a summation over the EPE profile, which is the natural way to look at the exposure component, together with the associated PD and LGD terms.

---

[4] In case explicit discount factors are required, care must be taken – for example, in an interest rate product where high rates will imply a smaller discount factor and vice versa. To account for this convexity effect technically means quantifying the underlying exposure using the 'T-forward measure' (Jamshidian 1989). By doing this, discount factors depend on expected future interest rate values, not on their distribution. Hence, moving the discount factor out of the expectation term (for exposure) can be achieved.

However, direct calculations of xVA terms can be more efficient in terms of computational time. Each simulation in the path-wise approach will require multiple valuations of the underlying portfolio according to the choice of the number of time intervals (m in Equation 17.3). Increasing m will improve the approximation of the integral, but likely at an increased computational cost due to the larger number of portfolio valuations required. It turns out that this can be quite inefficient.

In order to see this, we compare the convergence of the direct and path-wise implementations as a function of the number of valuations of the underlying portfolio that need to be made (since this is often the bottleneck of the CVA calculation). The CVA is calculated for an uncollateralised 10-year receiver interest rate swap with direct and path-wise approaches according to Spreadsheets 17.1 and 17.2. In the path-wise approach, 40 time steps are used, which corresponds to a quarterly grid. This means that for the case of 40,000 valuations, the path-wise method will use 1,000 simulations and 40 time steps, whereas the direct approach will use 40,000 different default times. Figure 17.4 shows the results, which illustrate that the direct approach converges much more quickly.

In order to be more precise about the improvement when using the direct method, the standard deviation of the CVA estimate with each approach (using 20 different calculations, each with a total of 40,000 valuations) is calculated (Figure 17.5).

The reason for the better computational performance of the direct method is that the path-wise simulation is slow to converge due to the autocorrelation between successive points in the simulation. For example, Figure 17.6 shows the strong relationship between successive valuation points in the path-wise simulation. This high positive correlation means that convergence, as a function of the total number of valuations, is slow.

The improvement is quite dramatic, with the standard deviation being six times smaller in the direct approach. Since Monte Carlo error is approximately proportional to the

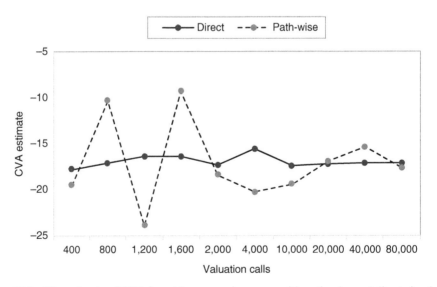

Figure 17.4   The estimate of CVA for a 10-year receiver swap with path-wise and direct simulation approaches as a function of the total number of valuation calls.

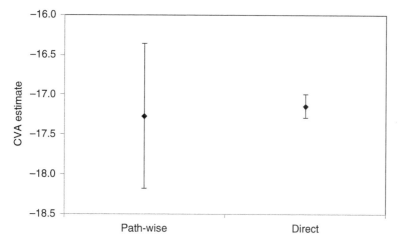

Figure 17.5   The estimate of CVA for a 10-year interest rate swap with path-wise and direct simulation approaches and a total of 100,000 valuations. The error bars showing one standard deviation are shown.

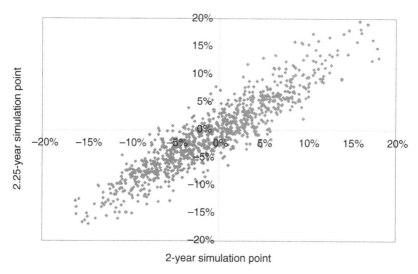

Figure 17.6   Correlation between valuations at successive points (two years, and two years and three months) in the path-wise CVA calculation.

square root of the number of simulations,[5] this actually represents a speed improvement of $6 \times 6 = 36$ times. In other words, we can do 36 times fewer valuations in the direct approach to achieve the same accuracy. Whilst this may sound appealing, it presumes that the valuation step will be a major bottleneck in the calculation. Amdahl's law (Amdahl 1967) gives a simple formula for the overall speed-up from improving one component of

---

[5] This is a consequence of the central limit theorem.

a calculation. This formula is $\left((1-P)+\frac{P}{S}\right)^{-1}$, where P is the percentage of the calculation that can be improved and S is the relative speed improvement. For example, if 90% ($P = 0.9$) of the time is spent on pricing function calls, and these can be sped up by 25 times, then the overall improvement is 7.3 times. There may also be additional overheads in the direct simulation, such as generating the entire path to the default time.[6]

A direct simulation approach for CVA may, therefore, be faster, but this will depend on the precise time spent on different components in the Monte Carlo model. This approach is also less obviously applied to portfolios with path dependencies, such as collateralised transactions and some exotics.

Another advantage of the direct approach may be in the modelling of WWR, discussed later in Section 17.6.

17.2.3   CVA as a Spread

For pricing purposes, it is often useful to calculate CVA – and indeed any xVA adjustment – as a running spread (per annum charge) so as to, for example, adjust a rate paid or received. One simple way to do this is to divide by a duration or annuity value for the maturity in question. However, this potentially ignores the 'CVA of the CVA'. Charging CVA will increase the value of the transaction which will, in turn, increase the total CVA. The correct result could be achieved by solving recursively for the spread that makes the value of the transaction including CVA equal zero. Vrins and Gregory (2011) show that the effect can be bounded by using both risky and non-risky annuity values (see Appendix 17B).

Another approximation to the above (Appendix 17C) assumes that the EPE is constant over time, which yields the following approximation based on the average EPE:

$$UCVA \approx -average\ EPE \times spread \qquad (17.4)$$

where the UCVA is expressed in the same units as the credit spread (which should be for the maturity of the instrument in question) and the average EPE is as defined in Figure 11.4.[7] This approximation generally works reasonably well, especially where the EPE profile (or default probability profile) is relatively constant over time. Whilst not used for actual calculations, the approximate formula in Equation 17.4 is useful for intuitive understanding of the drivers of CVA, as it separates the credit component (the credit spread of the counterparty) and the market risk component (the exposure, or average EPE).

Table 17.1 illustrates running CVA calculations for the interest rate swap considered in Section 17.2.2.

For relatively small CVA charges, such as in this example, the recursive effect is small, although Vrins and Gregory (2011) show that it is significant in certain cases (typically more risky counterparties and/or long-dated transactions). Note also that this effect is systematic: an xVA desk charging based on the first-order CVA will always lose money when the trade is booked – all other things being equal – due to the additional 'CVA on the CVA'.

---

[6] This would be required in some models and any path-dependent cases (e.g. collateralisation).

[7] This is the simple average of the EPE values in our example, although for non-equal time intervals it would be the weighted average. In the approximate formula, the undiscounted EPE is required, although in a low interest rate environment the discounting differences may be small, especially for short-dated transactions.

Table 17.1 Running CVA calculations.

	CVA (bps per annum)
Divide by risky annuity	−1.92
Exact (recursive)	−1.96
EPE approximation	−2.01

17.2.4 Special Cases

There are special cases where CVA can be calculated easily. For example, Figure 17.7 shows CVA for payer and receiver swaps as a function of the swap rate. As noted in Section 15.1.3, in the case where the transaction or portfolio is very in-the-money (ITM) (has a large positive value), the EPE can be approximated by the expected future value (EFV), which leads to a simplification in the calculation.

In such situations, it is possible to either use the CVA formula with the EFV, or alternatively to use a discounting approach, as discussed in Section 16.2.1.[8] This effect is showing the complex swap-like CVA calculations converging to a simpler case, as previously illustrated in Figure 17.1.

17.2.5 Credit Spread Effects

The *shape* of the credit curve can have a material impact on CVA. Section 12.1.3 considered upwards-sloping, flat, and inverted credit curves, all of which had the same

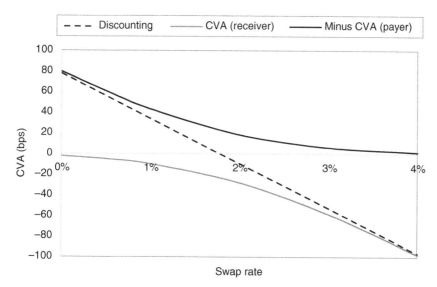

Figure 17.7 CVA for payer and receiver interest rate swaps as a function of the swap rate. Also shown is the analytical CVA calculated with the EFV. The CVA of the payer swap is shown as a positive value for display purposes.

---

[8] This would have to account for the LGD.

Table 17.2   CVA for 10-year receive fixed interest rate swap using the three credit curves in Figure 12.3. The five-year credit spread is assumed to be 150 bps and the LGD 60% in all cases.

	10 years
Upwards sloping	−24.6
Flat	−20.0
Inverted	−15.7

five-year credit spread of 150 basis points (bps). It was discussed how, whilst these curves gave cumulative default probabilities that were the same at the five-year point, the marginal default probabilities differed substantially. For a flat curve, default probability is approximately equally spaced, whilst for an upwards- (downwards-) sloping curve, defaults are back- (front-) loaded. We show the impact of curve shape on CVA in Table 17.2. The upwards-sloping curve gives the largest value, mainly due to having the largest extrapolated 10-year credit spread. The inverted curve gives the smallest CVA for the opposite reason.

Another important feature to understand is the change in CVA as credit spread widens, as shown in Figure 17.8. CVA generally increases with increasing credit spread. However, in default, CVA will converge to the exposure of the transaction (or portfolio), which may be zero. Whilst this is not apparent for relatively small credit spread changes, it leads to a large gamma for larger credit spread changes. This behaviour is also important for understanding jump-to-default risk, discussed in Section 21.2.5.

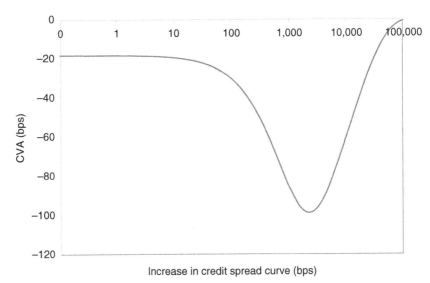

Figure 17.8   CVA for 10-year receiver swap as the credit spread curve is increased. A lognormal scale is used for clarity. The CVA for a very large credit spread change converges to zero since it is a par transaction.

17.2.6 Loss Given Default

Section 12.1.4 discussed the fact that LGD (or recovery rate) could be defined as either the settled or actual value. Substituting the default probability formula (Equation 12.1) into the CVA formula (Equation 17.3) gives:

$$UCVA(t) = -LGD_{actual} \sum_{i=1}^{m} EPE(t, t_i) \times \left[\exp\left(-\frac{s_{i-1}t_{i-1}}{LGD_{mkt}} \right) - \exp\left(-\frac{s_i t_i}{LGD_{mkt}} \right) \right] \quad (17.5)$$

where the 'actual' and 'market' LGDs, which should be expected values (although this is not always stated explicitly), are referenced explicitly. The former (LGD_{actual}) should reference the actual expected LGD that would be received in the event that the counterparty defaults. The latter (LGD_{mkt}) refers to the value to assume for calibrating market-implied default probabilities, which should, therefore, relate to the seniority of the underlying instrument used to determine the credit spread (usually senior unsecured for most CDS contracts). For example, BCBS (2011b) states that, for regulatory capital purposes:[9]

> It should be noted that this LGD_{mkt}, which inputs into the calculation of the CVA risk capital charge, is different from the LGD that is determined for the IRB [internal ratings-based approach] and CCR [counterparty credit risk] default risk charge, as this LGD_{mkt} is a market assessment rather than an internal estimate.

Whilst the above LGDs are different conceptually, if a derivatives claim is of the same seniority as that referenced in the CDS (as is typically the case), then one should typically assume that $LGD_{actual}= LGD_{mkt}$. Indeed, this is a requirement in the aforementioned regulatory capital framework (BCBS 2011b), since only LGD_{mkt} is referenced in the formula. In this case, the LGD terms in Equation 17.5 will cancel to first order, and there will be only moderate sensitivity to changing the LGD value.[10] The simple approximation in Equation 17.4 has no LGD input reflecting this cancellation.

Figure 17.9 illustrates the minimal impact of changing the LGD in this case. As expected, changing both LGDs has a reasonably small impact on CVA since there is a cancellation effect: increasing LGD reduces the market-implied default probability but increases the loss in the event of default. The net impact is only a second-order effect: for example, changing the LGD from 60% to 50% changes CVA by less than 2%.

Despite this, in certain cases institutions may consider it appropriate to use a different value for LGD_{actual}. These cases may include (in order of ease of justification):

- seniority in the exposure waterfall (e.g. trades with securitisation special purpose vehicles) or a significantly different LGD due to the structural nature of the counterparty (e.g. project finance-related transactions);

---

[9] We note that regulatory capital requirements are more prescriptive than accounting requirements, which is why we make reference to them here. However, it does not necessarily follow that accounting CVA must follow Basel standards. The future regulatory framework for computing CVA capital (BCBS 2017) will use a bank's accounting CVA for determining regulatory capital (standardised CVA, SA-CVA), which may completely align accounting standards with regulatory capital ones.

[10] This is because $\exp(-x) \approx 1 - x$ for small values of x. This is therefore more accurate for smaller spread values.

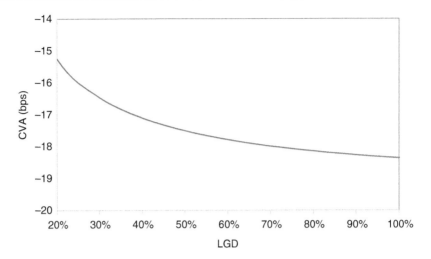

Figure 17.9   CVA as a function of the LGD used when $LGD_{actual} = LGD_{mkt}$

- credit enhancements such as margin or other forms of credit support; and
- the consideration that, due to their work-out process experience, they may achieve a higher recovery rate.

The first case – that of different seniority – is the most common and easy-to-justify reason for using a different LGD_{actual}. An example of this is:

> … estimated recovery rates implied by CDS, adjusted to consider the differences in recovery rates as a derivatives creditor relative to those reflected in CDS spreads, which generally reflect senior unsecured credit risk.[11]

This adjustment for seniority is also envisaged by regulatory capital rules – for example, BCBS (2015a) states:

> The market-implied ELGD [LGD_{actual}] value used for regulatory CVA calculation must be the same as the one used to calculate the market-implied PD from credit spreads [LGD_{mkt}] unless it can be demonstrated that the seniority of the derivative exposure differs from the seniority of senior unsecured bonds.

One common situation where lower LGDs are used is project finance. Project finance refers to the funding of infrastructure and industrial projects off-balance sheet, and based upon the projected returns from the project rather than from an underlying balance sheet. The majority of funding is usually via senior debt, with junior debt, equity, and grants also forming part of the financing. Senior debtors will aim for the project to produce sufficient cash flows to repay them in full, and will ensure that the legal structuring of the project will be such that they have priority over all material assets in a default scenario. Project finance is typically associated with strong credit underwriting principles and structural features

---

[11] J.P. Morgan (2015). Annual Report.

that enhance the position of senior debtors. This is generally seen via higher recovery rates (approximately 75% on average) in project finance compared to other types of unsecured lending (e.g. approximate 40% average for corporates). For example, Standard & Poor's (2016) states that 'project finance exhibits a strong average recovery rate of 77%, which is stronger compared to average recoveries observed in the corporate world'.

The impact of using different LGDs is shown in Figure 17.10.

One caveat to the above LGD 'override' process is that the LGD must not be a consideration in the credit curve construction process. In cases where different LGDs are used to reflect a more favourable recovery outcome, it is important to ensure that any credit spread proxy that has been determined on the basis of a rating has been done so only via reference to default probability. If this is not the case, then there is the potential for double-counting if the expectation of a relatively high recovery rate leads to a better rating. In such a case, this better rating would, in turn, lead to a lower credit spread, and it would therefore be inappropriate to reflect this a second time using a lower LGD. In order to avoid the above double-counting, it is important that any rating used for the basis of credit spread mapping should reflect only default probability and not expected loss. Standard & Poor's rating definitions are default probability based – for example, AA is defined as 'The obligor's capacity to meet its financial commitments on the obligation is very strong.'[12] On the other hand, Moody's definitions suggest that recovery rates may be part of the rating process, with, for example, Aa being defined as 'Obligations rated Aa are judged to be of high quality and are subject to very low credit risk.'[13]

Note that the xVA desk in a bank commonly assumes LGD risk in relation to actual defaults.[14] This risk is due to the potential difference between the value of LGD_{actual} and the LGD experienced after the work-out process.

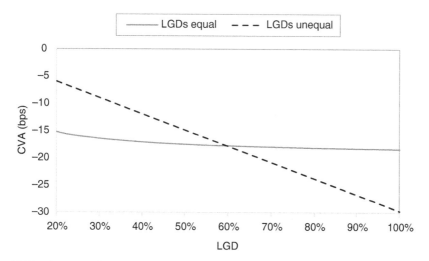

Figure 17.10 CVA as a function of the LGD used for equal ($LGD_{actual} = LGD_{mkt}$) and unequal (LGD_{actual} varied and $LGD_{mkt} = 60\%$) LGD assumptions.

---

[12] www.standardandpoors.com.
[13] www.moodys.com.
[14] International Association of Credit Portfolio Managers (IACPM) Survey (2018).

17.3   DEBT VALUE ADJUSTMENT

17.3.1   Accounting Background

A key assumption in the definition of CVA above was that the party making the calculation could not default. This may have seemed like a fairly innocuous and straightforward belief. Indeed, it is consistent with the 'going concern' accountancy concept, which requires financial statements to be based on the assumption that a business will remain in existence for an indefinite period. However, as mentioned in Section 5.3.3, international accountancy standards allow (indeed, potentially *require*) a party to consider its own default in the valuation of its liabilities. It is stated explicitly that an 'own credit' adjustment must be made. Furthermore, DVA could be interpreted as being part of the 'exit price' due to the fact that a counterparty will charge CVA. DVA is associated, via the expected negative exposure (ENE), with the liability position in the same way that CVA is associated with an asset via the EPE. The use of both CVA and DVA is generally referred to as 'bilateral CVA' (BCVA).

The use of BCVA has been largely driven by accounting practices and formally began in 2006 when the FAS 157 (Section 5.3.3) determined that banks should record a DVA entry. FAS 157 states:

> Because non-performance risk includes the reporting entity's credit risk, the reporting entity should consider the effect of its credit risk (credit standing) on the fair value of the liability in all periods in which the liability is measured at fair value.

This led to a number of large US (and some Canadian) banks reporting DVA in financial statements, with the BCVA taking the form of an exit price rather than a reserve. Most other banks did not report DVA adjustments at this time and still considered CVA to be a reserve (e.g. using historical default probabilities in the calculation).

Following the introduction of IFRS 13 from January 2013 (IFRS 2011), most other large banks have moved to BCVA reporting using market-implied parameters. IFRS 13 requires that transactions such as derivatives be reported at 'fair value', the definition of which includes the following comment:

> The fair value of a liability reflects the effect of non-performance risk. Non-performance risk includes, but may not be limited to, an entity's own credit risk.

The interpretation of auditors has generally been that IFRS 13 accounting standards require the use of market-implied default probabilities (via credit spreads) and both CVA and DVA components to be reported. This has led to a moderate convergence in recent years, although there are still some exceptions for regions where IFRS 13 has not been implemented, or banks where the CVA and DVA may be considered to be immaterial. However, these exceptions are becoming less common.[15]

Despite the general adoption of DVA in accounting, it is important to note that the precise implementation – like CVA – does not follow clear standards across the market (see ESMA 2017). It is also important to note that, whilst banks have generally adopted

---

[15] Davis, C. (2019). Japan banks face huge CVA hit, dealers say. *Risk* (21 January). www.risk.net.

DVA in financial reporting, this is somewhat undermined by their introduction of funding value adjustment (FVA), as discussed in Chapter 18.

DVA is a double-edged sword. On the one hand, it resolves some theoretical problems with CVA and creates a world where price symmetry can be achieved. On the other hand, the nature of DVA and its implications and potential unintended consequences are troubling. Indeed, as will be discussed in Chapter 18, market practice can be seen to generally disregard DVA in aspects such as pricing and replace it with funding considerations (FVA). However, it is still important to understand DVA from an accounting standpoint and its subsequent relationship to FVA.

17.3.2 DVA, Price, and Value

DVA will be discussed from the point of view of accounting, economic, and regulatory value introduced earlier (Section 5.3.1).

In order to understand the accounting rationale behind DVA, consider two parties with respective valuations of a certain portfolio: V_A and V_B. If these are base valuations (Section 5.2.1), then it is reasonable that the parties agree on a valuation (e.g. they use the same discounting approach) and therefore $V_A = -V_B$. If this is not the case, then value has been created or destroyed.

Now, if we bring CVA into the picture, then the valuations between the different parties will not agree since CVA is always a negative adjustment. However, by including DVA then:

$$V_A + CVA_A + DVA_A \text{ (party A point of view)} \tag{17.6a}$$

$$V_B + DVA_B + CVA_B \text{ (party B point of view)} \tag{17.6b}$$

With $CVA_A = -DVA_B$ and $DVA_A = -CVA_B$ ('my CVA is your DVA'), then once again it is possible for the actual valuations to agree.

From a pricing point of view, CVA has traditionally been a charge for counterparty risk that is levied on the end user (e.g. a corporate) by their counterparty (e.g. a bank). Historically, banks charged CVAs linked to the credit quality of the end user and the exposure in question. An end user would not have been able credibly to question such a charge, especially since the probability that a bank would default was considered remote (and, indeed, the credit spreads of banks were traditionally very small and their credit ratings strong). This changed during the global financial crisis, and the credit spreads of the 'strong' financial institutions became – and have since remained – material. This raises the question of whether banks, too, should be charged a CVA by their counterparties and how two banks could trade together in the interbank market.

One important feature of DVA is that it solves the above issues and creates 'price symmetry', where, in theory, parties can agree on prices. However, this raises the question of whether or not a party would be happy to include DVA in its pricing. Whilst this will not give rise to a loss (assuming DVA is also part of valuation), it may be questioned to what extent DVA has an *economic* value. Whilst there is a clear economic impact of counterparty default losses leading to CVA, the notion of own default leading to DVA gains is more problematic. Furthermore, from a hedging perspective, whilst CVA can be seen as relating to the cost of buying CDS protection on a counterparty, DVA would be linked to selling CDS protection on one's own credit.

A party that does not believe that DVA is part of economic value will be reticent to include it in their pricing. It is important to note that price symmetry is not generally a requirement for markets: for example, banks may determine prices for derivatives, and end users decide whether or not to transact at these quoted prices.

In line with the above view is the fact that regulation requires that DVA gains be derecognised from equity (Section 5.3.3), implying that DVA is not part of the regulatory value.

Rationalising the different accounting, economic, and regulatory DVA viewpoints can be done by considering the view of shareholders and bondholders. In the event of the default of an institution, shareholders receive nothing, whereas bondholders receive a residual – or recovery – value. Suppose a firm enters into an out-of-the-money (OTM) (negative value) transaction, for which it will receive an upfront payment and which will also have a significant DVA component. In the event of default, the other creditors will receive a portion of this amount, leading to a higher recovery rate, and therefore they may see the DVA as real.[16] The shareholders will not consider the DVA to be real since they receive nothing in default. Conflicts between shareholders and bondholders are well known in finance.

Since regulatory capital requirements set the required amount of shareholder equity, it is therefore not surprising that they require the derecognition of DVA. On the other hand, taking the view that financial reporting should reflect the total value of a firm (i.e. not only to shareholders) would support the reporting of DVA as a benefit to bondholders. In terms of pricing, taking a shareholder view would require the exclusion of DVA.

The above shareholder and bondholder view and the link to DVA will be discussed in more detail for FVA in Section 18.2.6.

17.3.3   Bilateral CVA Formula

Under the assumption that both the party making the calculation and its counterparty can default, a BCVA formula is obtained consisting of CVA and DVA components (Appendix 17D):

$$BCVA = CVA + DVA \tag{17.7a}$$

$$CVA(t) = -LGD_C \int_t^\infty \lambda_C D_{r+\lambda_C+\lambda_P}(t,u)EPE(t,u) \tag{17.7b}$$

$$DVA(t) = -LGD_P \int_t^\infty \lambda_C D_{r+\lambda_C+\lambda_P}(t,u)ENE(t,u) \tag{17.7c}$$

The suffixes P and C indicate the party making the calculation and its counterparty, respectively. The CVA term is similar to Equation 17.2, but with the factor $D_{r+\lambda_C+\lambda_P}(t,u) = \int_t^u \exp(-(r+\lambda_C+\lambda_P))ds$ representing the survival of both parties in the formula. This is sometimes known as the 'first-to-default' effect because it ensures that a default event is conditioned on the other party not defaulting first.

The DVA term above is the mirror image of CVA based on the ENE, the party's own default probability and the LGD. DVA is positive due to the sign of the ENE, and it will, therefore, oppose CVA as a benefit. The DVA term corresponds to the fact that in cases where the party itself defaults, it will make a 'gain' if it has a liability position

---

[16] Assuming the creditors for the transaction in question have no security or seniority over the other creditors.

(negative exposure). This gain is the opposite of the loss that the surviving counterparty experiences. Since ENE is equal and opposite to the counterparty's EPE, it can be seen that one party's DVA, theoretically, is equal and opposite to the other's DVA, and vice versa.[17]

As before, it is possible to discretise the above integrals:

$$CVA(t) = -LGD_C \sum_{i=1}^{m} EPE(t, t_i) \times PD_C(t_{i-1}, t_i) \times [1 - PD_P(0, t_{i-1})] \qquad (17.8a)$$

$$DVA(t) = -LGD_P \sum_{i=1}^{m} ENE(t, t_i) \times PD_P(t_{i-1}, t_i) \times [1 - PD_C(0, t_{i-1})] \qquad (17.8b)$$

Note that the CVA above is different from the previously defined unilateral CVA (UCVA) in Equation 17.3, and a similarly defined unilateral DVA (UDVA), because it contains the survival (no default) probability of the party making the calculation given by $[1 - PD_P(0, t_{i-1})]$. This will be discussed in Section 17.3.4.

Spreadsheet 17.3 CVA and DVA calculations.

Table 17.3 shows BCVA calculations for different interest rate swap transactions. In this example, the counterparty's credit quality is worse than the party's own credit quality.[18] The contingent values are smaller, as would be expected, although the impact on BCVA (or UCVA + UDVA) is not clear, since both individual values decrease but have opposite signs. There is a strong asymmetry for BCVA between pay and receive fixed swaps due to the skew in the exposure profiles (see Figure 15.24). This causes the BCVA of the receive fixed swap to be close to zero due to the relatively large DVA, in turn due to the size of ENE. A similar but larger effect is seen for off-market swaps: the OTM swap having a BCVA which is positive overall.

Table 17.3   Upfront CVA and DVA values (in bps) for 10-year interest rate swaps. The party's own credit spread is lower than the counterparty's, and both LGDs are assumed to be 60%. The ITM and OTM transactions are based on a swap rate of 1%, instead of the market rate of 1.49%.

	Pay fixed	Receive fixed	Pay fixed (ITM)	Receive fixed (OTM)
UCVA	−29.9	−17.2	−43.7	−9.9
UDVA	8.1	14.4	4.8	20.7
UCVA + UDVA	−21.8	−2.7	−39.0	10.8
CVA	−28.9	−16.6	−42.4	−9.6
DVA	7.4	13.2	4.3	18.9
BCVA	−21.5	−3.5	−38.1	9.4

---

[17] This assumes that the parties will make the calculations in the same way (e.g. models and parameters).
[18] The precise credit curves can be seen in Spreadsheet 17.3.

Whilst the BCVA price symmetry has some nice theoretical properties, it could be questioned to what extent market participants would actually price these benefits into transactions. For example, would it be realistic to charge so little for the receive fixed swap or to 'pay through mid'[19] to step into the OTM swap?

To understand BCVA price symmetry more easily, consider the simple formula in Equation 17.4. An obvious extension including DVA is:

$$BCVA \approx -average\ EPE \times Spread_C - average\ ENE \times Spread_P \qquad (17.9)$$

where the average ENE is similar to the average EPE defined in Section 11.1.5. Assuming that *average EPE = −average ENE*,[20] we obtain $BCVA \approx -EPE \times (Spread_C - Spread_P)$. A party could, therefore, charge its counterparty for the *difference* in its credit spreads (and if this difference is negative, then this party should pay their counterparty). Weaker counterparties would pay stronger counterparties in order to trade with them based on the differential in credit quality. Theoretically, this leads to a pricing agreement (assuming parties can agree on the calculations and parameters), even when one or both counterparties have poor credit quality. Practically, there are concerns with such an approach, based on the arguments in Section 17.3.2.

17.3.4   Close-out and Default Correlation

The above discussion and formulas for BCVA ignored or simplified three important and interconnected concepts:

- *Survival adjustment.* UCVA and UDVA are defined without reference to the survival probability of the other party, whilst CVA and DVA include survival probabilities. On one hand, it seems that the first-to-default effect – in that the underlying contracts will cease when the first party defaults and therefore there should be no consideration of the second default – would justify the inclusion of survival probabilities. However, this leads to CVA having sensitivity to a party's own credit quality, which may be seen as unnatural. Regulation may also prohibit doing this (Section 13.3.1).
- *Default dependency.* Related to the above, the default dependency between the party and its counterparty is not included. If such a dependency is significant, then this would be expected to change the CVA and DVA terms (the formulas above assume that the defaults are independent).
- *Close-out.* Finally, as discussed in Section 11.1.2, the definitions of EPE and ENE are typically based on standard valuation assumptions and do not reflect the actual close-out assumptions that may be relevant in a default scenario. In other words, in the event of a default, it is assumed that the underlying transactions will be settled at their base values (Section 6.3.4) at the default time, which is inconsistent with the reality of close-out that may reference actual values. For example, as discussed in Section 6.3.5, the 2002 ISDA documentation specifies that the claim 'may take into account the

---

[19] Meaning giving a better price than the case with no valuation adjustments, such as an interbank trade.

[20] This is sometimes a reasonable approximation in practice, especially for a collateralised relationship, but we will discuss the impact of asymmetry below.

creditworthiness of the Determining Party,' which seems to suggest that CVA/DVA may be a part of the close-out value and therefore should change EPE/ENE.

The above points have been studied by various authors. Gregory (2009a) shows the impact of survival probabilities and default correlation on BCVA, but in isolation of any close-out considerations. Brigo and Morini (2010) consider the impact of close-out assumptions in the unilateral (i.e. one-sided exposure) case.

Not only are close-out assumptions difficult to define, but quantification is challenging because it involves including the future BCVA at each possible default event in order to eventually determine the current BCVA. This creates a difficult recursive problem. Brigo and Morini (2010) show that, for a loan, the expectation that DVA can be included in the close-out assumptions ('risky close-out') leads to cancellation, with the survival probability of the party making the calculation. This means that the formula in Equation 17.8a without the survival probability term is correct in a one-sided situation with risky close-out. Gregory and German (2013) consider the two-sided case and find that a simple result does not apply, but that the bilateral formulas used in Equations 17.8a and 17.8b without survival probabilities are probably the best approximation in the absence of a much more sophisticated approach.

Generally, most market participants do not follow a more advanced approach and simply include survival probabilities (or not) directly. For example, in an Ernst & Young Survey in 2012,[21] six out of 19 respondents report making CVA and DVA 'contingent' (survival probability adjusted) and seven non-contingent, with the remainder not reporting DVA at the time. Anecdotal evidence (e.g. Totem, Section 5.3.5) seems to suggest that there is still a mix between participants that use contingent or non-contingent calculations. As discussed in Section 6.3.4, this problem is not specific to CVA and DVA, but is a general consideration for any xVA term.

17.3.5   The Use of DVA

The issue of DVA in counterparty risk is part of a broader issue: the general incorporation of credit risk in liability measurement. Accountancy standards have generally evolved to a point where 'own credit risk' can (and should) be incorporated into the valuation of liabilities. For example (relevant for the US), the Financial Accounting Standards Board (FASB) issued Statement of Financial Accounting Standards (SFAS) 157 in 2006 (which became effective in 2007), relating to fair value measurements. This permits a party's own credit quality to be included in the valuation of its liabilities, stating 'The most relevant measure of a liability always reflects the credit standing of the entity obliged to pay.' Amendments to IAS 39 by the International Accounting Standards Board (IASB) in 2005 (relevant for the European Union) also concluded that the fair value of a liability should include the credit risk associated with that liability. This position was reinforced with the introduction of IFRS 13 from the beginning of 2013.

DVA was a very significant question for banks in the years following the global financial crisis, since their own credit risk (via credit spreads) experienced unprecedented volatility. Banks reported massive swings in accounting results as their credit spreads widened and

---

[21] Ernst & Young (2012). CVA Survey. www.ey.com.

tightened. Articles reporting such swings did not seem to take them seriously, making statements such as:

> The profits of British banks could be inflated by as much as £4bn due to a bizarre accounting rule that allows them to book a gain on the fall in the value of their debt.[22]
>
> [DVA is] a counter-intuitive but powerful accounting effect that means banks book a paper profit when their own credit quality declines.[23]

There is logic to the use of DVA on own debt, since the fair value of a party's own bonds is considered to be the price that other entities are willing to pay for them. However, it is questionable whether a party would be able to buy back its own bonds without incurring significant funding costs. It therefore became typical for equity analysts to remove DVA from their assessment of a company's ongoing performance, with the view that DVA is no more than an accounting effect and of no interest to shareholders.

DVA in derivatives has probably received more scrutiny than that in own debt since derivatives valuation has received much attention and is based on rigorous hedging arguments. The criticism of DVA stems mainly from the fact that it is not easily realisable (Gregory 2009a). Other criticisms include the idea that the gains coming from DVA are distorted because other components are ignored. For example, Kenyon (2010) makes the point that if DVA is used, then the value of goodwill (which is zero at default) should also depend on a party's own credit quality. Losses in goodwill would oppose gains on DVA when a party's credit spread widens.

This debate really hinges on to what extent a party can ever *realise* a DVA benefit. Some of the arguments made in support of DVA have proposed that it can be monetised in the following ways:

- *Defaulting*. A party can obviously realise DVA by going bankrupt but, like an individual trying to monetise their own life insurance, this is a clearly not a very good strategy.
- *Unwinds and novations*. A party unwinding, novating, or restructuring a transaction might claim to recognise some of the DVA benefits since they are paid out via a CVA gain for the counterparty. For example, monolines derived substantial benefits from unwinding transactions with banks,[24] representing large CVA-related losses for the banks and associated DVA gains for the monolines. The monoline MBIA monetised a multibillion-dollar derivatives DVA in an unwind of transactions with Morgan Stanley.[25] However, these examples occurred since the monolines were so close to default that the banks preferred to exit transactions prior to an actual credit event. The banks

---

[22] Wilson, H. (2011). Banks' profits boosted by DVA rule. *Daily Telegraph* (31 October). www.telegraph.co.uk.

[23] Wright, W. (2011). Papering Over the Great Wall St Massacre. *Financial News* (26 October). www.fnlondon.com.

[24] Due to there being different accountancy standards for insurance companies, the monolines did not see this gain as a DVA benefit.

[25] Rappaport, L. (2011). MBIA and Morgan Stanley settle bond fight. *Wall Street Journal* (14 December). www.wsj.com. Although MBIA paid Morgan Stanley $1.1bn, the actual amount owed (as defined by Morgan Stanley's exposure) was several billion dollars. The difference can be seen as a DVA benefit gained by MBIA in the unwind, although MBIA may not have seen it like this.

would have been much less inclined to unwind in a situation where the monolines' credit quality had not been so dramatically impaired. Furthermore, if a transaction is unwound, then it would generally need to be replaced. All things being equal, the CVA charged on the replacement transactions should wipe out the DVA benefit from the unwind.

- *Close-out process.* As discussed above (Section 17.3.4), another way to realise DVA might be in the close-out process in the event of the default of the counterparty. In the bankruptcy of Lehman Brothers, these practices have been common, although courts have not always favoured some of the large DVA (and other) claims.[26]
- *Hedging.* An obvious way to attempt to monetise DVA is via hedging. The obvious hedging for CVA is to short the counterparty's credit risk. This can be accomplished by shorting bonds or buying CDS protection. It is possible that neither of these may be achievable in practice, but they are theoretically reasonable ways to hedge CVA. The CVA (loss) is monetised via paying the carry in the repo transaction (to finance the bond purchase) or the premiums in the CDS protection position. However, in order to hedge DVA, a party would need to go long its own credit risk. This could be achieved by buying back one's own bonds, which requires funding (see discussion in Section 18.2.5), or by selling CDS protection referencing one's own credit risk (which is not possible).[27] An alternative is, therefore, to sell protection on similar correlated credits. This clearly creates a major problem as banks would attempt to sell CDS protection on each other, and it is also inefficient to the extent that the correlation is less than 100%. An extreme example of the latter problem was that some banks had sold protection on Lehman Brothers prior to their default as an attempted 'hedge' against their DVA.

Most of the above arguments for monetising DVA are fairly weak. It is therefore not surprising that (although not mentioned in the original text), the Basel Committee (BCBS 2011d) determined that DVA should be derecognised from the CVA capital charge (Section 13.3.1). This would prevent a more risky bank having a lower capital charge by virtue of DVA benefits opposing CVA losses. This is part of a more general point with respect to the Basel III capital charges focusing on a regulatory definition of CVA and not the CVA (and DVA) defined from an accounting standpoint. Even accounting standards have recognised problems with DVA with the FASB – for example, determining that DVA gains and losses be represented in a separate form of earnings known as 'other comprehensive income'.

Market practice has always been somewhat divided over the inclusion of DVA in pricing, as shown in Figure 17.11, with many banks giving some, but not all, of the DVA benefit in pricing new transactions. Even those quoting that they 'fully' include DVA would not do this on all transactions (an obvious exception being where the DVA is bigger than the CVA and they would not pay through mid). Anecdotally, most banks' submissions to the Totem consensus pricing can be clearly seen to contain no DVA component (although they do contain FVA, as discussed in Section 18.2.5).

---

[26] PricewaterhouseCoopers (2017). Lehman Brothers International (Europe) – In Administration. Joint Administrators' eighteenth progress report, for the period from 15 March 2017 to 14 September 2017 (9 October). www.pwc.com.

[27] Either because it is illegal or because of the extreme WWR it will create (Section 17.6.5), meaning that no party should be willing to enter such a trade except at a very low premium.

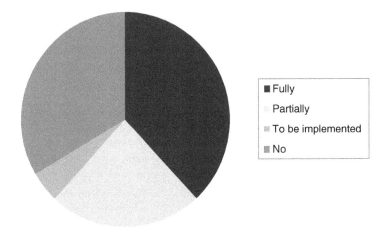

Figure 17.11   Market practice around including DVA in pricing. Source: Deloitte/Solum CVA Survey (2013).

Market practice has generally resolved the debate over DVA by considering it a funding benefit. Indeed, in the hedging argument above, buying back one's own debt could be seen as a practical alternative to the obviously flawed idea of selling CDS protection on one's own credit. However, buying back debt clearly requires that it is first issued, creating a link to funding which must, therefore, be considered. More broadly, it can be shown that different 'strategies' give rise to different valuation adjustments. Whilst there are strategies that support the use of DVA, these are hard to justify as being economically realistic.

When FVA is considered, it is possible to see DVA as a funding benefit. This will be discussed in more detail in Chapter 18.

17.4   CVA ALLOCATION

Risk mitigants, such as netting and margin, reduce CVA, but this can only be quantified by a calculation at the netting set level. It is, therefore, important to consider the allocation of CVA to the transaction level for pricing and valuation purposes. This, in turn, leads to the consideration of the numerical issues involving the running of large-scale calculations rapidly.

17.4.1   Incremental CVA

When there is a netting agreement, the impact will reduce CVA and cannot increase it (this arises from the properties of netting described in Section 11.3.1). It follows that, for a netting set (a group of transactions with a given counterparty under the same netting agreement):

$$CVA^{NS} \geq \sum_{i=1}^{N} CVA_i^{SA} \tag{17.10}$$

where CVA^{NS} is the total CVA of all transactions under the netting agreement and CVA_i^{SA} is the standalone CVA for transaction i (i.e. computed in isolation). The above effect (CVA becoming less negative) can be significant, and the question then becomes how to allocate the netting benefits to each individual transaction. Note that these netting benefits constitute a portfolio effect and will be strong for balanced and offsetting portfolios and weaker for directional portfolios (Section 15.2.3).

The most obvious way to allocate the portfolio netting effect is to use the concept of 'incremental CVA', analogous to the incremental EPE discussed in Section 15.6.3.[28] Here the CVA as a result of any trading behaviour (most obviously a new transaction) is calculated based on the incremental effect this transaction has on the netting set:

$$CVA^{NS \to NS^*} = CVA^{NS^*} - CVA^{NS} \tag{17.11}$$

where CVA^{NS} and CVA^{NS^*} represent the (portfolio) CVA before and after the change, respectively, and $CVA^{NS \to NS^*}$ represents the incremental effect of that change. The above formula ensures that the CVA of a new transaction is represented by its contribution to the overall CVA at the time it is executed. Hence, it makes sense when CVA needs to be charged to individual salespeople, traders, businesses, and, ultimately, clients. CVA depends on the order in which transactions are executed, but does not change due to subsequent transactions. An xVA desk (Chapter 21) charging this amount will directly offset the instantaneous impact on its total CVA from the change in CVA as a result of the new transaction. Note that Equation 17.11 may not only correspond to new transactions but also to:

- unwinding;
- restructuring transactions; and
- changes to contractual terms (e.g. margin agreements).

The above situations are all cases where it may be necessary to charge (or refund) a counterparty for the change in CVA, and where the incremental calculation is relevant.

As shown in Appendix 17E, it is possible to derive the following fairly obvious and intuitive formula for incremental CVA:

$$CVA^{NS \to NS^*} = -LGD \sum_{i=1}^{m} EPE^{NS \to NS^*}(t, t_i) \times PD(t_{i-1}, t_i) \tag{17.12}$$

which is the same as Equation 17.5 but with the incremental EPE replacing the standalone EPE. This assumes that the behaviour in question does not change the PD or LGD of the counterparty, which may be debated in some situations (e.g. a counterparty undertaking to post more margin may be more likely to default, although this would be captured in the credit spread). The quantification of incremental EPE was covered in detail in Section 15.6.3 and will require aggregations (Equation 15.2) at the netting set level. For new transactions this will just require comparing the netting set properties with and without the new transaction, whereas for more complex restructurings it will require a full calculation of the netting set EPE:

$$V^{NS}(s, t) = \sum_{k=1}^{K^{NS}} V(k, s, t) \tag{17.13}$$

---

[28] The reader may wish to refer back to the discussion around incremental exposure in this section as many of the points made there will apply to incremental CVA also.

Table 17.4   Incremental BCVA calculations (bps upfront) for a seven-year USD swap paying fixed with respect to different existing transactions and compared to the standalone value. The counterparty credit curve is assumed to be flat at 150 bps, the own credit curve is 100 bps and both LGDs are equal to 60%.

	Standalone	Directional	Neutral/Offsetting
CVA	−26.3	−25.1	−13.7
DVA	6.0	5.3	−2.5
BCVA	−20.3	−19.9	−16.3

Incremental EPE can be negative, due to beneficial netting effects, which will lead to CVA being positive; in such a case, it would be a benefit and not a cost (e.g. unwinding a transaction would be expected to lead to this effect).

It is worth emphasising that, due to the properties of EPE and netting, incremental CVA in the presence of netting will never be lower (more negative) than standalone CVA without netting. The practical result of this is that an institution with existing transactions under a netting agreement will be likely to offer conditions that are more favourable to a counterparty with respect to a new transaction. Cooper and Mello (1991) quantified such an impact many years ago, showing specifically that a bank that already has a transaction with a counterparty can offer a more competitive rate on a forward contract. Anecdotally, some clients in jurisdictions with debatable netting enforceability (Section 6.3.2) may note that they only trade with banks who deem netting to be enforceable, since the other banks are unable to price in any incremental benefits.

The treatment of netting makes the treatment of CVA a complex and often multidimensional problem. Whilst some attempts have been made at handling netting analytically (e.g. Brigo and Masetti 2005b, as noted in Section 15.1.3), CVA calculations incorporating netting accurately typically require a general Monte Carlo simulation for exposure (EPE) quantification. For pricing new transactions, such a calculation must be run more or less in real time.

An example of incremental CVA following the previous results for incremental exposure in Section 15.6.3 is shown in Table 17.4. The example is a seven-year EUR payer interest rate swap in directional and neutral/offsetting cases. The counterparty and party's own credit spreads are assumed to be 150 bps and 100 bps respectively, and an LGD of 60% is assumed for both.

Spreadsheet 17.4 Incremental CVA and DVA calculations.

Considering CVA or DVA in isolation, the above results are expected since the directional case leads to only a small reduction (in absolute terms), whilst the reduction in the neutral/offsetting case is much larger. Indeed, incremental DVA changes sign in this case, which might be described as offsetting, whereas CVA reduces but does not change sign, which might be more accurately defined as neutral.

Note that there is another important feature in this example, which is that BCVA does not change substantially due to a cancellation. Indeed, for equal credit spread, BCVA is

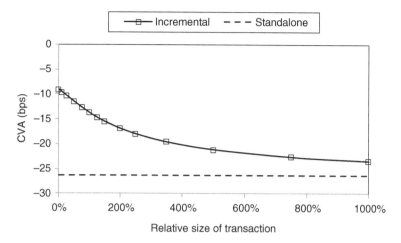

Figure 17.12   Incremental CVA (as a spread in bps per annum) for the balanced/risk-reducing case in Table 17.4.

always the same and has no incremental effect. This is analogous to a similar result for FVA, discussed in Section 18.3.3.

Another point to emphasise is that the benefit of netting seen in incremental CVA of a new transaction also depends on the relative size of the new transaction. As the transaction size increases, the netting benefit is lost, and CVA (or DVA) will approach the standalone value. This is illustrated in Figure 17.12, which shows incremental CVA for the seven-year swap in the last example, a function of the relative size of this new transaction. For a smaller transaction, CVA decreases to a lower limit of -6.2 bps, whereas for a large transaction size, it approaches the standalone value (-17.9 bps).

17.4.2   Marginal CVA

Following the discussion in Section 15.2.2, it is possible to define marginal CVA in a similar way by simply including marginal EPE in the relevant formula. Marginal CVA may be useful to break down CVA for any number of netted transactions into transaction-level contributions that sum to total CVA. Whilst it might not be used for pricing new transactions (due to the problem that marginal CVA changes when new transactions are executed, implying adjustment to the value of existing trades), it may be required for pricing transactions executed at the same time (perhaps due to being part of the same deal) with a given counterparty.[29] Alternatively, marginal CVA is the appropriate way to allocate CVA to transaction-level contributions at a given time – for example, for accounting purposes. This may be useful to give an idea of transactions that could be usefully restructured, novated, or unwound.

Table 17.5 shows incremental and marginal CVA corresponding to the same interest rate swap shown in Table 17.4 together with a cross-currency swap. DVA results are not shown but can be reproduced in Spreadsheet 17.5.

---

[29] This could also cover a policy where CVA adjustments are only calculated periodically and several trades have occurred with a given counterparty within that period.

Table 17.5 Illustration of the breakdown of CVA of an interest rate swap (IRS) and cross-currency swap (XCCY) via incremental and marginal allocation. The counterparty credit curve is assumed to be flat at 150 bps, and the LGD is 60%.

	Incremental (XCCY first)	Incremental (IRS first)	Marginal
IRS	−13.7	−26.3	−17.7
XCCY	−23.2	−10.7	−19.2
Total	−36.9	−36.9	−36.9

> **Spreadsheet 17.5 Marginal CVA and DVA calculations.**

Incremental CVA clearly depends very much on the ordering of the transactions, with the contribution from the second transaction being much smaller. The marginal allocation is more 'fair'. Clearly, the amount of CVA charged can be very dependent on the timing of the transaction. This may be problematic and could possibly lead to 'gaming' behaviour. However, this is not generally problematic for two reasons:

- a given client will typically be 'owned' by a single trader or salesperson and will, therefore, be exposed only to the total charge on a portfolio of transactions (although certain transactions may appear beneficial at a given time); and
- most clients will execute relatively directional transactions (due, for example, to their hedging requirements) and netting effects will therefore not be large.

17.5 IMPACT OF MARGIN

17.5.1 Overview

The impact of margin on CVA follows directly from the assessment of the impact of margin on exposure in Sections 15.6.5 and 15.6.6. As with netting, the influence of margin on the standard CVA formula given in Equation 17.3 is straightforward: margin only changes EPE, and hence the same formula may be used with EPE based on assumptions of collateralisation.

Whilst strong collateralisation would imply that CVA would be small and potentially negligible, it has become increasingly common for market participants to model the impact of variation margin, even when thresholds are zero. Although the minimum margin period of risk (MPoR) of 10 days applies only for regulatory capital purposes, it has become standard across other CVA calculations, such as for accounting purposes. Whilst margining may reduce CVA significantly, this reduction is not as strong as might be thought, as shown in Section 15.6.5. Furthermore, whilst CVA to 'collateralised counterparties' may be materially reduced, an institution may have more of such counterparties and/or bigger portfolios with them.

As an illustration of the above, consider the results in Figure 3.4 in Chapter 3. The bank in question has a material CVA to banks and 'other financial institutions', even though most of these counterparties would be expected to be strongly collateralised. It is therefore important to model the impact of margin on CVA.

It should be noted that the ability to charge collateralised counterparties for CVA may be limited. Whilst financial end users posting margin may still be charged some CVA, it is clearly not possible to charge interbank counterparties for the purposes of hedging. There is less incentive, therefore, to price collateralised CVA for pricing purposes.

17.5.2   Example

Figure 17.13 shows CVA for the same pay and receive interest rate swaps considered previously, using the aforementioned Spreadsheet 17.4, with a classical model for the MPoR (Section 15.5.3). The exposure profiles are shown in Figure 17.13 for the pay fixed swap and compared to the uncollateralised exposure. Since the MPoR modelling assumptions are symmetric, the receive fixed swap will be the opposite of this case. The MPoR is assumed to be 10 business days.

Table 17.6 shows CVA and DVA values for uncollateralised and collateralised interest rate swaps. Note that the collateralised values are more symmetric for pay and receive swaps (this may not be the case when more advanced modelling of cash flows is done, as discussed in Section 15.5.3). As shown in Appendix 15C, the simple formula of the reduction in CVA (via EPE) due to collateralisation would be about 8.4 times.[30] CVA reduction of the pay fixed swap (or DVA of the receive fixed swap) is better than this due to the positive skew of EPE (see Figure 15.24). CVA reduction of the receiver swap is lower due to the negative skew.

The fact that BCVA is small for collateralised transactions may provide some comfort as it may be difficult to charge such costs in these situations (e.g. interbank transactions).

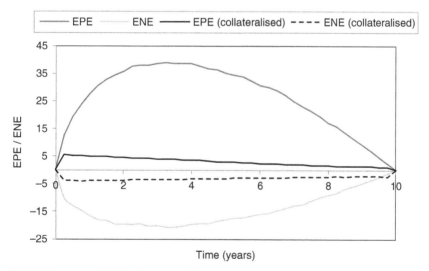

Figure 17.13   Incremental CVA (as a spread in bps per annum) for the balanced/risk-reducing case in Table 17.4.

---

[30] Using an MPoR of 10 days and a maturity of 10 years, and assuming 250 business days in a year, this comes from $\frac{8}{15} \times \sqrt{10 \times \frac{250}{10}} = 8.4$.

Table 17.6 Upfront CVA and DVA values (in bps) for 10-year uncollateralised and collateralised interest rate swaps.

	Pay fixed		Receive fixed	
	Uncollateralised	Collateralised	Uncollateralised	Collateralised
CVA	−28.9	−3.0	−16.6	−3.2
DVA	7.4	1.5	13.2	1.3
BCVA	−21.5	−1.5	−3.5	−1.9

However, note that the DVA calculation for collateralised counterparties is potentially even more controversial than for uncollateralised cases. This is because it stems from the implicit assumption that, 10 days prior to a party's own default, they would cease to make margin payments and this would, in turn, lead to a benefit. Even if present, this benefit would only be experienced by bondholders, for whom the margin not returned would enhance their recovery rate.

17.5.3   Initial Margin

As discussed in Section 15.5.4 and demonstrated in Section 15.6.6, the initial margin will reduce exposure – and therefore CVA/DVA – towards zero. Figure 17.14 illustrates this for CVA by showing the impact of a fixed initial margin or threshold.[31] Note that a threshold can be seen to be a negative initial margin and vice versa. For high thresholds, CVA tends to the uncollateralised value, whilst for high initial margin it tends to zero. As previously discussed in Section 15.5.4, the modelling of dynamic initial margins is a complex undertaking. Given that CVA in the presence of initial margin should be small, the degree of complexity that is warranted in order to calculate this is not clear. In terms of accounting

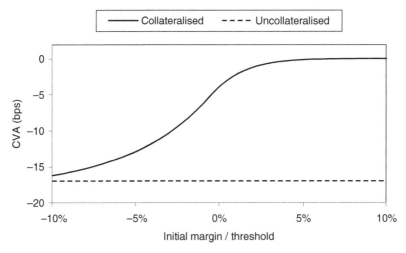

Figure 17.14   Impact of the initial margin and threshold (negative values) on the CVA of a 10-year receiver interest rate swap with an MPoR of 10 business days.

---

[31] A one-way margin agreement in favour of the party in question is assumed.

CVA, it may be that parties argue that where a high coverage of initial margin is held, CVA can be assumed to be zero. Alternatively, a party may ignore the benefit of initial margin, which will lead to a material CVA but avoid the complexity of the calculation.

Note that any initial margin posted would not show up in any of the above calculations as long as it is segregated (Section 7.2.5). However, it will represent a cost from the point of view of margin value adjustment (MVA) (Chapter 20).

17.5.4   CVA to CCPs

Episodes such as the recent Nasdaq default (Section 10.1.3) provide a reminder that central counterparties (CCPs) are risky. Of particular note is the fact that clearing members can make losses as a result of their default fund contributions, even if the CCP itself is not insolvent. Such default fund exposure would suggest that clearing members should attempt to quantify their CVA to a CCP. This is also in line with the fact that default fund-related capital requirements are relatively high (Section 13.6.3), reflecting this risk.

Nowadays, CVA is generally calculated for all counterparties, even those that are strongly collateralised (for example, see Figure 3.4), but the calculation of CVA to CCPs is not standard. However, it would seem that this is likely to become more routine, given the increasing use of CCPs and awareness of the risk. Accountants may also require such CVA calculations given the likely materiality of the numbers.

However, the calculation of CVA to a CCP is a very challenging problem since the underlying parameters for CVA – namely PD, EPE, and LGD – are hard to determine. In order to determine these inputs, the follow points need to be quantified.

- *Default probability*. This is the probability of one or more defaults amongst the other clearing members of the CCP. This would require the assessment of many different credit spread curves together with – in theory – assumptions regarding the dependency between the defaults. CVA will also be sensitive to the LGD used to imply default probability, since it will not cancel as it does in more traditional CVA calculations.
- *Total exposure*. In the event of one or more defaults, it would be necessary to determine the potential total loss in excess of the defaulter-pays resources. Note that the initial margin and default fund contributions of each individual member are generally not known, although there may be CCP disclosures regarding the aggregate amounts. Since CCP initial margins are taken to a high coverage, this may be expected to be small. However, the possibility of extreme market moves and difficulty in auctioning portfolios can create potentially large losses, as in the aforementioned Nasdaq case. It is not clear how – or if – it would be possible to model the likely efficiency of an auction.
- *Allocation of exposure*. Even knowing the total loss in a default fund, it would be necessary to estimate the proportion of this loss that would be experienced by a given clearing member. Methods such as rights of assessment (Section 8.3.4) are usually based on a pro rata allocation which is predictable. However, the possibility for heterogenous allocation via the use of auction incentive pools (Section 10.2.3) or other loss-allocation methods, such as variation margin gains haircutting (Section 10.2.4), further complicates this.
- *LGD*. The assessment of any recovery of losses will also be extremely difficult.[32]

---

[32] Karagiannopoulos, L. (2018). Clearing members warn recovering money after Nasdaq deal could take a long time. *Reuters* (16 November). www.reuters.com.

Another important consideration is the meaning of the CVA value to a given CCP. CVA, being an expected loss, is relevant in the event that the exposure is part of a diversified portfolio and/or is hedgeable. It could be argued that CVA to a CCP does not meet either of these criteria as there are few CCPs and a clearing member may have a material CVA to a given CCP that can be neither diversified nor hedged.

Regarding the computation of CVA to a CCP, Arnsdorf (2019) has proposed a simple approach based on the posted initial margin of the clearing member (and therefore not requiring detailed information about the structure of the CCP). This assumption holds if default fund requirements are linked to initial margin requirements and also if default fund losses are allocated homogenously, both of which are approximately true. Arnsdorf also proposed to use the credit spreads of the other clearing members to calculate default probabilities, and extreme value theory to calculate EPE based on the distribution of losses above the defaulter-pays resources.

17.6   WRONG-WAY RISK

17.6.1   Overview

So far, this chapter has described the calculation and computation of CVA under the commonly-made simplification of no WWR, which assumes that EPE, PD, and LGD are not related. WWR is the phrase generally used to indicate an unfavourable dependence between exposure (EPE) and counterparty credit quality: the exposure is high when the counterparty is more likely to default, and vice versa. Such an effect would have a clear impact on CVA and DVA. Moreover, certain WWR features can also apply to other situations and impact other xVA terms through dependencies related to collateral, funding, and other factors. WWR is difficult to identify, model, and hedge due to the often subtle macro-economic and structural effects that cause it.

Whilst it may often be a reasonable assumption to ignore WWR, its manifestation can be potentially dramatic. In contrast, 'right-way' risk can also exist in cases where the dependence between exposure and credit quality is a favourable one. Right-way situations will reduce CVA.

Losses due to WWR have also been clearly illustrated. For example, many dealers suffered heavy losses because of WWR during the Asian crisis of 1997/1998. This was due to a strong link between the default of sovereigns and of corporates and a significant weakening of their local currencies. A decade later (starting in 2007), the global financial crisis caused heavy WWR losses for banks buying insurance from so-called monoline insurance companies (Section 2.4.4).

WWR is often a natural and unavoidable consequence of financial markets. One of the simplest examples is mortgage providers who, in an economic recession, face both falling property prices and higher default rates by homeowners. In derivatives, classic examples of trades that obviously contain WWR across different asset classes are:

- *Put option*. Buying a put option on a stock (or stock index) where the underlying reference in question has fortunes that are highly correlated to those of the counterparty is an obvious case of WWR (e.g. buying a put on one bank's stock from another bank). Correspondingly, equity call options should be right-way products.

- *FX forward or cross-currency products.* Any foreign exchange (FX) contract should be considered in terms of a potential weakening of the currency and simultaneous deterioration in the credit quality of the counterparty. This would obviously be the case in trading with a sovereign and paying its local currency in an FX forward or cross-currency swap (or, more likely in practice, hedging this trade with a bank in that same region). Another way to look at a cross-currency swap is that it represents a loan collateralised by the opposite currency in the swap. If this currency weakens dramatically, the value of the 'margin' is strongly diminished. This linkage could be either way: first, a weakening of the currency could indicate a slow economy and hence a less profitable time for the counterparty. Alternatively, the default of a sovereign, financial institution, or large corporate counterparty may itself precipitate a currency weakening.
- *Interest rate products.* Here it is important to consider a relationship between the relevant interest rates and the credit spread of the counterparty. A corporate paying the fixed rate in a swap when the economy is strong may represent WWR for a bank receiving fixed, since interest rates would be likely to be cut in a recession. On the other hand, during an economic recovery, interest rates may rise and so paying fixed may represent a right-way situation.
- *Commodity swaps.* A commodity producer (e.g. a mining company) may hedge the price fluctuation to which it is exposed with derivatives. Such a contract *should* represent right-way risk since the commodity producer will only owe money when the commodity price is high, when the business should be more profitable. The right-way risk arises due to hedging (as opposed to speculation).
- *Credit default swaps.* When buying protection in a CDS contract, the exposure will be the result of the reference entity's credit spread widening, and the default probability will be linked to the counterparty's credit spread. In the case of a strong relationship between the credit quality of the reference entity and the counterparty, clearly there is extreme WWR. A bank selling protection on its own sovereign would be an obvious problem. On the other hand, with such a strong relationship, selling CDS protection should be a right-way trade.

There is also empirical evidence supporting the presence of WWR. Duffee (1998) describes a clustering of corporate defaults during periods of falling interest rates, which is most obviously interpreted as a recession, leading to both low interest rates (due to central bank intervention) and a high default rate environment. This has also been experienced in the last few years by banks on uncollateralised receiver interest swap positions, which have moved ITM together with a potential decline in the financial health of the counterparty (e.g. a sovereign or corporate). This effect can be seen as WWR creating a 'cross-gamma' effect (Section 21.2.3) via the strong linkage of credit spreads and interest rates, even in the absence of actual defaults. Regarding the FX example above, results from Levy and Levin (1999) look at residual currency values upon default of the sovereign and find average values ranging from 17% (triple-A) to 62% (triple-C). This implies the amount by which the FX rate involved could jump at the default time of the counterparty.

Regulators have identified characteristics of both general (driven by macro-economic relationships) and specific (driven by causal linkages between the exposure/margin and default of the counterparty) WWR, which are outlined in Table 17.7.

Table 17.7   Characteristics of general and specific WWR.

General WWR	Specific WWR
Based on macro-economic behaviour	Based on structural relationships that are often not captured via real-world experience
Relationships may be detectable using historical data	Hard to detect except by a knowledge of the relevant market, the counterparty, and the economic rationale behind their transaction
Potentially can be incorporated into pricing models	Difficult to model and dangerous to use naïve correlation assumptions; should be addressed qualitatively via methods such as stress testing
Should be priced and managed correctly	Should, in general, be avoided as it may be extreme

Specific WWR is particularly difficult to quantify since it is not based on any macro-economic relationships and may not be expected to be part of historical or market-implied data. For example, in 2010, the European sovereign debt crisis involved deterioration in the credit quality of many European sovereigns and a weakening of the euro. However, historical data did not bear out this relationship, largely since neither most of the sovereigns concerned nor the currency had ever previously been subject to any strong adverse credit effects.

17.6.2   Quantification of WWR in CVA

Incorporation of WWR in the CVA formula is probably most obviously achieved by simply representing the exposure *conditional* upon the default of the counterparty. For example, in the path-wise formula, this would simply involve replacing EPE in Equation 17.3 with $EPE(t, t_i | t_i = \tau_C)$, which represents EPE at time t_i, conditional on this being the counterparty default time (τ_C). This approach supports approaching WWR quantification heuristically by qualitatively assessing the likely increase in the conditional – compared to unconditional – exposure. An example of a qualitative approach to WWR is in regulatory capital requirements and the alpha factor (Section 13.4.5). A conservative estimate for alpha, together with the requirement to use stressed data in the estimation of the exposure, represents a regulatory effort partially to capitalise general WWR.

Appendix 17F shows a simple formula for the conditional EPE for a forward contract-type exposure (an extension of the previous unconditional case given in Appendix 11A). The relationship between EPE and counterparty default is expressed using a single correlation parameter. This correlation parameter is rather abstract, with no straightforward economic intuition, but it does facilitate a simple way of quantifying and understanding WWR.

Spreadsheet 17.6 Simple wrong-way risk example.

Figure 17.15 shows the impact of wrong-way (and right-way) risk on EPE. With 50% correlation, WWR approximately doubles the expected positive exposure (EPE), whilst with -50% correlation, the impact of right-way risk reduces it by at least half. This is

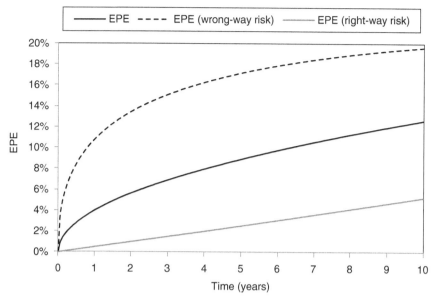

Figure 17.15 Illustration of wrong-way and right-way risk exposure profiles using a simple model with correlations of 50% and -50%, respectively.

exactly the type of behaviour that is expected: positive correlation between the default probability and exposure increases conditional EPE (default probability is high when exposure is high), which is WWR. Negative correlation leads to smaller EPE and so-called right-way risk.

The size of EPE will now depend on the counterparty default probability. Figure 17.16 shows EPE for differing counterparty credit quality, showing that the exposure increases as the credit quality of the counterparty increases. This result might at first seem counterintuitive, but it makes sense when one considers that for a better credit quality counterparty, default is a less probable event and therefore represents a bigger shock when it occurs. We note an important general conclusion, which is that WWR *increases* as the credit quality of the counterparty *increases*.

A more sophisticated approach to modelling the relationship between default probability and exposure will be harder to achieve and may introduce computational challenges. At a high level, there are a number of problems in doing this, which are:

- *Uninformative historical data.* Unfortunately, WWR may be subtle and not revealed via any empirical data, such as a historical time series analysis of correlations.
- *Misspecification of relationship.* The way in which the dependency is specified may be inappropriate. For example, rather than being the result of a correlation, it may be the result of causality – a cause-and-effect-type relationship between two events. If the correlation between two random variables is measured as zero, then this does not prove that they are independent.[33]

---

[33] A classic example of this is as follows. Suppose a variable X follows a normal distribution. Now choose $Y = X^2$. X and Y have zero correlation but are far from independent.

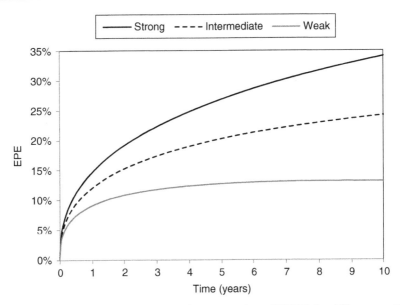

Figure 17.16   Illustration of exposure under the assumption of WWR for different credit quality counterparties.

- *Direction.* The direction of WWR may not be clear. For example, low interest rates may typically be seen in a recession, when credit spreads may be wider and default rates higher. However, an adverse credit environment where interest rates are high is not impossible.

17.6.3   Wrong-way Risk Models

An obvious modelling technique for WWR is to introduce a stochastic process for the credit spread and correlate this with the other underlying processes required for modelling exposure. A default will be generated via the credit spread ('intensity') process, and the resulting conditional EPE will be calculated in the usual way in either a path-wise or direct implementation (but only for paths where there has been a default). This approach can be implemented relatively tractably, as credit spread paths can be generated first, and exposure paths need only be simulated in cases where a default is observed. The required correlation parameters can be observed directly via historical time series of credit spreads and other relevant market variables.[34] This will be referred to as the intensity approach.

Spreadsheet 17.7 Direct simulation of wrong-way risk for an interest rate swap.

---

[34] Noting that the credit spread may be determined by some proxy or generic curve, in which case this historical time series should be used.

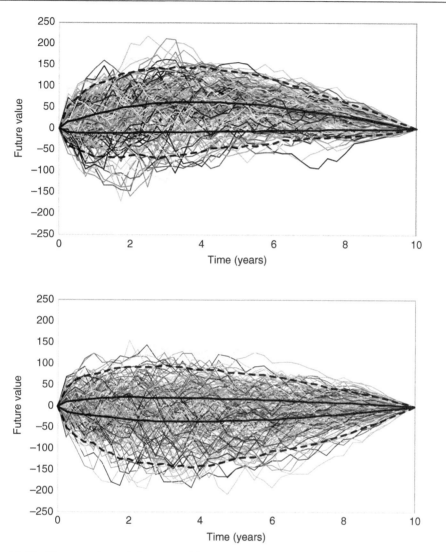

Figure 17.17 Future values of the swap with 90% (top) and -90% (bottom) correlation between credit spreads and interest rates. The potential future exposure (5% and 95%) is shown by the dotted black lines, and EPE and ENE are shown by the solid black lines.

This approach is illustrated for the interest rate swap example previously discussed in Section 15.6.1. Using a lognormal model for credit spreads correlated to the interest rate process, the exposure conditional on default in Equation 17.3 is calculated to be compared to the previous Figure 15.23. Figure 17.17 shows the swap values generated conditional on default for high positive and negative correlations.

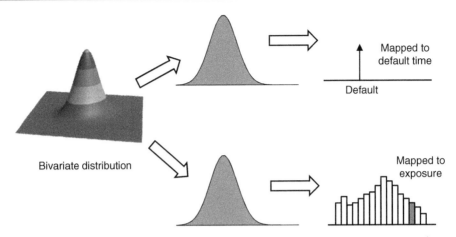

Figure 17.18   Illustration of the structural approach to modelling general WWR, assuming some underlying bivariate distribution.

Since this is a swap paying the fixed rate, a positive correlation with credit spreads leads to interest rates being higher in default scenarios, leading to a higher positive exposure (WWR). For a negative correlation, the negative exposure increases (right-way risk). The relationship between changes in interest rates and default rates has been empirically shown to be generally negative.[35]

Note that the above approach can be seen to generate only weak dependence between exposure and default, given that the correlations used are close to their maximum and minimum values. Hence, whilst this approach is the most obvious and easy to implement, it may underestimate the true WWR effect.

An even simpler and more tractable approach to general WWR is to specify a dependence directly between the counterparty default time and the exposure distribution, illustrated in Figure 17.18 (for example, see Garcia-Cespedes et al. 2010). In this 'structural approach', the exposure and default distributions are mapped separately onto a bivariate distribution. Positive (negative) dependency will lead to an early default time being coupled with a higher (lower) exposure, as is the case with WWR (right-way risk). Note that there is no need to recalculate the exposures as the original unconditional values are sampled directly. The advantage of this method is that pre-computed exposure distributions are used, and WWR is essentially added on top of the existing methodology. However, this is also a disadvantage since it may not be appropriate to assume that all the relevant information to define WWR is contained within the unconditional exposure distribution.

Spreadsheet 17.8 Exposure distribution using a Gaussian copula approach.

Figure 17.19 shows EPE of the payer swap with a structural model and a correlation of 50%, and compared to an intensity model with the same correlation.

---

[35] Longstaff and Schwartz (1995), Duffee (1998), and Collin-Dufresne et al. (2001).

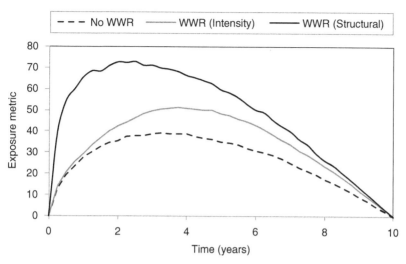

Figure 17.19 EPE of a payer interest rate swap calculated with WWR using intensity and structural models, each with a correlation of 50%.

Figure 17.20 shows CVA as a function of correlation for the intensity and structural approaches. Whilst both approaches produce a qualitatively similar result, with higher CVA for negative correlation, the effect is much stronger in the structural model.

The big drawback with the structural model is that the correlation parameter described above is opaque and, therefore, difficult to calibrate. Discussion and correlation estimates are given by Fleck and Schmidt (2005) and Rosen and Saunders (2010). More complex representations of this model are suggested by Iscoe et al. (1999) and De Prisco and Rosen

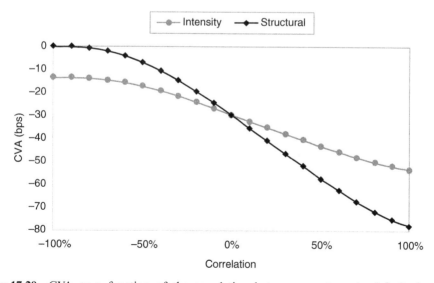

Figure 17.20 CVA as a function of the correlation between counterparty default time and exposure.

(2005), where the default process is correlated more directly with variables defining the exposure. Estimation of the underlying correlations is then more achievable.

One other possible approach to WWR is a more direct, parametric one. For example, Hull and White (2011) have proposed linking the default probability parametrically to the exposure using a simple, functional relationship. They suggest using either an intuitive calibration based on a what-if scenario, or calibrating the relationship via historical data. This latter calibration would involve calculating the portfolio value for dates in the past and examining the relationship between this and the counterparty's credit spread. If the portfolio has historically shown high values together with larger than average credit spreads, then this will indicate WWR. This approach obviously requires that the current portfolio of trades with the counterparty is similar in nature to that used in the historical calibration, in addition to the historical data showing a meaningful relationship.

17.6.4   Jump Approaches

Jump approaches for WWR may be more realistic, especially in cases of specific WWR. For example, this has been clearly shown to be relevant for FX examples where the CDS market gives some clear indication of the nature of FX WWR. Most CDSs are quoted in US dollars, but sometimes simultaneous quotes can be seen in other currencies. For example, Table 17.8 shows the CDS quotes for Italian sovereign protection in both US dollars and euros. These CDS contracts should trigger on the same credit event definitions, and thus the only difference between them is the currency of cash payment on default. There is a large 'quanto' effect, with euro-denominated CDSs being cheaper by around 30% for all maturities.

Figure 17.21 shows the historical evolution of the Japanese sovereign quanto basis, which also shows a considerable difference between the price of CDS protection purchased in US dollars and Japanese yen. The CDS market, therefore, allows WWR effect in currencies to be observed and potentially also hedged.

The above data seem to suggest that the relationship involved is a causal one and the FX rate 'jumps' around the time of a sovereign default. Indeed, it has been shown (Ehlers and Schönbucher 2006) that an intensity-type modelling approach, such as that described in Section 17.6.3, is not able to match the CDS data. In such an approach, there would be a correlation between the FX rate and the credit spread, but the effect that this produces is generally not strong enough, even with +/-100% correlation.

Table 17.8   CDS quotes (mid-market) for Italian sovereign protection in both US dollars and euros, from April 2011.

Maturity (years)	USD	EUR
1	50	35
2	73	57
3	96	63
4	118	78
5	131	91
7	137	97
10	146	103

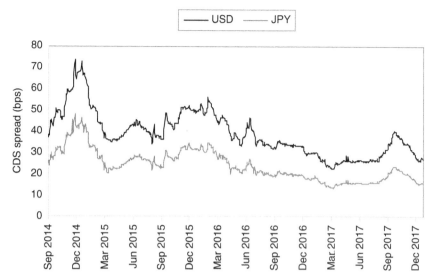

Figure 17.21   The Japan sovereign quanto basis for the dollar–yen pair. Source: Chung and Gregory (2019).

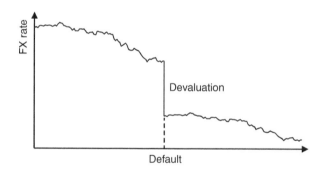

Figure 17.22   Illustration of the currency jump approach to WWR for FX products.

A simple jump approach was first proposed by Levy and Levin (1999) to model FX exposures with WWR. This assumes that the relevant FX rate jumps at the counterparty default time, as illustrated in Figure 17.22.

The nature of implied jumps related to sovereign defaults has been well characterised. Levy and Levin (1999) used historical default data on sovereigns and showed that the implied jump is larger for better-rated sovereigns – for example, 83% for AAA and 27% for BBB sovereigns. This is probably because their default results in or is caused by a more severe financial shock and the conditional FX rate, therefore, should move by a greater amount. For example, a default of a large corporation should be expected to have quite a significant impact on the local currency (albeit smaller than that due to sovereign default).

The RVs can also be implied from available CDS quotes. For example, the implied jumps for the euro against the US dollar for European sovereigns around the time of the sovereign debt crisis in Europe were 9%, 17%, 20%, and 25% for Greece, Italy, Spain, and Germany, respectively.[36] This is again consistent with a higher-credit-quality – and potentially more-systemically-important – sovereign, creating a stronger impact.

It is not surprising that the above jump effect is observed for sovereign counterparties. However, it can also be observed for other counterparties as well. For example, Chung and Gregory (2019) use data from the Japanese CDS market to show that there are material implied jumps for financial institutions (average 13.5%) and non-financial corporations (average 8%), as well as for the sovereign (average 38.4%).

Whilst there is rarely market data to illustrate the above effect, in the absence of CDS data, Finger (2000) suggests how non-sovereign counterparties might be modelled if the sovereign quanto effect is observed.

17.6.5   Credit Derivatives

Credit derivatives are a special case, as the WWR is unavoidable (buying credit protection on one party from another party) and may be specific (e.g. buying protection from a bank on its sovereign). A number of approaches have been proposed to tackle counterparty risk in credit derivatives, such as Duffie and Singleton (2003), Jarrow and Yu (2001), and Lipton and Sepp (2009).

Appendix 17G describes the pricing for a CDS with counterparty risk using a simple model, ignoring the impact of any collateralisation. Due to the highly contagious and systemic nature of CDS risks, the impact of margin may be hard to assess and indeed may be quite limited. It is interesting to calculate the fair price for buying or selling CDS protection as a function of the correlation between the reference entity and the counterparty (the counterparty is selling protection). Figure 17.23 shows the fair premium – i.e. reduced to account for CVA – that an institution should pay in order to buy CDS protection.[37] Selling protection will require an increased premium. We can observe the very strong impact of correlation: one should be willing only to pay around 200 bps at 60% correlation to buy protection, compared with 250 bps with a 'risk-free' counterparty. CVA in this case is 50 bps (per annum), or one-fifth of the risk-free CDS premium. At extremely high correlations, the impact is even more severe and CVA is huge. At a maximum correlation of 100%, the CDS premium is just above 100 bps, which relates entirely to the recovery value.[38] When selling protection, the impact of CVA is much smaller and reduces with increasing correlation due to right-way risk.[39]

---

[36] Moses, A. (2010). Quanto swaps signal 9 percent Euro drop on Greek default. *Bloomberg* (21 June). www .bloomberg.com.

[37] This is assumed to be free of counterparty risk. We assume that the reference entity CDS spread is 250 bps, whereas the counterparty CDS spread is 500 bps. Both LGDs are assumed to be 60%.

[38] The premium based only on recovery value (i.e. where there is no chance of receiving any default payment) is $250 \times 40\% = 100$ bps.

[39] For zero or low-correlation values, the protection seller may possibly suffer losses due to the counterparty defaulting when the CDS has a positive mark-to-market (requiring a somewhat unlikely tightening of the reference entity credit spread). However, for high correlation values, the mark-to-market of the CDS is very likely to be negative at the counterparty default time and (since this amount must still be paid) there is virtually no counterparty risk.

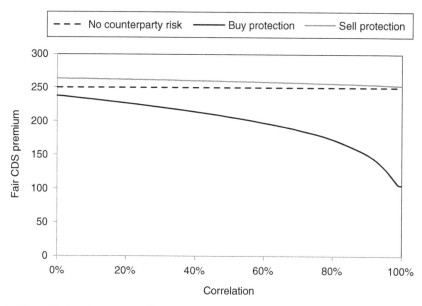

Figure 17.23   Fair CDS premium when buying protection subject to counterparty risk, compared with the standard (risk-free) premium. The counterparty CDS spread is assumed to be 500 bps.

17.6.6   Collateralisation and WWR

Margin is typically assessed in terms of its ability to mitigate exposure. Since WWR potentially causes exposure to increase significantly, the impact of margin on WWR is very important to consider. However, this is very hard to characterise because it is very timing dependent. If the exposure increases gradually prior to default, then margin can be received, whereas a jump in exposure deems margin useless. This is illustrated, for example, by Chung and Gregory (2019), who show that margining has very little impact on an FX portfolio under the jump approach described in Section 17.6.4.

   Not surprisingly, jump approaches tend to show collateralisation as being near useless in mitigating WWR, whereas more continuous approaches (such as the intensity and structural approaches described in Section 17.6.3) suggest that margin is an effective mitigant against WWR. The truth is somewhere in between, but is likely very dependent on the type of transaction and counterparty. Pykhtin and Sokol (2013) consider that the quantification of the benefit of margin in a WWR situation must account for jumps and a period of higher volatility during the MPoR. They also note that WWR should be higher for the default of more systemic parties, such as banks. Overall, their approach shows that WWR has a negative impact on the benefit of collateralisation. Interestingly, counterparties that actively use margin (e.g. banks) tend to be highly systemic and will be subject to these extreme WWR problems, whilst counterparties that are non-systemic (e.g. corporates) often do not post margin anyway.

   WWR may also be present in terms of the relationship between the value of margin and the underlying exposure. Consider a payer interest rate swap collateralised by a high-quality government bond. This would represent a situation of general WWR, since an interest rate rise would cause the value of the swap to increase, whilst the margin value would decline. In the case of a receiver interest rate swap, the situation is reversed and there would be a beneficial right-way margin position. Given the relatively low volatility of interest rates, this is not generally a major problem.

A more significant example of general wrong-way (or right-way) margin could be a cross-currency swap collateralised by cash in one of the two underlying currencies. If margin is held in the currency being paid, then an FX move will simultaneously increase the exposure and reduce the value of the collateral.

There can also be cases of specific WWR where there is a more direct relationship between the type of margin and the counterparty credit quality. An entity posting its own bonds is an example of this: this is obviously a very weak mitigant against credit exposure and CVA, although it may mitigate FVA, as discussed in Section 11.4.3. A bank posting bonds of its own sovereign is another clearly problematic example.

17.6.7   Central Clearing and WWR

Given their reliance on collateralisation as their primary protection via variation and initial margin, CCPs may be particularly prone to WWR, especially those that clear products such as CDSs. A key aim of a CCP is that losses due to the default of a clearing member are contained within resources committed by that clearing member (the so-called 'defaulter-pays' approach described in Section 8.3.4). A CCP faces the risk that the defaulter-pays resources of the defaulting member(s) may be insufficient to cover the associated losses. In such a case, the CCP would impose losses on its members and may be in danger of becoming insolvent itself.

CCPs tend to disassociate credit quality and exposure. Parties must have a certain *credit quality* (typically defined by the CCP and not external credit ratings) to be clearing members, but will then be charged initial margins and default fund contributions driven primarily by the *market* risk of their portfolio (that drives the exposure faced by the CCP).[40] In doing this, CCPs are in danger of implicitly ignoring WWR.

For significant WWR transactions such as CDSs, CCPs have the problem of quantifying the WWR component in defining initial margins and default funds. As with the quantification of WWR in general, this is far from an easy task. Furthermore, WWR increases with increasing credit quality, shown both quantitatively and empirically in Section 17.6.4. Similar arguments are made by Pykhtin and Sokol (2012) in that a large dealer represents more WWR than a smaller and/or weaker credit quality counterparty. These aspects perversely suggest that CCPs should require greater initial margin and default fund contributions from *better*-credit-quality and more-systemically-important members.[41]

Related to the above is the concept that a CCP waterfall may behave rather like a collateralised debt obligation (CDO), which has been noted by a number of authors, including Murphy (2013), Pirrong (2013), and Gregory (2014). The comparison,

---

[40] Some CCPs do base margins partially on credit quality, but this, if used, is not a large effect.
[41] Of course, better-credit-quality members are less likely to default, but the impact if they do is likely to be more severe.

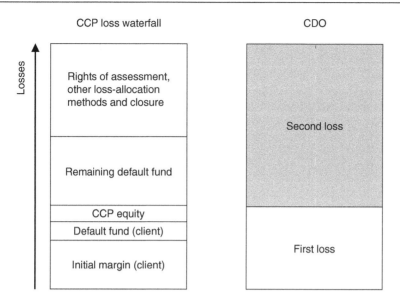

Figure 17.24 Comparison between a CCP loss waterfall and a CDO structure.

illustrated in Figure 17.24, is that the 'first loss' of the CDO is covered by defaulter-pays initial margins and default funds, together with CCP equity. Clearing members, through their default fund contributions and other loss-allocation exposures, have a second loss position on the hypothetical CDO. Of course, the precise terms of the CDO are unknown and ever changing, as they are based on aspects such as the CCP membership, the portfolio of each member, and the initial margins held. However, what is clear is that the second loss exposure should correspond to a relatively unlikely event, since otherwise it would imply that initial margin coverage was too thin.

The second loss position that a CCP member is implicitly exposed to is therefore rather senior in CDO terms. Such senior tranches are known to be heavily concentrated in terms of their systemic risk exposure (see, for example, Gibson 2004, Coval et al. 2009, and Brennan et al. 2009) as discussed in Section 10.2.2.

CCPs also face WWR on the margin they receive. They will likely be under pressure to accept a wide range of eligible securities for initial margin purposes. Accepting more risky and illiquid assets creates additional risks and puts more emphasis on the calculation of haircuts that can also increase risk if underestimated. CCPs admitting a wide range of securities can become exposed to greater adverse selection, as clearing members (and clients) will naturally choose to post margin that has the greatest risk (relative to its haircut) and may also present the greatest WWR to a CCP (e.g. a European bank may choose to post European sovereign debt where possible).

FVA

18.1 OVERVIEW

This chapter will describe the consideration of funding and its potential impact on price and valuation through funding value adjustment (FVA). The nature of funding costs and benefits will be described, together with underlying formulas and examples. The recent debate around the use of FVA in pricing and valuation and the link between FVA and debt value adjustment (DVA) will be addressed.

FVA can be broadly thought to be a consideration of funding for uncollateralised – and partially-collateralised – transactions. FVA, therefore, is a consideration alongside credit value adjustment (CVA) in many situations. From a quantification point of view, FVA is similar in many ways to CVA, and many of the components to calculate the two are shared. Transactions with large CVA (and DVA) components are also likely to have significant funding components.

Assets create funding costs, whereas liabilities provide funding benefits. In-the-money (ITM) positions and expected positive exposure (EPE) will, therefore, relate to funding costs, whilst out-of-the-money (OTM) positions and expected negative exposure (ENE) will lead to funding benefits.

FVA was not given much consideration prior to 2007 because unsecured funding for institutions such as banks was trivial and could be achieved at more or less 'risk-free' rates. However, such funding costs have increased considerably, which has led to their inclusion in pricing and valuation. This means that transactions – especially those that are uncollateralised – are now typically treated including the party's own funding as a component of their price. This is the role of FVA, although its use in valuation through accounting statements has been more controversial.

Despite the increased use of margining, a significant portion of transactions such as over-the-counter (OTC) derivatives remain uncollateralised (Figure 2.7). This arises mainly due to the nature of the counterparties involved, such as corporates and sovereigns, without the liquidity and/or operational capacity to adhere to frequent margin calls. In general, funding costs (and benefits) in derivatives portfolios can be seen as arising from the following situations:

- *Undercollateralisation*. Transactions that are undercollateralised give rise to funding costs (and potentially benefits). This includes transactions that are completely uncollateralised (no margin agreement), but also cases of partial collateralisation (e.g. a two-way margin agreement with a material threshold). One-way margin agreements are also a special case, since one party is collateralised whilst the other is not.
- *Non-rehypothecation and segregation*. Even if a party can receive margin, there is a question of whether or not this can be used. If the margin cannot be rehypothecated or reused and/or must be segregated, then this will prevent it from offsetting any funding position.

Note that FVA – as a definition – will not include margin value adjustment (MVA), which defines the funding of initial margin requirements. Whilst FVA represents the cost of being *undercollateralised*, MVA represents the cost of *overcollateralisation*. Generally, FVA is related to variation margin, whilst MVA (Chapter 20) is related to initial margin. FVA also considers debt funding, with capital value adjustment (KVA) (Chapter 19) being the cost of funding equity in relation to capital requirements.

In some sense, FVA is not a particularly new concept. Prior to the global financial crisis (GFC), it was common to use rates such as LIBOR (London Interbank Offered Rate) to discount cash flows, not because it was the risk-free rate (which is, in any case, a theoretical construct), but because it was a good approximation of a bank's short-term unsecured funding costs. Post-GFC, banks have simply realised that funding costs have increased and they cannot be as reliant on short-term (e.g. LIBOR) funding, and they have, therefore, sought to incorporate these higher costs through FVA.

18.2   FVA AND DISCOUNTING

18.2.1   Market Practice

Whilst collateral discounting (Section 16.1.3) is now seen as the correct valuation of collateralised transactions, the aftermath of the GFC created a parallel problem regarding the valuation of uncollateralised transactions. Banks started to incorporate funding costs into transactions by discounting at a funding rate. For example:

> Transactions secured with collateral are valued using a discount curve based on the overnight index spread. Transactions not secured with collateral are valued using a discount curve based on Euribor/Libor plus a spread that reflects market conditions. (Rabobank Interim Report 2015)

The difference between a standard (collateralised) valuation and one incorporating funding became known as FVA. FVA is generally seen by banks as an internal cost of financing their uncollateralised derivatives portfolios, and has correspondingly been reported in financial statements alongside CVA and DVA components. For example:

> … a fair-value adjustment was applied to account for the impact of incorporating the cost of funding into the valuation of uncollateralised derivatives. (Barclays Annual Report 2012)

FVA reporting has become standard amongst the largest banks, with many other banks following, and the total FVA reported now amounts to many billions of US dollars. Note that, whilst the rationale for FVA seems to stem from economic value considerations, its reporting in financial statements is justified by fair value and exit price considerations. Whilst it is clear that banks consider FVA to arise from their own internal costs of funding uncollateralised derivatives, there is some reference to market pricing. Although the exit price concept is not completely compatible with the view of FVA as an internal cost, it is acceptable to report FVA if the market practice is to incorporate this into pricing.

Hence, the inclusion of FVA (and indeed any other xVA component) in financial statements can be supported via a self-fulfilling prophecy. For example:

> The Firm implemented a Funding Valuation Adjustments ("FVA") framework this quarter for its OTC derivatives and structured notes, reflecting an industry migration towards incorporating the cost or benefit of unsecured funding into valuations. For the first time this quarter, we were able to clearly observe the existence of funding costs in market clearing levels. As a result, the Firm recorded a $1.5B loss this quarter. (J.P. Morgan, Fourth Quarter 2014)

FVA adjustments only consider uncollateralised (or partially collateralised) trades due to the special case of collateral discounting (Section 16.1.3). For example:

> The adjustment this quarter is largely related to uncollateralized derivatives, as ... [c]ollateralized derivatives already reflect the cost or benefit of collateral posted in valuations. (J.P. Morgan, Fourth Quarter Earnings Presentation 2013)

Finally, as mentioned above, funding costs can arise from the inability to reuse (rehypothecate) margin, as well as merely from situations where margin is not received:

> In general, FVA reflects a market funding risk premium inherent in the uncollateralized portion of derivative portfolios, and in collateralized derivatives where the terms of the agreement do not permit the reuse of the collateral received. (Citigroup Third Quarter 2014)

18.2.2   Source of Funding Costs and Benefits

One of the difficult aspects in defining FVA in relation to derivatives is that it may be considered to be related to the following:

- receiving or posting margin;
- paying or receiving cash flows; or
- holding assets or liabilities (defined by the value).

The above components are not mutually exclusive. For example, a strongly-collateralised transaction would seem to have funding considerations due to the need to post or receive variation margin. However, this will be offset by the cash flow payments or the transaction value, leading to no overall adjustment, as mentioned above.

Most banks probably see the economics of FVA as being driven by their margin requirements. This is because banks generally hedge most of their market risk, and so cash flow payments and valuations will be approximately offset by the equal and opposite values from hedges. Many banks, therefore, define the source of funding costs and benefits to be the posting and receipt of margin. However, this alone is not completely accurate and may misrepresent some components and special cases.

From this point of view, a high-level view of funding is represented in Figure 18.1. Since banks aim to run mainly flat derivatives books, market risk will generally be hedged, and

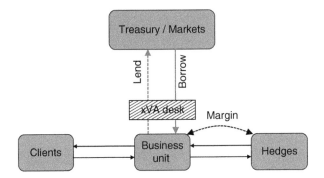

Figure 18.1   Illustration of the source of funding costs (and benefits) within a bank.

so there will not be a large mismatch with respect to cash flows. Generally, there is a mismatch between uncollateralised and collateralised derivatives, with the former usually being client transactions and the latter their associated hedges. A trading desk or business unit will need to have an ability to fund itself via its internal treasury and/or the market. Increasingly, the xVA desk may intermediate this relationship, as shown in Figure 18.1.

Historically, trading desks would carry such funding costs on an accrual basis, but as they have increased in magnitude, a more rigorous treatment has been seen as being important. The xVA desk may, therefore, facilitate better pricing, valuation, and risk management of FVA.

In the above example, and as previously shown in Figure 7.4, when a client trade is ITM from the bank's point of view, then they may not receive margin (collateral) but will be required to post margin on the equivalent OTM hedge(s) (due to being transacted with other banks bilaterally or in an exchange/CCP environment). Such margin must be funded for a reasonable period, either for reasons of good liquidity management or as a result of the net stable funding ratio (NSFR) (Section 4.3.4). The return paid on the margin will typically be the overnight indexed spread (OIS) rate (Section 7.2.4). Hence, unless the bank can fund the margin it posts at the OIS rate, there will be an associated cost. The funding rate will be the spread of the funding rate of the margin over its remuneration rate (typically the OIS rate). Note that when the trade moves in the opposite direction (i.e. the client is ITM), the reverse effect occurs and the bank receives funding. Note that this funding benefit requires the reuse of the margin (e.g. if required, rehypothecation must be allowed).

The above explanation is commonly used by banks to justify FVA. For example:

> Those [funding] costs arise when the trade is hedged with a collateralised transaction, meaning that when the dealer is in-the-money on the first trade it does not receive any margin from its client, but would be out-of-the-money on the hedge and required to post margin as a result.[1]

---

[1] Wood, D. (2012). Putting the fun in funding valuation adjustment. *Risk* (6 September). www.risk.net.

Although useful for explanation purposes, the above analogy must not be taken too literally, as it may suggest the wrong FVA in certain situations. For example:

- *The bank does not hedge the transactions in question.* Here, there may likely still be an FVA adjustment, even though there is no movement of margin.
- *Profit margin.* The profit that a bank makes on a transaction will not be a component of the value of the hedges and, therefore, will not be posted as margin, and yet an FVA will likely still include this amount.
- *Intermediation/novation.* Here a bank might effectively step in to a portfolio with an upfront payment, but any hedges executed would likely be at par (zero value) and, therefore, not require margin posting. This does not mean that there would be no FVA incorporated in the price.
- *Restriking a portfolio.* If a bank restrikes the value of a client portfolio, involving paying or receiving an upfront amount in cash, but again without impacting the hedges, then there are still FVA considerations (indeed, FVA may be one reason for doing this).
- *Change of margin terms.* If the bank and client change their credit support annexe (CSA) terms (e.g. move from a one-way to a two-way CSA), then there will be FVA considerations, even though the hedges are again not impacted.

The reason for the above problems is that they involve cash flows or valuation differences that are not captured by considering only margin movements. It is therefore important to capture these as consistently and easily as possible. Another consideration is currency: funding needs to take into account the currency of the transaction and/or margin, as different currencies can have rather different funding costs.

With the above in mind, there are the following options – in order of sophistication – in terms of defining the funding costs of a business (hereafter known as the 'funding profile'):

- *Uncollateralised value.* This is the simplest way to calculate funding costs and is based on the total net value of all uncollateralised transactions. However, it misses components such as thresholds and the correct impact of novations and restructurings, which involve cash payments.
- *Total margin posted.* This will correctly assess the cost of margin in each currency and also account for thresholds on collateralised trades. However, it will still incorrectly state the funding related to novations and restructurings. It will also not charge funding on a positive value on a client trade that does not lead to a margin posting requirement (e.g. a client swap with a positive value which is hedged with a collateralised par swap).
- *Collateralised value.* This involves assessing the value of all collateralised transactions. This will be an approximation to the above, but may be misleading in terms of funding currency (e.g. a euro swap collateralised in US dollars) and would also miss the impact of thresholds on collateralised trades.
- *Total value minus total margin.* This approach will capture all effects and is the most accurate metric. Strictly speaking, it should include all margin posted as a negative amount and all rehypothecable margin received as a positive amount (in practice, this may simply mean that any initial margin received should be ignored due to segregation).

The last approach above requires knowledge of the total valuation of all transactions and the total amount of margin. Simpler approaches may require only information on the total net margin amount or total net valuation.

Which of the above options to choose for calculating FVA is an important consideration. Considering only the uncollateralised value will be simpler but will mean that collateralised transactions (of which there will likely be a greater volume) will not need to be assessed. However, this will lead to certain assumptions which may not be correct.

The difficulty in defining FVA is that it relates to values, cash flows, and margin flows, but these are not mutually exclusive. Hence, it may be appropriate to focus primarily on one of these components but to capture the others. Depending on the nature of the underlying business of the party concerned, this might be done in different ways. For example, since banks generally hedge their market risk, cash flows and values tend to net, leading to margin flows being the primary measure of the funding of derivatives, as depicted in the example in Figure 18.1. However, this may lead to an incorrect conclusion, such as that an ITM transaction has a lower funding cost because the hedge will be a par transaction.

Taking the final definition above (total value minus total margin) as the best representation of funding is actually relatively simple and intuitive. Unsecured derivatives assets require funding since this is a value that has not been realised and, therefore, has to be funded. By contrast, unsecured derivatives liabilities represent funding benefits. Recalling the relationship given previously in Equation 11.7 and assuming the reuse of margin:

$$funding = value - margin \qquad (18.1)$$

Funding costs (benefits) arise when the above term is positive (negative). The analogy in Figure 18.1 can still be used, but any valuation differences between transactions (e.g. where the client transaction has a positive value, reflecting a profit, whereas the hedge is a par transaction) and cash payments (e.g. upfront cost of novating into a transaction) must be accounted for. Alternatively, the hedge should be assumed to be an idealistic hedge (i.e. exactly the opposite of the transaction at all times) performed under a perfect margin agreement (according to the terms at the start of Section 16.1.2).

Yet another way to think of this funding cost (benefit) is that a party would receive (pay) the positive exposure (negative exposure) in cash if a transaction was terminated and hence there would be a funding position in order to maintain the transaction.

The key point is that, regardless of how it is defined, exposure drives a funding cost, just as it drives CVA. By symmetry, negative exposure drives a funding benefit analogous (or perhaps identical) to DVA (Figure 11.24).

18.2.3   Definition of FVA

In order to understand FVA, consider a single, uncollateralised receiver interest rate swap transaction as an example. Figure 18.2 shows the cash flows and associated funding considerations for a payer interest rate swap, assuming an upwards-sloping yield curve. In the early stages of the swap, the fixed cash flows being paid are expected (on a risk-neutral basis) to be greater than the floating ones received. This creates a positive value (an asset) which needs to be funded and is real since cash is being paid out. The value increases

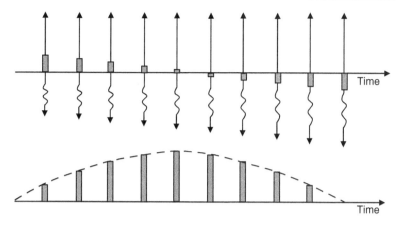

Figure 18.2 (Top) Illustration of the funding needs on a payer interest rate swap which arises due to the future cash flow differential. The grey bars show the net projected funding cost (based on a risk-neutral valuation). (Bottom) The cumulative effect over time of the cash flow differential and resulting funding profile.

cumulatively for the first five payment dates and then reduces as the projected floating payments start to exceed the fixed ones.[2]

The funding profile that arises is the same as the expected future value (EFV) of the transaction (for example, see Figure 15.24), as will be proved below. The corresponding receiver swap would have precisely the opposite profile, creating a funding benefit overall.

Intuitively, it would be expected that FVA be calculated by multiplying the future cost of funding by the funding profile above. This will be illustrated in Section 18.2.4.

18.2.4 Symmetric FVA Formula

As noted in Section 18.2.1, a simple way to include funding costs in a valuation is to discount using the cost of unsecured funding (note that this rate is implicitly symmetric, meaning that the party assumes it can both borrow cash and invest excess cash at this rate). It is important to understand what assumptions this corresponds to and under which conditions it is valid. As shown in Appendix 18A, the FVA discounting approach can be shown to be equivalent to a CVA-like formula:

$$FVA = -\sum_{i=1}^{m} EFV(t_i) \times [\exp(-FS(0, t_{i-1})t_{i-1}) - \exp(-FS(0, t_i)t_i)] \qquad (18.2)$$

For reasons that will become clear, this will be referred to as symmetric FVA. It is driven by EFV, which is the discounted expected amount that has to be funded (if positive), or that will create a funding benefit (if negative). $FS(0, t_i)$ is the funding spread for the time t_i with respect to the rate used for valuation (e.g. OIS). Note that the above formula is equivalent to the difference between discounting at a higher rate minus discounting at the base rate (see Appendix 18A).

---

[2] Note that the reduction in this case occurs exactly halfway through the profile. This is for illustration purposes only and the true profile depends on the precise shape of the yield curve.

The above can be written more intuitively in terms of a forward funding spread:

$$FVA = -\sum_{i=1}^{m} EFV(t_i) \times FS(t_{i-1}, t_i) \times (t_i - t_{i-1}) \tag{18.3}$$

$$FS(t_{i-1}, t_i) = \frac{\exp(-FS(0, t_{i-1})t_{i-1}) - \exp(-FS(0, t_i)t_i)}{(t_i - t_{i-1})}$$

$$\approx \frac{FS(0, t_i)t_i - FS(0, t_{i-1})t_{i-1}}{(t_i - t_{i-1})}$$

Compared to the CVA formula (Equation 17.3), the main differences in Equation 18.3 are that the funding spread of the bank (FS) replaces the counterparty credit spread, and (discounted) EFV replaces EPE. Note that the funding spread should be the difference between the cost of funding and the rate used for discounting (most obviously the OIS rate).

Equation 18.3 represents the overall economic value adjustment associated with respect to funding, without showing costs and benefits explicitly. This is not problematic in the completely uncollateralised and symmetric case,[3] but it does not give any insight into other cases such as partial collateralisation. However, a very simple transformation can produce a more intuitive formula. Recalling the definitions of EPE and ENE from Section 11.1.5, $EPE + ENE = EFV$, and so the above formula can be decomposed into two terms. Whilst at first glance this is unnecessarily complex, it does generalise the FVA formula and provide additional intuition. FVA is, therefore, typically defined as being driven by both funding costs (FCA) and benefits (FBA):

$$FVA = FCA + FBA \tag{18.4a}$$

$$FCA = -\sum_{i=1}^{m} EPE(t_i) \times FS(t_{i-1}, t_i) \times (t_i - t_{i-1}) \tag{18.4b}$$

$$FBA = -\sum_{i=1}^{m} ENE(t_i) \times FS(t_{i-1}, t_i) \times (t_i - t_{i-1}) \tag{18.4c}$$

In certain situations, this might complicate things unnecessarily, since EFV is relatively easy to compute, depending mainly on forward rates, whilst EPE/ENE are more complex to quantify and depend on factors such as volatilities. However, the EPE and ENE components above are readily calculated from a CVA/DVA framework, although these may differ in the event of non-rehypothecable margin, as will be explained later. Furthermore, the above representation can be extended to understand other situations.

The formula above does not include survival probabilities. It is possible to include these in a similar way to bilateral CVA (Section 17.3.3) – we will refer to this as 'contingent' FVA. Survival adjustments, as for CVA, should be considered based on aspects such as close-out assumptions (e.g. should the FVA decline as a counterparty approaches default?), as discussed in Section 6.3.4. Contingent FVA assumes that FVA vanishes at the default of one or either party: this is consistent with a risk-free close-out process using the base value. If a party thought that funding costs and benefits could be included in

---

[3] Meaning we consider funding costs and benefits to be associated with the same funding spread, which will be discussed more in Section 18.3.

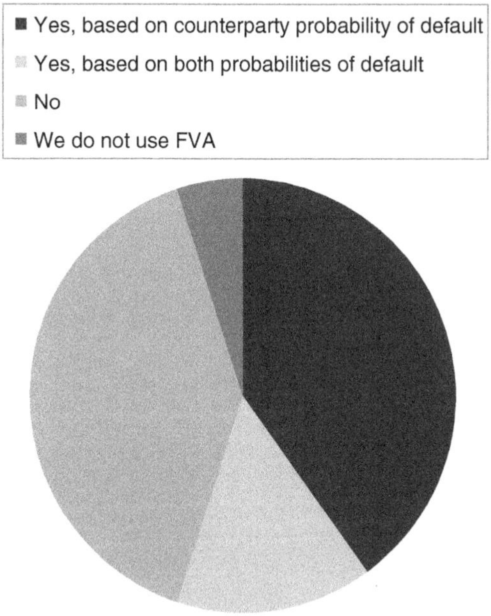

Figure 18.3   Market practice around including survival probabilities in FVA computation. Source: Solum CVA Survey (2015).

the close-out amount, then it would be more appropriate to ignore survival probabilities. Such assumptions may even be asymmetric – i.e. a party may assume that it would charge for funding costs in a close-out process but not pay funding benefits (Section 6.3.4). It is also important to consider that survival adjustments will create credit spread sensitivity in the FVA number. As shown in Figure 18.3, market practice is divided on which survival probabilities to adjust for in FVA calculation. Anecdotally, the Totem results (Section 5.3.5) show a similar divergence in market practice.[4]

Note that symmetric FVA is a trade-level quantity in this specification, and total FVA would simply be summed over all relevant trades. This is simpler than CVA, which is a counterparty-level (or, strictly speaking, netting set-level) calculation. This means that the FVA of a new transaction can be calculated on a standalone basis as there is no portfolio effect.

FVA can be either positive or negative depending on the relative size of the FCA and FBA terms above. This is consistent with the fact that discounting at a higher rate may lead to a higher or lower valuation depending on the nature of the trade (e.g. moneyness and cash flow timing).

Spreadsheet 18.1 Symmetric FVA calculation compared to discounting approach.

---

[4] The Totem submissions include counterparties of different credit quality, and so by examining the contributions across counterparties, it is possible to see if survival probabilities are being used.

Table 18.1   Upfront FVA value for interest rate swaps. The credit spreads and loss given defaults are the same as the previous example in Table 17.2. The cost of funding is the same as the party's own credit default swap curve.

	Pay fixed		Receive fixed	
	Non-contingent	Contingent	Non-contingent	Contingent
Discounting approach	−6.8		6.8	
FCA	−15.5	−14.0	−8.7	−7.9
FBA	8.7	7.9	15.5	14.0
FVA	−6.8	−6.1	6.8	6.1

Table 18.1 shows FVA for the interest rate swaps considered previously. The pay fixed swap has negative FVA due to positive EFV (Figure 15.24). The receiver swap has equal and opposite FVA. Note that the discounting approach (i.e. discounting at a rate with and without the cost of funding) corresponds exactly to 'non-contingent' FVA, as shown above.

The equivalence between the discounting and (non-contingent) FVA approach is illustrated in Figure 18.4. Note that the funding spread in FVA must be defined as the difference between the base rate used for valuation and the cost of funding.

The base rate above is, therefore, most obviously the margin rate, to be consistent with 'perfect collateralisation' (Section 16.1.2), although this is not necessary. For example, historically, some banks have used LIBOR discounting as a starting point (Figure 18.5). The funding spread used in Equation 18.3 must then be defined with respect to LIBOR. This is often consistent with internal policies of basing funding costs as a spread over LIBOR. However, the move away from LIBOR (Section 14.3.4) will make this increasingly less common and eventually obsolete.

The definition of the funding spread above requires that a 'funding' currency must be nominated and an associated curve or spread curve must be defined. This may be a single currency (e.g. if a bank primarily raises the bulk of its marginal funds in one currency and converts this pool of funds as needed to other currencies via FX markets), or there may be several curves defined from issuance levels in different currencies. One approach to calculating FVA is to use separate funding curves and EFV calculations for different currencies. Alternatively, a single currency could be used, with the associated cost of funding in other currencies being determined within the exposure simulation via the appropriate implied 'risky FX forwards' (Section 15.4.3).

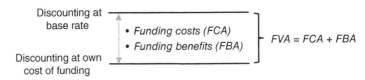

Figure 18.4   Illustration of equivalence between discounting at own cost of funding versus applying a symmetric FVA adjustment. Note that this adjustment can be positive or negative.

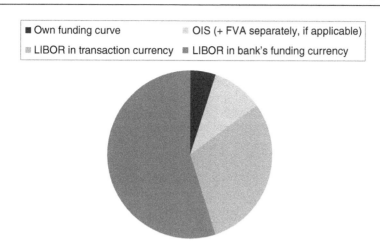

Figure 18.5   Market practice for valuing uncollateralised transactions. Source: Solum CVA Survey (2015).

18.2.5   CVA/DVA/FVA Framework

There is a generally agreed upon double-counting (e.g. Tang and Williams 2010) of DVA and FBA illustrated in Figure 18.6, meaning that only one (at most) should be considered. It is possible to see both DVA and FBA as the benefit of a negative exposure: the former because, in default, some of this is not paid, whilst the latter is a funding benefit. Morini and Prampolini (2010) show that the explicit inclusion of DVA leads to a duplication of the funding benefit in a transaction and, therefore, would be equivalent to discounting cash flows twice.

It is clear from banks' FVA reporting practices that they consider there to be an overlap between FVA (as it is typically referred to) and DVA. For example:

> The adjustment this quarter is largely related to uncollateralized derivatives receivables, as … [e]xisting DVA for liabilities already reflects credit spreads, which are a significant component of funding spreads that drive FVA. (J.P. Morgan Fourth Quarter Earnings Presentation 2013)

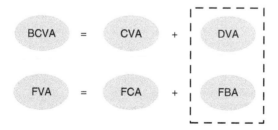

Figure 18.6   Illustration of the link between FBA and DVA.

FVA is considered the primary adjustment applied to derivative liabilities. The extent to which DVA and FVA overlap is eliminated from DVA. (RBS Annual Report 2016)

The FVA applies to both assets and liabilities, but largely relates to uncollateralized derivative assets given the impact of the Bank's own credit risk, which is a significant component of the funding costs, is already incorporated in the valuation of uncollateralized derivative liabilities through the application of debit value adjustments. (Toronto Dominion Annual Report 2016)

The double-counting of DVA and funding benefits is therefore generally agreed upon.

More rigorously, Burgard and Kjaer (2011a, 2011b) derive a framework for the economic cost of a derivative, including credit and funding. In addition to a CVA term, as given in Equation 17.7b, they derive a funding cost adjustment (FCA), which can be written as:

$$FCA(t) = -\int_t^\infty FS(t,u)D_{r+\lambda_P+\lambda_C}(t,u)EPE(t,u)du \qquad (18.5)$$

where $D_{r+\lambda_P+\lambda_C}(u)$ is a risky discount factor including survival probabilities as defined in Section 17.3.3, and $FS(u)$ represents the funding spread at time u. The above formula is the contingent (including survival probabilities) integral representation of the FCA summation term in Equation 18.4b where r is the risk-free interest rate, λ_P and λ_c are the default intensities of the party and counterparty, respectively.

In the Burgard and Kjaer framework, there is another term that is referred to as DVA:

$$DVA(t) = -LGD_P \int_t^\infty \lambda_P(u)D_{r+\lambda_P+\lambda_C}(t,u)ENE(u)du \qquad (18.6)$$

where LGD_P is the loss given default of the party making the calculation. The above term can be seen as a funding benefit which is monetised by using excess cash to buy back bonds, with the FCA being a symmetric term that arises from the equivalent cost of issuing bonds to generate cash. The DVA term in Equation 18.6 can equivalently be seen as the previously-defined funding benefit (Equation 18.4c) under the following two assumptions:

- *Same spread.* Equivalence between the risk-neutral default probability derived from the credit default swap (CDS) market and the cost of funding, which would be more obviously linked to a bond yield spread. This amounts to $FS = LGD_P\lambda_P$ and is the case in the Burgard and Kjaer framework, since they consider the existence of bonds only and there is, therefore, a single credit spread that can be seen as defining own credit risk and funding costs.
- *Portfolio effect.* DVA should be applied at the netting set level with respect to the close-out process in a default. A funding benefit would not have this additivity since it does not relate to the default process. In the funding strategy considered by Burgard and Kjaer,[5] this condition is met since all terms (CVA, FCA, and DVA) are additive at the netting set level (Burgard and Kjaer 2015).

---

[5] Burgard and Kjaer (2013) call this 'Strategy 1' and do consider alternative strategies such as discussed in Section 18.3.

To avoid a double-counting of funding benefits, there are two obvious frameworks for treating counterparty risk and funding consistently. These will be known as:

- CVA and symmetric funding (CVA + FCA + FBA).
- Bilateral CVA and asymmetric funding (CVA + DVA + FCA).

The symmetric funding case would be more consistent with Basel III capital rules where DVA cannot be recognised, but inconsistent with accounting requirements (e.g. IFRS 13) where DVA must be included (Section 5.3.3). This may also be more closely aligned to the treatment of funding in a bank where a treasury department considers both funding costs and benefits, and considers that two hedged transactions with the same margin terms (but potentially different counterparties) have a net-zero funding cost, as their benefits and costs cancel perfectly.[6] It also allows the xVA desk to consider CVA but ignore DVA, which may be considered to be a benefit that is hard to monetise. Not surprisingly, the majority of market practitioners could be seen to adopt this framework for pricing (CVA + symmetric funding) fairly early in the development of FVA (Figure 18.7).

The symmetric funding version of FVA fits the simple discounting approach mentioned in Section 18.2.4 for completely uncollateralised transactions, as shown by Piterbarg (2010) and also considered by Fries (2011). One way to see this simplification is that the quantity *EFV* is largely model independent, unlike the components *EPE* and *ENE*. Under these assumptions, uncollateralised derivatives can be valued via an appropriate choice of discount factor, rather than via the need to calculate an explicit FVA adjustment. This has been useful for banks to implement funding adjustments in a relatively straightforward manner (see the first quote in Section 18.2.1). This symmetry also means that FVA is additive across transactions, meaning that pricing can be done at a transaction level.

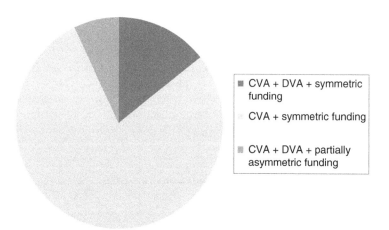

Figure 18.7   Market practice on pricing CVA, DVA, and funding. Source: Deloitte Solum CVA Survey (2013).

---

[6] Aside from the time delay in receiving margin, which is usually ignored in such situations.

In the symmetric funding framework, the simpler discounting approach can be used, and there is no obvious need to implement the more complex formulas in Equation 18.4. Collateralised transactions can be discounted at the margin rate and uncollateralised ones at the cost of funding. However, given that EPE (and ENE) need to be calculated for CVA purposes, it may be that this formula approach is preferred. A disadvantage of the discounting approaches (without a separate FVA adjustment) is that they make the following implicit assumptions about the nature of funding for a bank – either in general or with respect to individual trades:

- Trades are assumed to be completely uncollateralised, and there is no ability to represent partially-collateralised (e.g. non-zero-threshold) or one-way collateralised trades.
- Costs and benefits are completely symmetric so that funding benefits are equal and opposite to funding costs. Whilst this is true to some degree (e.g. two exactly opposite trades under the same margin terms must represent a zero-funding cost strategy), it might not always be the case at a high level.
- There are no additional constraints on the funding strategy of a bank. In reality, this may not be the case due to aspects of the liquidity coverage ratio (LCR) and NSFR requirements.

A simple discounting approach is not appropriate in cases of partial collateralisation (e.g. a margin agreement with a threshold or one-way margin agreement). In such cases, the formula in Equation 18.4 can be used together with the relevant EPE and ENE modelling, similar to those required for CVA computation. For example, Burgard and Kjaer (2013) show that a one-way margin agreement (where the counterparty does not post) only leads to a CVA and FCA term. Not surprisingly, the funding benefit (or DVA) is absent due to the need to post margin. More generally, evaluating funding using the two explicit terms in Equation 18.4 will capture effects such as high thresholds and one-way collateralisation. However, such cases will require calculations to be made at the margin set level for all transactions covered by the same margining terms (this portfolio-level calculation is similar to CVA).

To properly account for aspects such as partial collateralisation, it is necessary to model EPE/ENE consistently with the margin terms in question. This has been discussed already for CVA computation in Section 17.5. There are caveats with respect to modelling EPE/ENE for CVA and FVA purposes, which were discussed previously in Section 11.4.2. It may, therefore, be necessary to change certain assumptions for modelling EPE/ENE for FVA compared to calculating CVA in these cases:

- *Margin period of risk*. One important difference is regarding the MPoR. In CVA/DVA calculations, the MPoR reflects the relevant time horizon to consider over the default and close-out period (Section 7.2.3), and is typically taken to be 10 business days or more. For FVA purposes, the equivalent time horizon should only be the time taken to receive margin in a normal (not default) scenario and would therefore be assumed to be much shorter. Note that small funding costs theoretically occur in the zero-threshold, two-way CSA case, since OIS discounting alone requires continuous margin posting and zero minimum transfer amounts. However, market practice is generally to ignore such impacts. In other words, for a zero-threshold margin agreement, CVA but not FVA may be calculated.

- *Rehypothecation.* Whilst non-reusable margin will still reduce CVA, it will not mitigate funding and so would need to be ignored in an EPE simulation for FVA, but not CVA.
- *Wrong-way risk.* Another important distinction between CVA and FVA modelling is the treatment of wrong-way risk, which is generally conditioned on default and therefore of relevance for CVA. However, there may be situations of wrong-way funding risk (Section 18.3.7).

Following Equation 18.2, it is possible to write a more general formula for FVA:

$$FVA = -\sum_{i=1}^{m} E\left[\left(\sum_{trades\ j} V^j_{t_i} - C_{t_i}\right)\right] \times FS(t_{i-1}, t_i) \times (t_i - t_{i-1}) \qquad (18.7)$$

where $V^j_{t_i}$ represents the value of a given trade at the future date t_i, and C_{t_i} represents the total amount of reusable margin held (probably variation margin only, since any initial margin will probably be segregated). As noted above, this formula would now need to be calculated at the counterparty level (strictly speaking, the margin set level if there is more than one agreement). The above can be decomposed into FCA and FBA, although this is not required. The term inside the expectation will become total EFV when there is no margin.

Note that the above has used the complete definition of funding as being 'total value minus total margin', as discussed in Section 18.2.2. However, it is possible to ignore strongly-margined counterparties (zero threshold and small minimum transfer amounts) in this representation, where as a general rule $\sum_{trades\ j} V^j_{t_i} = C_{t_i}$ will always hold as a good approximation.

Table 18.2 shows CVA, FCA, and FBA in the case of a one-way margin agreement. Whilst there is a small CVA when receiving margin, FCA is zero. A one-way agreement in favour of the party (i.e. the party has an infinite threshold and the counterparty has a zero threshold), therefore, has FBA and no FCA, whilst the reverse is true when the agreement is in favour of the counterparty.

The above formulas, together with appropriate modelling of EPE and ENE, can also be used in cases where there is a material threshold in the margin agreement. For example, Figure 18.8 shows FCA and FBA for a receive fixed interest rate swap as a function of the threshold in the margin agreement. A positive exposure will create a funding cost only up

Table 18.2 Upfront CVA and FVA (non-contingent) values for interest rate swaps for cases of one-way collateralisation, compared to the uncollateralised (UC) case. Assumptions are as for Table 18.1, but the MPoR for calculating FCA and FBA is zero.

	Pay fixed			Receive fixed		
	UC	One-way (in favour)	One-way (against)	UC	One-way (in favour)	One-way (against)
CVA	−29.9	−1.2	−30.8	−17.2	−0.8	−18.4
FCA	−15.5	–	−16.0	−8.7	–	−9.4
FBA	8.7	9.4	–	15.5	16.0	–
Total	−36.6	8.2	−46.8	−10.3	15.2	−27.8

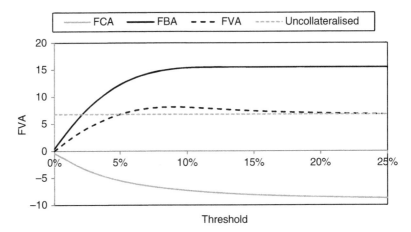

Figure 18.8 Upfront FCA and FBA for a receive fixed interest rate swap as a function of the threshold (which is the same for the party and counterparty). Assumptions are as for Table 18.1, but the MPoR for calculating FCA and FBA is zero.

to the threshold amount, after which margin would be taken, and the exposure above the threshold would essentially be capped, reducing the FCA term. Correspondingly, the negative exposure defining the funding benefit would also be capped (at a potentially different threshold), reducing the FBA term. FCA and FBA increase (in absolute terms) monotonically with increasing threshold, with their sum tending – although not completely monotonically – to uncollateralised FVA for high thresholds.

Table 18.3 shows CVA and FVA for two-way margin agreements where the margin can and cannot be rehypothecated (or generally reused). In cases where reuse is not possible, CVA is mitigated but FCA remains. This situation is relatively uncommon,[7] but it is one of the cases used in Totem (Section 5.3.5). Note that in the case of the receiver swap, total CVA and FVA in the case of no reuse is more negative than the uncollateralised case.

Table 18.3 Upfront CVA and FVA (non-contingent) values for interest rate swaps for cases of collateralisation with and without reuse of margin, compared to the uncollateralised (UC) case. Assumptions are as for Table 18.1, but the MPoR for calculating FCA and FBA is zero.

	Pay fixed			Receive fixed		
	UC	Two-way	Two-way (no reuse)	UC	Two-way	Two-way (no reuse)
CVA	−29.9	−3.0	−3.0	−17.2	−3.2	−3.2
FCA	−15.5	–	−15.5	−8.7	–	−8.7
FBA	8.7	–	–	15.5	–	–
Total	−36.6	−3.0	−18.5	−10.3	−3.2	−11.9

---

[7] It is uncommon contractually, although it could occur also when receiving securities which cannot be repoed or used as margin in another agreement.

Note that there are other funding strategies that can give rise to different results. For example, Burgard and Kjaer (2012) discuss a strategy where a party can completely hedge out all its own and its counterparty's default risks, and there is no FCA term. However, Burgard and Kjaer argue that the funding strategy required for this result is not practical since a party would have to trade freely in and out of its own bonds of different seniorities as a delta hedge (effectively buying back junior bonds and issuing senior ones). Another way to recover a CVA and DVA result is to assume (again impractically) that the transactions can be repoed (with zero haircut and at the margin remuneration rate) so as to be 'self-funding'. In this case, an asset would be repoed for an amount of cash equal to its value and, therefore, there would be no FCA. This point is important since some transactions (such as the purchase of treasury securities) do not have analogous funding costs due to the presence of an active repo market. However, transactions such as derivatives cannot be repoed and so this argument does not hold.

It should be noted that the form of the Totem xVA consensus pricing (Section 5.3.5) makes it possible to extract information of xVA terms and potentially determine the assumptions being made by a contributing bank. For example, suppose the quotes in Table 18.4 were seen, and assume a symmetric FVA framework. It is possible to back out the xVA terms as follows:

- FCA can be determined from the first bilateral agreement with segregation (since in this case CVA only would be mitigated, as discussed in Section 11.4.2).
- The unilateral agreement in favour of the bank would lead to only FBA (or DVA).
- The unilateral agreement in favour of the counterparty would lead to CVA and FCA. These three quotes allow determination of CVA, FCA, and FBA, as shown.
- Finally, these can be checked against the uncollateralised transaction, which is the sum of these three terms.

The above hypothetical values would be consistent with a bank that was pricing using CVA, FCA, and either FBA or DVA (but not both). Furthermore, by looking at the

Table 18.4 Hypothetical upfront xVA prices in bps for different types of collateralisation.

Collateralisation	Interpretation in symmetric FVA framework	Price
Bilateral (counterparty posts to segregated account)	FCA	−25.5
Unilateral, in favour of bank	FBA	15.4
Unilateral, in favour of counterparty	CVA + FCA	−62.3
Uncollateralised	CVA + FCA + FBA	−46.9
Implied xVA values in symmetric FVA framework	CVA	−36.8
	FCA	−25.5
	FBA	15.4
	Check (sum of three above terms)	−46.9

opposite transaction (e.g. a receive versus pay fixed swap), if FCA and FBA values for the opposing transactions were equal and opposite, then this would confirm the use of symmetric FVA and mean that the bank was categorically not pricing in DVA. Anecdotally, this can be seen for a number of the Totem contributors.

18.2.6   The FVA Debate

To some, FVA is problematic, since including a party's individual funding cost in the price breaks the price symmetry of CVA/DVA and goes against basic foundations of valuation and the 'law of one price'. FVA also suggests that parties may be unable to agree on a price due to their unique funding costs, and that arbitrage opportunities will, therefore, be present in the market.

Early on in the use of FVA, Hull and White (2012a) put forward a view that FVA should not be considered in the pricing or valuation of derivatives. Specifically, they state 'we argue that FVA should not be considered when determining the value of the derivatives portfolio, and it should not be considered when determining the prices the dealer should charge when buying or selling derivatives'. In general, their arguments stem from very well-established principles in finance, such as the risk-neutral valuation principle and the Modigliani–Miller theorem. For example, Hull and White (2014) argue that the use of FVA in pricing would lead to arbitrage opportunities whereby an end user could buy options from a bank and sell the same options to a bank with a higher funding cost. This could be countered by taking the view that there is no 'market' for uncollateralised derivatives (Kenyon and Green 2014).

Some authors have countered the Hull and White arguments (for example, see Carver 2012, Castagna 2012, and Laughton and Vaisbrot 2012, with a response in Hull and White 2012b), in general, by arguing that inefficiencies make Hull-and-White-type arguments not perfectly valid, and that FVA is real. Some of the arguments can be circular – for example:

- *Against FVA*. Discounting should be at the risk-free rate since this is required by the risk-neutral valuation principle.
- *For FVA*. Funding costs show that the standard risk-neutral valuation principle is incorrect because it assumes risk-free borrowing and lending.

The Hull and White argument can be seen to relate to a setup where there is CVA, DVA, and FCA, but where FCA is cancelled by another term, which they call DVA2.[8] DVA2 is a benefit that arises because a party may default on its general funding liabilities (e.g. bonds), as opposed to DVA, which is the benefit of defaulting on derivatives liabilities. Hence, FCA can be seen as a cost to shareholders, with the equivalent gain accruing to creditors (via DVA2), and so the firm as a whole would not see a cost from FCA. This leads to a CVA and DVA framework, compared to the CVA and symmetric FVA one (Table 18.5).

It is important to realise that the debate around the reality of DVA and DVA2 stems primarily from the shareholder or bondholder views introduced in Section 17.3.2.

---

[8] Albanese et al. (2015) make a similar argument around what they call 'funding debt adjustment' (FDA) and Elouerkhaoui (2016) discusses a similar term, the 'fair-value option' (FVO).

Table 18.5 Valuation adjustments in the no-FVA and FVA regimes.

	No FVA (e.g. Hull and White 2012a)	FVA (e.g. Burgard and Kjaer 2011a)
Terms	CVA + DVA + FCA + DVA2 = CVA + DVA	CVA + FCA + FBA = CVA + FVA
Interpretation	Total firm value (shareholders and creditors)	Shareholder value

The consideration of shareholder value leads to the CVA and FVA framework, whereas the total firm value (shareholders and creditors) leads to CVA and DVA. A new deal may, therefore, increase the total firm value but reduce shareholder value due to the related funding costs. Andersen et al. (2016) illustrate that the CVA and FVA framework can be seen as a pricing result where the objective is to maximise shareholder value. Albanese et al. (2013, 2015) also agree that incremental FVA can be included in entry prices under the assumption that these are set with shareholders' interests in mind.[9] Burgard and Kjaer (2012) note that derivatives funding strategies can result in windfalls or shortfalls to bondholders in the case of a firm's default.

There is probably little or no theoretical debate around the use of FVA in pricing subject to the shareholder point of view being relevant. In practical terms, FVA pricing is clearly seen in clearing prices and Totem consensus pricing (Section 5.3.5). The remaining debate is more in relation to valuation; one argument (Albanese et al. 2015) is that, for accounting purposes, bilateral CVA (CVA and DVA) should be used.[10] Andersen et al. (2016) also support this view. This requires the argument that fair value should represent the combined value to both shareholders and creditors. This does lead to potential issues with fair value being defined as exit price: one solution being to argue (probably unrealistically) that the best price would come from a party with negligible funding costs. This accounting approach would also involve a bank posting a net profit or loss due to the incremental funding and DVA adjustments. Withholding or prematurely releasing profits may be undesirable, as discussed in Section 5.4.5. Since exit price represents another party's entry price, the shareholder-driven view that seems to be adopted by most banks is not surprising.

Even in the total firm value view of funding, there would still be a component of FVA, which is the component of the funding cost that is not related to the credit risk of the party concerned. As explained in Morini and Prampolini (2011), this funding would be a market funding risk premium or liquidity component (Section 14.3.2). Assuming the CDS spread is a 'pure credit spread', then the liquidity premium component of the credit spread could be estimated from bond yields or the 'CDS-bond basis' (CDS spread minus the bond yield spread), although this term can become negative. Indeed, Hull and White (2014) state that FVA is 'justifiable only for the part of a company's credit spread that does not reflect default risk'. Note that some theoretical studies treat funding costs as

---

[9] Note that Albanese et al. (2015) also propose a different version of FVA which is asymmetric and will be discussed in Section 18.3.

[10] With some additional adjustments for the 'first-to-default' effect.

exogeneous and may assume implicitly that the bond-CDS basis is zero, and so will not identify any specific components as being attributable to default risk and liquidity effects.

An important question that remains is the correct definition of fair value and whether this should focus only on shareholders, or rather look at the combined view of shareholders and bondholders. In the former case, an FVA accounting adjustment is relevant (as is currently market practice), but in the latter, there need be no adjustment since FVA (apart from the liquidity component mentioned above) represents an internal transfer from shareholders to bondholders.

There are other debates around the implementation of FVA that relate to the funding strategy assumed and whether excess cash can always be recycled, as is the case in the symmetric FVA framework. This is discussed in Section 18.3.

18.2.7   Funding Costs and FVA Accounting

As discussed in Section 14.3.2, a funds transfer pricing (FTP) framework will probably define a fixed curve for transfer pricing funding costs, which may be determined from the treasury, potentially via the xVA desk. Such a framework usually represents an assessment of the average funding cost of the balance sheet of the party in question, rather than being specific to a counterparty. To take a quote from a market practitioner:

> Kok [ING Bank] also argues there is a double-count between CVA and FVA, because poor-quality derivatives counterparties could drive up a bank's funding costs.[11]

Potentially related to the FVA debate (Section 18.2.6) is the fact that FVA may not capture the true *incremental* cost of funding a transaction given its type and counterparty, but will rather capture a static cost based on the average balance sheet cost. This is probably a necessary approximation given the situation, but it may lead to ad hoc adjustments for special cases (e.g. triple-A counterparties). This point is made by Hull and White (2014), who state that a bank should consider its incremental funding cost when entering into a transaction and, if appropriately considered, this cost should be zero. Morini (2014) argues that this is not completely correct as it is based on three crucial assumptions:

- that the market has instantaneous efficiency;
- that the funding of a deal happens after the market knows about the deal; and
- that the effect of a new deal on the funding costs of a bank is linear.

In other words, the market may not react appropriately and efficiently, for example, when a bank is raising funds against business with high credit quality counterparties.

FVA is generally seen by banks as an internal cost of financing their uncollateralised derivatives portfolios (which involves their own cost of funding). Calculating FVA using a bank's own cost of funding does not sit well with the accounting concept of exit price (which would involve another party's funding costs). Accounting standards require that fair value should not be entity specific. For example, FAS 157 emphasises that 'fair value is

---

[11] Becker, L. and N. Sherif (2015). FVA: How six smaller banks do it. *Risk* (2 April). www.risk.net.

a market-based measurement, not an entity-specific measurement', which implies that fair value should be based on the assumptions that market participants would use in pricing. This is why many banks use a 'blended market cost of funds' (Figure 18.9) within their FVA valuation, which represents an average level of banks funding charges that would be relevant from an exit price point of view. It is not unreasonable for a bank to use its own cost of funding if this can be shown to be representative of average market funding cost levels. If taken literally, then this leads to further problems: in exiting a derivative with a larger FCA (FBA), it is optimal to find a counterparty with a lower (higher) cost of funding. This would imply that funding spreads would be transaction specific and change with market factors.

Lou (2015) has suggested a point of view that removes this problem by pricing funding at the counterparty's funding spread. The rationale for this is that a counterparty should be indifferent to collateralising a derivative as long as the margin earns an interest rate commensurate with the cost of its own debt. This argument does not seem to be borne out in practice: for example, it has not been the norm for multilateral development banks with close to zero funding costs to move willingly to two-way margin agreements, nor are they charged zero FCA.

Not surprisingly, for pricing, some banks do use their own funding costs (Figure 18.9). This obviously creates a mismatch with the accounting treatment, especially if the bank has a relatively high or low funding cost, but this mismatch should converge over time.[12]

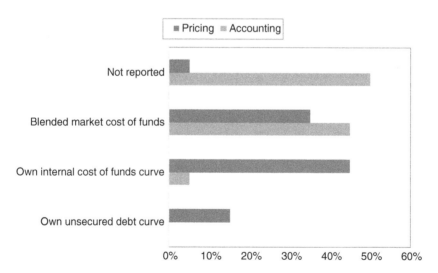

Figure 18.9   Market practice on determining funding costs for FCA valuation and pricing.[13]
Source: Solum FVA Survey (2014).

---

[12] For example, banks with high funding costs will realise a day one profit if they charge more FCA than they value. However, this will be lost in a negative carry over time as they borrow from the treasury. The net result is to encourage the right trades.
[13] The question focused on FCA due to the potential overlap of FBA and DVA.

An example of the scaling of a bank's funding costs to meet market levels is as follows (emphasis added):

> The FFVA [FVA] incorporates a <u>scaling factor</u> which is an estimate of the extent to which the cost of funding is incorporated into observed traded levels … The effect of incorporating this scaling factor at 31 December 2014 was to reduce the FFVA by <u>£300m.</u> (Barclays Annual Report 2014)

Another accounting problem arises from the treatment of the overlap between DVA and FBA, as banks may price the funding benefit component of FVA but then have to report a DVA benefit under accounting standards.

Let us also use the case of J.P. Morgan to illustrate an important aspect of banks reporting FVA.[14] J.P. Morgan reported an FVA charge of $1.5bn in its fourth quarter earnings in 2013 (as discussed below, this charge is likely to be more akin to what is defined here as FCA) and noted that future FVA/DVA volatility was expected to be significantly lower as a result. In order to understand this statement, assume that J.P. Morgan used an effective funding spread of 60 bps in the calculation. This would, therefore, imply a sensitivity of -$25m per basis point.[15] In the same period, J.P. Morgan's DVA had changed by $536m (a loss), since their CDS spread had tightened from 93 bps to 70 bps. This suggests an opposite $23m per basis point sensitivity for DVA.[16] Hence, if J.P. Morgan's credit spread widens by 1 bp, then they can expect to lose approximately $25m due to increased funding cost, but gain $23m in DVA benefit.[17] It therefore appears as if FVA is being used to partially cancel the impact of DVA.

For most banks, accounting FVA is mainly applied to derivatives assets (receivables) and therefore constitutes mainly FCA (for example, see comments as the start of Section 18.2.5). Assuming the bank believes that it should be reporting FBA instead of DVA, there is a question of whether or not this will be treated imperfectly, or whether there are further adjustments within FVA for this. For example, whilst some banks treat this problem imperfectly, others report using terms such as 'incremental FBA' (Solum FVA Survey 2014), which is defined as the difference between FBA and DVA. This would lead to the following:

$$CVA + DVA + FCA + \overbrace{(FBA - DVA)}^{'FVA'} = CVA + FVA$$

The above definition of FVA can be seen as adding FCA and then effectively removing the DVA component and replacing it with FBA, and it is partially justified by evidence such as Totem submissions (see discussion in Section 18.2.5: some banks' Totem quotes can be clearly shown to contain no DVA).

---

[14] This analysis is based on market information and the statements of J.P. Morgan and is not their own analysis.

[15] The loss of $1.5bn divided by the assumed funding spread of 60 bps.

[16] The loss of $536m divided by the change in CDS of −23 bps.

[17] Ignoring any basis between their own CDS and funding costs.

Given the presence of FVA in accounting statements alongside CVA, it has been common practice for the xVA desk of a bank to own the profit and loss volatility of FVA and to manage it alongside that of CVA. However, whilst FVA has become a relatively standard adjustment in the financial reports of banks, it is not yet part of market risk capital rules and is, therefore, not recognised as part of the value of a derivative by regulation. Not surprisingly, given the number of banks reporting FVA in their accounting statements, the Basel Committee has launched an FVA project to determine its position with respect to this adjustment.[18] There is also the question of whether or not a bank would need to derecognise DVA from its equity (Section 5.3.3) in the event that it was – effectively – not reporting DVA.

18.3   ASYMMETRIC FVA

18.3.1   Overview

Recall that the assumption for the symmetric FVA introduced in Section 18.2.4 is that funding is symmetric: required cash has to be funded, but available cash is assumed to earn an equivalent funding rate, either by buying back bonds or by recycling cash for other funding needs. Note that this symmetry is inconsistent with the NSFR, which assigns 100% RSF (required stable funding) to net derivatives assets, but 0% ASF (available stable funding) to net derivatives liabilities (and also the potential 100% RSF charge for 20% of derivatives liabilities and the ineligibility of non-cash variation margin, as discussed in Section 4.3.4). This does not mean that a bank cannot use a symmetric FVA approach, but just that this approach will tend to be at odds with the bank maintaining a strong NSFR. We will illustrate this with an NSFR invariance FVA (Section 18.3.4).

More generally, the form of FVA is linked to a funding strategy, and alternative funding strategies will lead to different FVA terms and overall economic values to shareholders. In particular, there is a potential alternative (or extension) to FVA which treats funding asymmetrically.

The key defining point for the correct funding strategy is the rates at which a business can borrow and lend funds, either via its own internal treasury or externally with the market. There are a number of possibilities and resulting outcomes:

- borrow and lend at the overnight rate (no FVA);
- borrow and lend at the same unsecured rate (symmetric FVA);
- borrow at an unsecured rate but lend at the overnight rate (asymmetric FVA); or
- borrow at an unsecured rate but lend at a shorter-term unsecured rate (partially asymmetric FVA).

This section will deal with the latter two possibilities, where FVA is asymmetric or partially asymmetric. If it is not possible to monetise net funding benefits at the same rate as net funding costs, there will be an asymmetry in the funding. Note that funding must, in this situation, be calculated for the aggregate portfolio level. This is because there is a difference between funding benefits that offset funding costs and those that create outright funding benefits. Asymmetric funding is illustrated in Figure 18.10.

[18] Becker, L. (2015). Basel Committee Launches FVA Project. *Risk* (24 April). www.risk.net.

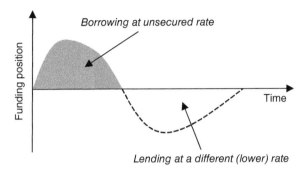

Figure 18.10 Illustration of the impact of asymmetric funding assumptions. The total funding requirement (or benefit) of the portfolio is depicted.

To understand the motivation behind the asymmetric funding considerations above, recall that derivatives variation margin is paid on a daily basis. Therefore, the assumption that this can be used to buy back own bonds (for example) is potentially aggressive, since the variation margin may need to be returned one day later. On the other hand, margin posted against long-dated transactions could be required for a long period of time and – on a conservative basis – may give rise to long-term funding requirements.

If there is asymmetry over funding, then the funding profile of the portfolio in question is important. Asymmetry would tend to be more of a problem if this profile is a liability – and not asset heavy (Figure 18.11). However, due to the nature of client trading activity (e.g. long-dated cross-currency swaps with more ENE against short-dated transactions with more EPE), it is possible for the profile to change sign. At the time of writing, many banks have an asset-heavy derivatives book, but there are definitely banks with all of the characteristics shown in Figure 18.11. To some extent, the form of a bank's funding profile may be changeable (e.g. by restructuring or incentivising certain client trading). However, this may be limited due to certain systematic factors (e.g. a low interest rate environment coupled with predominantly receiving the fixed rate on uncollateralised trades). Note that asset-heavy portfolios are still sensitive to asymmetric funding assumptions, although less so than those with larger relative liability components.

18.3.2   Asymmetric FVA

Albanese and Iabichino (2013) and Albanese et al. (2015) propose the view that excess cash for derivatives books is an unstable source of funding and should be assumed to earn only the risk-free lending rate.[19] Burgard and Kjaer (2012) also assume asymmetry regarding unsecured borrowing and lending, where unsecured lending may be assumed to yield only the risk-free rate,[20] whilst borrowing will require the unsecured term funding rate. In this setup, FVA should be considered at the 'funding set' level, defined as a

---

[19] Furthermore, in Burgard and Kjaer (2012), symmetric funding arises when a zero-coupon bond is a sole funding instrument, whilst asymmetric funding is a consequence of assuming that a single bond with recovery is freely tradable.

[20] Of course, unsecured lending can yield more than the risk-free (or OIS) rate, but this then involves taking additional credit risk.

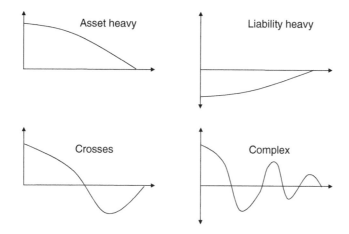

Figure 18.11 Possible funding profiles.

collection of transactions which can be combined from the point of view of funding. In the funding set, reusable variation margin received can be freely rehypothecated to meet the funding requirements of other transactions. However, this rehypothecation cannot be done outside the funding set. An obvious interpretation of a funding set is that it is the entire OTC derivatives book of the party in question.[21] A positive cash position in the funding set is not rehypothecated across funding sets but invested at the risk-free rate. This assumes that a net benefit on a funding set cannot be used to reduce funding costs across any other activity (different funding set) of the bank.

In this situation, a bank would have only an FCA term, which would be a portfolio-level (funding set) calculation:

$$FCA_p = -\sum_{i=1}^{m} E\left[\left(\sum_{trades} V_{t_i}^j - \sum_{margin} C_{t_i}^k\right)^+\right] \times FS_b(t_{i-1}, t_i) \times (t_i - t_{i-1}) \qquad (18.8)$$

where $V_{t_i}^j$ is the value of trade j, and $C_{t_i}^k$ is the value of rehypothecable[22] margin k (both discounted). $FS_b(t_{i-1}, t_i)$ now represents the appropriate funding spread for borrowing. The summation above needs to be across all trades and margin agreements in the funding set. However, it may be necessary first to sum over counterparty-level information to capture:

- counterparty survival probabilities (if desired); and
- thresholds in margin agreements.

Note that the calculation of the above term requires a consistent simulation of the total funding set (e.g. the entire OTC derivatives book), although, as mentioned previously, it

---

[21] In an earlier version of Albanese et al. (2015) they state 'we propose that excess collateral on OTC books should be considered as an unstable source of funding, not fungible with bank debt'.
[22] If received.

may be relevant to leave out strongly collateralised counterparties where the trade value will be cancelled by the margin held.

This is clearly quite challenging in terms of processing time and memory requirements and could mean that pricing one transaction would involve resimulation of the entire funding set. To understand this intuitively, note that, under asymmetric funding assumptions, it is necessary to know if a future funding benefit reduces overall funding requirements in the funding set or increases benefits (in the former case, there is a benefit, and in the latter, there is not). This was illustrated in a stylised fashion in Figure 18.10. The larger the asymmetric region in Figure 18.11, the greater the deviation will be between the symmetric and asymmetric FVA approaches.

More generally, it is not necessary to assume that lending is done at the risk-free rate and there is an equivalent FBA formula:

$$FBA_p = -\sum_{i=1}^{m} E\left[\left(\sum_{trades} V_{t_i}^j - \sum_{margin} C_{t_i}^k\right)^-\right]$$
$$\times FS_l(t_{i-1}, t_i) \times (t_i - t_{i-1}) \qquad (18.9)$$

where the only difference is the collateralised ENE term and the funding spread for lending. With respect to this spread, there are three possibilities:

- Symmetric: $FS_b = FS_l$
- Asymmetric: $FS_b > 0, FS_l = 0$
- Partially asymmetric: $FS_b > FS_l > 0$

An immediate consequence of the (partially) asymmetric assumption is that FCA (and FBA, if relevant) will not be additive across transactions or counterparties (note that FCA is negative):

$$\sum_{trades} FCA_j \leq FCA_p \leq \sum_{trades} FVA_j \qquad (18.10)$$

Spreadsheet 18.2 Asymmetric FVA calculation.

In order to give an example of this, an asset-heavy portfolio is used with exposure profiles, as shown in Figure 18.12. The funding spread is as used in the previous example in Section 18.2.4.

For the partially asymmetric case, the lending spread is assumed to be half the borrowing spread. Table 18.6 shows FVA for this portfolio in the three different cases. Since the portfolio is asset heavy, asymmetric FVA is only slightly less negative than symmetric FCA. Fully asymmetric FVA is about 18% larger than symmetric FVA, with partially asymmetric being in between the two. Note that asymmetric FVA is different even though EFV for the portfolio is always positive at all maturities.

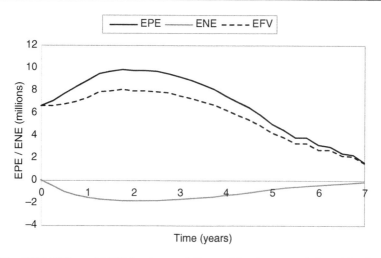

Figure 18.12   EFV, EPE, and ENE for the portfolio used for the example in Table 18.6.

Table 18.6   Different FVA calculations for the portfolio characterised in Table 18.12.

	Symmetric (portfolio level)	Partially asymmetric	Asymmetric
FCA	−181,984	−181,984	−181,984
FBA	27,384	13,769	–
FVA	−154,600	−168,215	−181,984

18.3.3   FVA Allocation

Like CVA, it is important to be able to allocate FVA to transaction level for pricing and valuation purposes. One advantage of the symmetric framework is that FVA is additive across transactions: there is no difference between reducing funding cost and accruing funding benefits. In the symmetric framework, the allocation is trivial as all calculations can be made at the trade level. The only exception to this is partial collateralisation – such as one-way margin agreements – where FVA would need to be calculated at the counterparty (margin agreement) level to account for these features. In symmetric cases, this approach (Equation 18.4) will correctly represent overall funding costs across transactions. For example, consider the total funding cost of a non-collateralised transaction hedged via a partially-collateralised transaction represented via the sum of the relevant FVAs. Suppose an uncollateralised receiver swap has an overall funding benefit. By symmetry, the payer hedge will have an equal and opposite funding cost. However, this cost will be smaller due to the ability to receive collateral above the threshold. Hence, the combination of the two transactions has an overall funding benefit. This can be seen as the benefit from receiving margin above the threshold on the hedge but not posting margin on the uncollateralised transaction, minus the cost from posting on the hedge and not receiving.

Spreadsheet 18.3 FVA allocation.

However, in an asymmetric FVA framework, funding costs and benefits are assessed differently. There is the difference between a funding benefit that will reduce an existing funding cost and one that will add to existing funding benefit. When pricing a transaction, it will be important to know if the existing portfolio has a net cost or benefit at a given tenor and the impact a new transaction has on this. Incremental pricing of FVA would be similar to that for CVA (Section 17.4.1), except that FVA would then need to be considered at the overall portfolio level. This would lead to very significant computational requirements for pricing new transactions and allocating FVA to existing ones, as, for example, discussed by Albanese and Iabichino (2013).

Pricing asymmetric FVA, therefore, requires a full simulation approach at the portfolio level. It will generally (but not always) lead to a more negative (higher-cost) FVA than a symmetric approach. To illustrate this, consider a typical funding-beneficial trade, a cross-currency swap paying the lower rate of interest which, therefore, has a large ENE (and, therefore, potentially large FBA) component. The standalone EPE/ENE of this can be seen in the previous Figure 15.27 (bottom). Incremental FVA for this new transaction is shown in Table 18.7 and the relevant exposure profiles in Figure 18.13. The cross-currency swap has a large funding benefit term under symmetric FVA due to large ENE, which causes portfolio EFV to reduce (Figure 18.13, top). However, this EFV reduction is a result of an increase in EPE but a larger reduction (more negative) in ENE (Figure 18.13, bottom). Hence, an asymmetric FVA framework, where ENE is not relevant, shows only a cost due to the increase in EPE and FCA. In a symmetric FVA world, there is, therefore, a benefit of 26,231, whereas in an asymmetric one, there is a cost of -15,166. Note that incremental FVA in the symmetric case is exactly equal to standalone FVA (but this is not true for FCA and FBA).

Whilst asymmetric FVA is always worse (more negative) than symmetric FVA, this may not be the case for incremental charges (although it almost always is). Asymmetric FVA can give more beneficial pricing for risk-reducing trades where there is a large loss in the funding benefit, and the framework without FBA is more beneficial. This difference will be large for a liability-heavy portfolio where the loss in FBA benefit can be more substantial. This is illustrated in Table 18.8 and Figure 18.14. Symmetric FVA leads to an incremental cost resulting from the loss of funding benefit. On a standalone basis, this is

Table 18.7 Incremental pricing of a five-year cross-currency swap for symmetric and asymmetric FVA regimes.

	Standalone	Incremental	
		Symmetric	Asymmetric
FCA	−64,391	−15,155	−15,166
FBA	90,622	41,397	–
FVA	26,231	26,231	−15,166

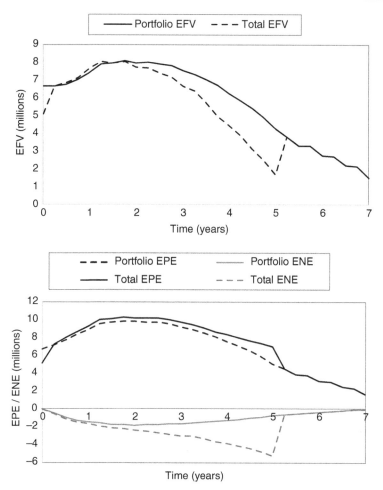

Figure 18.13 EFV (top) and EPE and ENE (bottom) profiles for the portfolio and total (portfolio plus cross-currency swap).

Table 18.8 Incremental pricing for a risk-reducing trade according to the profiles in Figure 18.14.

	Standalone	Incremental	
		Symmetric	Asymmetric
FCA	−46,225	9,770	9,770
FBA	10,332	−45,664	−
FVA	−35,893	−35,893	9,770

equivalent to the cost of FCA being larger (in absolute terms) than FBA. In an asymmetric FVA framework, there is no loss of funding benefit and the overall incremental effect is positive due to a reduction of FCA.

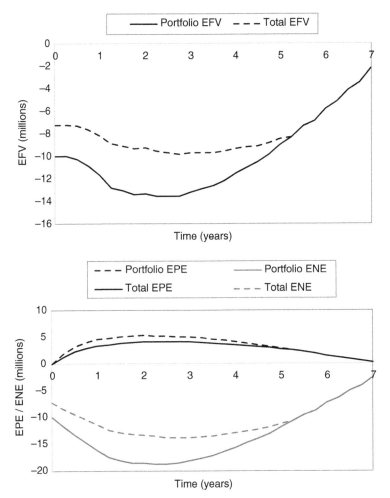

Figure 18.14   EFV (top) and EPE and ENE (bottom) profiles for a risk-reducing trade (portfolio is pay fixed, and new trade is receive fixed).

18.3.4   NSFR Invariance

The examples in Section 18.3.3 illustrate that it may be relevant for banks to adapt their FVA pricing so as to avoid paying excessively for funding benefits. This will be further amplified with the implementation of the NSFR (Section 4.3.4). The NSFR contains elements that will skew the funding requirements of a derivatives business:

- Net derivatives payables have a 0% ASF weight. This means that a bank with a derivatives book that provides funding overall will not gain any benefit from this in terms of an increase in its NSFR. This is broadly consistent with the completely asymmetric representation in Equation 18.8.
- 20% of total standalone derivatives liabilities (payables) have 20% ASF. This means that even funding benefits have an associated funding cost under NSFR (the intention of

this is to reflect the large variability in derivatives exposures and the fact that a funding benefit can quite quickly become a cost).

- Margin received can only reduce the funding cost of a derivative if it is cash in the currency of the transaction.[23] This means that collateralised transactions, which are generally thought of as having little or no FVA, may still have a large contribution to the NSFR if, for example, bonds are held as collateral.

The concept of invariance pricing was introduced in Section 5.4.3. Not surprisingly, NSFR invariance FVA pricing (i.e. pricing funding to maintain a given NSFR) requires asymmetric FVA. If the funding cost for the high-quality liquid assets (HQLAs) is different from the standard funding cost, then there should be a (scaling) adjustment made. However, even transfer pricing via asymmetric FVA will deteriorate a bank's NSFR. To price to maintain the NSFR ('NSFR invariance'), the following terms would need to be included:

- an adjustment for the increase in liabilities in relation to the 20% charge;
- an adjustment for non-cash variation margin; and
- a scaling factor corresponding to the bank's desired NSFR.

This is illustrated in Table 18.9 for the cross-currency swap example above (Table 18.7), assuming that the bank's desired NSFR is 120% and 20% of derivatives liabilities are given an RSF charge. A further assumption is that the bank's cost of funding HQLAs is the same as its normal unsecured funding cost. Note that NSFR invariance approximately doubles the cost of the trade compared to an asymmetric FVA framework.

Since NSFR applies only at the bank level, there is the question of whether a bank would allow derivatives to be partly subsidised by other activities or require them to be NSFR compliant on a standalone basis, as the NSFR invariance price above implies. Some banks, especially those with relatively small derivatives businesses, are likely to allow this cross-subsidisation and may be more competitive on certain trades as a result.

For allocation for valuation purposes, asymmetric FVA would require a calculation of marginal FVAs following the discussion in Section 15.2.2, whereas symmetric FVA is a trivial allocation. Table 18.10 shows marginal FVA for symmetric and asymmetric cases for the four transactions discussed previously for marginal EPE (see Figure 15.31). Note that the difference allocation is quite different in the two cases and not completely

Table 18.9 NSFR invariance incremental pricing for the five-year cross-currency swap compared to the symmetric and asymmetric FVA regimes.

	Symmetric	Asymmetric	NSFR invariance
FCA	−64,391	−15,166	−18,199
FBA	90,622	−	−
Liability RSF	−	−	9,935
Total	26,231	−15,166	−28,134

---

[23] For more detail, see BCBS (2014b), Paragraph 35. www.bis.org.

Table 18.10 Marginal FVA in symmetric and asymmetric cases for the transactions considered previously in Section 15.6.2.

	Symmetric	Asymmetric
7Y Payer IRS	−50,895	−59,786
5Y Payer IRS	−17,947	−18,152
5Yx5Y Long Payer Swaption	−85,758	−76,380
5Y USDJPY XCCY	26,231	−42,832
Total	−128,369	−197,150

predictable. For example, whilst asymmetric FVA is generally more negative, the swaption has a less negative contribution due to having very little ENE.[24]

18.3.5   Funding Strategies

It is important to align FVA with the funding costs actually experienced. In the illustration in Figure 18.1, FVA appears as the cost of all the future funding charges experienced by the xVA desk from the treasury. This means that the daily cost of funding charged to the xVA desk will be offset by a profit resulting from the reduction in FVA held. Changes in FVA due to market variables can also be hedged (this will be discussed in more detail in Section 21.2).[25] However, a misalignment between FVA charges and the funding costs experienced (e.g. symmetric versus asymmetric) will lead to profits or losses (probably the latter) being experienced by the xVA desk, which is probably not in line with its intended mandate.

A symmetric FVA approach is clearly desirable since it makes pricing and valuation easy and generally leads to more competitive pricing. However, there is a question of whether symmetric FVA is consistent with paying for funding benefits, when this may not align with the funding strategy and the NSFR. Banks with asset-heavy portfolios may feel that they are close to a symmetric FVA regime, but this may also incentivise the liability-heavy transactions, such as the example above (Table 18.7), that may create a portfolio with more FBA, which may be difficult to monetise.

An asymmetric funding policy used internally in a bank creates an incentive to maintain a derivatives book that is asset heavy to simplify pricing and valuation and to be able to pay funding benefits.[26] This could be achieved, for example, by executing large zero-coupon swaps or novating into uncollateralised derivatives positions with a positive value, which can be seen as lending to the counterparty at an unsecured rate (rather than lending internally at a lower rate). It is, therefore, important to consider the incentives that arise from the treatment of funding and the consequences for pre-deal FVA.

The asymmetric framework arises from the view that excess funding benefits (in the form of variation margin, for example) do not represent term funding due to the daily nature of the margining process. However, if the funding costs in Figure 18.1 seem to be

---

[24] It is a physically-settled swaption and so there is some ENE arising after the exercise date, but this is small.

[25] Any changes in the funding spread of the bank will be more difficult to hedge.

[26] Noting that paying funding benefits will potentially lead to trades which are antithetic to maintaining an asset-heavy book.

based on the current funding requirement of a business, this may, therefore, implicitly off-set short-term funding benefits (e.g. an OTM short-dated transaction) against long-term funding costs (e.g. an ITM cross-currency swap). It may, therefore, be desirable for the treasury to charge funding across the entire EFV profile and incorporate this into their Asset Liability Management (ALM) process. This will be discussed in more detail in Section 21.3.1.

The process in Figure 18.1 may also treat funding costs as fixed, irrespective of aspects such as the type of counterparty. This means that the funding of a new transaction will be priced at something like the average funding cost of the bank, and FVA charges would not be sensitive to the counterparty type. In reality, it is the incremental cost of funding new business that is relevant. Trading with poor-quality counterparties will likely drive up funding costs and vice versa. To create the right incentives, an xVA desk may incorporate this into pricing in an ad hoc manner by charging less FCA to high-quality counterparties and vice versa. However, this will potentially misalign with the funding costs experienced from the treasury. The true economic cost of funding a new transaction is very hard to assess as it is driven by the change in the funding cost of the balance sheet that this creates. The xVA and treasury setup is only approximating the true effect by considering the average cost of funding that balance sheet at the current time.

18.3.6   LCR Costs

Contingent FVA could occur due to rating triggers within the margin agreement and the requirement to pre-fund with HQLAs any outflows in relation to a downgrade (e.g. three notches, Section 4.3.3) of a bank's own credit rating. In order to assess FVA in such a situation, it is necessary to define rating transition probabilities. These can be estimated from historical default data, although such estimates are long-term averages of mainly corporations and the rating changes cannot be hedged.

For example, suppose a given trade is uncollateralised, but the bank is contractually obliged to post variation margin in the event that it is downgraded. The FVA representation – which would amount to an LCR invariance price since it would charge the funding cost of new HQLAs – would have the following components:

- the current cost of HQLAs that would need to be held against a negative value (this would reduce the funding benefit component arising from an ENE-like term in the event that the downgrade trigger is not breached); and
- an actual funding cost when the trigger is breached, leading to variation margin being posted (or some modelling of the dependency between the rating process and the funding cost).

Note that the above would be one sided and a cost, since only the downgrade of the bank must be considered (no benefit can be achieved as a result of the counterparty being downgraded). The adjustment for this contingent FVA (CFVA) could be written as:

$$CFVA = \sum_{i=1}^{m} E[(C_{t_i}^*)^-] \times [1 - Q(0, t_i)] \times FS_{HQLA}(t_{i-1}, t_i) \times (t_i - t_{i-1})$$

$$+ \sum_{i=1}^{m} E[(C_{t_i})^-] \times Q(0, t_i) \times FS_b^{dg}(t_{i-1}, t_i) \times (t_i - t_{i-1}) \qquad (18.11)$$

where $C_{t_i}^*$ is the hypothetical variation margin that would have to be pre-funded under the LCR, and FS_{HQLA} is the funding spread for the HQLA cost (conditional on no ratings trigger). The term C_{t_i} is the actual variation margin that would be posted in the event of the downgrade, and FS_b^{dg} is the funding spread in this downgraded state. The term $Q(0, t_i)$ gives the probability of the contingent outflow (e.g. three-notch downgrade). Assuming the threshold for contingent margin posting is zero, $C_{t_i}^*$ and C_{t_i} will be equivalent to the value of the transaction V_{t_i} and the expectation term becomes an ENE. Furthermore, since the above two terms are of similar form, it is possible to use a blended funded spread:

$$FS^{av} = [1 - Q] \times FS_{HQLA} + Q \times FS_b^{dg} \qquad (18.12)$$

Note that it would be unrealistic for this funding spread to be higher than the base funding spread (assuming the funding of HQLAs is lower), since the latter value should include the possibility of rating downgrades. This leads to:

$$CFVA = \sum_{i=1}^{m} ENE(t_i) \times FS^{av}(t_{i-1}, t_i) \times (t_i - t_{i-1}) \qquad (18.13)$$

In a symmetric FVA framework, this can, therefore, be seen as a reduction in the funding benefit term, which occurs intuitively due to the need to post variation margin if the rating trigger occurs, or holding HQLA against the amount if not:

$$FBA = -\sum_{i=1}^{m} ENE(t_i) \times [FS(t_{i-1}, t_i) - FS^{av}(t_{i-1}, t_i)] \times (t_i - t_{i-1}) \qquad (18.14)$$

In an asymmetric FVA framework, the CFVA components need to be included, with any LCR component related to ratings triggered captured at the counterparty level and aggregated to the full portfolio level.

An example of this is given in Table 18.11, with the same assumptions used in Section 18.3.2.[27] The HQLA funding cost is assumed to be 50% of the standard funding cost, and the annual probability of the rating trigger being breached is 5%. In the symmetric case with LCR costs, total FVA is the sum of FCA, FBA, and CFVA cost, or equivalently FCA and modified FBA. In this example, CFVA cost is the same in both frameworks, as the example is for a single counterparty. In a full portfolio case, this would not be the case for asymmetric FVA.

The above calculations become more involved when there are multiple rating triggers (e.g. different threshold levels in the margin agreement depending on the rating). In such cases, there are multiple possible rating states, with different HQLAs and funding costs. In the event of a downgrade, there is a potential increase in funding cost due to the need to post variation margin, but a potential reduction in HQLA cost since this is no longer a contingent component.

---

[27] The portfolio considered is the one used in Section 18.3.2, including the cross-currency swap; the total EPE and ENE can be seen in Figure 18.13 (total).

Table 18.11 Total FVA adjustments with and without LCR costs related to a downgrade trigger. Note that with LCR costs, the total FVA can be seen as either FCA + Modified FBA or FCA + FBA + CFVA Cost.

	Symmetric (portfolio level)		Asymmetric	
	Base	With LCR cost	Base	With LCR cost
FCA	−197,150	−197,150	−197,150	–
FBA	68,781	68,781	–	–
CFVA cost	–	−42,714	–	−42,714
Modified FBA	–	26,065	–	–
FVA	−128,369	−171,085	−197,150	−239,866

18.3.7   Funding and Wrong-way Risk

In the context of funding, wrong-way risk (WWR) is a positive relationship between an institution's funding spread and other market variables. There may also be WWR funding implications, although these may be less severe and more easily captured compared to CVA WWR. This is because, unlike CVA, funding is not related to default events. CVA WWR can be the result of causal relationships between defaults and other market variables that may be hard to capture and model (e.g. the FX example discussed in Section 17.6.4). On the other hand, WWR in FVA may occur primarily as a result of more observable macro-economic relationships.

An obvious example of WWR in FVA is the correlation between funding spreads and interest rates. Consider the interest rate swap example presented in Section 17.6.3. Table 18.12 shows the symmetric and asymmetric FVA calculations for positive and negative correlations between interest rates and funding spreads. A positive correlation causes the swap to be more ITM when funding spreads are high, leading to higher FCA and lower FBA. The reverse is true for the negative correlation case, and the receive fixed swap shows the opposite behaviour. Note also that in the symmetric FVA case, WWR has a larger impact due to simultaneously changing FCA and FBA in the same direction (e.g. FCA becomes more negative and FBA becomes less positive).

WWR in funding may also be important for FX products where a devaluation in a bank's local currency may be linked to an increase in funding spreads. This is discussed in more detail by Turlakov (2012).

Table 18.12 Upfront (non-contingent) FVA value for interest rate swaps with a correlation between interest rates and funding spreads.

	Pay fixed			Receive fixed		
	−50%	No WWR	+50%	−50%	No WWR	+50%
FCA	−11.5	−15.5	−21.8	−4.7	−8.7	−12.0
FBA	11.9	8.7	4.2	21.3	15.5	11.3
Symmetric FVA	0.4	−6.8	−17.6	16.7	6.8	−0.7
Asymmetric FVA	−11.5	−15.5	−21.8	−4.8	−8.7	−12.0

19

KVA

19.1 OVERVIEW

Banks have historically charged capital to transactions, at least implicitly, by setting limits on capital usage or requiring a certain capital hurdle to be achieved. Whilst these actions discourage capital intensive transactions to a degree, they do not properly price in the lifetime costs associated with holding capital. Recent years have seen banks become increasingly focused on return on capital (ROC). Capital is a cost because investors require a return on their investment. High capital ratios make banks more resilient but potentially reduce their ROC (profit/capital). Whilst the Modigliani–Miller theorem (Section 14.1) suggests that a firm should be indifferent to how it is financed, the reality is that banks generally find capital expensive compared to debt.

Whilst businesses have always had ROC targets and hurdles, these have often been relatively easy to achieve and treated rather softly when compared with other components such as the net profit of a trading desk. ROC metrics have also often been based on 'economic capital' (Section 14.2.1) and not regulatory capital requirements. However, the size of regulatory capital components and the cost of raising new capital have created a greater need to price regulatory capital into transactions more explicitly. The greater focus on capital costs for banks can be seen to be driven by a number of components:

- the requirement for banks to have higher capital ratios and a greater proportion of high-quality capital (Section 4.2.2);
- additional capital requirements such as the credit value adjustment (CVA) capital charge (Section 13.3); and
- other capital constraints such as the leverage ratio (LR) (Section 4.2.7), capital floors (Section 4.2.8), and bank stress tests (Section 4.2.10).

Whilst the above apply to all activities of a bank, derivatives are particularly expensive with respect to counterparty risk-related regulatory capital requirements and their relatively conservative treatment. Capital is seen as a scarce resource, and there is, therefore, a strong need to 'match' the profit in a transaction to the associated capital requirements.

Additionally, the more rigorous treatment of other xVA components, in terms of quantification and management, has led to similar approaches being applied to capital. For example, capital requirements for derivatives can be relatively volatile and, therefore, the correct lifetime cost of capital, instead of merely a current (spot capital) or approximate profile, may be considered.

In terms of pricing, it is clear that capital costs need to be factored in, at least to a degree. Capital value adjustment (KVA) is commonly used to define such costs. In one sense, KVA is just another way to express a minimum ROC hurdle. However, whilst ROC hurdles have been historically used as soft hurdles for derivatives businesses, more rigorous KVA charges are becoming more common.

In terms of valuation, including capital costs is more contentious. On the one hand, it can be seen as the cost of funding equity, and there is, therefore, an analogy with debt funding and funding value adjustment (FVA) (and margin value adjustment, MVA). On the other hand, it is possible to see capital not as a direct cost per se but as merely representing the ownership of a bank, with the owners being paid a dividend contingent on the bank's profitability. KVA accounting is, therefore, a subject of much debate.

19.2   CAPITAL VALUE ADJUSTMENT (KVA)

19.2.1   Return on Capital

Banks have used metrics such as return on risk-adjusted capital (RORAC) for many years as a benchmark of the performance of a trade or project. RORAC is often defined as:

$$RORAC = \frac{Income - Costs}{Capital} \tag{19.1}$$

Formulas such as the above often do not consider multiple periods, which is reasonable if the underlying is either of short maturity (e.g. one year or less) or if the capital is fairly constant over time.

For situations where the underlying time horizon is long and/or the amount of capital required is variable, it is necessary to consider multiple periods. In such situations, it is common to use an internal rate of return (IRR) formula to evaluate the profitability of a project. IRR is typically defined as an interest rate that makes the net present value of a project equal to zero. For example, IRR is the return that is the solution to the formula:

$$0 = \sum_{i=0}^{n} CF_i \exp(-IRR \times t_i) \tag{19.2}$$

where CF_i represents the cash flow at a time t_i.

In order to use the above formula to consider the ROC, it is necessary to consider the appropriate cash flows. At time zero ($i = 0$), there will be a profit (P) on the transaction minus the current amount of capital that will need to be held (K_0). The cash flows at any subsequent date will relate to the change (usually a release) in the amount of capital required, ($K_{i-1} - K_i$). IRR is then the solution to:

$$P - K_0 + \sum_{i=0}^{n} [K_{i-1} - K_i] \exp(-IRR \times t_i) = 0 \tag{19.3}$$

It can be shown (Appendix 19A) that the above can be rewritten as being approximately:

$$P \approx IRR \sum_{i=0}^{n-1} K_i.(t_i - t_{i-1}). \exp(-IRR.t_i) \tag{19.4}$$

where the term $K_i.(t_i - t_{i-1})$ can be interpreted as representing the future cost of capital for the period in question, and $\exp(-IRR.t_i)$ can be seen as a discounting term. If we now consider IRR to be a pre-determined rate, then this formula is intuitive in that the profit required must be the amount of capital required over time multiplied by the cost of holding that capital (IRR) discounted at the cost of capital. However, in this simple representation, cash and capital were not treated differently, and there was only a single rate that represented a return and also gave rise to a discount factor.

19.2.2   KVA Formula

A KVA formula (e.g. Green et al. 2014) can be written as:

$$KVA = -\sum_{i=1}^{m} ECP(t_i) \times CC(t_{i-1}, t_i) \times (t_i - t_{i-1}) \qquad (19.5)$$

where $ECP(.)$ denotes the discounted expected capital profile, which is the amount of capital that is expected to be held, $E[K_t]$, at a given time t in the future multiplied by an appropriate discount factor, and $CC(.)$ is the cost of holding this capital (previously the IRR term in Equation 19.4). The formula is essentially integrating over all capital costs over the lifetime of the transaction or portfolio in question. It can be seen as defining the profit that is required to generate the required return on the capital deployed.

Note that the above formula is defined to be a negative value, which interprets KVA as a cost, although this is only a convention. It can also be written as an integral similar to CVA and FVA:

$$KVA = -\int_0^\infty D_{r+\lambda_B+\lambda_C}(t, u).CC(u).E[K(u)]du \qquad (19.6)$$

where the term $D_{r+\lambda_B+\lambda_C}(t, u)$ is as defined for CVA in Section 17.3.3. As discussed in Section 14.2.3, the capital cost (CC) term is a relatively subjective parameter and may depend on aspects such as the nature of the business in question, the dividend policy of the bank, and the competition. Whilst numbers in the range 8–10% may often be mentioned, 'efficiency' and tax effects (since dividends are paid post-tax) are often included to make the actual gross number bigger (Green and Kenyon 2015 consider tax more explicitly and derive a tax valuation adjustment). The hurdle may also increase so as to penalise longer-dated transactions where more business and regulatory uncertainty exists. It may also be that the CC is actually not an input but rather an output in certain cases – for example, knowing the potential profit of a transaction, equating this to KVA and solving for the CC that gives this KVA.

The expected capital profile (ECP) term is a more quantitative challenge, similar to expected positive exposure (EPE) and expected negative exposure (ENE) terms required for CVA/DVA (debt value adjustment) and FVA calculations. However, this is also directly linked to the underlying regulatory capital requirements, both at the current time and in the future. It therefore requires a strong appreciation of the regulatory rules over the lifetime of the portfolio in question. This will be discussed in Section 19.2.3.

In Equation 19.5, unlike Equation 19.4, there are different rates for the cost of capital and the discount factor. The question on the discounting to apply and/or the use of survival probabilities will be discussed in Section 19.3.3.

KVA is likely to differ substantially between different banks for a number of fundamental reasons:

- *Capital requirements*. Banks may be subject to different overall capital requirements due to regional rules or other aspects (e.g. the requirement for globally-systemically-important banks (G-SIBs) to hold additional capital).
- *Capital methodologies*. Different banks may use different methodologies in capital calculations (e.g. internal models versus standardised formulas).
- *Return on capital*. Banks may have different business models and, therefore, have differing ROC hurdles (e.g. a large commercial bank may accept making a low ROC on a relatively small derivatives business on the basis that this is provided as a service to clients).

Hence, the KVA calculation is highly subjective and may differ substantially between banks. It may also, like MVA, be computationally expensive due to the need to simulate market scenarios in order to calculate the ECP. This is particularly the case where a bank has internal model approval since this would involve a secondary Monte Carlo simulation. In practice, banks may sometimes hope that approximating using a projected capital profile (i.e. one in which there is only one market scenario) may be reasonable. Indeed, the error in doing this may be relatively insignificant compared to some of the other problems mentioned above, such as future changes in capital requirements and methodologies.

19.2.3   Capital Profiles

In order to calculate KVA, it is necessary to be able to generate capital profiles over time for the different methodologies in question. When calculating capital profiles, the first problem is the differing regulatory requirements and associated methodologies that exist. Capital is made up of a number of different components which may all need to be considered:

- *Credit risk*. This is a charge for the counterparty default risk (Section 13.2).
- *CVA capital charge*. The capital, introduced under Basel III, for the volatility of a bank's CVA (Section 13.3).
- *Leverage ratio*. A minimum capital requirement based on a regulatory definition of leverage (Section 13.4.6).
- *Market risk*. Market risk capital requirements may often be small, as derivatives transactions will generally be hedged. However, some residual requirements due to basis risks (for example) may exist. This has also been shown by Kenyon and Green (2014) to be potentially significant, where back-to-back hedges may create spurious capital charges due to being ineligible hedges, as discussed in Section 13.3.6. This may have less of an impact in the future, with more aligned regulatory methodologies such as standardised CVA (SA-CVA).
- *Prudent valuation (EBA 2013)*. Additional capital requirements for aspects such as the uncertainty of CVA calculations required in the European Union (EU).

Note that some capital components will not be explicitly considered since they are not easily 'matched' to a precise transaction. Examples would include minimum capital requirements for operational risk and any capital buffers. Such components can potentially be captured implicitly by increasing the CC term in the KVA formula (Equation 19.5). Of the above five components, most banks will rigorously capture the impact of the first two, with the other three being taken into account by some banks and in some situations.

Furthermore, given the timescales for implementation of regulation and changes to regulatory methodologies, it is important to consider the evolution of the underlying capital requirements over time. Some of the important aspects in this respect are:

- *Standardised approach for counterparty credit risk (SA-CCR).* The new methodology for banks without internal models, which also applies to other regulations (Section 13.4.3).
- *Leverage ratio.* The simple backstop to capital requirements using the above SA-CCR methodology (Section 4.2.7).
- *Fundamental Review of the Trading Book (FRTB).* Changes to the market risk capital rules (Section 4.2.4).
- *FRTB-CVA.* Changes to the CVA capital charge in line with the above market risk changes (Section 13.3).
- *Capital floors.* Capital floors using standardised methodologies for banks with internal models (Section 4.2.8).
- *CVA capital exemption.* The EU exemption for CVA capital charges, which may be removed at some point in the future (Section 4.2.5).
- *Hedging effectiveness.* The impact of CVA hedges, which currently may produce adverse capital costs, but under future SA-CVA regulation may lead to substantial benefits for CVA hedges (Section 13.3.6).

KVA is clearly the most subjective xVA component.[1] This is amplified due to the difficulty of predicting future regulatory regimes and the behaviour of counterparties. Capital requirements can also be region specific, with different regulatory bodies differing in terms of the timescales for implementation and the precise rules applied (CVA capital exemption being a significant example of the latter). In some cases, changes in regulation may be known with certainty (implementation details and dates), and in others there may be some uncertainty. However, banks will typically attempt to calculate capital costs based on the best available information at the time in question. Clearly, there will be components that are too uncertain to quantify (such as the fact that the regulatory regime in a decade may be very different from the one now).

As an example to illustrate the above, Figure 19.1 illustrates the future capital costs that a bank may attempt to capture. Note that capital charges depend very much on the situation in question and this is only one possible example. There are changes to ECP driven by the introduction of SA-CCR, the possible removal of CVA capital charge exemption (EU banks) and the introduction of the new FRTB-related CVA capital charge methodologies. There is also a potential consideration due to the implementation of the LR. Since a bank only needs to meet this requirement overall, the question arises as to whether it is a necessary consideration. The dotted line shown in Figure 19.1 represents what will

---

[1] Sherif, N. (2015). KVA: Banks wrestle with the cost of capital. *Risk* (2 March). www.risk.net.

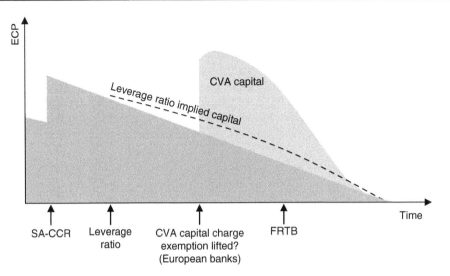

Figure 19.1   Qualitative example of the approach to capturing regulatory capital costs over time.

later be defined as a leverage ratio invariance capital charge (Section 19.2.6), and a bank is leverage ratio constrained when the normal capital requirement is below this line. Note that on removal of CVA capital charge exemption, the bank assumes it will have to hold more capital, and, therefore, the LR becomes less of a concern at this point.

As a real example, the credit risk-related capital charges for a 1,000 notional uncollateralised 10-year maturity interest rate swap through time are shown in Figure 19.2.[2] All profiles decay to zero as the swap approaches maturity, with the current exposure method (CEM) approach being rather inelegant due to the simple add-ons used (Table 13.8). Note that the SA-CCR result is significantly higher than that of the internal model method (IMM). An implication of this is that an IMM bank may be more sensitive to the LR since its normal capital requirements will be lower.

The above example only showed a projected capital profile over time. In reality, it is necessary to model a particular transaction and also account for the volatility of market factors. This requires including capital calculations within the underlying exposure simulation in order to calculate the capital requirement at each point in the future. For methodologies such as SA-CCR, this is relatively straightforward since it is based on simple formulas. It is more of a problem for IMM approaches, which are themselves simulation based, and this, therefore, represents quite a significant computational problem.

Spreadsheet 19.1 KVA calculation for interest rate swap.

---

[2] A default probability of 0.1% is assumed in an internal ratings-based (IRB) approach (Section 13.2.2). We assume a par swap at all times and so this does not capture the expected future value profile of the swap, which will be shown below. See Spreadsheet 13.4 for the calculation of this and other methodologies.

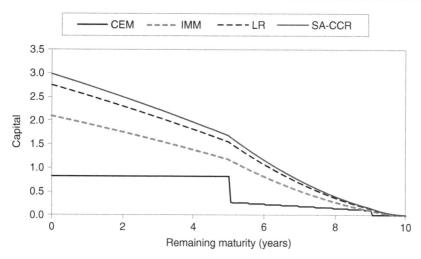

Figure 19.2 Total credit risk capital charge through time for a 10-year interest rate swap of notional 1,000, using the CEM, SA-CCR and IMM methodologies. The LR-implied capital charge assuming a 5% requirement is shown.

Figure 19.3 illustrates the evolution of the counterparty risk-related capital charges using SA-CCR and standardised CVA capital charge methodologies.[3] Both projected[4] and expected (ECP) values are shown. The capital is variable and can both increase and decrease, largely driven by the swap moving in- and out-of-the-money. The downward move in the capital is limited since it cannot become negative, and also due to the floor used in the SA-CCR approach (Equation 13.21). This makes capital quite convex and means that ECP is significantly higher than the (more easily calculated) projected profile. The variability of the future capital requirements potentially suggests the need to hedge counterparty risk capital requirements (discussed later in Section 21.3.2).

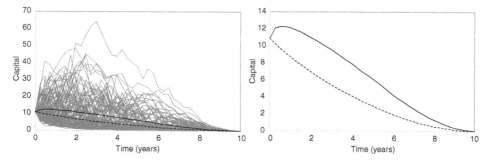

Figure 19.3 Simulations showing the evolution of counterparty risk capital for a 10-year interest rate swap with notional 1,000, using SA-CCR and SA-CVA capital charges. The dotted line shows the projected value, and the solid line the expected capital profile (ECP).

---

[3] A weight of 0.8% for a single-A counterparty is used in the CVA capital charge formula, and the same assumptions as in Footnote 2 are used for the SA-CCR methodology.

[4] This takes a single deterministic capital requirement projected in the future via current forward rates.

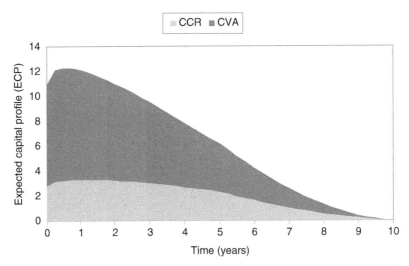

Figure 19.4 Expected capital profile (ECP) from Figure 19.3 broken down into credit (CCR) and market risk (CVA) charges.

The above graphs show the aggregate capital across both credit risk (CCR) and market risk (CVA). ECP showing the breakdown between the two capital charges is illustrated in Figure 19.4. Note that the CVA capital charge represents the largest contribution, as is often the case, and that CVA capital also has a different shape over time.

Note that the capital profile does not always amortise as in the above examples. For the case of a forward transaction, since there are no periodic cash flows, the capital will project approximately flat. Similar behaviour will also be seen for cross-currency swaps (although they will likely amortise slightly due to the interest rate cash flows).

The above examples are for a single transaction, but in reality ECP would need to be calculated for a bank's entire portfolio. Whilst the credit risk (CCR) capital charge is additive across netting sets, the CVA capital charge is a portfolio-level calculation in both the standardised and advanced versions (and the future basic CVA (BA-CVA)/SA-CVA methodologies). This will represent a potential computational challenge for pricing KVA on new transactions, especially in an IMM approach. Note also that, ideally, the impact of any capital-reducing hedges should be included in the ECP profile. As stated in Section 19.2.2, this requires certain subjective assumptions about how much capital relief can actually be achieved.

19.2.4   KVA Example

KVA calculations for the same swap discussed in Section 19.2.3 are now shown and compared to the CVA value, which has previously been discussed (Table 17.3). For KVA, the parameters are as used in Section 19.2.2, with a required ROC of 8%. KVA will be discounted with the cost of capital, which is discussed in more detail in Section 19.3.3.

It is first important to emphasise the need to capture the correct ECP rather than to approximate it using a projected profile based on just a single scenario (Figure 19.3). As shown in Table 19.1, KVA approximated via the projected profile is much smaller than true KVA.

Table 19.1 KVA calculations (in bps upfront) for the 10-year swap using the correct ECP compared to the more approximate projected capital profile.

	Using ECP	Using projection (approximation)
KVA	−38.8	−23.7

Table 19.2 CVA and KVA calculations for the 10-year swap on an upfront (basis points) or running (basis points per annum) basis.

	Upfront	Running
CVA	−17.9	−2.0
KVA (CCR)	−12.8	−1.4
KVA (CVA)	−26.0	−2.9
KVA (total)	−38.8	−4.3

Table 19.3 Standalone and incremental CVA and KVA calculations for the 10-year swap.

	Standalone	Incremental	Reduction
CVA	−17.9	−10.3	35%
KVA	−38.8	−27.8	29%

KVA is also shown broken down according to credit risk (CCR) and market risk (CVA) capital charges in Table 19.2. Note that full KVA is around double the CVA value.

Consider now the impact of the same swap but on an incremental basis on an existing portfolio. The portfolio is dominated by trades in a different currency, which gives rise to a reasonable netting impact. However, from the point of view of capital, the SA-CCR approach does not allow potential future exposures (PFEs) to offset across different currencies (Section 13.4.3). This reduces the portfolio effect for the purposes of calculating KVA because there is no netting effect with respect to the PFE term of the new transaction in SA-CCR, although there is a netting effect with respect to the replacement cost (RC) term (see Equation 13.16). Standalone and incremental EPE and ECP are shown in Figure 19.5, with the former showing a larger portfolio effect, as expected.

The result of the above profiles on CVA and KVA is shown in Table 19.3. The incremental reduction is smaller for KVA due to the aforementioned lack of netting when calculating the PFE term across different currencies in the SA-CCR methodology.

19.2.5 Implementation of KVA

It is quite natural to leverage the implementation of exposure simulation (Chapter 15) for CVA and FVA purposes in order to calculate KVA. For standardised regulatory methodologies – such as SA-CCR – ECP is a relatively simple function of the value of the underlying portfolio. It is, therefore, necessary to simply implement this methodology within the exposure simulation and call it repeatedly in each simulation path as required.

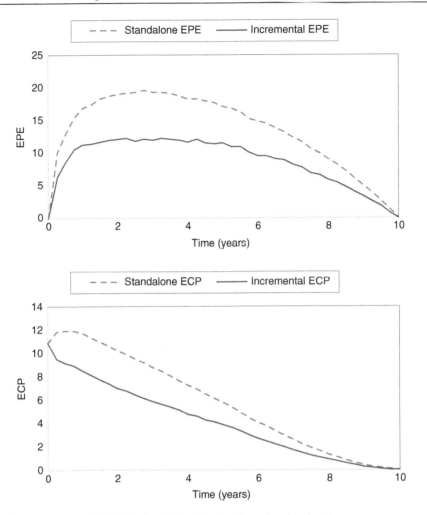

Figure 19.5   Incremental EPE (top) and ECP (bottom) profiles for the 10-year swap.

This has been previously discussed in Section 15.1.1 (see Table 15.1) and is the approach implemented in Spreadsheet 19.1.

For more complex capital methodologies, where the capital is not a simple function of the value of the portfolio at a given point in time, this leads to computation challenges. This applies for the following methodologies:

- *IMM (Section 13.4.5)*. This is typically implemented using a Monte Carlo simulation and, therefore, would represent a 'Monte Carlo within a Monte Carlo' for KVA calculations. Adding to this problem is the fact that IMM implementations are often real-world based, but exposure simulations for CVA/FVA purposes are generally risk neutral (this has been previously discussed in Section 15.3.3).
- *Advanced CVA capital risk charge (Section 13.3.4)*. This also requires a Monte Carlo simulation, although it will be replaced by SA-CVA.

- *SA-CVA (Section 13.3.5).* This does not require another simulation but is based on portfolio sensitivities that would need to be calculated in each underlying scenario within the exposure simulation. This is potentially a challenging and computationally insensitive problem.

There is also the question of whether or not KVA should be calculated using a risk-neutral simulation (as for CVA/FVA) or whether a real-world simulation is more appropriate. One answer to this depends on the likely management of KVA, most importantly whether or not it will be hedged (see later discussion in Section 21.3.2). The difference between KVA calculated with real-world and risk-neutral simulations can be significant in some cases. For example, Figure 19.6 shows EPE and ECP for a foreign exchange (FX) forward under these different assumptions. In the historical calibration, the volatility is flat, and EPE will follow a familiar 'square root of time' shape and the projected capital will be roughly flat. Using implied volatility will change the shape of EPE, making it lower in the short term and higher in the longer term. This means that ECP also increases over time.

The above differences between real-world and risk-neutral parameterisations are important. Since terms such as CVA and FVA are generally hedged and reflected in financial statements, risk-neutral calibrations are relevant. However, KVA is typically not (yet) charged directly to desks, hedged, or reflected in accounting statements. Hence, there is a question as to whether pricing KVA with risk-neutral parameters is relevant. Of course, a bank may have a view that KVA will be hedged at some point in the future, in which case a risk-neutral approach to capital calculations may be preferable.

19.2.6   The Leverage Ratio

Minimum regulatory capital requirements – often defined in terms of risk-weighted assets (RWAs) – have generally represented the binding balance sheet constraint in banks' derivatives portfolios. However, the introduction of the LR potentially adds a new constraint. As discussed in Section 4.2.7, a bank must comply with both minimum regulatory capital requirements and the LR, with the latter not being credit-quality sensitive. Furthermore, the calculation of derivatives exposures in the LR can be more penalising than the exposure for capital purposes (Section 13.4.6). High credit quality and/or collateralised counterparties and transactions with certain features (such as non-cash collateralisation) will, therefore, have relatively high implied LR capital requirements.

Since the LR is a binary condition, it is not completely clear how a bank would incorporate this constraint into pricing. A primary consideration is whether or not the bank has RWA requirements or the LR as their binding constraint. A broker-dealer is more likely to find that the LR is a binding constraint since they have a relatively high proportion of low-risk assets and large, more complex businesses such as repos, derivatives, and client clearing. On the other hand, a commercial bank is more likely to be, through its lending activities, RWA constrained and may not see the need to focus on the LR.

The pricing of KVA above follows the idea that the return on a given transaction or portfolio must be commensurate with the amount of underlying regulatory capital. Whilst a bank which naturally meets its LR requirement may see little reason to price in the LR, other banks may see this as important in order to create the right incentives (Section 5.4.1). An obvious way to do this is via an invariance approach (Section 5.4.3). This would

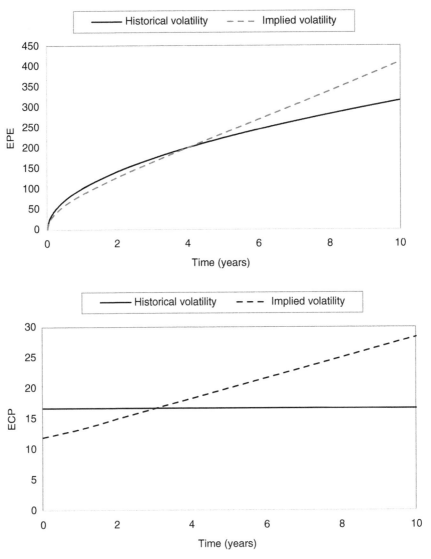

Figure 19.6 Expected exposure (EPE) (top) and projected capital charge (bottom) for a 10-year forward transaction using historical and implied volatility. The implied volatility is upwards sloping.

require that the ROC is calculated on a capital amount which is consistent with a bank's LR staying constant. Since a bank must meet both standard capital requirements and the LR constraint, this would likely amount to pricing in the maximum capital requirement of the two at any given point in time. This may be expressed as:

$$\max(CCR\ capital + CVA\ capital, \alpha \times Exposure) \tag{19.7}$$

where the second term simply arises from solving for capital in the LR formula (Equation 4.1). Note that the above requires that a bank needs to achieve a return on its counterparty risk regulatory capital requirements or meet LR invariance, whichever is the highest number. In the event that the regulatory capital requirements are the binding constraint, the LR of the bank will actually increase, and in the latter case it will stay the same.

The above may be more complex than net stable funding ratio invariance FVA pricing (Section 18.3.4), which may always be considered to be more conservative than traditional FVA pricing and where a comparison of different funding strategies is not, therefore, necessary. To illustrate this, the ECP profile is shown for three cases as the maximum of the minimum capital requirement (defined by CCR and CVA capital) and the implied LR capital (assuming a requirement of $\alpha = 5\%$). The SA-CCR methodology is used for the LR capital calculations. Figure 19.7 shows three different cases:

- *Uncollateralised swap.* This is the example of the 10-year swap previously shown in Section 19.2.3. Since the total capital requirement is relatively high, the LR invariance has very little impact on ECP.[5]
- *As above, but assuming a CVA capital exemption.* This case is as above, but without pricing in CVA capital. In this situation, with a lower minimum capital requirement, the LR becomes more important, as discussed in Section 19.2.3.
- *Collateralised swap.* This case is the same example, but assuming collateralisation where the counterparty has the right to post non-cash margin. Since such margin cannot be used to reduce the LR exposure (both current and PFE), it also has an important impact.

19.3   MANAGEMENT OF KVA

19.3.1   Current Treatment of KVA by Banks

Beyond the definition and calculation of KVA, there is difficulty in the underlying calculation and the treatment of KVA alongside components such as CVA and FVA. One aspect that is important to consider is that KVA is, unlike components such as CVA and FVA, not an expected future cost per se, but rather a profit that is expected (at some point) to be paid to shareholders, and possibly employees. Note that this shareholder profit is not guaranteed: equity investors may be paid lower returns in times of poor profitability and vice versa.

Although CVA and FVA have been embraced from not only a pricing but also a valuation perspective, the same is not yet true of KVA. From a pricing point of view, KVA is potentially the oldest valuation adjustment, as banks have long used the notional of capital hurdles in assessing new trades. However, there is currently no evidence of KVA – like CVA and FVA – being reflected as a valuation adjustment in the financial reporting of banks. This means that KVA is generally managed differently than terms such as CVA. Some of the important contrasting features (which are inter-related) are as follows:

- KVA is generally not transfer priced to an internal xVA desk, and so not meeting a target KVA (ROC) will not create a loss.

---

[5] The reason for the small impact is that, under SA-CCR, a negative mark-to-market value is not recognised as being risk reducing (Section 13.4.6).

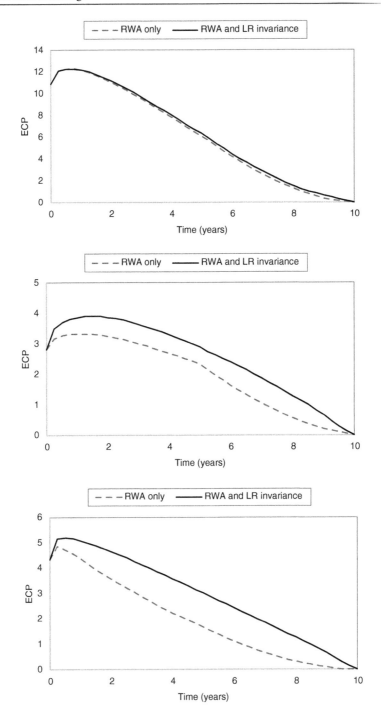

Figure 19.7   Illustration of ECP profile using traditional regulatory capital requirements (RWA only) and also using the LR capital requirement (RWA and LR invariance). The cases shown are an uncollateralised trade (top), the same trade assuming no CVA capital (middle), and the same trade collateralised with non-cash margin (bottom).

- KVA is not – anecdotally – fully seen in the entry price ('clearing price') of client trades.
- Profits of transactions that relate to KVA are paid out immediately, irrespective of the lifetime of the transaction.

The above treatment creates different incentives when managing KVA, such as shown in Figure 19.8 (which is a more specific version of Figure 5.3, discussed previously). Here, CVA and FVA are priced at entry into a transaction and owned by the xVA desk. This desk is axed to pay out (the now different) CVA/FVA upon exit of the trade and will offset CVA/FVA charges (e.g. charged by another counterparty in a novation). In the event that it is possible to exit a trade with lower charges than CVA/FVA at that time, this will lead to a profit at the time of exit. This gives traders and salespeople the incentive to try and restructure client portfolios, as this can lead to real profit benefits.

However, whilst KVA may be priced into the transaction at entry, it is released as profit and is not part of the economic consideration upon exiting. This implies that it may only be possible to exit transactions at a loss (in order to pay the KVA charged) and raises the related problem of how a bank could incentivise staff to restructure portfolios so as to reduce regulatory capital costs.

The above has a number of implications for the pricing of KVA. One is that banks are more likely to incorporate structural features such as non-mandatory break clauses (Section 7.1.1) into KVA pricing, even though they would not be considered to mitigate CVA and FVA. This is because there is no ownership of KVA profit and loss (P&L) that is related to the decision as to whether or not to break. CVA and FVA actually change profit, but KVA only changes the required profit. Related to this is the fact that banks may also incorporate certain behavioural factors into their assessment of future capital requirements. For example, a client may be expected to unwind a transaction early, and this may lead to a reduced KVA charge. This will, of course, be related to the motive

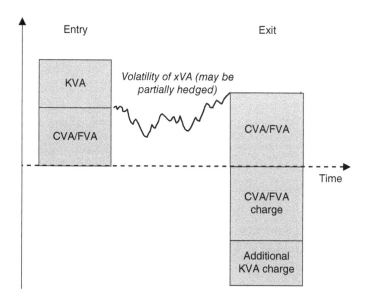

Figure 19.8   Illustration of CVA/FVA and KVA charges at entry and exit of a transaction.

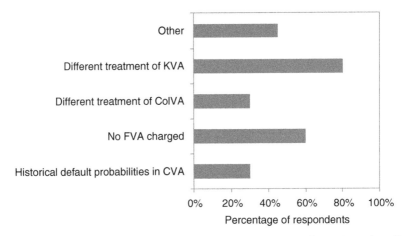

Figure 19.9   Market view of the most significant causes of divergence in market prices. Source: Solum CVA Survey (2015). See Glossary for definitions.

and past behaviour of the client: a hedge fund is likely to unwind transactions, whilst a corporate hedging debt issuance is not. The lack of ownership of KVA in a bank is why, as mentioned above, KVA is not fully part of entry pricing in the way that CVA and FVA generally are. The pricing of capital, despite the birth of KVA, represents one of the biggest divergences of pricing within over-the-counter derivatives (Figure 19.9).

19.3.2   Optimal KVA Management

The fundamental problem is that many derivatives, especially the most profitable ones, have maturities that are greater than the period (e.g. quarterly or annually) with which a bank remunerates shareholders and employees. Hence, when a bank makes a profit on a given transaction, it is typically paid out in the first year, and yet the transaction may exist for many years after this. Hence, long-dated transactions contribute to a large ROC in the first year and then represent a 'drag' on ROC for their subsequent lifetime, where the required capital does not have any associated return. Whilst ROC may change through the business cycle, large fluctuations are probably not desirable.

The question is whether or not KVA is a valuation adjustment or just a measure of profitability. Related to this is whether or not there should be a delay in recognition of profits, which represent the ROC. The debate around the treatment of KVA stems from whether or not capital is a cost. Consider a simple balance sheet and related funding with debt and equity (Figure 19.10). Debt repayments must be made to avoid default and are typically fixed. Equity dividends are discretionary and depend on the profitability of the firm. When ROC is low, equity holders can decide whether to accept this or redeploy their capital elsewhere. Whilst debt funding is a clear cost, there is a question as to whether equity funding is a cost or not.

A further problem is how to – if desired – withhold KVA profits and prevent them from being paid into the dividend (and bonus) stream. It is obviously not acceptable to arbitrarily reserve, which may be seen as an artificial way to prevent profits from being recognised. KVA clearly needs to be somehow held aside in the financial reporting of a

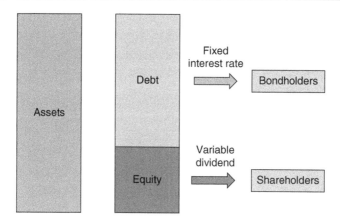

Figure 19.10   Simple illustration of the funding of a balance sheet with debt and equity.

bank, either by the explicit reporting of KVA (like FVA before) or some other method, such as within retained earnings.

With respect to the above, there seem to be (at least) three views regarding KVA management and accounting:

- *KVA is profit.* In this view, KVA is a profit which should not be treated as a valuation adjustment or withheld in any way. Proponents of this approach probably do not consider that the term KVA is relevant and that it should instead be referred to as an ROC or hurdle rate.
- *KVA is retained earnings.* In this view (Albanese et al. 2015), KVA is a profit that should be withheld but not hedged or treated in the same way as other valuation adjustments. Shareholders would be paid higher dividends if total KVA increased, and suffer lower dividends or possibly dilutions if KVA declined in value. Banks' derivatives businesses would accept some element of cyclicality, increasing and reducing hurdle rates with changes in their total KVA pool. In this approach, the total profit of a transaction would be realised eventually, although potentially in a heterogeneous fashion, suggesting that KVA should be part of retained earnings and not hedged.
- *KVA is a valuation adjustment.* In this approach, KVA is treated as a valuation adjustment like CVA and FVA and is managed in a similar manner. For example, Green et al. (2014) state that 'The most appropriate approach would be to manage KVA alongside CVA and FVA.' This would also imply that KVA should be reported in financial statements, which would probably lead to the need to hedge KVA.

The first approach above will generate a high ROC in the first period (e.g. quarter/year) and then zero ROC thereafter. After the first year, capital costs will not be covered. This means that either the ROC in subsequent years will not be achieved or revenues will have to increase – probably unsustainably – in order to meet the required ROC. The more long-dated the transaction, the more acute this problem will be.

KVA – as in the second and third approaches above – can potentially correct the unsustainability problem and create more aligned incentives: the decay of KVA will release profits over the lifetime of trades/portfolios.

Consider the two latter approaches where KVA will be released over the lifetime of the transaction. In order to understand the implication of this, we use the interest rate swap from previous examples. The evolution of the regulatory capital requirements in three scenarios is examined: an average scenario corresponding to the expected future value (EFV) profile, and two more extreme scenarios represented by the 5% and 95% PFE. The exposure profile (seen before in terms of EFV/EPE/ENE for the opposite swap in Figure 15.24) and capital profiles are shown in Figure 19.11. In the average scenario (EFV), the capital decays to zero relatively predictably, whereas in the other scenarios the behaviour is

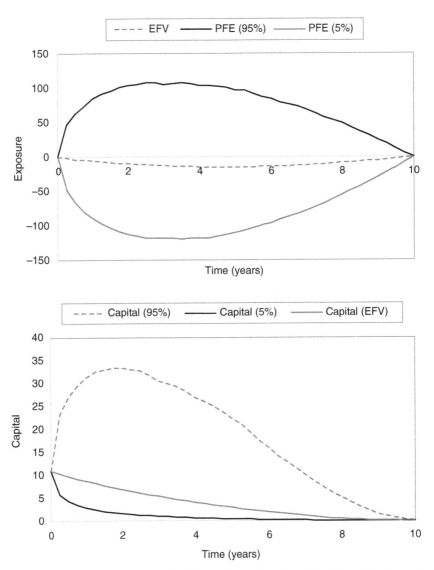

Figure 19.11 Exposure (top) and capital (bottom) profiles for the 1,000 notional receive fixed interest rate swap.

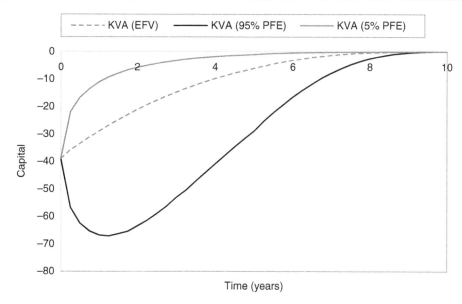

Figure 19.12   Evolution of KVA in the three scenarios shown in Figure 19.11.

quite different. In the 5% PFE scenario, the capital declines rapidly due to the transaction being OTM. In the 95% PFE scenario, the capital increases for the first two years, due to the transaction moving in-the-money (ITM), and then gradually declines to zero over the remaining lifetime.

The behaviour of KVA in the three scenarios is now examined (Figure 19.12). Whilst KVA decays to zero in all scenarios, meaning that it will be released at some point during the lifetime of the transaction, this again occurs in materially different ways. In particular, in the 95% PFE scenario, KVA initially becomes more negative as the underlying capital requirements increase.

The result of the above is very different ROC for each year over the life of the transaction, as shown in Figure 19.13. The three scenarios can be understood as follows:

- *EFV*. In this average scenario, the ROC is approximately constant each year, with the average ROC being about 10%. Note that this is higher than the 8% return included in the KVA calculation for this transaction because of the convexity of capital (Figure 19.3).
- *5% PFE*. In this scenario, the ROC is very high, especially in the early years, due to the low capital requirements for the OTM transaction. The average ROC is about 16%.
- *95% PFE*. Here, there is a large negative ROC in the first year due to the more negative KVA driven by higher capital requirements for the ITM transaction. After this, there is relatively low positive ROC for the remainder of the transaction. The average ROC is only 3%.

The above example illustrates that whilst KVA represents the amount of profit that is required on average to generate a given ROC, the actual ROC will be extremely volatile, driven by the underlying volatility in regulatory capital. Whilst the above example is for

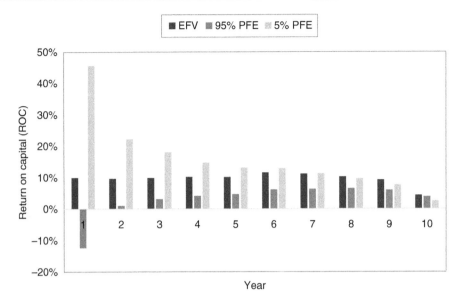

Figure 19.13   Annual ROC in the three scenarios shown in Figure 19.11.

a single transaction, it could reflect the general position for a bank in the case where its client business is quite directional (e.g. corporates wanting to pay the fixed rate in uncollateralised interest rate swaps to hedge floating borrowing). Whilst a bank may accept that ROC in a business such as derivatives may be cyclical and potentially balanced by other businesses, the variability is quite significant. Assuming this is not desirable, there are two obvious ways to mitigate the above volatility in the ROC:

- *Balanced portfolio*. A bank could aim to have a fairly balanced portfolio so that higher capital requirements on some transactions would be offset by lower requirements in others. For example, a bank predominantly receiving fixed in uncollateralised interest rate swaps would need to pay fixed in similar transactions. This may be easier for global banks compared to smaller and/or more regionally-focused ones.
- *Hedging*. A bank could seek to 'lock in' a given ROC by hedging KVA, in a similar way to CVA and FVA. This would mean additional hedging profits (losses) as future capital requirements increase (decrease). For example, in a scenario where regulatory capital requirement dropped (due to the transaction moving OTM, as in the 5% PFE case above), profits would be offset by losses on KVA hedges, although the ROC would be maintained. In examples such as the 95% PFE above, KVA hedge profits would increase the ROC to the desired level. The initial profits and hedging P&L would be less relevant metrics as they would simply provide the mechanism to attain a given ROC. Clearly, a bank cannot hedge for the change in regulatory methodologies or a change in its required ROC.

It remains to be seen which of the above (or other) approaches is adopted by the industry or if banks follow different business models.

The topic of KVA hedging is discussed in more detail in Section 21.3.2.

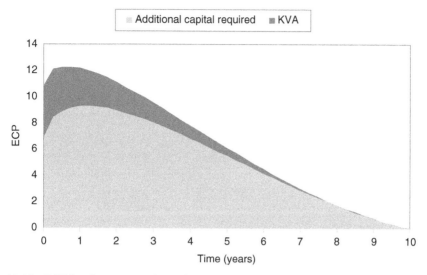

Figure 19.14   ECP for the example shown in Section 19.2.4, assuming that KVA is not released as a profit and, therefore, forms part of the required regulatory capital.

19.3.3   Discounting

In the example in Table 19.1, ECP was discounted at the cost of capital, which led to KVA of -38.8 basis points. Without discounting at this higher rate, KVA is larger in absolute terms at -49.1 basis points. As with all xVA formulas, the precise assumptions to use depend on the underlying strategy and payoffs.

For KVA, discounting at cost of capital is appropriate if KVA is counted towards the regulatory capital requirements (see, for example, Albanese et al. 2016 and Kjaer 2018). This would then follow the IRR approach in Equation 19.4, where there is a single rate. For this to be appropriate, KVA-related profits would have to be withheld, either as retained earnings or via another accounting adjustment, such as an explicit KVA valuation adjustment. This would, therefore, apply to the second and third cases described at the start of Section 19.3.2. This point is also considered by Garcia Munoz et al. (2016), who consider that the use of KVA as capital creates a recursive problem.

The use of KVA as capital is illustrated in Figure 19.14, which shows the ECP of the previous interest rate swap example. The fact that KVA itself forms part of the regulatory capital can be seen to reduce the capital cost, which, in turn, improves the ROC and rationalises the lower initial KVA. In the example shown, KVA is reduced by around 20% in the case where it is not released and forms part of regulatory capital.

19.3.4   KVA Accounting

In general, individual xVA components initially developed as non-standard adjustments to prices but then developed into standard and rigorous charges with accounting implications. Given the increasing prominence of KVA, it is natural to ask whether or not it will eventually be seen as an accounting adjustment, like CVA and FVA before it.

It is hard to extract the precise magnitude of KVA in clearing prices, but there is a general consensus that KVA or a hurdle rate calculation is included in entry prices for derivatives. However, it appears as though only a portion of KVA is charged, or equivalently that the required ROC is quite low. At the time of writing, no bank appears to have taken a generic accounting reserve for KVA (although some banks have done so in certain specific cases). It is not market practice for KVA to be managed or reserved internally by banks, although some banks are clearly moving in this direction.

There is a debate over whether or not banks should and can report KVA in financial statements. One argument is that this can be justified via the exit price, since another bank will require KVA when entering a transaction. This would also be in line with an estimate of the cost of liquidating the business, although this is unlikely to be a desirable or practical strategy. The idea is also supported by the fact that capital costs measured by KVA (cost of funding equity) have similarities to the funding costs represented by FVA (cost of funding debt), as shown in Figure 19.10.

The potential benefits of KVA accounting are:

- *Return on capital.* When KVA is only a hurdle, this implies that the ROC in the first year will be very strong since it will be based on the total profit of a transaction, but will then drop to zero for the remaining lifetime. Taking KVA as an accounting item would allow profits to be released over the lifetime of the transaction, thereby generating the required ROC.
- *Incentives.* With capital hurdles, sales and trading in a bank will still gain from the entire profit of a transaction at inception. Taking KVA as an accounting item would allow profits to be deferred and released over the lifetime of a transaction, arguably creating the right incentive for front-office staff.
- *Management.* Like other xVAs, KVA could be transfer priced to a central xVA desk and managed accordingly. Without this, a bank may suffer from extremely volatile return on capital numbers.

However, given that most banks have relatively long-dated derivatives books, the one-off adjustment that would be required to achieve the above would be large compared to the fairly significant FVA reported values discussed in Section 18.2.1. It is, therefore, difficult to see how a bank would satisfy its staff and shareholders by making such a fundamental change, especially if competitors were not also doing so.

On the other hand, there are arguments that KVA should not be an accounting adjustment as KVA represents profits and not costs. This is also supported by the lack of a standard and well-defined KVA calculation across the market, which negates the ability truly to define KVA in this fashion. In particular, the inputs for KVA are extremely subjective due to:

- different ROC requirements for different banks;
- different capital requirements (e.g. additional charges for G-SIB banks or the EU capital charge exemption);
- contrasting approaches to pricing capital (e.g. banks pricing in the LR);
- different (current) capital methodologies (e.g. banks pricing in economic instead of regulatory capital or the use of SA-CCR versus IMM); and
- different approaches to pricing in future regulatory change (see Figure 19.1).

Some of the above have parallels with the accounting of FVA – for example, the choice of the cost and symmetry of funding (Section 18.3.2). However, KVA valuation is much more subjective than FVA, and it would be difficult to decide what the market-standard KVA calculation for exit price purposes should be.

Another problem with FVA accounting is that there are potential overlaps between KVA and other xVA terms. Regulatory capital could be used as funding, in which case KVA seemingly overlaps with FVA, or it could be used to absorb default losses, in which case it seemingly overlaps with CVA. We will discuss these aspects in Section 19.4.

19.4   KVA OVERLAPS

19.4.1   CVA and KVA

The calculation of CVA using risk-neutral default probabilities as implied by regulation and accounting standards is the theoretical cost of hedging counterparty risk (Section 3.1.7). Due to a credit risk premium (Figure 12.1), this is expected to be higher than both:

- the actual loss experienced with respect to counterparty defaults; or
- the CVA calculated using historical default probabilities (see discussion in Section 12.1.2).

If it were possible to hedge most of the variability associated with CVA, then the above would be of limited interest. However, hedging CVA (discussed later in Section 21.2) is not straightforward. This is particularly true for hedging credit risk, with single-name credit default swaps (CDSs) being especially illiquid, meaning – somewhat perversely – that hedging actual counterparty defaults is often not possible.

Another related problem is that regulatory and accounting frameworks are not har-monised. Whilst regulators make efforts to introduce risk-sensitive capital methodologies without double-counting (e.g. the subtraction of 'incurred CVA' in Basel capital rules, discussed in Section 13.4.1), inefficiencies inevitably exist. One example can be seen in the internal ratings-based (IRB) capital formula shown in Equation 13.1. Here, the subtrac-tion of the probability of default (PD) term envisages that an expected loss has been taken as an accounting adjustment. However, in this framework the PD concerned would be a historical estimate, whereas the CVA accounting adjustment usually involves the higher risk-neutral PD. The PD subtracted is, therefore, too small.

Another example of the lack of harmonisation of regulatory and accounting CVA frameworks is the treatment of CVA hedges, and related capital relief, in capital method-ologies. Under the current regulatory rules, CVA hedges may not reduce capital charges in line with economic risk reduction and may even increase capital in some situations (see Section 13.5.3). This has created some problems for banks managing CVA. For example, a large bank reported significant CVA losses associated with its capital reduction pro-gramme (Carver 2013).

For ease of exposition, it is useful to define two idealistic approaches to counterparty risk and related capital requirements:

- *Counterparty risk warehousing.* In this approach, there is no CVA hedging, and there is the economic cost of counterparty defaults, which are provisioned for via an expected

Table 19.4 Pricing for CVA and KVA under the two stylised frameworks and a more realistic partial hedging approach.

	α	β	Result
Credit risk warehousing	0	1	EL + KVA
Fully hedged	1	0	CVA
Partial hedging	0–1	?	$(1 - \alpha)EL + \alpha CVA + \beta KVA$

loss (EL), and associated capital requirements (KVA). CVA accounting – especially with risk-neutral parameters – is not desirable since this creates accounting volatility.
- *Fully hedged.* Here, CVA is hedged perfectly, and there is no residual risk and, consequently, no capital requirements.

Whilst the above approaches are stylised, they have led to banks pricing in consideration of the overlap between CVA and KVA – for example, by charging the higher of the warehousing (EL + KVA) or hedging approaches (CVA). This is discussed by Morini and Prampolini (2015) and is similar to the approach where an ROC hurdle is defined according to Equation 19.1, but EL, and not CVA, is subtracted from the revenue as a cost. Such an approach may be a compromise to respond to the complaint (sometimes from salespeople in banks, or clients) that, by charging CVA and KVA, a bank is charging the cost of hedging counterparty risk and the capital requirement in relation to not hedging it.

More generally, Kenyon and Green (2014) describe a framework where a bank could be at some point between the two above extremes of credit risk warehousing and perfect hedging. In this framework, the cost of counterparty risk and capital can be defined as $(1 - \alpha)EL + \alpha CVA + \beta KVA$, where α represents the amount of credit hedging that is being done and β accounts for the impact of CVA hedges on regulatory capital. The two stylised frameworks in this representation, together with a more realistic partial hedging approach, are shown in Table 19.4.

The first two representations above are stylised since they (at the very least) assume a perfect harmonisation of accounting CVA and capital requirements. In reality, accounting standards and the need for a CVA desk with an appropriate governance structure prevent a bank from completely warehousing counterparty risk. On the other hand, it is not possible to hedge perfectly, and regulatory capital definitions prevent a bank from achieving full capital relief. It is useful to consider two more practical situations:

- *Partial hedging (capital increasing).* In this case, CVA hedges actually increase regulatory capital requirements ($\beta > 1$), which, as explained in Section 13.3.6, is likely the current situation for many banks.
- *Partial hedging (capital reducing).* Here, CVA hedges reduce regulatory capital requirements ($\beta < 1$).

These scenarios are compared to the stylised cases in Figure 19.15. We note that this representation is only qualitative and does not consider certain factors, such as the cost of CVA accounting volatility and the associated benefit of reducing it through CVA hedges.

The representation in Figure 19.15 explains the reluctance of some banks to account for and actively manage CVA. This is because the increased hedging cost of moving away

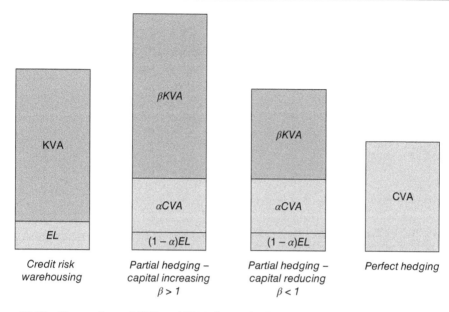

Figure 19.15   Comparison of CVA and KVA for partial hedging scenarios.

from the credit risk warehousing approach is undesirable, unless it is associated with a reduction in KVA ($\beta < 1$) that is recognised within the bank. Indeed, at the current time, it is quite possible that the current value of β can be greater than unity due to the fact that market risk hedges actually consume, rather than reduce, CVA capital.

However, looking to the future, the introduction of the FRTB-CVA capital rules may create different incentives. Under the more advanced SA-CVA approach (Section 13.3.5), most CVA hedges, which reduce P&L volatility, will achieve regulatory capital relief. In such a situation, a bank is more incentivised to follow a hedging approach. In this situation, the appropriate pricing approach would probably be $CVA + \beta KVA$.[6] In other words, the bank would charge CVA and seek to achieve a return on the residual capital requirement after factoring in the likely achievable capital relief. The value of β in this situation is probably counterparty specific (e.g. due to the liquidity of the single-name CDS market) and is probably, at best, an estimate (since a bank's CVA hedging strategy and its ultimate performance is not known precisely *a priori*).

Note that, from a KVA point of view, it is the situation in the future, not just at the current time, that is important. Hence, the future capital methodologies, KVA strategy, and values of α and β are important.

19.4.2   FVA and KVA

Another potential overlap is due to the ability to use capital as a source of funding which would – depending on the representation – lead to a reduction of either FVA or KVA.

---

[6] Since CVA is an accounting adjustment, we assume a bank would consider this the economic cost rather than the more stylised $(1 - \alpha)EL + \alpha CVA$ component.

Albanese et al. (2015, 2016) consider a full funding cost environment, but where regulatory capital is used for funding which is also FVA reducing. The use of regulatory capital to reduce funding requirements is also discussed by Green et al. (2014).

In order to benefit from any such overlap, this would have to be part of the relationship between the xVA desk and the treasury in a bank. This would amount to calculating the holistic and incremental cost of funding a given transaction across both equity and debt funding. The relationship between the xVA desk and the treasury will be discussed in more detail in Section 21.3.1. This approach can be seen as optimisation of xVA (Section 21.3.4).

20

MVA

20.1 OVERVIEW

This chapter follows on from the discussion of funding in Chapter 18 and discusses the specific funding cost of posting initial margin (IM). It also considers the potential benefit of receiving IM, in terms of reduction of credit value adjustment (CVA) and capital value adjustment (KVA).

As previously discussed, IM considerations are of growing importance due to two significant aspects of regulatory reform:

- *The clearing mandate.* This requires that standardised over-the-counter (OTC) derivatives transactions are cleared through central counterparties (CCPs) (Section 4.4.1). CCPs impose various financial resources requirements and contractual commitments on their members for the benefit of their own risk management. The most significant of these is IM to cover a severe scenario at a high confidence level, which must be paid upfront and will vary during the life of a portfolio depending on the output of the CCP IM model. CCPs will only invest IM conservatively, if at all, and so the return paid on cash IM is typically low. A benefit of central clearing for banks is that the capital charges against CCPs are relatively favourable (Section 13.6). CCPs also require other financial commitments, notably via the default fund contributions and rights of assessment (future default fund contributions). Such requirements are definitely costly since, like IM, default funds are held by the CCP or third party and are not remunerated at anything more than an overnight rate (and typically less). It would seem logical to include the cost of default fund contribution alongside IM in margin value adjustment (MVA). Rights of assessment and other contingent loss-allocation methods are unfunded and potentially heavily capitalised (Section 13.6.3) and so would more likely appear via KVA.
- *Bilateral margin rules.* From September 2016, non-centrally cleared transactions have become increasingly subject to bilateral margin requirements (Section 4.4.2). This means that both parties to a transaction must post IM, which partially mimics the CCP treatment. This IM must be segregated and cannot typically be rehypothecated (except potentially in one limited situation mentioned in Section 7.4.1) and so will be costly due to the need for segregation. The Standard Initial Margin Model (SIMM) is becoming market standard for the calculation of these amounts (Section 9.4.4). The IM must be held with an unaffiliated third-party custodian, and no return will be paid on cash.

The above rules apply, in general, to major players in the OTC derivatives market, and small end users are, broadly speaking, exempt (see Section 4.4.3).

Note that all of the above requirements are costly since they involve posting high-quality IM that is usually not rehypothecated, but is rather segregated and therefore remunerated at a low return. Furthermore, even if the IM was allowed to be rehypothecated, a higher return may be achievable, but it would then create additional counterparty risk via CVA.

Not all IM is regulatory driven, with a substantial amount of discretionary IM also being posted (see ISDA 2018). Note that – historically at least – such IM has often gone by the name of 'independent amount'. Whilst there is, strictly speaking, no difference between IM and independent amount, the latter tends to be a non-regulatory, one-way payment without segregation and is often based on simple metrics such as percentage of notional (Table 20.1). The use of rating triggers is common with discretionary IM, but this is not allowed with regulatory IM, with the amounts being independent of credit rating.

An important feature is the increased complexity of risk-sensitive, model-based IM methodologies, such as the proprietary models used by CCPs and the International Swaps and Derivatives Association (ISDA) SIMM (Section 9.4.4). This dynamic feature is important because the computation of xVA in the presence of IM depends on the ability to simulate IM requirements in the future.

Some margin agreements require contingent posting in certain situations, most commonly upon a rating downgrade (see example in Table 7.4). Regulatory rules in the liquidity coverage ratio (LCR) require banks to hold a liquidity buffer to cover such outflows in the event of a three-notch ratings downgrade, and such an outflow, therefore, needs to be pre-funded (Section 4.3.3). Note that it may be beneficial for a bank to actually post a smaller IM[1] (than would be required in the event of the trigger) in order to have such rating-based triggers removed, since the IM needs to be held in high-quality liquidity assets (HQLAs) in the bank's liquidity buffer anyway. Sometimes there may be alternatives to contingent IM posting, such as transactions being terminated or novated; this is even more of a challenge to quantify since it would require the estimation of the price charged by a replacement counterparty. Note that a bank does not generally derive any benefit from contingent triggers in its favour because the prudent LCR rules would require the assumption that these triggers were not breached. As seen from Figure 20.1, market

Table 20.1   Differences between discretionary and regulatory IM.

	Discretionary	Regulatory
Nature	Usually one-way and sometimes called 'independent amount'	Two-way
Segregation	Uncommon	Required
Calculation	Often simple metrics or proprietary models	Standard schedule or ISDA SIMM
Determinants	Often linked to rating triggers	No linkage

---

[1] Although ideally this should then be segregated to avoid creating additional CVA.

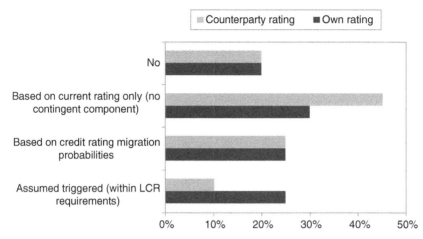

Figure 20.1 Market practice around pricing contingent funding requirements. Source: Solum CVA Survey (2015).

practice is divided on the treatment of such contingent liquidity requirements, but many banks do price them in, especially in relation to their own potential rating downgrade.

In terms of the incorporation of IM into xVA measures, there are two main considerations:

- the extent of risk reduction due to receiving IM from bilateral counterparties; and
- the cost of posting IM to bilateral counterparties and CCPs.

The latter component generally gives rise to MVA costs, whilst the former may lead to a reduction in counterparty risk, seen via lower CVA and KVA components. However, this also depends on whether or not the IM is segregated (Table 20.2). Non-segregated IM will create a cost for the poster due to an increase in counterparty risk, but an associated benefit for the receiver in the form of a funding benefit. Segregation will remove these cost and benefit components. The benefit of segregation, with the loss of funding benefit, is that IM can only reduce, and not increase, counterparty risk. Due to the bilateral margin requirements, segregation of IM is becoming increasingly common.

Table 20.2 IM impact on xVA. Note that regulatory IM must be segregated, but discretionary IM need not be.

	Posted IM		Received IM	
	Non-segregated	Segregated	Non-segregated	Segregated
Counterparty risk (CVA and KVA)	Cost	–	Benefit	
Funding (MVA)		Cost	Benefit	–

20.2   INITIAL MARGIN FUNDING COSTS

20.2.1   Introduction

MVA, like funding value adjustment (FVA), represents a funding cost, although there are fundamental differences between the two (Table 20.3) and it is therefore probably relevant mainly to consider them separately. In general, FVA is associated with being uncollateralised and therefore making and receiving cash flow payments and their impact on the underlying valuation without any associated and offsetting margin flows. As discussed in Section 18.2.2, FVA is not really driven by margin posting per se, although it is sometimes explained in this context. Nevertheless, FVA is largely a result of imperfect variation margin posting. MVA is the cost of posting IM, which is to a large extent not related to cash flows and valuation, but rather to the future risk of the position. MVA is also simpler than FVA in that it is only a cost and there is no question over symmetry (Section 18.3.2). There will, however, be the question of overlap between FVA and MVA, which will be considered in Section 21.3.1. Unlike FVA, which has cost and benefit components, MVA is a cost only, due to the fact that regulatory IM received must typically be segregated and so provides no funding benefit.

Since cash IM is remunerated at only a short-term rate (if at all), there is a significant funding or opportunity cost, similar to the situation for FVA. Indeed, the fact that IM is generally remunerated at a sub-overnight-indexed-spread rate means that it is unlikely to be optimal to post cash and that eligible securities (such as government bonds), effectively providing remuneration at the repo rate, are a more natural asset to use. The relative ease of segregating securities over cash also supports their use for IM posting. The cost of IM naturally leads to MVA representing the lifetime cost of posting IM against a transaction or portfolio.

20.2.2   MVA Formula

A formula for MVA (Kenyon and Green 2015) can be written as:

$$MVA = - \int_0^\infty E[IM(u)]FS(u)du \approx \sum_{i=1}^m EIM(t_i) \times FS(t_{i-1}, t_i) \times (t_i - t_{i-1}) \qquad (20.1)$$

with $FS(u)$ being the funding spread, and $E[IM(u)] = EIM(u)$ being the discounted expected initial margin profile over time. The funding spread should reflect the type of

Table 20.3   Differences between FVA and MVA.

	FVA	MVA
Nature	Funding assets, cash flows and variation margin	Funding IM posting
Symmetry	Potentially symmetric (asset and liability)	Asymmetric due to segregation (liability only)
Cost/benefit	Potentially a cost and benefit	Cost only
Reference	Remuneration rate (typically overnight indexed spread) or repo rate	Remuneration rate (typically sub-overnight indexed spread) or repo rate

margin being posted (currency, type) and any related remuneration (cash) or repo rate (securities). There will be cheapest-to-deliver optionality (Section 16.2.3) with respect to the posting of IM, since both bilateral and CCP requirements will typically permit IM to be posted in different currencies and types of securities (this is in contrast to variation margin, which is often in cash in the currency of the transaction). This optionality would be most obviously accounted for in the estimation of the funding cost term. Note that received IM may also constitute a cost since it will typically have to be segregated, and this segregation cost may be viewed as contributing to MVA. This would involve computation of expected initial margin (EIM) on the reverse portfolio.

The $EIM(u)$ term above represents the expected IM posted at a given future time u. This is complex to quantify since the underlying IM calculation methodology may be sensitivity or simulation based and subject to unpredictable changes in model assumptions and calibration choices. There are also components – as with KVA (Section 19.2.3) – which are impossible to quantify (except perhaps qualitatively) since they relate to changes in the underlying IM methodology. Examples of this are the decision of a CCP to change its IM calculation methodology or the recalibration of the SIMM (Section 9.4.4). Unlike FVA, MVA is therefore not trivially calculated alongside CVA and requires additional work and potential computation challenges.

For centrally-cleared transactions, as noted above, it may be relevant to include any default fund contribution with the IM requirement in Equation 20.1. Furthermore, the relatively small capital charges arising from IM and default fund contributions may be incorporated qualitatively at this stage or assessed more accurately via KVA.

20.2.3   EIM Term

Future IM requirements can evolve in many different ways, depending on a number of factors:

- Changes in the portfolio composition as transactions mature (excluding new transactions, which can be priced as they occur). Note that the profile may actually increase when transactions that are offsetting more longer-dated transactions in the portfolio mature.
- Continuous changes in the look-back period for historical simulation (in particular when important days drop in and out of the data set) and the periodic recalibration of the parameters in the ISDA SIMM.
- Alterations in methodology, such as changes in underlying assumptions and changes in the stress periods used. For example, several years ago, most CCPs switched from the assumption of 'relative returns' to 'absolute returns' (Section 9.3.3) for interest rate movements, which is usually more conservative in a falling interest rate environment.

The main challenge of MVA is calculating the EIM term in Equation 20.1. Ideally, doing this would capture:

- the specific IM methodology being applied;
- the ageing of the portfolio;
- modelling the entire portfolio of transactions together;
- the variability of future IM requirements; and
- potential changes in the IM methodology.

Table 20.4   Balanced and directional portfolios of interest rate swaps for IM analysis.

	Balanced portfolio				Directional portfolio			
	Maturity	Notional	Pay/Rec	Currency	Maturity	Notional	Pay/Rec	Currency
Trade 1	3 years	250m	Rec	USD	3 years	50m	Pay	USD
Trade 2	5 years	100m	Pay	GBP	5 years	30m	Pay	USD
Trade 3	7 years	50m	Pay	USD	7 years	30m	Pay	USD
Trade 4	10 years	30m	Rec	EUR	10 years	30m	Pay	USD

The importance of the above points will be highlighted using two portfolios (Table 20.4) of interest rate swaps, one of which is balanced across pay fixed and receive fixed positions, and the other which is (relatively) directional, being all pay fixed, although in different currencies. IM calculations will use the ISDA SIMM methodology as described in Section 9.4.4. Note that the same SIMM parameters are used for the entirety of the simulation. In reality, there is an annual recalibration of these parameters, but this is difficult to model.

The forward IM is first shown based on a single scenario based on ageing the portfolio through time and calculating the future IM using forward rates. For single trades and directional portfolios, the IM usually behaves in a predictable fashion, often simply decaying to zero, as can be seen for the directional portfolio in Figure 20.2. For balanced portfolios, this is often not the case as shorter-dated trades age and drop out of the portfolio, potentially changing its overall directionality. This is the case for the balanced portfolio in Figure 20.2. The portfolio initially has a negative sensitivity to interest rate movements (as interest rates increase, the portfolio loses value) and so it represents a receive fixed position overall. This means that the ageing impact of the large, short-dated (three-year) receive fixed swap is initially beneficial and reduces IM, since the portfolio becomes more balanced. However, at approximately the two-year point, the overall interest rate sensitivity of the portfolio – mainly due to the ageing of the large three-year

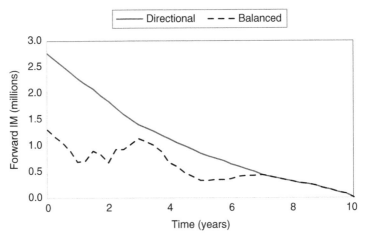

Figure 20.2   Forward IM for the balanced and directional interest rate swap portfolios under the SIMM methodology.

swap – becomes positive. As a result, the further ageing of this swap starts to increases the future IM.

Capturing the variability of future IM requirements is challenging due to the need to run the underlying methodology (ISDA SIMM, in this case) many times in different future scenarios. The scenarios are generated using the same simulation methodology, as described for the exposure simulations in Section 15.6. In certain situations, using simulation is not particularly important as the variability is small, as shown for the balanced portfolio in Figure 20.3. In this case, IM at the 5% and 95% confidence levels is only slightly higher and lower than the EIM value. In such cases, forward IM represents an accurate approximation to the EIM profile, and there is minimal variation around this.

There are two reasons for the above being a relatively simple case with only a small variation in future IM requirements. First, the underlying portfolio is simple and has approximately linear risk-factor sensitivity (delta and not gamma or vega). Second, the underlying calculation methodology (SIMM) is assumed to remain fixed (in reality, SIMM would update, but only annually when the parameters are recalibrated). These points together mean that the only variability in future IM arises from a change in the underlying sensitivities of the swap portfolio. The change in these sensitivities is relatively small and broadly symmetric (a certain increase in rates reduces the sensitivity, and a corresponding rates decrease leads to an increase in the sensitivity by about the same amount).

One case where the above is not true is for a non-linear transaction such as an option. Figure 20.4 shows future IM for a long position in a physically-settled, five-year, European-style swaption on a five-year payer swap using SIMM methodology. In this case, future IM before the five-year point is very variable due to the potential for the swaption to be very in-the-money (high delta contribution in SIMM) or out-of-the-money (low delta contribution in SIMM). The contribution from the vega component in SIMM is smaller and more linear. After the five-year point, the profile is also variable due to possibility of the swaption being exercised (in which case there will be an IM requirement on the underlying swap) or not exercised (in which case there will be zero IM). EIM during the last five years, therefore, represents an average over paths, some with and

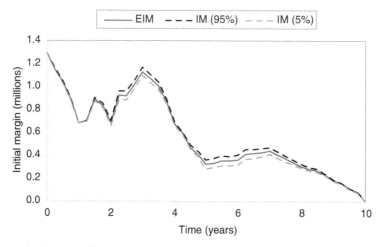

Figure 20.3 Distribution of future IM quantified by EIM and high and low quantiles for the balanced swap portfolio under the SIMM methodology.

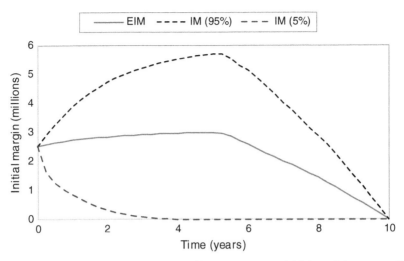

Figure 20.4 Distribution of future IM quantified by EIM and high and low quantiles for a physically-settled payer swaption under SIMM methodology.

some without IM requirements. For the same reason, the forward IM is not accurate in such a case and will be zero after the exercise date if the swaption is OTM.

This swaption example with SIMM methodology is more relevant than the swap example above because many swaps are now centrally cleared, leaving a significant number of bilaterally-cleared swaption transactions with associated IM tied to the SIMM methodology.

Whilst future IM for cleared trades should be simpler to calculate for the reasons shown above (e.g. linearity), CCP IM methodologies are more difficult to capture. These methodologies are typically more complex and use approaches such as historical simulation with 'look-back' periods that continuously update as new data becomes available. They may also include data from stressed periods which may sometimes be changed. Whilst other changes in CCP methodologies are impossible to predict, the continual updating with new data can be modelled by including the simulated scenario data within the future CCP IM calculation.

To illustrate the above effect (Figure 20.5), an IM methodology based on 99% value-at-risk (VAR) and a 10-year look-back period are assumed. When simulating future IM, the look-back period will incorporate the simulated data. For example, IM in two years will be based on the last eight years of known data, plus the two that have been generated in the scenario in question. This is essentially a historical simulation within a Monte Carlo simulation. Using this approach, Figure 20.5 shows future IM distribution for a centrally-cleared interest rate swap assuming a CCP-like methodology. There is material variation in the future initial paths, mainly caused by sharp increases driven by relatively volatile scenarios which increase IM via their future inclusion in the historical look-back period. Note that IM cannot reduce substantially due to the use of a high quantile, and reductions only occur due to data dropping out of the look-back period.

Note that the above effect makes future IM, like capital (Section 19.2.4), more likely to increase than reduce. It may be important to quantify such 'convexity' of IM for pricing and management purposes. It may also need to be calculated for the LCR (Section 4.3.3).

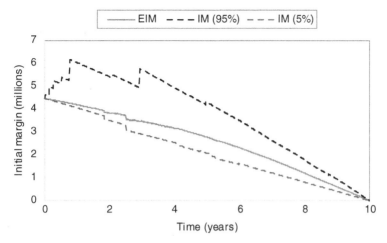

Figure 20.5 Distribution of future IM quantified by EIM and high and low quantiles for an interest swap using a typical CCP methodology based on VAR and historical simulation.

Recall that MVA computation also raises the question of whether or not to use the P- or Q-measure for the underlying simulation (Section 15.3.3). In the above example, the historical-simulation IM calculation represents a physical (P-measure) calculation. Choosing to use the risk-neutral (Q-measure) for the simulation would be consistent with the calculation of other metrics such as CVA and FVA. However, it would be inconsistent with the fact that future IM requirement is largely unhedgeable. It also means that future IM is driven partially by historical data and partly by risk-neutral data (from the prior simulation path). A simulation using the physical measure would be more natural, but would then require different scenarios compared to those used for CVA and FVA.

20.2.4   Computation Challenges

IM requirements for derivatives are increasingly being calculated using measures such as VAR or expected shortfall (ES): this is the case for both CCP and bilateral transactions. A typical methodology uses historical simulation and a VAR or ES metric at the 99% confidence level or more over a time horizon of five (CCP) or 10 (bilateral) business days. It is now common for a stressed period of data to be included in the calculation to dilute any procyclical problems where consistent periods of low volatility may lead to excessively low IMs. Examples of centrally-cleared and bilateral markets in this regard are:

- *Bilateral.* BCBS-IOSCO[2] (2015) recommends IM to be based on a 99% confidence level with a 10-day time horizon and calibrated to a period including financial stress.
- *CCP.* SwapClear[3] uses historical simulation with a five-day time horizon calibrated to a long-time period, with the IM defined by the average of the worst six moves in this period. This equates to an ES at a high (more than 99.5%) confidence level.

---

[2] Basel Committee on Banking Supervision and Board of the International Organization of Securities Commissions.

[3] www.lch.com.

The form of MVA as an integral over the EIM profile leads to computation problems, since a traditional approach would require a Monte Carlo simulation similar to the exposure methodology but with IM calculations at each point. Noting that an IM calculation itself may require another simulation, this leads to a classic computational bottleneck. There are a number of methods that can be used to solve this, including:

- *Simple amortisation assumptions.* The simplest approach is to approximate by making amortisation assumptions based on current IM. However, this may not be a good approximation, as shown in Figure 20.2.
- *Approximation with forward IM.* This approach involves calculating only forward IM (i.e. a single path), which may be a good approximation for some portfolios (e.g. Figure 20.3) and not others (e.g. Figure 20.4).
- *Using a quantile of the exposure distribution.* Since IM is generally a certain quantile, a reasonably simple and cheap approach is to use a quantile of the exposure distribution to approximate this quantile, essentially reusing the simulation data.
- *Regression methods.* A more sophisticated approach is to estimate IM via regression (also known as American Monte Carlo; see Section 15.3.2). This is discussed by, for example, Green and Kenyon (2015) and Caspers et al. (2017). Such approaches generally require scaling so as to reproduce the current IM. A fixed scaling is often not accurate, and Anfuso et al. (2017) suggest a scaling function with a parametric form.
- *Adjoint algorithmic differentiation (AAD).* In the case of SIMM, IM is driven mainly by sensitivities and aggregation rules, with the former representing the bottleneck of the calculation. Hence, a method such as AAD – which calculates sensitivities (partial derivatives) directly – is useful.

20.2.5   Pricing and MVA Example

Note that the IM term (EIM) in Equation 20.1 will also be typically defined for a portfolio of transactions with a bilateral counterparty or CCP. In particular:

- *Bilateral.* The bilateral margin rules require IM to be calculated across four asset classes (currency/rates, equity, credit, commodities). If a model-based approach is being used, then there will be a portfolio IM for all transactions within a given asset class. Due to the nature of SIMM, this can be further broken down into risk contributions (e.g. delta risk, vega risk).
- *Centrally cleared.* CCPs generally net ('cross-margin') IM across transactions in the same asset class (e.g. rates in different currencies), although they may not net across asset classes. This means that there will be a total IM requirement for all CCP-netted transactions.

The portfolio shown in Table 20.4 – being all interest rate products – would, therefore, be cross-margined with respect to a given bilateral counterparty or CCP. The above means that there will be a need for an 'incremental MVA', similar to the incremental CVA defined in Section 17.4.1. This increases the computational requirements further, since it will be necessary to calculate a portfolio MVA with and without the impact of a new transaction.

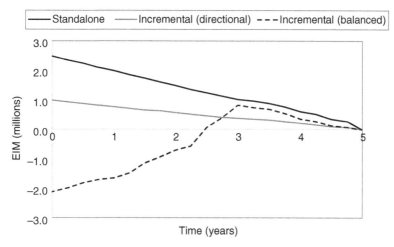

Figure 20.6   Incremental EIM profiles for the five-year swap in the portfolios shown in Table 20.4. Note that all cases are scaled to a notional of 100 million for illustration.

As with other xVAs, the magnitude of incremental MVA that would be required for pre-deal pricing depends on the size and directionality of the underlying portfolio. To illustrate this, consider adding the five-year swap in Table 20.4 to the remainder of the portfolio. Figure 20.6 shows EIM for adding this transaction to the other three swaps in the (relatively) directional and balanced portfolios, and compared to the standalone profile. For the directional portfolio, there is a relatively predictable reduction in EIM due to the fact that the currency of the swap is different. For the balanced portfolio, EIM has a more complex shape and is mainly negative, which is indicative of the overall portfolio IM being reduced by the addition of this swap.

The corresponding MVA values for the EIM profiles in Figure 20.6 are shown in Table 20.5, assuming a funding spread of 100 bps per annum. For the directional port-folio, MVA is substantially reduced. This can be seen as the portfolio being dominated by USD swaps, making the cost of transacting a GBP swap cheaper due to a portfolio effect. For the balanced portfolio, incremental MVA is positive, representing a benefit. Such benefits, if material, may be important to capture in order to make pricing more competitive.

Table 20.5   Incremental MVA for the five-year swap in the balanced and directional portfolios shown in Table 20.4, compared to the standalone calculation. A funding spread of 100 bp pa is assumed.

	MVA (bps upfront)
Standalone	−6.7
Incremental (directional portfolio)	−2.6
Incremental (balanced portfolio)	2.5

20.3   MVA

20.3.1   A Need to Charge MVA?

Banks internally calculate the cost of funding IM posting and are clearly paying more attention to pricing MVA. It would seem likely that the costs of funding IM, via MVA, will become more standard adjustments to the accounting of fair value of derivatives, in a similar way to the current use of FVA for funding costs of uncollateralised derivatives. Banks are generally directing the responsibility for pricing IM costs towards the xVA desk. However, there are a number of reasons why MVA may not be as necessary and viable as other traditional valuation adjustments, such as CVA and FVA. Note that MVA primarily arises on interbank trades and trades with financial institutions above the regulatory threshold (Section 9.4.1). It represents the cost of overcollateralisation, as opposed to more traditional terms such as CVA and FVA, which are the result of undercollateralisation.

In general, where other xVA terms have become standard adjustments both in pricing and valuation, the following points generally apply:

- *End user clients.* The standard xVAs apply mainly to relatively unsophisticated, non-margin posting, end user clients. Such clients – depending on jurisdiction and the precise level of their derivatives usage – are often exempt from the mandates that give rise to IM and therefore MVA.
- *Directionality.* Related to the above, the underlying portfolio is likely to be directional, driven by the hedging requirements of the client. This will limit netting benefits and make xVA prices close to their standalone values.
- *Lack of optimisation opportunities.* The client will be unlikely to want to restructure transactions or margin terms. Nor will there be portfolio compression (Section 6.2.4) opportunities due to directionality and the client's standalone need for transactions (e.g. for cash flow accounting purposes).

MVA tends to arise with more sophisticated clients that may not have directional portfolios and may want, or be willing, to restructure transactions at some point in the future. Such optimisations will recover previous incremental MVA, which may suggest that it does not need to be charged, or accounted for, in the first place. Hence, MVA charges are only really necessary where there is clear directionality with respect to a new trade such that the cost cannot be offset in the future. Regional banks tend to experience such directionality, whilst many global banks do not as they are able to balance their portfolios. It is important to note that bilateral IM requirements will create more need to attempt to balance bilateral portfolios with counterparties and consider opportunities for optimising IM and utilising central clearing (discussed later in Section 21.3.4).

When MVA is important, it might not be directly chargeable. The hedges of a trade may have associated MVA components that often cannot be charged directly (since the counterparty will likely be another bank). Hence, in certain circumstances, an end user may be charged MVA, in addition to CVA and KVA components, representing a cost associated with the hedging of their trade.

There is also the question of the pricing of MVA where the €50m threshold has been utilised in the contractual terms. The threshold rules imply that a firm must have in place a system to identify the exposure to a counterparty across an entire group. It would then be necessary to decide how to identify the benefit created by the threshold. It could be allocated across entities *a priori* or used on a first-come-first-served basis. In such a case, MVA would not – in theory – be necessary until IM breaches the threshold, whereupon the pricing with respect to a given counterparty may change materially. It is probably best not to treat such a situation in a completely binary fashion.

At the current time, banks often do not have the capability to rigorously and industrially calculate MVA for all situations, and may only consider it material for large client trades (either directly or with respect to the hedges of uncollateralised trades). On the one hand, this could be seen as being due to a lack of development of procedure and analytics to handle this (similar to CVA, which many years ago was only considered on significant trades). On the other hand, the fact that IM is harder to charge and may not always be directional (leading to potential optimisation opportunities) may not require an advanced treatment of MVA. Time will tell whether or not MVA becomes more rigorously treated or whether this is seen as overkill.

20.3.2   Accounting MVA

When it comes to including MVA in valuation, there are similarities with the FVA debate (Section 18.2.6). For example, Andersen et al. (2016) illustrate the same wealth transfer from shareholders to creditors, illustrating that the total value of a bank is invariant to IM payments. This has accounting implications, and these authors suggest that – like FVA – MVA should not be a component of financial reporting. Nevertheless, shareholders need to be compensated for the wealth transfer, and so MVA can be charged.

IM actually represents another form of wealth transfer between creditors, as described by Gregory (2016). Derivatives creditors (CCPs and bilateral counterparties) become more senior by virtue of holding IM that can be used in default scenarios. By symmetry, other creditors, such as unsecured senior bondholders, become less senior and should expect to experience larger default losses (lower recovery rates). Hence, the funding costs associated with IM may increase due to the worse payoff afforded to non-derivatives creditors. Andersen et al. (2016) argue that the total value of a firm has no net MVA component. This requires a net consideration of shareholders, other creditors, and derivatives creditors, with only the last category seeing any benefit.

Leaving aside some of the above differences, it would seem that if the cost of funding is included in financial reporting for FVA, then the cost of IM, via MVA, should also be accounted for. There is already some evidence for this,[4] although the adoption of MVA is proceeding more slowly than the equivalent adoption of FVA from around 2012 onwards. The likely reason for the slower adoption of MVA accounting is the inability to charge it in most situations.

20.3.3   Contingent MVA

Due to the LCR (Section 4.3.3), there may also be the need to consider contingent IM posting alongside actual (non-contingent) requirements (Figure 20.7). This can arise due

---

[4] The 2018 International Association of Credit Portfolio Managers (IACPM) survey suggested that around 50% of the participants were charging MVA, 30% were transferring profit and loss in relation to MVA (to an xVA desk), and just under 20% were accounting for MVA.

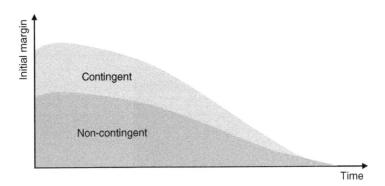

Figure 20.7   Illustration of MVA with both contingent and non-contingent components.

to the need to hold HQLAs against additional IM requirements in the liquidity stress period envisaged by the LCR, and is analogous to the case already discussed for FVA (Section 18.3.6). Most obviously, such requirements arise in relation to the three-notch downgrade, where contractual terms require additional IM (or 'independent amount') in the event of such credit rating changes. These contractual clauses are not market standard but do exist in certain relationships. Additionally, there is a need to consider the contingent IM that would arise from the potential 'recalibration' of the underlying methodology in such a stress period. This is difficult to quantify but is most significant for CCP methodologies, which are very dynamic and potentially volatile (for example, see Figure 20.5) compared to SIMM, which is more static and subject only to an annual recalibration. Note, therefore, that whilst non-contingent CCP IM may be generally lower than the equivalent SIMM values, contingent CCP IM may be more expensive.

20.3.4   CCP Basis

The CCP basis is a price differential that exists due to IM costs for dealers clearing a swap at one CCP versus another. For a given trade that could clear at more than one CCP, a dealer will have a preferred choice. This choice may well be related to the fact that the dealer already clears most of its business with this CCP.

Consider the case where a party wishes to trade with a dealer and clear at CCP1, but where the dealer's optimal clearing venue is CCP2 (Figure 20.8). From the dealer's perspective, there is a potential cost of IM at CCP1 due to the original trade, and another potential cost due to the hedge at CCP2. One or both of these incremental IM costs is likely to be material.

Taking the situation where the party is happy to clear at the favoured CCP (Figure 20.9), the dealer can clear both the original trade and the hedge at this CCP and would expect no additional IM requirement (unless the portfolio was subject to a concentration or liquidity multiplier; see Section 9.1.5). The ability to perform compression at the CCP may also cancel the two cleared transactions, from the dealer's perspective, at a later point in time.

The above shows that the dealer would prefer to clear the underlying trade at CCP2 (Figure 20.9), compared to CCP1 (Figure 20.8). Despite the underlying contracts being equivalent, they may, therefore, quote a different price for clearing at different CCPs. This

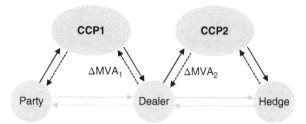

Figure 20.8   Illustration of the origin of the CCP basis where a party trades with a dealer and wants to clear at CCP1, but where the dealer clears most of its business (including the hedge) with CCP2. The grey lines indicate the original executed bilateral trades and the black lines the cleared trades.

Figure 20.9   Illustration of the origin of the CCP basis where a party trades with a dealer and clears at the dealer's favoured CCP. The grey lines indicate the original executed bilateral trades and the black lines the cleared trades.

price would be driven by MVA and be specific to the dealer in question, depending on the nature of the business cleared at the CCPs in question. Note that MVA is not directly visible via the CCP basis.

In some situations, the CCP basis might not represent a particular problem. A party may want to clear a trade at CCP1 and may – through choosing the best price available – naturally select the dealer that prefers this CCP.[5] When executing a different trade, a different dealer may prove to provide the optimal price. In such situations, whilst a CCP basis would exist for some dealers, it would not be a systematic charge across all participants, and would not need to be experienced by a party able to execute with the dealer giving the best price.

However, due to the hedging needs of similar clients and inherent directionalities and concentrations in the market, the CCP basis may persist across all dealers. For example, consider that a group of clients all want to do the same type of trade (e.g. pay the fixed rate). Furthermore, assume that all of these clients prefer a certain 'local' CCP, either due to regulatory (they are required to clear at this venue) or economic (this CCP allows a broad range of eligible margin) reasons. Suppose that all major dealers tend to use another 'global' CCP and have cleared the majority of their portfolios at this CCP. In such a case,

---

[5] There may be other components of the price that may lead to a different choice. However, in cleared markets, initial margin costs are likely to be a key component of prices.

there will be a persistent CCP basis in pricing seen across all participants. This has been seen to be the case in practice.[6]

Note that a given transaction cleared at two different venues is economically the same instrument but with a potentially different price. Since International Financial Reporting Standards (IFRS) 13 requires banks to measure derivatives fair values based on exit prices for accounting purposes, it is relevant to report the fair value of cleared trades by using rates specific to the respective CCPs. This results in a volatile profit and loss (P&L) of accounting fair values of the CCP basis position due to changes of the CCP basis in the market.

20.4   LINK TO KVA

20.4.1   Overview

KVA and MVA are not mutually exclusive (Table 20.6). In a bilateral margin regime, posting IM will lead to MVA, but received IM may lead to capital relief and a lower KVA, although there may be a significant modelling challenge to being able to quantify this.[7] In this respect, a part of the IM received can be seen as fulfilling the loss-absorbency role of capital. In a centrally-cleared regime, IM is not received, but there are potentially lower capital charges due to the perceived safety of the CCP.

The above implies that it is important to be able to capture KVA reduction in a bilateral margin or clearing regime, and to consider the offset of this component with the MVA cost. This also implies that KVA should be treated equivalently to MVA in terms of pricing and valuation. If this is not the case, then a bank may incorrectly incentivise opportunities such as 'backloading' portfolios to a CCP or posting 'discretionary' IM, which increase MVA but provide a more than offsetting KVA benefit, or vice versa. For example, suppose there is an opportunity to restructure a portfolio by posting and receiving more IM. This will create the following effects:

- reduced cost of equity (lower regulatory capital); and
- increased cost of debt (funding the required IM).

Both of the above need to be reflected in the valuation of KVA and MVA and the way in which this is transfer priced to the business. Without this, businesses will make decisions that do not reflect the actual cost of funding by the treasury, which will reflect sub-optimal choices for the bank as a whole.

Table 20.6   Impact of IM regimes on MVA and KVA.

	MVA	KVA
Bilateral	Cost of posting IM	Benefit of receiving IM, potentially leading to lower capital costs
Central clearing		Benefit of lower capital costs for cleared trades

---

[6] Wood, D. (2019). CCP basis and the future of cleared swap pricing. *Risk* (7 August). www.risk.net.
[7] This is also true for CVA, but this component will likely be small even without IM.

20.4.2   Example

To illustrate the above overlap between MVA and KVA, consider a 10-year interest rate swap in a bilateral margin regime. Regulatory capital is calculated using the standardised approach for counterparty credit risk (SA-CCR) methodology, which is equivalent to the results in Section 13.5.1. The regulatory IM is calculated under SIMM and considers IM requirements in a range around this value. The cost of capital is assumed to be 12%, and the funding cost of IM is 80 bp pa (0.8%). The MVA and KVA results as a function of bilateral IM are shown in Figure 20.10.

Obviously, the cost of posting IM will increase linearly with the amount, but the received IM will correspondingly produce a reduction in KVA. The gain in KVA is limited in the SA-CCR case due to the relative conservatism of this approach (e.g. the size of the add-ons and the 5% floor discussed in Section 13.4.3) There is a law of diminishing returns with KVA: every unit of initial margin received has a smaller relative impact.

The above example shows the reduction of KVA (under SA-CCR methodology) that occurs in combination with an increase in MVA with the bilateral IM amount. In this example, it is actually optimal to post a small, bilateral IM since the KVA reduction is slightly larger than the MVA increase. However, posting the regulatory IM amount (100% multiplier) is not optimal.

The above results depend on the bank's assessment of the cost of capital and funding IM. Figure 20.11 shows a similar example, but where the bank's cost of capital is perceived to be higher and its cost of funding lower. In this case, a larger bilateral IM posting is optimal, and the regulatory requirement is not far away from this optimum.

It may be expected that IM posting would be more favoured under internal model method (IMM) approaches, since the capital relief achievable may be better (although the capital requirements without IM will also be lower).

Note that the above result is not spurious – for example, due to the Modigliani–Miller theorem (Section 14.1) – and is largely driven by the nature of regulatory capital rules.

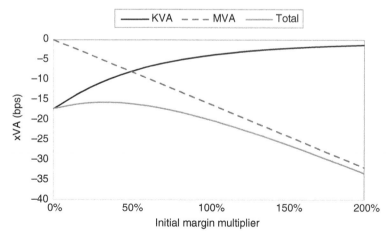

Figure 20.10   KVA and MVA in bps upfront for a 10-year interest rate swap, as a function of the bilateral IM posted with a 100% multiplier corresponding to the SIMM result. A cost of capital of 12% is assumed, with a funding cost of IM of 80 bp pa.

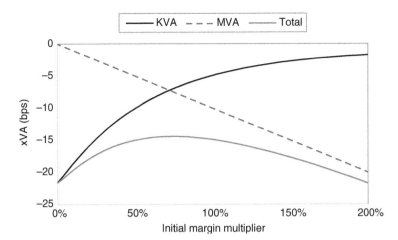

Figure 20.11 As in Figure 20.10, but with a cost of capital of 15% and a funding cost of IM of 50 bp pa.

However, clearly, the cost of funding debt and equity should be carefully chosen to represent correctly the impact of funding the balance sheet of the bank in question.

In general, regulatory bilateral IM requirements (which require a conservatively high amount to be exchanged) are not favoured purely via a reduction in KVA. This is not surprising, as this would imply a form of regulatory arbitrage where it is cheaper for banks to give each other capital than to hold it themselves.

Actively Managing xVA and the Role of an xVA Desk

21.1 THE ROLE OF AN xVA DESK

In this chapter, we look at the ways in which banks and other significant derivative users manage counterparty risk, funding, collateral (margin), and capital. Large banks have generally had 'CVA desks' for many years to facilitate the pricing and hedging of counterparty risk. These units have evolved into 'xVA desks', with a broader mandate including aspects such as funding, margin optimisation, and capital reduction. Smaller banks have, in recent years, embarked on the same process, driven by aspects such as IFRS 13 and Basel III. Even other financial institutions (e.g. supranationals) and non-financials (e.g. large corporates) have had the need to build some sort of xVA specialisation driven by accounting needs and pricing optimisation.

Most institutions have recognised the efficiencies of centralising xVA for both pricing and risk management. This allows risk to be managed across different business lines and also provides a centralised place for inception pricing. A key role of this centralised desk is to neutralise the overall xVA profit and loss (P&L) impact with respect to market movements. This has led to some xVA desks moving from a passive to a more active risk management role. This represents a significant challenge, as an xVA desk is essentially a cross-asset credit hybrid trading business with components that are difficult or impossible to hedge, such as illiquid credit risk and cross-gamma.

21.1.1 Motivation

Historically, derivatives pricing and valuation were thought to relate only to cash flows; aspects such as credit risk, funding, margin, and capital were ignored. In line with this, derivatives trading and risk management were siloed according to asset class (e.g. rates, foreign exchange (FX), commodities, equities, and credit) with the associated expertise. xVA is now a large part of derivatives pricing and valuation.

As xVA components have become more important, there has been a clear need to change approaches to pricing and valuation. However, xVA is not asset class specific and requires broad knowledge, not only of all asset classes, but also of underlying credit, margin, funding, and capital implications. It has been common to have an xVA desk (also known as a 'central desk' or 'scarce resource desk') to perform this function. This set-up is partly defined by a historical development: asset class-specific trading desks operate in much the same way, and the xVA desk picks up all of the complexities that have developed in recent times. However, this separation is also partly justified by the fact that xVA adjustments are often portfolio-level quantities and are not mutually exclusive, and their calculations are complex.

In general, the role of an xVA desk can be seen to address the following primary needs:

- *Pricing.* xVA arises heterogeneously, with long-dated trades, and lower quality and uncollateralised counterparties being the most significant contributors. It is important to charge the correct xVA to each transaction, taking into account the underlying incremental impact on counterparty risk, margin, funding, and capital. Failure to incorporate xVA correctly represents a failure to price properly. This, in turn, means that the correct compensation is not achieved for future costs. It is also important to consider aspects such as the restructuring of transactions and option exercising as part of the xVA pricing process. This creates the right incentives in terms of the utilisation of the balance sheet of a bank.
- *Valuation.* It follows that any xVA component in pricing should ideally be reflected in valuation so as to avoid spurious P&L being reported. It is also important to correctly capture and explain the volatility of xVA components. A general aim may be that the xVA priced at trade inception is 'locked in' over the lifetime without any additional costs (or benefits).
- *Optimisation.* Whilst some xVAs may represent hard costs, there are also situations where xVA can be optimised beneficially. Activities such as compression (Section 6.2.5), restructuring transactions, or margining terms can have a beneficial effect in terms of xVA reduction. The xVA desk is the best place to understand the benefits of such optimisation, especially where it may involve reducing one component (e.g. capital) at the increased cost of another (e.g. initial margin).
- *xVA management.* New transactions have impacts on credit limits, margin, funding, and capital requirements. These aspects are unpredictable and can also give rise to significant mark-to-market (MTM) volatility. It is, therefore, necessary for the xVA desk to own and – where desirable and possible – manage this underlying volatility.

An xVA desk is generally set up as a central unit within an institution. There is a benefit in centralising all the required expertise and systems in one place. It is also difficult to separate xVA components from pricing data (such as information on clearing prices, where a bank may have lost out on certain competitive transactions), but at least a centralised xVA desk should be able to aim to understand this. There are also cases where xVA components will be seen to interact and may not be additive, examples being:

- *Credit risk warehousing.* Due to the belief that warehousing credit risk will generate profits and, therefore, a lower credit value adjustment (CVA) can be charged (see also the comments in Section 19.4.1).
- *Workout process.* The assumption of a lower loss given default (LGD) from the view that the claim is more senior or will benefit from some form of structural support (Section 17.2.6).
- *Capital relief.* Reduction in capital value adjustment (KVA) due to the capital relief achieved from hedging – for example, with credit default swap (CDS) indices. See also the discussion in Section 13.3.6.

The above must be clearly rationalised and balanced against accounting policy, especially with respect to CVA, where accounting requirements are relatively prescriptive. For example, charging a lower CVA due to the view that LGD may be lower may lead to accounting losses due to the inability to include this assumption in the accounting CVA calculation.

21.1.2   Charging Structure and Coverage

It is informative to consider the historical development of CVA and how it has been managed in banks over the last three decades. In most major banks, there has been a historical development, which has involved the following activities in roughly the order presented below:

- *Pricing*. The need to correctly charge and not originate credit risk in derivatives too cheaply would tend to cause a bank to start to price CVA, potentially in line with the origination of credit risk in other areas, such as the corporate lending business. At this point, CVA would still be revenue but would provide a hurdle to entering a transaction.
- *Passive reserving*. Once CVA is clearly part of pricing, it makes sense to reserve these amounts so that they do not form part of revenue. Such a reserve can be used to absorb losses in the event of a counterparty default. However, in the absence of sufficient defaults, it will be released back to revenue. Whether this is done heterogeneously (CVA paid back at the transaction level) or more generally, the originating business will still see CVA as potentially being revenue.
- *Accounting*. The passive reserving eventually becomes a more rigorous accounting for CVA in financial reporting, potentially driven by accounting standards such as IFRS 13 and Financial Accounting Standards Board (FASB) 157 (Section 5.3.3).
- *Hard transfer*. There is a hard transfer of P&L from the originating business to the xVA desk in relation to underlying CVA. This is associated with the transfer of counterparty risk, which immunises the originating business against the risk of counterparty default. Typically, CVA would not ever be paid back unless the transaction was later unwound or restructured in some way.
- *Active management*. The final stage of the process is often the move towards active management of CVA, where xVA P&L is hedged so as to minimise accounting volatility. This has associated capital implications that must be considered (Section 13.3.6).

As previously mentioned, most major banks have already embraced all of the above in their approach to CVA – and, more broadly, xVA – pricing, valuation, and management. However, some smaller regional banks may still identify as being at an intermediate stage in the above developments.

An xVA desk is responsible for some or all of the below components, which collectively represent the cost of holding an over-the-counter (OTC) derivative to maturity:

- *Counterparty risk*. The most common and fundamental role of the xVA desk is to own the counterparty risk in the event of a counterparty default, but also to manage the MTM volatility of CVA.
- *Margin optimisation*. The xVA desk may be involved in margin optimisation by choosing the most efficient margin to post in line with pricing the 'cheapest-to-deliver' collateral (Section 16.2.3). Margin also mitigates various xVA components such as CVA, funding value adjustment (FVA), and KVA and, therefore, the negotiation and renegotiation of margin terms is a critical component of managing xVA.
- *Funding and margin*. The xVA desk may be responsible for managing funding and initial margin posting requirements and costs – for example, via hedging internally with a treasury department. The overlap between CVA, debt value adjustment (DVA), and FVA (Section 18.2.5) is also important in this respect.

Table 21.1   Consideration of xVA terms in different types of transaction.

	Uncollateralised	Collateralised	Overcollateralised
CVA	Yes	Partly	Partly
FVA	Yes	–	–
ColVA	–	Yes	Maybe
MVA	–	–	Yes
KVA	Yes	Yes	Yes

- *Capital.* Capital requirements for counterparty risk can be large and there are associated aspects such as the leverage ratio (Section 13.4.6). There may be a responsibility to manage the potential increase in capital requirements and reduce capital usage, for example, by hedging CVA with CDSs.

Note that some of the above roles are complementary. For example, hedging counterparty risk with CDSs with respect to either default events (single-name CDSs), or generic credit spread movements (index CDS) would also be expected to provide capital relief. However, these aspects are not always complementary, as discussed later.

Since xVA arises in different combinations for different types of transactions, the consideration of different xVA terms requires evaluation of a different sub-portfolio of derivatives transactions (Table 21.1). CVA and FVA are mainly concerned with uncollateralised transactions, although there may be some need to quantify CVA on collateralised or even overcollateralised portfolios. Collateral valuation adjustment (ColVA) exists only on collateralised and overcollateralised portfolios, although in the latter case, simplifications of the margin agreement may mean that it is less relevant. Margin value adjustment (MVA) is relevant only for overcollateralised portfolios where initial margin is present. KVA is relevant for all cases, although in some situations (e.g. central clearing) it may be considered far less relevant due to favourable capital requirements.

It is also important to constantly challenge xVA assumptions with anecdotal feedback from the salesforce and pricing resources such as the Totem xVA service (Section 5.3.5). This may avoid assumptions that may materially over- or underestimate xVA charges compared to peers and market practice.

A challenge for an xVA desk, especially in the early stages of development, is the coverage of transactions. It is important to address the biggest xVA users, which tend to be uncollateralised, long-dated transactions. For CVA assessment, it is possible to ignore many transactions, such as those that are well collateralised or with high-quality counterparties. However, the biggest xVA-related losses for banks in the global financial crisis arose from transactions with monoline insurers (Section 2.4.4), which were generally ignored for these reasons. Furthermore, xVA generally applies to every transaction in some way, and it is important to assess all components correctly.

From a pricing perspective, broadly speaking, there are two roles that an xVA desk can perform:

- *Transfer pricing.* Here, xVA pricing is similar to buying insurance. The xVA desk requires a hard transfer of cash, at inception, from a trading or sales desk, with respect to a given new transaction. The trading or sales desk, in turn, will charge this to the client, and any margin it can make on top of this is generally realised. It is hard for the originator (e.g. the trading desk) to avoid passing on the charge in full, since this would likely lead to them generating a loss (in limited situations they may do this in order to build the client relationship). The xVA is only returned in the event that the transaction is restructured or unwound and is, therefore, a real cost (or benefit).

• *Hurdles*. In this case, the xVA desk only sets a hurdle for the trading or sales desk to achieve, and there is no actual transfer of profit or risk. The originating desk is guided but not forced to charge this full amount to the client. Any charge is likely still to appear as revenue, and there is a reduced incentive to restructure transactions unless this can generate direct profit (as opposed to profit from xVA reduction).

Historically, xVA has tended to migrate from the latter to the former category as xVA desks have been built out. Smaller banks tend to follow more of a hurdle approach, whilst larger and more sophisticated ones transfer price. The increasing impact of accounting standards (e.g. IFRS 13), regulatory rules (Basel III capital requirements, leverage ratio), and market practice (FVA, MVA) have increased the need for active management of xVA, which, in turn, has led to the need for transfer pricing. However, not all xVA components are routinely transfer priced: the obvious current exception is capital (KVA), where hurdles to achieve the correct return on capital (ROC) are defined, but most banks have not yet moved to upfront transfer pricing of KVA. In the current environment, transactions may be executed even though their KVA is not sufficient to meet the relevant ROC hurdle. This situation will not materialise immediate losses, but will lead to poor returns compared to the required regulatory capital actually deployed over the lifetime of the transaction. This will be discussed in more detail in Section 21.3.2.

In the transfer pricing regime, xVA charges are typically not returned to the point of origination, even in the event of favourable outcomes (e.g. counterparties not defaulting). Such xVA charges are instead used indirectly or to offset other costs. For example, an xVA desk may use CVA premiums to buy options: this is not offsetting CVA per se, but is one component in managing CVA volatility. However, any other economic decision in relation to the trade (e.g. unwind, restructuring, option exercise – including cancellation – termination, or change in risk mitigants) should trigger an xVA adjustment. Indeed, in recent years, optimisation via various restructurings (e.g. unwinds, change in margining terms) has been proactively used by banks to minimise costs and maximise returns. An xVA desk should price such restructurings and pay out any xVA reduction so as to give trading and sales desks the right incentive in such situations.

In a hurdle-based regime, it is harder to incentivise the correct behaviour, since an xVA cost increase is not explicitly charged when entering a transaction and, by construction, cannot be paid out when exiting. However, in such a regime, it is easier to apply qualitative adjustments to xVA charges, such as the belief that a client will restructure or early-terminate transactions.

Note also that, when pricing a new transaction, aspects such as hedging activities have become increasingly important. For example, suppose a client executes a swap, which in turn is hedged with the reverse swap. Since this hedge is likely with a financial counterparty, it will give rise to initial margin costs either bilaterally or due to the requirement for central clearing. The cost of this initial margin may be charged to the original client, even though they themselves may be exempt from posting initial margin. At the current time, banks may only consider this to be important for large transactions, but it may become more standard to capture these components more rigorously.

21.1.3   Time Decay

An important aspect to understand in the management of xVA, in general, is the time decay ('theta') that is experienced against a real cost or benefit experienced in the future. This occurs because – all things being equal – the movement of time will cause xVA to become slightly smaller as the portfolio reduces in maturity. In opposition to this theta gain will be a future cost that is experienced over time in an unpredictable way. xVA components that are benefits will have a theta loss offsetting a potential future gain. The unpredictable nature of the cost or benefit leads to xVA volatility, some of which can be hedged and some of which is unhedgeable (Table 21.2).

Regarding CVA, the accrual cost comes from defaults, which usually cannot be hedged directly (unless there is a single-name CDS or similar contract available). The market risk in relation to CVA volatility can be hedged, although the credit spread risk may only be partially hedgeable. For ColVA, the theta term arises from (positive or negative) carry from the margin securities, together with the return from any margin transformation trades (e.g. repos). The cash component of this can be partly hedged, but the part involving securities may be unhedgeable. For funding (FVA/MVA) and capital (KVA), there are borrowing costs which are largely unhedgeable, but market risk which, as for CVA, can be hedged.

The performance of an xVA desk will ultimately be a balance between the carry component versus hedging costs (Table 21.3), together with other uncertain and unhedgeable components such as methodology changes. It is very important that the xVA desk has a clear mandate that is implemented via relevant metrics such as risk limits. A more aggressive strategy will tend to lead to lower P&L volatility but higher losses, due to the theta benefit being offset by the cost of hedging. On the other hand, a passive strategy – whilst cheaper in the long term – will create more short-term P&L volatility, which may not be acceptable.

Changes in documentation terms – such as the introduction of break clauses, thresholds or margin eligibility/terms, segregation, and initial margin – can all have material impacts on the risk characteristics of the exposure and, therefore, xVA. It is important that the xVA desk is a stakeholder in any documentation changes. It is also often the case that

Table 21.2 Accrual costs in opposition to xVA time decay.

	Accrual cost	Hedgeable components	Unhedgeable component
CVA	Defaults	Market risk	Defaults (usually), credit spread risk (partly)
ColVA	Remuneration of margin and transformation trades (e.g. repos)	Cash remuneration rates	Remuneration of securities
FVA/MVA	Funding costs	Market risk	Cost of funding
KVA	Dividends to shareholders	Market risk	Cost of capital/ regulatory change

Table 21.3 Example performance breakdown of an xVA desk.

P&L component	Gain/Loss	Comment
Net theta	37.3	Time decay of portfolio
New trades charged	4.2	Difference between charged amount and incremental xVA due to new trades (e.g. due to extra charges for hedging costs)
Cost of hedging	(17.3)	CDS hedging, vega hedging, bid/offer spreads
Defaults	(12.3)	Loss following workout process
Changes in methodology, static data and illiquid parameters	(6.5)	Rating changes change in recovery marks
Net P&L	5.4	

the xVA desk incentivises the salesforce to introduce these risk-mitigating factors into documentation by paying out the resulting reduction in CVA (and FVA).

Wrong-way risk (WWR) is present in all asset classes and embedded in all xVA portfolios. It is easily observable in hindsight, but dependency between a client exposure and market risk factors can evolve over time and be poorly represented by standard measures such as correlation. An example of a macro or general WWR can be represented as increased defaults when interest rates are low, which can be the worst time for a bank in terms of increased exposure in a one-directional receive fixed interest rate position. Specific WWR or tail risk is normally a result of concentrated exposures across multiple counterparties or oversized structural positions. Specific WWR can lead to severe negative cross-gamma losses, even when the client does not default.

The main challenge of WWR or tail risk is to identify and define scenarios in order to better understand the impact on xVAs and hence the P&L. This type of analysis, also described as stress testing, presents choices to better risk-manage the portfolio, to diversify the business away from a particular WWR scenario, or incentivise risk-reducing trades.

21.1.4   Profit Centre or Utility?

Another question is whether or not an xVA desk is a 'profit centre' or a 'utility', although these terms are generally not that distinct. It is generally agreed[1] that an xVA desk should be a utility function with a zero (or even slightly negative)[2] P&L target. This partially mitigates challenges such as when an xVA desk may be perceived to charge excessive prices, leading to reduced client revenue and lost business opportunities. A zero P&L target should also incentivise good behaviour for an xVA desk compared to a traditional trading desk. There should be no incentive to overcharge (or undercharge) xVA, and active management via hedging and paying out for risk-reducing transactions is encouraged. In an ideal world, xVA would represent the total cost of a transaction, and there would be no chance of the institution in question experiencing future losses in excess of this amount. The utility approach also implies that the xVA desk is not undertaking proprietary trading

---

[1] International Association of Credit Portfolio Managers (IACPM) Survey 2018.

[2] Due to hedging costs.

activity and would, for example, support a 'risk-mitigating hedging' exemption under the Volker rule in the US.[3]

Obviously, the above ideal is impractical as hedging xVA is imperfect. It is, therefore, important for a given institution to define its risk appetite to xVA. In general, the more one seeks to reduce the volatility of xVA, the greater will be the long-term cost. This is particularly true for counterparty risk: warehousing credit risk will lead to large CVA volatility, but expected long-term gains as actual credit losses are smaller than those priced in via risk-neutral default probabilities (Section 12.1.1). Banks traditionally warehouse credit risk arising from lending activities and have often looked at counterparty risk from derivatives in a similar fashion. This is particularly true for smaller and regional banks, and is especially relevant since the relative illiquidity of the CDS market makes hedging of counterparty risk on a single-name basis impossible in most cases. The warehousing approach to CVA has become increasingly difficult over the years due to developments such as IFRS 13 and Basel III. An xVA desk will need to have a carefully defined limits structure so that it cannot run significant open risks. That said, it should also have leeway to make tactical decisions when hedges might be expensive and inefficient and, subject to its limits, it may prefer to warehouse the risk. Some components will be relatively easy to hedge, some less so and some will be unhedgeable, as discussed in Section 21.2.4. Future capital requirements may create even more incentive to hedge CVA, with the greater recognition of CVA hedges as being capital reducing (Section 13.3.5).

With respect to other components, such as FVA, the incentive to hedge may or may not be stronger. On the one hand, without any potential benefit, such as the credit risk premium, hedging would seem natural. On the other hand, potential additional capital requirements for the hedges (since only CVA is considered explicitly in regulatory capital requirements) can be problematic. This is discussed in more detail in Section 21.2.9.

Reducing P&L volatility is one of the primary purposes of an xVA desk's hedging activity, although capital considerations can also sometimes play a part in this process. Due to the relative illiquidity of many of the hedging instruments, it is important to have a practical balance between minimising volatility and trading costs. Hedging is, to a degree, discretionary in nature due to the complexity of the xVA risk and the significant transaction costs, especially with respect to credit risk.

The key to running a successful xVA desk is to find the right balance between inception pricing, risk taking, and active hedging. Although xVA may be hedged to avoid dramatic P&L swings, it is not possible to hedge perfectly, and the residual risks and resultant P&L need to be understood by stakeholders and senior management. As an xVA desk has a P&L component, it is normal to view the desk as a trading desk; however, unlike most trading desks, it is typically not expected to be a profit centre. The zero or negative P&L target implies requiring a balance between xVA prices charged at inception to cover the risk and the general interests of the firm in advancing its business.

Given that xVA hedging is sometimes not possible or desirable, whilst an xVA desk may have a zero P&L target, it is important to consider the allocation of potential excess gains or losses periodically in some way. Some of these losses or gains may be accounting driven

---

[3] This may only be relevant for US banks. Non-US banks may have a TOTUS (trading outside the United States) exemption for their xVA desks.

(e.g. from a credit spread widening), whilst some will be actually realised (e.g. default losses). In the former case, a homogenous allocation back to the point of origination would be most obvious, potentially weighted by the xVA charge (i.e. those paying the most xVA will experience most of the excess gains or losses). In some scenarios, such as defaults, it may be appropriate to consider a more heterogeneous allocation to the point of origination. Otherwise, there is a potential adverse selection problem that the originating salesperson or trader may choose to transact with the wrong type of clients (e.g. lower credit quality), based on the fact that all risks are perceived to be passed fully to the xVA desk. In some client relationships, the originating trader or business may be best placed to understand the nature of the underlying risk, especially in relation to complex aspects such as WWR. Of course, this type of allocation may also be seen as unfair in some situations.

In the event of default, the workout process (the process of negotiating claims with a defaulted counterparty) is also important, and the xVA desk should be an active participant, managing its claims optimally.

21.1.5 Pricing

The xVA charge is often the key determinant in the price of a derivative, in particular for many end user transactions, and especially if they are long-dated and/or uncollateralised. A key aspect of the transfer pricing of xVA is, therefore, that there must be a robust and industrialised process in place for the calculation of xVA charges in real time. To do this properly is complex from both an operations and a systems point of view, and simple methods are sometimes used by necessity. The ways in which real-time pricing is implemented vary in sophistication, as below:

- *Static definitions*. A static definition, such as a lookup grid with dimensions of product type, maturity, and counterparty credit quality, will provide an easy estimate of an xVA charge. Such calculations cannot, of course, account for trade specifics or risk mitigants, but they do make for a very simple, rapid, and transparent approach. There may be little or no consideration of the nature of the counterparty. Such approaches are required in many markets where price quotation has to be either immediate (electronic trading) or rapid. Of course, in such markets, xVA will be low or immaterial due to the level of collateralisation and the short-dated maturity of the underlying transaction.
- *Standalone calculations*. Standalone xVA pricing for given products can be implemented relatively simply (e.g. in spreadsheets) and does capture more transaction-specific aspects, but ignores potential risk mitigants. For directional transactions, this is sometimes not as problematic, as components such as netting may be only weak.
- *Full simulation-based pricing*. Incorporation of all aspects (especially netting and margining) can only be done accurately with simulation-based approaches that can run the entire portfolio of transactions. This needs to consider counterparty-specific terms, but also aggregate at the appropriate portfolio level (which depends on the xVA term in question). Practically, this requires a simulation engine that can generate all relevant market variables and compute values of the current portfolio and the new transaction in all required scenarios through time. This requires very rapid processing power and/or the use of significant data storage.

Full simulation-based pricing is a requirement for accurate incremental pricing at the counterparty or portfolio level. As discussed previously (see Figure 15.15), the aggregation level is important here. In particular:

- *CVA and DVA*. CVA and DVA are typically required at the netting set level. This will usually be the same as the counterparty level, but could, in theory, be different if there is more than one netting agreement for the counterparty.
- *FVA*. Depending on the nature of the margin agreement and the underlying assumptions, FVA may need to be calculated at the standalone (transaction) level or potentially the entire portfolio level (Section 18.3.2).
- *MVA*. The computation of initial margin for bilateral transactions will be at the portfolio level (unless a simple methodology, such as the standardised schedule shown in Table 7.11, is used). For centrally-cleared transactions, the initial margin will be calculated depending on the extent of the cross-margining at the central counterparty (CCP). Typically, this means that all transactions within an asset class at the same CCP will constitute the portfolio for the calculation.
- *KVA*. The counterparty credit risk (CCR) capital charge (Section 13.2) is linear across netting sets and, therefore, follows a similar calculation to CVA. The leverage ratio depends on a similar methodology. However, due to the portfolio-level assumptions for CVA capital, this element of KVA would, in theory, constitute a calculation for the whole portfolio.

The requirement for near real-time calculations with a flexible level of aggregation requires relatively sophisticated systems implementations, which will be discussed below. In most banks, the volume of pricing requests is too large for them all to be funnelled through the xVA desk (although the particularly large ones may well be),[4] which means that the implementation also needs to be robust enough to be useable by non-xVA specialists.

Note that it is not only new transactions that need to be priced. Anything that represents a choice and has an economic implication for xVA needs to be considered, such as:

- restructuring (of transactions or portfolios);
- novations (the replacement of a party in a transaction or portfolio, which may involve reducing or taking on new exposure);
- changing margining terms or credit support annexe (CSA) renegotiation; or
- moving bilateral transactions to a CCP ('backloading').

All of these factors will have an impact on one or more xVA terms and may need to be quantified on a dynamic basis. From a bank's perspective, the above situations are usually proactively used to reduce xVA. The xVA desk will be able to incentivise them by at least partially paying out any accounting xVA gains (see Figure 5.3). Two further related situations are:

- option exercise (including cancellation); and
- exercise of a break clause.

---

[4] Usually defined in terms of a metric such as the delta of the transaction, which combines size and maturity as the key determinants.

A break clause such as an additional termination event (ATE) or 'mutual put' (Section 7.1.1) may be easier to deal with quantitatively since it will typically cause xVA to be cancelled, and it is, therefore, always optimal to break where possible (unless the overall xVA is seen as a benefit). Indeed, banks are much more likely nowadays to terminate such transactions or charge clients for not doing so (and communicate upfront to clients that they will do this). However, if break clauses are linked to a trigger event, such as a rating downgrade, then they are much more difficult to quantify and impossible to hedge.

Option exercises are complex because they involve the overall value of the underlying, not merely xVA, and essentially xVA changes the exercise boundary. For example, the exercise of a physically-settled swaption should be done optimally with respect to the xVA components of the underlying swap. Failure to do so may lead to sub-optimal exercising, where the base value of the swap is positive, but the xVA-adjusted value is not. Ideally, an xVA desk would impose a cost or refund on any economic decision to avoid this. This may translate into a conditional xVA charge for exercising an option, or a rebate for cancelling a transaction, so as to achieve the correct exercise boundary.

Banks will also sometimes incorporate behaviour-driven adjustments in xVA, such as charging less for a transaction in anticipation of future, more profitable transactions, or the assumption that it will be unwound or restructured later and lifetime xVA costs will not, therefore, be realised. Note that, when the xVA term is considered as a transfer price rather than a hurdle (Section 21.1.2), this is more difficult to achieve, as the xVA desk will be unable to accept a loss in the hope or expectation of a later xVA benefit. Indeed, this is why, currently, banks may be willing to apply behavioural assumptions to ROC (KVA) but not CVA or FVA costs.

21.2   HEDGING

21.2.1   Overview

The increasing volatility of xVA has led more banks to consider some sort of hedging strategy. A key aspect of xVA, as mentioned first in Section 5.2.1, is the ability to separate the basic valuation of a derivative from xVA adjustments. The same applies to hedging (Figure 21.1): whilst the market risks on a derivative may be hedged by a trading desk in isolation, the xVA desk will seek to hedge its own market risk. This separation of xVA is relevant due to the asset-specific nature of different classes of derivatives, combined with the fact that xVA generally depends on counterparty risk, margin, funding, and capital. Additionally, whilst the basic valuation of any derivative portfolio is additive, xVAs generally are not. This requires special treatment of xVA hedging at the portfolio level. Furthermore, xVA tends to be more complex than basic valuation, often involving components such as volatility and cross-gamma, which may be dramatically more complex, especially for simple products.

An xVA portfolio will experience sensitivity to every single market parameter for the underlying transactions in every currency, asset class, and product type. Furthermore, there will be sensitivities specific to xVA, such as where volatility risk arises from non-volatility-sensitive products. It is possible to compare xVA management to managing a book of options. For example, the Sorensen–Bollier analogy that represents swap exposure as a series of European swaptions (Section 15.1.3) implies that the problem of

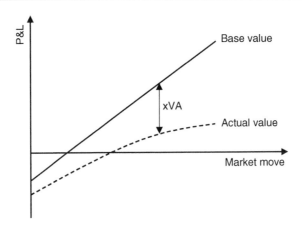

Figure 21.1   Illustration of xVA hedging.

hedging should be approached in a similar way to that of hedging options. Furthermore, this 'option book' is fairly complex, with aspects such as cross-asset exposure and moneyness being important considerations.

It is important to be pragmatic and bear in mind that some components can be hedged, some can be hedged with difficulty, leading to residual basis risks, and some cannot be hedged at all. In order to understand this, take a simple example of hedging xVA on an interest rate swap. xVA is sensitive to interest rates, interest rate volatility, and credit spreads, and so to hedge could require an interest rate swap, single-name CDS, and interest rate swaption. In theory, these hedges would not be single transactions (e.g. one would hedge with a series of swaptions to match the vega profile). The single-name CDS that would ideally be used is likely to be illiquid, and so some index or another proxy must be utilised. The hedges will also require frequent rebalancing as market movements occur. Finally, even if xVA is hedged on rates and credit, a simultaneous move where interest rates go down and credit spreads widen can cause significant P&L movements (cross-gamma).

It is also important to emphasise that xVA hedging for reducing P&L volatility alone may not be the only consideration. There are at least three different aspects here:

- *Actual economic risk.* The actual underlying financial risk (e.g. defaults).
- *Accounting xVA.* The changes in xVA driven by the accounting practices (e.g. credit spread widening).
- *Regulatory capital.* The regulatory capital requirements.

In an ideal world, the above would be perfectly aligned but, in reality, the misalignment can be significant. For example, DVA is a component of accounting xVA that is not generally recognised as being economically realistic (Section 17.3.5). Banks generally view FVA as being an important consideration (Section 18.2.1), but it is not yet mentioned in accounting standards or regulatory capital rules. Different banks will have a different focus on the above: a bank that is capital constrained may primarily aim to reduce capital, whereas another may focus on reducing accounting volatility. There are also potential issues with some xVA hedges increasing regulatory capital requirements, as discussed in Section 21.3.2.

Finally, any change in funding and capital costs will potentially impact the P&L of the xVA desk. However, this generally reflects internal parameters, such as a return on equity (ROE) target or a funds transfer pricing (FTP) curve. These parameters are likely to be semistationary, although indirectly driven by continuously evolving market rates. Any changes here will cause a P&L move that is very difficult to hedge, and it is probably not relevant to continuously remark such parameters, since this will merely cause spurious P&L volatility for the xVA desk. However, when such rates are changed, there will be a P&L change that may have to be absorbed by the xVA desk.

21.2.2   Sensitivities

In general, xVA can be represented as a combination of market risk and some underlying credit, margin, funding, or capital cost. It is possible to discuss the hedging of xVA in general without specific reference to the terms under consideration.

The market risk sensitivity of xVA can be broadly broken down into:

- *Spot/forward rates*. The sensitivity to spot and forward rates, such as interest rates and FX. This is generally hedgeable, with the underlying hedging instruments being liquid, potentially exchange-traded or centrally cleared.
- *Volatility*. The sensitivity to implied volatility, such as FX options or interest rate swaptions. This is also hedgeable, although the underlying instruments will generally be bilateral OTC products and may be illiquid and unavailable in some cases. For example, hedging long-dated volatility may not be possible.
- *Correlation*. The sensitivity to the correlation between different exposure variables (such as two different interest rates). This is generally unhedgeable, except via exotic products such as quantos, basket options, and spread options, which are not usually liquid.

Note that market risk will be hedged on aggregate and not at the counterparty level, and it is also helpful to combine market risk hedges across some or all xVA terms. For example, an interest rate hedge may exist because an increase in rates could cause both CVA and FVA to increase. If an xVA desk does not have the mandate to hedge the change in a particular component (e.g. capital costs via KVA), then this would obviously not be included in its P&L.

The number of sensitivities that the above categories can constitute is large, even in some rather simple cases, let alone for large portfolios of trades. Due to the cross-asset nature of xVA, the number of sensitivities (or Greeks) can become very large, even for vanilla trades. For example, a single vanilla cross-currency swap will give rise to the following CVA risks:

- interest rate risk (for the two currencies);
- interest rate basis risk;
- interest rate volatility (for the two currencies);
- FX spot risk;
- FX vega risk;
- cross-currency basis risk;
- credit delta;

- gamma/jump to default (JTD) risk (the impact of a large credit spread movement or default); and
- cross-gamma (correlation) between market risk factors themselves (interest rates and FX), and between credit risk and market risk factors (interest rates and FX to credit risk).

All hedges should also ideally be considered across the term structure, which is often impractical as it leads to increasing numbers of hedging transactions. Other xVA terms will introduce more sensitivities, such as the relationship to the cost of funding in the case of FVA. There is also the need to consider the sensitivity to credit spreads and other components such as funding costs.

A general representation of xVA Greeks is set out below:

$$\partial x VA = \frac{\partial x VA}{\partial S} \Delta S + \frac{\partial x VA}{\partial E} \Delta E + \frac{\partial x VA}{\partial t} \Delta t + \frac{\partial^2 x VA}{\partial S \, \partial E} \Delta S \, \Delta E \qquad (21.1)$$

xVA sensitivity with respect to spreads

xVA sensitivity with respect to exposure

xVA sensitivity with respect to time (theta)

Cross-gammas

In general, sensitivities can be seen to be broken down into exposure (E) components (such as interest rate and FX deltas) and vegas, spread (S) components (such as credit deltas), and cross-gamma components. Not shown in the above are cross-gammas between exposure terms (e.g. interest rate and FX) and second-order (gamma) terms in general.

From a hedging point of view, it is possible to consider – broadly speaking – four categories:

- *Liquid hedges.* Where the underlying risk is reasonably straightforward to hedge and where the underlying costs of doing this are only small or moderate due to liquid hedging instruments. An example of this is interest rate and FX delta hedges.
- *Illiquid hedges.* Where the underlying risk can be hedged but the associated hedging costs are relatively high, such as when hedging vega, which would involve, for example, buying swaptions and FX options.
- *Proxy hedges.* Where the underlying risk can only be hedged using instruments that are correlated to the underlying sensitivity, such as when using CDS indices to hedge credit delta or buying out-of-the-money (OTM) options so as to hedge 'tail risk'.
- *No hedge.* Where the underlying risk cannot be practically hedged, such as with respect to correlations or cross-gamma, except on a completely bespoke basis.

It is also important to note that there may be exposure to multiple currencies, FX pairs, etc. In such cases, it may be relevant to actively hedge certain components that are linked to large exposures, but treat other, less significant components less dynamically or not hedge them at all. There may also be proxies used for calibration, such as using swaptions in one currency to calibrate interest rate volatility for another currency where there is no volatility market. In these cases, it may be possible to reduce accounting volatility by hedging, although this may not provide regulatory capital relief.

Whilst market risk hedging is reasonably practical, the hedging of credit and funding aspects is less straightforward. Credit hedging is clearly more difficult due to the illiquidity of the underlying CDS market. Potential hedging instruments are:

- *Single-name CDS.* If liquid, then this is the ideal hedge against counterparty credit quality. However, there is a difference between hedging the credit spread and the JTD risk. In the former case, the focus is on a small credit spread change, and the latter on an actual default event (Section 17.2.5). Ideally, one should buy protection from a high-quality counterparty with minimal correlation to the original counterparty (if the CDS is centrally cleared, then this may be viewed as resolving this problem).
- *Single-name proxy CDS.* Hedging using a similar credit may be viewed as efficient, although this obviously depends on the underlying credit spread correlation. Also important is whether the proxy credit would default in the same situations. In some situations, this may be the case (e.g. the proxy is a sovereign that would always support the counterparty in question) and in some cases not (e.g. a name in a similar region and sector).
- *Index CDS.* Credit indices are more liquid and can be used to provide a macro-hedge of a general credit spread widening, but do not provide any protection against actual counterparty default.[5] The benefit of index hedging (and associated capital relief) also depends heavily on there being a significant correlation between the index and single-name CDS, which may not always be observed in practice.[6]

Due to the above, most institutions would consider some credit hedging to be relevant in order to avoid excessive fluctuation in their accounting CVA. They may also use, where possible, credit options to manage convexity and single-name CDSs to hedge large exposures.

Hedging of funding costs is generally not possible, but in case the xVA desk is responsible for these costs, credit indices would be one potential proxy. This depends on the policy for setting the funding cost for FVA purposes. Capital costs are also largely unhedgeable.

In an xVA context where multiple terms may be hedged in aggregate (e.g. CVA and DVA or CVA and FVA), different sensitivities may either be additive or will offset one another. In general, exposure deltas (e.g. interest rate and FX delta hedges) will tend to be in the same direction for all xVA terms, leading to a larger overall sensitivity. On the other hand, credit deltas and vegas will tend to offset, since CVA/FCA (funding cost adjustment) hedges would tend to involve buying vega and credit protection, whilst DVA/FBA (funding benefit adjustment) hedges would sell vega and credit protection.

As an example, Table 21.4 shows the Greeks for a receiver interest rate swap. An increase in interest rates will cause the swap to be more OTM, which will reduce expected positive exposure (EPE) and increase expected negative exposure (ENE). This will, in turn, make CVA less negative and DVA more positive, both of which are positive effects. In the case of a vega, both the EPE and the ENE will increase, and the effect will be offsetting (CVA impact negative, DVA positive). The credit spread sensitivity causes a similar effect to that of the vega. The impact on FCA and FBA follows that of CVA and DVA, respectively.

---

[5] Except implicitly because the name happened to be referenced in the index.
[6] Sherif, N. (2015). CDS de-correlation a threat to CVA hedging, traders warn. *Risk* (3 September). www.risk.net.

Table 21.4 xVA Greeks for a 100 million notional receive fixed 10-year interest rate swap. The deltas are with respect to a parallel shift of the curve (of 1 bp), whilst the vega is calculated based on a 1% increase in the implied volatility.

	Interest rate delta (DV01)	Interest rate vega	Credit spread delta (CS01)
CVA	1,083	−3,848	−1,487
DVA	1,271	1,640	2,252
FCA	540	−2,022	−1,507
FBA	1,400	1,750	2,328

As discussed in Section 15.3, the calculation of xVA is computationally demanding due (usually) to the use of Monte Carlo simulation and the need to evolve the portfolio across the entire lifetime of trades (which in turn require full revaluation). If sensitivities are calculated using a finite-difference 'bump-and-run' approach, then there is potentially adverse linear scaling with respect to computation time and the total number of sensitivities required. Whilst optimisations are possible,[7] this does require a significant degree of computational power, unless a method such as adjoint algorithmic differentiation (AAD) is used.[8] It is often important to limit the sensitivities that will be calculated to ones that are required for hedging purposes, or in order to be able to explain materially-important P&L movements. Furthermore, in the case of curves, it is important to choose a relatively compact representation of the risk to minimise the number of sensitivity calculations required. Note that simplifying assumptions such as constant basis (Section 15.4.2) keep the required number of sensitivities low, as they essentially mean that the sensitivity to multiple curves is calculated altogether.

Banks may also choose to calculate a number of important sensitivities on a daily basis, and some less important ones less frequently (e.g. weekly basis). This may also apply to running stress scenarios, which may represent large and/or simultaneous moves in various risk factors. Since such scenarios define the general directionality and risk of an xVA portfolio, they do not typically need to be recalculated on a very frequent basis.

In the event that the xVA calculation assumes independence between the exposure and spread components (no WWR), credit-related sensitivity calculations are greatly simplified. This is because defaults are not simulated and the calculation is based only on an analytical calculation of default probabilities (e.g. Equation 12.1). This also applies to cross-gamma components, including credit risk elements. An example of this would be that – in a no-WWR setting – a credit delta calculation should be very fast, as it would not require the Monte Carlo simulation to be rerun. Credit rates cross-gammas would also be easy to calculate, as long as they were evaluated alongside the relevant interest rate bump scenario.

Technical problems with xVA models can also cause hedging problems. For example, potential instability of calibrated parameters can cause day-to-day swings in xVA and the

---

[7] For example, only updating valuations for trades which are sensitive to a given risk factor change. This can be implemented algorithmically (e.g. if a valuation does not change in a given simulation, then other instances in other simulations are not revalued) or via a mapping of each trade to the dependent market data.

[8] AAD uses the chain rule to compute derivatives automatically within a computer algorithm. It has been implemented by some banks to provide an efficient calculation of many xVA Greeks at a fixed cost (see Section 21.3.3).

associated sensitivities. Clearly, it is desirable to reduce such effects, which is why simple and more parsimonious xVA models are often preferred. Another example is that the time discretisation of the xVA integral can be problematic moving from one day to another, as cash flows move between discretisation dates. This is less easy to control and is often simply accepted as creating background noise.

Most banks compute xVA for collateralised counterparties based on assumptions around the close-out process and the value of the margin period of risk (MPoR). However, this is an inherently quite subjective and noisy calculation due to the precise assumptions regarding the margin exchange and cash flows within the MPoR, and can be particularly problematic where cash flow payments fall inside the MPoR. As a consequence, many banks are less concerned with hedging and with P&L explain of such counterparties, which may also make up only a relatively small fraction of the total xVA.

21.2.3   Gamma, Cross-gamma, Tail Risk, and Rebalancing

Gamma refers to the change in the delta, and a large gamma will, therefore, make a required delta hedge change significantly with market conditions. Where there is significant gamma or convexity with respect to a delta-hedged parameter, it may be helpful to construct a profile that better matches this gamma (e.g. buying swaptions against interest rate sensitivity). This would be more expensive upfront, but would reduce the need to balance the delta position frequently.

Whilst gamma generally refers to a large move in an underlying variable, cross-gamma refers to the joint move of two variables. Even if the two variables are hedged or explained independently, their *joint* move may have a material impact. Cross-gamma components are typically unhedgeable, but can be sizeable for xVA portfolios, especially the credit-related cross-gamma terms. As an illustration of cross-gamma, Figure 21.2 shows the credit spread sensitivity (CS01) for a receive fixed interest rate swap for different levels of interest rates. As interest rates increase, the swap moves OTM and the credit

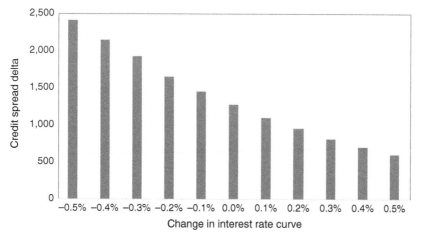

Figure 21.2   CVA credit spread sensitivity (parallel CS01) as a function of different parallel interest rate moves for an interest rate swap. Note that the CS01 is defined by a negative shift of one basis point and is, therefore, a positive number.

delta reduces, and vice versa. In practical terms, cross-gamma might be experienced as a result of a major market movement, such as interest rates falling, together with a credit spread widening. In such a situation, the larger uncollateralised exposures on receiver swap positions will then require more credit hedges, but the cost of these hedges will not be funded by gains on existing interest rate hedges, unless these accounted for the underlying cross-gamma effect.

Cross-gamma is often realised when there is a significant move in two underlying variables that effectively amounts to a delivered correlation of close to +/-100%, associated with large volatility. This often occurs in the aftermath of a significant event: for example, the vote in the European Union referendum on 23 June 2016. This event led to GBP swap rates tightening and credit spreads widening. For interest rate swaps receiving the fixed rate, this would have led the swap to have a larger exposure, coupled with a deterioration in the underlying credit quality, leading to losses even if interest rates and credit spreads were delta hedged on an individual basis.[9]

Cross-gamma is generally unhedgeable, but can be partially neutralised in various ways:

- Finding a direct hedge. For example, it is possible to trade CDS protection in two currencies (Section 17.6.4) against a reference entity which allows a hedge against a potential credit/FX WWR and, therefore, cross-gamma.
- Overhedging or underhedging the relevant deltas based on the known directionality of the position, together with a market view. Due to the over- or underhedging, this leads to more P&L volatility in normal scenarios, but a lower change in a more extreme scenario.
- Buying options referencing one or both underlying risk factors. Hedging of these types of risk typically involves buying OTM options which have a low delta but more significant gamma.

Individually and jointly stress testing each of the market input variables used in calculating xVA allows the xVA desk to gain an understanding of the portfolio behaviour in various environments. When an adverse scenario is identified (e.g. internet rate tightening and credit spread widening), consideration should be given to how to best manage the scenario by either adopting a hedging strategy or incentivising risk reduction and diversification by the business.

Due to the relative illiquidity of xVA hedges, rebalancing must be done pragmatically, with the underlying bid-offer costs taken into account. Being able to hedge some convexity components may be an efficient way to reduce rebalancing costs if the convexity hedges are not prohibitively expensive. For example, some banks will use swaptions together with a normal delta hedge to manage their interest rate sensitivity, the advantage being that the hedges remain relatively stable for moderate moves in the underlying.

As noted above, banks often charge xVA to mid. Due to hedging costs, this will be likely to lead to P&L losses, which should at the least be understood. Sometimes – and where systems are sophisticated enough – there will be additional charges for approximate rehedging costs. This requires an incremental calculation of the hedging costs, as illustrated for credit delta (which is likely to be the most significant) in Table 21.5. Here, a bank may charge for a certain bid-offer for the rehedging. For example, if the bid-offer

---

[9] Sherif, N. (2016). CVA desks suffer Brexit double whammy. *Risk* (30 June). www.risk.net.

Table 21.5 Illustration of the calculation of rehedging costs.

Tenor	CS01 (before)	CS01 (after)	CS01 change
6 months	−11,380	−7,988	−3,390
1 year	13,845	8,458	5,387
2 years	4,000	631	3,371
3 years	2,732	2,341	391
4 years	5,959	7,278	−1,319
5 years	11,427	11,472	−44
7 years	9,824	9,676	148
10 years	5,501	5,384	117
Total	41,912	37,249	4,661

were 10 basis points (bps) and the duration of the portfolio was four years, then a charge of half the bid-offer times the net CS01 sensitivity times the duration would be 4,661 × 5 × 4 = 93,220, which may be added to the other incremental xVA components. This envisages a hedge of only the overall sensitivity. If all tenors were to be rehedged, then the gross CS01 change would be more relevant (although, given the liquidity of the CDS market, this is unlikely).

21.2.4   Market Practice

Many large banks now have a fairly long history of hedging CVA. Hedging is generally, to a degree, discretionary in nature (Figure 21.3), due to the complexity of CVA risk and the underlying illiquidity or lack of availability of hedges. Market risk hedges are most common, which is not surprising due to the underlying instruments being the most liquid and not being subject to significant additional counterparty risks. Credit spread risk is the next most commonly hedged, but it is less liquid and, as noted above, banks would

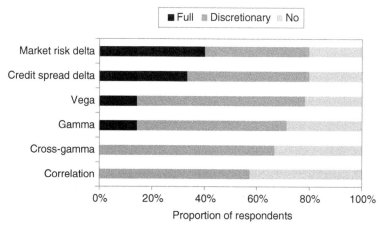

Figure 21.3   Market practice on hedging of CVA Greeks. Source: Deloitte/Solum CVA Survey (2013).

Table 21.6 Summary of market practice with respect to xVA hedging.

Risk factor	Practicality of hedging	Market practice
DV01s (interest rate, FX, inflation, etc.)	• Liquid	• Usually hedged
Volatility (swaptions, FX options, etc.)	• Less liquid • Long-dated and OTM volatility harder to access	• May be hedged (e.g. major currencies and FX pairs)
Credit CS01	• Relatively liquid (indices) • Illiquid (single-name CDS)	• May be hedged or partially hedged with credit indices
Correlation and cross-gamma (e.g. rates–rates, rates–FX)	• Not liquid	• Only hedged in special and bespoke circumstances

prefer in general to warehouse some counterparty risk. Not surprisingly, vegas, gammas, and other terms are less commonly hedged.

Most banks hedge the market risk of CVA in aggregate with FVA, although a small number still hedge CVA and DVA. An xVA desk will pay the mid-to-bid or mid-to-offer when hedging its positions, as illustrated in Table 21.5. This is a real cost, since standard xVA pricing will usually be calculated at mid. Whilst bid/offer of standard rates and FX hedging instruments may be quite small, CDS bid-offer spreads are quite significant, even for index hedges.

A summary of the market practice on hedging is given in Table 21.6. Exposure delta (DV01) risk is hedged by most banks (in full or in part) and on the most frequent basis. This is due to underlying hedges being the most liquid. Interest rate hedges are generally liquid, with futures being the cheapest hedges for directional risk. Swaps for hedging curve risk are quite liquid in major currencies for all tenors of the swap curve up to 10 years. Long-dated swaps can sometimes be less liquid. Due to the number of different interest rate curves (London Interbank Offered Rate, overnight indexed spread, short-term interest rates – STIRs), basis risk can be material, giving rise to some P&L volatility. Spot FX markets for most currency pairs are also quite liquid.

An xVA book is almost always short volatility risk (vega). Vega is more difficult to hedge and is, therefore, not hedged as frequently, except in situations where the underlying sensitivity is very large. In some specific cases, buying vega can be a macro-hedge for managing WWR in situations where the currency is correlated to the creditworthiness of large companies in those countries. It can also allow a closer match to the profile and, therefore, requires a less frequent rebalancing of DV01 hedges.

Correlation and cross-gamma hedges are completely illiquid and are only done in special circumstances.

Credit risk delta (CS01) is sometimes hedged, but it can generally only be done on a macro basis, given the illiquidity of the single-name CDS market (especially for typical uncollateralised counterparties such as non-financial corporations). Proxy single-name hedges (e.g. a parent company or sovereign) may be available and used for some counterparties, but single-name CDSs are generally illiquid, except for large counterparties, and even then they are generally available only for financial institutions and sovereigns (see discussion in Section 12.2.2). Due to the relative illiquidity of most

Table 21.7 Summary of market practice with respect to hedging CVA (and potentially DVA, if relevant) credit risk.

Hedging instrument	Practicality	Market practice
Index CDS	• Reasonable liquidity • Spread hedging • Benefit linked to mapping methodology	• Hedged for P&L volatility reduction and capital relief
Proxy single-name CDS	• Limited liquidity • Spread hedge • Possible partial JTD hedge	• Sometimes used for P&L volatility reduction
Single-name CDS	• Very limited liquidity • Spread hedge • JTD hedge	• Hedged where liquid for P&L volatility reduction, capital relief, and JTD hedging

CDS tenors, there is also a balance between hedging curve risk and minimising bid-offer costs. Due to the better liquidity in five-year CDS maturities, xVA desks tend to build up a 'steepener' position over time, which must be managed by, for example, rolling index hedging into the on-the-run index after each index roll and rehedging single-name CDS positions periodically.

In addition, most banks ideally do not want to hedge credit risk, since this is often seen as being profitable (due to the inherent risk premiums). Hence, the hedging of credit is generally driven by the need to reduce P&L volatility (and possibly capital), rather than to reduce actual economic risk. The key considerations relating to credit risk hedging for CVA are set out in Table 21.7 below.

21.2.5   Jump to Default Risk

Whilst credit hedging is primarily done to minimise P&L volatility, xVA desks also need to analyse potential default scenarios, especially for distressed counterparties. As discussed in Section 17.2.5, the impact of a sudden default for a delta-hedged counterparty can be either positive or negative, depending on the current exposure.

A calculation of JTD P&L can be represented as follows:

$$-Current\ exposure \times Assumed\ LGD$$

$$+Notional\ of\ CDS\ hedge^{10} \times Assumed\ CDS\ LGD \qquad (21.2)$$

$$-Current\ xVA\ contribution\ for\ counterparty$$

When the above term is negative, it provides an estimate of the potential loss in the event of default, considering exposure, recovery rates, CDS notional, and xVA release.

---

[10] Note that this should reference the counterparty directly, but can include protection via being long an index, where the counterparty is one of the reference names.

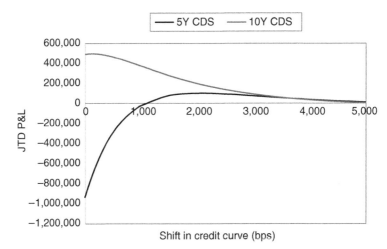

Figure 21.4 JTD P&L as a function of the positive shift in the credit curve for a 10-year ITM interest rate swap, assuming a hedge of the credit spread sensitivity with a single-name CDS hedge of either five- or 10-year maturity.

For in-the-money (ITM) portfolios that do not have single-name CDS hedges, JTD risk is always negative and driven by the size of the current exposure less the xVA contribution (which is generally small in comparison). When there is a single-name CDS hedge, JTD risk is more complex and depends on the level of the current exposure and the maturity of the portfolio and CDS hedge. As an example, Figure 21.4 shows JTD P&L for an ITM receive fixed interest rate swap, which is assumed to be delta hedged with a single-name CDS. For the 10-year CDS, there is JTD risk, which reduces as the credit spread widens. With the five-year CDS, a larger notional is required to neutralise the credit spread volatility, which makes JTD P&L positive. As the credit spread widens and the counterparty moves towards default, JTD tends to zero, but not necessarily in a monotonic fashion.

JTD risk can only realistically be hedged by adjusting the credit spread delta by tenor (e.g. buying short-term protection). Whilst this is often not possible, it is good practice to report and monitor JTD values for each counterparty and consider acting if these become relatively large and/or the credit quality deteriorates.

21.2.6 Beta Hedging

The potential for hedging with indices or proxy single-name CDS raises the question of the efficiency of such a hedge. The hedging of one underlying with another different but correlated asset is often known as beta hedging.

A simple analysis (see Appendix 21A) shows that the optimal amount to hedge within this situation is driven by the level of the correlation between the counterparty exposure and the hedging instrument. With this optimal hedge, the residual variability (standard deviation) is $\sqrt{1 - \rho^2}$. This means that, for a correlation of $\rho = 50\%$, the residual variability would be 87%.[11] Such a hedge appears fairly inefficient unless the correlation is very high. However, for a portfolio, there is a greater benefit since the idiosyncratic risk is diversified away, making the resulting hedging of systematic risk

---

[11] $\sqrt{1 - 50\%^2} = 0.866$

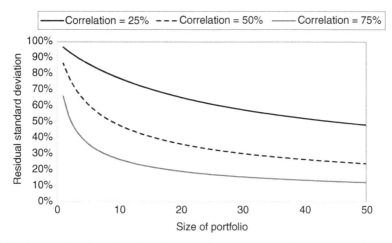

Figure 21.5 Potential hedging benefit with a credit proxy, depending on correlation and (equal) portfolio size.

more efficient. This makes the residual variability lower, as illustrated in Figure 21.5 (see Appendix 21A for a more detailed description). This means that hedging a portfolio of 50 equal counterparties with an index that is 50% correlated to all of them leaves a residual variability of only 23%. This suggests material reduction of accounting volatility and capital relief from index CDS hedges, as will be discussed below.

When the credit spread sensitivity of xVA (mainly CVA)[12] is hedged, it is necessary to estimate the 'beta' to the index (or indices) that is used for hedging. Such betas will be partly driven by the mapping methodology used to define illiquid credit curves (Section 12.3) and partly by actual empirical data. They can be estimated by examining the historical relationship between xVA volatility and that of the associated index. This is a subjective process, with the length of the time series and the frequency of updating being important considerations. If the beta is too high (low), then the credit spread volatility will be overhedged (underhedged), leading to xVA gains (losses) when credit spreads widen. The correct beta will be a function of the correlation between index and counterparty credit spreads and their associated volatilities. This can clearly change quite dynamically and is a challenge to predict accurately, especially as past behaviour may not be a good guide as to future relationships.

21.2.7 Risk Limits and P&L Explain

It is important to have limits in place to define the appetite for P&L volatility for the various different Greeks (Figure 21.6). Delta limits for market risk should generally be reasonably small so as to incentivise the hedging of these relatively liquid risk factors. Vega limits may be higher given the more limited liquidity and potential costs of buying options. Credit spread delta limits are probably the most important to define, since, whilst it may be profitable to warehouse credit risk, this is usually the biggest driver of accounting volatility. Credit spread hedging is, therefore, a balance between reducing the volatility of xVA and not 'paying away' the full credit risk premium. It is also important to have JTD

---

[12] Depending on calculation assumptions, such as whether survival probabilities are included, other xVA terms can have a small sensitivity to credit spread changes.

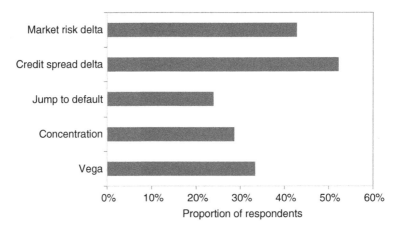

Figure 21.6   Market practice on CVA limits. Source: Deloitte/Solum CVA Survey (2013).

limits (to avoid a single counterparty exposure being too high) and concentration limits (e.g. with respect to a given region).

It is important to be able to predict and explain P&L changes in relation to xVA. This is a common requirement for trading desks to understand the performance of their hedging and the source of any material unhedged moves. P&L explain or predict is generally performed at the end of each trading day. It aims to predict the actual P&L based on changes in risk factors and then explain the actual observed change in xVA (which should be available the next day).

The illustration in Table 21.8 shows total xVA P&L calculated as the difference between xVA on day T-2 and xVA on day T-1 that needs to be explained. The attribution to credit, rates, and FX P&L is based on xVA sensitivities to the respective market factors (i.e. delta × market move). Unexplained P&L (UX) is the residual P&L that is not explained by changes to market risk factors. In the absence of any other changes to the portfolio (e.g. new trades or rating changes), this represents gamma and cross-gamma (and in the case shown, vega also, since it is not included).

The P&L explain may be aggregated in different ways. For example, from a credit point of view, it is useful to view by counterparty, but for most factors (e.g. interest rate risk), the entire portfolio view is relevant. It is also important to be able to decompose by xVA term (e.g. CVA and FVA). Whilst a small UX number is acceptable, if this number consistently exceeds a fraction of the overall daily P&L, it shows that material risks are not being captured. In such situations, the P&L explain may be expanded, even if the risk being explained cannot be hedged (e.g. cross-gamma). This will require more sensitivity calculations.

Table 21.8   Example P&L explain.

xVA T-2	xVA T-1	Total P&L	Theta	Credit delta	Rates delta	FX delta	UX
−58,381,190	−61,607,070	−3,225,880	120,960	−1,800,820	−1,610,770	279,335	−214,585

An alternative way to perform a P&L explain process is to shift risk factors sequentially, which, by construction, will explain total P&L. This approach may be favoured by finance departments, but it is not in line with the way in which an xVA desk sees and hedges its sensitivities.

Additionally, portfolio changes (new trades, novations, restructurings, etc.) should also ideally be incorporated in the P&L explain process, together with methodology changes (e.g. internal rating changes). Sometimes this is a manual process, with these components initially appearing to be unexplained and the formal P&L report being manually adjusted.

In summary, the following components may be part of a P&L explain process:

- changes in risk factors:
  - theta (time decay);
  - deltas (rates, FX, etc.);
  - implied volatility;
  - credit spread delta;
  - gamma;
  - cross-gamma;
  - defaults; and
  - funding and capital costs.
- portfolio changes:
  - new trades;
  - novations;
  - unwinds/terminations; and
  - exercise decisions.
- counterparty changes:
  - consolidation of netting terms;
  - changes to the margin agreement;
  - rating changes (leading to a change in spread mapping, for example);
  - credit events; and
  - model changes.

21.2.8 Examples

In order to give an insight into hedging xVA, Figure 21.7 shows the change in xVA driven by both interest rates (in the main currency driving the exposure) and credit spreads. In this case, the combination of CVA and FVA is being hedged. The performance of the hedges in each case and the overall effect is also shown. The interest rate hedges work well, with the total P&L variability being quite low. There is a small amount of noise due to curve movements and hedging frequency (the hedges are generally updated only periodically and/or when there is a material change in the sensitivity). For the credit spread hedges, the performance is worse, which should be expected due to the nature of 'beta hedging' (Section 21.2.6). There is a fairly systematic negative bias with respect to the credit hedges, which is partly due to bid-offer costs and partly due to the beta being slightly overstated. With respect to the latter, the general credit spread tightening regime leads to overall losses due to buying too much index protection (the xVA desk is, therefore, seen in hindsight to be short credit risk).

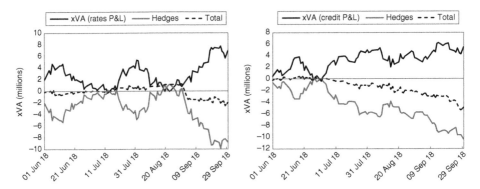

Figure 21.7   Hedging performance for xVA desk (CVA and FVA), showing behaviour with respect to interest rates (left) and credit spreads (right).

21.2.9   Impact on Capital

For some banks, alongside reducing P&L volatility, there is the question of the impact of xVA hedges on regulatory capital. In some cases, banks have even favoured regulatory capital reduction over P&L volatility control. Depending upon the regulatory approach and the type of hedging instruments used, there are different treatments with respect to regulatory capital relief.

Since capital relief can be gained with index CDSs, from a pure ROC – as opposed to an accounting volatility – point of view, there is an optimal point. This point occurs when the cost of buying index CDS protection is less than the capital benefit achieved. If the index CDS spreads are low enough, then hedging CVA capital will be optimal. This is illustrated in Figure 21.8, which shows the ROC as a function of CDS index hedge size for different spread regimes. If index spreads are too high, then it will not be optimal to hedge, but as for lower levels, an improvement in ROC can be achieved.

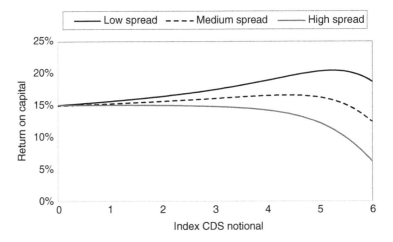

Figure 21.8   Overall ROC when using index CDS to hedge CVA capital.

Note that only single-name CDS hedges can provide capital relief against the CCR capital charge. However, this must reference the correct legal entity and have a cross-default provision so that bond default would be triggered in the event of derivative default. The main discussion over hedging relates to the CVA capital charge, where market risk hedges are potentially capital reducing.

The first point to make is that, under both current and future regulatory environments, the market risk of the actual value is not capitalised, but instead treated as the two components that have been previously referred to as base value and xVA (Equation 5.1).

Firstly, there are traditional trading book (TB) market risk capital requirements that generally can be seen to apply to the 'base value'. Relatively sophisticated banks have used value-at-risk (VAR) methodology to quantify such requirements under an internal model approach, and there are more basic approaches for other banks. These requirements are in the process of being overhauled as a result of the Fundamental Review of the Trading Book (FRTB) regulation (BCBS 2019a).

Secondly, there are independent CVA-related capital charges. These are also subject to regulatory change with regards to, for example, the future FRTB-CVA rules, as has been discussed in detail in Section 13.3.

The market risk and CVA capital charges are independent, despite both being subject to incoming FRTB requirements. One reason for this is that CVA is seen as inherently more complex and, therefore, requiring more simplistic methodologies. Indeed, the most sophisticated methodology under the market risk FRTB rules is the internal model approach (IMA), with a standardised approach (SA) being a simpler methodology. However, for CVA, there is no IMA, and the standardised approach (SA-CVA) is the most sophisticated choice, with a less complex basic approach (BA-CVA) being the alternative.

The first obvious problem with the separate treatment of market risk and CVA-related capital requirements is that they cannot offset one another. It is not uncommon that a CVA desk may naturally have CVA-related market risk that offsets market risk in the TB of the bank (e.g. the TB has a negative sensitivity to interest rates, and the CVA desk has a positive sensitivity). However, the regulatory capital requirements of such a bank would not recognise this offset and would double-count the capital requirement. Since banks hedge their market risk actively and their residual risk is second order, whereas CVA desks often have first-order outright risk due to the hedging challenges, this point may not be seen to be particularly problematic by most banks.

A second more difficult point regarding the separate treatment revolves around eligible hedges (Figure 21.9). The CVA capital framework incentivises active management of CVA by giving capital relief for CVA hedges that are captured by the methodology and are, therefore, eligible. Such hedges do not need to be captured within the market risk framework, and in the event that they are risk increasing – and not risk reducing – this may lead to a larger CVA capital charge. Suppose, as shown in Figure 21.9, that an uncollateralised transaction is hedged back to back with a collateralised transaction. Note that the market risk capital framework may see no net market risk (if the same discount rates are used). There is, of course, xVA associated with this situation. However, any xVA market risk hedges are not recognised in the CVA capital charge and must, therefore, be recognised under the standard market risk rules, where they will increase capital. Non-eligible hedges must be treated as TB instruments and captured within the market risk capital rules.

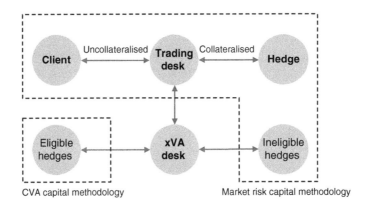

Figure 21.9 Illustration of the impact of eligible and non-eligible xVA hedges.

Table 21.9 gives an overview of the eligibility of xVA hedges under the current and future regulatory regimes and for the different capital methodologies (discussed previously in Section 13.3). The first point to note is that all non-CVA hedges are ineligible, since they have no associated regulatory capital requirements. In the event that xVAs are captured naturally within the base value via a discounting approach (e.g. ColVA, discussed in Section 16.2.1, or symmetric FVA, as discussed in Section 18.2.4), then this will not raise any issue since the value and hedges will all be reflected within the TB. However, hedges for specific components such as FVA will be ineligible.

Secondly, not all CVA hedges are eligible for capital relief. Under the current rules and future BA-CVA methodology, the capital charge for CVA volatility is driven solely by credit spread movements and, consequently, only credit hedges can achieve capital relief; only single-name and index CDS hedges are eligible, with all other hedges (including

Table 21.9 Eligibility of xVA hedges under current and future CVA regulatory capital rules.

	Current regulation			Future regulation (FRTB-CVA)		
	Standardised	Advanced	Ineligible	BA-CVA	SA-CVA	Ineligible
CVA	Single-name CDS		Proxy single-name CDS	Single-name CDS (including proxies)	Most CVA hedges	Non-IMA hedges
	Index CDS		All other market risk hedges	Index CDS		
Other xVA	N/A		All	N/A		All

proxy single-name CDSs) being ineligible.[13] Single-name CDS hedges are obviously most effective, as they can reduce both CCR capital and CVA capital (Section 13.3.6). Under the future SA-CVA methodology, most hedges will be eligible, except those not included in the IMA for market risk under the FRTB (e.g. tranched credit derivatives).

The non-capitalisation on other (non-CVA) xVA hedges has the problem that, since there is no xVA-specific capital requirement, the overall capital requirements of a bank may be over- or understated depending on whether the xVA hedges reduce or increase the TB market risk of the bank. There is, therefore, a strong argument for allowing banks to more properly reflect the risk in this situation by, for example, capturing xVA sensitivities alongside hedges in their market risk capital. Whilst there is no general Basel guidance on this point, local regulators are starting to address this.[14] This also means that the xVA desk may need to separate some hedges (e.g. interest rate) into CVA and FVA components so as to properly recognise capital relief. The hedging of accounting xVA (e.g. CVA and FVA) may appear to over- or underhedge accounting CVA depending on the behaviour of non-CVA. For example, FBA or DVA will reduce the size of vega hedges but increase delta hedges for accounting xVA terms (see Table 21.4 and related discussion).

For ineligible CVA hedges, and given that there is a specific capital charge, the problem is mainly related to over- and not undercapitalisation, where ineligible CVA hedges consume TB capital rather than reducing CVA capital. The European Banking Authority (EBA 2015b) reports that banks are sensitive to these capital-consuming hedges, with interest rate swaps, FX forwards, interest rate options, and cross-currency swaps being mentioned in particular. This conservative treatment may not be as concerning for regulators, but has been criticised by banks for creating the incentive not to hedge CVA risks. In response to this, US and Canadian regulators have moved to exempt CVA-related market risk hedges and thus prevent them from at least adding to capital (although they would still provide no capital relief). Such a route requires a qualitative demonstration that these hedges are risk reducing and not risk increasing. A more robust approach is to allow CVA sensitivities to be included in the market risk capital calculation, which some local regulators have allowed banks to do.

A better solution to the above problem would be to integrate the CVA capital charge methodology – together with other xVA terms as appropriate – into the market risk methodology, but this is currently viewed by regulators as being too complicated, and this is not a provision of even future regulatory rules.

Finally, recall that even eligible hedges may not provide optimal capital relief, as discussed in Section 13.5.3. The relative conservatism of methodologies such as SA-CCR means that a CVA hedge for accounting volatility would typically be seen as being an underhedge from a regulatory capital perspective. In contrast, choosing the optimum hedge for regulatory capital minimisation would overhedge the accounting volatility. Whilst the future SA-CVA should align regulatory and accounting CVA (if not xVA), it still poses problems with index hedges, as previously shown in Figure 13.20.

---

[13] Some more complex credit hedges such as swaptions are allowable, although they are generally very illiquid. Becker, L. (2014). CVA hedge losses prompt focus on swaptions and guarantees. *Risk* (28 October). www.risk.net.

[14] APRA (2019). Derivative valuation adjustments - frequently asked questions. Australian Prudential Regulatory Authority (8 May). www.apra.gov.au.

21.2.10   Pushing xVA into Base Value

Given the problems with xVA adjustments such as those related to the capital (Figure 21.9), there may be an incentive to try and characterise xVA as much as possible as being within the base value (Equation 5.1), where it may be more straightforward to deal with from a quantification and management point of view. As noted previously (Section 5.4.7), this can only be easily done for situations where xVA is a simple, transaction-level quantity, just requiring, for example, a change in discounting. Whilst xVA cannot usually be generally represented like this, except in special cases, there is a potential hybrid approach which involves capturing most of the xVA within the base value with a small, more complex adjustment.

For example, with respect to asymmetric FVA, which is a portfolio-level quantity (Section 18.3.2), it could be broken down into the sum of:

- a symmetric FVA calculated using cost of funds discounting (Section 18.2.4); and
- an adjustment reflecting the difference between the real FVA and the above.

The symmetric FVA component would be captured within the base value and would naturally net with FVA hedges from a market risk capital perspective (Figure 21.9). The adjustment would reflect aspects such as asymmetries and thresholds. This approach would create additional operational costs in capturing FVA via two different cal-culations, ensuring consistency (e.g. in terms of trade population) and aggregation (e.g. consolidation of risk numbers). However, it would offer strong numerical efficiency, as only the adjustment component would need to be captured via simulation, and this may also largely retain the benefit of the market risk treatment of hedges. This approach may be advantageous for a bank that wants to use asymmetric FVA but believes that the adjustment term would generally be small. This would be the case for an 'asset-heavy' portfolio (Figure 18.11).

21.3   OPERATION OF AN xVA DESK

21.3.1   Interaction with a Treasury

From a CVA-ownership perspective, an xVA desk can potentially work in isolation and manage risk by executing internal or external market and credit risk hedges. However, the same is not true of margin, funding, and capital components. The management and trans-fer pricing of these components in a bank is usually managed by a central 'treasury' unit, and so the way in which this unit passes on costs is clearly key to defining the underlying adjustments.

It is sub-optimal for an individual desk to manage its funding, and it is better to manage this centrally on the xVA desk, which may have access to treasury funding on a portfolio basis (see Figure 18.1). The xVA desk then becomes responsible for charging compo-nents such as inception FVA in line with the FTP costs defined by the treasury. The time decay (Section 21.1.3) that the xVA desk accrues should then act as a profit, offsetting the charges from the treasury. The associated xVA volatility has two main components:

- *Market risk.* This can be hedged alongside the analogous CVA market risk volatility, although there will be capital implications, as discussed in Section 21.2.9.

- *Funding risk.* This probably cannot be hedged. If the treasury increases (reduces) the cost of funding via the FTP curve, then this may create losses (profits) for the xVA desk.

From the point of view of managing funding risk, there are different ways in which the xVA desk can interact with the treasury:

- *Accrual based.* In this scenario, funding would be charged on the current borrowing on a periodic basis. Whilst the xVA desk is able to hedge the market risk, it carries the risk of changes in the funding cost, and it is not possible to hedge the treasury-determined FTP or term liquidity premium (TLP) curve. An implication of this is that a given point on the curve used to calculate FVA should represent the expected cost of funding that would be charged at that point in the future. The treasury would know the current funding requirement, but may not have visibility over future needs.
- *Term based.* In this scenario, funding would be charged across the whole term structure of the funding profile. This creates an alignment between the curve used to calculate FVA and the FTP curve of the treasury. It also means that the derivatives funding could be a more integrated part of the asset-liability management (ALM) process. However, it does mean that the treasury is providing funding on the basis of expected cash and margin flows, and there could be large changes in the funding profile which may have led to only small changes in the accrual-based approach (however, from an ALM point of view, it may be important to capture this).

As discussed in Section 18.3.5, there is also the important question of the symmetry of funding. Whilst funding will always be done at a certain level, with costs and benefits naturally netting and offsetting one other, there is the question of symmetry at the portfolio level, with the choices being:

- *Symmetric.* Here, the treasury would consider funding costs and benefits to be equal and opposite (on a net basis), and so there would be a return when the xVA desk lends cash (overall), which would also be remunerated at the same rate as when the xVA desk is borrowing to the same term. The advantage of this approach is that it is very simple, and every trade can be considered in isolation (symmetric FVA is discussed in Section 18.2). The disadvantage of this approach is that the treasury may struggle to monetise funding benefits unless they are offsetting funding costs. When borrowing against net derivatives assets, the treasury may naturally see this – prudently – as a term funding cost. However, net derivative liabilities may be seen as an unstable source of funding and, therefore, difficult to monetise at a similar rate. Furthermore, charging symmetrically is antithetical to the net stable funding ratio (NSFR) (Section 4.3.4), which charges 100% required stable funding for net derivatives assets but gives 0% available stable funding for net liabilities (and, indeed, charges for a percentage of such liabilities). Depending on how granular a bank decides to be over NSFR costs and to what extent its business and funding strategy is naturally NSFR compliant, this may be an important consideration.
- *Asymmetric.* In this setting, the treasury would remunerate derivatives assets and liabilities differently, paying a lower return on the latter. This makes the calculation of funding costs by the xVA desk much harder, as an accurate consideration can only be made at the portfolio level. However, it more closely aligns with a conservative funding

strategy, which would term fund derivatives assets but not term lend against derivatives liabilities. Such a strategy is also more consistent with the NSFR rules. In an asymmetric funding regime, there is also a question of defining the underlying portfolio to be funded and whether, within this portfolio, there are offsets from different requirements, such as variation margin received and initial margin posted. It is also important not to create the wrong incentives – for example, to novate into ITM portfolios as a way to lend to derivatives counterparties rather than the internal treasury of the bank.

There is also a need for margin optimisation in terms of aspects such as the 'cheapest-to-deliver' option (Section 16.2.3) and the pool of high-quality liquid assets (HQLAs) (Section 4.3.2). This optimisation can be owned by either the xVA desk or the treasury. It is clearly important to align this with pricing so that the remuneration of the margin posted/received is in line with the remuneration rate used in discounting. If this is not the case, then there will be accrual losses faced by the bank. This suggests that both pricing and ownership of margin optimisation should be done by the xVA desk. However, it is important to bear in mind that the treasury will also have its own derivatives transactions (for hedging the interest rate and FX risk in its borrowing and lending arrangements) that will have margining implications.

21.3.2   Capital

Whilst capital is a form of funding, it is not managed in most banks in a similar way to funding from FVA, as discussed in 19.3.1. This is probably in large part due to the fact that derivatives are marked-to-market and any profits are recognised on day one, which is beneficial to shareholders and employees, who benefit from such profits in the form of dividends and bonuses. Although deferring such profits may provide long-term benefits and incentives, it is not of interest to investors, such as shareholders, with relatively short-term views.

Whilst xVA desks have started to assume responsibility for charging KVA, this may be seen as a formalisation of setting ROC hurdles, which has long been a practice within banks. In order to understand whether practices might change in this respect, we consider three possible scenarios with respect to KVA pricing and management, which are roughly in line with the three proposals in Section 19.3.2. Consider that a five-year transaction has KVA of 50 units (in excess of any other xVA cost). Broadly, there are three ways in which this KVA could be released as profit, as illustrated in Table 21.10.

Table 21.10   Different approaches for releasing a KVA profit of 50 units on a five-year transaction.

	Method A	Method B	Method C Scenario 1	Method C Scenario 2
Year 1	50	10	30	5
Year 2	0	10	50	3
Year 3	0	10	40	2
Year 4	0	10	20	1
Year 5	0	10	10	0
Total	50	50	150	11

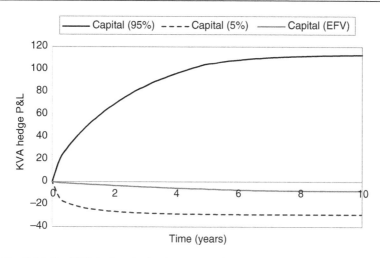

Figure 21.10 P&L for KVA hedges in the three scenarios shown in Figure 19.11.

Method A is – more or less – the approach still used at most banks, since there is no accounting adjustment for KVA and so any capital charge will automatically be released as profit immediately. This has obvious problems, such as creating the wrong incentives, as illustrated previously in Figure 19.8. Method B releases KVA in some defined way, which has the advantage of aligning revenue more with capital and risk. However, the arbitrary nature of the release is not in line with the definition of KVA and so would need to form some accounting adjustment, such as retained earnings. Method C is a full KVA approach, with the profit being driven by the time decay of the KVA term, together with the P&L from any associated hedges. The reason that this approach does not return a total profit of 50 is due to the KVA hedging.

A more real example will be provided by returning to the previous case in Figure 19.11, which considered the change in KVA in different market scenarios. Figure 21.10 shows the P&L for the KVA hedges in the three scenarios considered previously. In scenarios when the derivatives move OTM (ITM), there will be losses (gains) on KVA hedges so as to produce the desired ROC. The 95% and 5% potential future exposure (PFE) examples are roughly in line with scenarios 1 and 2 under method C in Table 21.10.

Method A in Table 21.10 locks in the P&L of the transaction but shows a variable ROC over the lifetime (as previously illustrated in Figure 19.13). Method C locks in the ROC and shows a variable P&L (including KVA hedges). Method B achieves neither and is probably more of an intermediate step towards method C and active KVA management.

Whether and how quickly banks might transition towards method C and the management of KVA in line with other valuation adjustments such as CVA and FVA remains to be seen.

21.3.3 Systems and Quantification

The quantification of xVA is a challenging task in terms of architecture and computational requirements due to a number of aspects, such as:

• the underlying data requirements;
• the high dimensionality and non-linearities;

- the need for real-time calculations;
- data aggregation at different levels (trade, counterparty, full portfolio); and
- the requirement for sensitivities and scenario analysis.

This has led banks, other financial institutions, and software vendors to invest heavily in xVA systems and infrastructure. The building blocks of an xVA system are:

- *Data.* Most institutions have multiple systems for legal, trade, market, and historical data. Data collection and storage is substantial and must be obtained from various front-office trading and back-office systems and external sources. Having a 'golden source' of market data, counterparty data, trade data, netting information, and margin terms can be useful. Data requirements cover the following aspects:
  o trade population (including hedges);
  o legal entities;
  o netting agreements;
  o margin agreements;
  o market data;
  o historical data;
  o credit ratings, default probabilities, and LGDs (internal and external); and
  o credit spreads.
- *Simulation engines.* The heart of the xVA calculation is typically a Monte Carlo simulation that must be able to efficiently generate the evolution of all relevant risk factors with an underlying correlation structure. It may also be necessary to generate additional scenarios, maintaining 'scenario consistency' – for example, in order to run an intraday calculation without rerunning an entire netting set or portfolio.
- *Revaluation functionality.* After generating a large number of scenarios, it is necessary to revalue every single transaction in each scenario. Whilst most common products are fast to value, the scale is huge, with potentially trillions of valuation calls required. Valuations can be speeded up significantly by applying both financial and computational optimisations.
- *Collateralisation.* It must be possible to track existing margin, whether this is in cash or other securities, calculate the projected future margin in each simulation, and calculate the impact of this (together with current margin) on exposure. This must include impacts such as segregation, and must also be able to simulate future initial margin.
- *Reporting.* Reporting functionality such as xVA for financial statements, limit breaches, P&L explain, and scenario analysis should be available.
- *Greeks.* Hedging and P&L explain require Greeks for all relevant risk factors, covering both market and credit risk. Due to the number of Greeks, calculation by finite-difference ('bump-and-run') methods may be extremely time consuming.
- *Scenario analysis and stress-testing tools.* The ability to run scenarios to test the behaviour of xVA in extreme scenarios.

It is inevitable that some optimisation will be required in order to manage the volume of calculations and likely requirements for near real-time xVA. Such optimisations can be in relation to hardware, software, or numerical methods. Typical methods used are:

- *Pre-calculations.* Pre-calculations on the existing portfolio can speed up pre-deal pricing of xVA. This does, however, require significant data storage and rapid retrieval, and will probably become less common as processing power and other optimisations become more common.

- *Numerical optimisations*. Relatively straightforward numerical approximations such as random number generation (low discrepancy sequences and using the same random numbers each day to avoid unnecessary noise) and cash flows bucketing (Section 15.3.2).

- *Fast revaluations*. Methods that speed up the revaluation of the portfolio, which is generally the major bottleneck of the xVA calculation. See, for example, Laris and Ruiz (2018) and Ferguson and Green (2018).

- *American Monte Carlo*. As mentioned in Section 15.3.2, American Monte Carlo (AMC) is an approach to optimisation quite commonly used in the industry (e.g. Cesari et al. 2009). This produces speed improvement, since the pricing overhead is absorbed within the simulation via regressing with respect to the relevant market variables. There is significant implementation work involved in AMC, and the specification of the regressions is not trivial. AMC can be particularly advantageous for portfolios with significant numbers of exotics (especially those with embedded Bermudan-style optionality).

- *Adjoint algorithmic differentiation (AAD)*. One of the more recent but increasingly popular applications to xVA, AAD is specific to the generation of sensitivities (Greeks) and requires significant implementation and architecture design. However, AAD allows the calculation of an arbitrary number of Greeks at a cost that is a small fixed multiple, often claimed to be in the region of four (see Capriotti and Lee 2014). For large portfolios where the number of required sensitivities is large (potentially in the hundreds), the additional overhead in implementing AAD is possibly worthwhile. However, it is important to bear in mind that AAD will probably result in all xVA calculations being slower, even when sensitivities are not required. It should be considered that all future developments of the xVA system (e.g. adding new products) will need to be done in an AAD-compliant way.

- *Processors*. The use of parallel processing involves splitting xVA computations across different processors. However, it is important to balance splitting calculations evenly and avoiding repeating calculations (such as calibrations). Additionally, some implementations have relied on more specialised hardware solutions such as graphics processing units (GPUs), which offer potential speed-up of traditional CPUs but with more implementation effort and additional expense.

Different xVA calculations also require varying amounts of complexity. First-generation xVAs such as CVA and FVA require only the calculation of the portfolio value in each scenario. However, more recent terms such as KVA and MVA often require more complex calculations, such as portfolio sensitivities, in each scenario. This additional complexity makes methods such as AMC and AAD even more important for dealing with computation demands.

Within an institution, there may be a number of different areas with xVA-related requirements, notably:

- *Front-office*. The calculation of xVA for pricing purposes.
- *Finance*. Daily valuation of transactions and the representation of this both internally for management purposes and externally for financial reporting (accounting) purposes.
- *Risk and regulatory*. The measurement of xVA against risk limits and the calculation of regulatory capital.

In an ideal world, the above would be addressed via a single holistic solution but, in practice, it is not uncommon to see separate implementations. Given the general convergence of standards and regulations such as SA-CVA (where accounting and regulatory CVA must be aligned), it would seem more likely that a greater amount of systems unification would occur. This is not always completely optimal (e.g. it is desirable to be able to modify front-office systems rapidly with a fast release cycle, but this is not possible when they have a strong regulatory role).

One area that may remain distinct is for banks with an internal model method (IMM) approval (Section 13.4.5). Such implementations calculate metrics such as PFE and effective EPE (EEPE), often use historical calibrations (including stress periods), and require backtesting. However, a few banks have aligned their CVA and IMM implementations (see Section 15.3.3).

Over the past decade, a number of software vendors have invested significantly in the development of counterparty risk and xVA solutions. Some of the significant vendors in this respect are CompatibL, Fincad, IBM (previously known as Algorithmics), IHS Markit (previously known as QuIC), Murex, Numerix, Pricing Partners, Quantifi, FIS Global (previously SunGard), and TriOptima. Not surprisingly, vendor solutions differ significantly, with two clear axes of differentiation being:

- *Sophistication.* Some vendors offer cheaper and less sophisticated solutions, whereas others offer greater sophistication at a higher cost.
- *Application.* Vendors are more focused on a particular implementation (e.g. front-office or risk).

Large banks have tended to build xVA systems internally, driven by economies of scale and the desire to maintain full control over the framework and its development. Smaller banks and financial institutions have tended to use external vendor solutions that may offer time savings. Additionally, in-house builds are generally preferred for more bespoke front-office xVA implementations, with vendor implementations being more common for risk and regulatory functionality.

An internally-developed solution can offer greater control over the development process and future flexibility. On the other hand, internal development from a limited starting point can be a substantial undertaking and may require significant time and resources, especially with respect to aspects such as achieving a satisfactory coverage of the many underlying products. A vendor system may offer a faster implementation route without the need to 'reinvent the wheel'.

The following is a list of the broad considerations when choosing a vendor-based xVA solution:

- modelling:
  o availability of different models and calibration across each asset class;
  o modelling of collateralisation;
  o treatment of resets and break clauses; and
  o treatment of specific and general WWR.
- calculation:
  o methodology for calculating xVA in real time;

- o approach for exotic payoffs and/or path dependency where the computation time for valuation is prohibitive (e.g. AMC);
- o what sensitivities can be calculated and how the calculation is implemented (e.g. finite difference, AAD);
- o whether a P&L explain is implemented;
- o ability to calculate terms such as MVA and KVA, and include initial margin in the calculation of CVA and KVA;
- o approach for scenario analysis and stress testing; and
- o speed and recommended hardware requirements for the portfolio in question.
- data and implementation:
  - o approaches for data capture (market, legal) and data maintained by vendor (e.g. market conventions and calendars);
  - o product coverage and how non-standard payoffs can be represented (e.g. generic scripting language); and
  - o reporting functionality and feeding of downstream systems (e.g. accounting, general ledger).
- general:
  - o other institutions that use the system and for what purposes;
  - o cost structure (upfront, costs per licence, computing services, consultants cost per day); and
  - o likely implementation time.

Not surprisingly, any incumbent vendor solutions for other purposes (risk, back-office) are also a major consideration in most cases.

21.3.4   xVA Optimisation

In addition to pricing and management, optimisation of xVA has been an important topic for banks. Optimisation of xVA in the interdealer market is active, with traditional portfolio compression (Section 6.2.4) and more advanced approaches seeking to reduce new components, such as bilateral initial margin. This is an area mainly limited by innovation, as all participants have similar goals and can benefit mutually.

Optimisation with respect to end users is more difficult for banks as the goals are not aligned and can only be agreed via a trade-off of benefits, such as one party making a cash payment. Some uncollateralised end users have experienced problems when hedging transactions that have moved heavily against them. Not only does this increase a bank's xVAs, but it may also cause credit limit breaches and lead to a bank being unable to transact and provide hedges any more. One potential solution in this situation is to 'restrike' transactions, so they are less ITM for the bank. This is similar at the outset to the effect of entering into a margin agreement, but without the uncertainty of future margin requirements and related liquidity costs. Basic, one-off optimisations such as restrikes can reduce xVA for an ITM portfolio and do not require any ongoing changes to contractual terms. Beyond this, changes to margining agreements can reduce xVA, which is advantageous for the bank but costly for the client. However, some clients have agreed to this as a means of achieving better prices and/or monetising gains from moving legacy portfolios. Moving beyond this, moving voluntarily to bilateral margining or central clearing will make xVA costs for clients smaller at the expense of initial margin posting.

Not surprisingly, a number of major end users of derivatives have actively considered the pros and cons of changing the way in which they transact, usually in the form of changing the level of collateralisation. For example, Danmarks Nationalbank (2015) gives an account of a move to two-way collateralisation and its costs and benefits. Nakashima et al. (2016) make a similar analysis and state that:

> In the case of Canada, our analysis shows that an asymmetric CSA [one-way margin agreement] is unlikely to be the most desirable margining structure, because it carries the highest risk charges and pass-through of bank dealer costs. The symmetric variation margin scenarios [two-way margin agreement] have lower risk and, with rehypothecation, result in lower pass-through of both the bank dealers' funding costs and Basel capital charges. The analysis appears to be consistent with the practices of certain OIs [official institutions], some of which have moved to more symmetric structures.

There are also potential regulatory arbitrages that arise from the above, where a bank may lend money to an end user in order for them to restrike their derivative portfolio. This can be seen as converting an ITM derivative portfolio into an at-the-money (ATM) derivative portfolio plus a loan. This practice is incentivised by regulation, since a bank does not experience anything analogous to the CVA capital charge for a loan, and so essentially can reduce KVA without changing the real economic risk it faces. The EBA (2015b) comments on this as follows:[15]

> From the point of view of the bank, there is a transformation of counterparty risk (coming from the derivatives) into credit risk (coming from the loan). But assuming the loan will roll over until the maturity of the derivative contracts, the overall level of risk has not changed. However, the net level of capital has.

Many end users have not traditionally posted margin due to the liquidity implications. For example, the EBA (2015b) notes:

> It is however more difficult to convince counterparties without collateral [margin] agreements to operate on a collateralised basis because most of them do not have the treasury function to exchange collateral on a frequent basis.

Nevertheless, in recent years, a number of parties have been under pressure to move towards transacting under two-way CSAs, driven by the large costs experienced by banks for uncollateralised transactions. Before entering into a margin arrangement, it would naturally be important to make an analysis of the funding implications that may arise, and to put in place a 'liquidity buffer' to mitigate the risk of having to post a substantial amount of liquid margin in a relatively short space of time. In sizing this liquidity buffer, there are subjective questions, such as what time horizon should be considered and what form

---

[15] Note that the comment on the loan rolling is relevant if the end user is entering into a margin agreement, rather than just restriking the derivative.

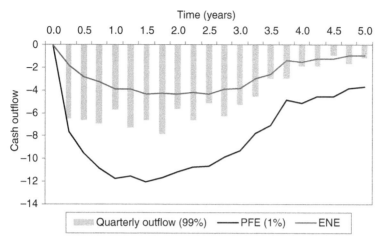

Figure 21.11   Worst-case (99% quantile) quarterly outflow for a two-way margin agreement with zero threshold, compared to ENE and PFE.

of cash and/or securities should make up the buffer. As an example of the type of analysis that might be used, Figure 21.11 shows the worst-case quarterly margin outflow for a client's portfolio, compared to ENE and PFE. Note that, with a zero threshold assumed, ENE and PFE represent approximately the expected and unexpected (to a confidence level) cumulative amount of margin posted. For parties with low costs of funding, such as sovereigns, supranationals, and agencies (SSAs), even funding a conservatively-large liquidity buffer may be optimal compared to paying the xVA costs of banks.

One feature of the clearing mandate and bilateral margin rules are that they only impact future and not existing transactions. However, the question arises as to whether or not it may be optimal to 'backload' legacy transactions to a CCP and voluntarily post initial margin against bilateral transactions that were transacted before the bilateral rules, or which are within the specified €50m threshold. It may be that certain users considering posting margin actually consider such routes, rather than the middle ground of bilateral trades without initial margin.[16]

A final aspect of optimisation is to correctly account for any overlaps or double-counting within the hierarchy of xVA terms. Whilst assessing the true impact of a new derivative on the balance sheet of a bank is very hard to do, it can be better approximated by assessing the impact of overlaps. For example, Albanese et al. (2015) argue that banks use a lower 'blended rate' to account implicitly for the possibility of using capital for funding purposes and, therefore, to avoid double-counting.

---

[16] Stafford, P. (2017). Dutch debt agency looks at derivatives clearing. *Financial Times* (23 June). www.ft.com.

Glossary

AAD	Adjoint algorithmic differentiation
AIG	American International Group
AIP	Auction incentive pools
ALM	Asset-liability management
AMC	American Monte Carlo
ASF	Available stable funding
ATM	At-the-money
AVA	Additional valuation adjustment
ATE	Additional termination event
Basel III	Basel III International Banking Regulatory Framework
BA-CVA	Basic CVA
BCBS	Basel Committee on Banking Supervision
BCVA	Bilateral CVA
BMR	Bilateral margin requirements
BRIC	Brazil, Russia, India, and China
CAPM	Capital Asset Pricing Model
CBOT	Chicago Board of Trade
CC	Capital cost
CCAR	Comprehensive Capital Analysis and Review
CCP	Central counterparty
CCR	Counterparty credit risk
CDS	Credit default swap
CDO	Collateralised debt obligation
CEEMEA	Central and Eastern Europe, Middle East and Africa
CE	Current exposure
CEM	Current exposure method
CET1	Common Equity Tier 1
ColVA	Collateral valuation adjustment
CLS	Continuous linked settlement
CME	Chicago Mercantile Exchange
ColRA	Collateral received adjustment
ColPA	Collateral posted adjustment
CRD IV	Capital Requirements Directive IV
CRIF	Common Risk Interchange Format
CSA	Credit support annex
CVA	Credit value adjustment
Dodd-Frank	Dodd–Frank Wall Street Reform and Consumer Protection Act
D-SIB	Domestic systemicallyimportant bank
DVA	Debt value adjustment

EAD	Exposure at default
EBA	European Banking Authority
ECB	European Central Bank/Expected collateral balance
ECP	Expected capital profile
EE	Expected exposure
EEE	Effective expected exposure
EFV	Expected future value
EIM	Expected initial margin
EMIR	European Market Infrastructure Regulation
ENE	Expected negative exposure
EPE	Expected positive exposure
EEPE	Effective expected positive exposure
ES	Expected shortfall
EU	European Union
EURIBOR	Euro Interbank Offered Rate
EWMA	Exponentially-weighted moving average
FAS	Financial Accounting Standards
FASB	Financial Accounting Standards Board
FBA	Funding benefit adjustment
FCA	Funding cost adjustment
FHS	Filtered historical simulation
FMI	Financial market infrastructure
FRTB	Fundamental Review of the Trading Book
FSB	Financial Stability Board
FTP	Funds transfer pricing
FVA	Funding value adjustment
FX	Foreign exchange
G7	Group of Seven Countries (Canada, France, Germany, Great Britain, Italy, Japan, and the US)
G20	Group of Twenty Countries (Argentina, Australia, Brazil, Canada, China, France, Germany, India, Indonesia, Italy, Japan, Mexico, Russia, Saudi Arabia, South Africa, South Korea, Turkey, United Kingdom, and the US. The European Union is also a member)
GAAP	Generally Accepted Accounting Principles
GFC	Global financial crisis
GPU	Graphical processing unit
G-SIB	Globally-systemically-important bank
G-SIFI	Globally-systematically-important financial institutions
HBOS	Halifax Bank of Scotland
HVAR	Historical value-at-risk
HQLA	High-quality liquid asset
IAS	International Accountancy Standards
IASB	International Accounting Standards Board
IBOR	Interbank Offered Rate
IFRS	International Financial Reporting Standards
IM	Initial margin
IMA	Internal model approach

IMM	Internal model method
IRB	Internal ratings-based (approach)
IRR	Internal rate of return
IRS	Interest rate swap
ISDA	International Swaps and Derivatives Association, Inc.
JTD	Jump to default
KVA	Capital value adjustment
LCR	Liquidity coverage ratio
LGD	Loss given default
LHP	Large homogeneous pool
LIBOR	London Interbank Offered Rate
LSOC	Legally separated; operationally commingled
LR	Leverage ratio
MDB	Multilateral development bank
MTA	Minimum transfer amount
MVA	Margin value adjustment
MTM	Mark-to-market
MPoR	Margin period of risk
NCB	Negative collateral balance
NDF	Non-deliverable forward
NEE	Negative expected exposure
NGR	Net gross ratio
NSFR	Net stable funding ratio
OSFI	Office of the Superintendent of Financial Institutions
OIS	Overnight indexed spread
OTC	Over-the-counter
P&L	Profit and loss
PAI	Price alignment interest
PAIRS	Portfolio Approach to Interest Rate Scenarios
PCA	Principal component analysis
PCB	Positive collateral balance
PD	Probability of default
PFE	Potential future exposure
PVP	Payment versus payment
ROC	Return on capital
ROE	Return on equity
QCCP	Qualifying CCP
QIS	Quantitative impact study
RFR	Risk-free rate
RMBS	Residential mortgage-backed securities
RORAC	Return on risk-adjusted capital
RSF	Required stable funding
RWA	Risk-weighted asset
SA-CCR	Standardised approach for counterparty credit risk (regulatory capital)
SA-CVA	Standardised CVA
SEF	Swap execution facility
SIFI	Systemically-important financial institution

SIMM	Standard Initial Margin Model
SLR	Supplementary leverage ratio
SME	Small and medium-sized enterprise
SPAN	Standard Portfolio Analysis of Risk
SPV	Special purpose vehicle
SSAs	Sovereigns, supranationals, and agencies
STM	Settle-to-market
TLAC	Total loss-absorbing capital
TLP	Term liquidity premium
TMT	Technology, media, and telecommunications
UCVA	Unilateral CVA
US	United States
UMR	Uncleared margin requirements/rules
VAR	Value-at-risk
VMGH	Variation margin gains haircutting
WACC	Weighted average capital cost
WWR	Wrong-way risk
xVA	CVA, DVA, FVA, ColVA, MVA, KVA, LVA, etc.

References

Albanese, C., F. D'Ippoliti, and G. Pietroniero (2011). In the margins. *Wilmott* (September).

Albanese, C. and S. Iabichino (2013). The FVA-DVA Puzzle: Risk Management and Collateral Trading Strategies. Global Valuation Ltd. No date given on paper.

Albanese, C., L. Andersen, and S. Iabichino (2015). FVA Accounting, Risk Management and Collateral Trading. *Risk* (30 January). www.risk.net.

Albanese, C., S. Caenazzo, and S. Crepey (2016). Capital Value Adjustment and Funding Value Adjustment. Working paper (9 March).

Altman, E. (1968). Financial Ratios, Discriminant Analysis and the Prediction of Corporate Bankruptcy. *Journal of Finance* 23 (4): 589–609.

Altman, E. (1989). Measuring Corporate Bond Mortality and Performance. *Journal of Finance* 44 (4): 909–922.

Altman, E. and V. Kishore (1996). Almost Everything You Wanted to Know About Recoveries on Defaulted Bonds. *Financial Analysts Journal* 52: 57–64.

Amdahl, G. M. (1967). Validity of the Single Processor Approach to Achieving Large-Scale Computing Capabilities. *AFIPS Conference Proceedings* 30: 483–485.

Andersen, L. and V. Piterbarg (2010a). *Interest Rate Modelling Volume 1: Foundations and Vanilla Models*. London: Atlantic Financial Press.

Andersen, L. and V. Piterbarg (2010b). *Interest Rate Modelling Volume 2: Term Structure Models*. London: Atlantic Financial Press.

Andersen, L. and V. Piterbarg (2010c). *Interest Rate Modelling Volume 3: Products and Risk Management*. London: Atlantic Financial Press.

Andersen, L., M. Pykhtin, and A. Sokol (2017a). Rethinking Margin Period of Risk. *Journal of Credit Risk* 13 (1): 1–45.

Andersen, L., M. Pykhtin, and A. Sokol (2017b). Does Initial Margin Eliminate Counterparty Risk? *Risk* (9 May). www.risk.net.

Andersen, L., D. Duffie, and Y. Song (2019). Funding Value Adjustments. *Journal of Finance* 74 (1): 145–192.

Anfuso, F., D. Aziz, P. Giltinan, and K. Loukopoulos (2017). A Sound Modelling and Backtesting Framework for Forecasting Initial Margin Requirements. *Risk* (19 January). www.risk.net.

Armakolla, A. and B. Bianchi. The European Central Counterparty (CCP) Ecosystem. IFC-National Bank of Belgium Workshop on Data Needs and Statistics Compilation for Macroprudential Analysis (18–19 May 2017). www.bis.org.

Arnsdorf, M. (2019). Central Counterparty CVA. *Risk* (3 April). www.risk.net.

Artzner, P., F. Delbaen, J-M. Eber, and D. Heath (1999). Coherent Measures of Risk. *Mathematical Finance* 9 (3): 203–228.

Australian Prudential Regulation Authority (APRA) (2016). Counterparty risk for ADIs. Discussion paper (15 September).

Arvanitis, A. and J. Gregory (eds.) (2001). *Credit: The Complete Guide to Pricing, Hedging and Risk Management*. London: Risk Books.

Arvanitis, A, J. Gregory, and J-P. Laurent (1999). Building Models For Credit Spreads. *Journal of Derivatives* 6 (3): 27–43.

Baird, D. G. (2001). *Elements of Bankruptcy (3rd edition)*. New York: Foundation Press.

Basurto, M. S. and M. Singh (2008). Counterparty Risk in the Over-the-Counter Derivatives Market. IMF working papers (1 November). www.imf.org.

Bates, D. and R. Craine (1999). Valuing the Futures Market Clearinghouse's Default Exposure during the 1987 Crash. *Journal of Money, Credit & Banking* 31 (2): 248–272.

BCBS (2004a). *Basel II: International Convergence of Capital Measurement and Capital Standards: a Revised Framework*. Basel: Basel Committee on Banking Supervision. www.bis.org.

BCBS (2005a). An Explanatory Note on the Basel II IRB Risk Weight Functions (5 July). www.bis.org.

BCBS (2005b). The Application of Basel II to Trading Activities and the Treatment of Double Default Effects. Consultative document (July). www.bis.org.

BCBS (2006). *Basel II: International Convergence of Capital Measurement and Capital Standards, A Revised Framework – Comprehensive Version*. Basel: Basel Committee on Banking Supervision. www.bis.org.

BCBS (2009a). *Revisions to the Basel II market risk framework*. Basel: Basel Committee on Banking Supervision. www.bis.org.

BCBS (2009b). Strengthening the resilience of the banking sector. Consultative document (17 December). www.bis.org.

BCBS (2010a). *Basel III: A global regulatory framework for more resilient banks and banking systems*. Basel: Basel Committee on Banking Supervision. www.bis.org.

BCBS (2010b). Sound practices for backtesting counterparty credit risk models (10 December). www.bis.org.

BCBS (2010c). Capitalisation of bank exposures to central counterparties. Consultative document (20 December). www.bis.org.

BCBS (2011a). *Revisions to the Basel II market risk framework*. Basel: Basel Committee on Banking Supervision (11 February). www.bis.org.

BCBS (2011b). *Basel III: A global regulatory framework for more resilient banks and banking systems1 June*. Basel: Basel Committee on Banking Supervision. www.bis.org.

BCBS (2011c). Capitalisation of bank exposures to central counterparties. Second consultative document (2 November). www.bis.org.

BCBS (2011d). Application of own credit risk adjustments to derivatives. Consultative document (21 December). www.bis.org.

BCBS (2011e). Basel III counterparty credit risk – Frequently asked questions (21 November). www.bis.org.

BCBS (2012a). Fundamental review of the trading book. Consultative document (3 May). www.bis.org.

BCBS (2012b). *Capital requirements for bank exposures to central counterparties*. Basel: Basel Committee on Banking Supervision (25 July). www.bis.org.

BCBS (2012c). Basel III counterparty credit risk and exposures to central counterparties - Frequently asked questions (28 December). www.bis.org.

BCBS (2013a). *Basel III: The Liquidity Coverage Ratio and liquidity monitoring tools*. Basel: Basel Committee on Banking Supervision (7 January). www.bis.org.

BCBS (2013b). *Supervisory framework for measuring and controlling large exposures*. Basel: Basel Committee on Banking Supervision (25 March). www.bis.org.

BCBS (2013c). The non-internal model method for capitalising counterparty credit risk exposures. Consultative document (28 June). www.bis.org.

BCBS (2013d). Capital treatment of bank exposures to central counterparties. Consultative document (28 June). www.bis.org.

BCBS (2013e). Fundamental review of the trading book: A revised market risk framework. Consultative document (31 October). www.bis.org.

BCBS (2014a). *Basel III leverage ratio framework and disclosure requirements*. Basel: Basel Committee on Banking Supervision (12 January). www.bis.org.

BCBS (2014b). *Basel III: The Net Stable Funding Ratio*. Basel: Basel Committee on Banking Supervision (12 January). www.bis.org.

BCBS (2014c). *The standardised approach for measuring counterparty credit risk exposures*. Basel: Basel Committee on Banking Supervision (31 March). www.bis.org.

BCBS (2014d). *Capitalisation of bank exposures to central counterparties*. Basel: Basel Committee on Banking Supervision (10 April). www.bis.org.

BCBS (2014e). *Supervisory framework for measuring and controlling large exposures*. Basel: Basel Committee on Banking Supervision (15 April). www.bis.org.

BCBS (2014f). Regulatory Consistency Assessment Programme (RCAP) Assessment of Basel III regulations – Canada. Implementation report (13 June). www.bis.org.

BCBS (2014g). Capital floors: the design of a framework based on standardised approaches. Consultative document (22 December). www.bis.org.

BCBS (2015a). Review of the Credit Valuation Adjustment Risk Framework. Consultative document (1 July). www.bis.org.

BCBS (2015b). Regulatory Consistency Assessment Programme: (RCAP) – Report on risk-weighted assets for counterparty credit risk (CCR). Implementation report (1 October). www.bis.org.

BCBS (2016). Reducing variation in credit risk-weighted assets – constraints on the use of internal model approaches. Consultative document (24 March). www.bis.org.

BCBS (2017). Basel III: Finalising post-crisis reforms. Consultative document (7 December). www.bis.org.

BCBS (2019a). *Minimum capital requirements for market risk*. Basel: Basel Committee on Banking Supervision (14 January). www.bis.org.

BCBS (2019b). *Leverage ratio treatment of client cleared derivatives*. Basel: Basel Committee on Banking Supervision (26 June). www.bis.org.

BCBS (2019c). *Credit Valuation Adjustment Risk: targeted final revisions* (November). Consultative document.

BCBS-IOSCO (2012). Margin requirements for non-centrally cleared derivatives. Consultative document (July). www.bis.org.

BCBS-IOSCO (2013a). Margin requirements for non-centrally cleared derivatives. Second consultative document (February). www.bis.org.

BCBS-IOSCO (2013b). Margin requirements for non-centrally cleared derivatives. Final report (September). www.bis.org.

BCBS-IOSCO (2015). *Margin requirements for non-centrally cleared derivatives*. Basel: Basel Committee on Banking Supervision and Board of the International Organization of Securities Commissions. www.bis.org.

BCBS-IOSCO (2019a). *Margin requirements for non-centrally cleared derivatives*. Basel: Basel Committee on Banking Supervision and Board of the International Organization of Securities Commissions. www.bis.org.

BCBS-IOSCO (2019b). *Minimum capital requirements for market risk*. Basel: Basel Committee on Banking Supervision and Board of the International Organization of Securities Commissions. www.bis.org.

Bernanke, B. (1990). Clearing and Settlement in the Crash. *Review of Financial Studies* 3 (1): 133–151.

Berrahoui, M., O. Islah, and C. Kenyon (2019). Revising SA-CCR. *Risk* (April). www.risk.net

BIS (Bank for International Settlements) (2018). Two defaults at CCPs, 10 years apart. *BIS Quarterly Review* (December). www.bis.org.

BIS (2010). Standards for Payment, Clearing and Settlement Systems: Review by CPSS-IOSCO. Press release (2 February). www.bis.org.

BIS (2013a). OTC derivatives statistics at end-December 2012. Statistical release (May). www.bis.org.

BIS (2013b). Macroeconomic impact assessment of OTC derivatives regulatory reforms. Press release (26 August). www.bis.org.

BIS (2018). OTC derivatives statistics at end-June 2016 (31 October). www.bis.org.

Bank for International Settlements (BIS), 2018, "Two defaults at CCPs, 10 years apart", Quarterly Review, December. www.bis.org.

Bliss, R. and R. S. Steigerwald (2006). Derivatives Clearing and Settlement: A Comparison of Central Counterparties and Alternative Structures. Federal Reserve Bank of Chicago Economic Perspectives (Fourth Quarter), pp. 22–29.

Bliss, R. and G. Kaufman (2005). Derivatives and Systemic Risk: Netting, Collateral, and Closeout. FRB of Chicago working paper no. 2005–03 (10 May).

Black, F. and J. Cox (1976). Valuing Corporate Securities: Some Effects of Bond Indenture Provisions. *Journal of Finance* 31 (2): 351–67.

Black, F. and M. Scholes (1973). The Pricing of Options and Corporate Liabilities. *Journal of Political Economy* 81 (3): 637–654.

Bluhm, C., L. Overbeck, and C. Wagner (2003). *An Introduction to Credit Risk Modeling*. London: Chapman and Hall.

Borovkova, S. and H-L. El-Mouttalibi (2013). Systemic Risk and Centralized Clearing of OTC Derivatives: A Network Approach. *SSRN* (11 December). papers.ssrn.com.

Boudoukh. J., M. Richardson, and R. Whitelaw (1998). The Best of Both Worlds. *Risk* 11 (5): 64–67. www.risk.net.

Brace, A., D. Gatarek, and M. Musiela (1997). The Market Model of Interest Rate Dynamics. *Mathematical Finance* 7 (2): 127–154.

Brady, N. (1988). Report of the Presidential Task Force on Market Mechanisms. Washington DC: US Government Printing Office.

Brennan, M. J., J. Hein, and S-H. Poon (2009). Tranching and Rating. *European Financial Management* 15 (5): 891–922.

Brigo, D. and F. Mercurio (2001). A Deterministic-Shift Extension of Analytically-Tractable and Time-Homogeneous Short Rate Models. *Finance and Stochastics* 5 (3): 369–388.

Brigo, D., K. Chourdakis, and I. Bakkar (2008). Counterparty Risk Valuation for Energy-Commodities Swaps: Impact of Volatilities and Correlation. Working paper (24 June).

Brigo, D. and M. Masetti (2005a). Risk Neutral Pricing of Counterparty Risk. In Pykhtin, M. (ed.) (2005). *Counterparty Credit Risk Modelling*. London: Risk Books.

Brigo, D. and M. Masetti (2005b). A Formula for Interest Rate Swaps Valuation under Counterparty Risk in presence of Netting Agreements. Working paper (9 May).

Brigo, D. and M. Morini (2010). Dangers of Bilateral Counterparty Risk: the fundamental impact of closeout conventions. Working paper (15 November).

Brigo, D. and M. Morini (2011). Closeout convention tensions. *Risk* (8 December). www.risk.net.

Brigo, D., M. Morini, and A. Pallavicini (2013). *Counterparty Credit Risk, Collateral and Funding: With Pricing Cases for All Asset Classes*. Chichester: Wiley.

Brigo, D., N. Pede, and A. Petrelli (2015). Multi Currency Credit Default Swaps Quanto Effects and FX Devaluation Jumps. Working paper (22 December).

Brouwer, D. P. (2012). System and Method of Implementing Massive Early Terminations of Long Term Financial Contracts. US Patent 8,306,905 B2, filed 3 August and issued 10 December 2012.

Burgard, C. and M. Kjaer (2011a). Partial Differential Equation Representations of Derivatives with Counterparty Risk and Funding Costs. *The Journal of Credit Risk* 7 (3): 1–19.

Burgard, C. and M. Kjaer (2011b). In the balance. *Risk* (24 October). www.risk.net.

Burgard, C. and M. Kjaer (2012). A Generalised CVA with Funding and Collateral via Semi-Replication. Working paper (6 December).

Burgard, C. and M. Kjaer (2013). Funding Costs, Funding Strategies. *Risk* (29 November). www.risk.net.

Burgard, C. and M. Kjaer (2015). Derivatives Funding, Netting and Accounting. Working paper (1 February).

Callsen, G. and A. Hill (2018). The European Corporate Single Name Credit Default Swap Market. International Capital Market Association (1 February).

Capriotti, L. and J. Lee (2014). Adjoint credit risk management. *Risk* (August).

Carver, L. (2012). Traders close ranks against FVA critics. *Risk* (September).

Carver, L. (2013). Capital or P&L? Deutsche Bank losses highlight CVA trade-off. *Risk* (October).

Caspers, P., P. Giltinan, R. Lichters, and N. Nowaczyk (2017). Forecasting Initial Margin Requirements - A Model Evaluation. *Journal of Risk Management in Financial Institutions* 10 (4): 365–394.

Castagna, A. (2012). Yes, FVA is a Cost for Derivatives Desks. Working paper (30 August).

Cesari, G., J. Aquilina, N. Charpillon, Z. Filipovic, G. Lee, and I. Manda (2009). *Modelling, Pricing, and Hedging Counterparty Credit Exposure*. Berlin: Springer Finance.

CGFS (Committee on the Global Financial System) (2010). *The role of margin requirements and haircuts in procyclicality*. CGFS Paper No. 36 (23 March). www.bis.org.

CGFS (2013). Asset encumbrance, financial reform and the demand for collateral assets (27 May). www.bis.org.

Cheyette, O. (2001). Markov Representation of the Heath-Jarrow-Morton Model. Working paper (26 March).

Chourdakis, K., E. Epperlein, M. Jeannin, and J. McEwen (2013). A cross-section across CVA. Nomura (19 February).

Chung, B. and J. Gregory (2019). CVA wrong-way risk: calibration using a quanto CDS basis. *Risk* (July). www.risk.net.

Clark, I. (2016). Modeling Pegged Currencies - Examples from 2015: EURCHF, USDCNY, and USDARS. *Wilmott* 82: 51–59.

Collin-Dufresne, P., R. S. Goldstein, and J. S. Martin (2001). The Determinants of Credit Spread Changes. *Journal of Finance* 56 (6): 2177–2207.

Condat, A-L., A. Puce, and C. Nommels (2018). EMIR data and derivatives market policies. Financial Conduct Authority Research Note (6 August). www.fca.org.uk.

Cooper, I. A. and A. S. Mello (1991). The Default Risk of Swaps. *Journal of Finance* 46 (2): 597–620.

Cont, R., R. P. Mondescu, and Y. Yuhua (2011). Central Clearing of Interest Rate Swaps: A Comparison of Offerings (March 11).

Cont, R. (2018). Margin Requirements for Non-cleared Derivatives. ISDA working paper (25 April). www.isda.org.

Coval, J., J. Jurek, and E. Stafford (2009). Economic Catastrophe Bonds. *American Economic Review* 99 (3): 628–666.

Cox, N., N. Garvin, and G. Kelly (2013). Central Counterparty Links and Clearing System Exposures. Research Discussion Paper (October). Reserve Bank of Australia. www.rba.gov.au.

CPSS-IOSCO (2004). Recommendations for central counterparties. Committee on Payment and Settlement Systems and the Technical Committee of the International Organization of Securities Commissions (November). www.bis.org.

CPSS-IOSCO (2010). Guidance on the Application of the 2004 CPSS-IOSCO Recommendations for Central Counterparties to OTC Derivatives CCPs: Consultative Report. Committee on Payment and Settlement Systems and the Technical Committee of the International Organization of Securities Commissions (May). www.bis.org.

CPSS-IOSCO (2012). Principles for financial market infrastructures. Committee on Payment and Settlement Systems and the Technical Committee of the International Organization of Securities Commissions (April). www.bis.org.

Dagher, J., G. Dell'Ariccia, L. Laeven, L. Ratnovski, and H. Tong (2016). Benefits and Costs of Bank Capital. IMF Staff Discussion Note (March). www.imf.org.

Danielsson, J. and J-P. Zigrand (2003). On time scaling of risk and the square root of time rule. Discussion paper number 439 (3 November). Financial Markets Group. London School of Economics and Political Science.

Danmarks Nationalbank (2016). Credit risk management: transaction to two-way collateral agreements. Danish Government Borrowing and Debt 2015, Ch. 4 (24 February). www.nationalbanken.dk.

Das, S. (2008). The Credit Default Swap (CDS) Market - Will It Unravel? *Wilmott* (16–18 May).

Das, S. and R. Sundaram (1999). Of Smiles and Smirks, A Term Structure Perspective. *Journal of Financial and Quantitative Analysis* 34 (2): 211–239.

De Prisco, B. and D. Rosen (2005). Modelling Stochastic Counterparty Credit Exposures for Derivatives Portfolios. In Pykhtin, M. (ed.) (2005). *Counterparty Credit Risk Modelling*. London: Risk Books.

Deloitte and Solum Financial LLP (2013). Counterparty Risk and CVA Survey (1 February). www.solum-financial.com.

Downing, C., S. Underwood, and Y. Xing (2005). Is liquidity risk priced in the corporate bond market? Rice University working paper (11 June).

Duffee, G. R. (1998). The Relation Between Treasury Yields and Corporate Bond Yield Spreads. *Journal of Finance* 53 (6).

Duffee, G. R. (1996a). Idiosyncratic Variation of Treasury Bill Yields. *Journal of Finance* 51 (2): 527–551.

Duffee, G. R. (1996b). On Measuring Credit Risks of Derivative Instruments. *Journal of Banking and Finance* 20 (5): 805–833.

Duffie, D. (1999). Credit Swap Valuation. *Financial Analysts Journal* 55 (1): 73–87.

Duffie, D. and M. Huang (1996). Swap Rates and Credit Quality. *Journal of Finance* 51 (3): 921–950.

Duffie, D. and K. J. Singleton (2003). *Credit Risk: Pricing, Measurement, and Management*. New Jersey: Princeton University Press.

Duffie, D. and H. Zhu (2011). Does a Central Clearing Counterparty Reduce Counterparty Risk? *Review of Asset Pricing Studies* 1 (1): 74–95.

Duffie, D. (2011). On the clearing of foreign exchange derivatives. Working paper (22 June). Rock Center for Corporate Governance at Stanford University Working Paper Series No. 102.

Duffie, D., A. Li., and T. Lubke (2010). Policy Perspectives on OTC Derivatives Market Infrastructure. FRB of New York Staff Report No. 424.

Duffie, D., M. Scheicher, and G. Vuillemey (2014). Central Clearing and Collateral Demand. ECB working paper no. 1638 (February).

EBA (2013). EBA FINAL draft Regulatory Technical Standards on credit valuation adjustment risk for the determination of a proxy spread and the specification of a limited number of smaller portfolios under Article 383(7) of Regulation (EU) No 575/2013 (Capital Requirements Regulation – CRR). European Banking Authority (20 December). www.eba.europe.eu.

EBA (2015a). EBA FINAL draft Regulatory Technical Standards on prudent valuation under Article 105(14) of Regulation (EU) No 575/2013 (Capital Requirements Regulation — CRR). European Banking Authority (23 January). www.eba.europe.eu.

EBA (2015b). On Credit Valuation Adjustment (CVA) under Article 456(2) of Regulation (EU) No 575/2013 (Capital Requirements Regulation - CRR). European Banking Authority (25 February). www.eba.europe.eu.

EBA (2015c). Draft Regulatory Technical Standards on risk-mitigation techniques for OTC-derivative contracts not cleared by a CCP under Article 11(15) of Regulation (EU) No 648/2012. Second consultation paper (10 June). www.eba.europe.eu.

EBA (2017). EBA FINAL draft Regulatory Technical Standards for determining proxy spread and limited smaller portfolios for credit valuation adjustment under Article 383(7) of Regulation (EU) No 575/2013 (the Capital Requirements Regulation – CRR). European Banking Authority (21 June). www.eba.europe.eu.

Ernst & Young (2014). Credit valuation adjustments for derivative contracts (3 April). www.ey.com.

Ehlers, P. and P. Schönbucher (2006). The Influence of FX Risk on Credit Spreads. Working paper (March).

Elliott, D. (2013). Central counterparty loss-allocation rules. Financial Stability Paper No. 20 (29 April). Bank of England. www.bankofengland.co.uk.

European Commission (2010). Regulation on OTC derivatives, central Counterparties and trade repositories. Proposal (15 September). www.eba.europe.eu.

EMIR (2012). Draft technical standards under the Regulation (EU) No 648/2012 of the European Parliament and of the Council of 4 July 2012 on OTC Derivatives, CCPs and Trade Repositories. European Securities and Markets Authority (September). www.eba.europe.eu.

ESMA (2015). Review on the efficiency of margining requirements to limit Procyclicality. EMIR Review Report no. 2 (13 August). www.esma.europa.eu.

ESMA (2017). Review of Fair Value Measurement in the IFRS financial statements (12 July). www.esma.europa.eu.

ESMA (2018). Draft Guidelines on Anti-Procyclicality Margin Measures for Central Counterparties. Consultation paper (8 January). www.esma.europa.eu.

FASB (2006). Statement of Financial Accounting Standards No. 157 (September). Financial Accounting Standards Board. www.fasb.org.

Ferguson, R. and A. Green (2018). Deeply learning derivatives. Working paper (17 October).

FIA (2018). Central Clearing: Recommendations for CCP Risk Management. Futures Industry Association (27 November). www.fia.org.

Finger, C. (2000). Towards a Better Understanding of Wrong-way Credit Exposure. *The Journal of Risk Finance*, 1 (3), 43–51.

Fleck, M. and A. Schmidt (2005). Analysis of Basel II Treatment of Counterparty Risk. In Pykhtin, M. (ed.) (2005). *Counterparty Credit Risk Modelling*. London: Risk Books.

Fleming, M. J. and A. Sarkar (2014). The Failure Resolution of Lehman Brothers. *Federal Reserve Bank of New York Economic Policy Review* 20 (2): 175–206. www.ny.frb.org.

FMA (2012). Rundschreiben: zu Rechnungslegungsfragen bei Zinssteuerungs-derivaten und zu Bewertungsanpassungen bei Derivaten gemäß §57 BWG. Finanzmarktaufsicht. www.fma.gv.at.

Fons, J. S. (1987). The Default Premium and Corporate Bond Experience. *Journal of Finance* 42 (1): 81–97.

Fries, C. (2011). Discounting Revisited: Valuation Under Funding, Counterparty Risk and Collateralization. Working paper (12 June).

FSB (2013). OTC derivatives market reforms: fifth progress report on implementation. Financial Stability Board (15 April).

FSB (2014). Reforming Major Interest Rate Benchmarks. Financial Stability Board (22 July). www.fsb.org.

Fujii, M. and A. Takahashi (2011). Choice of Collateral Currency. *Risk* (7 January). www.risk.net.

Gabillon, J. (1991). The Term Structure of Oil Futures Prices. Oxford Institute for Energy Studies working paper.

Garcia-Cespedes, J. C., J. A. de Juan Herrero, D. Rosen, and D. Saunders (2010). Effective Modelling of Wrong-Way Risk, CCR Capital and Alpha in Basel II. *Journal of Risk Model Validation* 4 (1): 71–98.

García M., L. Manuel, P. Burdeus, J.Esteban, and F. de Lope Contreras (2016). The recursive nature of KVA: KVA mitigation from KVA. Working paper (19 April).

Geman, H. and V. N. Nguyen (2005). Soybean Inventory and Forward Curve Dynamics. *Management Science* 51 (7): 1076–1091.

Geman, H. (2009). *Commodities and Commodity Derivatives: Modeling and Pricing for Agriculturals, Metals and Energy*. Chichester: Wiley.

Gemmill, G. (1994). Margins and the Safety of Clearing Houses. *Journal of Banking and Finance* 18 (5): 979–996.

Gibson, M. (2004). Understanding the risk of synthetic CDOs. Finance and Economics Discussion Paper 2004–36. Federal Reserve Board (23 July).

Gibson, M. (2005). Measuring Counterparty Credit Risk Exposure to a Margined Counterparty. In Pykhtin, M. (ed.) (2005). *Counterparty Credit Risk Modelling*. London: Risk Books.

Giesecke, K., F. Longstaff, S. Schaefer, and I. Strebulaev (2010). Corporate Bond Default Risk: A 150-Year Perspective. *Journal of Financial Economics.* 102 (2), 233–250.

Glasserman. P. and B. Yu (2002). Pricing American Options by Simulation: Regression Now or Regression Later? In Niederreiter, H. (ed.) (2002). *Monte Carlo and Quasi-Monte Carlo Methods.* Berlin: Springer Finance.

Glasserman, P. and J. Li (2005). Importance Sampling for Portfolio Credit Risk. *Management Science* 51 (11): 1643–1656.

Glasserman, P. and Q. Wu (2017). Persistence and Procyclicality in Margin Requirements. Office of Financial Research working paper (21 February).

Gordy, M. (2004). Granularity Adjustment in Portfolio Credit Risk Management. In Szegö, G. P. (ed.) (2004). *Risk Measures for the 21st Century.* Chichester: Wiley.

Green, A. D., C. Kenyon, and C. Dennis (2014). KVA: Capital Valuation Adjustment. *Risk* 27 (12).

Green, A. D. and C. Kenyon (2015). MVA: Initial Margin Valuation Adjustment by Replication and Regression. Working paper (12 January).

Green, A. D. (2015). *XVA: Credit, Funding and Capital Valuation Adjustments.* Chichester: Wiley.

Gregory, J. (2008). A free lunch and the credit crunch. *Risk* (1 August). www.risk.nct.

Gregory, J. (2009a). Being two faced over counterparty credit risk. *Risk* 22 (2): 86–90.

Gregory, J. (2009b). *Counterparty Credit Risk: The New Challenge for Global Financial Markets (1st edition).* Chichester: Wiley.

Gregory, J. (2010). *Counterparty Casino: The Need to Address a Systemic Risk.* European Policy Forum working paper. www.epfltf.org

Gregory J. (2011). Counterparty risk in credit derivative contracts. In Lipton, A. and A. Rennie (eds.). *The Oxford Handbook of Credit Derivatives.* Oxford: Oxford University Press.

Gregory, J. (2012). *Counterparty Credit Risk and Credit Value Adjustment: A Continuing Challenge for Global Financial Markets (2nd edition).* Chichester: Wiley.

Gregory, J. and I. German (2013). Closing out DVA. *Risk* (7 January). www.risk.net.

Gregory, J. (2014). *Central Counterparties: Mandatory Central Clearing and Initial Margin Requirements for OTC Derivatives.* Chichester: Wiley.

Gregory, J. (2016). The impact of initial margin. Working paper (8 June).

Gregory, J. (2019). A Note on the behaviour of single-name proxy CDS hedges in the BA-CVA formula. Working paper (14 August).

G-20 (2009). Leaders' Statement: The Pittsburgh Summit. Group of 20 (25 September). www.g20ys.org.

G-20 (2010). The G-20 Toronto Summit Declaration. Group of 20 (27 June). www.g20ys.org.

Hagan, P., D. Kumar, A. Lesniewski, and D. E. Woodward (2002). Managing Smile Risk. *Wilmott* 1: 84–108.

Hardouvelis, G. and D. Kim (1995). Margin Requirements: Price Fluctuations, and Market Participation in Metal Futures. *Journal of Money, Credit and Banking* 27 (3): 659–671.

Hartzmark, M. (1986). The Effects of Changing Margin Levels on Futures Market Activity, the Composition of Traders in the Market, and Price Performance. *Journal of Business* 59 (2): S147–S180.

Heckinger, R. (2012). MF Global: A Case Study of Liquidity Risks. *Journal of Financial Market Infrastructures* 3 (2): 79–96.

Heller D. and N. Vause (2012). Collateral Requirements for Mandatory Clearing of Over-The-Counter Derivatives. BIS working paper no. 373 (6 March).

Hille, C., J. Ring, and H. Shimanmoto (2005). Modelling Counterparty Credit Exposure for Credit Default Swaps. In Pykhtin, M. (ed.) (2005). *Counterparty Credit Risk Modelling.* London: Risk Books.

Hills, B., D. Rule, and S. Parkinson (1999). Central counterparty clearing houses and financial stability. Bank of England Financial Stability Review (June).

Hull, J. (2010). OTC Derivatives and Central Clearing: Can All Transactions Be Cleared? *Banque de France Financial Stability Review* 14: 71–78.

Hull, J. (2015). *Risk Management and Financial Institutions (4th edition)*. Chichester: Wiley.

Hull, J. and A. White (1990). Pricing Interest-rate Derivative Securities. *The Review of Financial Studies* 3 (4): 573–592.

Hull, J. and A. White (2011). CVA and Wrong Way Risk. *Financial Analysts Journal*, 68 (5), 58–69.

Hull, J. and A. White (2012a). The FVA Debate. *Risk* 25th anniversary edition, pp. 83–85.

Hull, J. and A. White (2012b). The FVA debate continues: Hull and White respond to their critics. *Risk* (5 October). www.risk.net.

Hull, J. and A. White (2014). Valuing Derivatives: Funding Value Adjustments and Fair Value. *Financial Analysts Journal* 70 (3), 46–56.

Hull, J., M. Predescu, and A. White (2004). The Relationship Between Credit Default Swap Spreads, Bond Yields, and Credit Rating Announcements. *Journal of Banking & Finance* 28 (11): 2789–2811.

Hull, J., M. Predescu, and A. White (2005). Bond Prices, Default Probabilities and Risk Premiums. *Journal of Credit Risk* 1 (2): 53–60.

Hull, J., A. Sokol, and A. White (2014). Modeling the Short Rate: The Real and Risk-Neutral Worlds. Rotman School of Management working paper no. 2403067 (3 July).

IMF (2010). Making over-the-counter derivatives safer: the role of central counterparties. Global Financial Stability Report, Ch. 3 (April).

IFRS (2011). International Financial Reporting Standard 13 - Fair Value Measurement (12 May). www.ifrs.org.

ISDA (International Swaps and Derivatives Association) (2003). Counterparty Risk Treatment of OTC Derivatives and Securities Financing Transactions (June). www.isda.org.

ISDA (2009). *ISDA close-out amount protocol*. New York: International Swaps and Derivatives Association. www.isda.org.

ISDA (2010). Market Review of OTC Derivative Bilateral Collateralization Practices (1 March). www.isda.org.

ISDA (2012). Initial margin for non-centrally cleared swaps: understanding the systemic implications (27 November). www.isda.org.

ISDA (2013a). CDS Market Summary: Market Risk Transaction Activity. Research note (October). www.isda.org.

ISDA (2013b). Risk sensitive capital treatment for clearing member exposure to central counterparty default funds (2 April). www.isda.org.

ISDA (2013c). ISDA Margin Survey (21 June). www.isda.org.

ISDA (2013d). CCP Loss Allocation at the End of the Waterfall (8 August). www.isda.org.

ISDA (2013e). *Standardised initial margin model for uncleared derivatives*. New York: International Swaps and Derivatives Association. www.isda.org.

ISDA (2014a). ISDA Margin Study 2014 (10 April). www.isda.org.

ISDA (2014b). *The Value of Derivatives*. New York: International Swaps and Derivatives Association. www.isda.org.

ISDA (2014). Interest Rate Derivatives: A Progress Report on Clearing and Compression. Research note (February). www.isda.org.

ISDA (2015). ISDA Margin Study 2015 (11 August). www.isda.org.

ISDA (2016). ISDA SIMM™: From Principles to Model Specification (3 March). www.isda.org.

ISDA (2017a). *ISDA SIMM™ Methodology, version R1.3*. New York: International Swaps and Derivatives Association. www.isda.org.

ISDA (2017b). *ISDA SIMM™ Methodology, version 2.0*. New York: International Swaps and Derivatives Association. www.isda.org.

ISDA (2017c). ISDA Margin Study 2017 (25 April). www.isda.org.

ISDA (2018). ISDA Margin Survey Full Year 2017 (25 April). www.isda.org.

ISDA-AFME (2017). ISDA-AFME Position Paper CRD 5 / CRR 2: The Standardized Approach for Counterparty Credit Risk (March). www.isda.org.

ISDA-SIFMA (2018). Initial margin for non-centrally cleared derivatives: Issues for 2019 and 2020 (19 July). www.isda.org.

Iscoe, I., A. Kreinin, and D. Rosen (1999). An Integrated Market and Credit Risk Portfolio Model. *Algo Research Quarterly* 2 (3): 21–38.

Jamshidian, F. (1989). An Exact Bond Option Pricing Formula. *Journal of Finance* 44 (1): 205–209.

Jamshidian, F. and Y. Zhu (1997). Scenario Simulation: Theory and methodology. *Finance and Stochastics* 1 (1): 43–67.

Jarrow, R. and S. M. Turnbull (1992). Drawing the analogy. *Risk* 5 (10): 63–70.

Jarrow, R. and S. M. Turnbull (1995). Pricing Options on Financial Securities subject to default risk. *Journal of Finance* 50 (1): 53–85.

Jarrow, R. and S. M. Turnbull (1997). When swaps are dropped. *Risk* 10 (5): 70–75.

Jarrow, R. and Y. Yildirim (2003). Pricing Treasury Inflation Protected Securities and Related Derivatives using an HJM Model. *Journal of Financial and Quantitative Analysis* 38 (2): 409–430.

Jarrow, R. and F. Yu (2001). Counterparty Risk and the Pricing of Defaultable Decurities. *Journal of Finance* 56 (5): 1765–1799.

Jorion, P. (2007). *Value-at-Risk: The New Benchmark for Managing Financial Risk (2nd edition)*. New York: McGraw-Hill.

J.P. Morgan (1996). RiskMetrics – Technical Document (Fourth edition) (17 December).

Kenyon, C. (2010). Completing CVA and Liquidity: Firm-level positions and collateralized trades. Working paper (17 September).

Kenyon, C. and A. D. Green (2012). Will Central Counterparties become the New Rating Agencies. Working paper (28 November).

Kenyon, C. and A. D. Green (2013). Collateral-Enhanced Default Risk. Working paper (31 January).

Kenyon, C. and A. D. Green (2014a). CVA under Partial Risk Warehousing and Tax Implications. Working paper (11 July).

Kenyon, C. and A. D. Green (2014b). Regulatory Compliant Derivatives Pricing is Not Risk-Neutral. Working paper (13 August).

Kenyon, C. and A. D. Green (2015). Warehousing Credit (CVA) Risk, Capital (KVA) and Tax (TVA) Consequences. Working paper (16 January).

Kenyon, C., A. Green, and M. Berrahoui (2015). *Which measure for PFE? The Risk Appetite Measure A*. Working paper (19 December).

Kjaer, M. (2018). KVA unmasked. Working paper (19 March).

Kroszner, R. (1999). Can the Financial Markets Privately Regulate Risk? The Development of Derivatives Clearing Houses and Recent Over-the-counter Innovations. *Journal of Money, Credit and Banking* 31 (3): 569–618.

Kupiec P. (1995). Techniques for Verifying the Accuracy of Risk Management Models. *Journal of Derivatives* 3 (2): 73–84.

Laughton, S. and A. Vaisbrot (2012). In Defence of FVA: a Response to Hull and White. *Risk* (6 September). www.risk.net.

Laris, M. Z. M. and I. Ruiz (2018). Chebyshev Methods for Ultra-efficient Risk Calculations. Working paper (2 May).

LCH (2017). LCH Limited Default Rules (1 September). www.lch.com.

Levy, A. and R. Levin (1999). Wrong-way exposure. *Risk* (July).

Li, D. X. (2000). On Default Correlation: A Copula Function Approach. *Journal of Fixed Income* 9 (4): 43–54.

Lipton, A. and A. Sepp (2009). Credit Value Adjustment for Credit Default Swaps via the Structural Default Model. *Journal of Credit Risk* 5 (2): 123–146.

Longstaff, F. A. and S. E. Schwarz (2001). Valuing American Options by Simulation: A simple Least Squares Approach. *The Review of Financial Studies* 14 (1): 113–147.

Lou, W. (2015). Coherent CVA and FVA with Liability Side Pricing of Derivatives. Working paper (25 October).

MAGD (2013). Macroeconomic impact assessment of OTC derivatives regulatory reforms report issued by the Macroeconomic Assessment Group on Derivatives (MAGD) (26 August). www.bis.org.

Meese, R. and K. Rogoff (1983). Empirical Exchange Rate Models of the Seventies. *Journal of International Economics* 14 (1–2): 3–24.

Mackenzie, D. (2006). *An Engine, Not a Camera: How Financial Models Shape Markets*. Cambridge, Massachusetts: MIT Press.

Mello, A. and J. Parsons (2013). Margins, Liquidity, and the Cost of Hedging. *Journal of Applied Corporate Finance* 25 (1), 34–43.

Mercurio, F. (2010). A LIBOR Market Model with Stochastic Basis. Working paper (5 April).

Merton, R. C. (1974). On the Pricing of Corporate Debt: The Risk Structure of Interest Rates. *Journal of Finance* 29 (2): 449–70.

Modigliani, F. and M. Miller (1958). The Cost of Capital, Corporation Finance and the Theory of Investment. *American Economic Review* 48 (3): 261–297.

Moody's Investors Service (2007). Corporate Default and Recovery Rates: 1920–2006. Moody's Special Report (February).

Morini, M. (2014). *XVAs without Double Counting*. WBS Fixed Income Conference, Barcelona.

Morini, M. and A. Prampolini (2010). Risky Funding: A unified framework for counterparty and liquidity charges. Working paper (30 August).

Murphy, D. (2012). The doom loop in sovereign exposures. *FT Alphaville Blog* (12 April). ftalphaville.ft.com.

Murphy, D. (2013). *OTC Derivatives: Bilateral Trading and Central Clearing: An Introduction to Regulatory Policy, Market Impact and Systemic Risk*. London: Palgrave Macmillan.

Nakashima, T., M. Cosma, and B. Plong (2016). A Framework in Search of an Optimal Margining Policy for Official Institutions: The Canadian Experience. Bank of Canada Staff Discussion Paper 2016–9 (March). www.bankofcanada.ca.

Norman, P. (2011). *The Risk Controllers: Central Counterparty Clearing in Globalised Financial Markets*. Chichester: Wiley.

O'Kane, D. (2017). Optimising the Multilateral Netting of Fungible OTC Derivatives. *Quantitative Finance* 17 (1): 1–12.

Ong, M. K. (ed.) (2006). *The Basel Handbook: A Guide for Financial Practitioners (2nd edition)*. London: Risk Books.

Picoult, E. (2002). Quantifying the Risks of Trading. In Dempster, M. A. H. (ed.) (2002). *Risk Management: Value at Risk and Beyond*. Cambridge: Cambridge University Press.

Picoult, E. (2005). Calculating and Hedging Exposure, Credit Value Adjustment and Economic Capital for Counterparty Credit Risk. In Pykhtin, M. (ed.) (2005). *Counterparty Credit Risk Modelling*. London: Risk Books.

Pindyck, R. (2001). The Dynamics of Commodity Spot and Futures Markets: A Primer. *Energy Journal* 22 (3): 1–29.

Pirrong, C. (1998). A Positive Theory of Financial Exchange Organization with Normative Implications for Financial Market Regulation. Working paper (6 October).

Pirrong, C. (2010a). The Economics of Clearing in Derivatives Markets: Netting, Asymmetric Information, and the Sharing of Default Risks Through a Central Counterparty. University of Houston working paper (11 February).

Pirrong, C. (2010b). The Inefficiency of Clearing Mandates. Cato Institute Policy Analysis (21 July).

Pirrong, C. (2011). The Economics of Central Clearing: Theory and Practice. ISDA Discussion Papers Series Number One (23 May).

Pirrong, C. (2014). A Bill of Goods: Central Counterparties and Systemic Risk. *Journal of Financial Markets Infrastructures* 2 (4): 55–85.

Piterbarg, V. (2010). Funding beyond discounting: Collateral agreements and derivatives pricing. *Risk* 24 (2): 97–102.

Piterbarg, V. (2012). Cooking with collateral. *Risk* (26 July). www.risk.net.

Piterbarg, V. (2013). Stuck with collateral. *Risk* (25 October): 60–65.

Pykhtin, M. (2012). Model foundations of the Basel III standardised CVA charge. *Risk* (8 August). www.risk.net.

Pykhtin, M. and A. Sokol (2013). Exposure under systematic impact. *Risk* (20 August). www.risk.net.

Pykhtin, M. and S. Zhu (2007). A Guide to Modelling Counterparty Credit Risk. *GARP Risk Review* 37: 16–22.

Rebonato, R. (1998). *Interest Rate Options Models (2nd edition)*. Chichester: Wiley.

Reimers, M. and M. Zerbs (1999). A Multi-factor Statistical Model for Interest Rates. *Algo Research Quarterly* 2 (3): 53–64.

Reserve Bank of Australia (RBA) (2017). Assessment of LCH Limited's SwapClear Service (December). www.rba.gov.uk.

Rosen, D. and M. Pykhtin (2010). Pricing Counterparty Risk at the Trade Level and CVA Allocations. *Journal of Credit Risk* 6 (4): 3–38.

Rosen D. and D. Saunders (2010). Risk Factor Contributions in Portfolio Credit Risk Models. *Journal of Banking and Finance* 34 (2): 336–349.

Rowe, D. (1995). Aggregating Credit Exposures: The Primary Risk Source Approach, in *Derivative Credit Risk*. Risk Publications, pp. 13–21.

Rowe, D. and M. Mulholland (1999). Aggregating Market-driven Credit Exposures: A Multiple Risk Source Approach, in *Derivative Credit Risk* (2nd edition). Risk Publications, pp. 141–147.

Sarno, L. and M. P. Taylor (2002). *The Economics of Exchange Rates*. Cambridge: Cambridge University Press.

Sarno, L. (2005). Viewpoint: Towards a Solution to the Puzzles in Exchange Rate Economics: Where do we Stand? *Canadian Journal of Economics* 38 (3): 673–708.

Segoviano, M. A. and M. Singh (2008). *Counterparty Risk in the Over-the-Counter Derivatives Market*. IMF working paper (1 November).

Sidanius, C. and F. Zikes (2012). OTC derivatives reform and collateral demand impact. Bank of England Financial Stability Paper No. 18 (1 October). www.bankofengland.co.uk.

Singh, M. and J. Aitken (2009a). Deleveraging after Lehman: Evidence from Reduced Rehypothecation. IMF working paper (23 March). www.imf.org.

Singh, M. and J. Aitken (2009b). Counterparty Risk, Impact on Collateral Flows and Role for Central Counterparties. IMF working paper 09/173 (1 August). www.imf.org.

Singh, M. (2010). Collateral, Netting and Systemic Risk in the OTC Derivatives Market. IMF working paper (1 April). www.imf.org.

Sorensen, E. H. and T. F. Bollier (1994). Pricing Swap Default Risk. *Financial Analysts Journal* 50 (3): 23–33.

Sokol, A. (2010). A Practical Guide to Monte Carlo CVA. In Berd, A. (ed.) (2010). *Lessons From the Crisis*. London: Risk Books.

Sokol, A. (2014). *Long-Term Portfolio Simulation - For XVA, Limits, Liquidity and Regulatory Capital*. London: Risk Books.

Soros, G. (2009). My three steps to financial reform. *Financial Times* (17 June). www.ft.com.

Sourabh, S., M. Hofer, and D. Kandhai (2018). Liquidity Risk in Derivatives Valuation: An Improved Credit Proxy Method. *Quantitative Finance* 18 (3): 467–481.

Standard & Poor's (2007). *Ratings Performance 2006: Stability and Transition*, New York, S&P (16 February). www.spglobal.com.

Standard & Poor's (2008). Default, Transition, and Recovery: 2008 Annual Global Corporate Default Study And Rating Transitions (2 April). www.spglobal.com.

Standard and Poor's (2016). Annual Global Project Finance Default and Recovery Study, 1980–2014 (June). www.spglobal.com.

Tang, Y. and A. Williams (2010). Funding benefit and funding cost. In Canabarro, E. (ed.) (2010). *Counterparty Credit Risk*. London: Risk Books.

Tennant, J., K. Emery, and R. Cantor (2008). *Corporate one-to-five-year rating transition rates.* Moody's Investor Services Special Comment.

Thompson, J. R. (2010). Counterparty Risk in Financial Contracts: Should the Insured Worry About the Insurer? *The Quarterly Journal of Economics* 125 (3): 1195–1252.

Turlakov, M. (2012). Wrong-way risk in credit and funding valuation adjustments. Working paper (27 August).

Van Duyn, A. and F. Guerrera (2008). Banks face $10bn monolines charges. *Financial Times* (10 June). www.ft.com.

Vasicek, O. (2002). The distribution of loan portfolio value. *Risk* 15 (12): 160–162.

Vrins, F. and J. Gregory (2011). Getting CVA up and running. *Risk* 11: 76–79.

Wilde, T. (2001). In ISDA's response to the Basel Committee On Banking Supervision's Consultation on The New Capital Accord (Annex 1) (May).

Wilde, T. (2005). Analytic Methods for Portfolio Counterparty Risk. In Pykhtin, M. (ed.) (2005). *Counterparty Credit Risk Modelling*. London: Risk Books.

Zangari, P. (1994). Estimating volatilities and correlations. RiskMetrics - Technical Document (2nd edition) pp: 43–66.

Zeron, M. and I. Ruiz (2018). *Dynamic Initial Margin via Chebyshev Spectral Decomposition*. Working paper (24 August).

Index